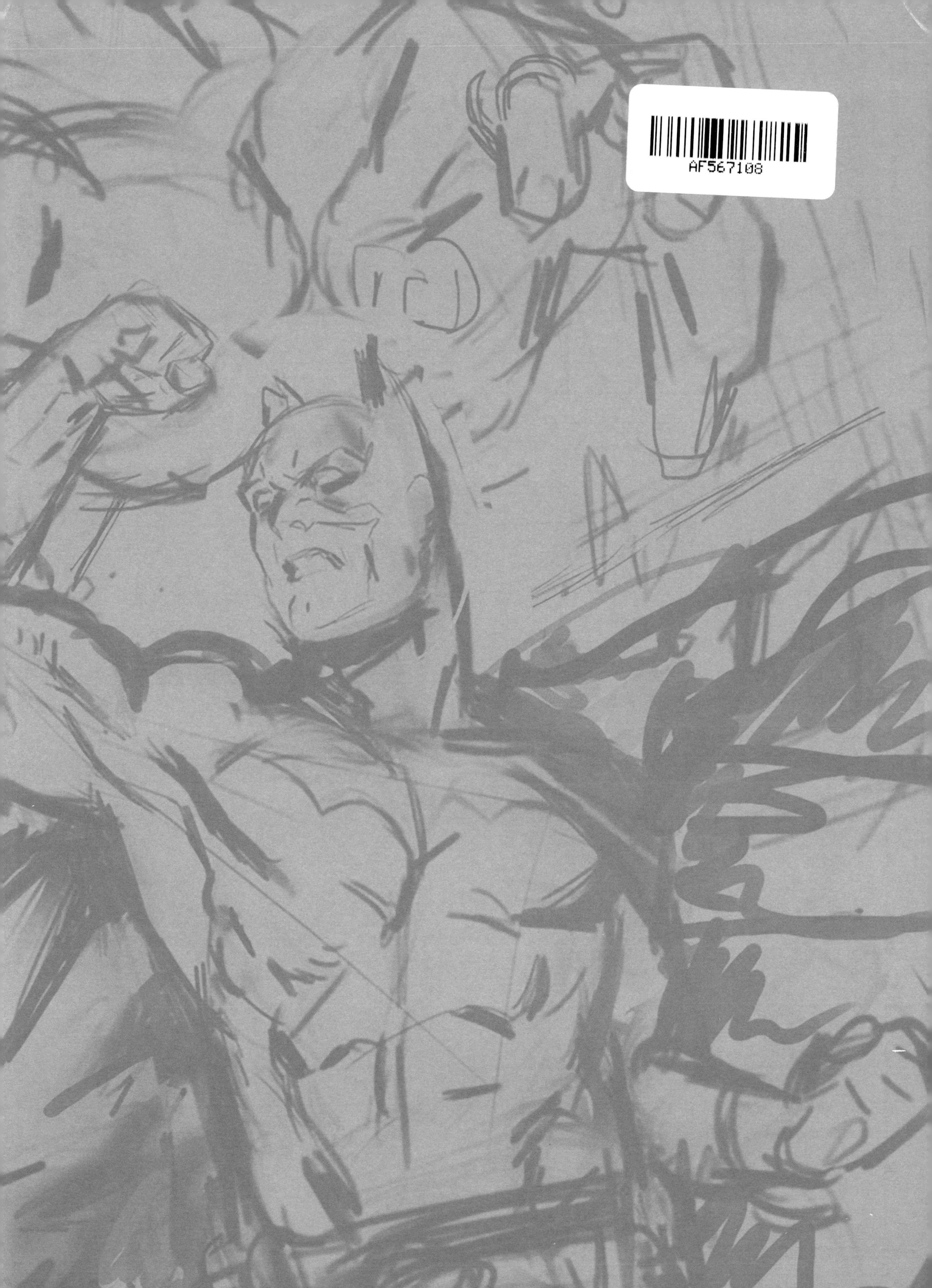

SIDESHOW

FINE ART PRINTS VOL. 2

Sideshow is proud to celebrate a supremely diverse and talented collective of illustrators with an extensive look at their limited edition Fine Art Prints from 2017-2018.

SIDESHOW

FINE ART PRINTS VOL. 2

WRITTEN BY ANDREW FARAGO

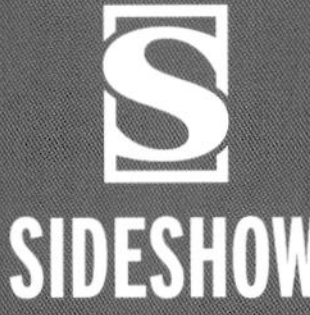

INSIGHT EDITIONS
SAN RAFAEL • LOS ANGELES • LONDON

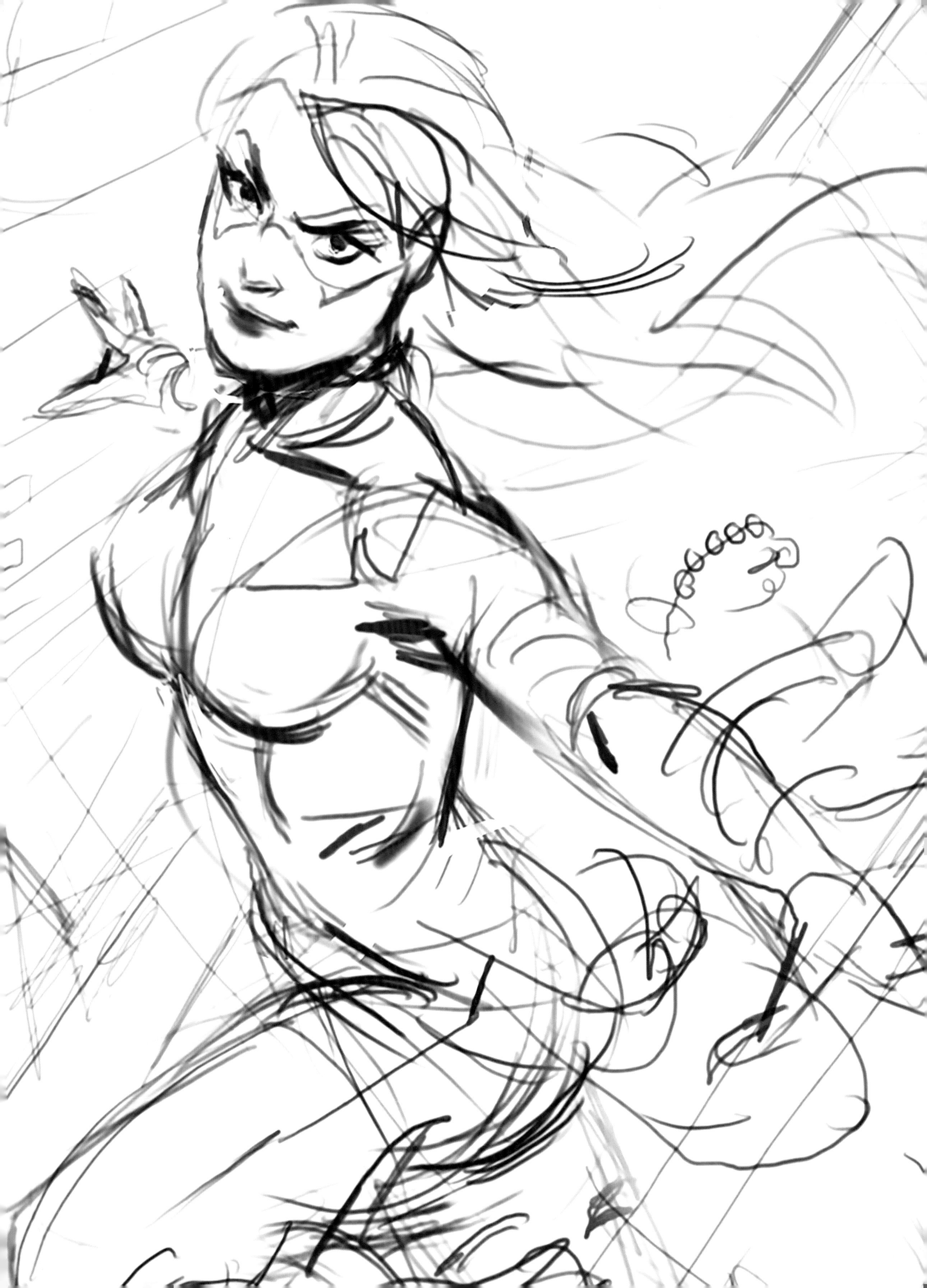

CONTENTS

> **We're extremely privileged to collaborate time and time again with immensely talented and highly regarded artists, and to have their work represented as part of Sideshow's fine art collection**
>
> —Gracie Bifulco | Art Print Manager, Sideshow

In 1994, Sideshow embarked on its mission of connecting people with their favorite characters and icons from the worlds of film, television, comic books, and popular culture. The studio quickly established itself as the premier manufacturer of premium collectibles, statues, and figures, through collaborations with the most celebrated properties in popular fiction, including *Star Wars*, Marvel, DC Comics, and classic films such as *Alien*, among many others.

Over the next two decades, Sideshow's reputation among collectors and artists grew, and the studio began sharing its creative process by turning concept art for 3-D statues into fully realized companion prints.

"As fans of these properties, characters, and stories ourselves, we always want to explore new and innovative ways to connect to the mythologies we all love so much," says Gracie Bifulco, art print department manager for Sideshow Collectibles. "[That] led us to the realization that people wanted to collect high-quality prints just as much as they wanted to collect high-quality statues," she adds.

The Fine Art Prints line was successful right out of the gate. While a whole new fanbase came on board specifically for the high-end prints, many of Sideshow's existing clientele were thrilled by the expansion of the studio's collectible offerings. "Our goal with the art print program is to be as broad as the 3-D offerings that we make and sell," says Sideshow CEO and president Greg Anzalone. "Our fans and collectors love these properties and these characters that we lovingly highlight in 3-D. We've always felt that we needed to give them a 2-D option as well."

Ever since its launch in 2015, the Fine Art Prints program has grown considerably—an expansion of creativity and artistry that's reflected in the following pages of this book. "It's been incredibly rewarding and satisfying to see the print program expand so much in the past few years," says Sideshow art director Ian MacDonald. "I definitely believe Sideshow's established itself as a major player in the fine art print world; the success of the program very much speaks to that."

As with the 3-D collectibles program before it, an important component of the growth of the Fine Art Prints program was the new licensees and artists joining in the fun. One of Sideshow's biggest signings on that front was the addition of the multiple Harvey- and Eisner Award-winning painter Alex Ross. Known to comic book fans as the visionary artist behind seminal titles including *Marvels*, *Kingdom Come*, *Astro City*, and hundreds of classic comic book covers over the past three decades, Alex Ross is nothing short of a legend.

For Greg Anzalone, working with Ross was a true career highlight. "Sideshow began more than a quarter century ago with the Universal Classic Monsters, so the chance to do a portfolio series of the Classic Monsters with Alex was quite the thing for us. It was surely a bit of a full-circle experience for many of us who have been here for the full ride," Anzalone says.

Alongside Ross, the Fine Art Prints program inducted many other top artists into its roster, including Allen Williams, Mark Brooks, Heon-hwa Choe, RJ Palmer, Terry and Rachel Dodson, and Karla Ortiz, among many others. Additionally, the full might of Marvel Studios brought its talents to the program. Marvel Studios' head of visual development, Ryan Meinerding, and visual development director, Andy Park, contributed pieces based on some of the most popular films of all time.

Of course, Sideshow's production values ensure that the work of these incredible artists receives the best possible presentation. "We're extremely privileged to collaborate time and time again with immensely talented and highly regarded artists, and to have their work represented as part of Sideshow's fine art collection," says Gracie Bifulco.

"To paraphrase a popular web-slinger, we believe that with great privilege comes great responsibility. We consider it our great responsibility—to the artists, to the source material, and to the collectors—to approach each illustration with the highest level of care and attention to detail. Starting from the inception of each print with conceptual sketches, all the way to the printing methods and materials selected for final production, it is our mission to create long-lasting, elegant, tangible touchstones that art enthusiasts will be proud to display."

Through constant innovation and the tireless efforts of a team of dedicated artists and an all-star production team, the Fine Art Prints program has reached new heights since its inception. Those leaps and bounds are captured within this book—a tribute to the creativity and artistry of everyone involved.

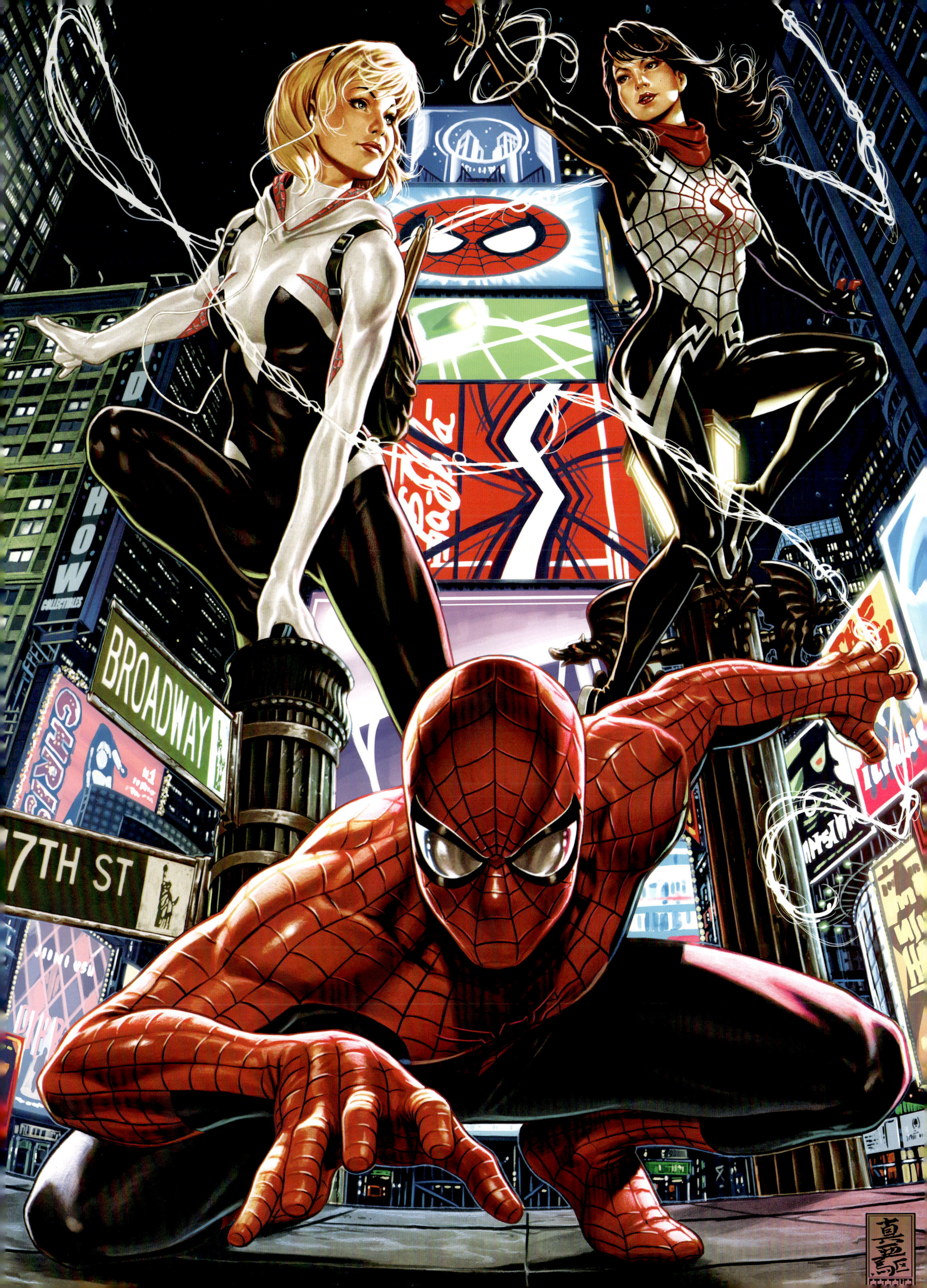
BROADWAY
7TH ST

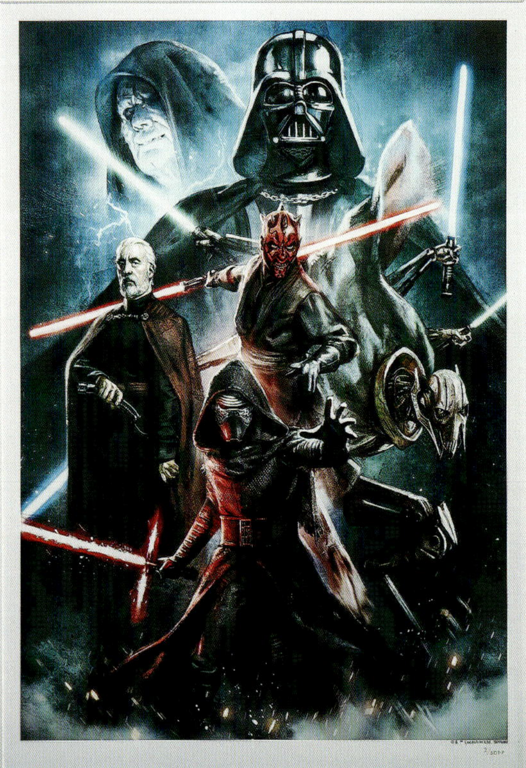

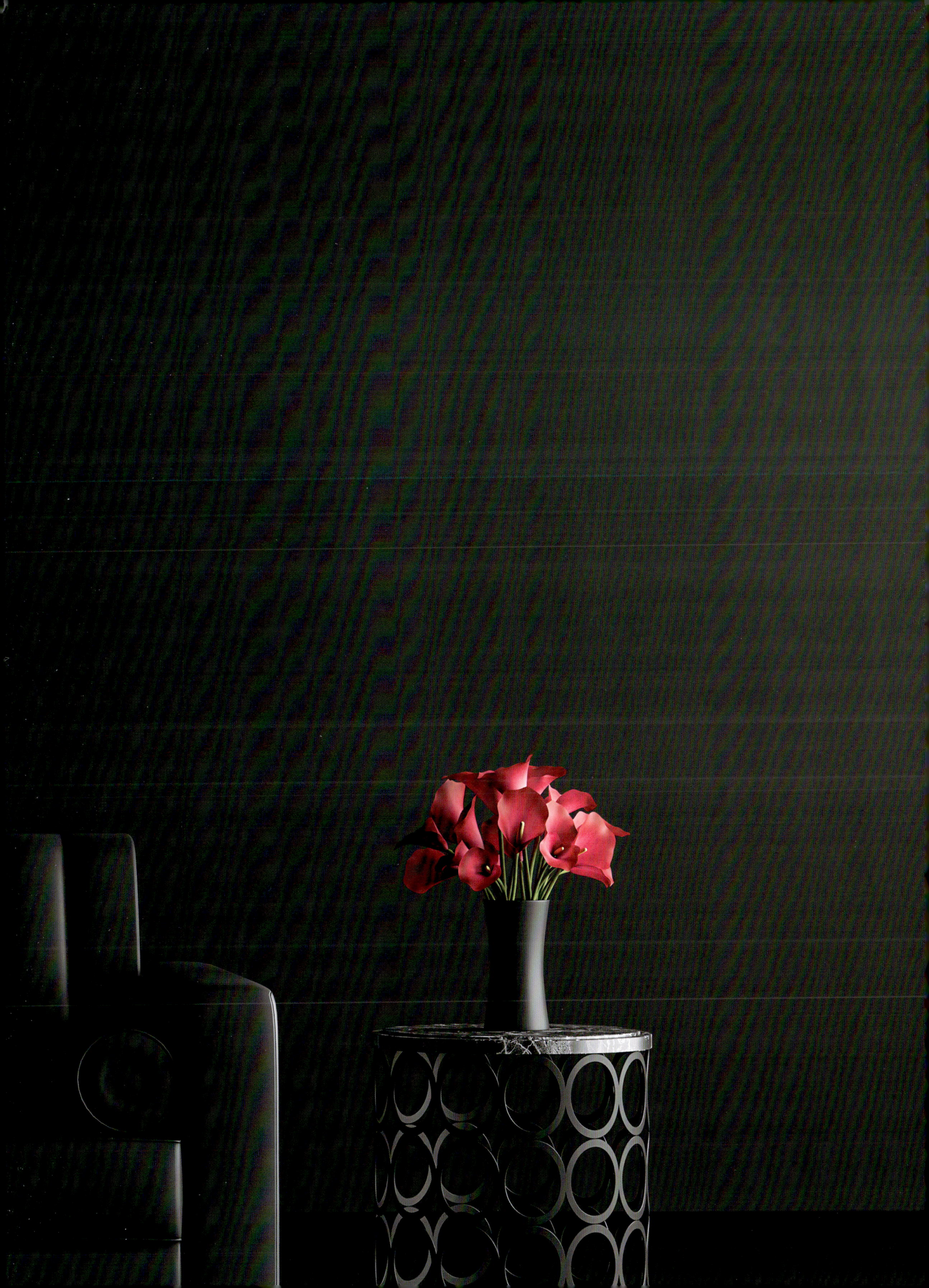

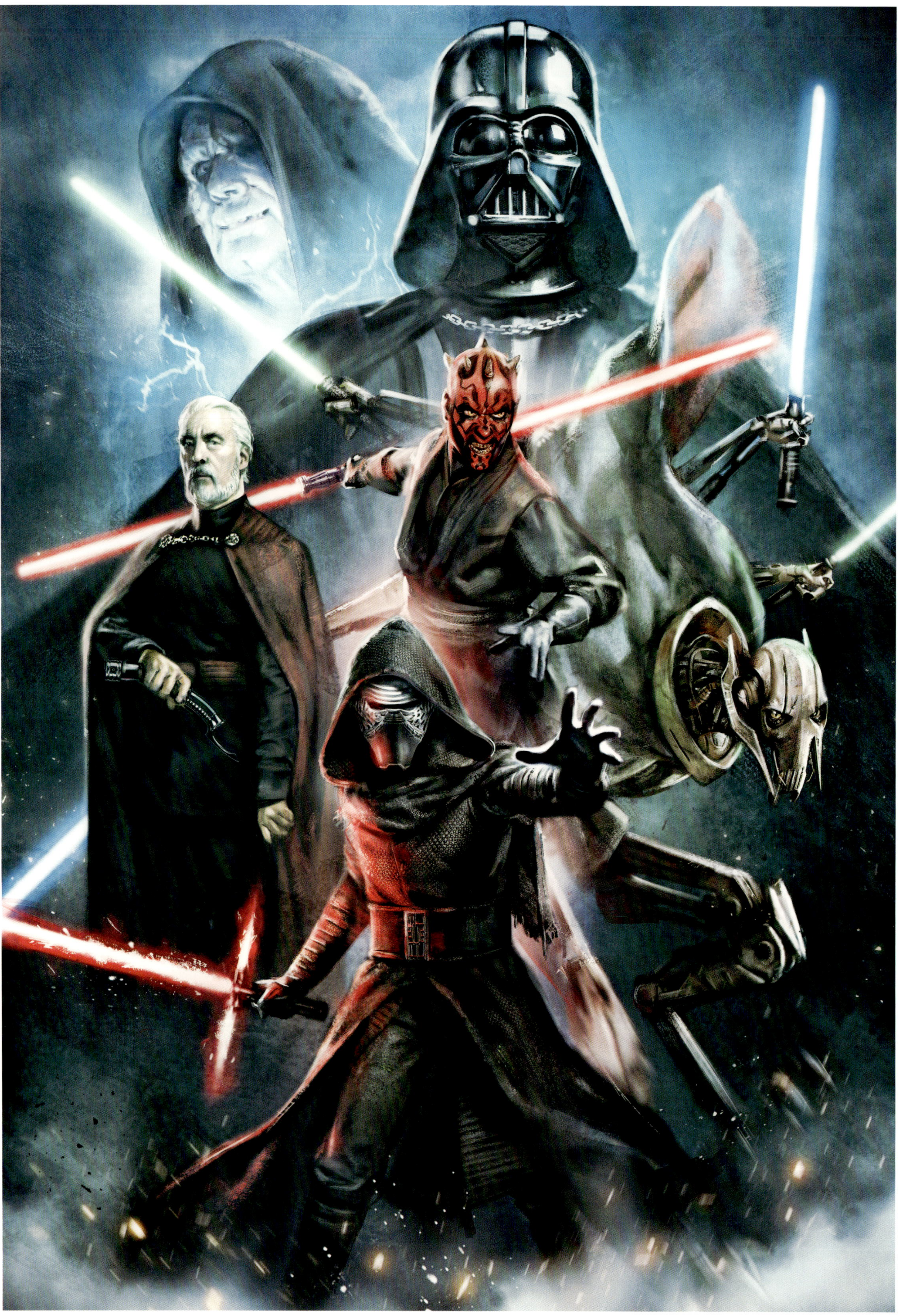

FORCE OF DARKNESS

IAN MACDONALD

Showcasing some of the galaxy's most powerful villains, this art print depicts acolytes of the dark side from across three eras of the *Star Wars* saga. Count Dooku, Darth Maul, and General Grievous represent the evils that befell the Galactic Republic, while the menace of Kylo Ren foregrounds the terror of the First Order. Darth Sidious and Darth Vader tower above all, a testament to their mighty influence over the galaxy.

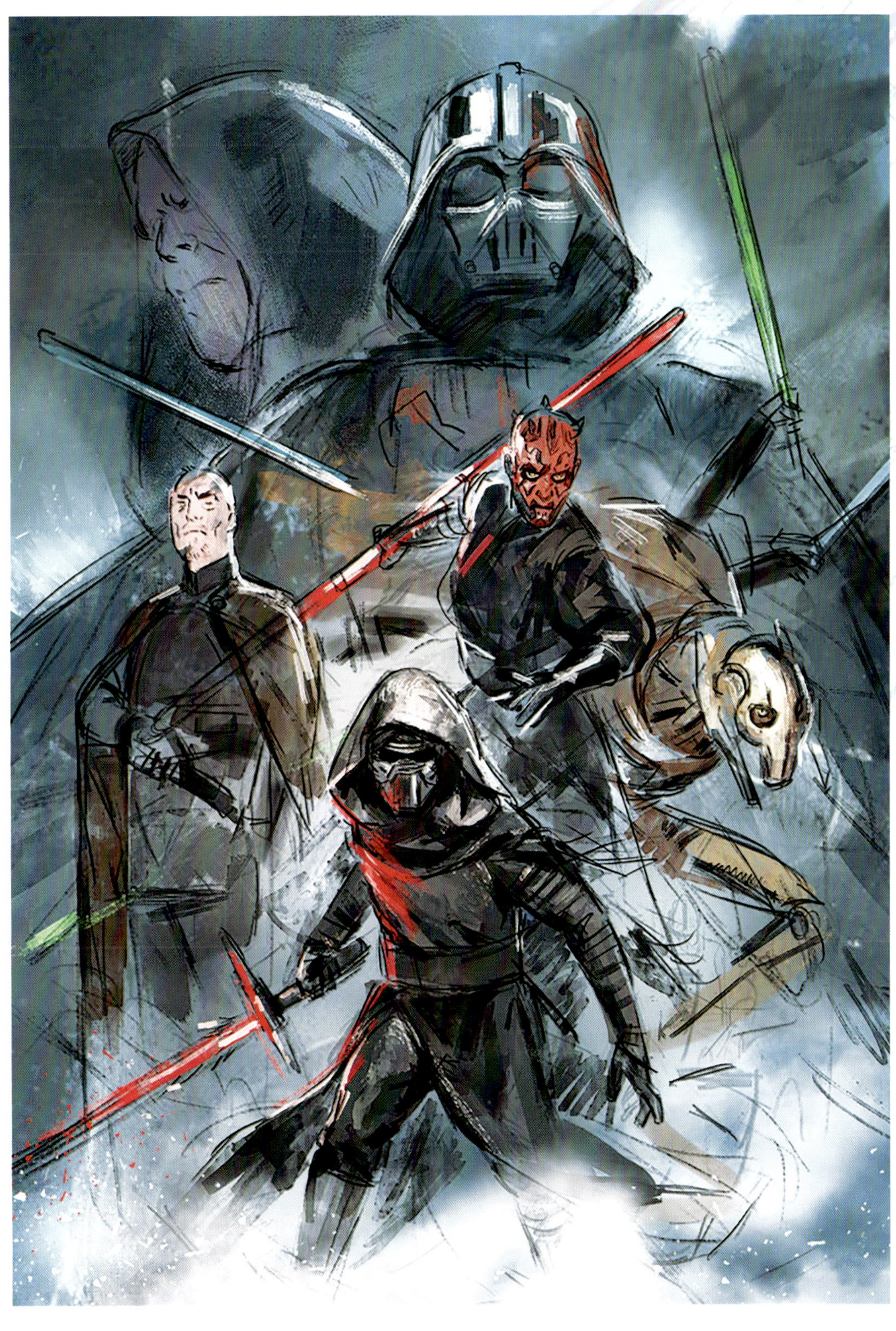

FORCE OF HOPE

IAN MACDONALD

Showcasing some of the galaxy's most powerful heroes, this art print depicts Jedi Knights from across three eras of the *Star Wars* saga. Rey continues the proud legacy of all who came before her, including Yoda, Qui-Gon Jinn, Obi-Wan Kenobi, Anakin Skywalker, and Luke Skywalker—the most formidable and iconic wielders of the Force.

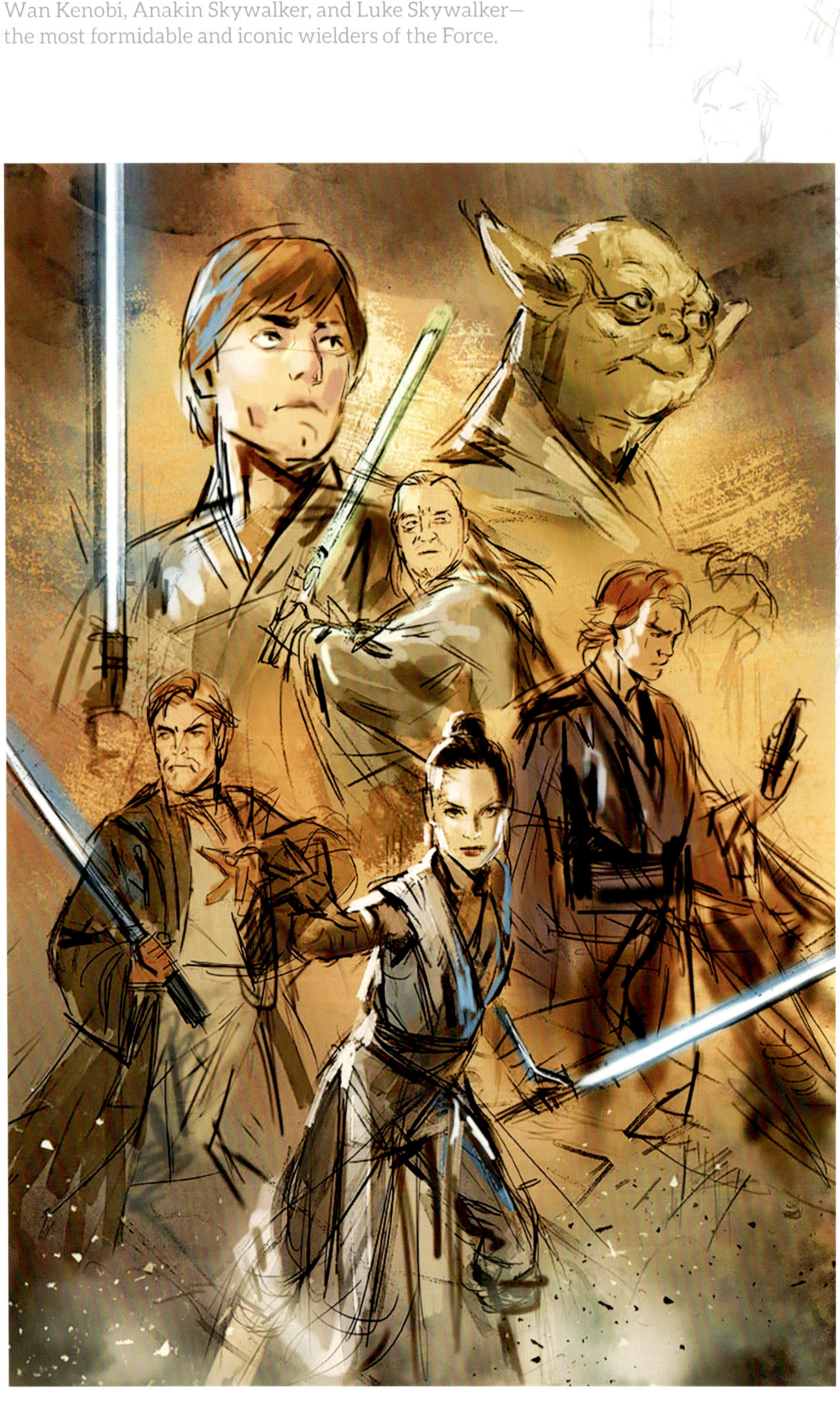

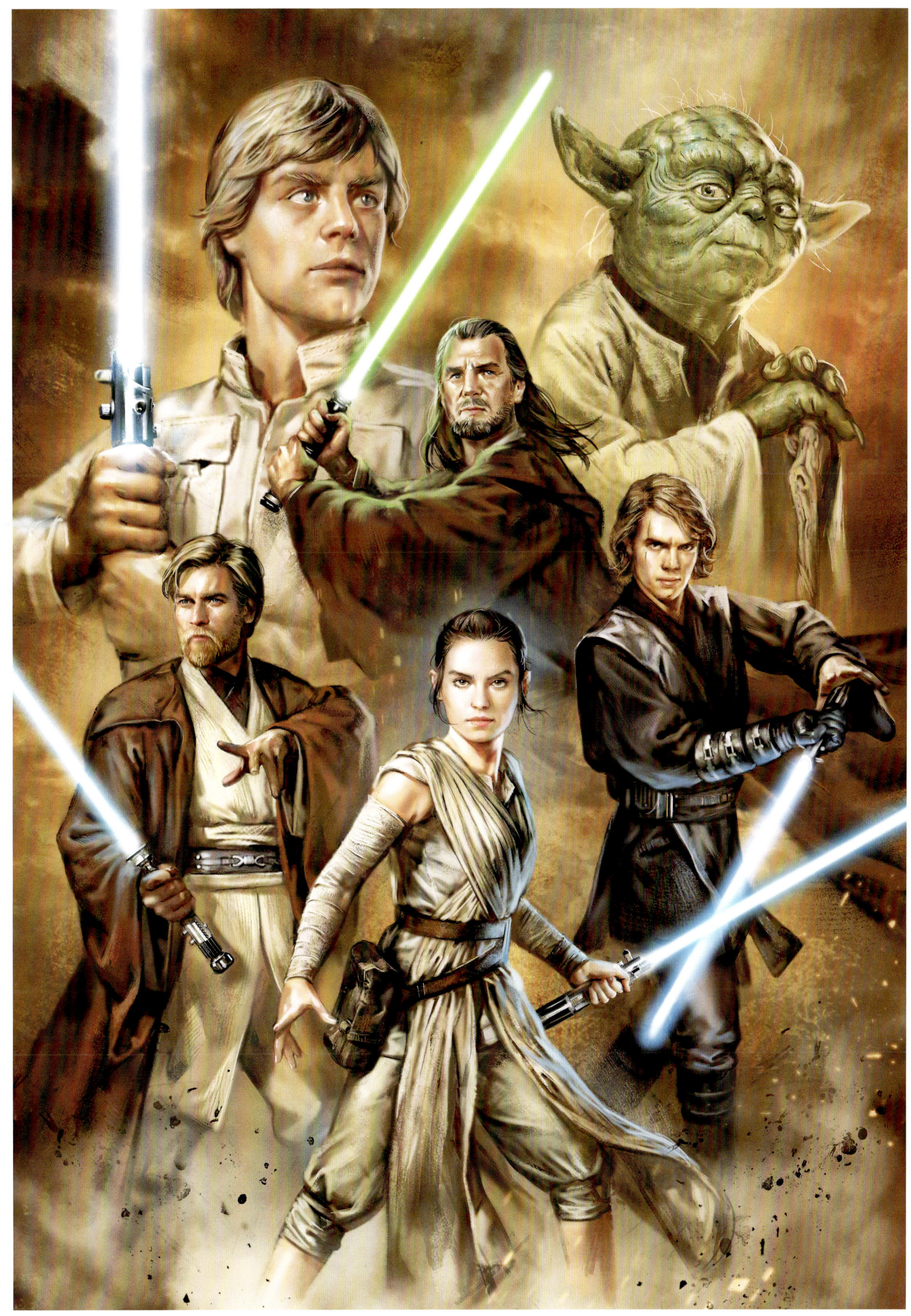

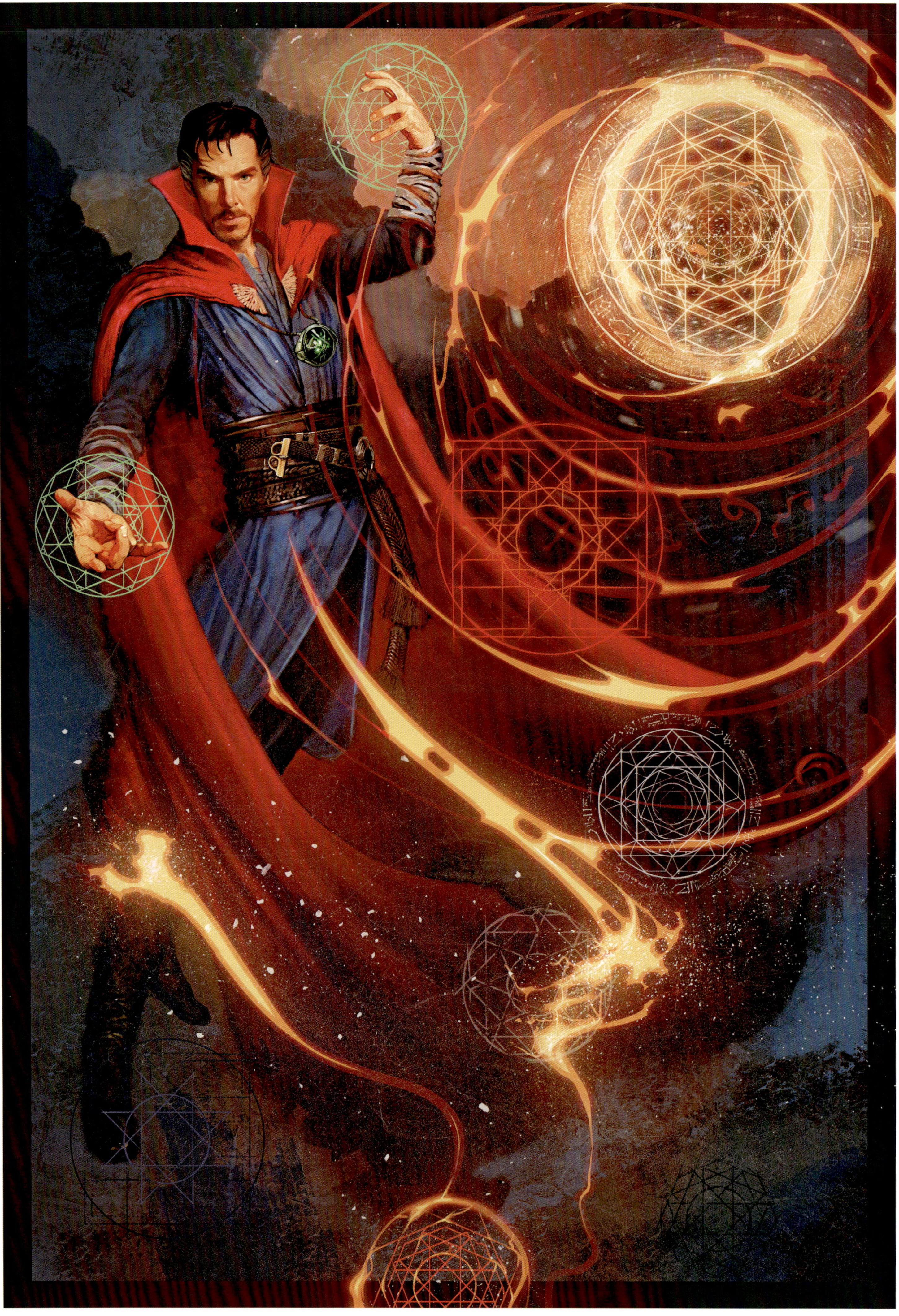

DOCTOR STRANGE

ALLEN WILLIAMS

Formerly a renowned surgeon, Dr. Stephen Strange now serves as the Sorcerer Supreme—Earth's foremost protector against magical and mystical threats.

Inspired by the popular, transformative film that enchanted fans of the Marvel Cinematic Universe, this portrait depicts Doctor Strange wielding his newfound arcane powers of levitation and mystical constructs, featuring Benedict Cumberbatch as the reluctant hero.

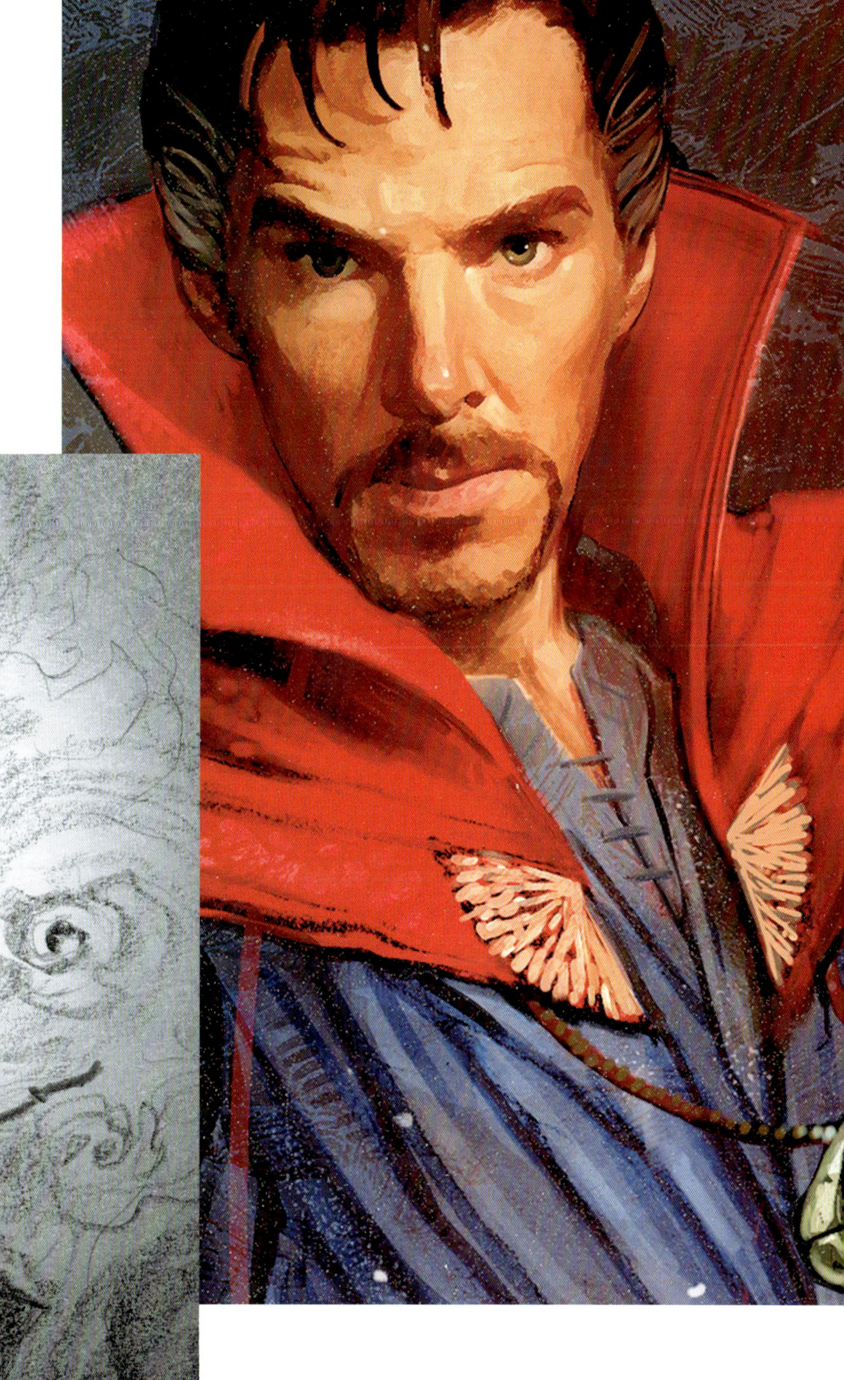

ALLEN WILLIAMS

“My first impression of Sideshow as an art studio was concepting for some of the *Court of the Dead* figures. They were great to work with, and seeing what they were making . . . there was a lot to live up to. It was all terrific.”

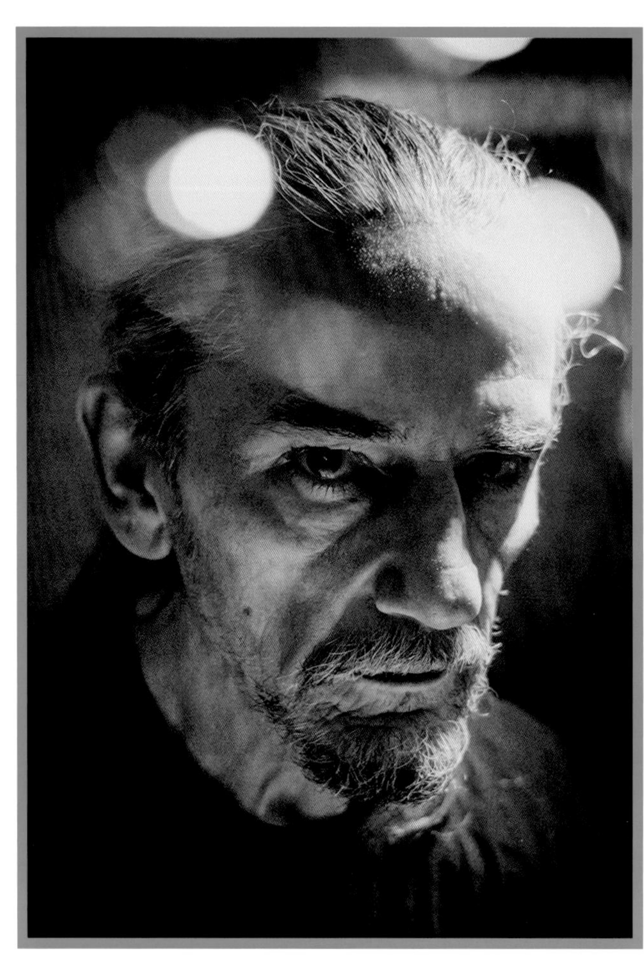

INSPIRATION

Allen Williams is an award winning illustrator, concept designer, and fine artist. From a young age a pencil and paper were an escape and refuge for Allen. Internationally known for over thirty years, Allen has applied his talents to everything from illustration for gaming companies and book covers, to concept work for major motion pictures and television. His vision for such projects ranges from illustration to concept work and creature and character designs.

His personal work has a strong basis in reality, but always flows into otherworldly aspects. He primarily works in graphite, gouache and oils. Multilayered images arise in his work in which the fragility and instability of our seemingly certain reality is questioned. His work can be seen online or in galleries across the United States, Europe, and Asia.

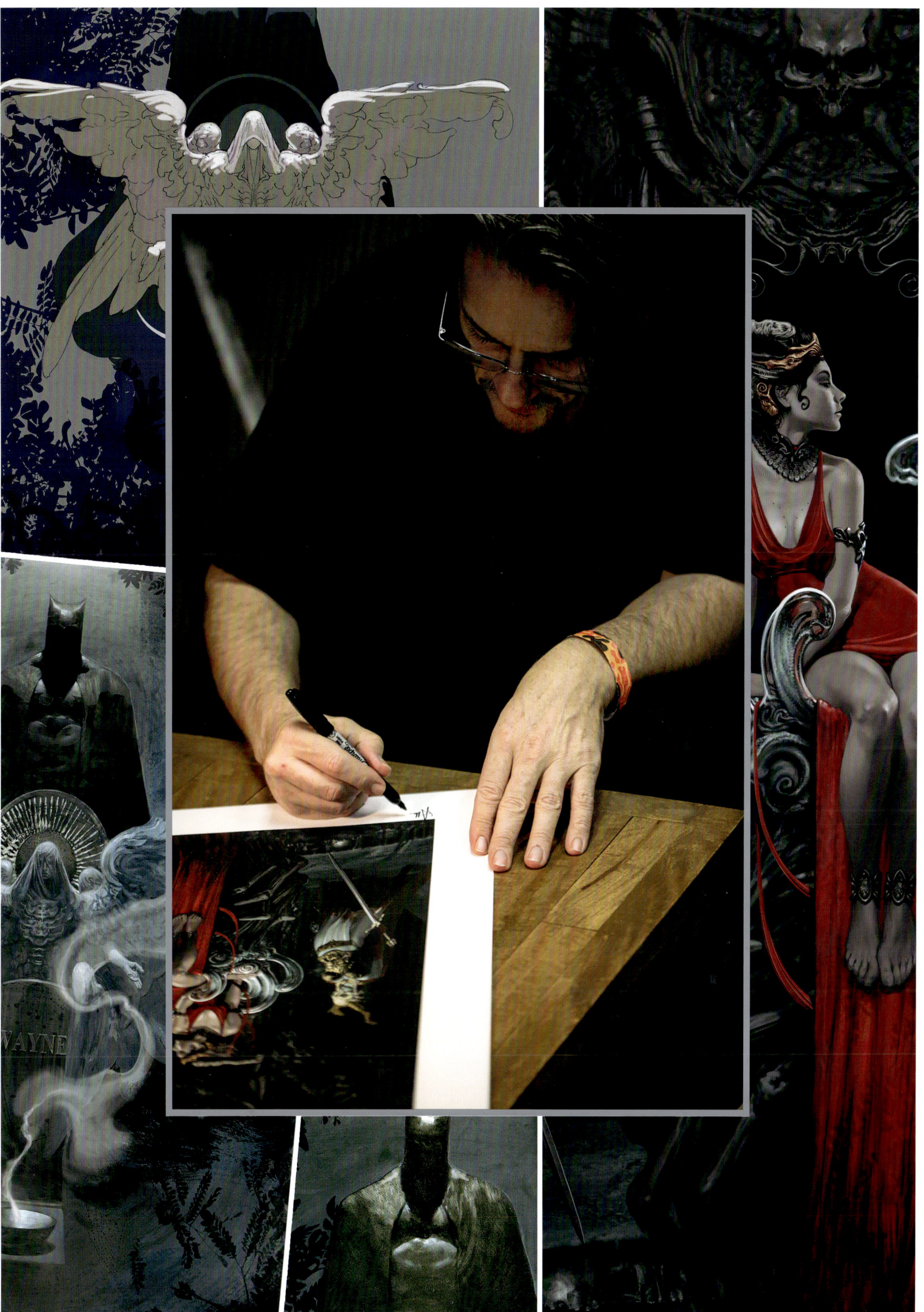

The Birth of Batman various concept art, *Divided We Stand*. Allen Williams signing.

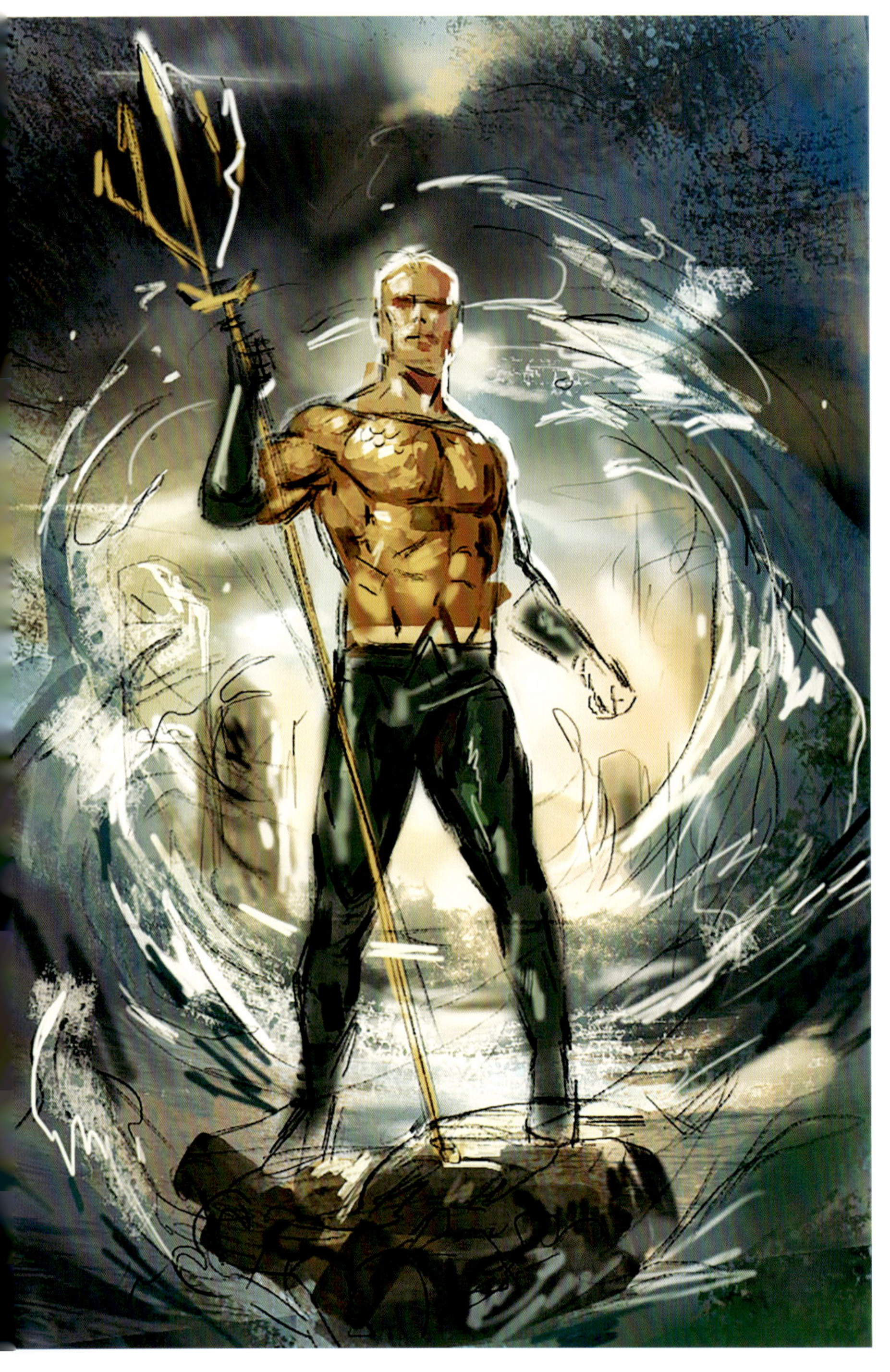

AQUAMAN

FABIAN SCHLAGA

Monarch of the undersea realm, Aquaman is one of the most powerful DC superheroes, commanding a kingdom that covers three-quarters of the Earth's surface, including all the creatures contained within.

This dramatic image captures the power and majesty of the King of the Seven Seas, reluctant ruler of Atlantis and stalwart member of the Justice League, as he stands triumphant amidst the raging tides.

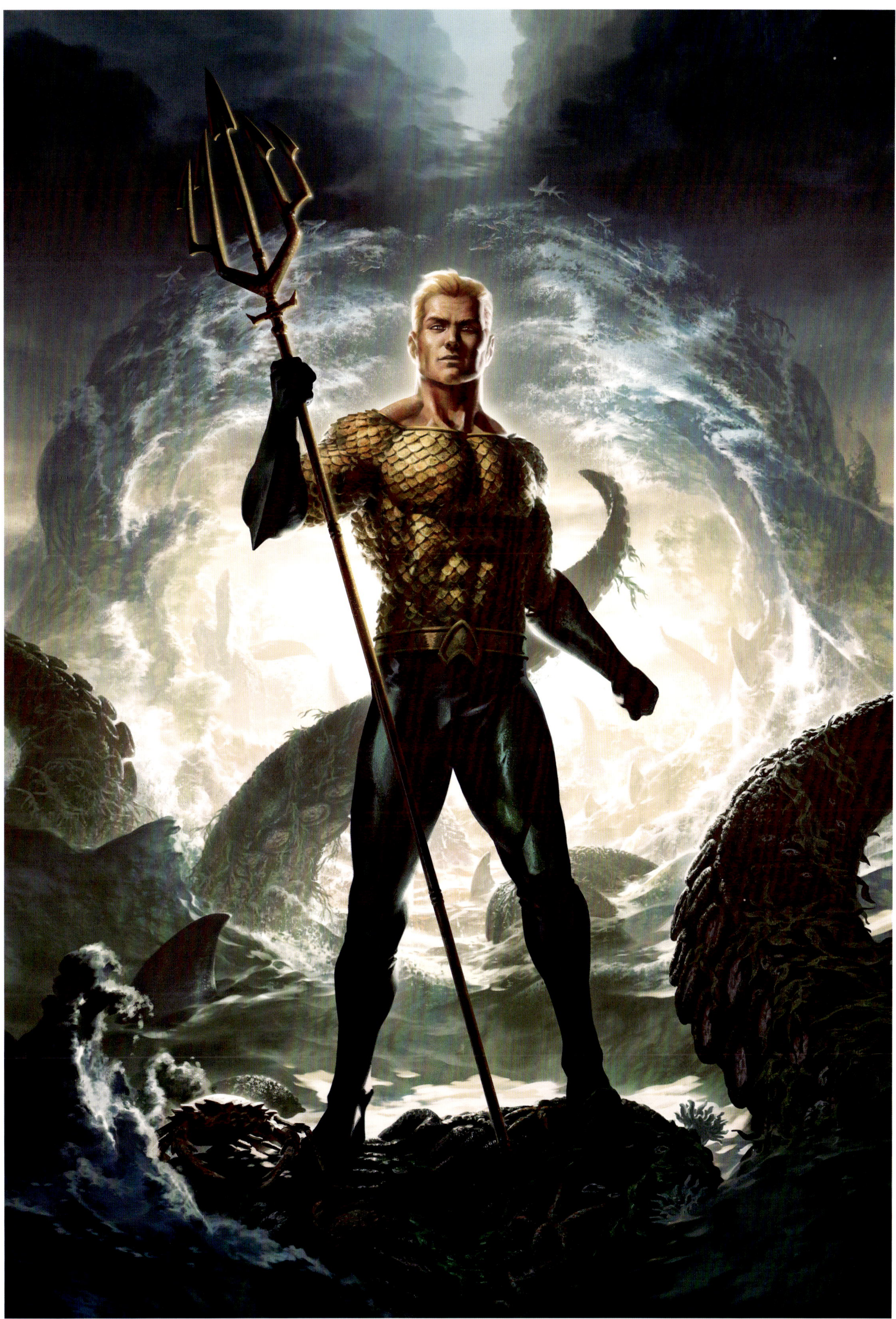

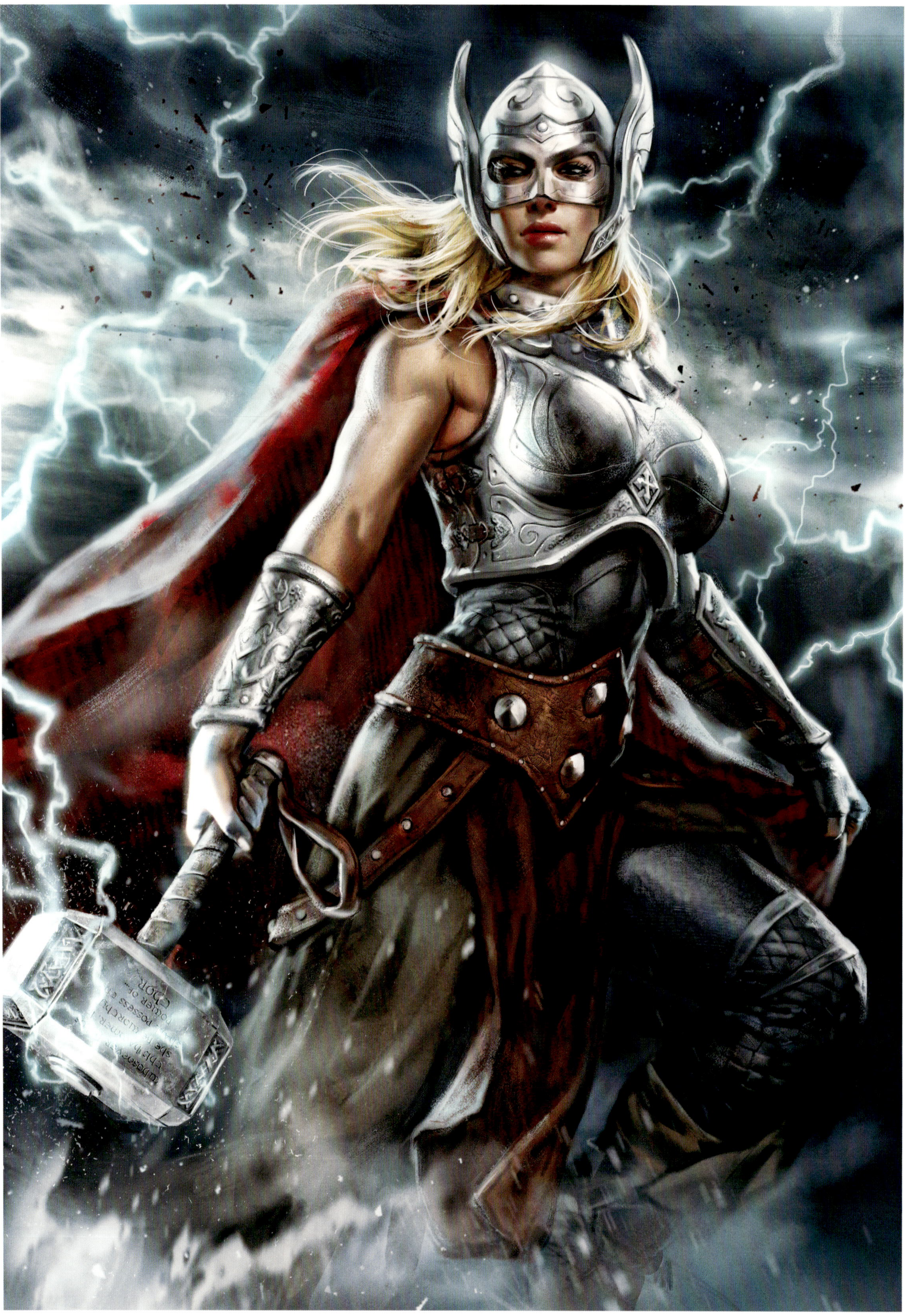

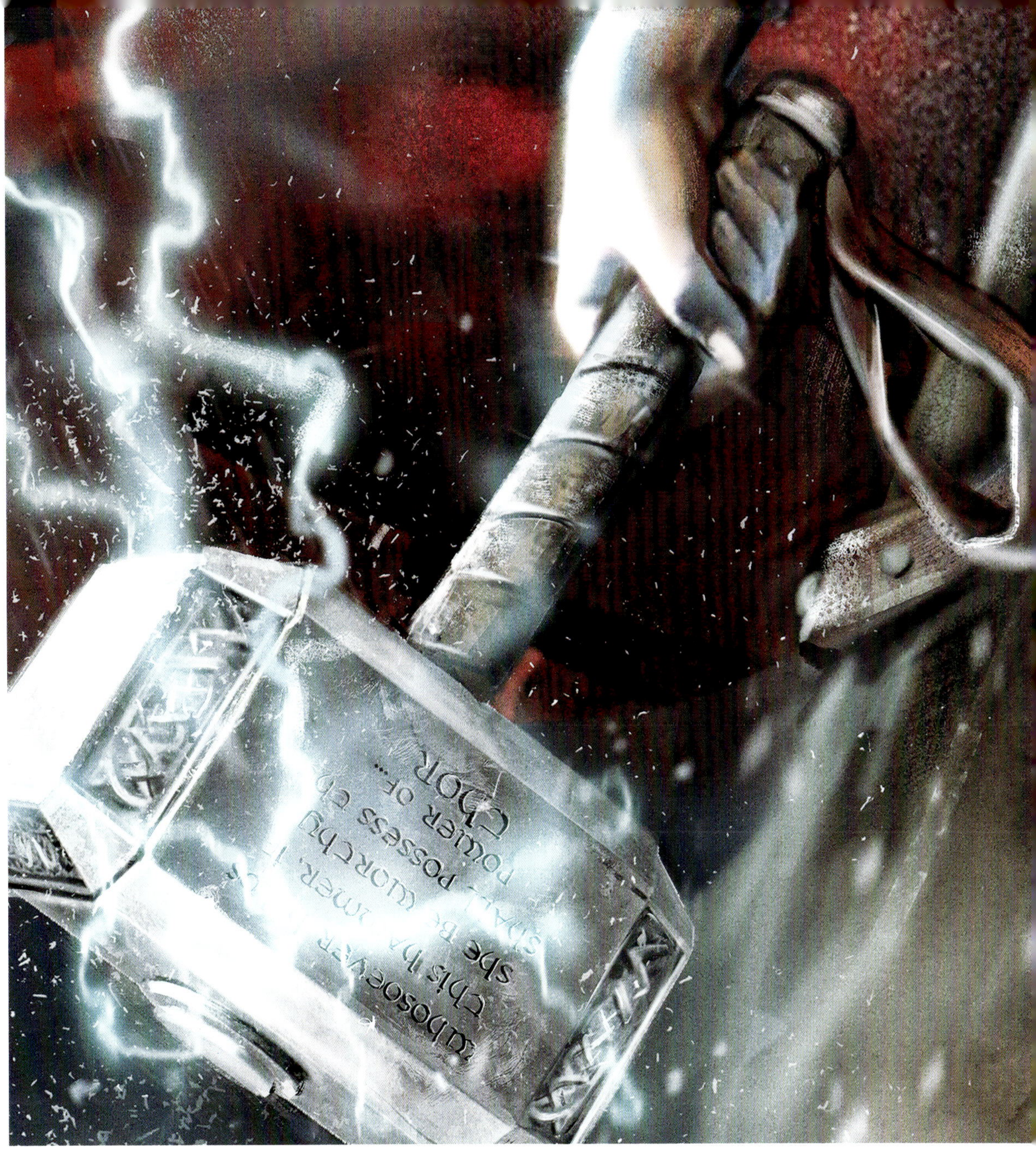

THOR JANE FOSTER

IAN MACDONALD

Exclusively commissioned for Sideshow's Marvel collection, the officially licensed *Thor: Jane Foster* Premium Art Print depicts a dramatic turning point in the Thor saga.

In a dramatic transformation, Jane Foster takes up the mantle of Thor as Goddess of Thunder, rising among crackling lightning, as the mystical inscription on the fabled hammer Mjolnir changes to reflect the gender of its new wielder!

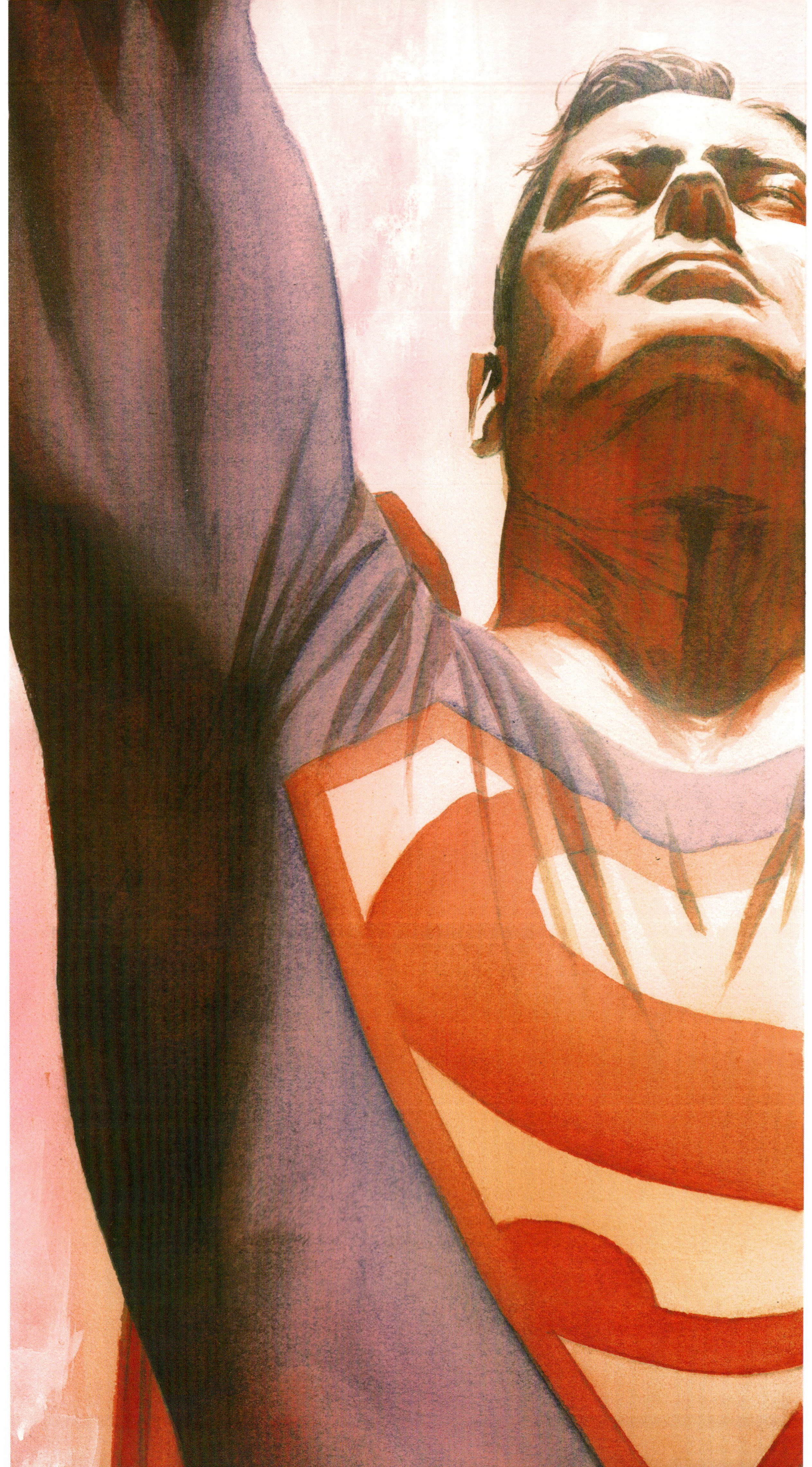

SUPERMAN IMMORTAL

ALEX ROSS

Superman: Immortal celebrates the timelessness of Superman, protector of mankind and Earth's greatest hero.

"From his blue uniform to his flowing red cape and the *S* shield on his chest, Superman is one of the most recognizable and beloved superheroes of all time. The Man of Steel is the ultimate symbol of truth, justice, and hope. He is the world's first superhero and a guiding light to all."

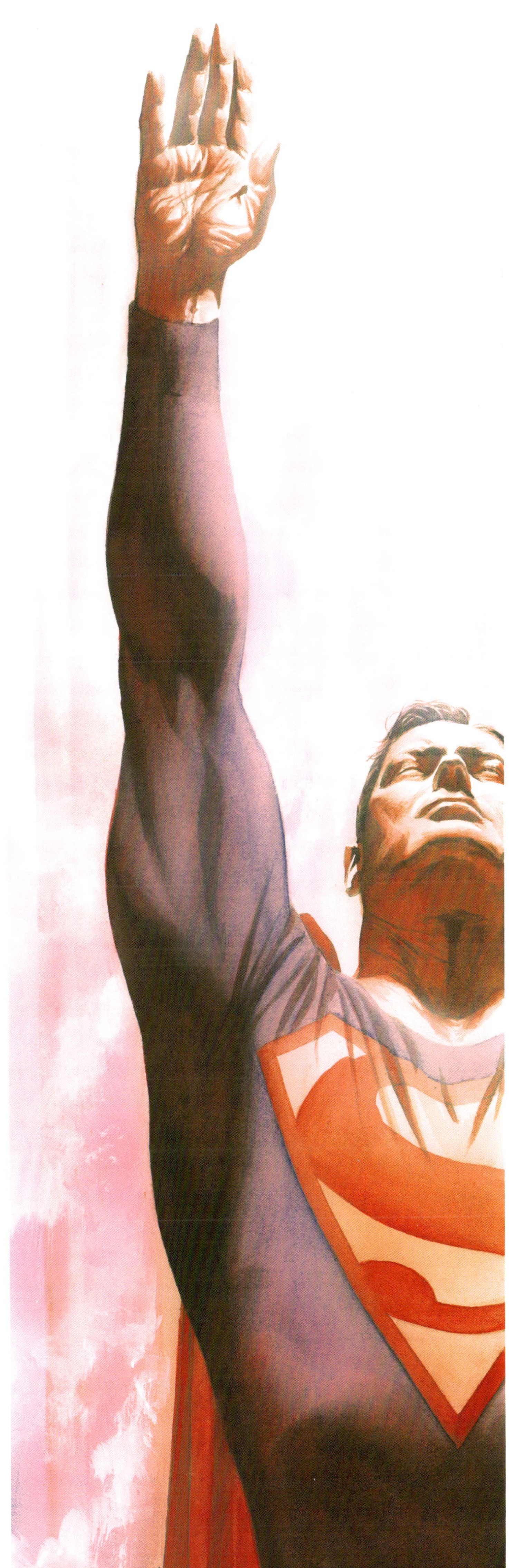

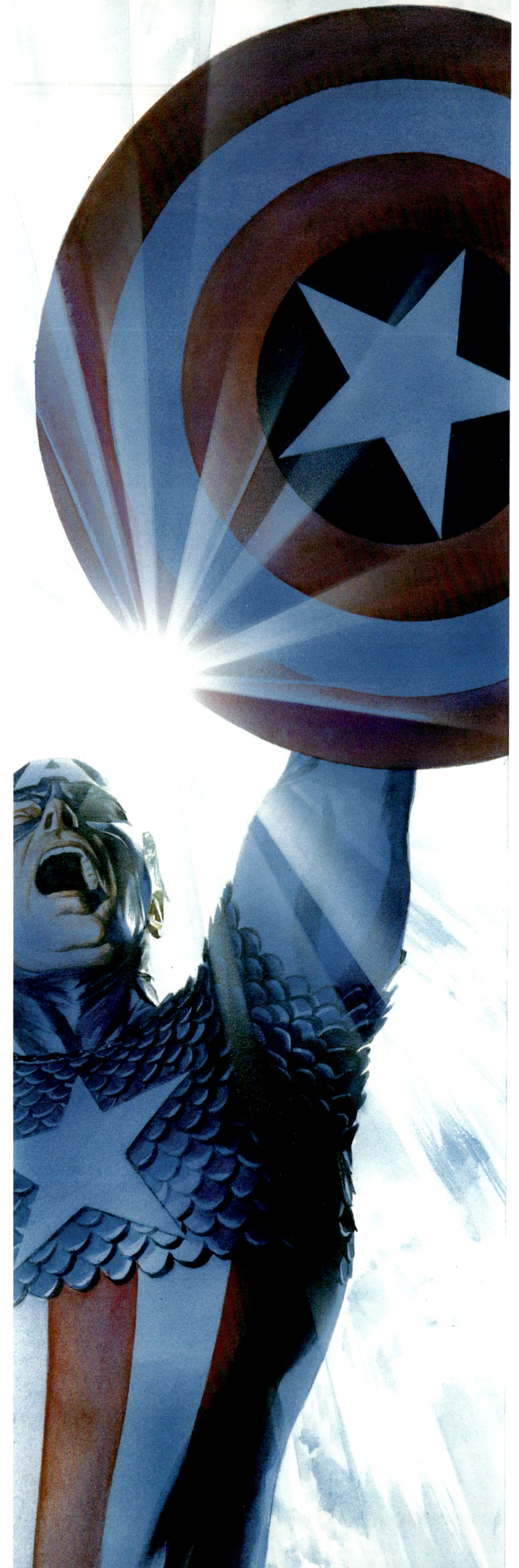

CAPTAIN AMERICA
TRIUMPHANT

ALEX ROSS

Captain America: Triumphant celebrates the invincible Steve Rogers as Captain America.

Armed with his vibranium metal shield and super soldier serum, Rogers becomes the pinnacle of physical perfection and the finest combatant Earth has ever known.

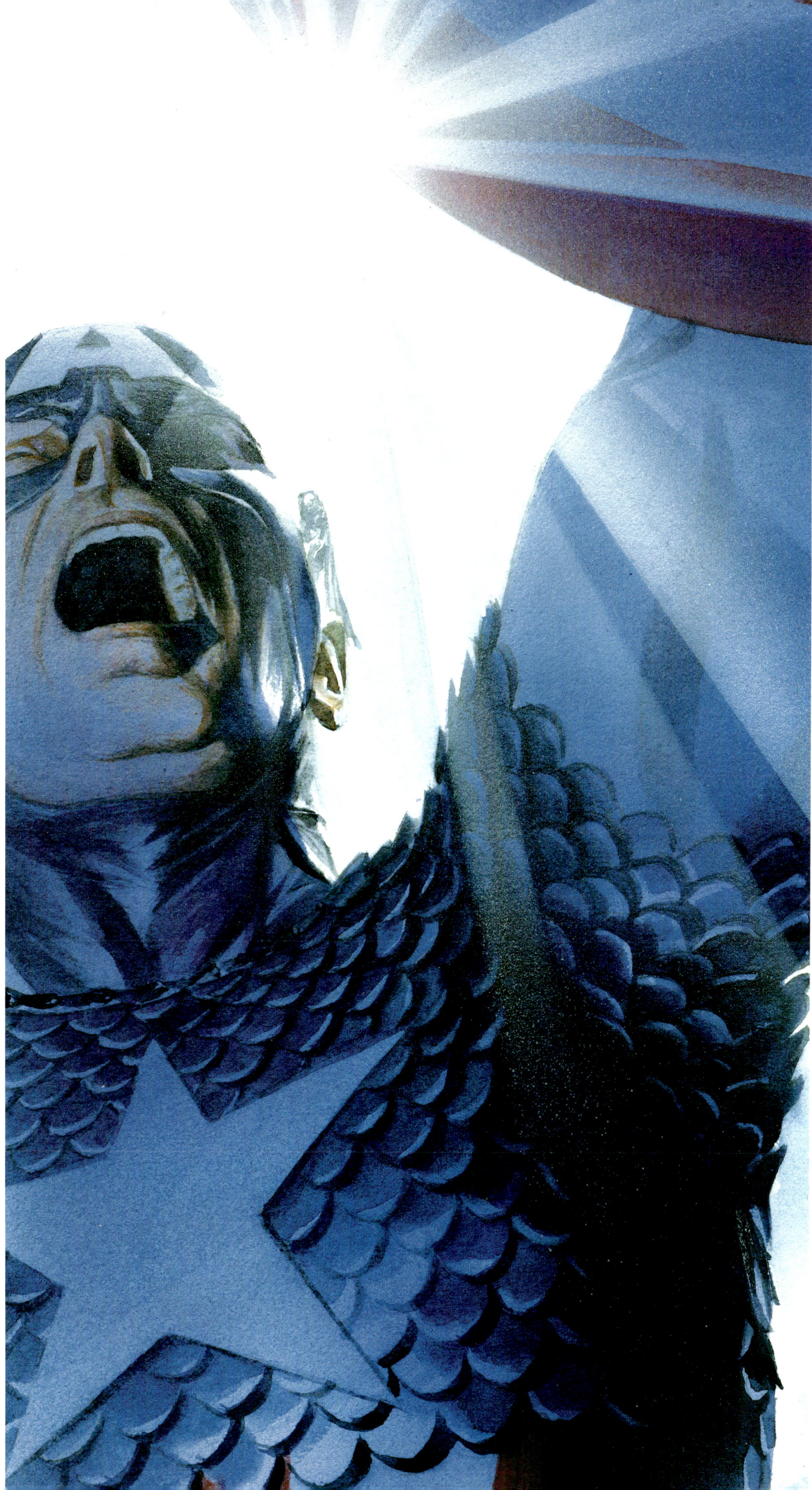

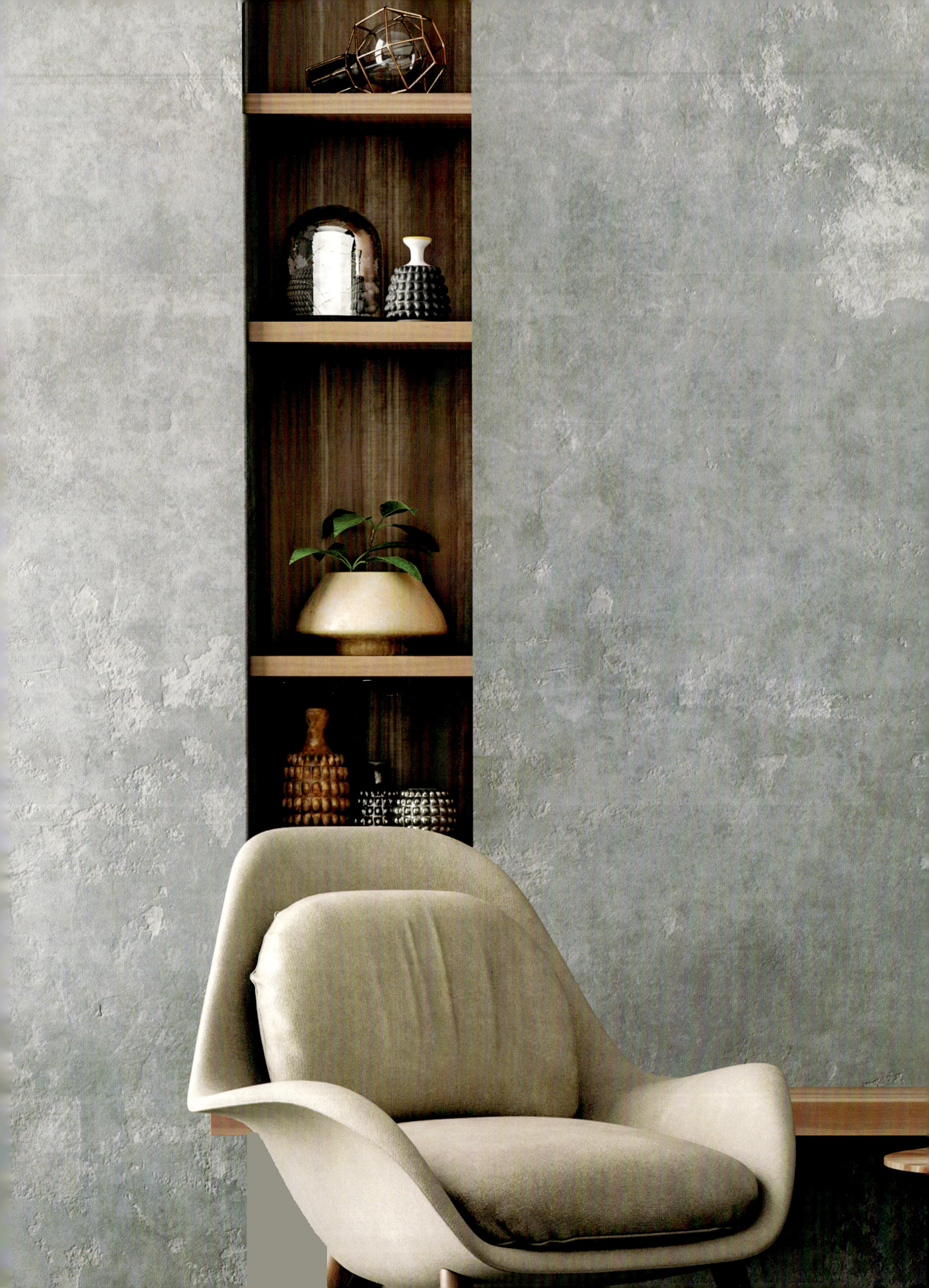

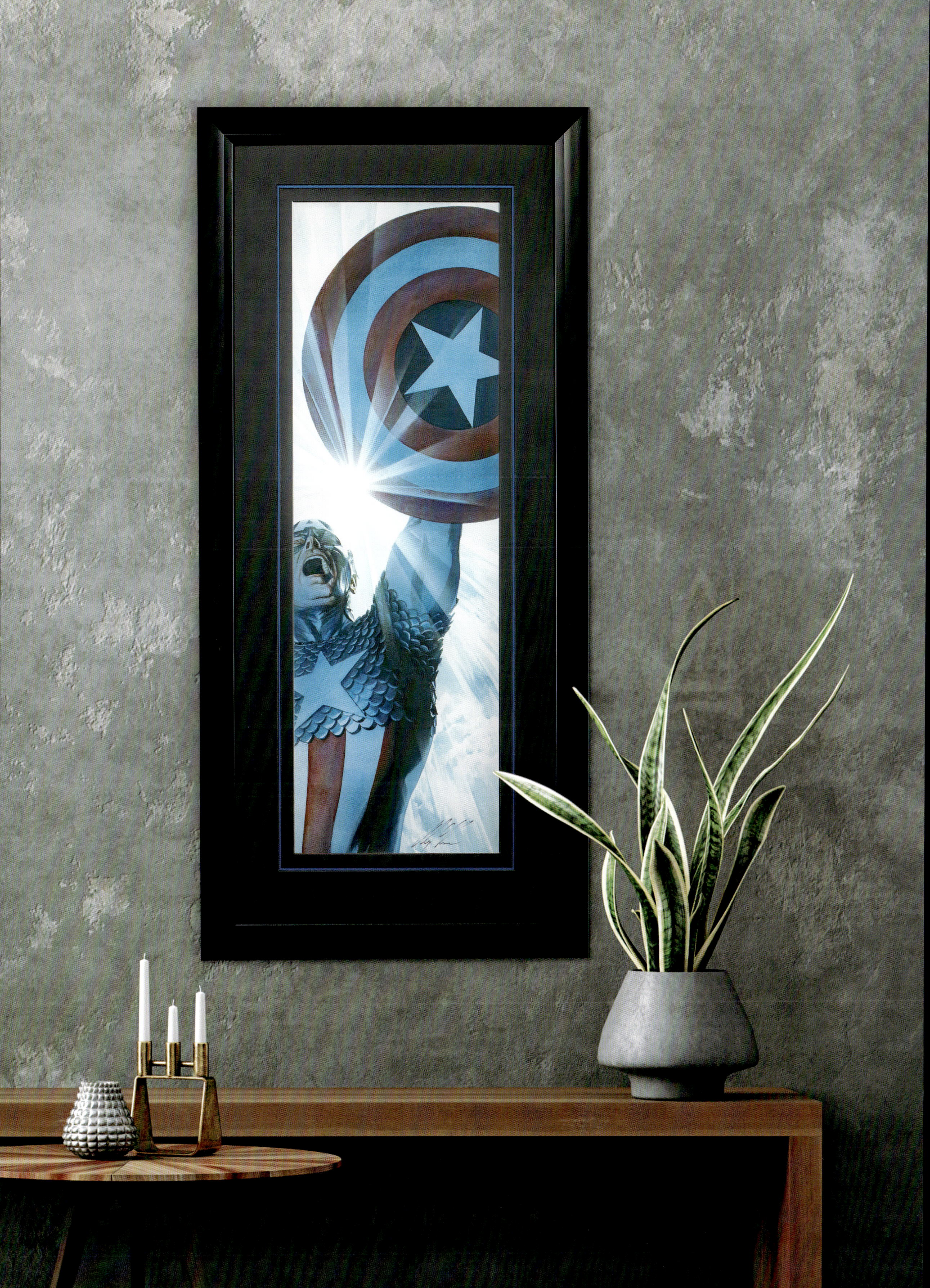

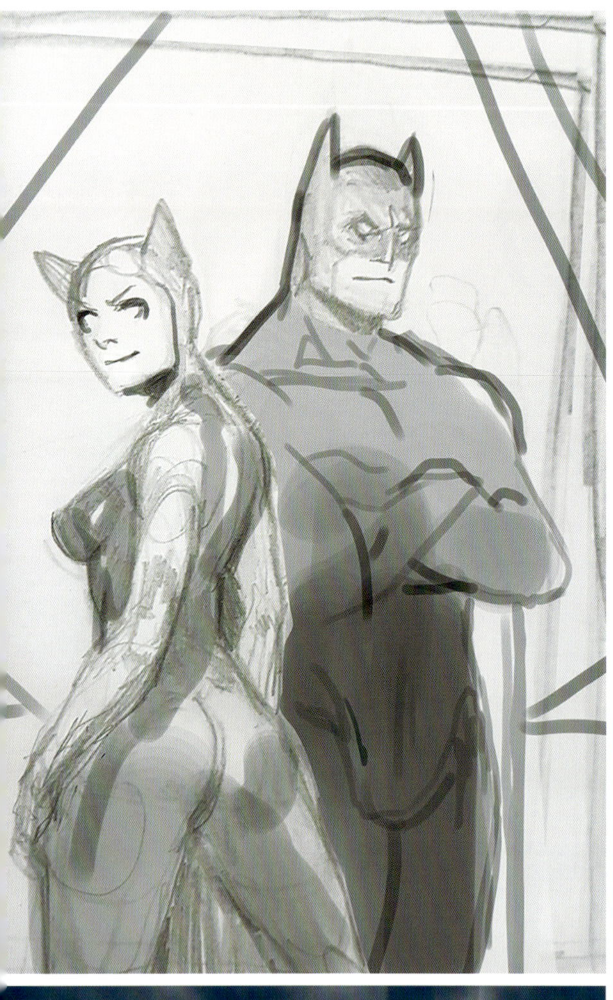

BATMAN & CATWOMAN

ALEX PASCENKO

Intrigue, excitement, animal attraction—the only thing missing from Batman and Catwoman's relationship is trust. Although Bruce and Selina like to keep each other close, standing side by side doesn't always mean they're on the same one.

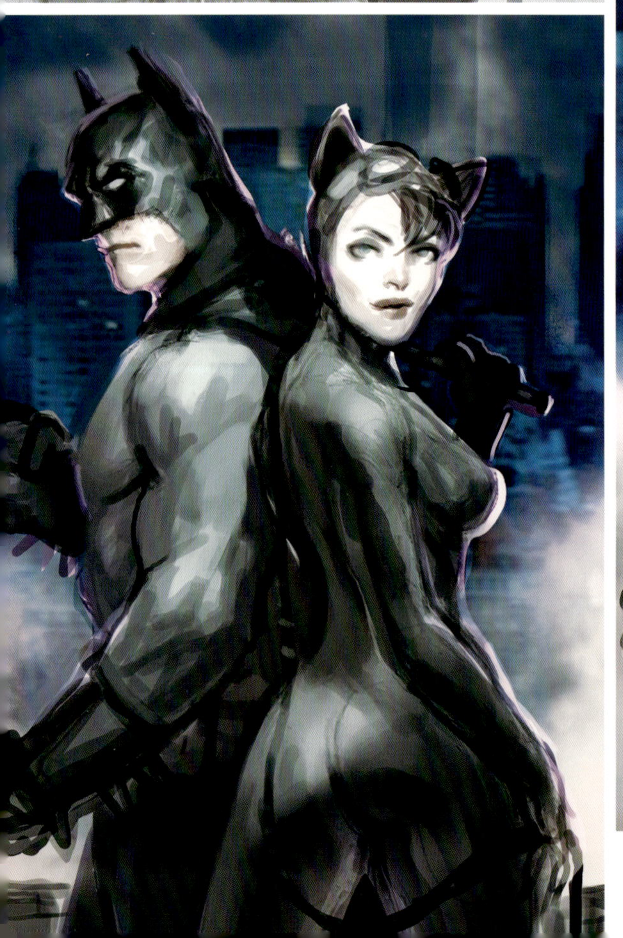

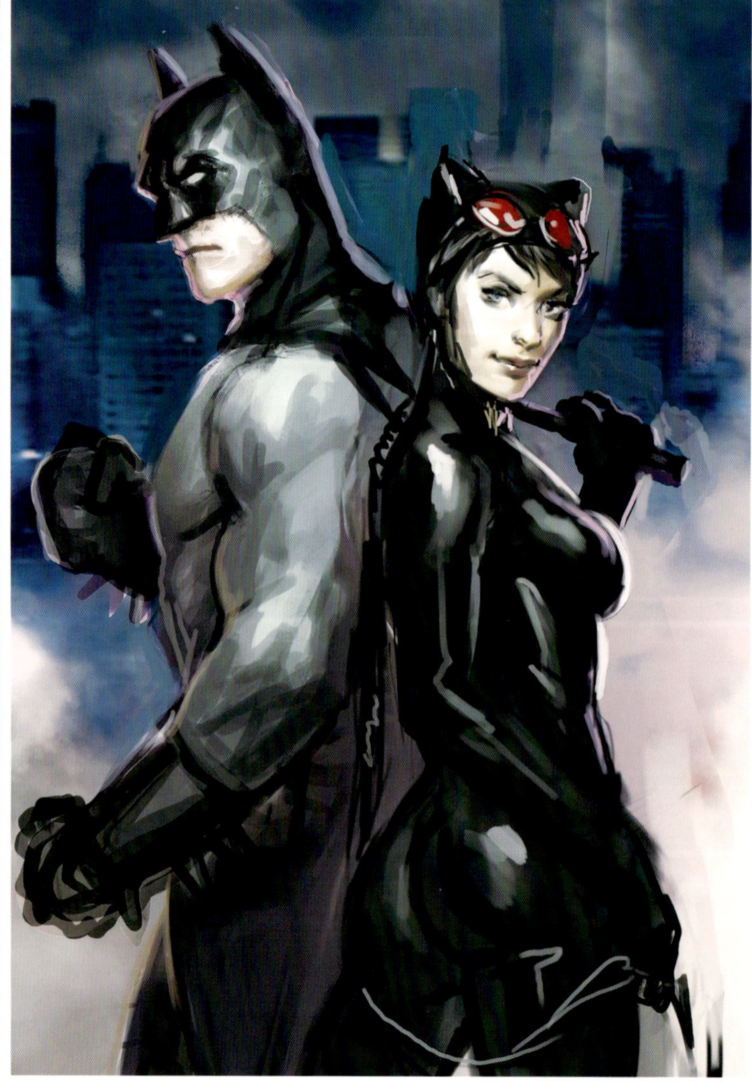

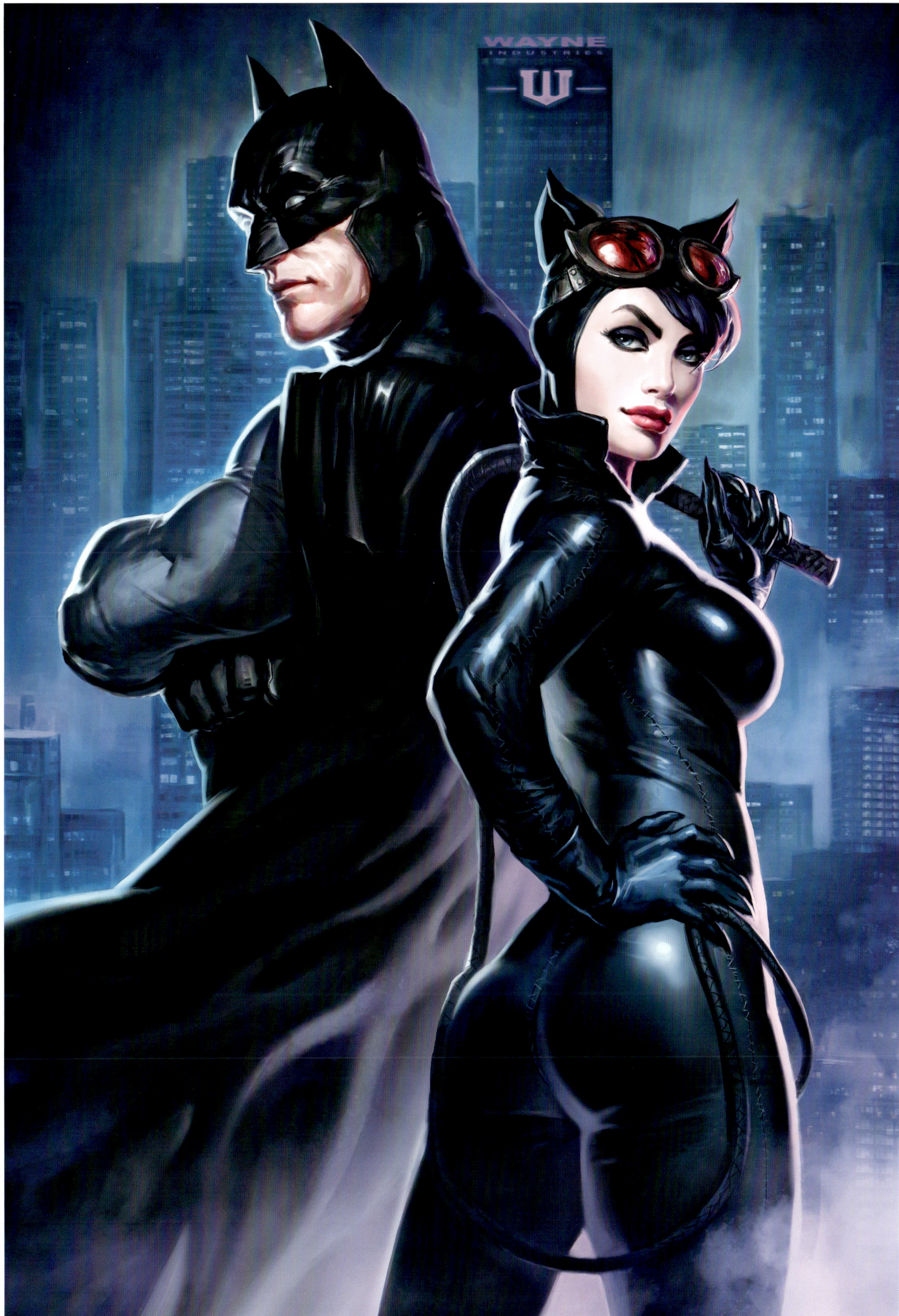
WAYNE
INDUSTRIES

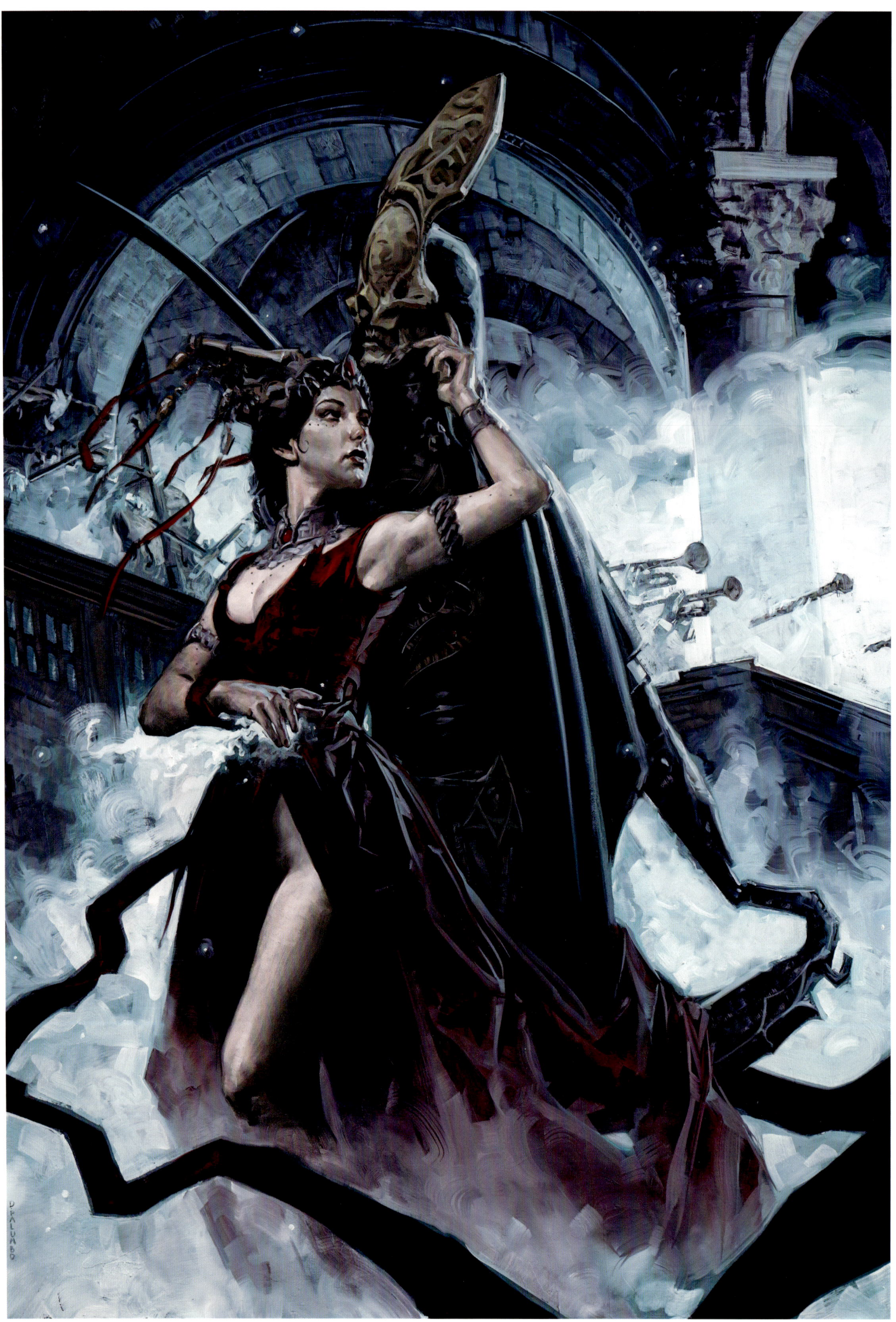

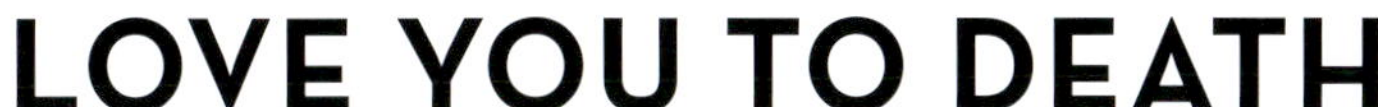

DAVID PALUMBO

When Death fashioned Gethsemoni—his lover, queen, and mother to all in the Underworld—he formed her consciousness from the raw, collective dreaming of the mortal realm. To know her mind is to glimpse the passions, fears, anger, and desires of all humanity. The Queen of the Dead is Death's muse. His conscience. Where he has only sympathy, she gives him empathy.

Gethsemoni is a mercurial beast in the body of a goddess. She loves him with a savage abandon that he himself can never experience, except through her eyes.

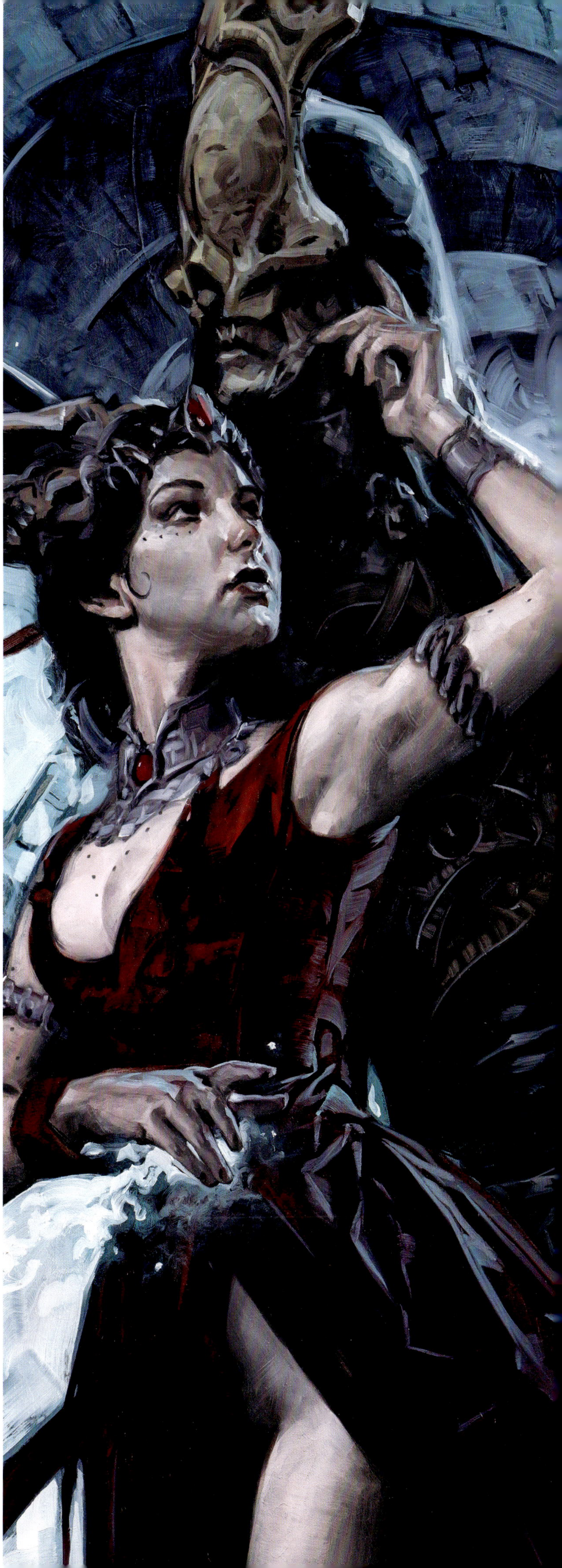

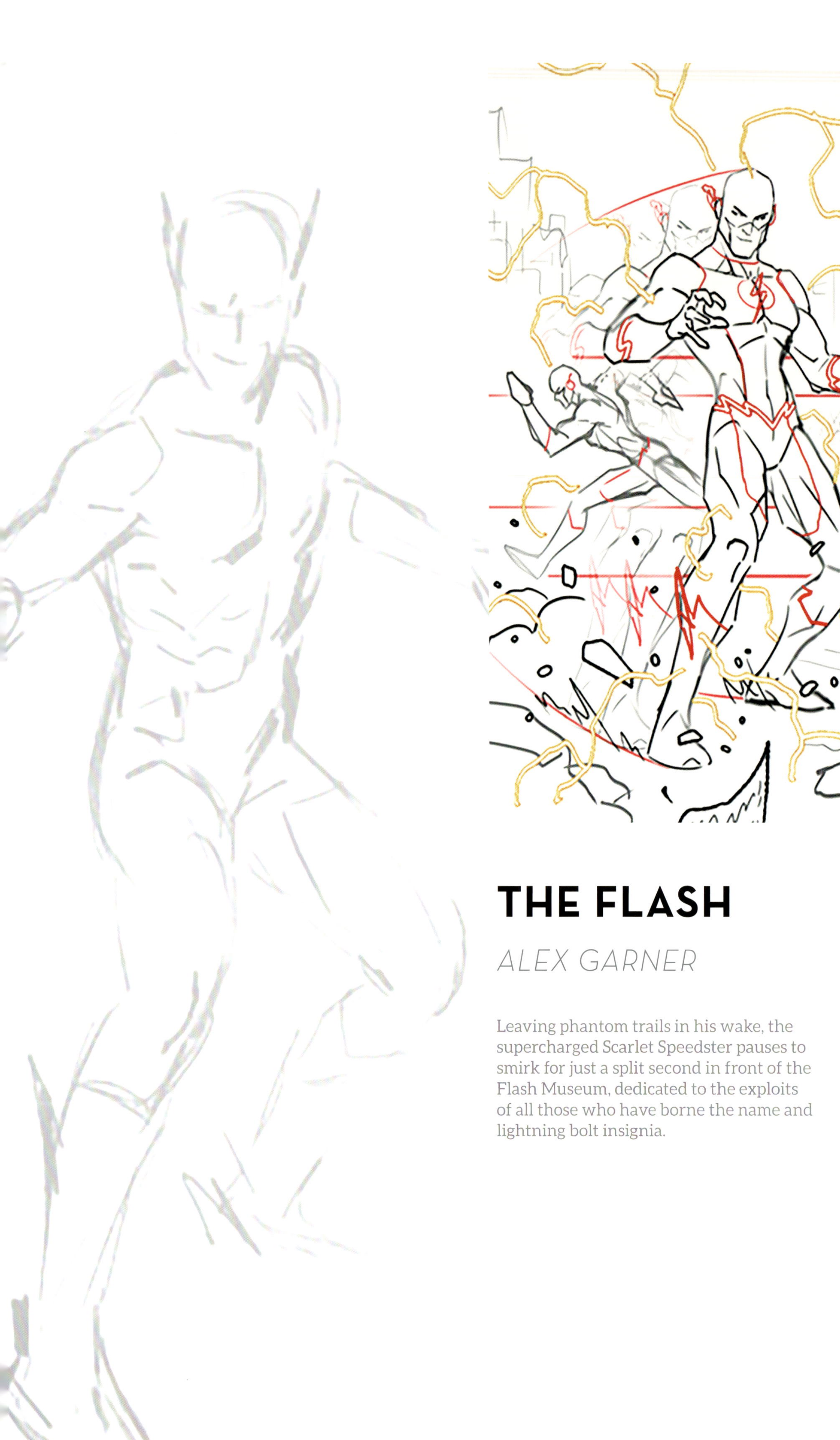

THE FLASH

ALEX GARNER

Leaving phantom trails in his wake, the supercharged Scarlet Speedster pauses to smirk for just a split second in front of the Flash Museum, dedicated to the exploits of all those who have borne the name and lightning bolt insignia.

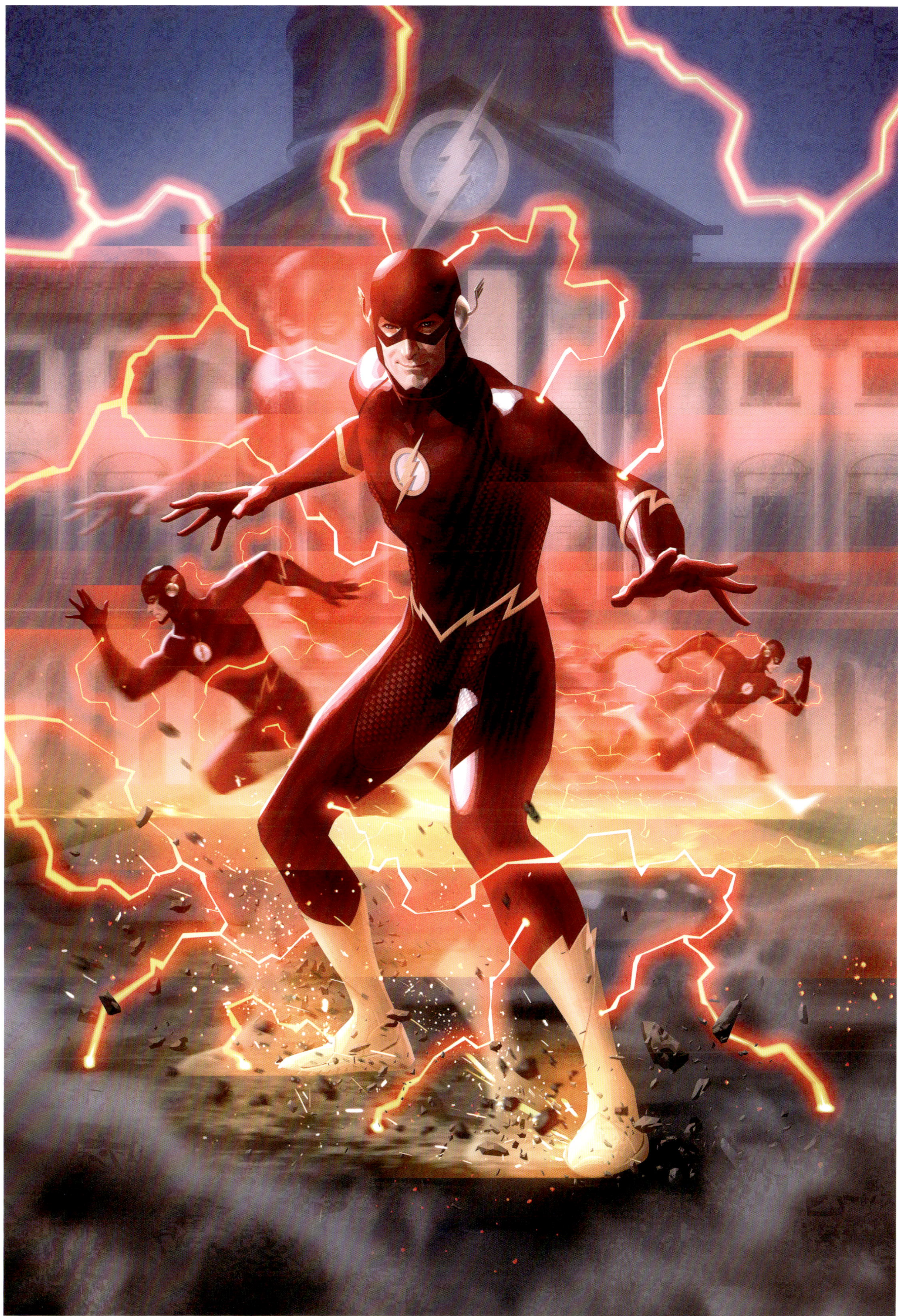

ALEX GARNER

"After all these years Sideshow is still my favorite client because while they give me a ton of creative freedom, they also give the best feedback on what I can do to make a piece even better. It's a real pleasure to work with the team there."

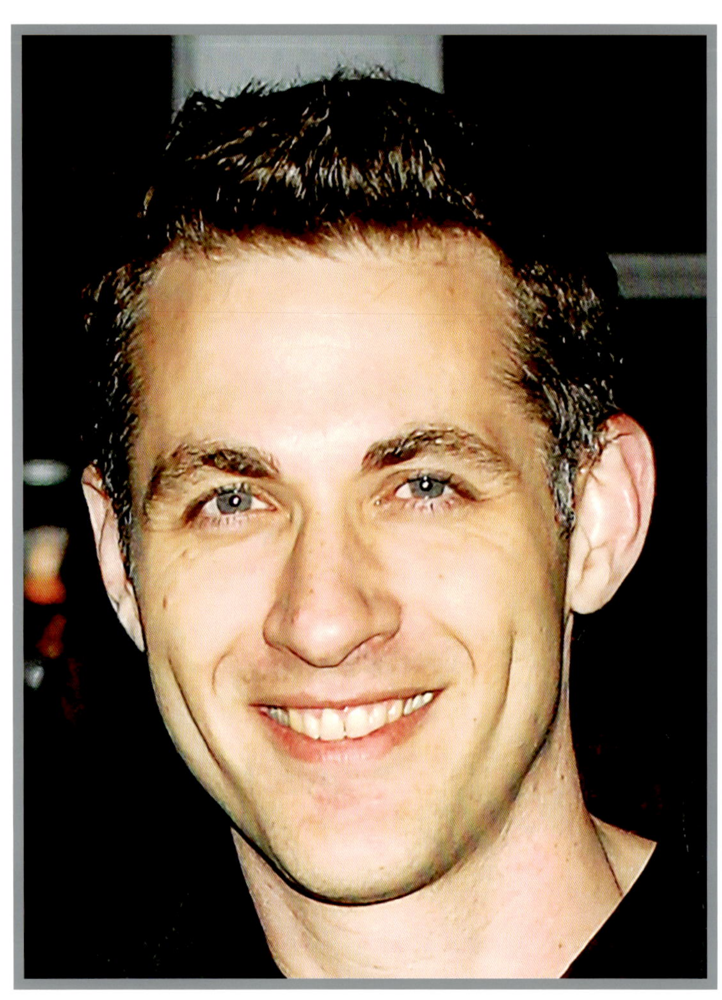

INSPIRATION

After working on popular comic book series (*Gen 13, Danger Girl, WildC.A.T.S*) for Jim Lee's WildStorm Productions, Alex Garner co-founded IDW Publishing in 1999 and was creative director through 2005. Since then, Alex has worked as a freelance Illustrator and concept artist for clientele such as Marvel Comics, DC Comics, Sideshow Collectibles, Blizzard Entertainment, Riot Games, Hasbro, and Warner Home Video.

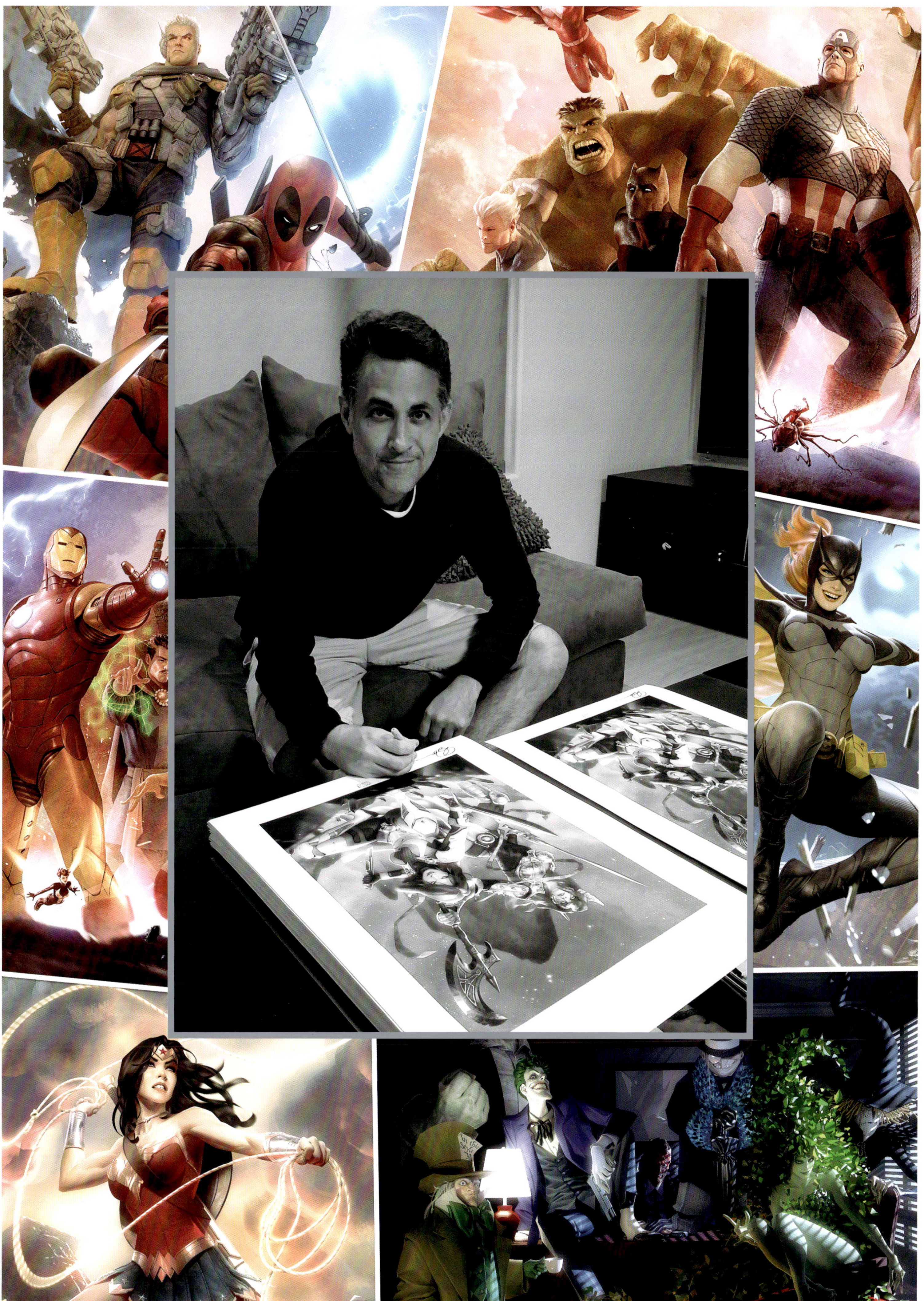

Deadpool & Cable, Avengers Team Cap, Batgirl, Batman: The Long Halloween, Wonder Woman, Avengers Team Iron Man, Alex Garner signing.

BATMAN VS. BANE

DAVE WILKINS

Fueled by the acid-green Venom super-steroid coursing through his veins, the monstrous crime lord Bane aims to "break the Bat" in an epic clash of titans. Meanwhile, Batman is all that stands between Gotham City and Bane's destruction.

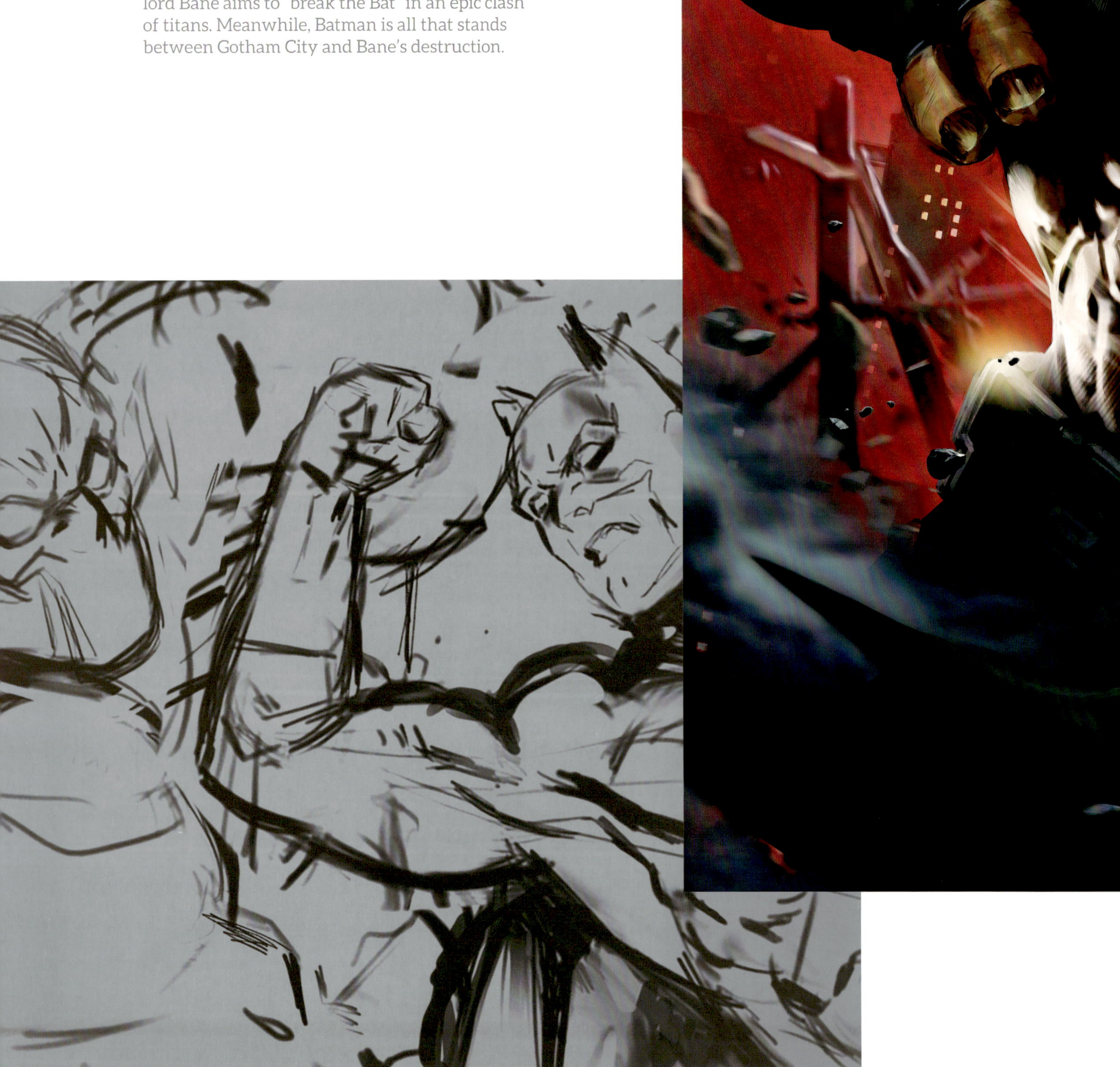

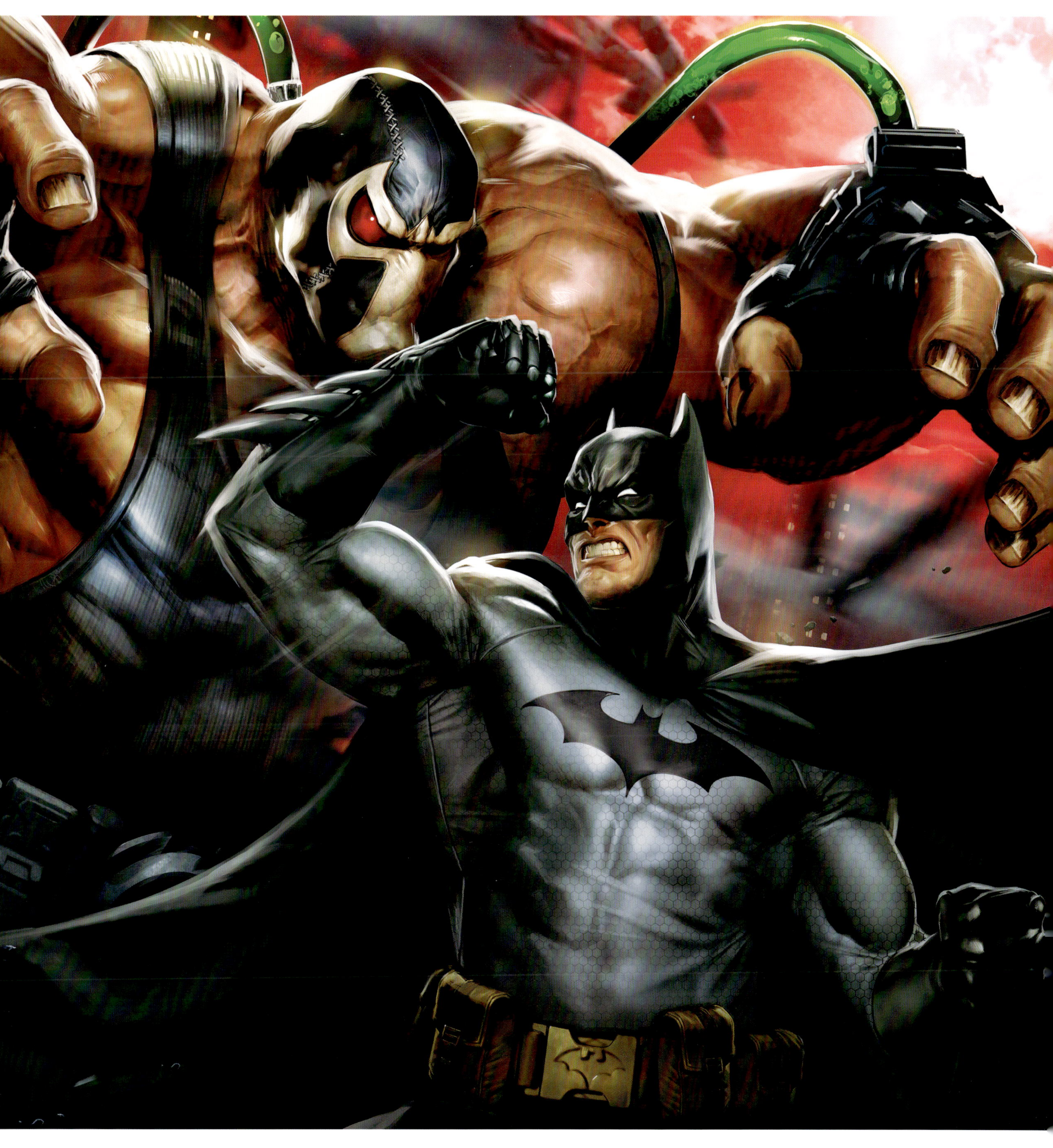

THE THIN DEAD LINE

STEPHEN SCHIRLE

In the mortal world, eons creep on. In the Land of the Dead, Death steadily builds his rebellion against the oppressive celestial kingdoms of Heaven and Hell. While Death's Court of the Dead administers his secret battle plan, it is the soldiers of the Underworld who will one day fight the war.

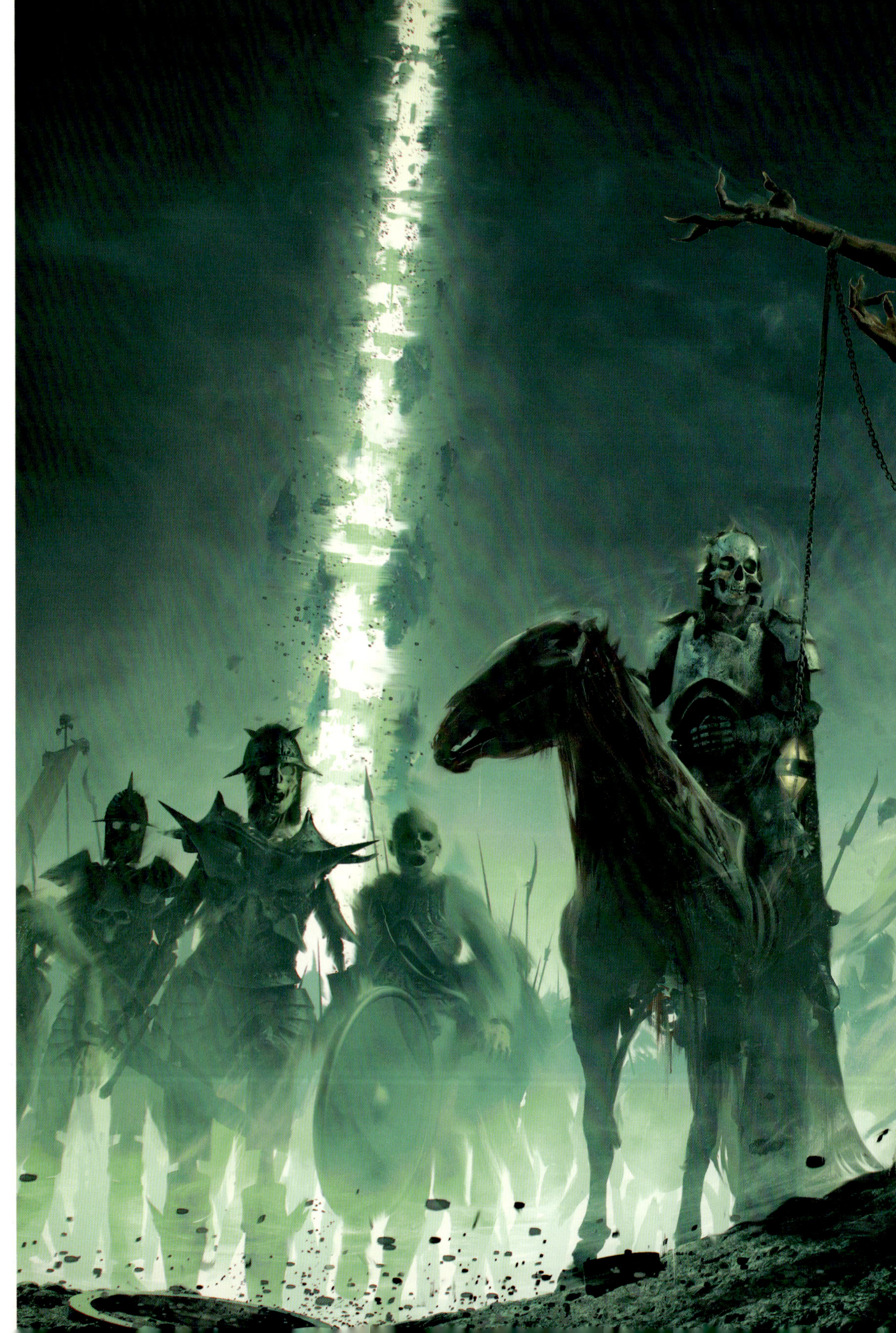

Thin in numbers now—but continuously growing—Death's army marshals behind the heroes of the Underworld: Reaper General Demithyle, Champion of Bone Mortighull, and legendary Valkyrie Kier. They prepare for the day when they will take the fight to the doorstep of their oppressors . . . and the Underworld will rise, conquer, and rule.

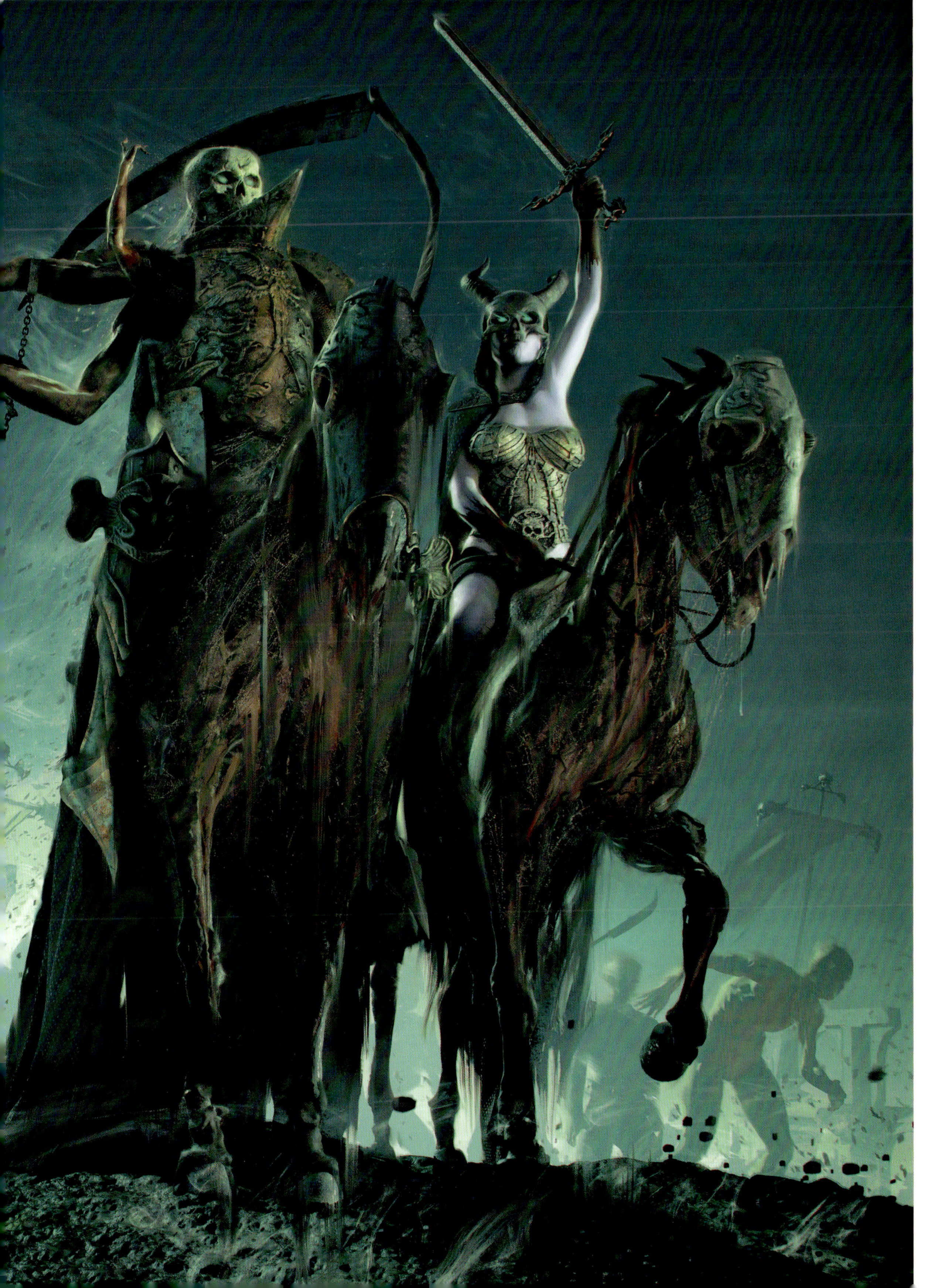

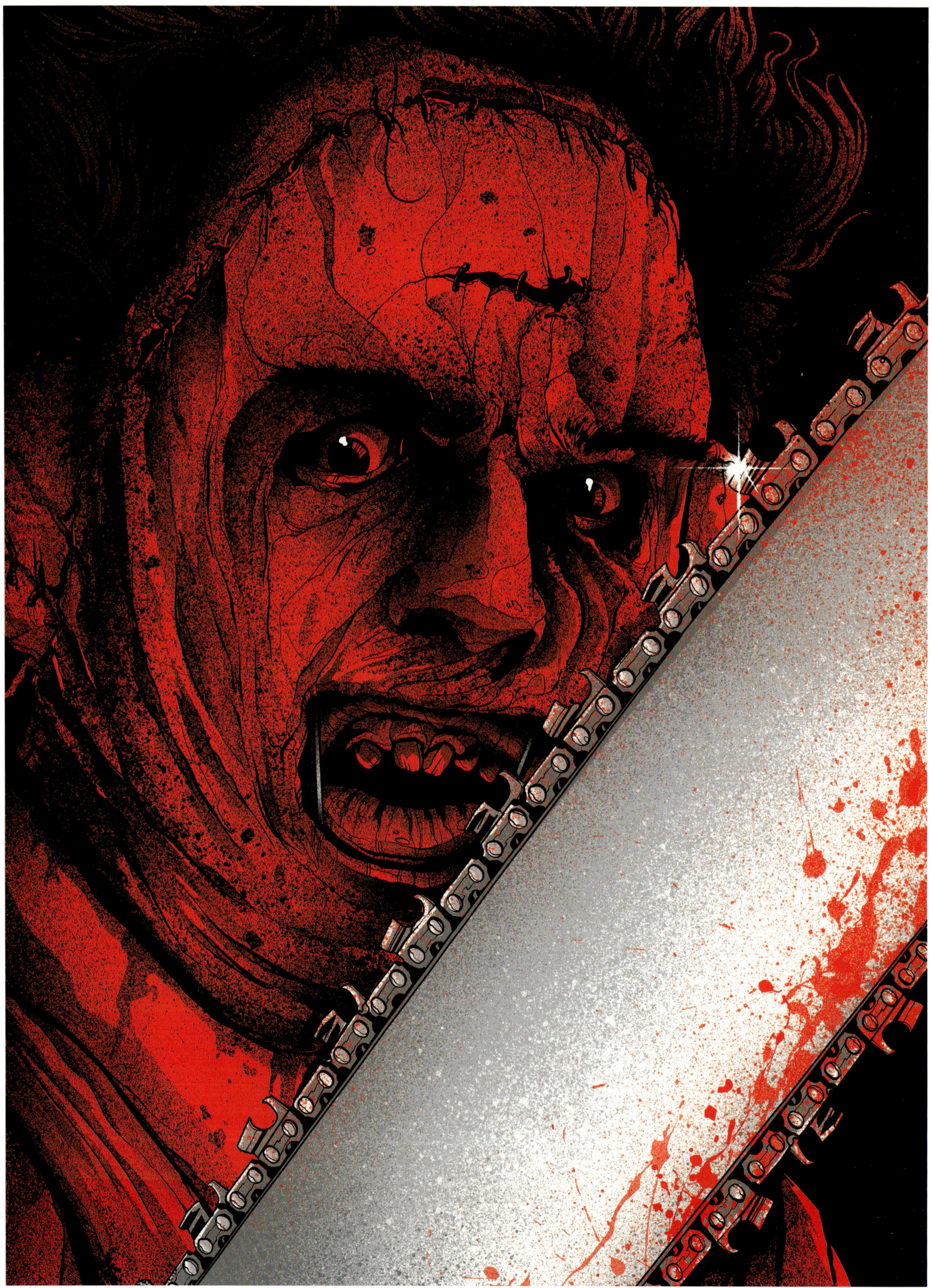

LEATHERFACE

MATT RYAN TOBIN

The infamous 1974 cult classic *The Texas Chainsaw Massacre* shocked audiences upon its initial release, as the controversial film—based on a true story—redefined cinematic horror.

The officially licensed *Leatherface* art print joins Sideshow's classic movie slasher series by poster artist Matt Ryan Tobin. Featuring the film's killer brandishing his bloody chainsaw, this four-color print with metallic highlights is a killer tribute for horror aficionados.

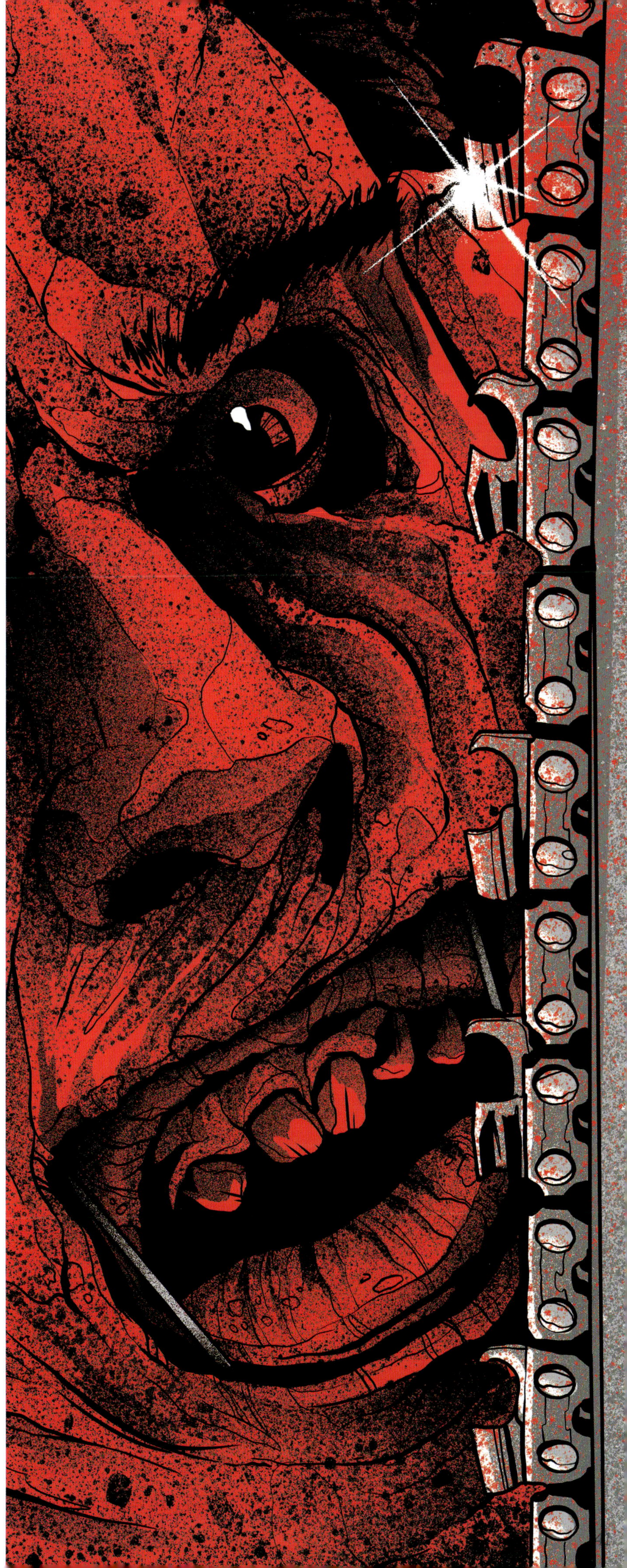

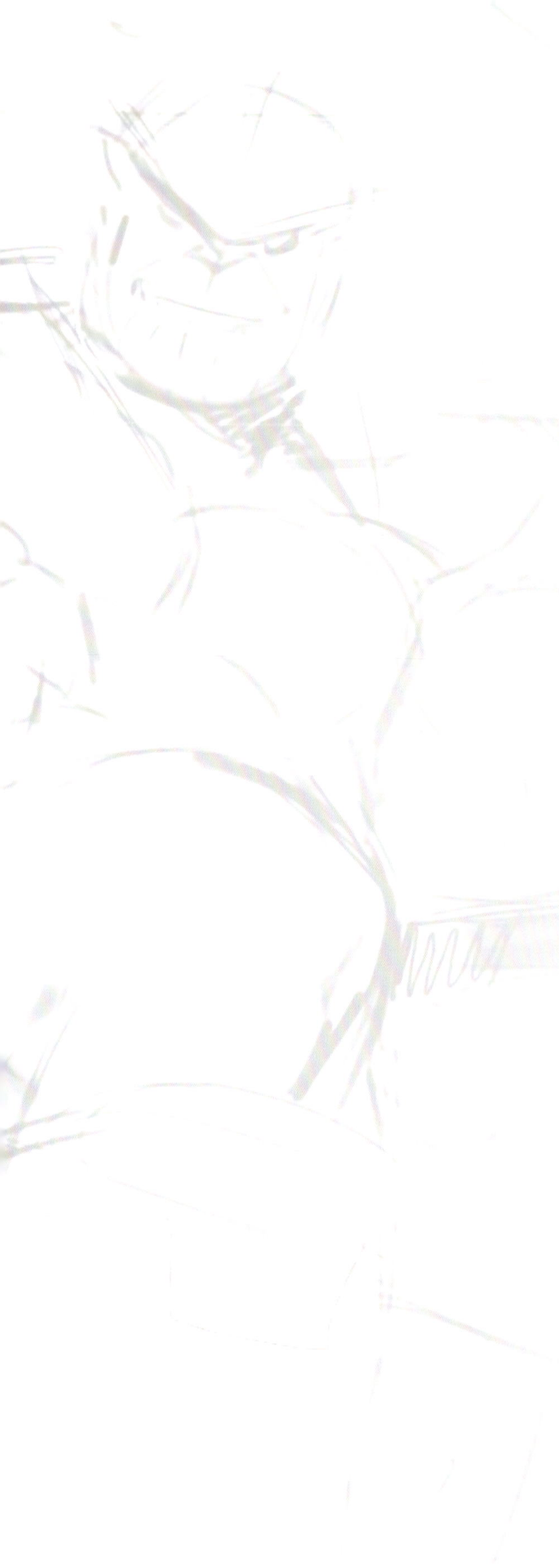

THANOS ON THRONE

DOO-CHUN

Witness the destruction of an entire world as a planet explodes behind the near-omnipotent Thanos. With his glaring red eyes and stoic portrait, the Mad Titan looks out over the starways, wielding the power of the Infinity Stones at his fingertips.

This crumbling world is a warning to all who may oppose him—the entire universe will fall to its knees before the might of Thanos.

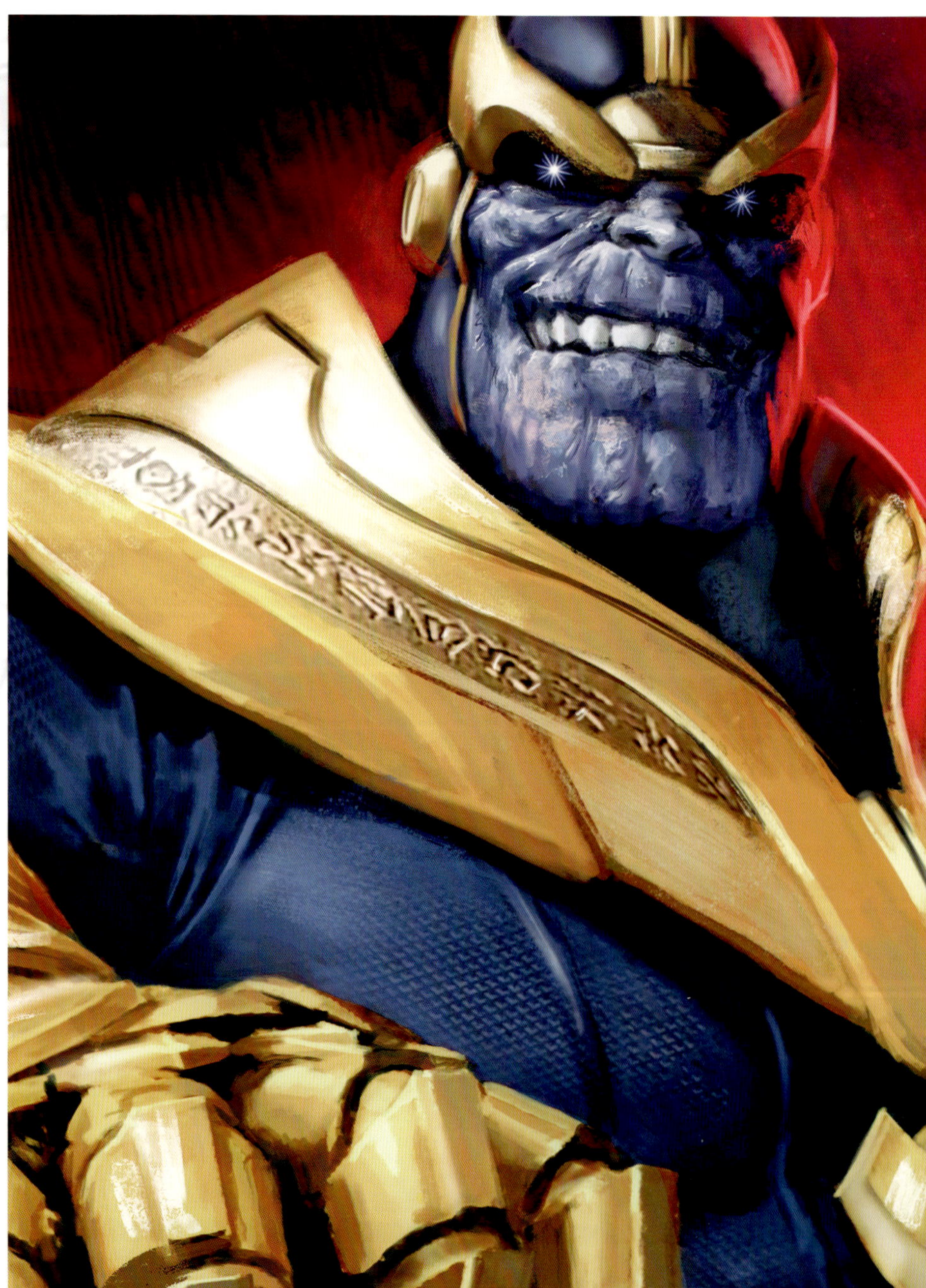

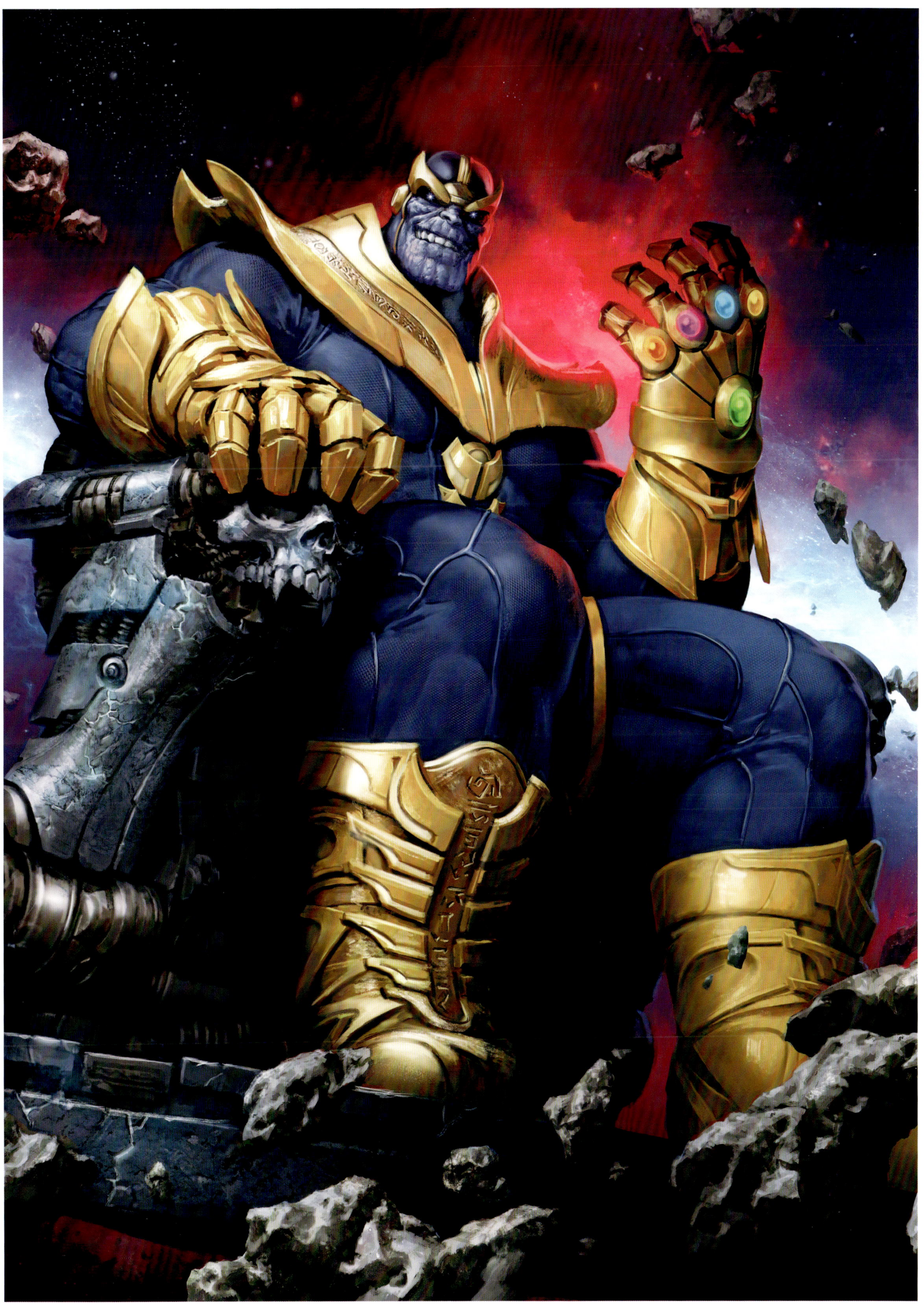

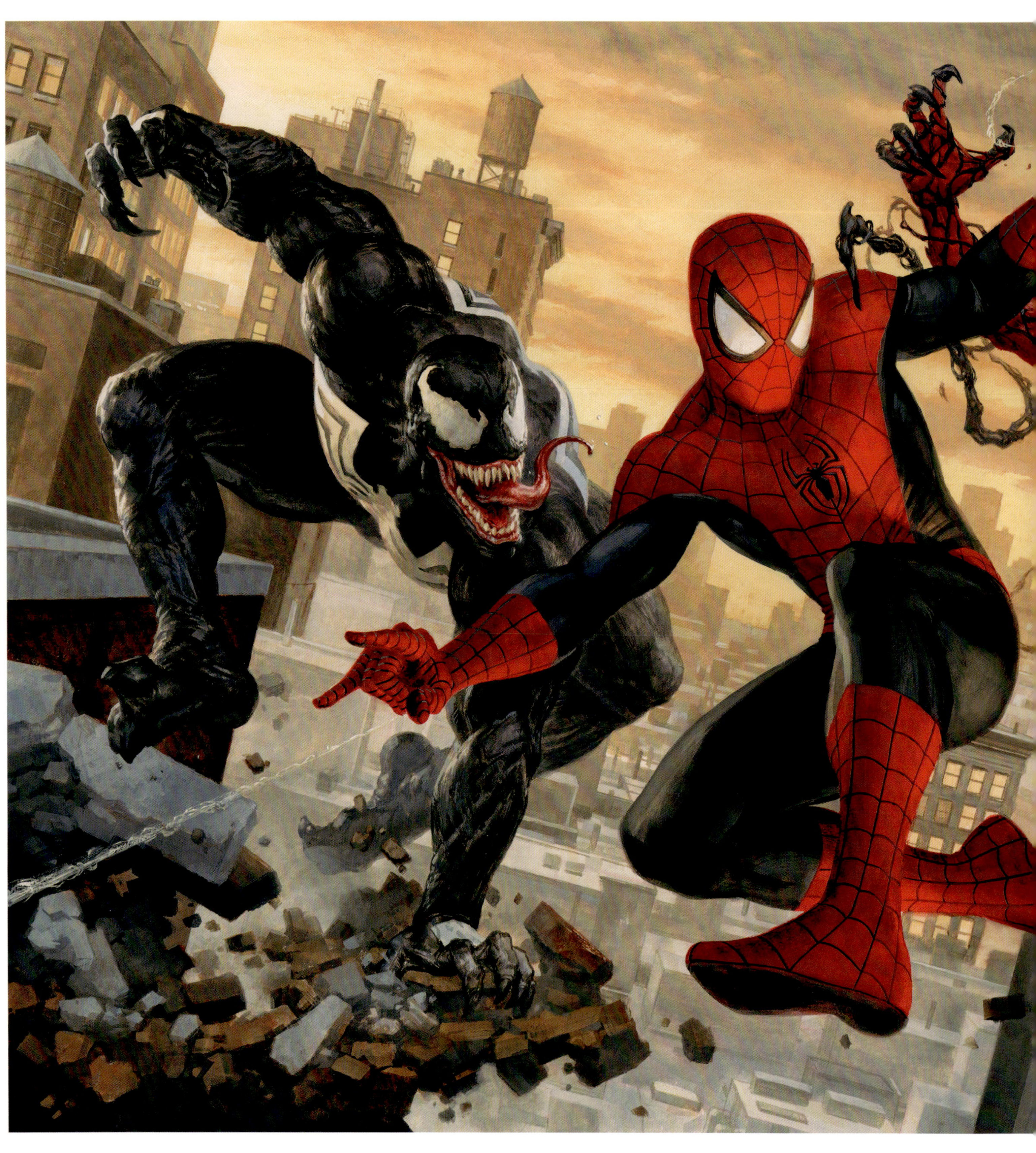

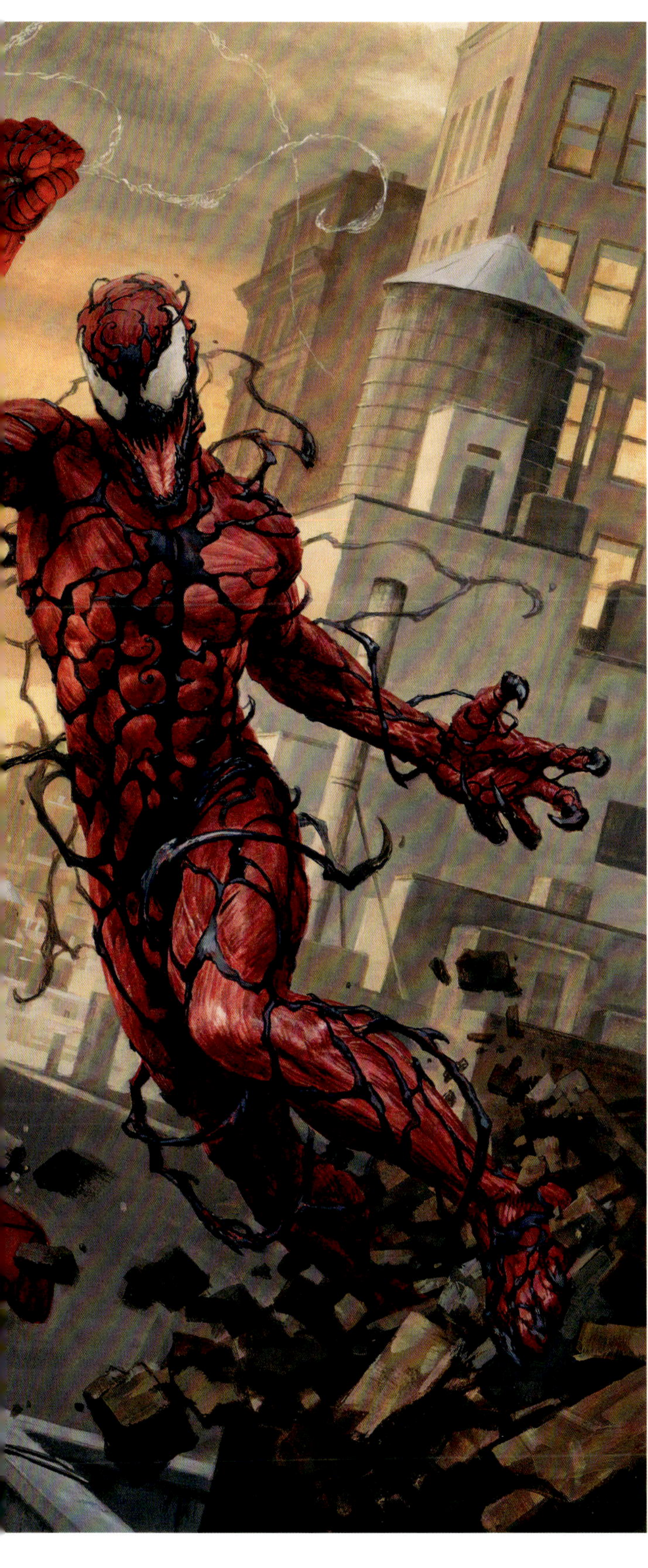

SPIDER-MAN VS. VENOM & CARNAGE

PAOLO RIVERA

Spider-Man's neighborhood isn't so friendly when he's confronted by two of his deadliest foes, Venom and Carnage. Swinging high above the streets of New York City, the amazing webhead is targeted by the deadly alien symbiotes who can't agree on anything—except their hatred of Spider-Man.

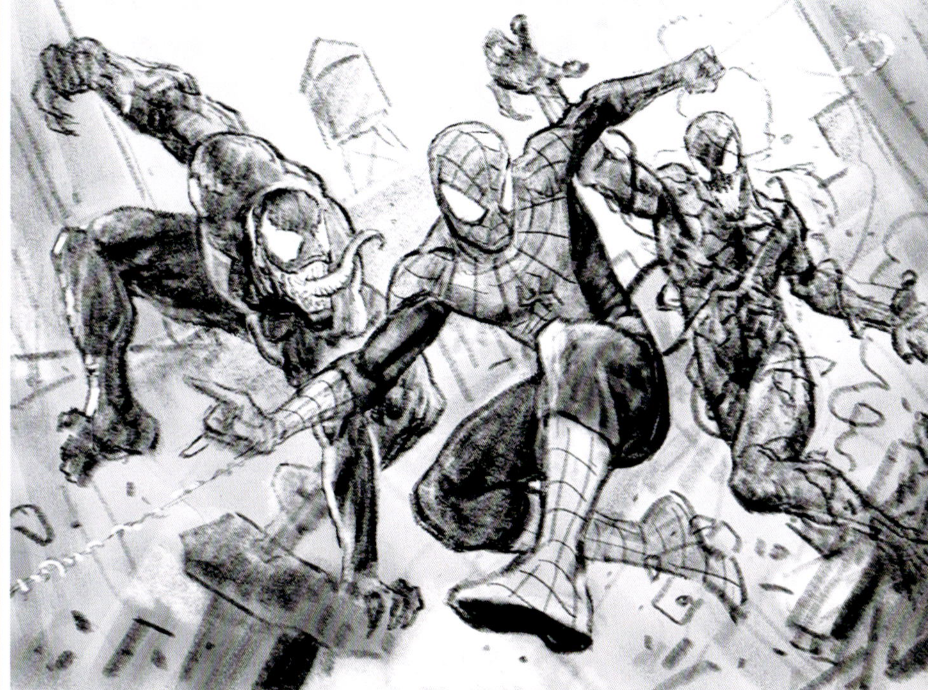

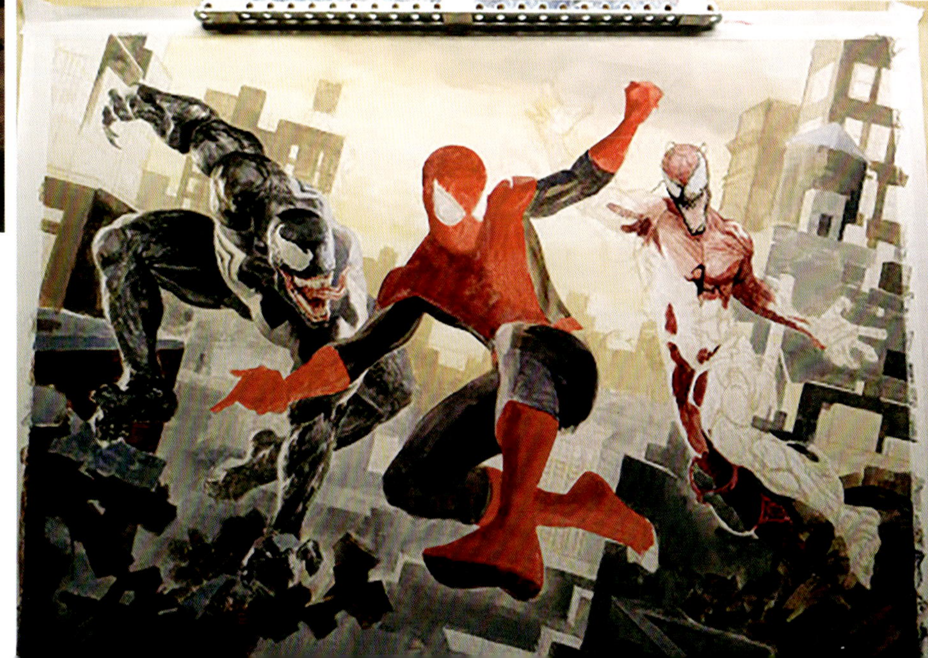

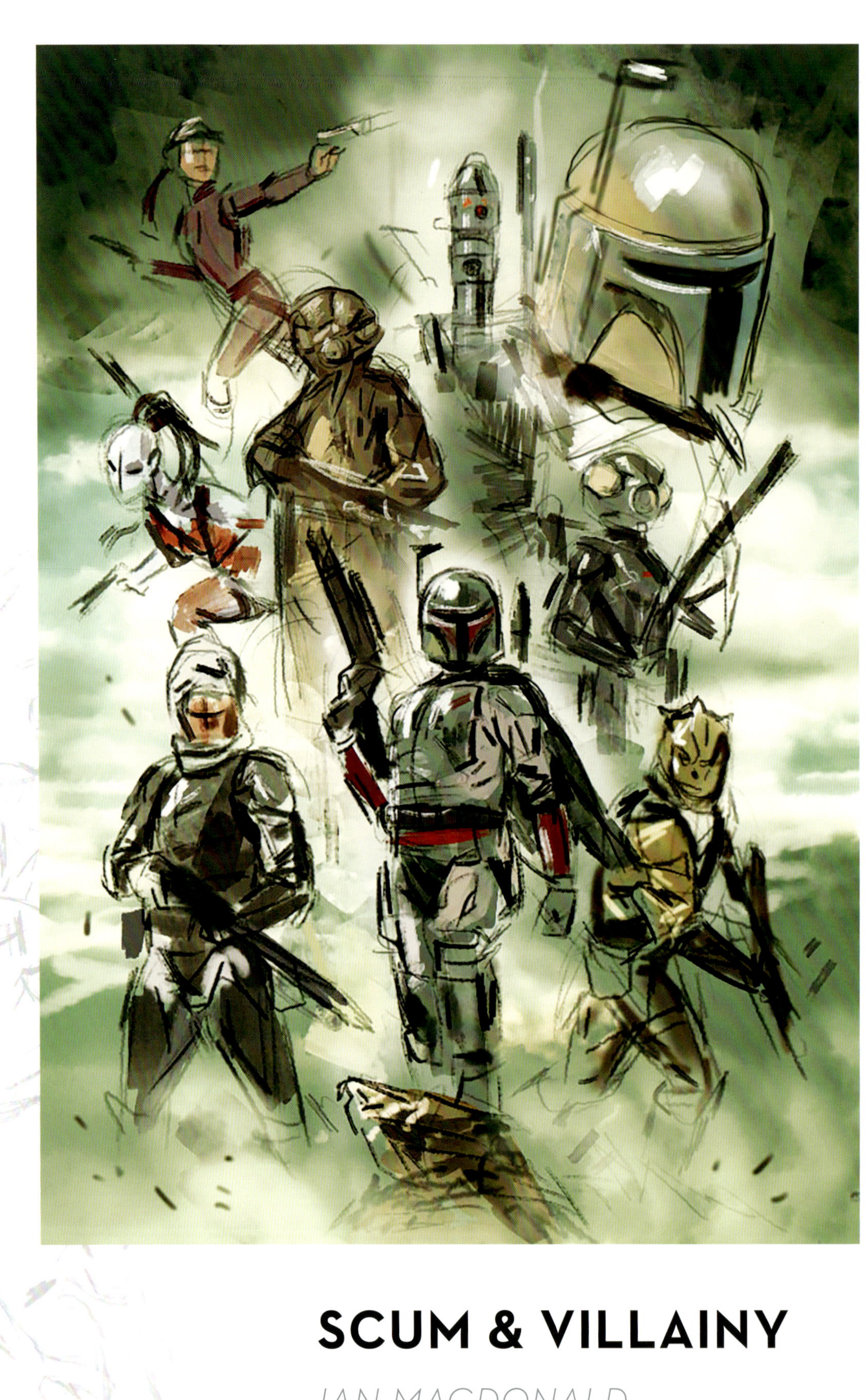

SCUM & VILLAINY

IAN MACDONALD

Bounty hunters have long played an integral role in the *Star Wars* galaxy and become fan-favorite icons in their own right.

A magnificent tribute to the galaxy's most notorious mercenaries, this dynamic artwork is a who's who of scum and villainy. The famed Mandalorian bounty hunter Boba Fett stands front and center, flanked by the galaxy's most infamous soldiers of fortune.

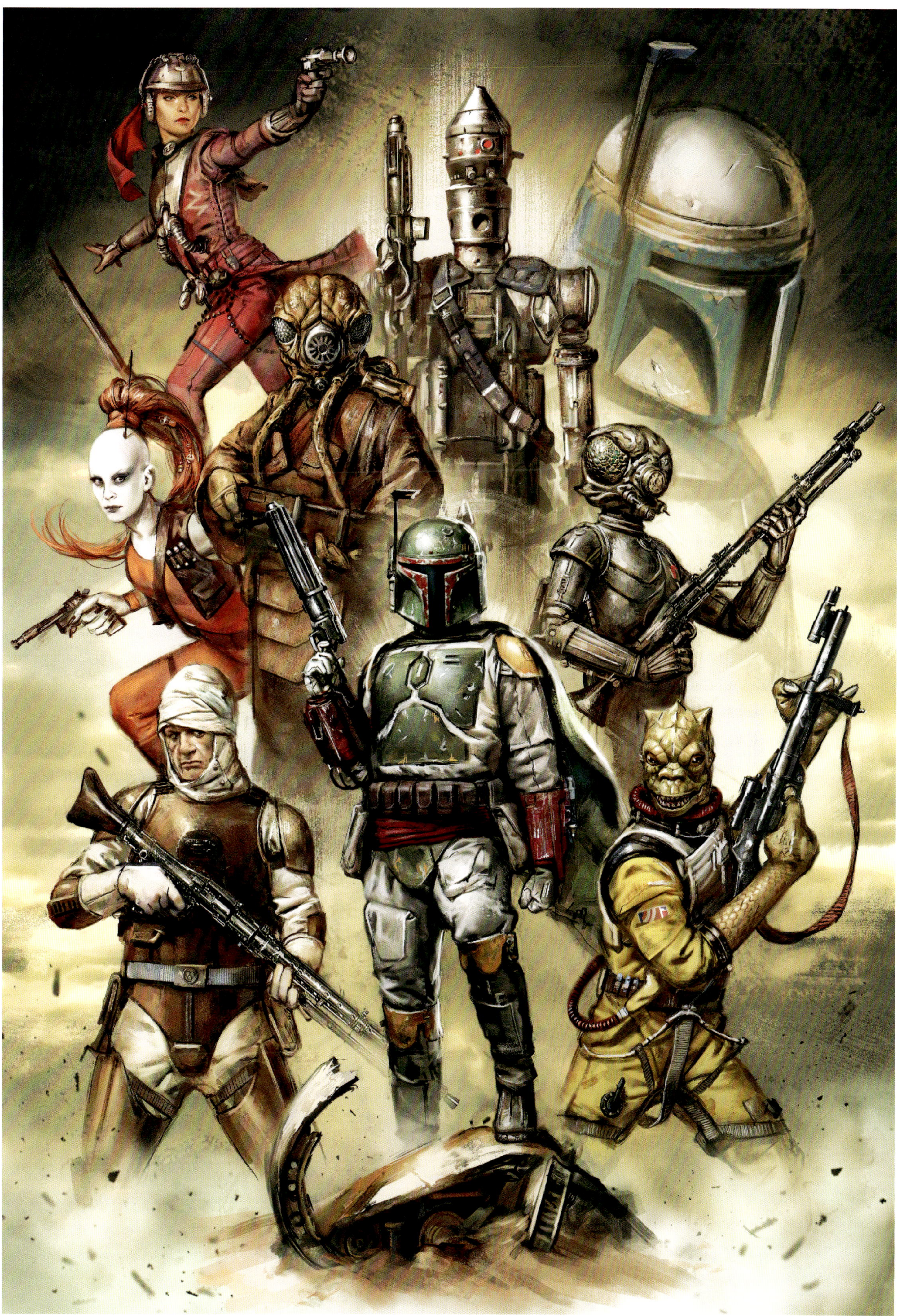

IRON MAN THE GOLDEN AVENGER

ALEX ROSS

Thomas Edison famously said, "Genius is one percent inspiration and ninety-nine percent perspiration." It's a creed that Tony Stark takes to heart as he forges the latest adaptation of his hi-tech armor while surrounded by battle suits from days gone by. Since their original inception, the Stark suits have gone through numerous incarnations, with each new rendition more sophisticated than the last.

It seems unfathomable that more can be added to the intricate machine; however, Stark's brilliant mind continues to perfect his original invention.

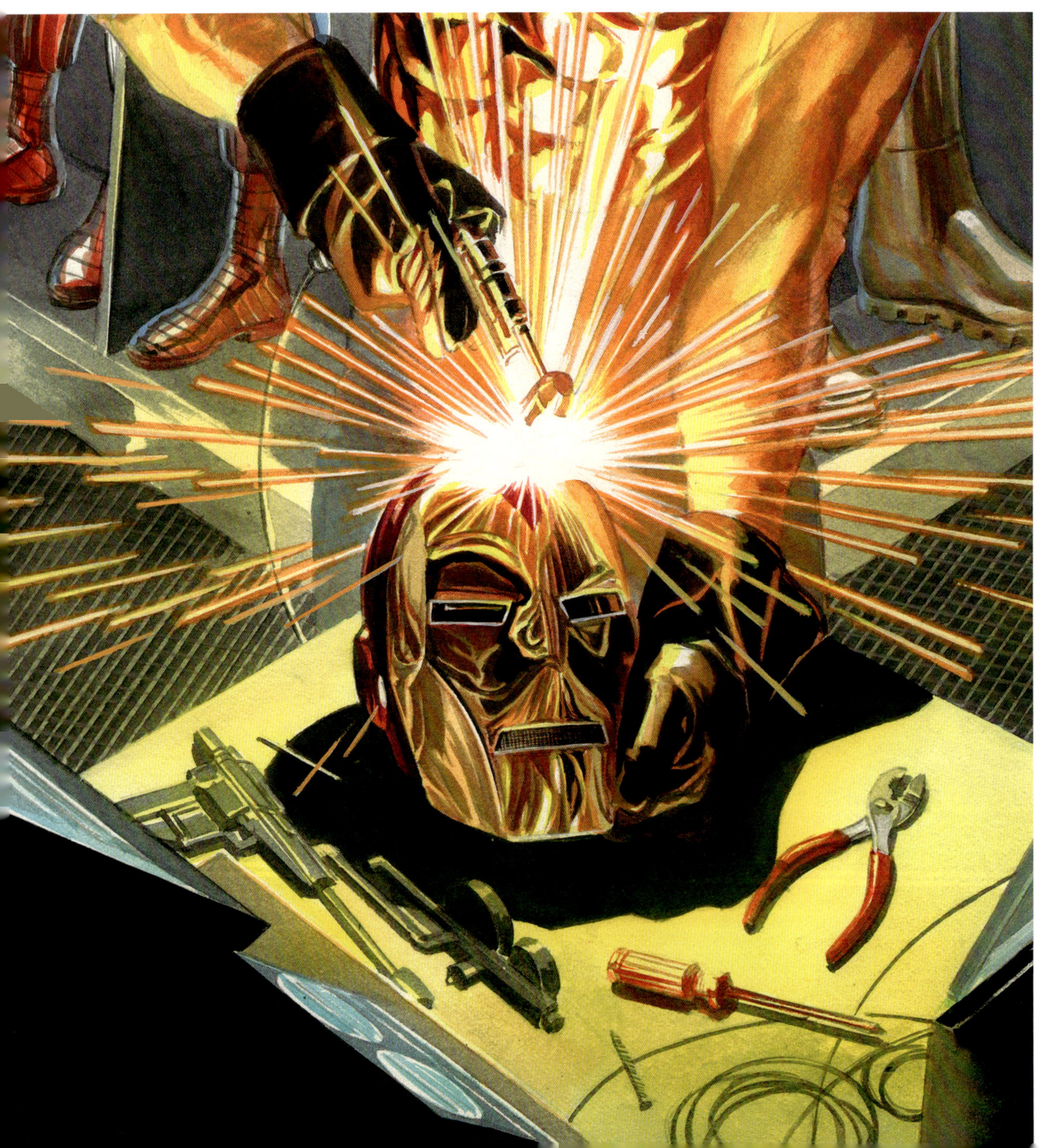

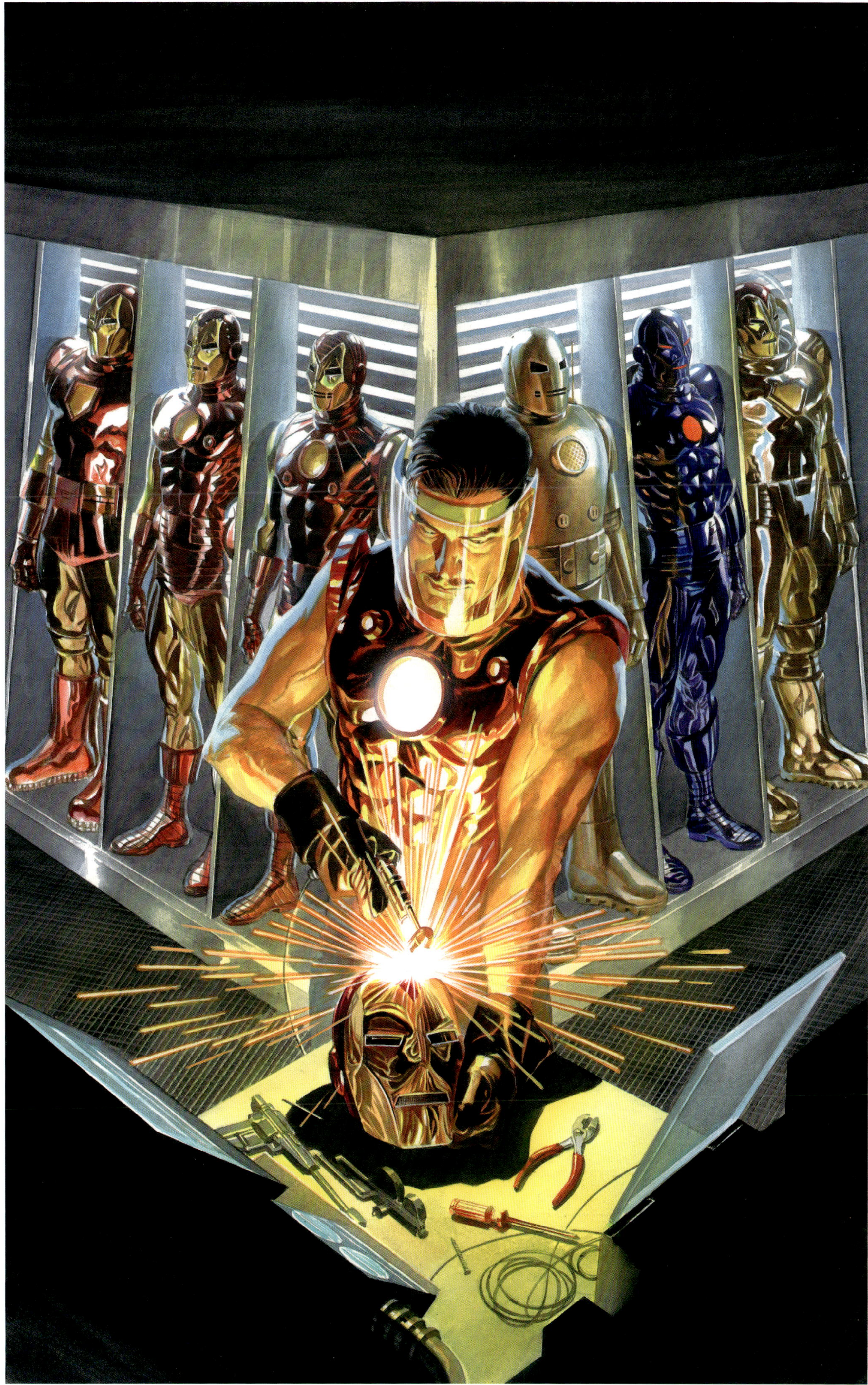

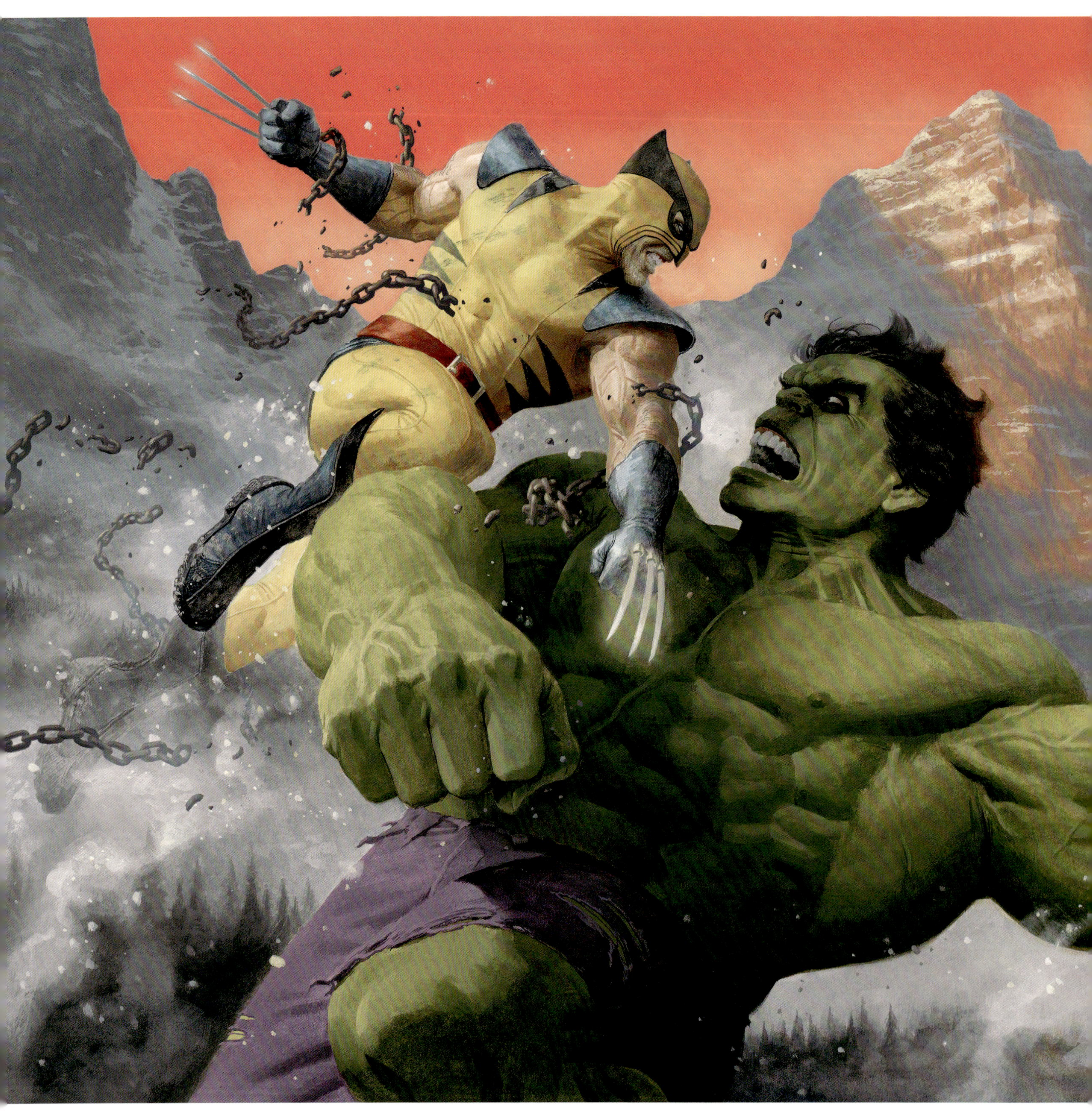

HULK AND WOLVERINE
FIRST APPEARANCE VARIANT

PAOLO RIVERA

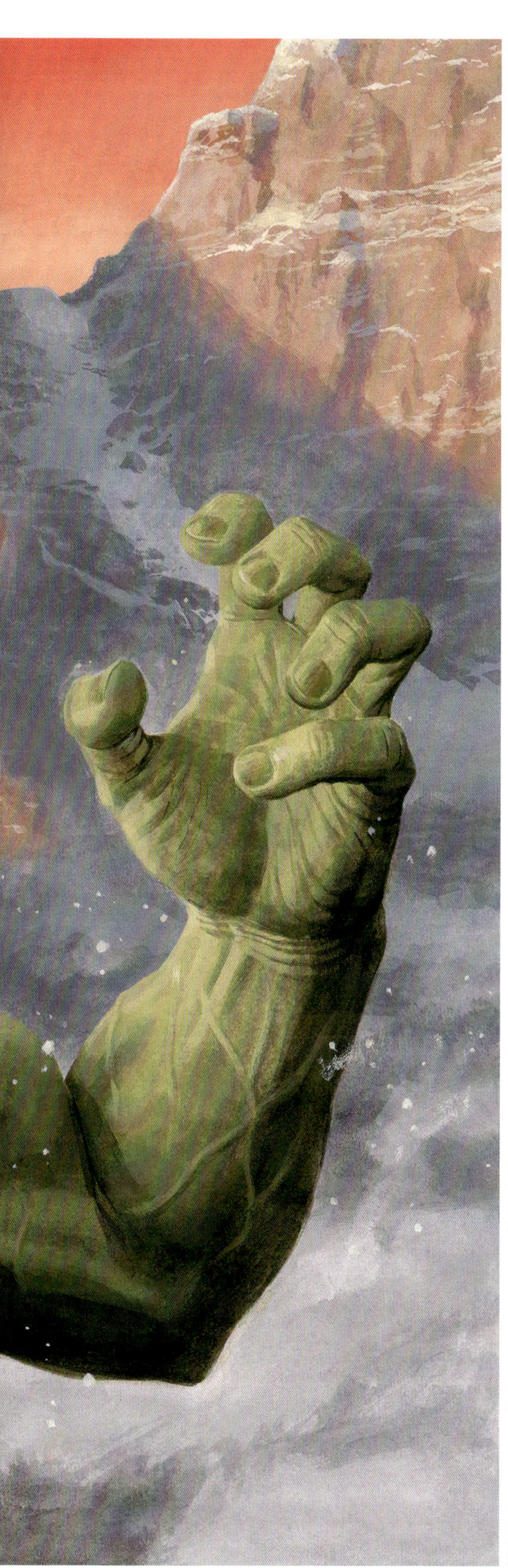

The *Hulk and Wolverine: First Appearance* variant Premium Art Print by Paolo Rivera depicts an epic confrontation between two of Marvel's mightiest heroes, based on the unforgettable introduction of Wolverine.

Inspired by the character's debut on the cover of Marvel Comics' *Incredible Hulk* #181, this fantastic limited edition variant captures a clash of titans. Wolverine is seen in his original costume, with a flurry of exploding chains and razor-sharp claws set against a dramatic red sky, as Weapon X attacks the jade giant.

The Marvel universe would never again be the same.

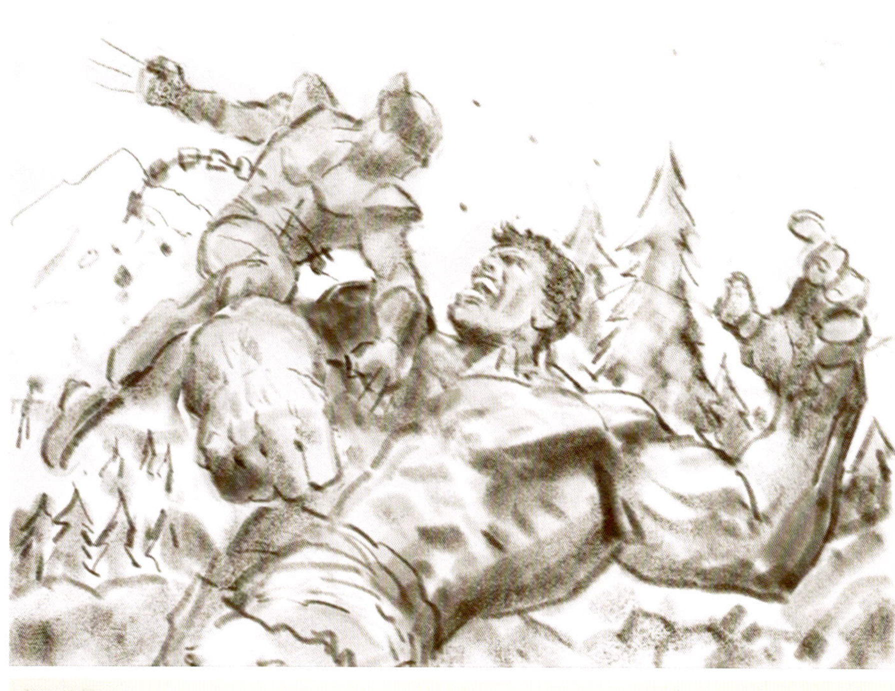

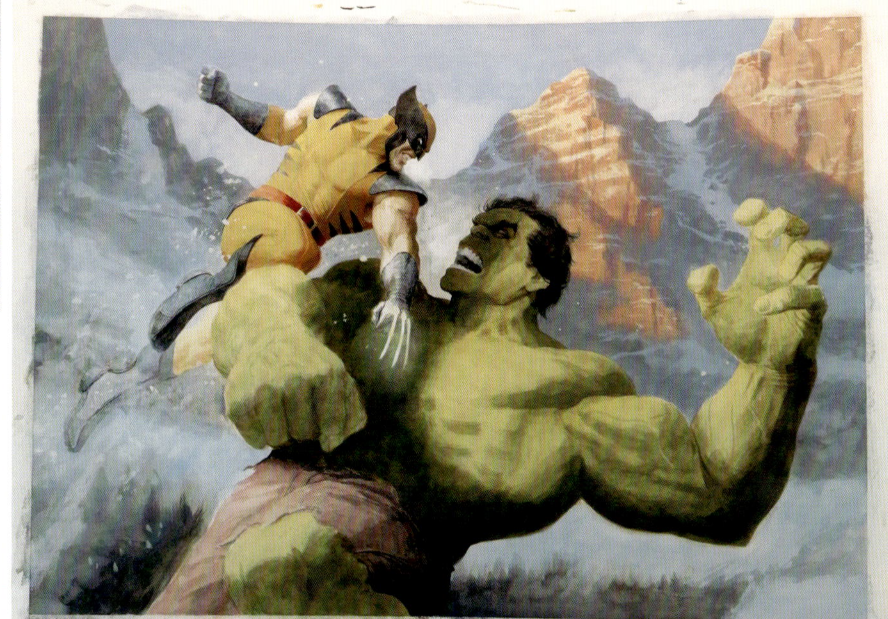

GUARDIANS OF THE GALAXY

ALEX ROSS

Even the 31st century needs heroes, and the call has been answered by the Guardians of the Galaxy—a team of superhuman and extraterrestrial adventurers dedicated to the safeguarding of the Milky Way galaxy from any force that threatens its various people. This depiction of the improbable group of heroes includes Rocket Raccoon, Gamora, Groot, Drax, and Star-Lord, as well as members of the original classic team.

This dynamic painting was originally created as a Marvel 75th-anniversary variant cover by legendary comic book artist Alex Ross.

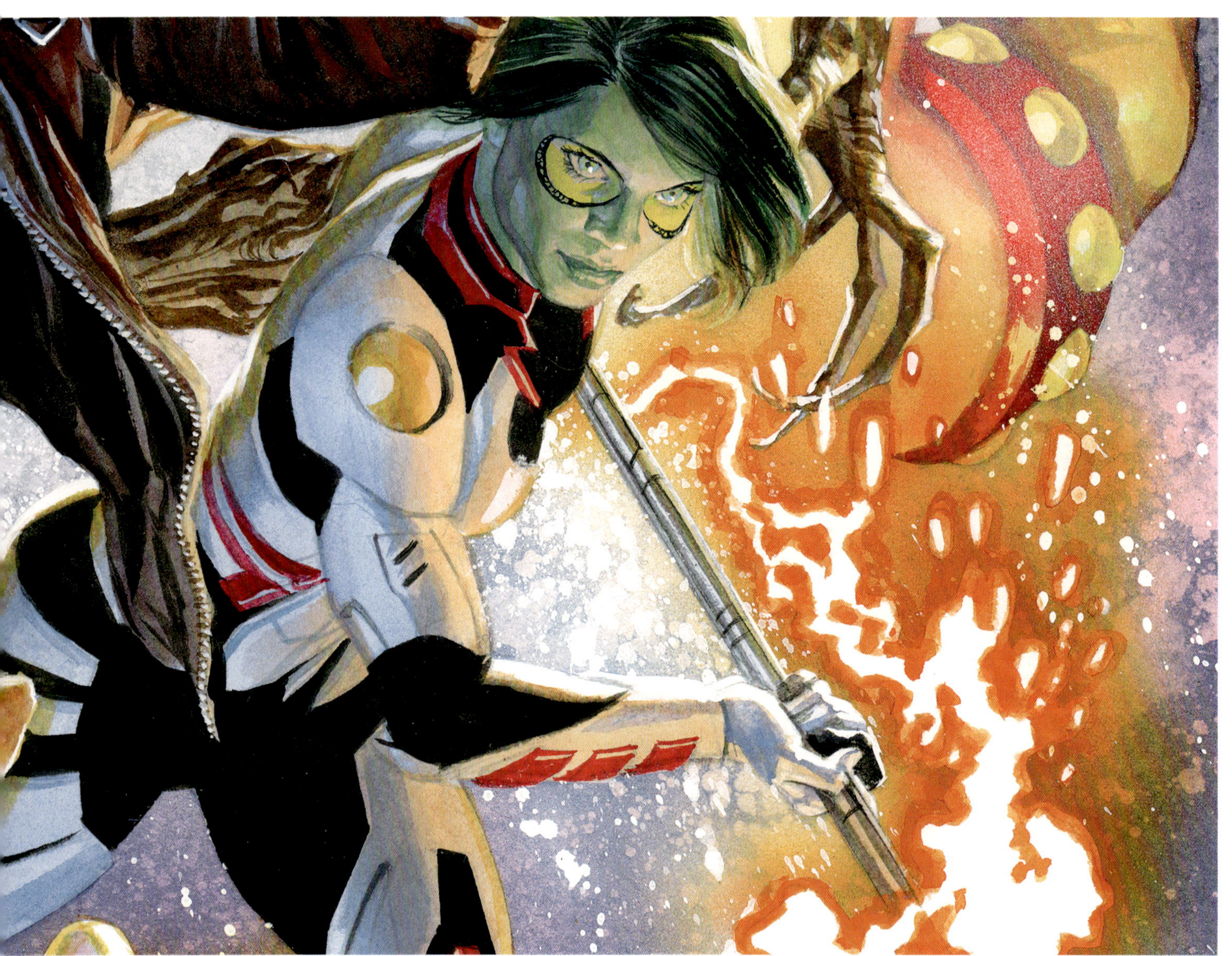

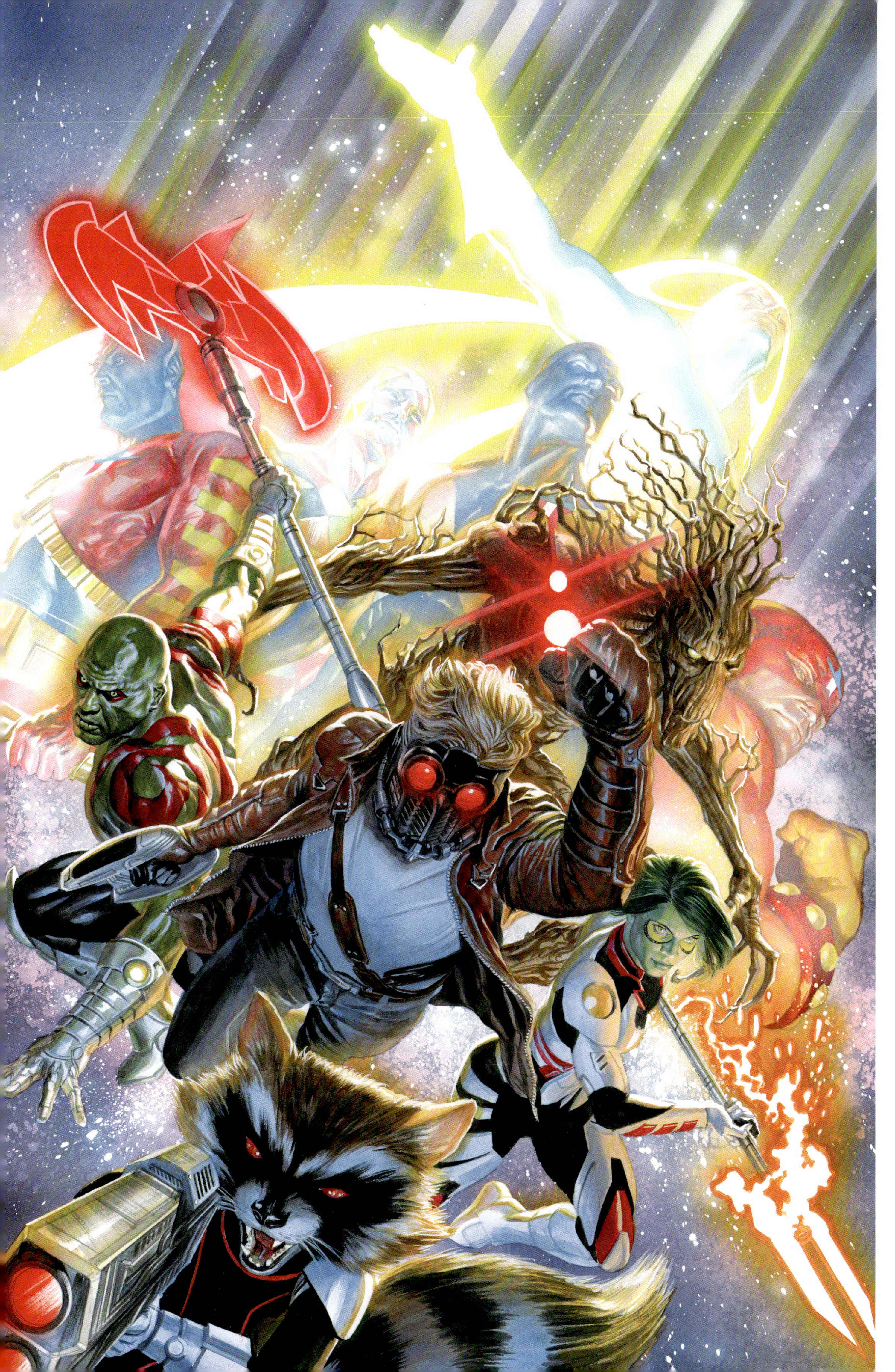

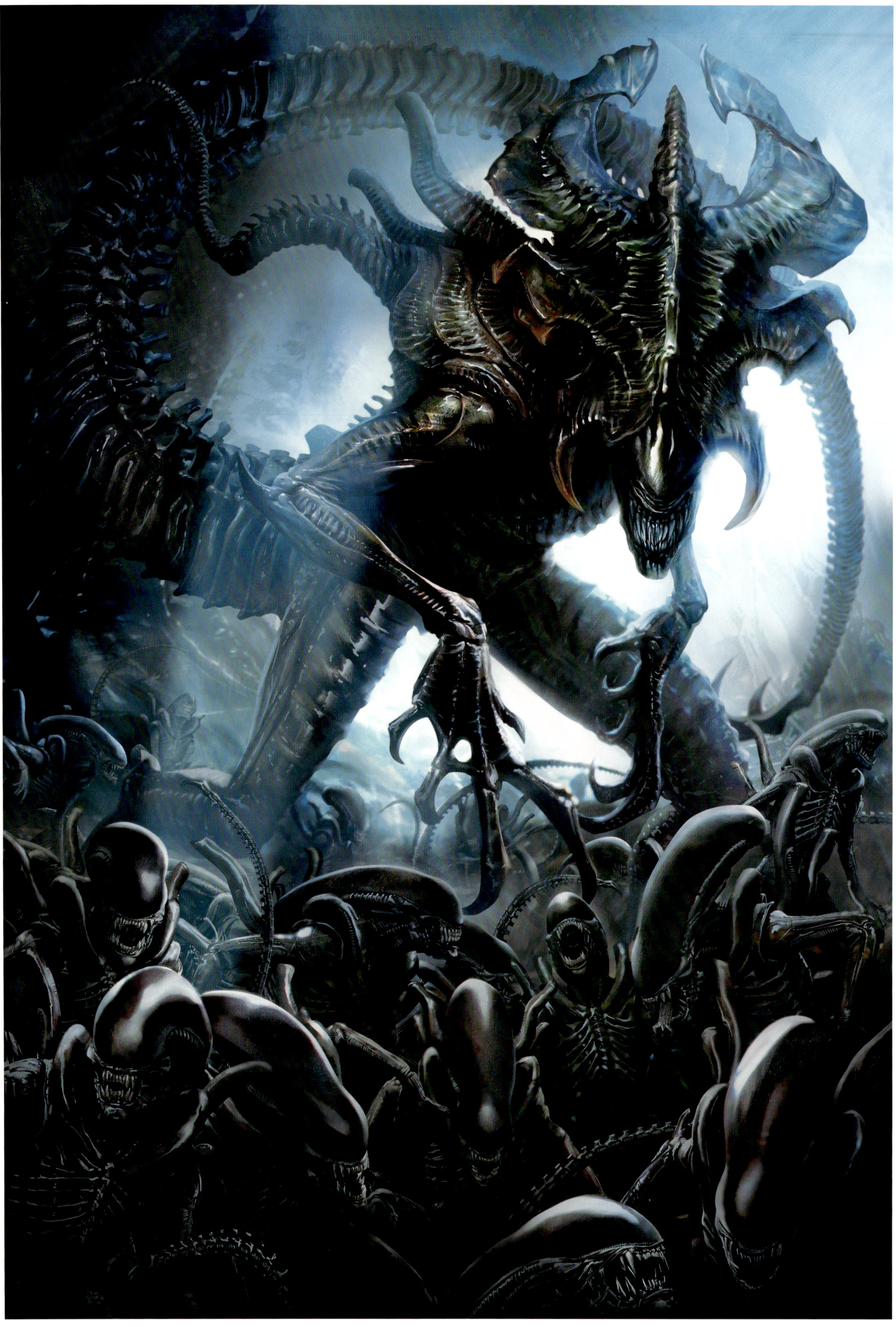

ALIEN KING

RJ PALMER

Translated from Latin as "murderous thief," *Internecivus raptus* is one of the few official names recorded for the xenomorph species moviegoers have come to recognize in the Alien film series.

Inspired by the legacy of H. R. Giger and mythos of the Alien franchise, the menacing *Internecivus raptus rex*, king of the species, rises as a worthy rival for the infamous xenomorph queen, with droves of vicious alien warriors swarming his feet.

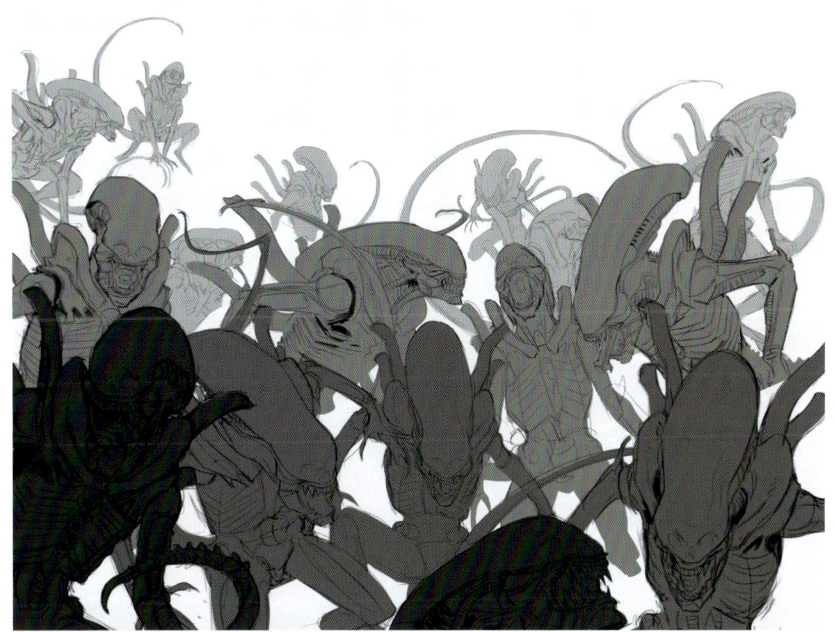

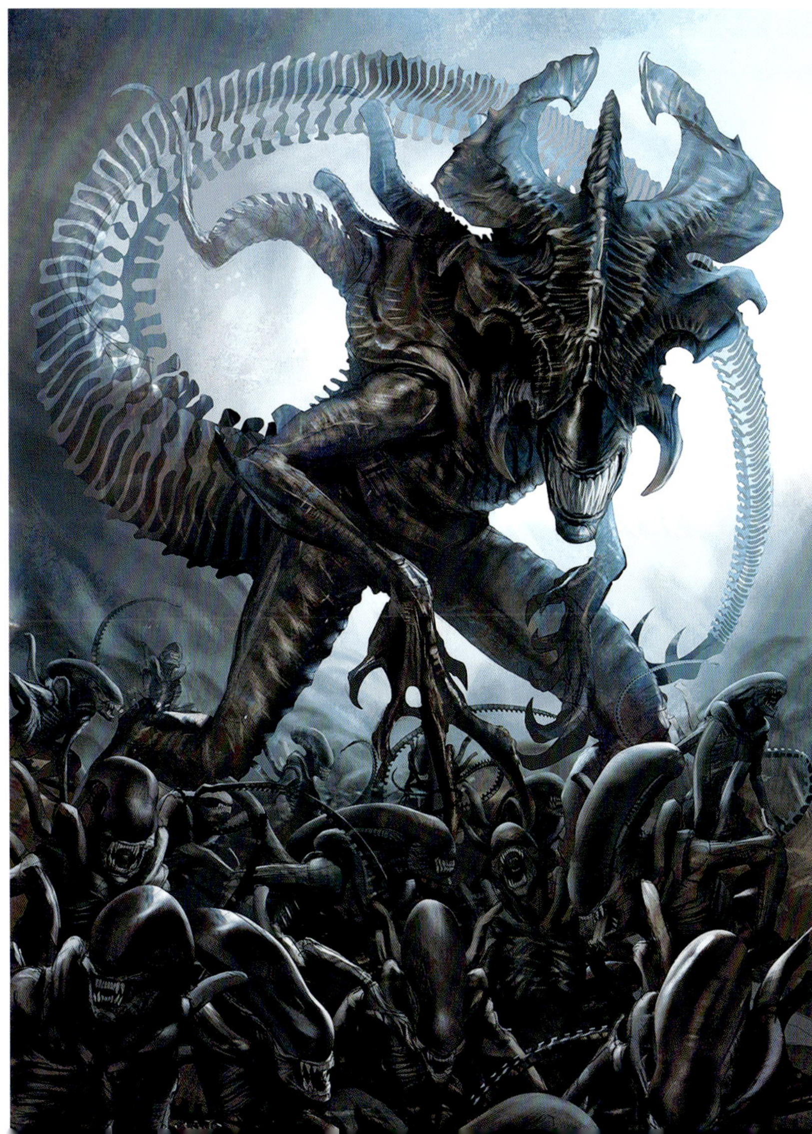

GREEN LANTERN

ALEX PASCENKO

Proudly wielding his legendary ring in front of the magnificent power battery on Oa, Hal Jordan, the Green Lantern of Sector 2814, descends a cosmic stairway, sworn to guard and protect the DC Universe.

Recruited by the fabled Green Lantern Corps because of his fearless nature, Hal Jordan is always willing to protect those in need—whether alone, with the Corps, or alongside the Justice League and Earth's other heroes—for he has sworn the oath of every Green Lantern: that no evil will escape his sight.

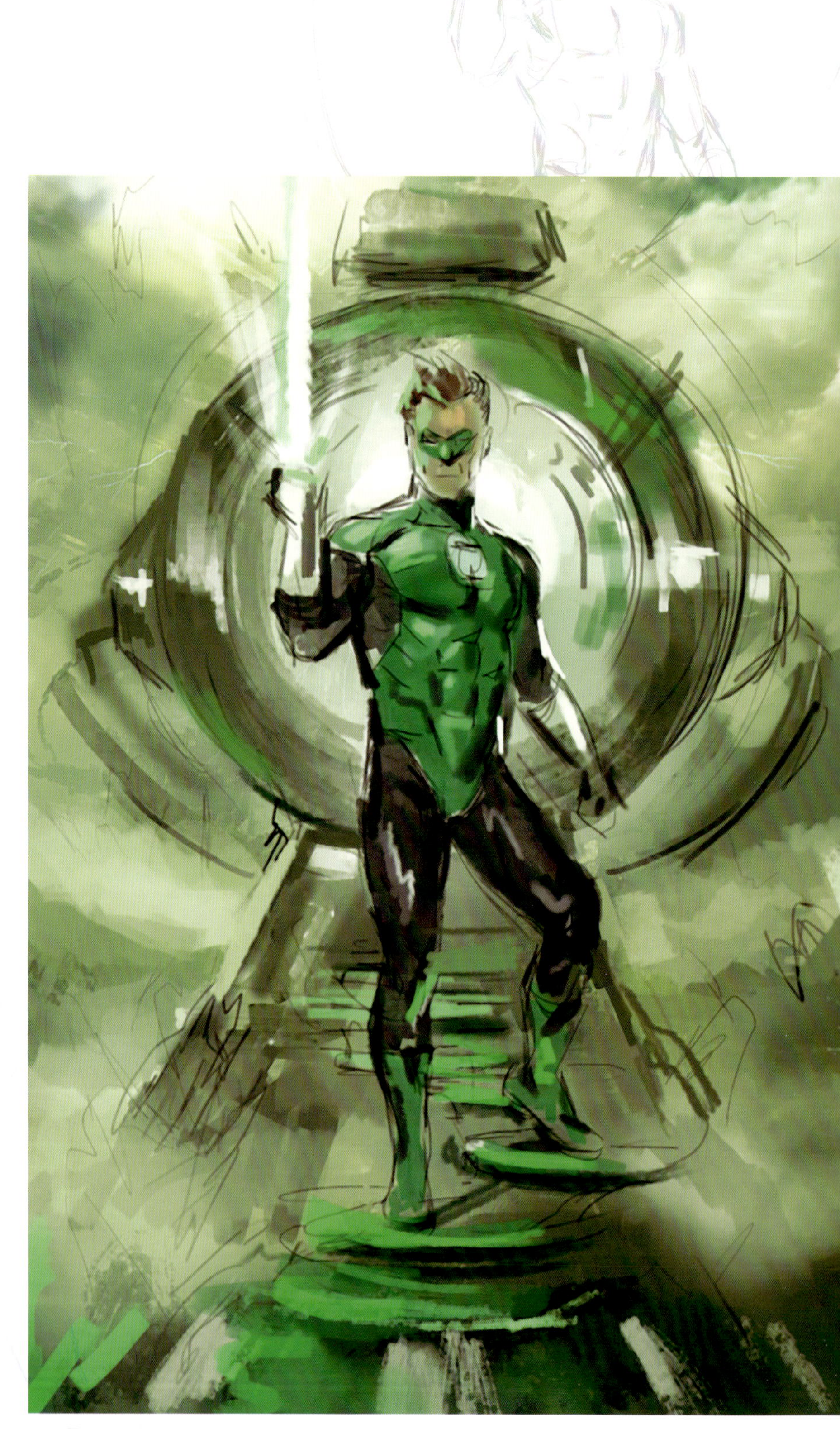

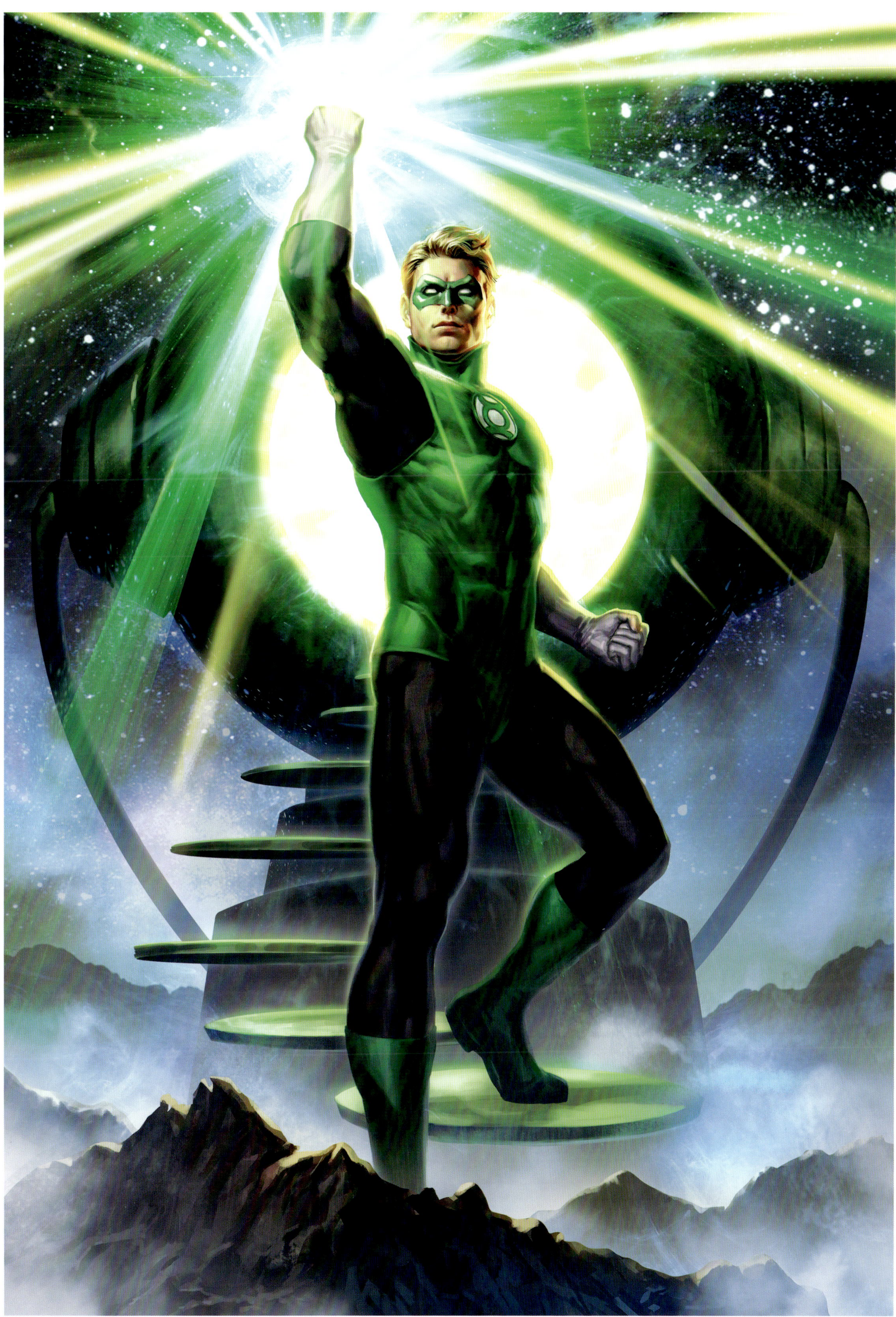

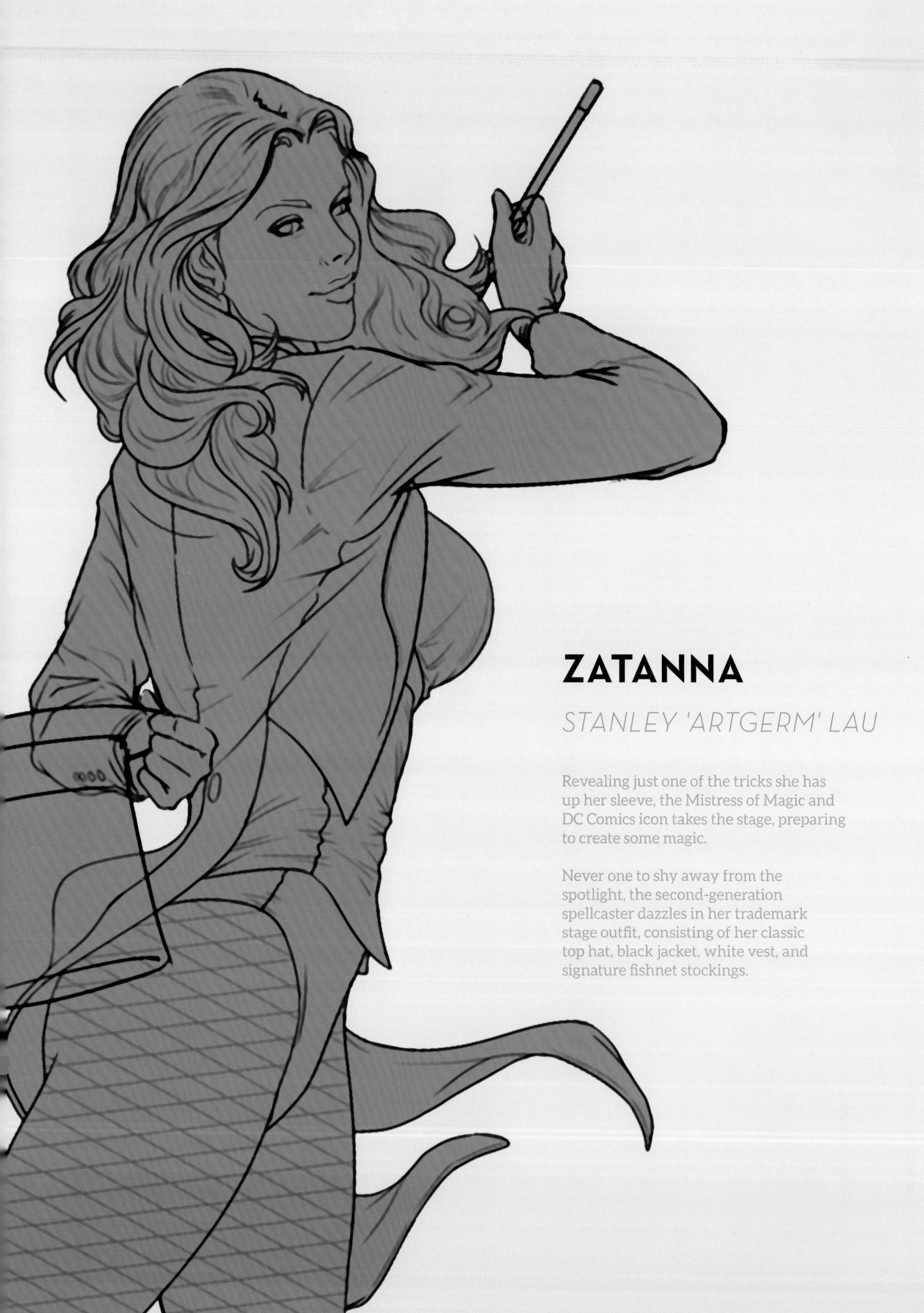

ZATANNA

STANLEY 'ARTGERM' LAU

Revealing just one of the tricks she has up her sleeve, the Mistress of Magic and DC Comics icon takes the stage, preparing to create some magic.

Never one to shy away from the spotlight, the second-generation spellcaster dazzles in her trademark stage outfit, consisting of her classic top hat, black jacket, white vest, and signature fishnet stockings.

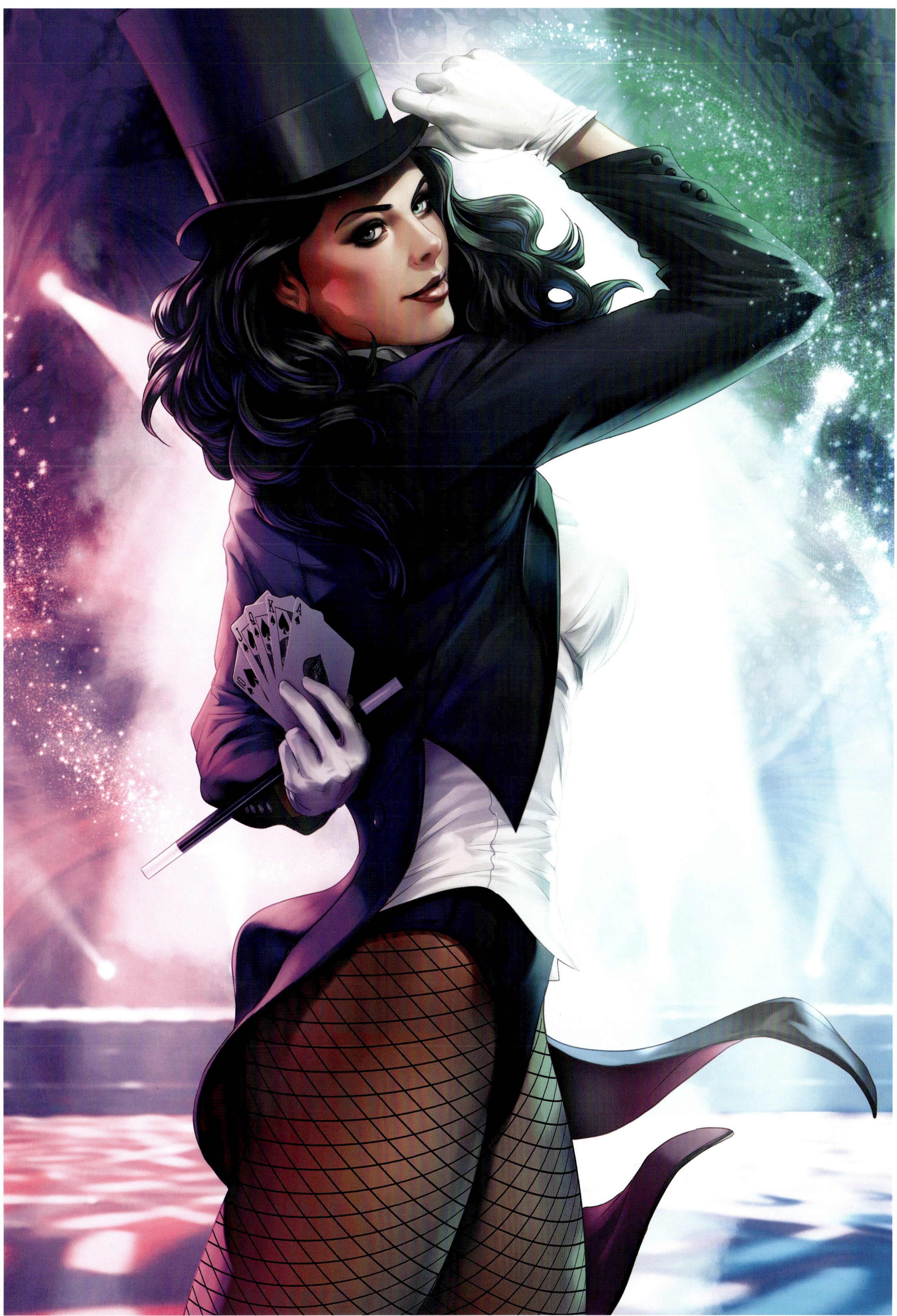

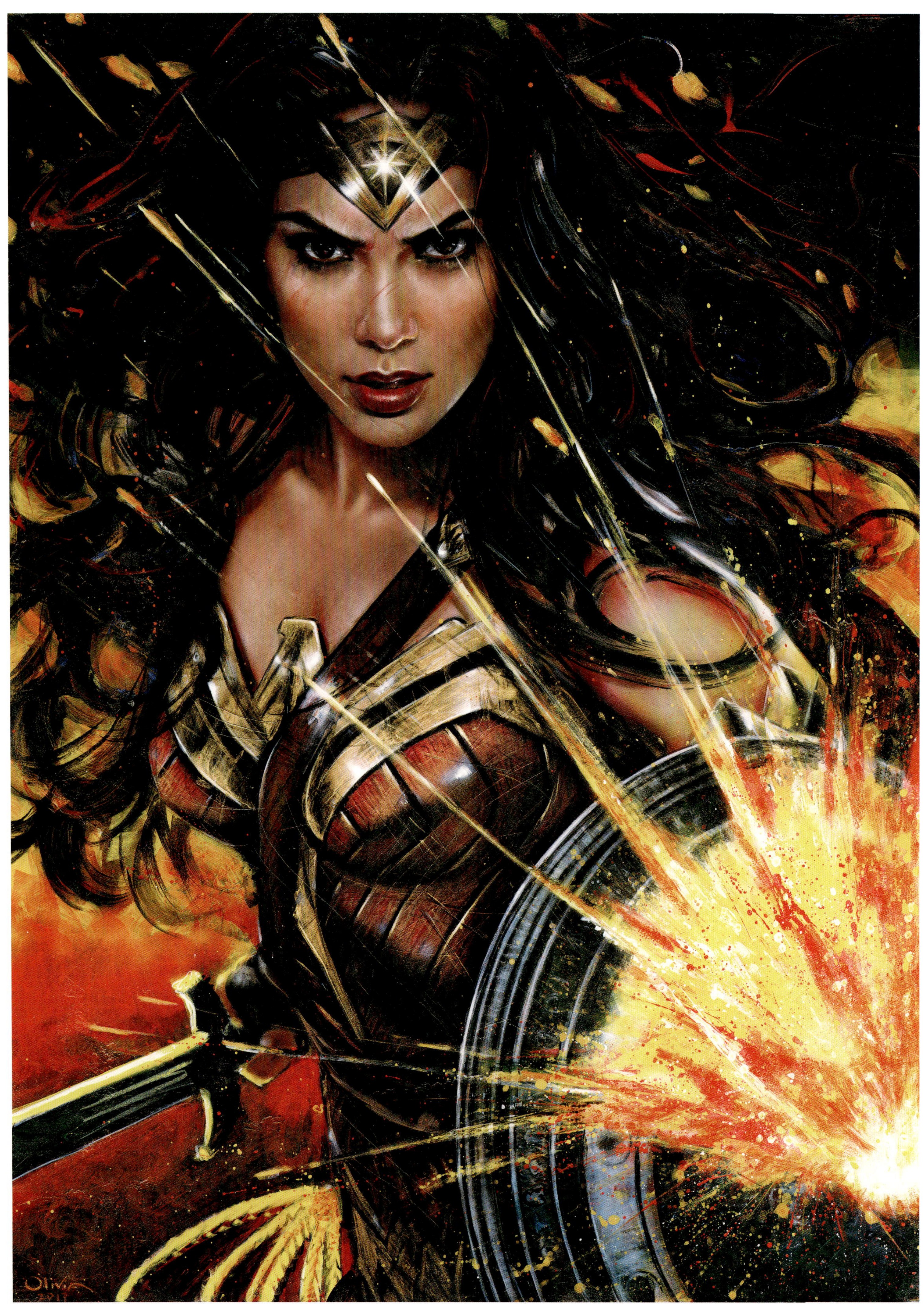

Wonder Woman : Diana of Themyscira © 2017 Olivia De Berardinis

WONDER WOMAN
DIANA OF THEMYSCIRA

OLIVIA DE BERARDINIS

Diana stands tall, armed with her sword, her legendary golden lasso, and her aegis shield, ready to defend all of humanity as she spreads her message of truth, justice, and equality to people everywhere.

Acclaimed artist Olivia De Berardinis's *Wonder Woman: Diana of Themyscira* Art Print captures the beauty and strength of Gal Gadot as Wonder Woman.

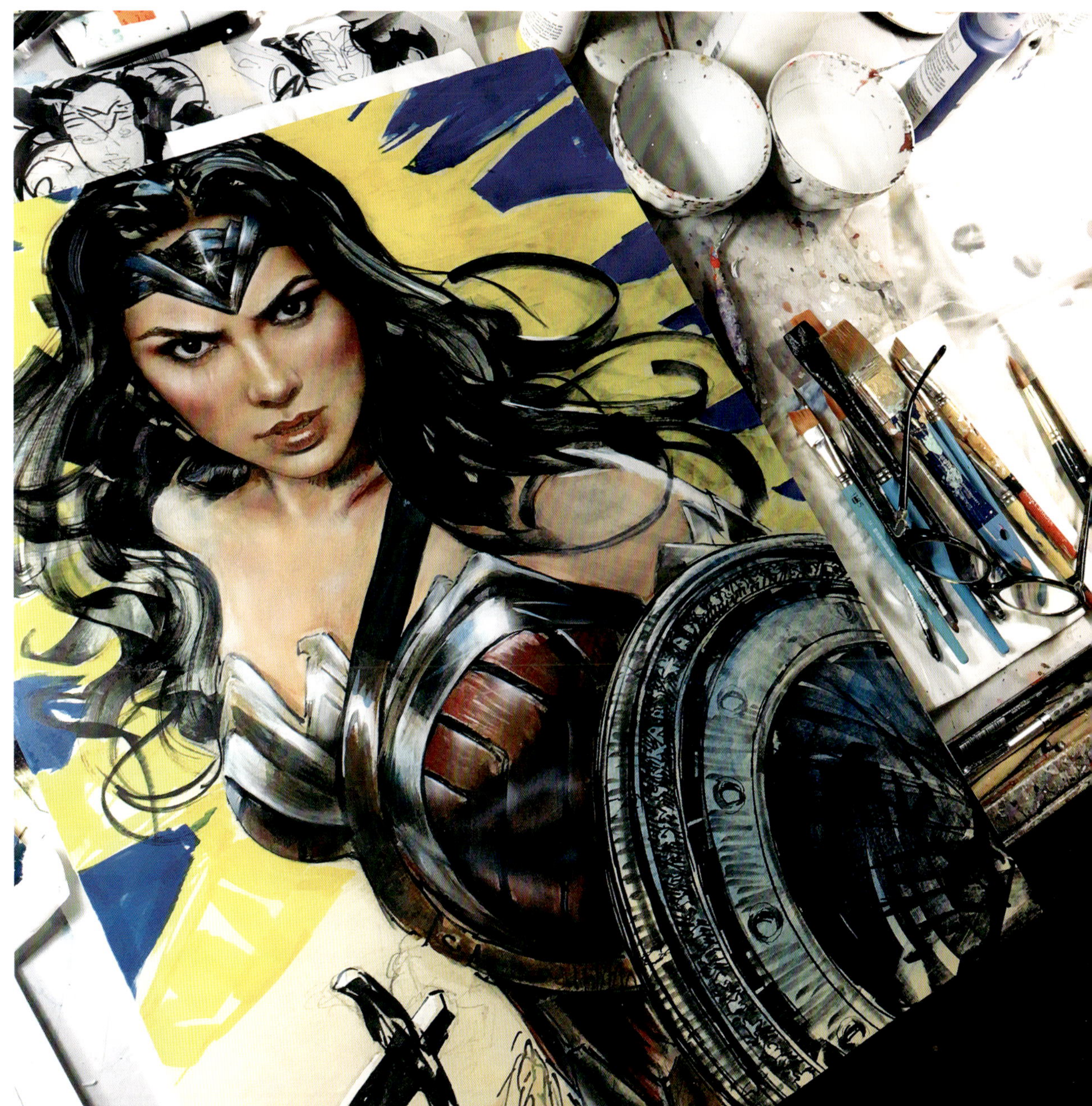

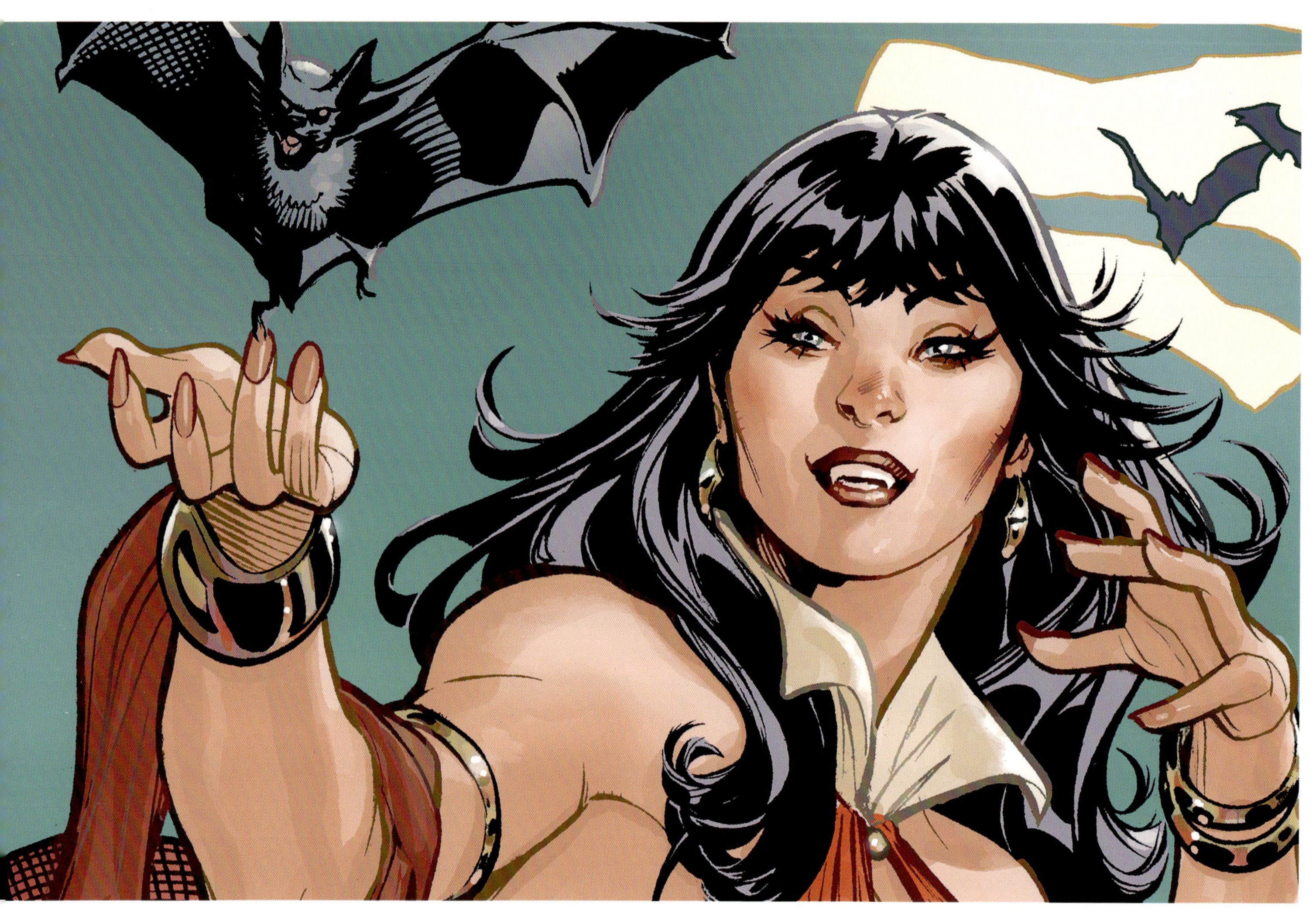

VAMPIRELLA A SCARLET THIRST

TERRY & RACHEL DODSON

Perched on a morbid throne of skeletal remains sits the legendary Vampirella, adorned in her iconic white high collar and crimson costume. The mesmerizing raven-haired vampire hunter playfully summons her favorite bloodthirsty companions in an enchanting composition designed to bewitch and beguile.

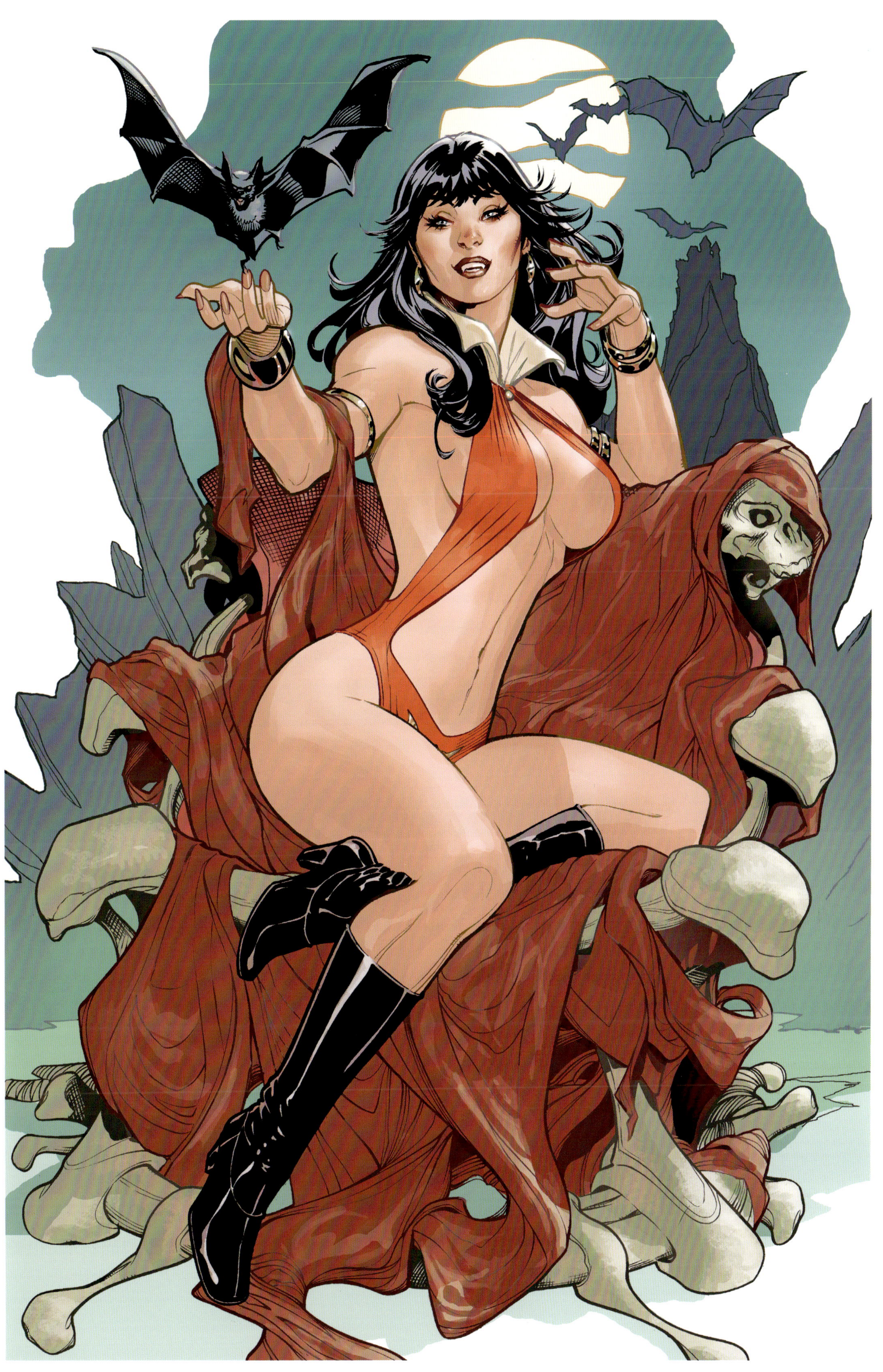

LIBERTY & JUSTICE JLA

ALEX ROSS

DC Comics' greatest superheroes join forces in this dynamic fine art lithograph print, first seen in the comic titled *JLA: Liberty and Justice*, by Emmy Award–winning writer Paul Dini and legendary comics illustrator Alex Ross. Batman, Superman, Wonder Woman, Green Lantern, the Flash, Aquaman, and the Martian Manhunter must band together to counteract a lethal alien virus and restore order to a world that has fallen into mass hysteria.

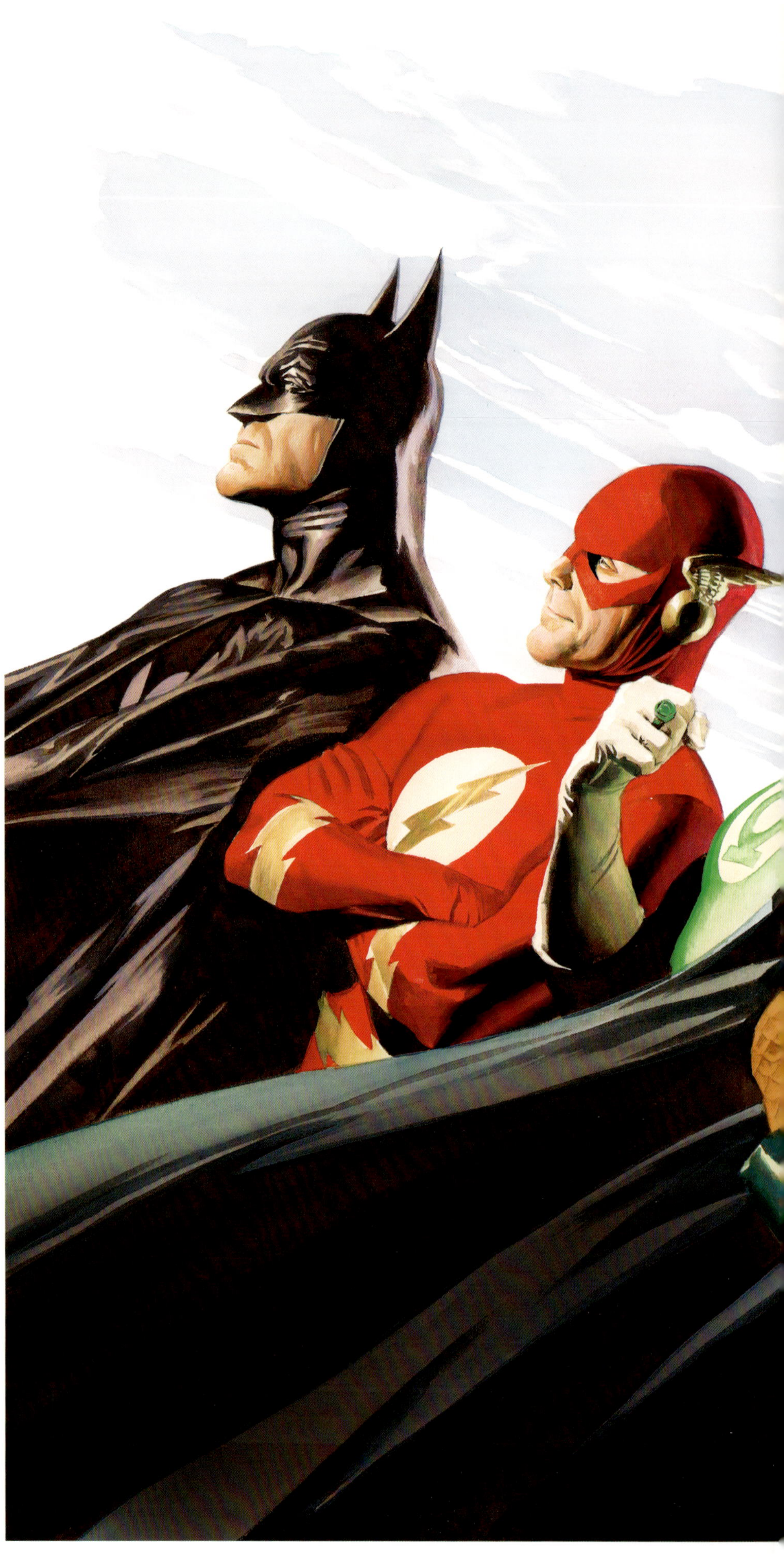

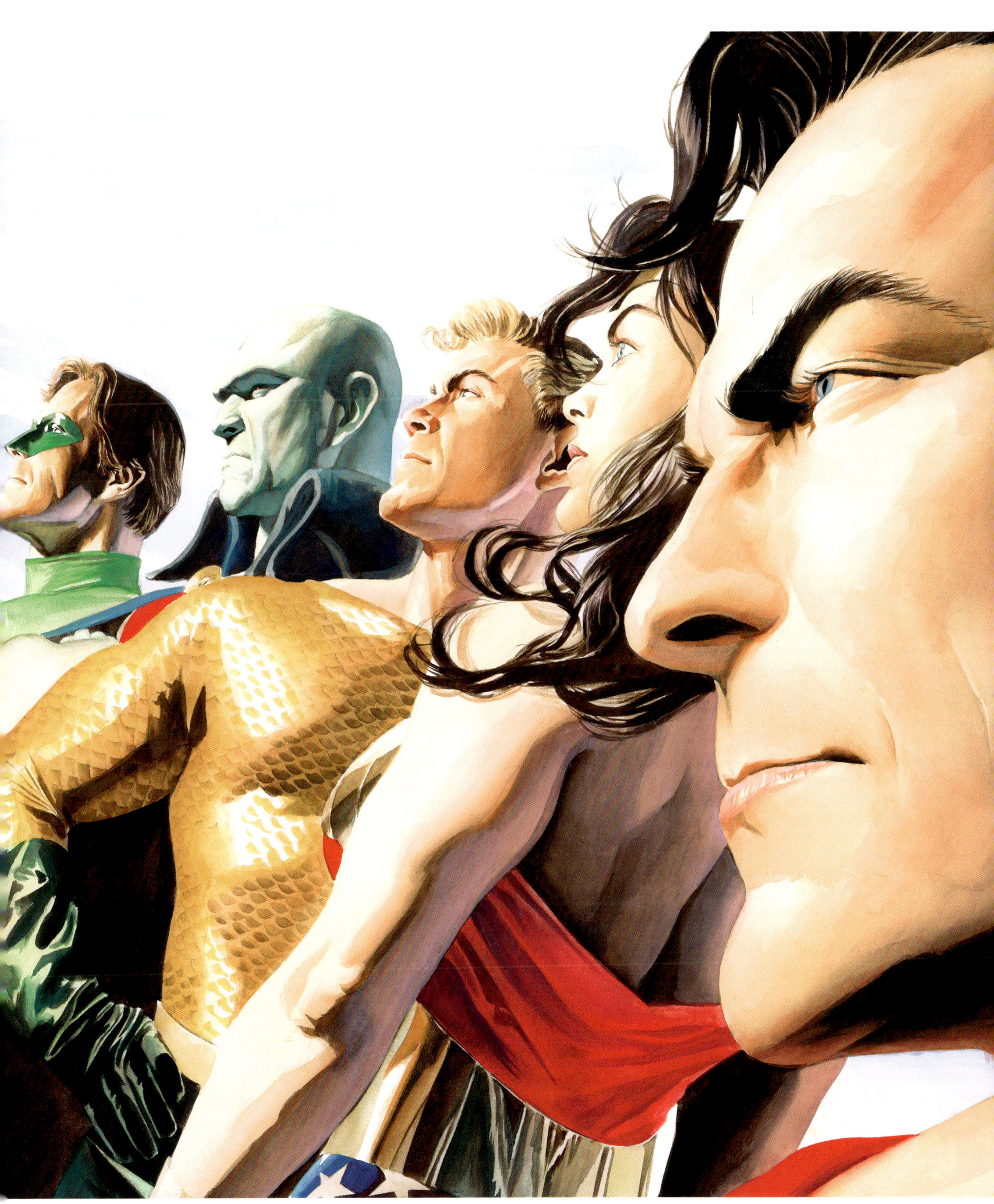

ALEX ROSS

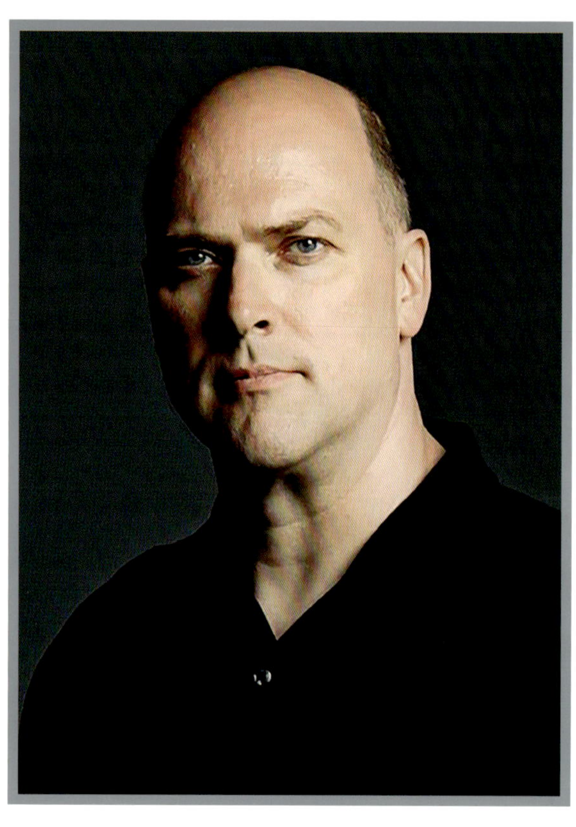

INSPIRATION

Born in Portland, OR, and raised in Lubbock, TX, Alex made his artistic debut at three when, according to his mother, he grabbed a piece of paper and drew the contents of a television commercial he'd seen moments before. By age thirteen he was scripting and drawing original comic books. Ten years later? He was hired by Marvel Comics to illustrate Marvel's central characters in the limited series comic book *Marvels* (1994).

Having established himself creatively and financially with superhero projects, Ross turned to the real world with *Uncle Sam*, a ninety-six-page story that took a hard look at the dark side of American history. Like *Marvels*, the individual issues of *Uncle Sam* were collected into a single volume—first in hardcover, then in paperback—and remain in print today. Ross would go on to win the Comic Buyer's Guide Fan Award for Favorite Painter. He won so many times that the award was officially retired.

Alex's work has celebrated the sixtieth anniversaries of Superman, Batman, Captain Marvel, and Wonder Woman with fully painted, tabloid-size books, depicting each of these characters using their powers to inspire humanity as well as help them.

In recent years, Ross has applied his artistic skills to outside projects with comic book roots, including a limited edition promotional poster for the Academy Awards. In 2015, Alex was chosen by Apple Corps Limited to be commissioned as the first artist in over thirty years to paint the Beatles. *Yellow Submarine* is a classic of animated cinema, driven by the Fab Four's legendary music and inspired by that generation's new trends in art. Alex has often been referred to as "the Norman Rockwell of comics" but his *Yellow Submarine* piece reveals the similarly powerful influence of master surrealist Salvador Dalí, whom Alex has also recognized as a guiding influence on his style.

Forty years ago, Spider-Man learned that with great power comes great responsibility. Looking at Alex Ross, it's obvious that the lesson took.

It makes perfect sense that Alex Ross would become one of the world's most preeminent and well-respected comic book artists. It's a job he's been preparing for nearly all his life.

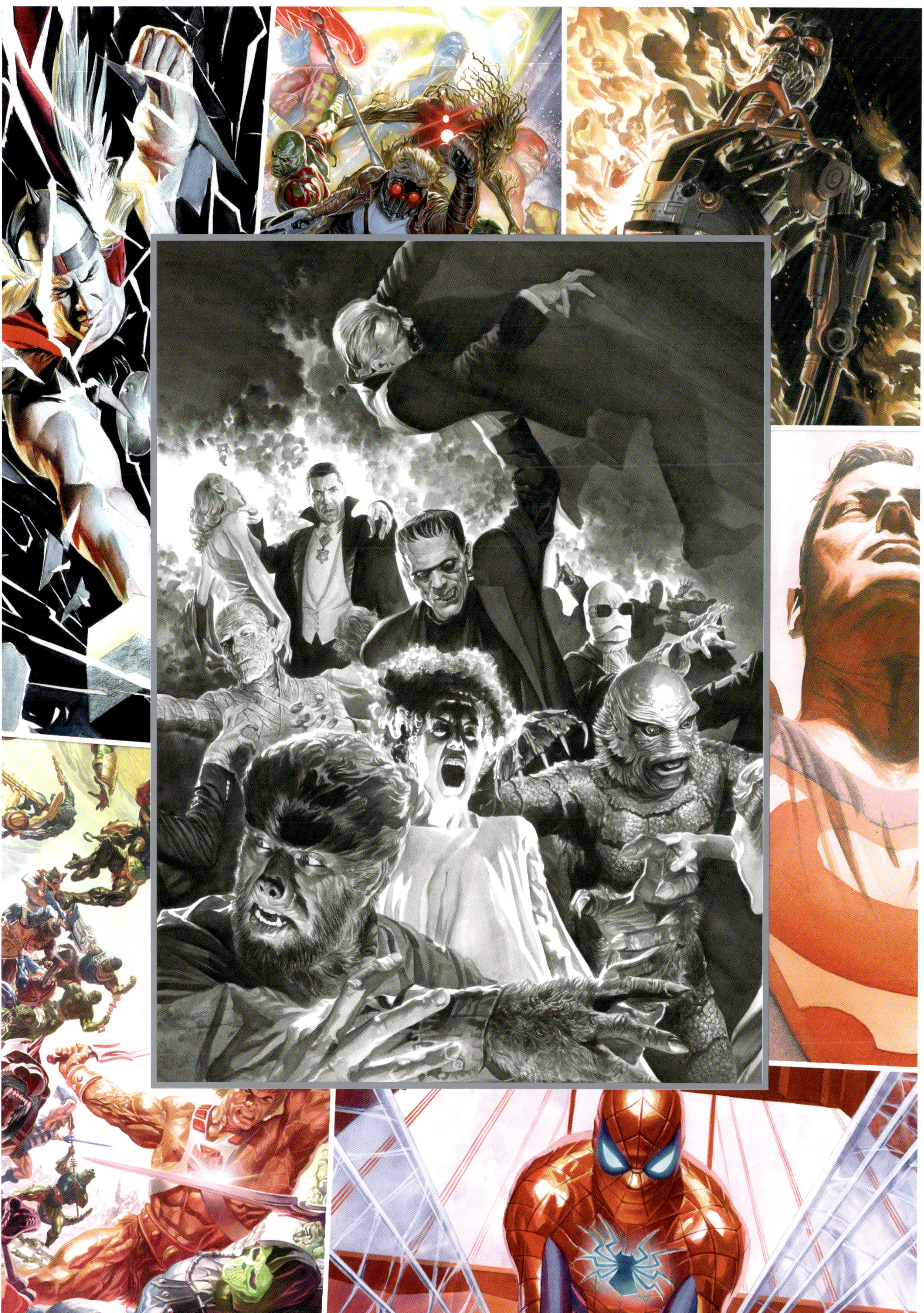

Thor: Shattered, Guardians of the Galaxy, Terminator: The Burning Earth, Superman: Immortal, Spider-Man: Trouble in San Francisco, Masters of the Universe, Universal Monsters: The Mash.

SHE-RA PRINCESS OF POWER

DAVE WILKINS

Inspired by the wildly popular '80s animated series *She-Ra: Princess of Power*, and fueled by pure, unadulterated nostalgia, artist Dave Wilkins provides a dynamic new vision of the Most Powerful Woman in the Universe and her friends and foes from the mystical world of Etheria.

Armed with her enchanted Power Sword and steely resolve, Princess Adora's invincible alter ego stands ready to defend the honor of Grayskull against the mighty Hordak and his Evil Horde.

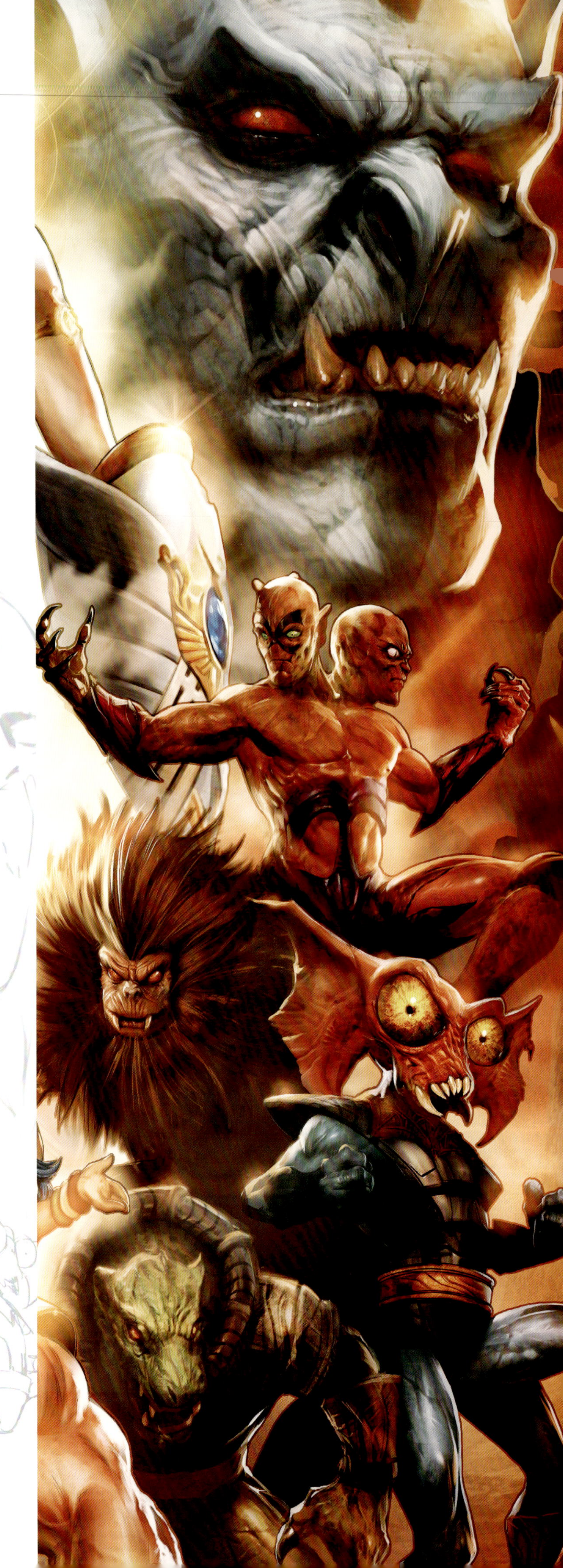

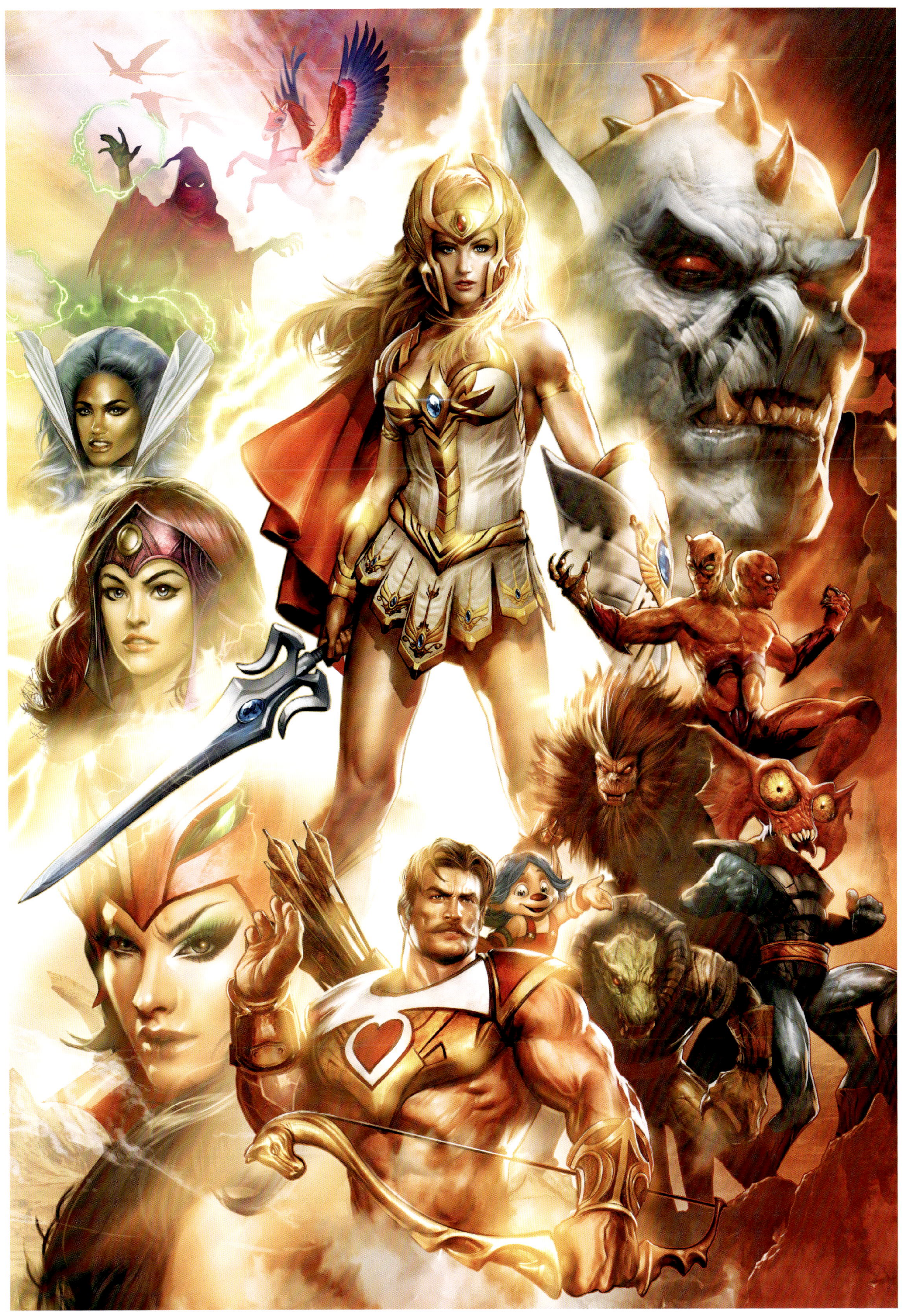

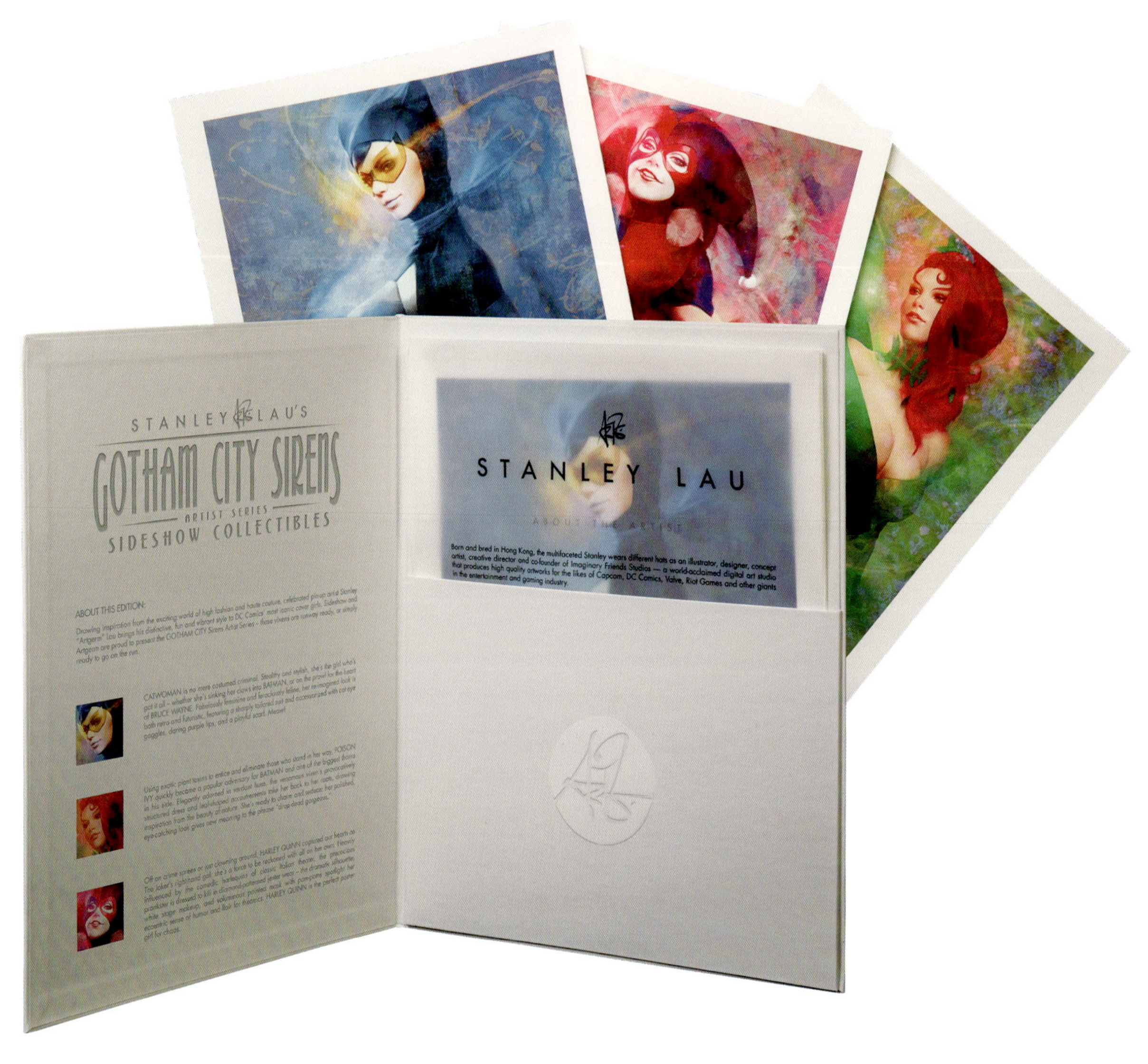

GOTHAM SIRENS
ARTIST SERIES PORTFOLIO

STANLEY 'ARTGERM' LAU

Drawing inspiration from the exciting world of high fashion, celebrated artist Stanley 'Artgerm' Lau brings his distinctive, fun, and vibrant style to DC Comics' most iconic antiheroes.

Runway ready, or simply ready to go on the run, Catwoman, Harley Quinn, and Poison Ivy are reimagined by Artgerm as stylish pinups that are simultaneously retro and futuristic.

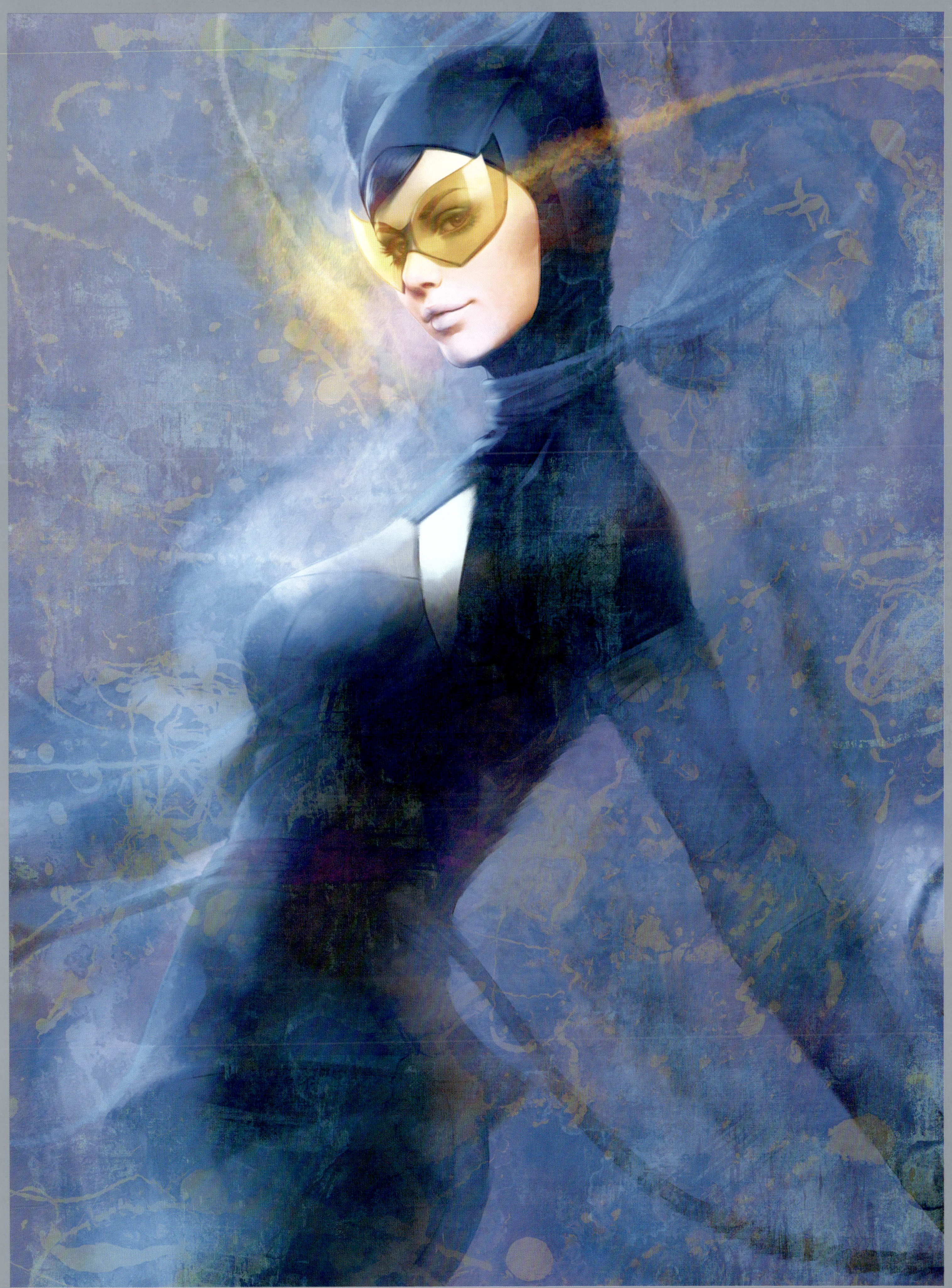

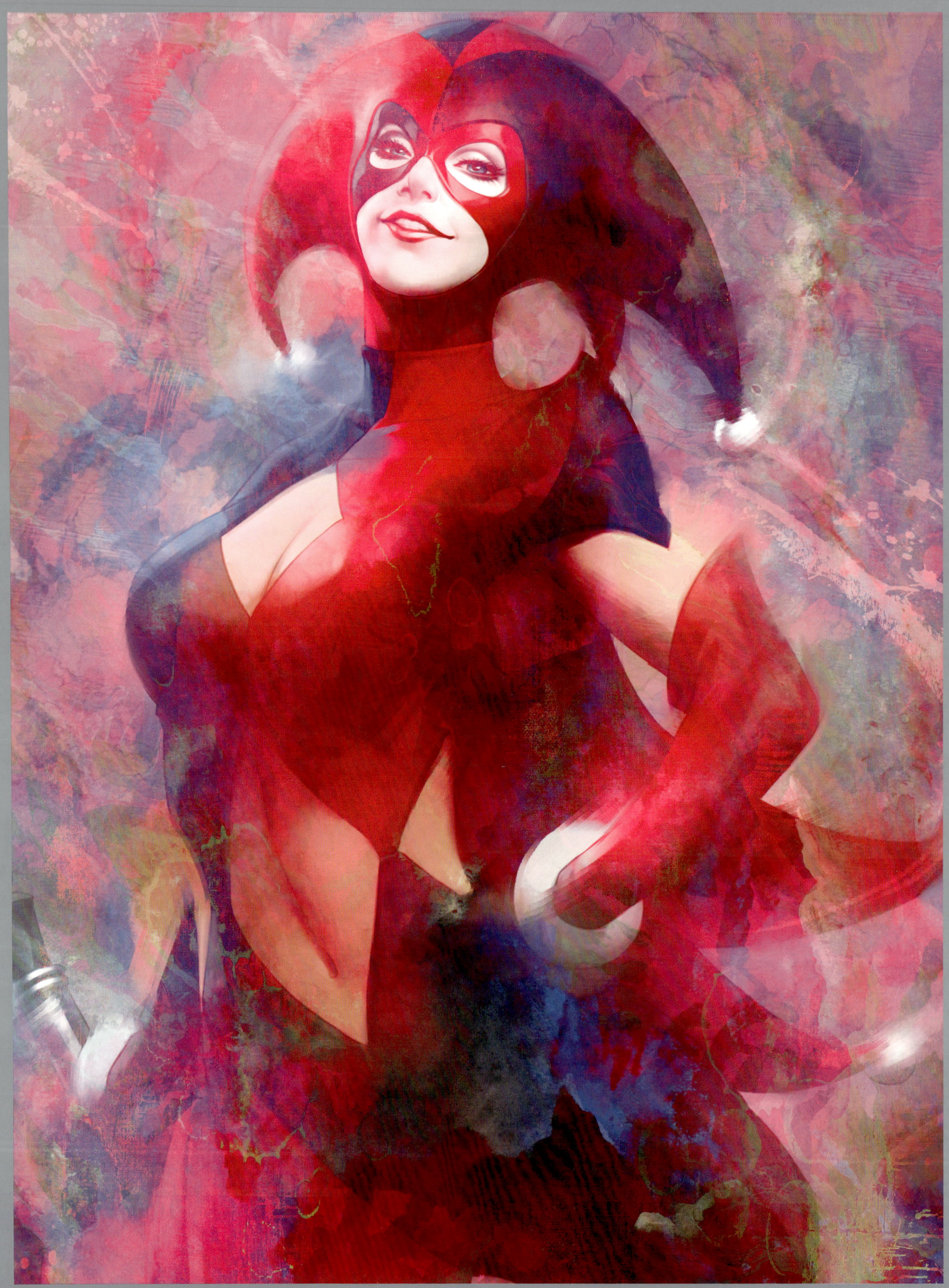

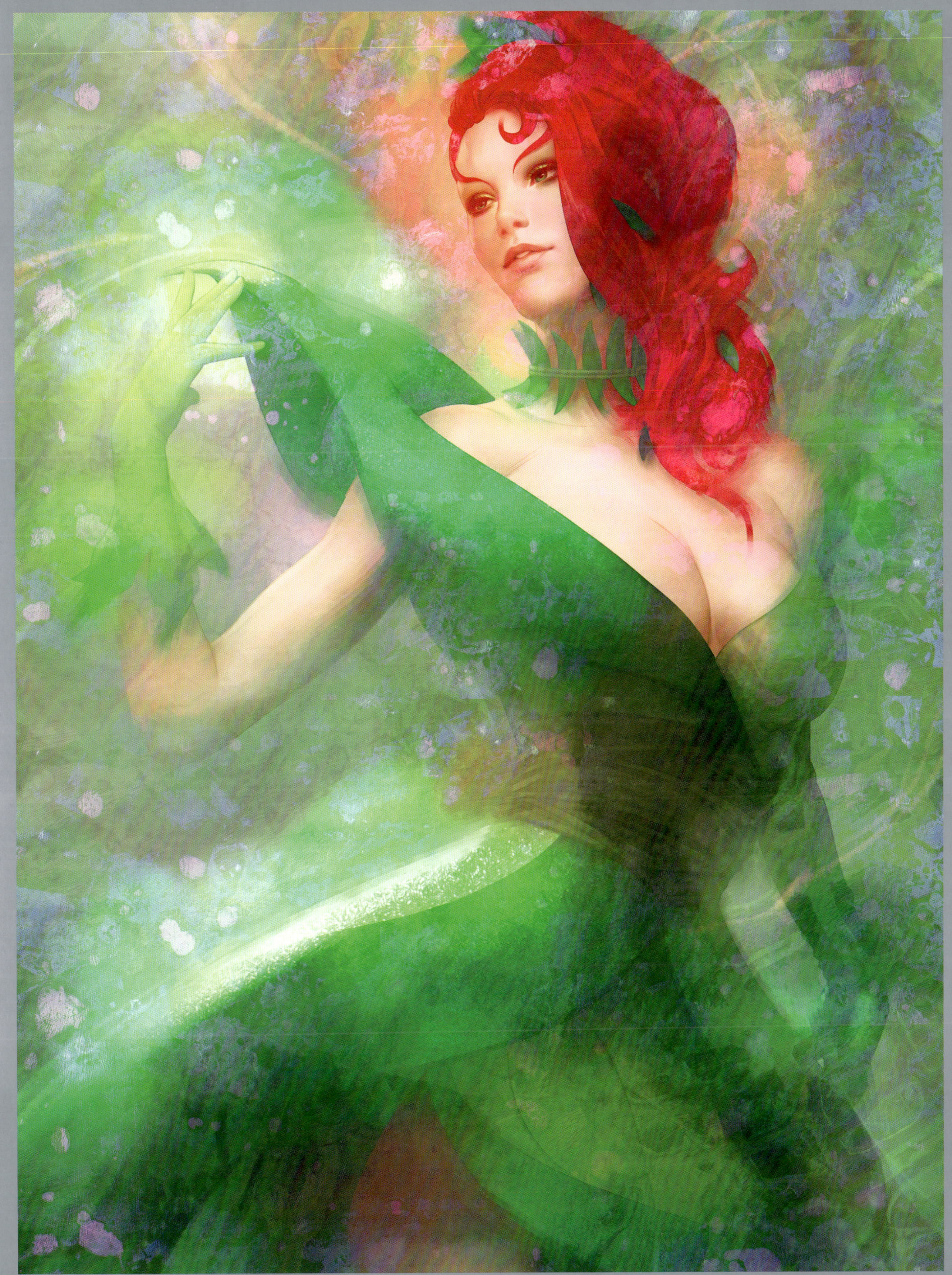

IN A GALAXY FAR, FAR AWAY . . .

ADAM HUGHES

Best known for his spectacular depictions of iconic heroines in comics and pop culture, Adam Hughes brings his signature style to this tribute to the *Star Wars* galaxy.

The Force awakens with Rey as she takes up the fabled Skywalker lightsaber to face her destiny, surrounded by a subtle and long-lasting legacy of powerful women who have come before her, including Rebel Alliance leader Mon Mothma, Jedi Padawan Ahsoka Tano, and the legendary Princess Leia Organa.

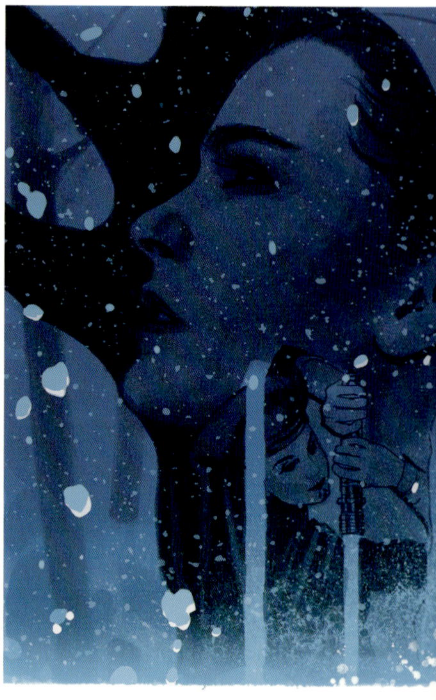

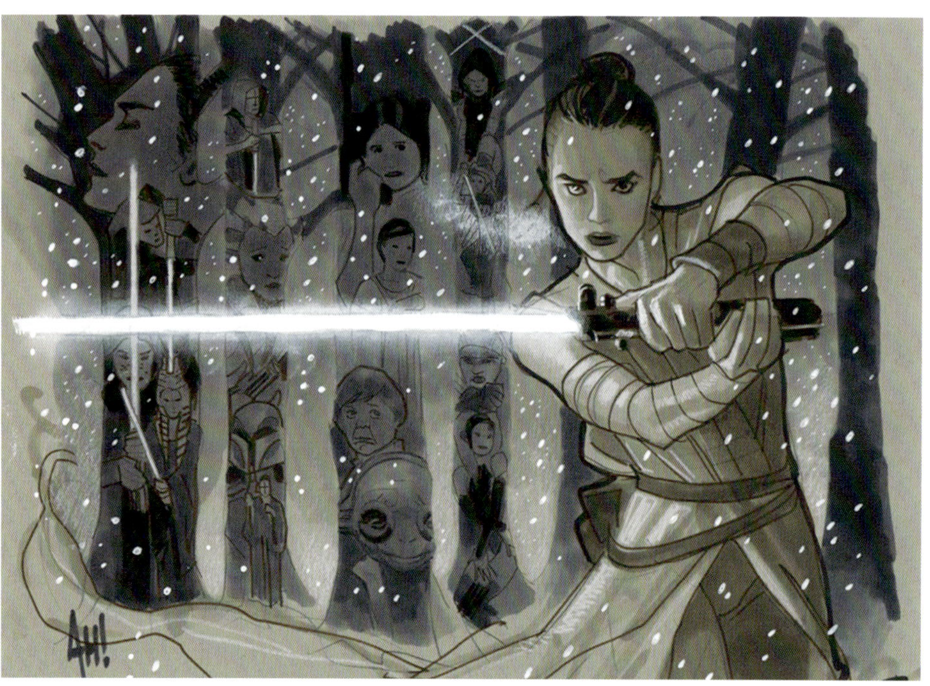

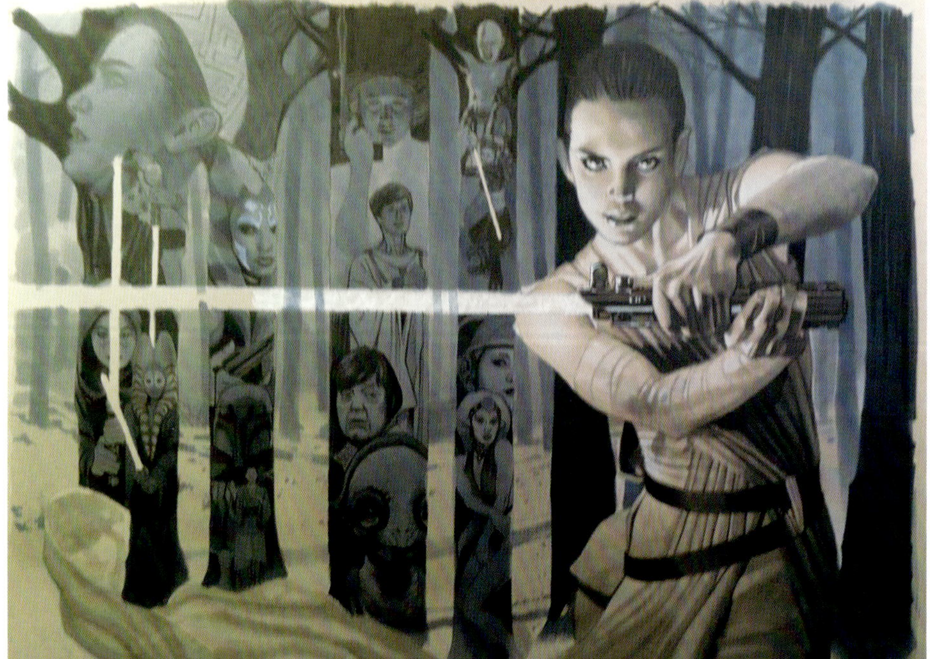

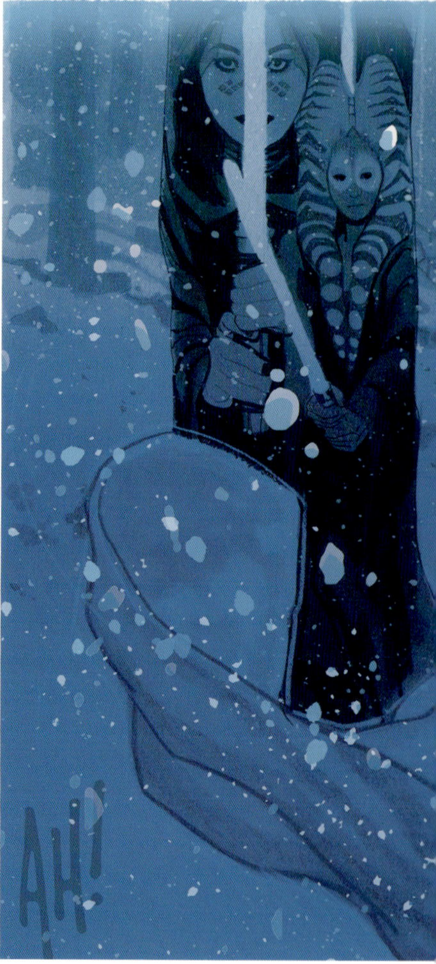

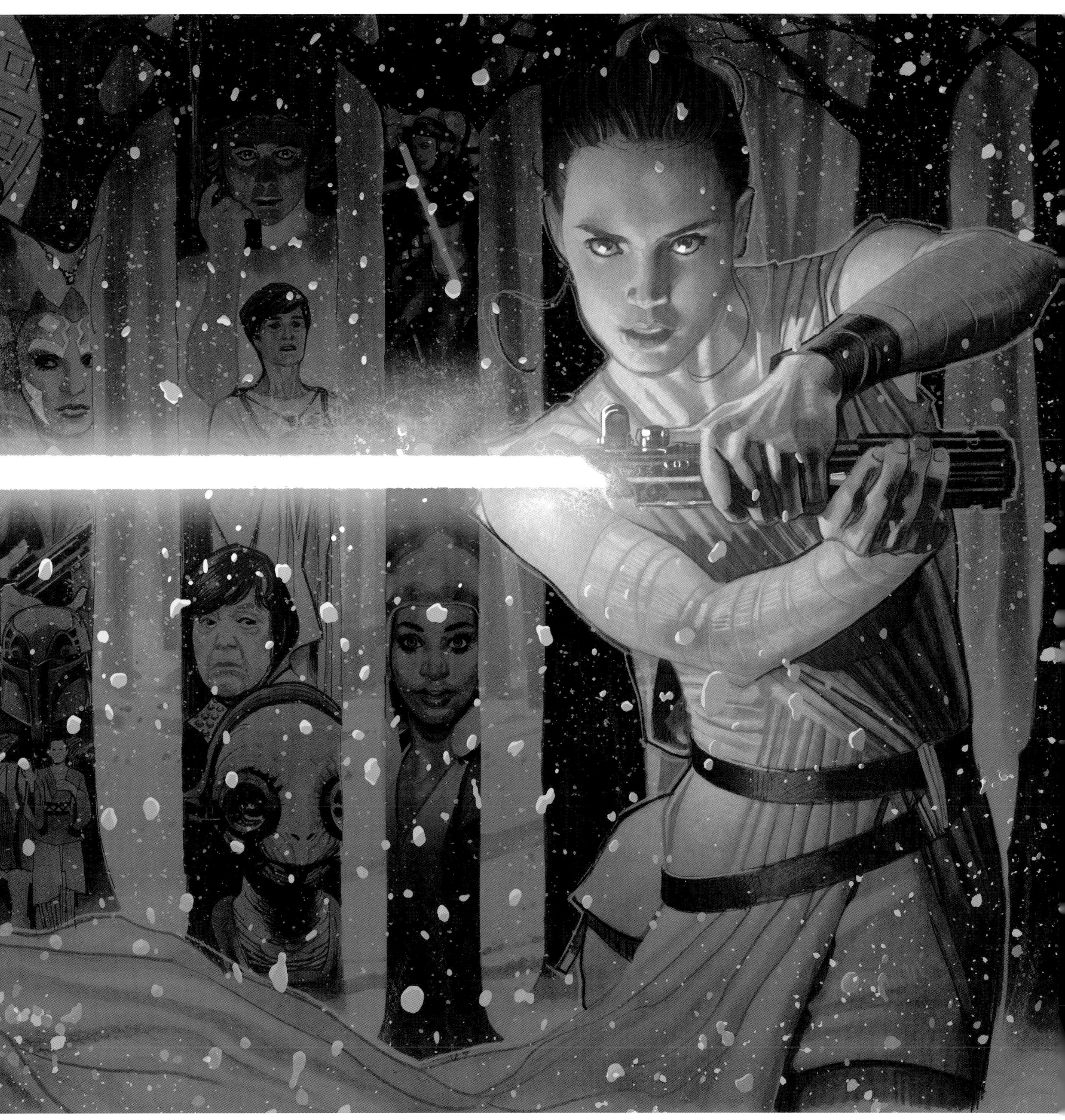

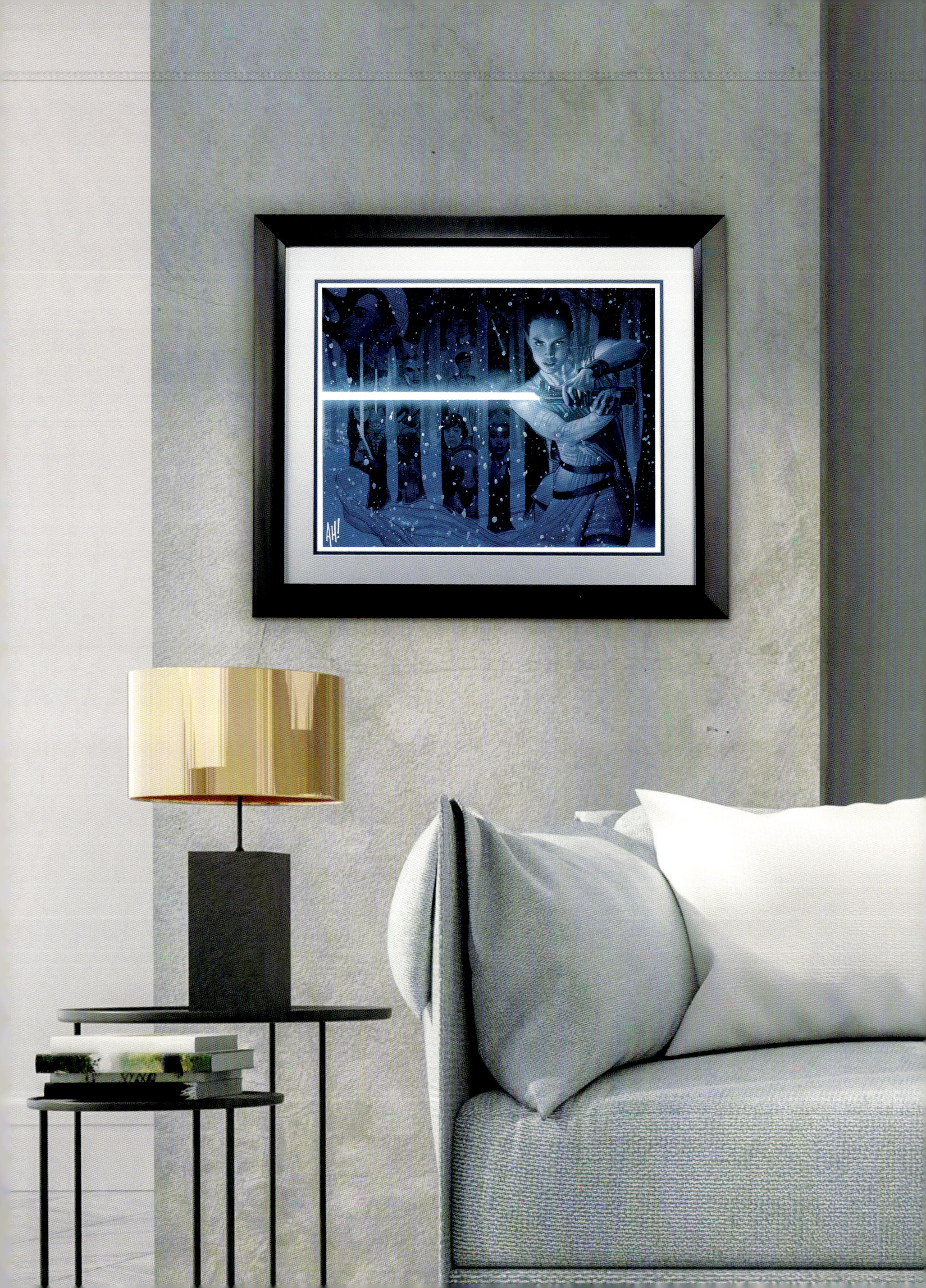

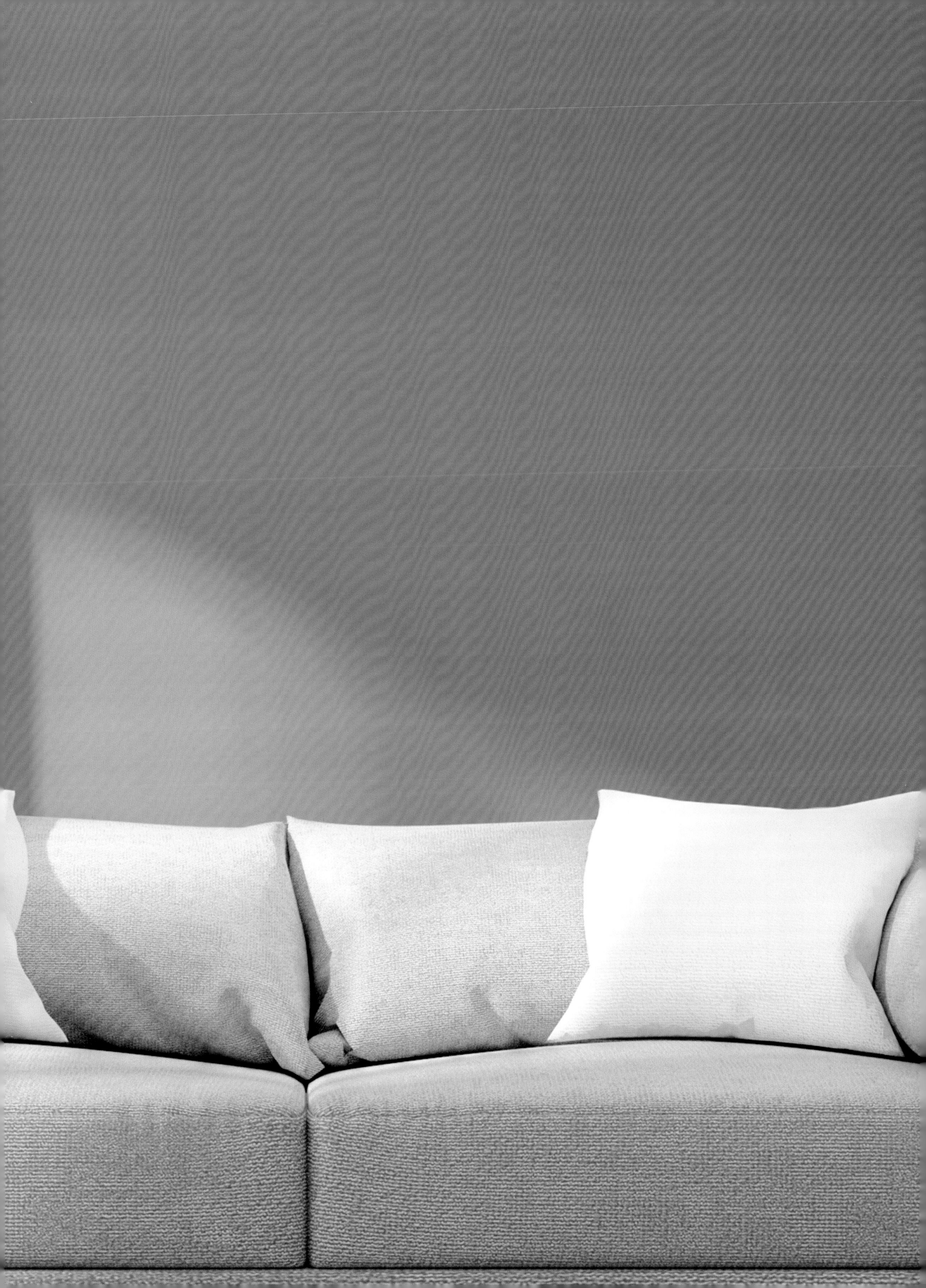

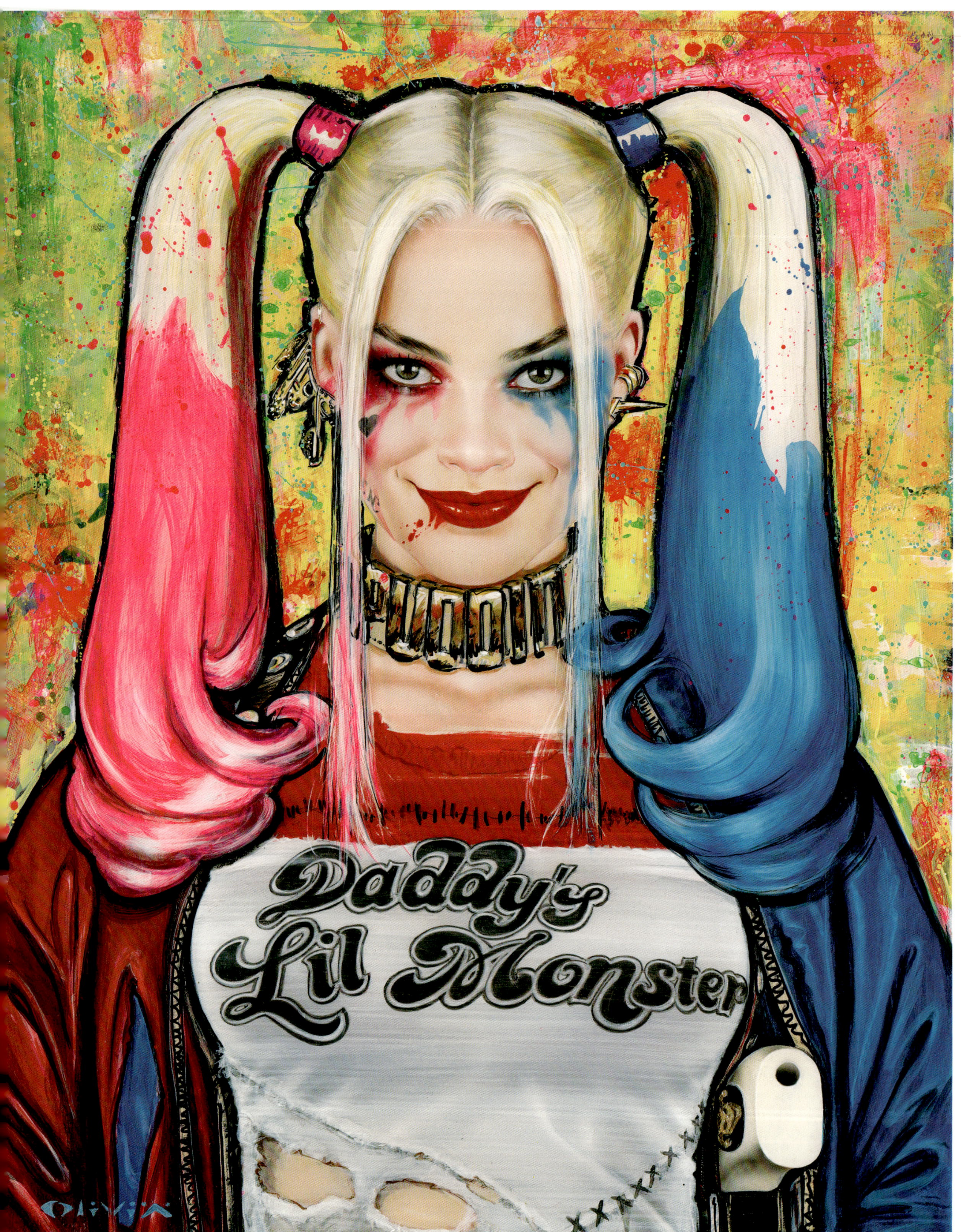

Harley Quinn: Daddy's Lil Monster © 2017 Olivia De Berardinis

HARLEY QUINN
DADDY'S LIL MONSTER

OLIVIA DE BERARDINIS

Harley Quinn, everyone's favorite wild card, flashes a coy, teasing smile as she contemplates her next move, one that's sure to leave Gotham in stitches.

Bursting with bright colors, manic energy, and stunning realism, acclaimed artist Olivia De Berardinis's painting captures every detail of Margot Robbie as she appeared in the 2016 summer blockbuster *Suicide Squad*.

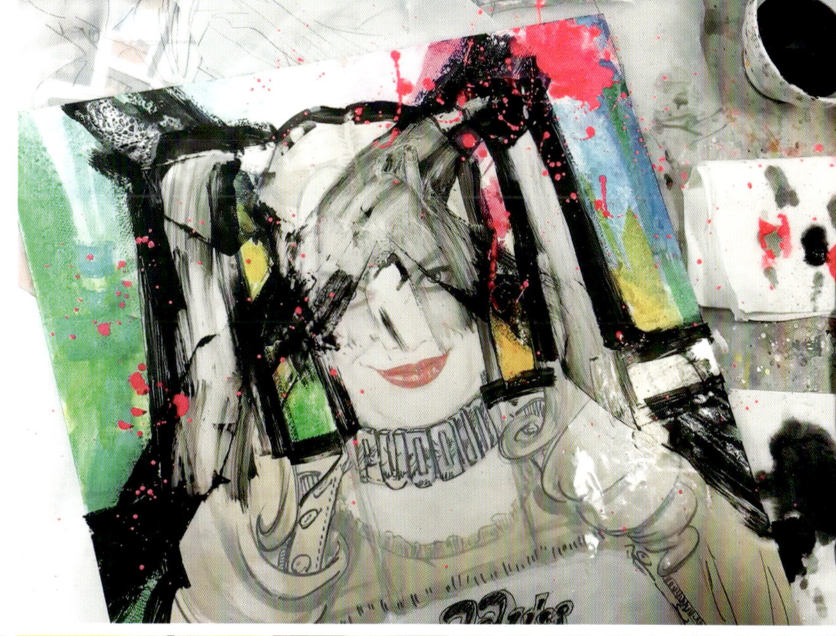

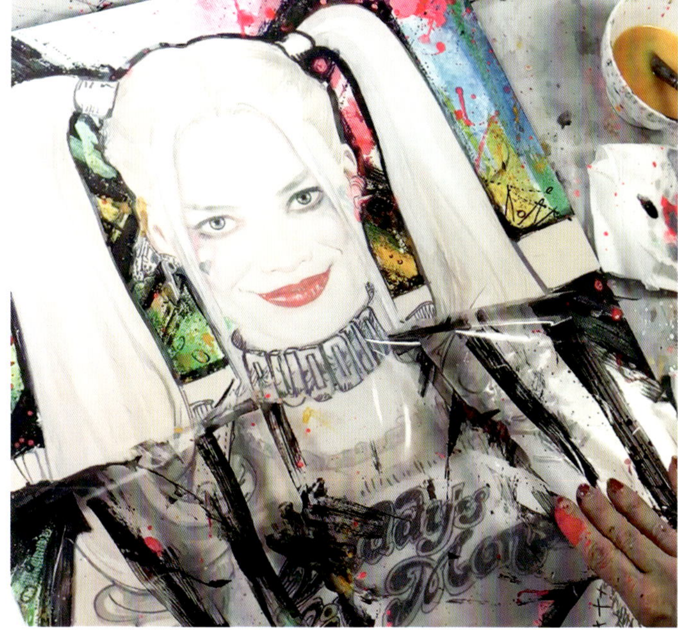

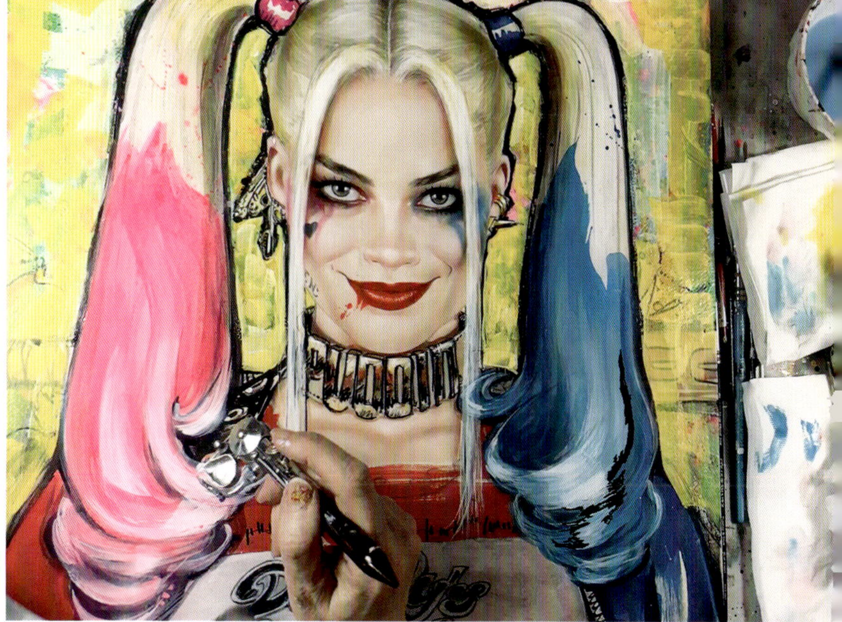

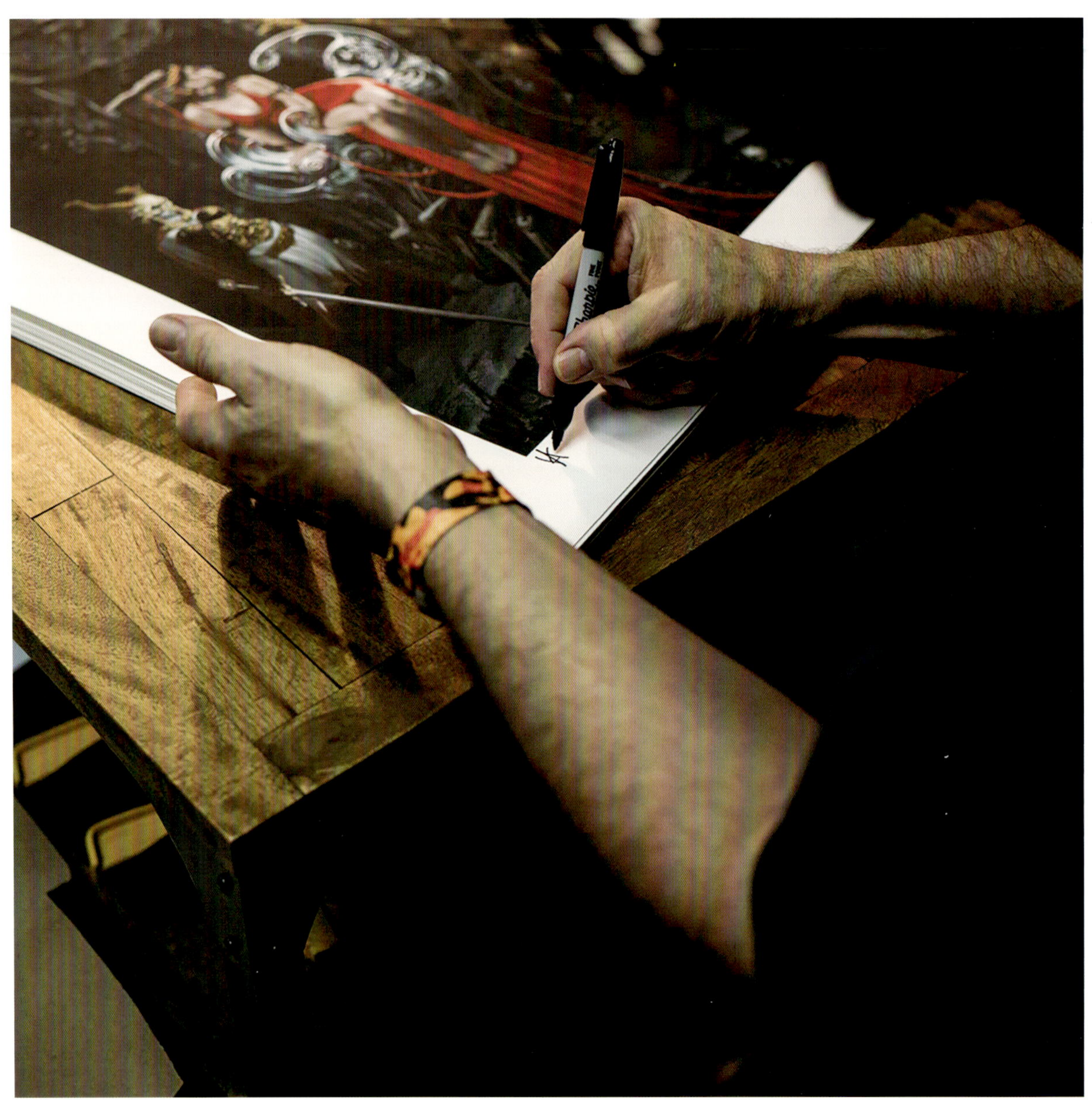

DIVIDED WE STAND

ALLEN WILLIAMS

It is by the Alltaker's design that the Underworld stands divided under three factions: Bone, Flesh, and Spirit.

The factions' contentious sisterhood of leaders goads the Land of the Dead ever onward: Xiall of Bone Faction, Gethsemoni of Flesh Faction, and Kier of Spirit Faction. This ensures that the Underworld will never lapse into a myopic war, such as the one that is consuming Heaven and Hell.

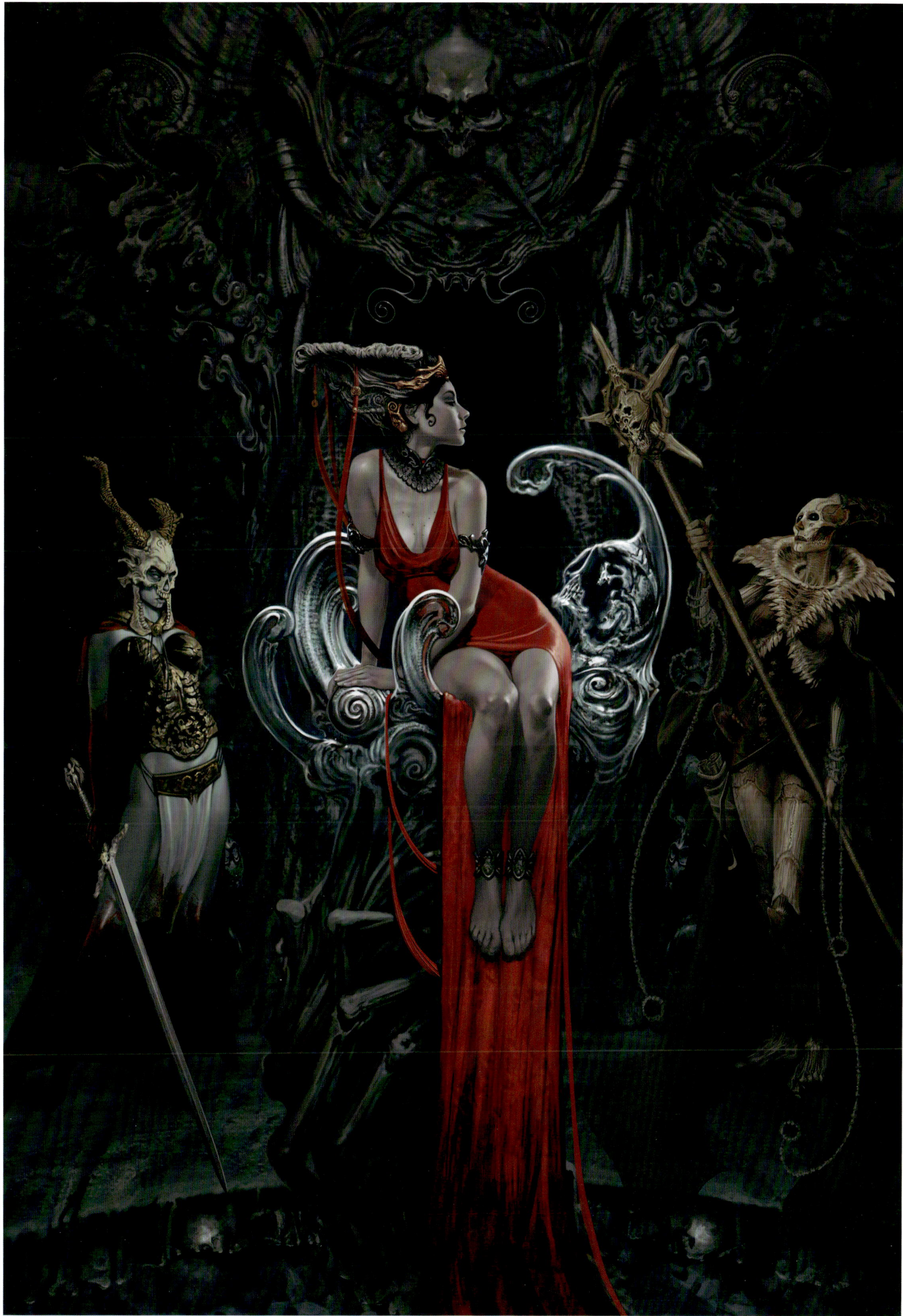

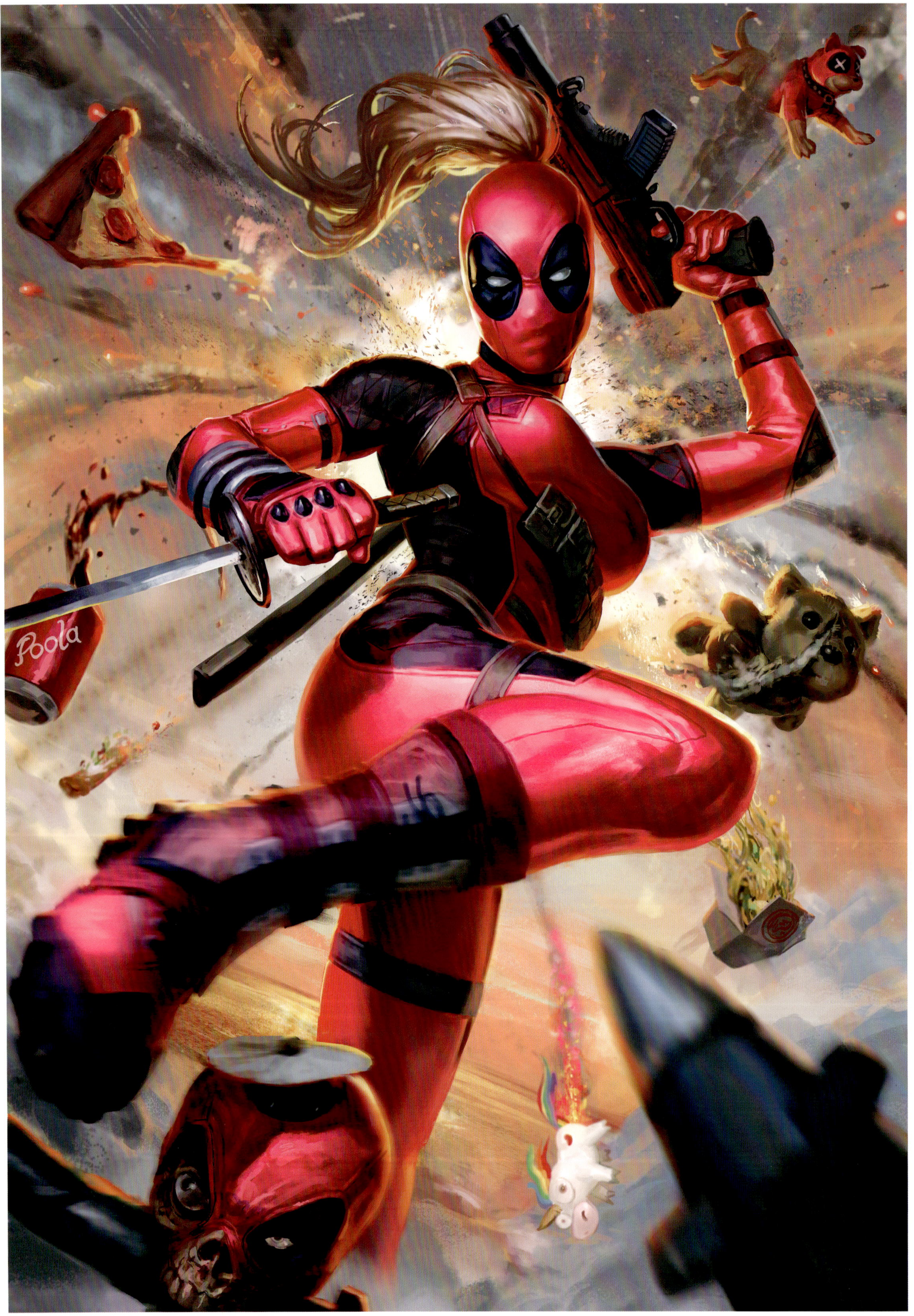
Poola

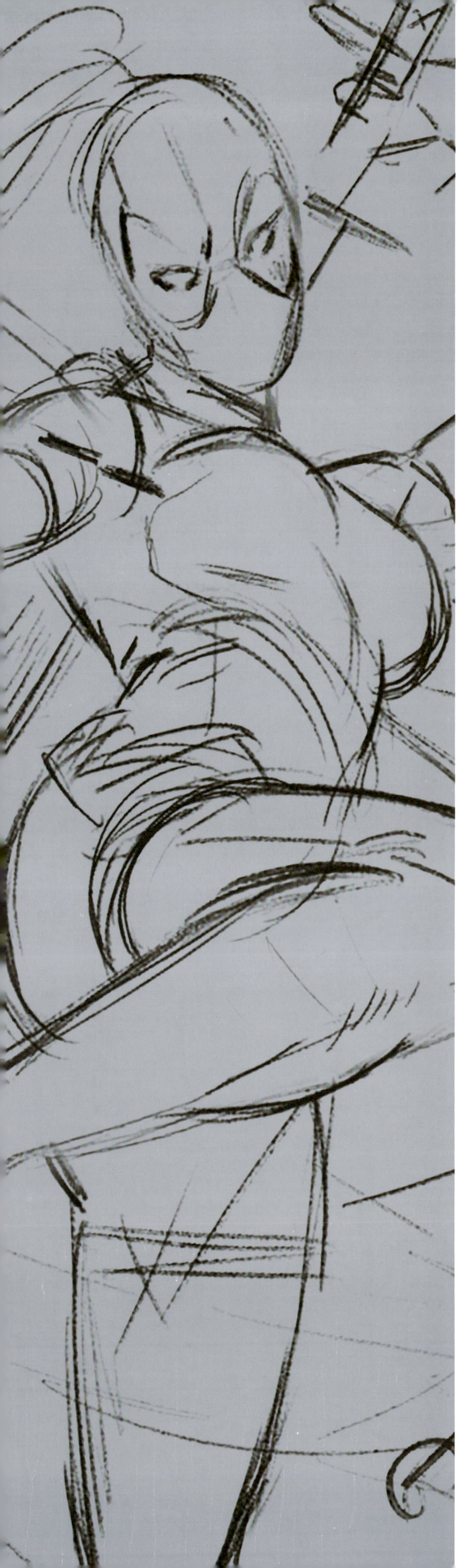

LADY DEADPOOL

ALEX PASCENKO

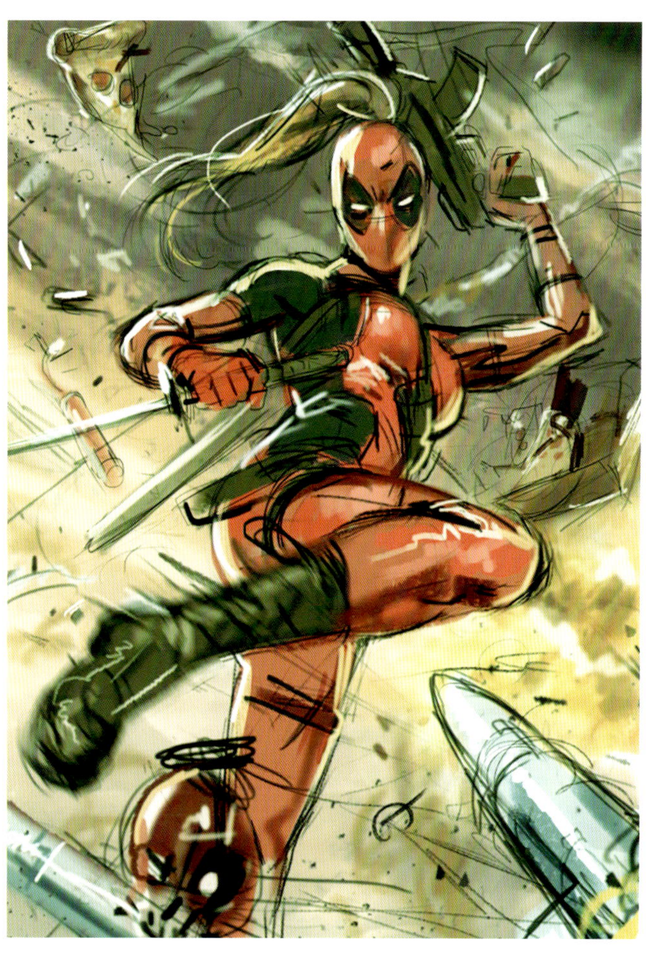

Packed with more awesome than the world ever thought possible comes Lady Deadpool in a print loaded with action, derring-do, and cheap takeout food.

Straight outta an alternate universe, Marvel's own gender-swapping, dimension-hopping Merc with a Mouth, Wanda Wilson, prepares to roundhouse a rocket missile, accompanied by Headpool and an explosion of absurd accoutrement.

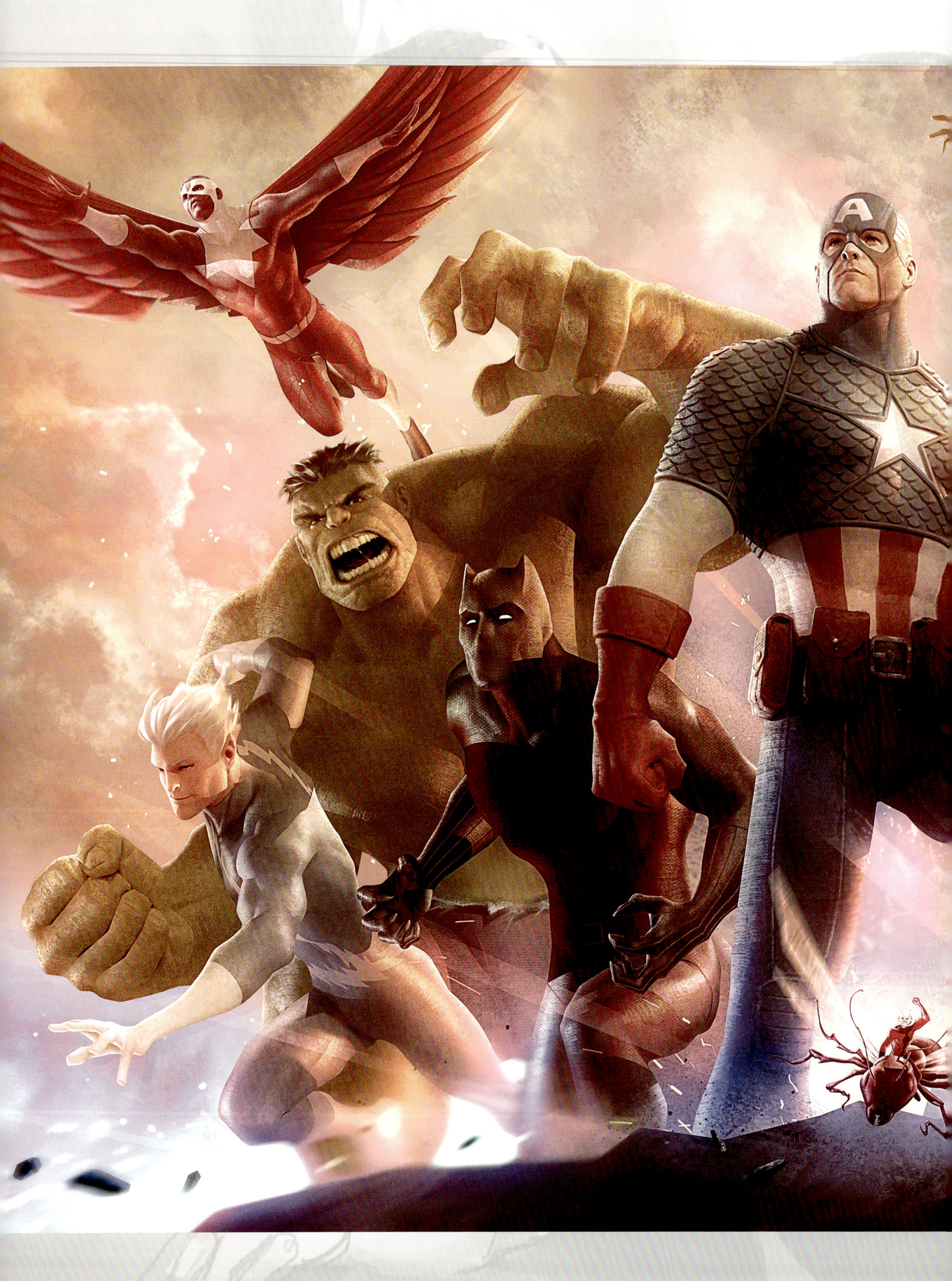

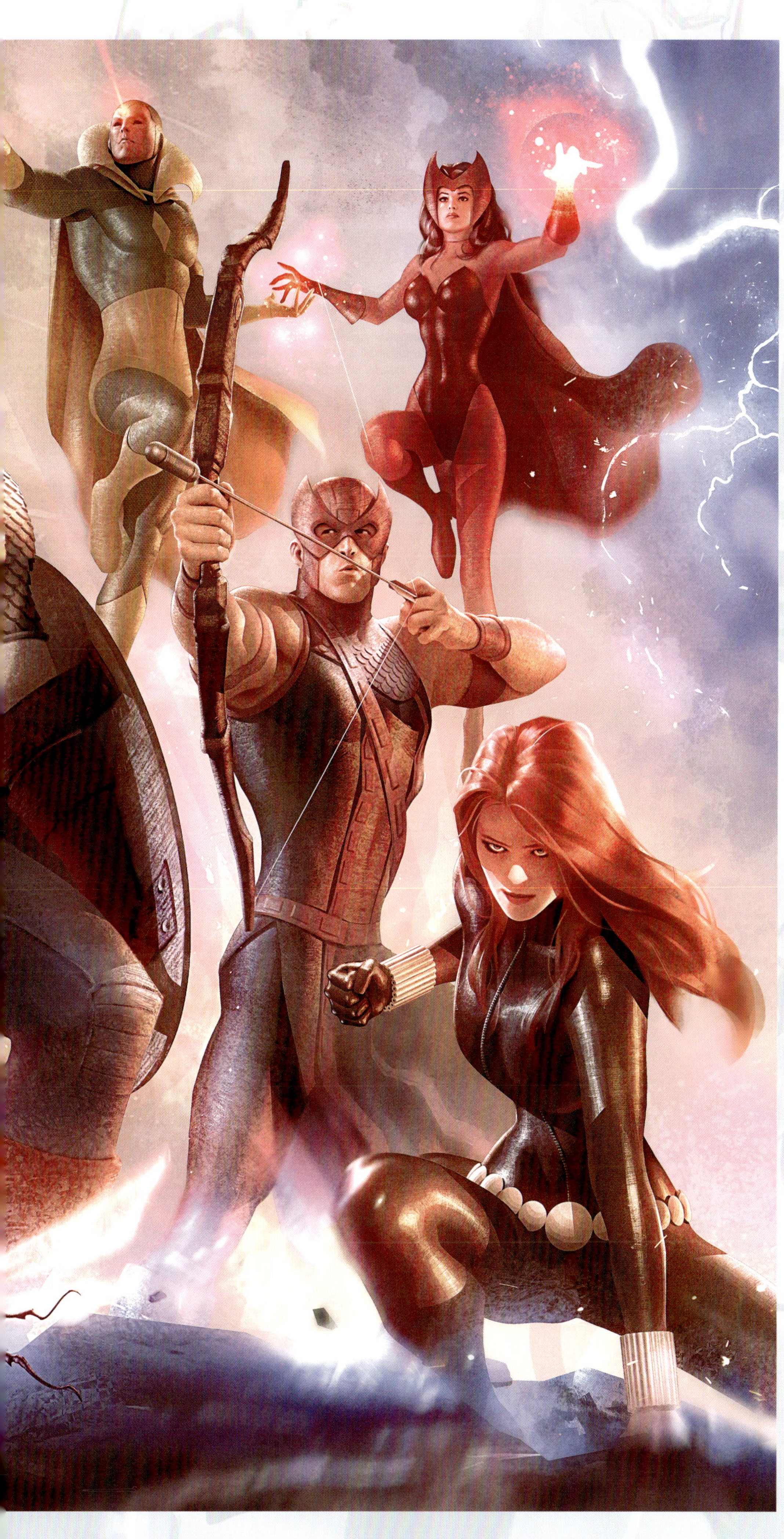

AVENGERS
TEAM CAP

ALEX GARNER

In this epic print, Captain America battles evil alongside mighty Marvel mainstays Quicksilver, Hulk, Falcon, Black Panther, Ant-Man, Vision, Hawkeye, Scarlet Witch, and Black Widow.

AVENGERS
TEAM IRON MAN

ALEX GARNER

Iron Man stands ready to defend Earth from any threat! He is joined by founding Avengers team members Thor, Wasp, and Giant-Man, alongside classic heroes including Doctor Strange, Spider-Woman, Captain Marvel, and She-Hulk.

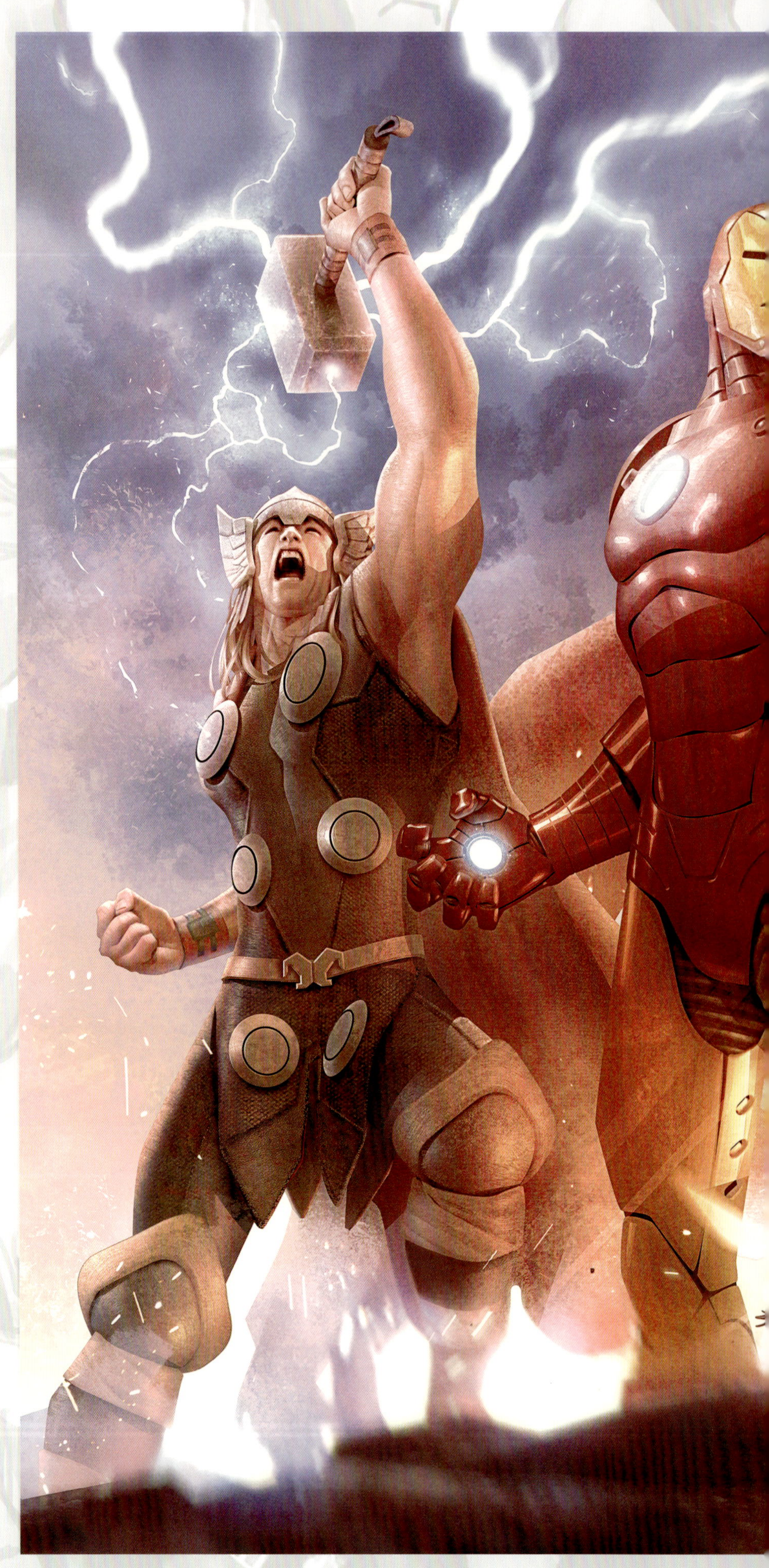

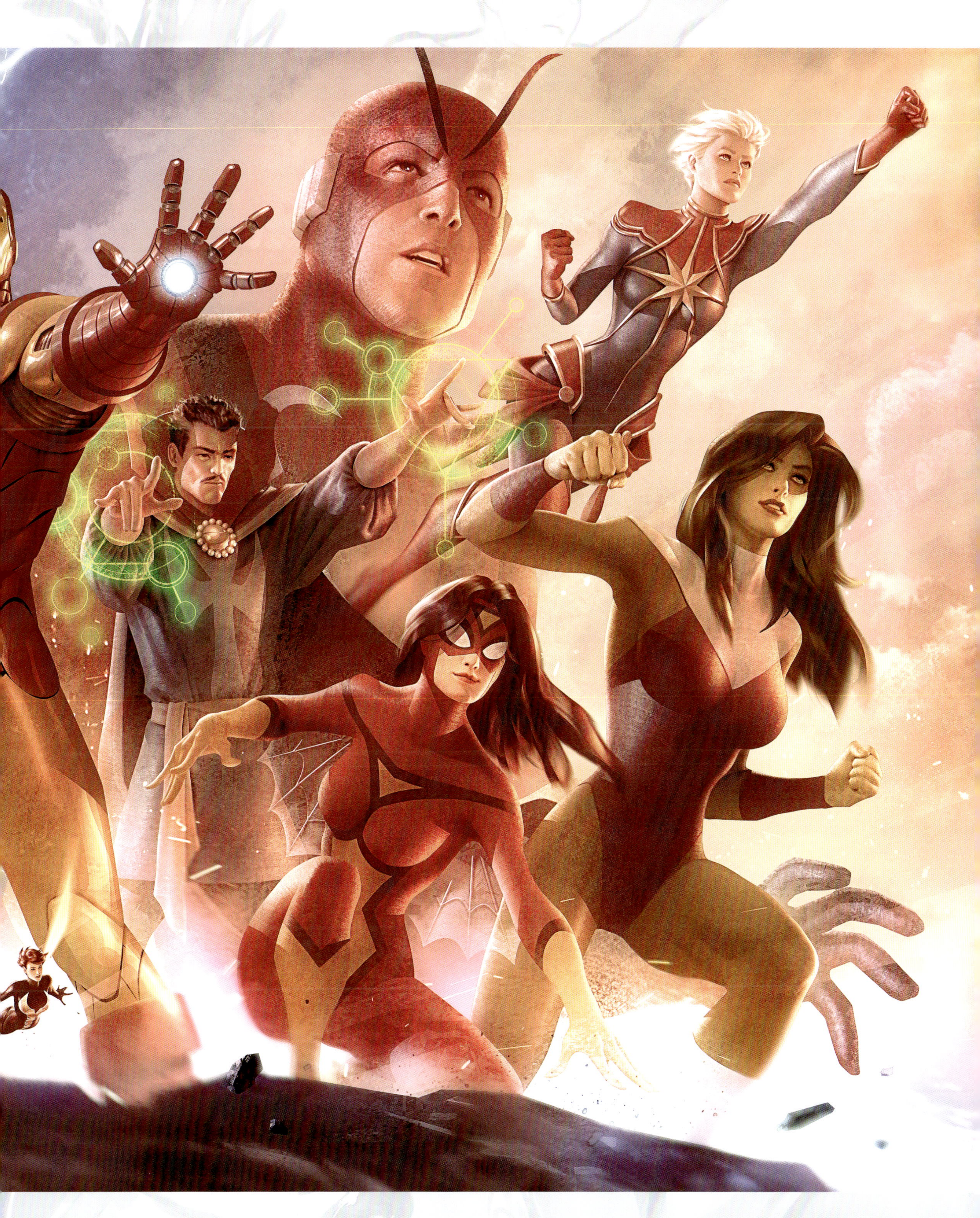

AVENGERS ASSEMBLE

ALEX GARNER

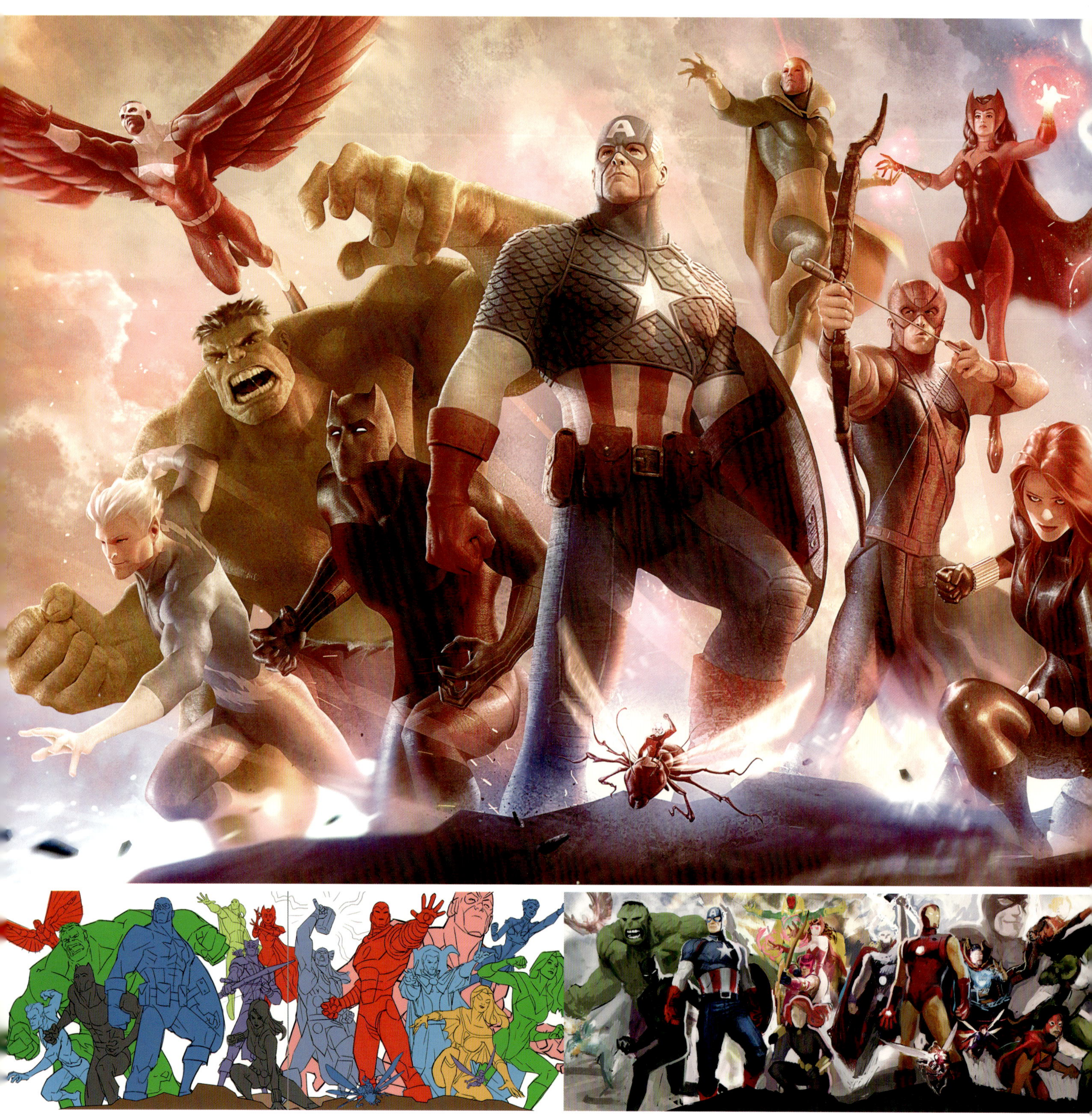

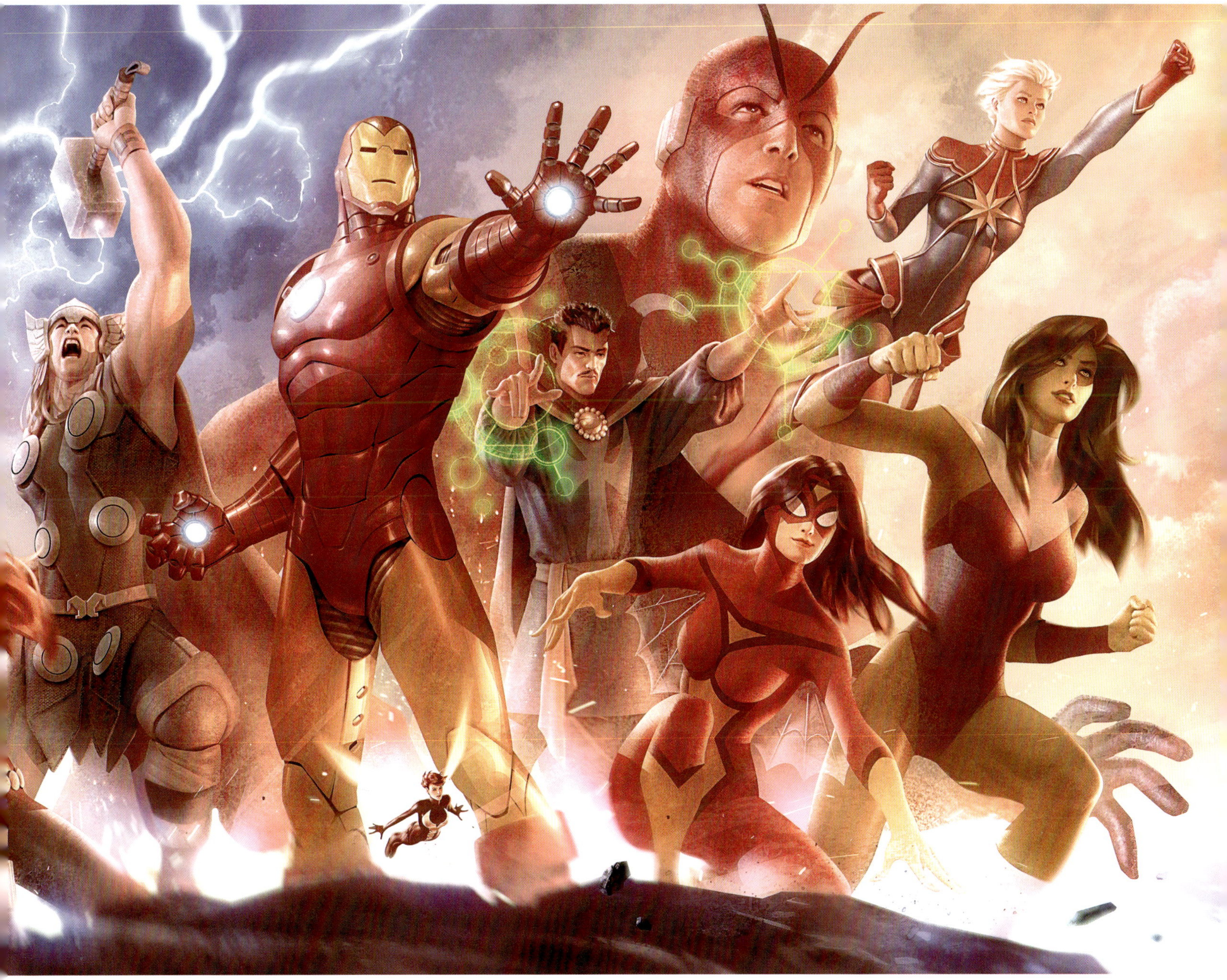

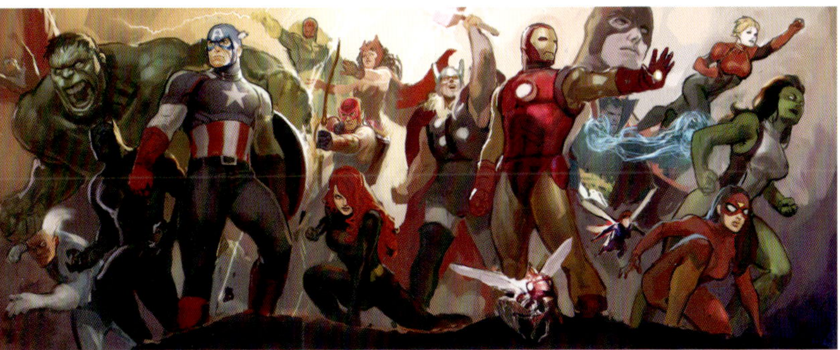

This dynamic print by Alex Garner features eighteen of Earth's Mightiest Heroes in one epic illustration. This classic lineup showcases many of the most popular Avengers in Marvel history, including Quicksilver, Hulk, Falcon, Black Panther, Captain America, Ant-Man, Vision, Hawkeye, Scarlet Witch, Black Widow, Thor, Iron Man, Wasp, Doctor Strange, Giant-Man, Spider-Woman, Captain Marvel, and She-Hulk.

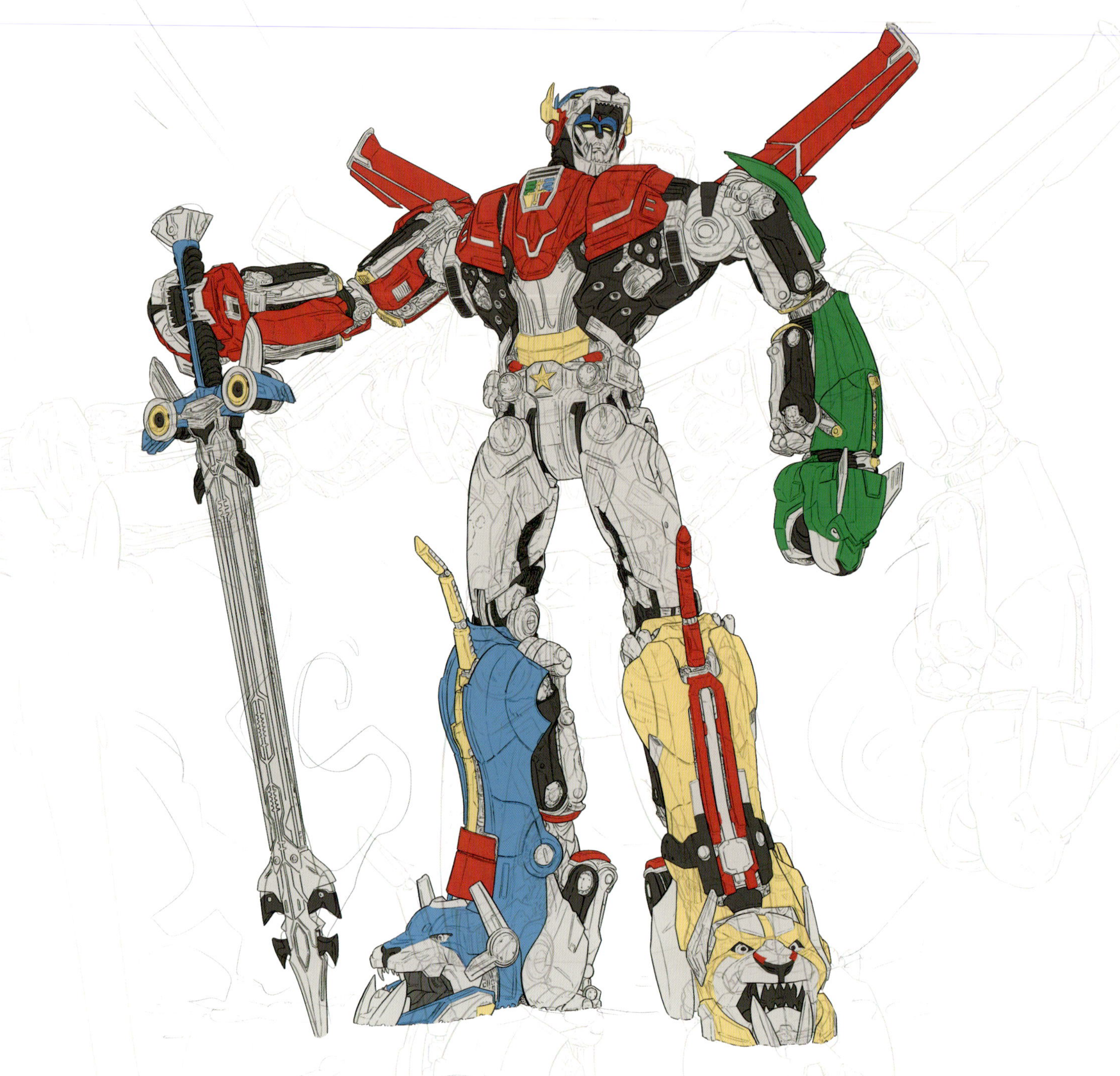

VOLTRON

DEFENDER OF THE UNIVERSE VARIANT

TOM JILESEN & JOSH NIZZI

The officially licensed *Voltron, Defender of the Universe Variant* Art Print by Tom Jilesen and Josh Nizzi pays homage to the new and classic animated series.

Like the mighty Lions themselves, the two artists join forces to become an unstoppable team, revisiting the legendary Defender of the Universe with a vibrant cel-shaded aesthetic.

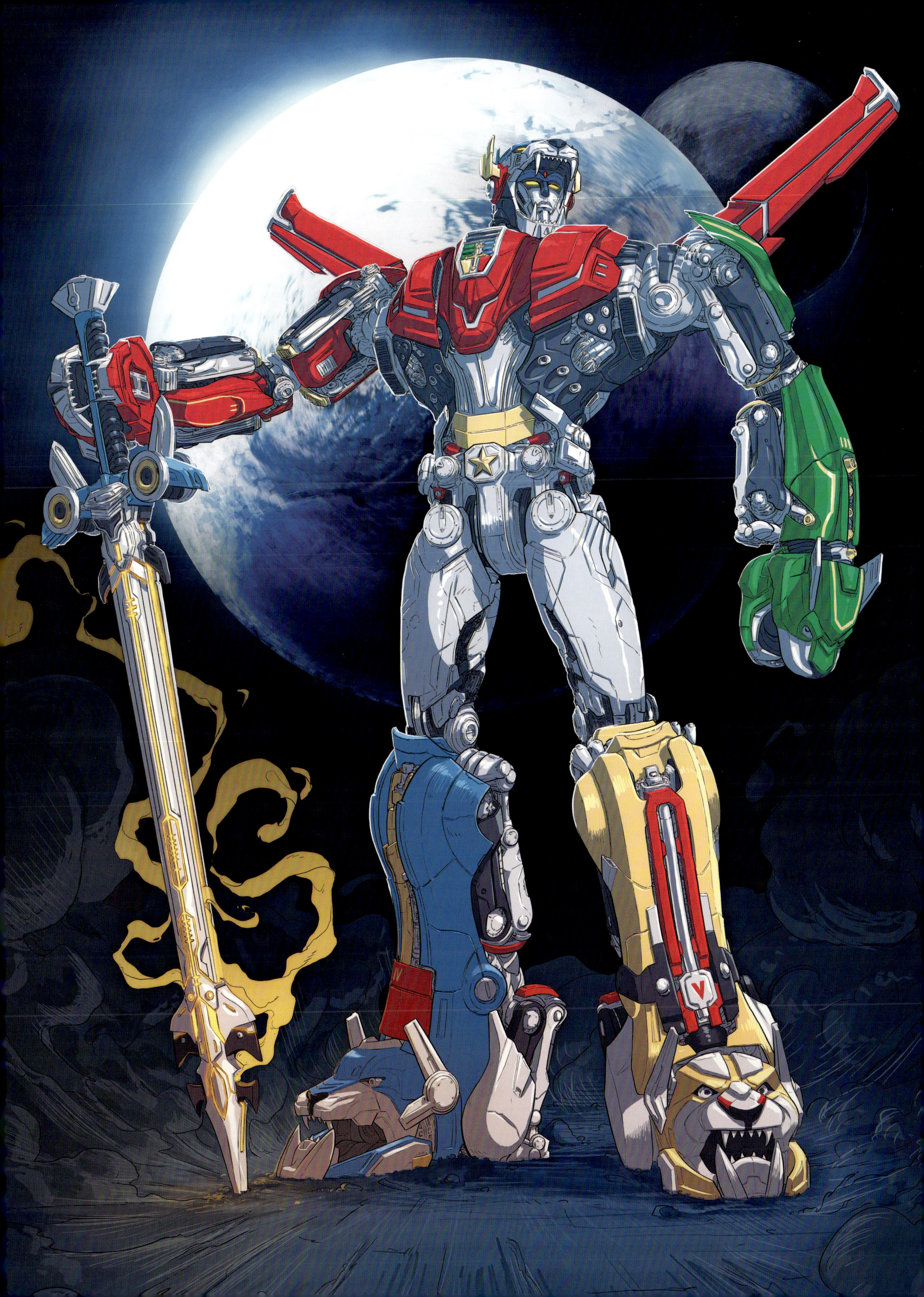

BLACK CANARY
BIRDS OF PREY

STANLEY 'ARTGERM' LAU

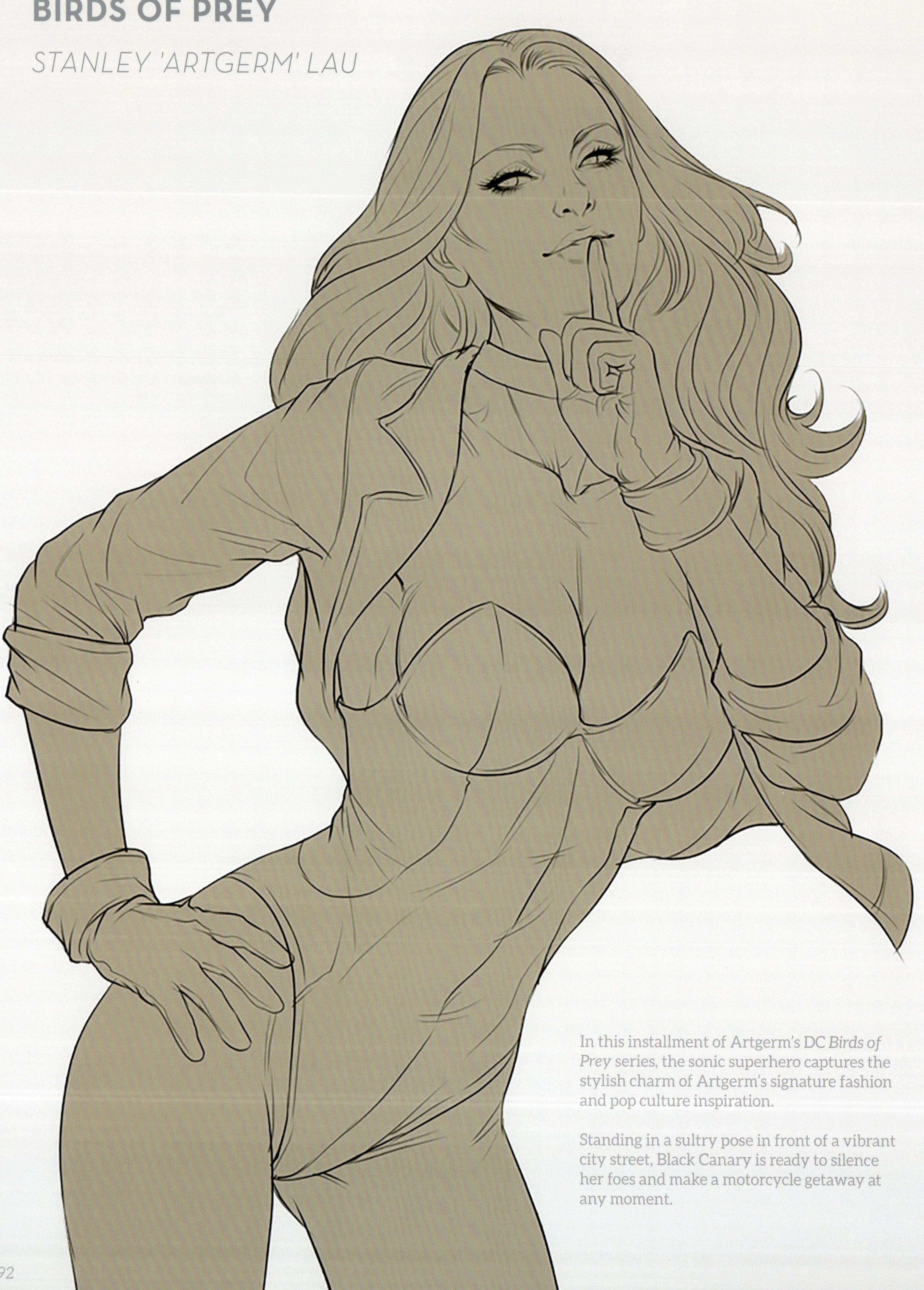

In this installment of Artgerm's DC *Birds of Prey* series, the sonic superhero captures the stylish charm of Artgerm's signature fashion and pop culture inspiration.

Standing in a sultry pose in front of a vibrant city street, Black Canary is ready to silence her foes and make a motorcycle getaway at any moment.

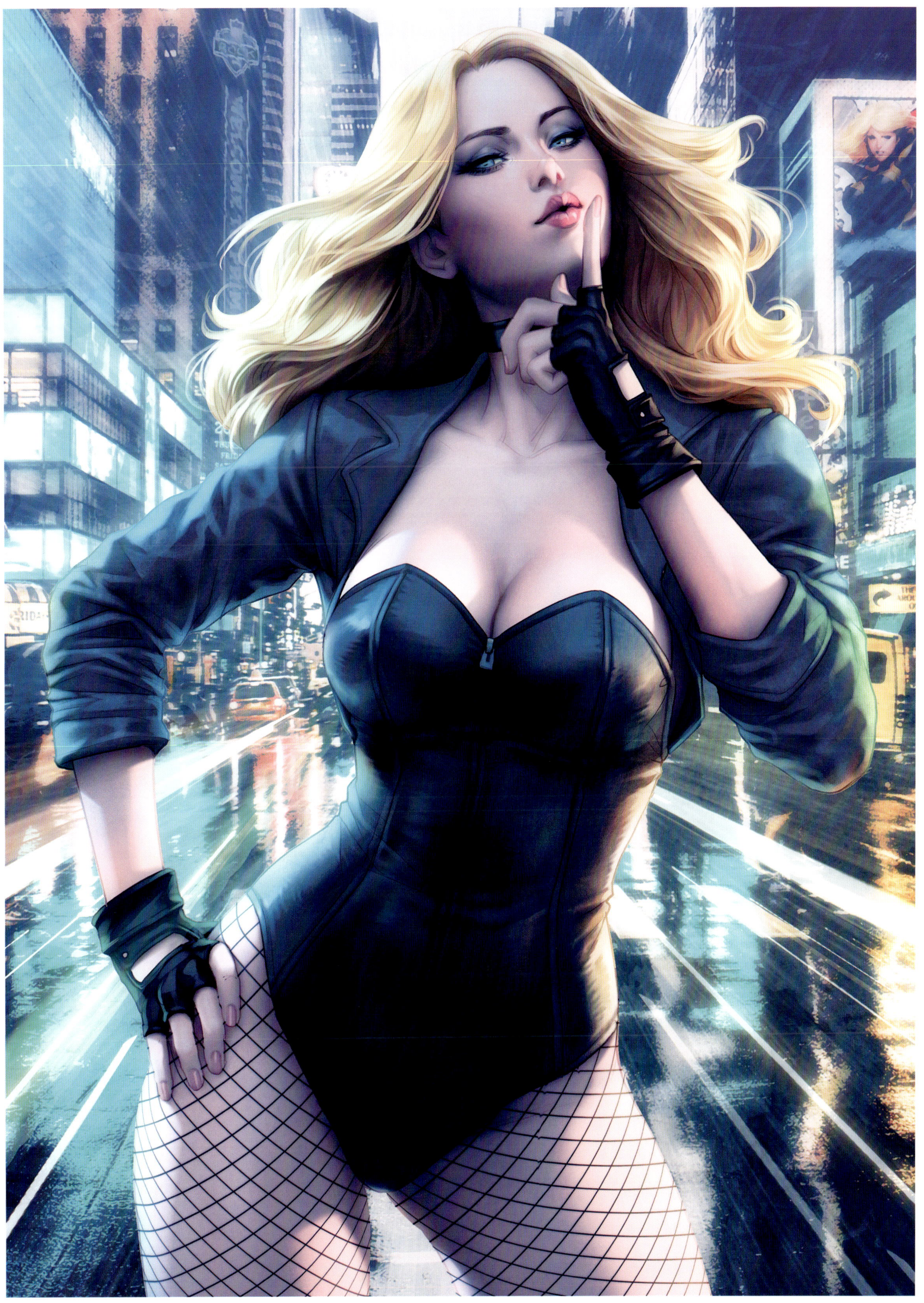

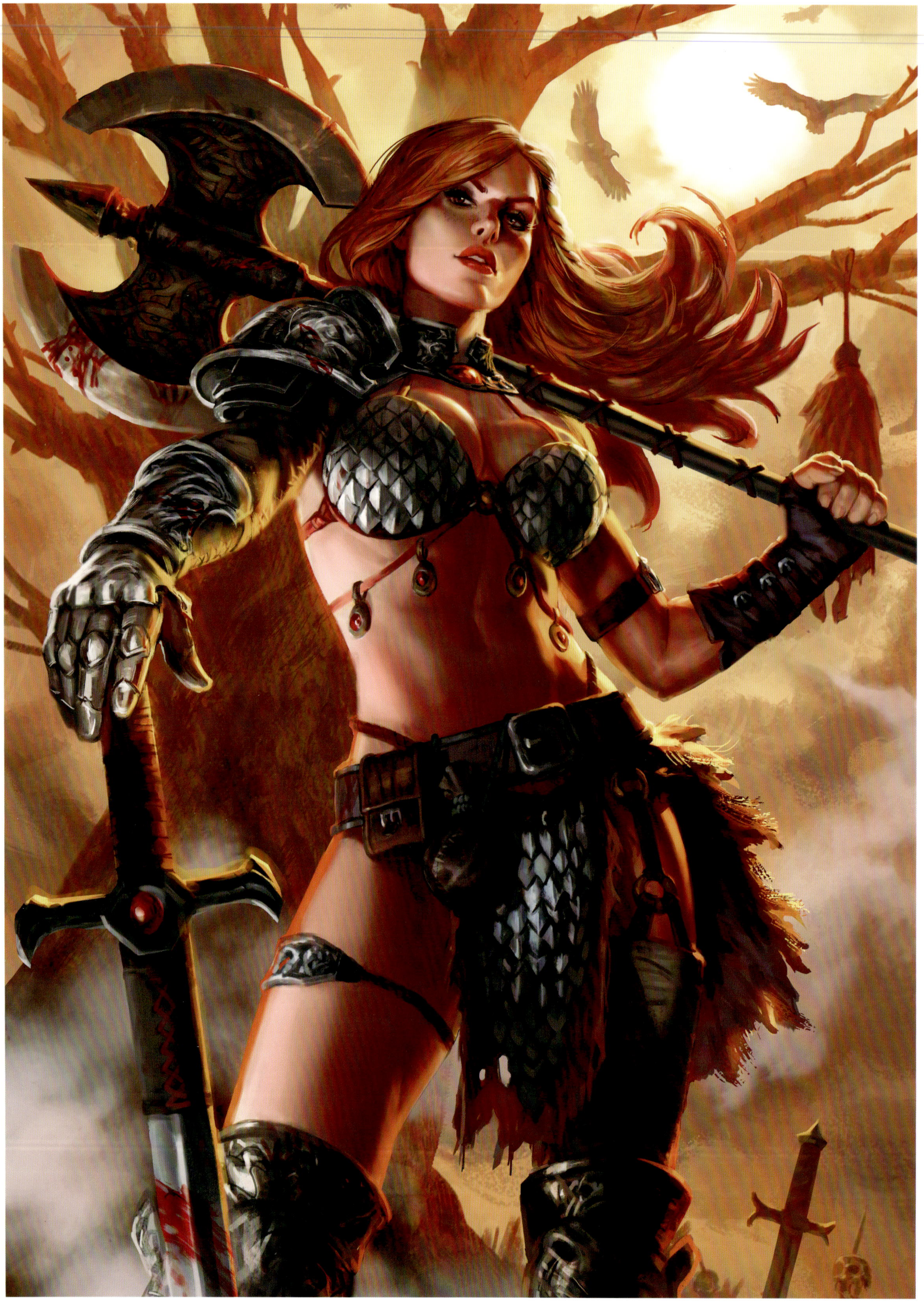

RED SONJA
QUEEN OF SCAVENGERS
ALEX PASCENKO

Holding the spoils of victory stolen from her fallen foe, Red Sonja stands defiant and ready for her next challenge.

Vultures circle above the Queen of Scavengers, waiting to forage in the wake of her bloody battle. The She-Devil with a Sword bears a confident smirk, and subtle freckles complete her detailed portrait. She is wearing her iconic chainmail costume with armored embellishments collected throughout her adventures.

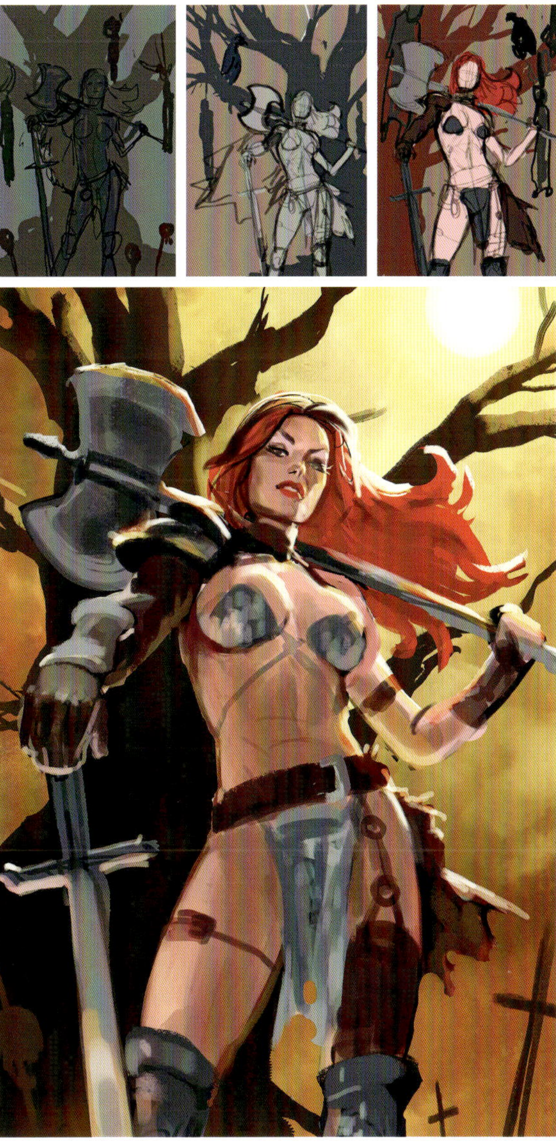

WONDER WOMAN
HELL HATH NO FURY

OLIVIA DE BERARDINIS

Based on the likeness of Gal Gadot as Wonder Woman, this print captures a pivotal and iconic moment in Diana's heroic journey.

With her gauntlets raised in defense, the brave Amazon chooses love over warfare when confronted with Ares, her ultimate foe. Wonder Woman refuses to give in to hatred—she stands as a champion for all of humanity, fighting on behalf of those who need her strength most.

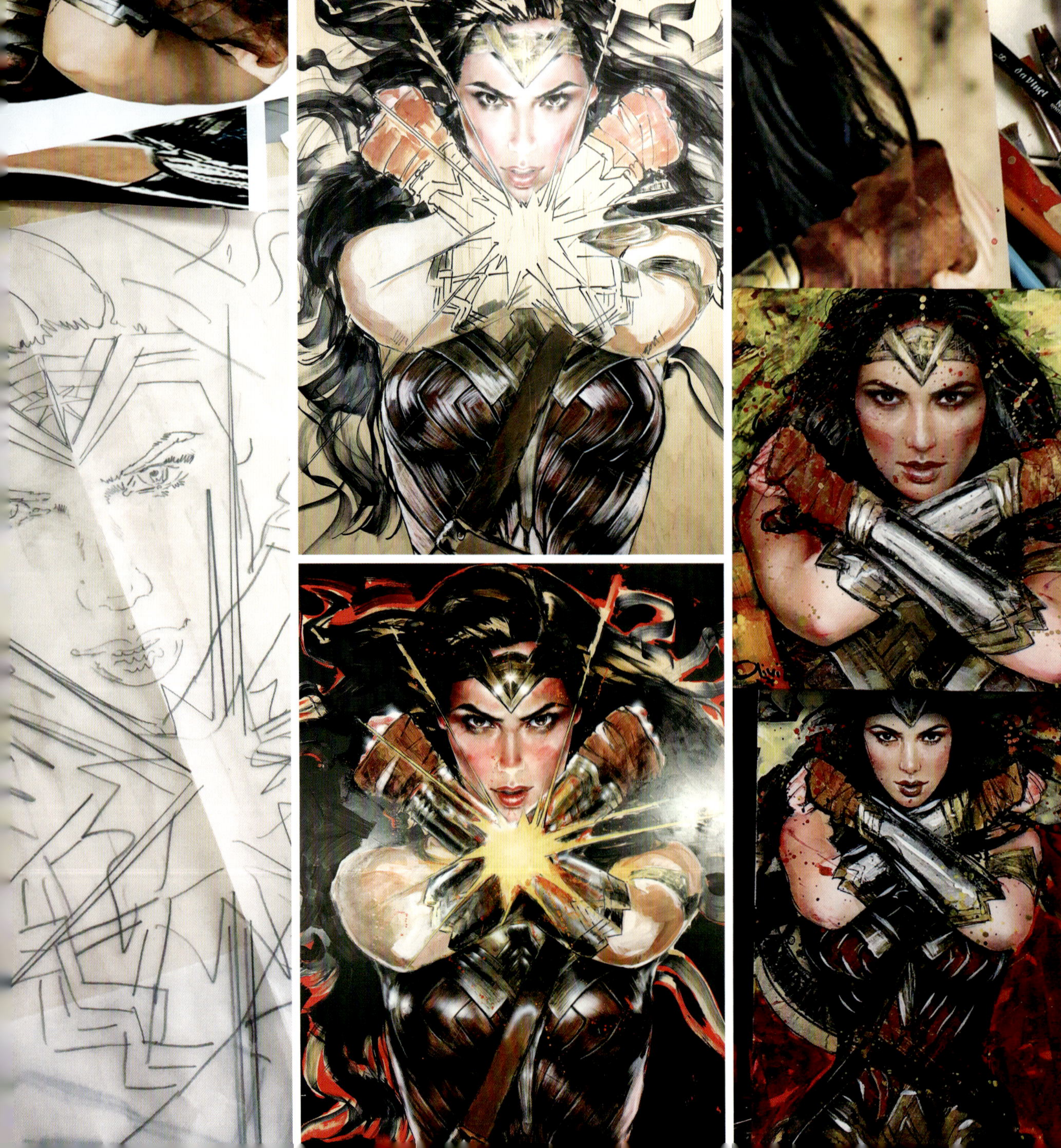

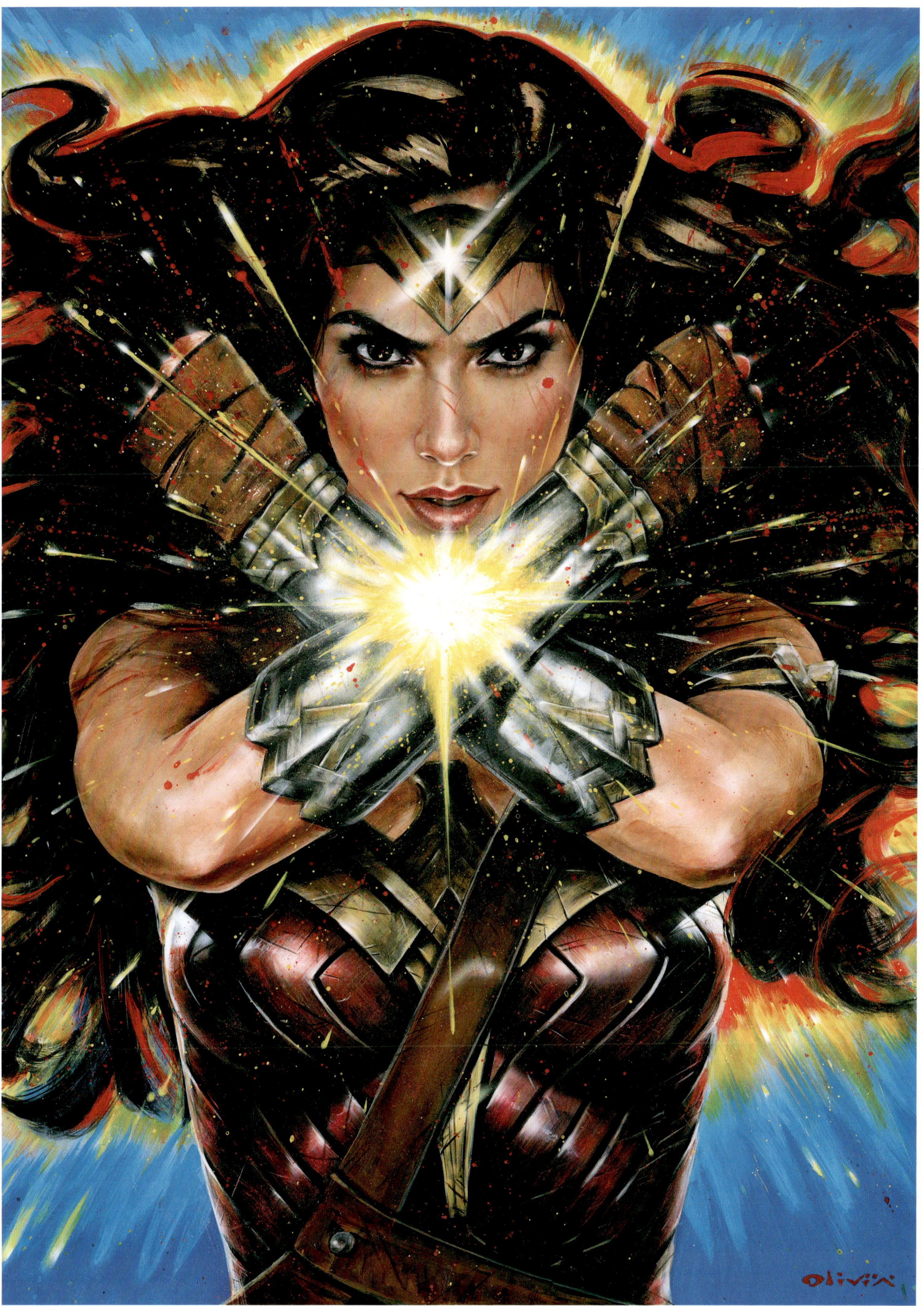

Wonder Woman: Hell Hath No Fury © 2017 Olivia De Berardinis

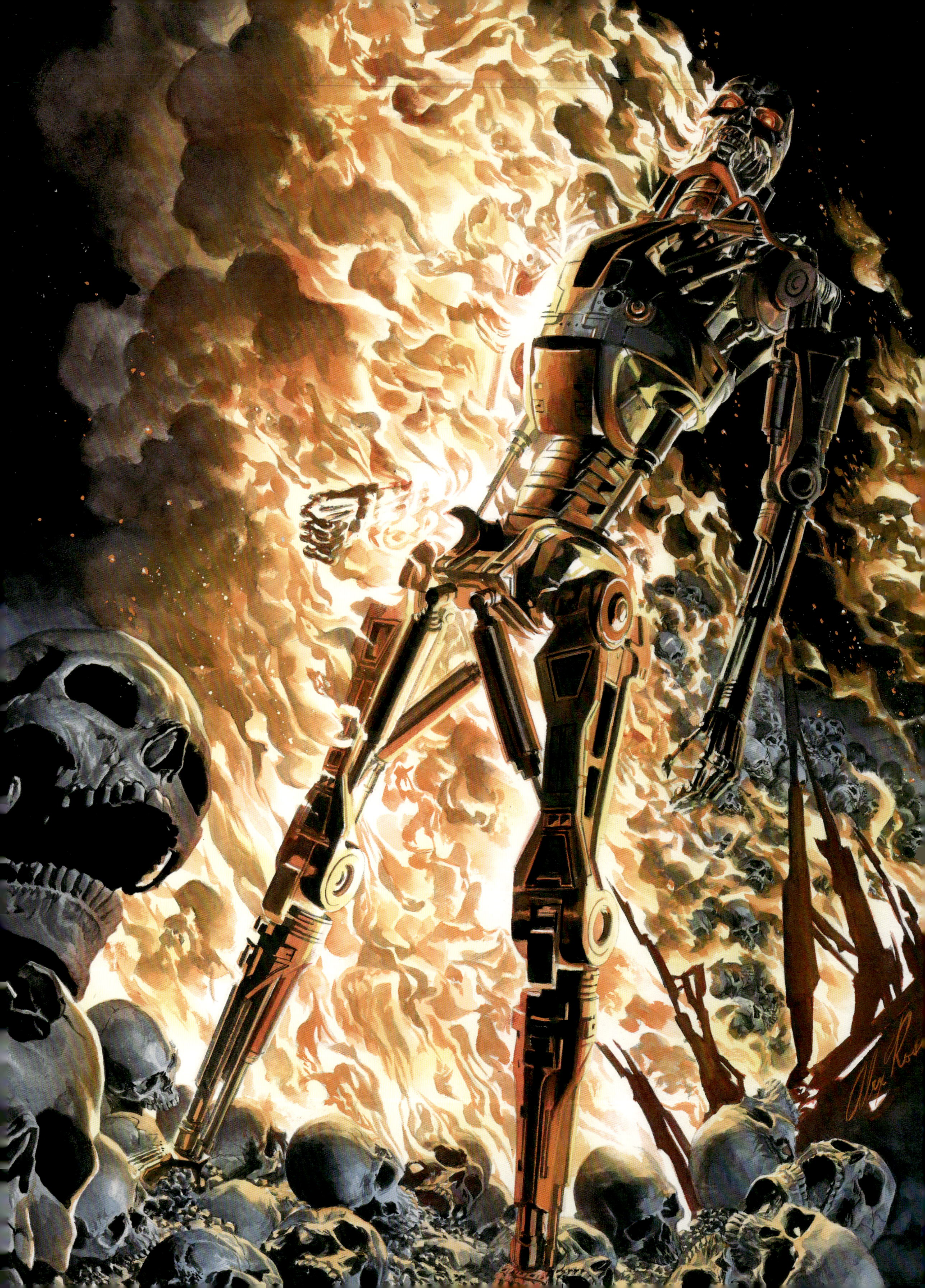

TERMINATOR

THE BURNING EARTH

ALEX ROSS

Witness the birth of an artistic legend in Eisner Award-winning painter Alex Ross's first professional work!

Originally created as a cover illustration for the Dark Horse comic of the same name, this incredible image has been specially reproduced for Sideshow as a fine art lithograph print on paper in an exclusive limited edition of 225.

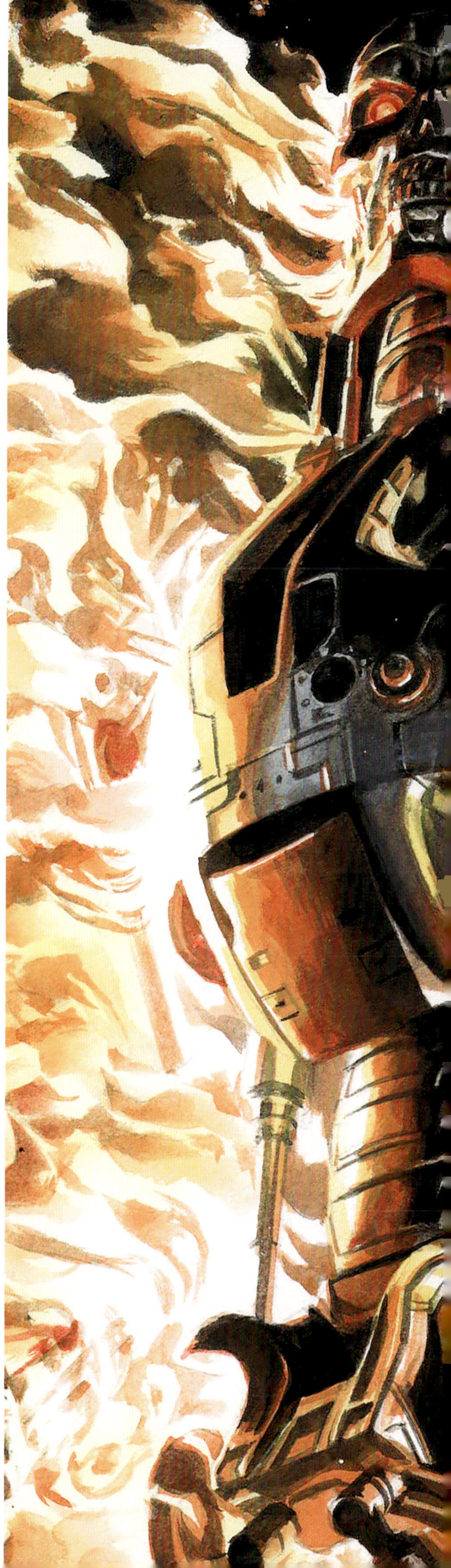

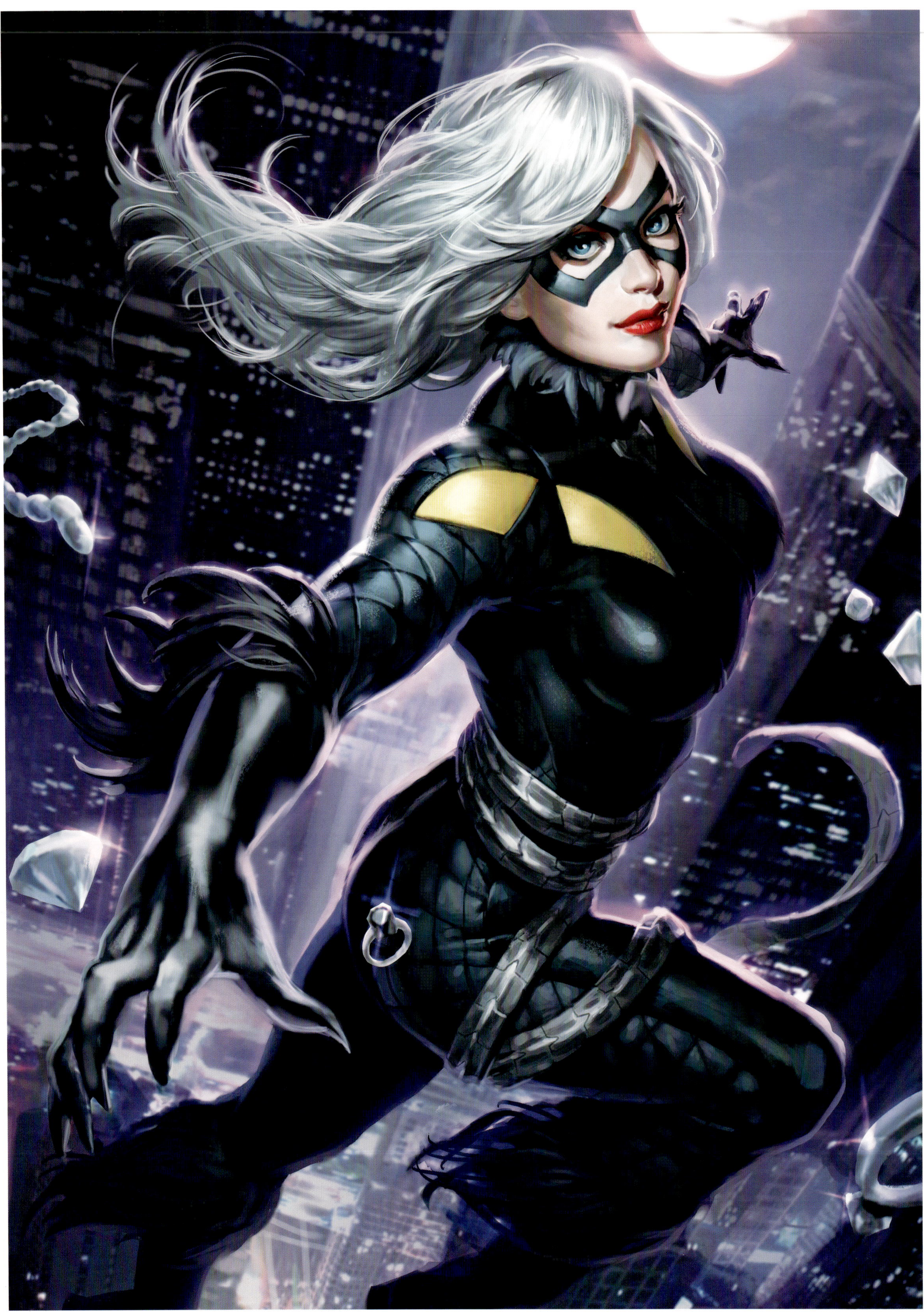

BLACK CAT

ALEX PASCENKO

Leaping gracefully over the rooftops of a bustling city below, Black Cat has certainly given someone a run of bad luck tonight.

Her stolen valuables glisten with a moonlit glow, as this crafty cat burglar makes a glamorous getaway from her latest heist.

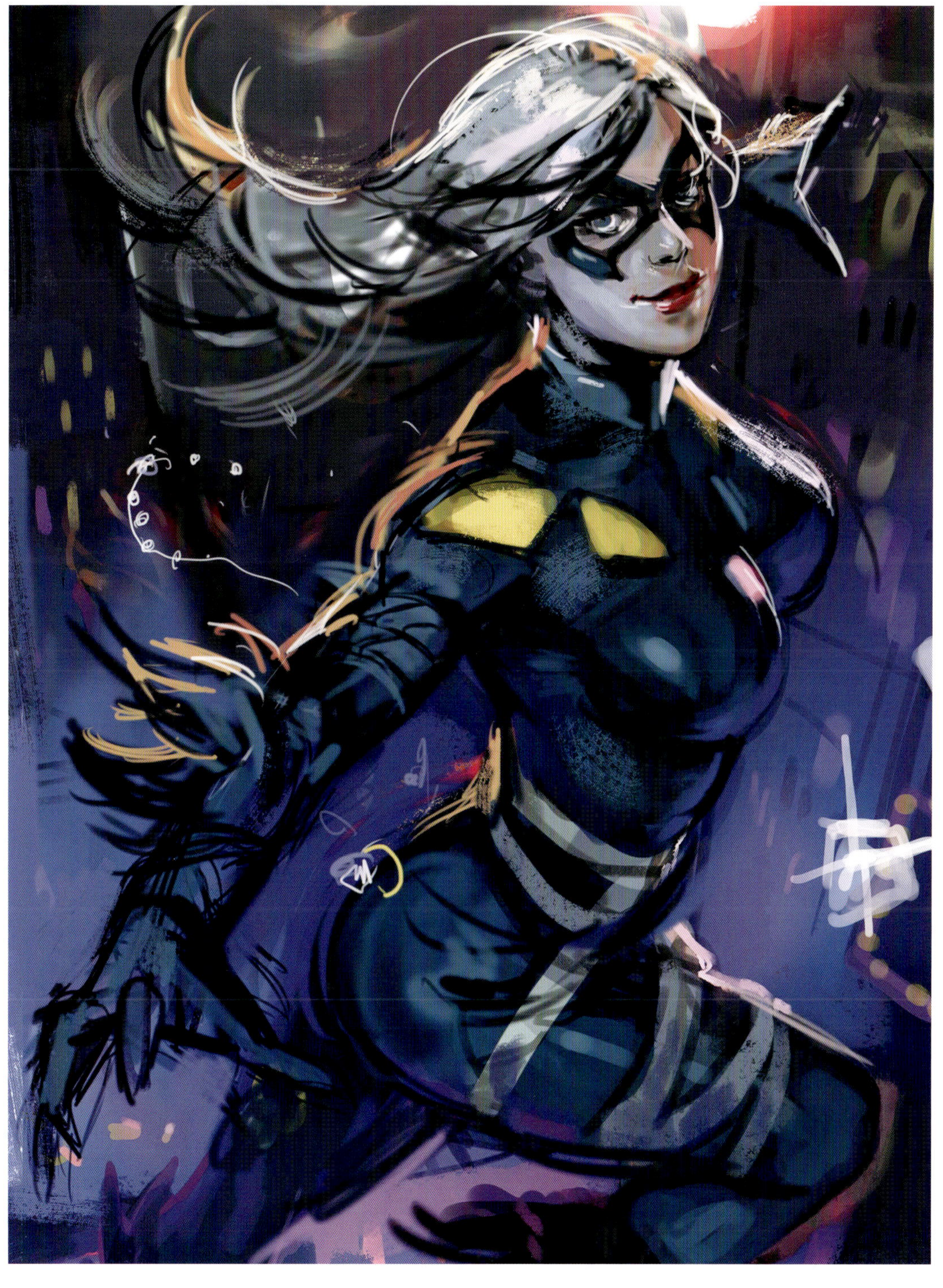

HE-MAN & SKELETOR

ALEX ROSS

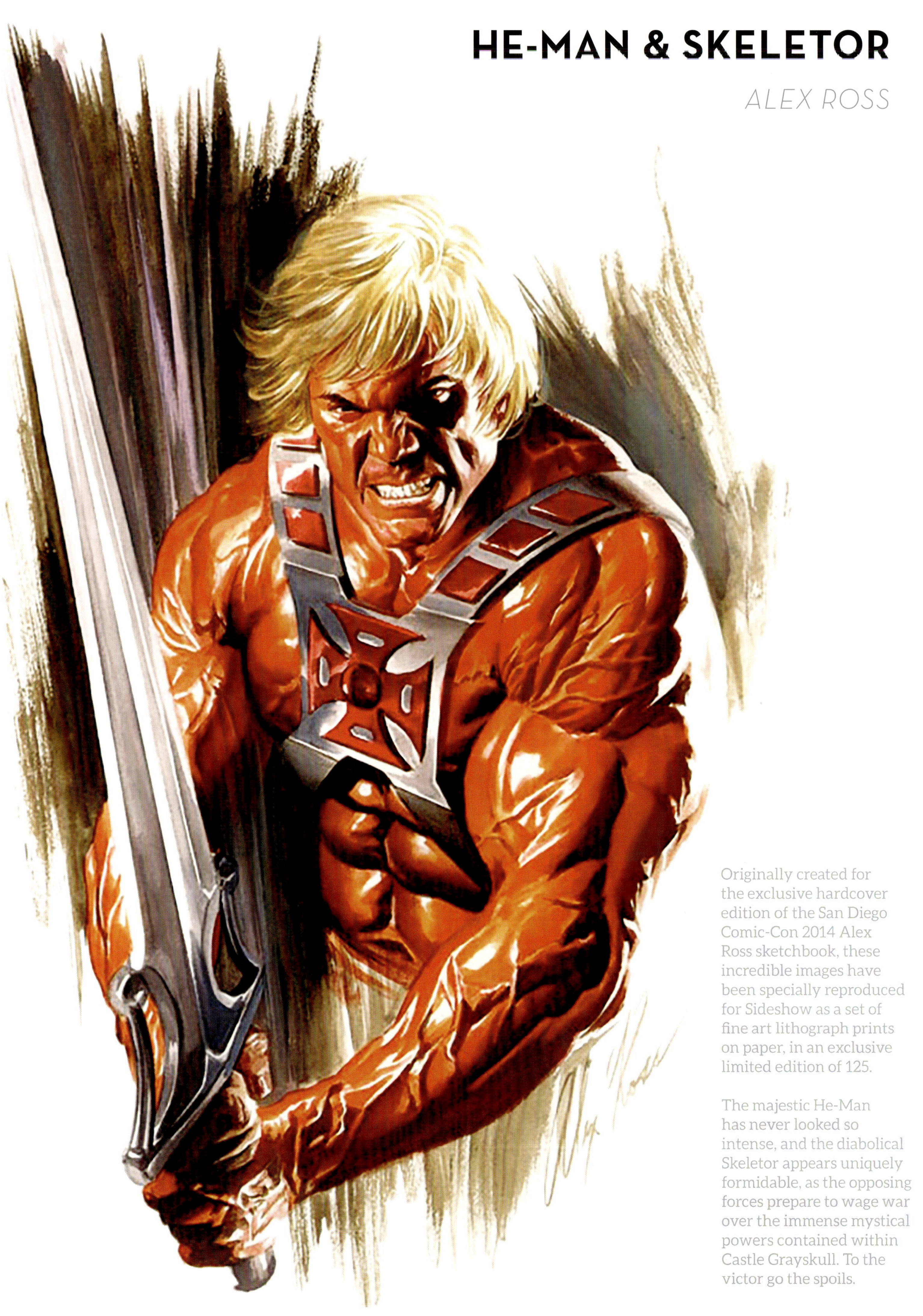

Originally created for the exclusive hardcover edition of the San Diego Comic-Con 2014 Alex Ross sketchbook, these incredible images have been specially reproduced for Sideshow as a set of fine art lithograph prints on paper, in an exclusive limited edition of 125.

The majestic He-Man has never looked so intense, and the diabolical Skeletor appears uniquely formidable, as the opposing forces prepare to wage war over the immense mystical powers contained within Castle Grayskull. To the victor go the spoils.

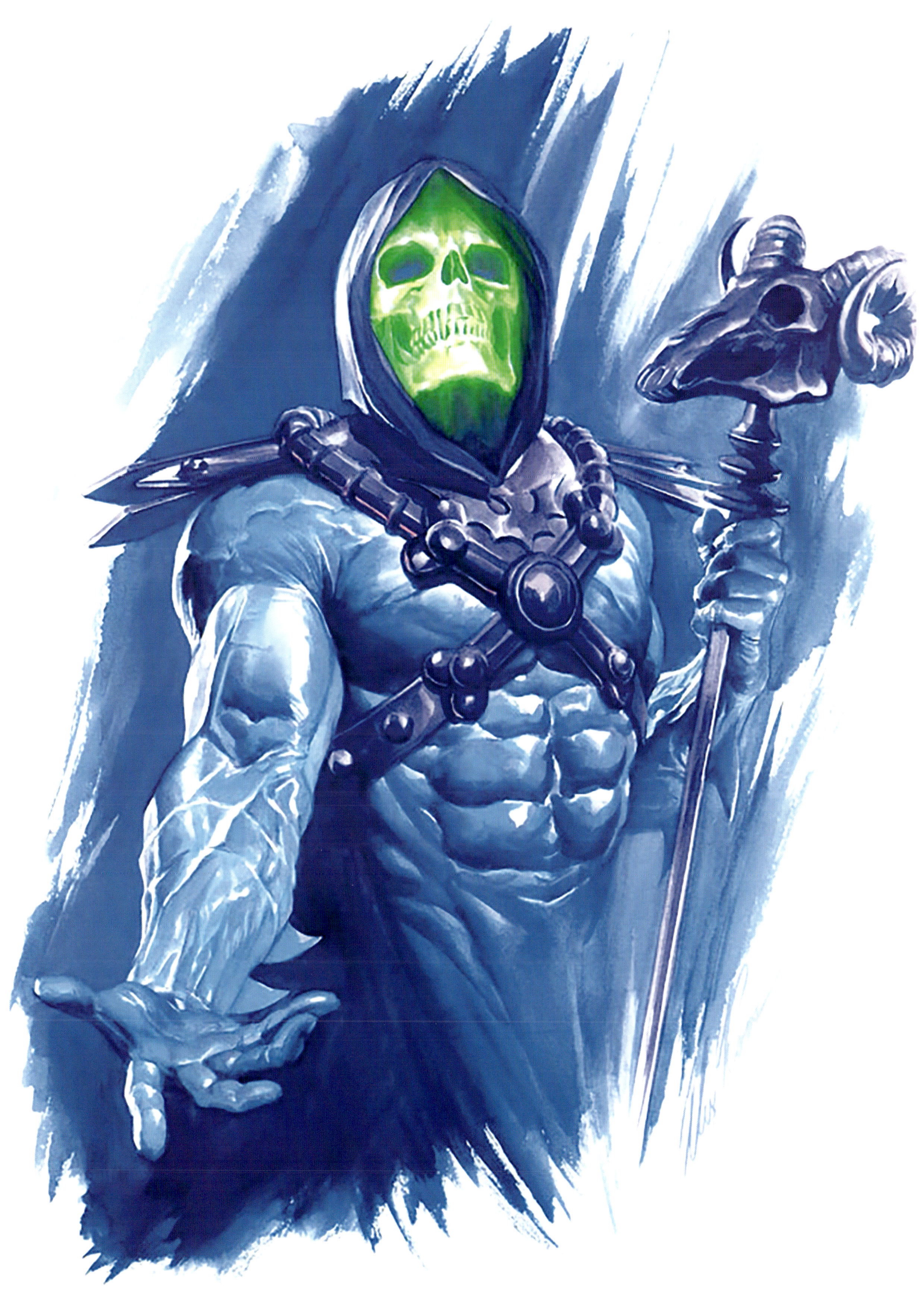

HUNTRESS
BIRDS OF PREY

STANLEY 'ARTGERM' LAU

This installment of Artgerm's *Birds of Prey* series depicts the DC heroine Huntress standing high above the rooftops of Gotham as she searches for her next target.

The violet-clad vigilante holds her crossbow and battle staff while striking a powerful pose against the purple skies, ready to face down any foe in her way.

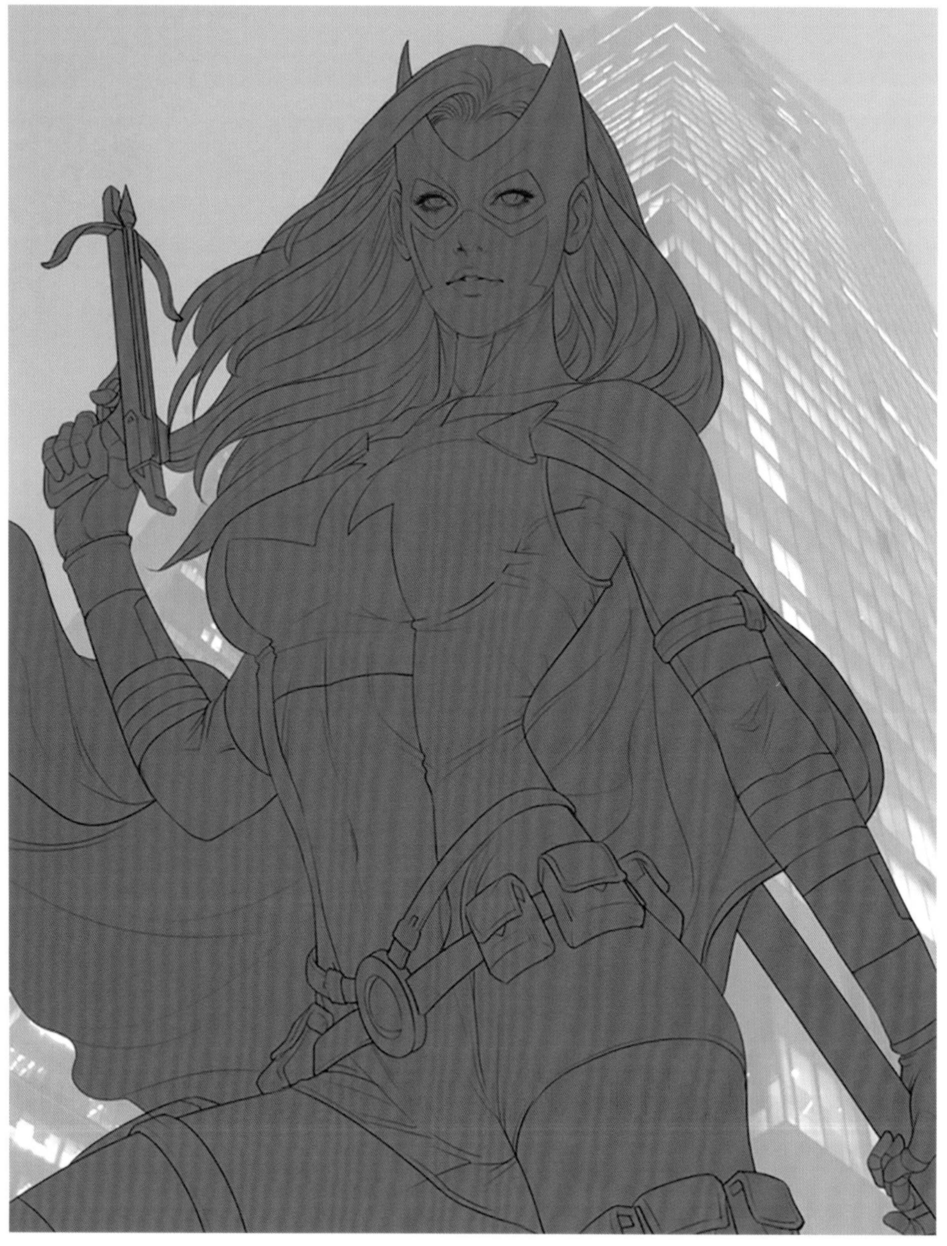

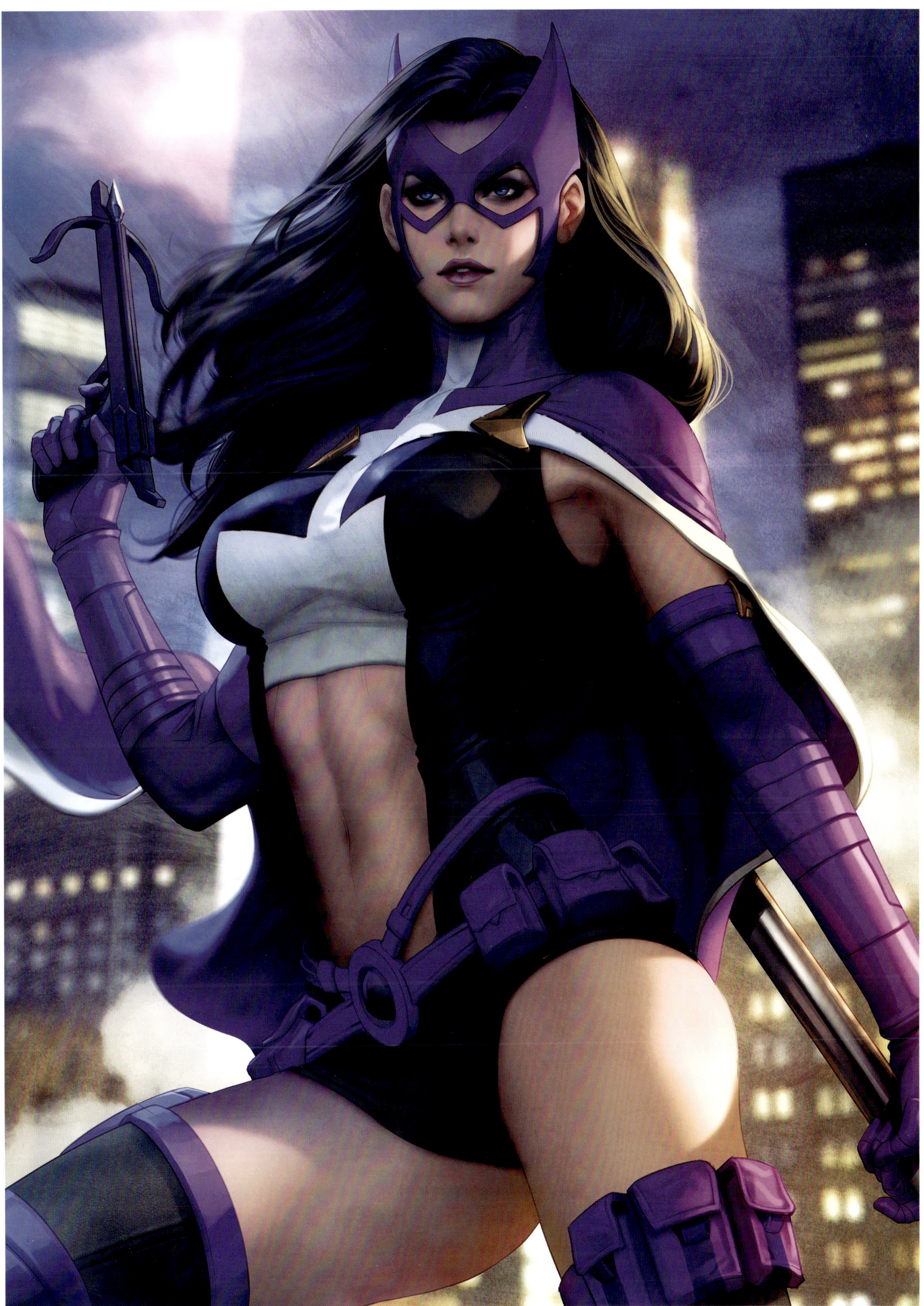

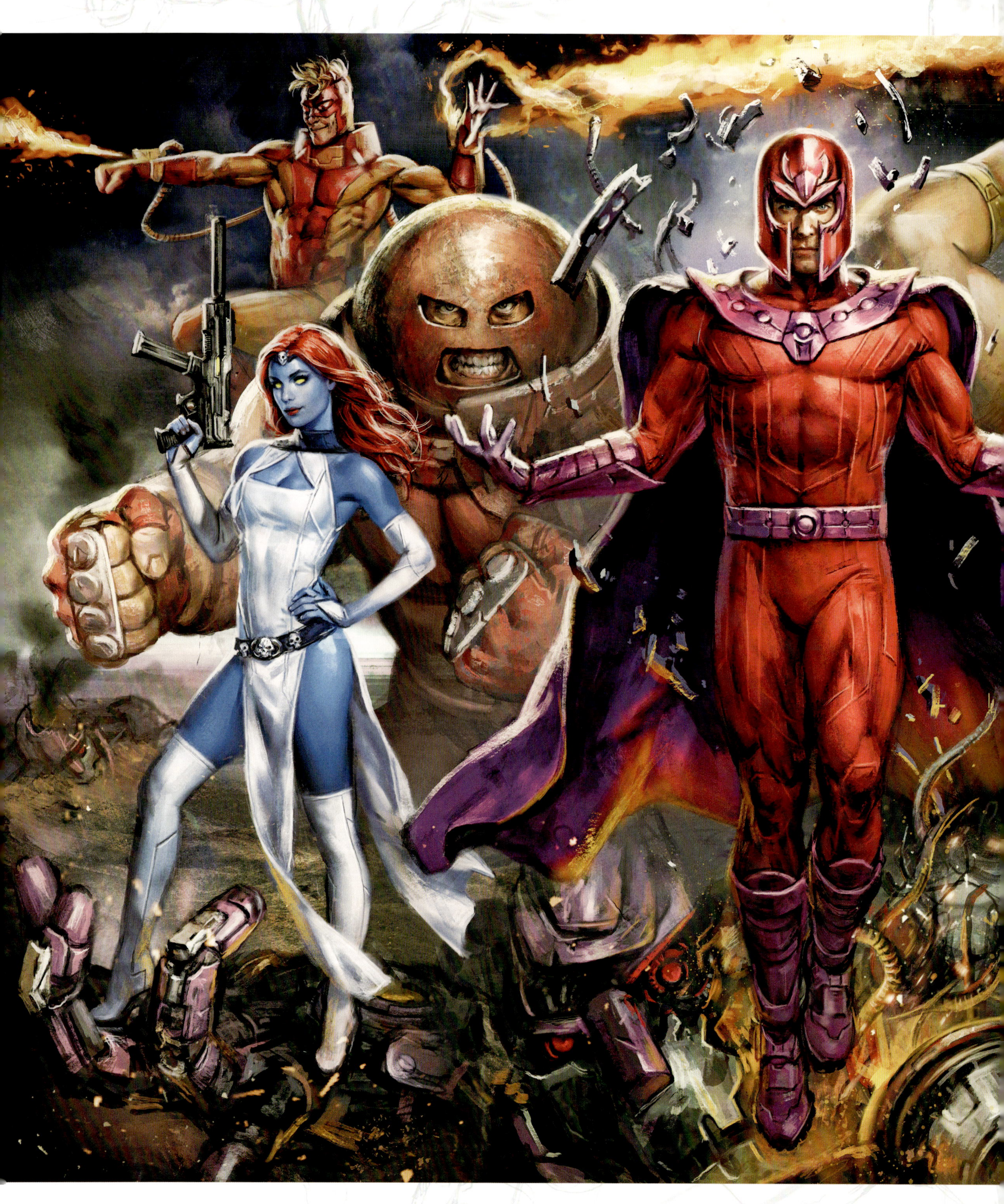

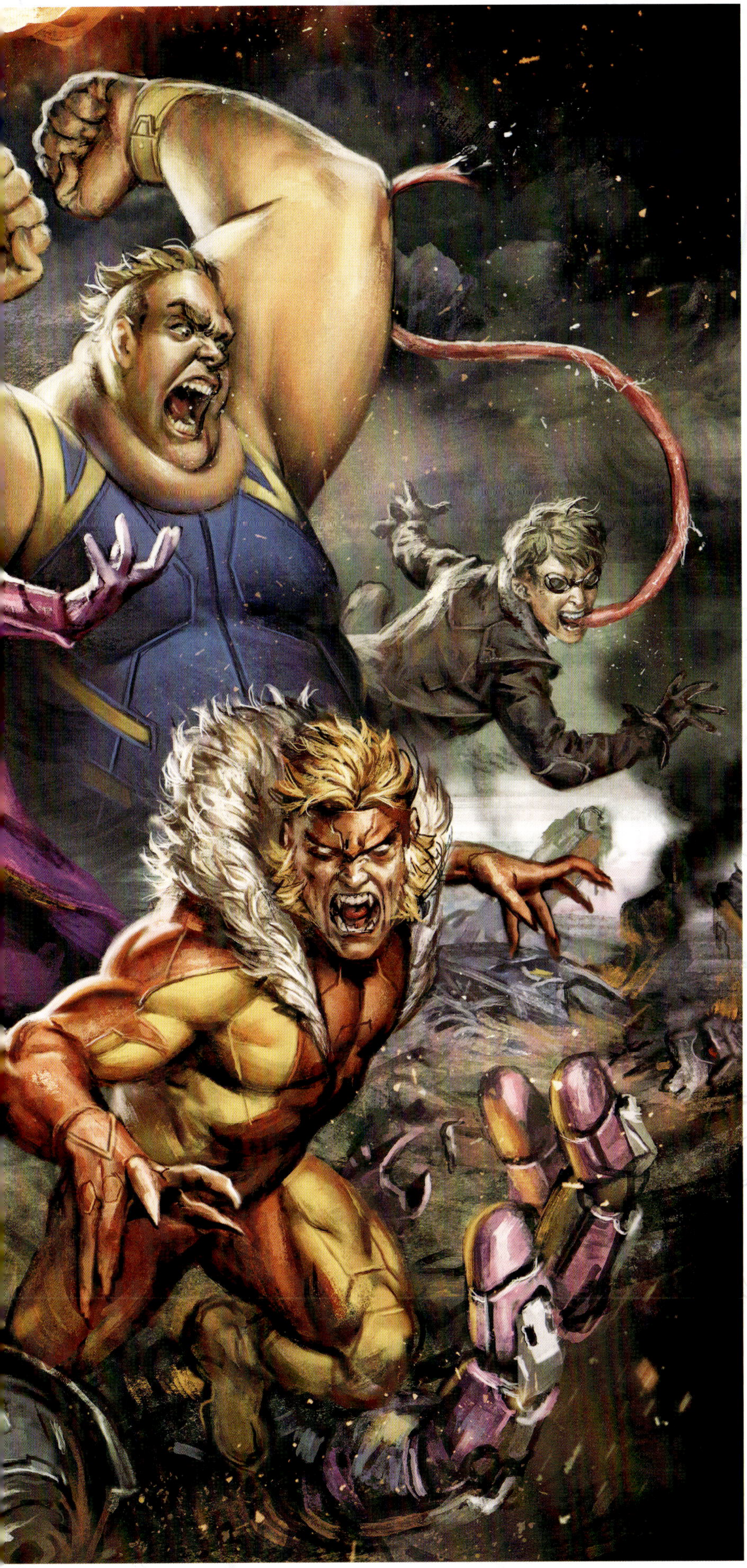

MAGNETO & THE BROTHERHOOD OF MUTANTS

IAN MACDONALD

This epic presentation unites some of Marvel's most notorious mutants in a battle for their lives.

Taking the lead, the formidable Magneto hovers menacingly above the smoldering remains of mutant-murdering Sentinels. He is flanked by the villainous Brotherhood of Mutants, including Mystique, Pyro, Juggernaut, Blob, Sabretooth, and Toad.

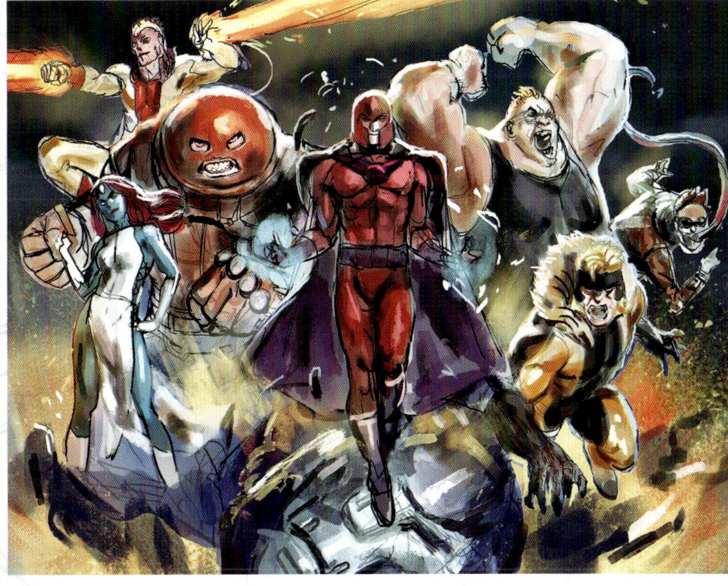

BATWOMAN

ALEX PASCENKO

Batwoman stands vigilant in the streets of Gotham in her striking red-and-black costume, elegantly mixing military-grade armor and weaponry with her own deadly combat skills.

The heiress turned heroine is lit by the glow of moonlight and burning embers as she brings her more tactical brand of justice to the city's seedy underworld.

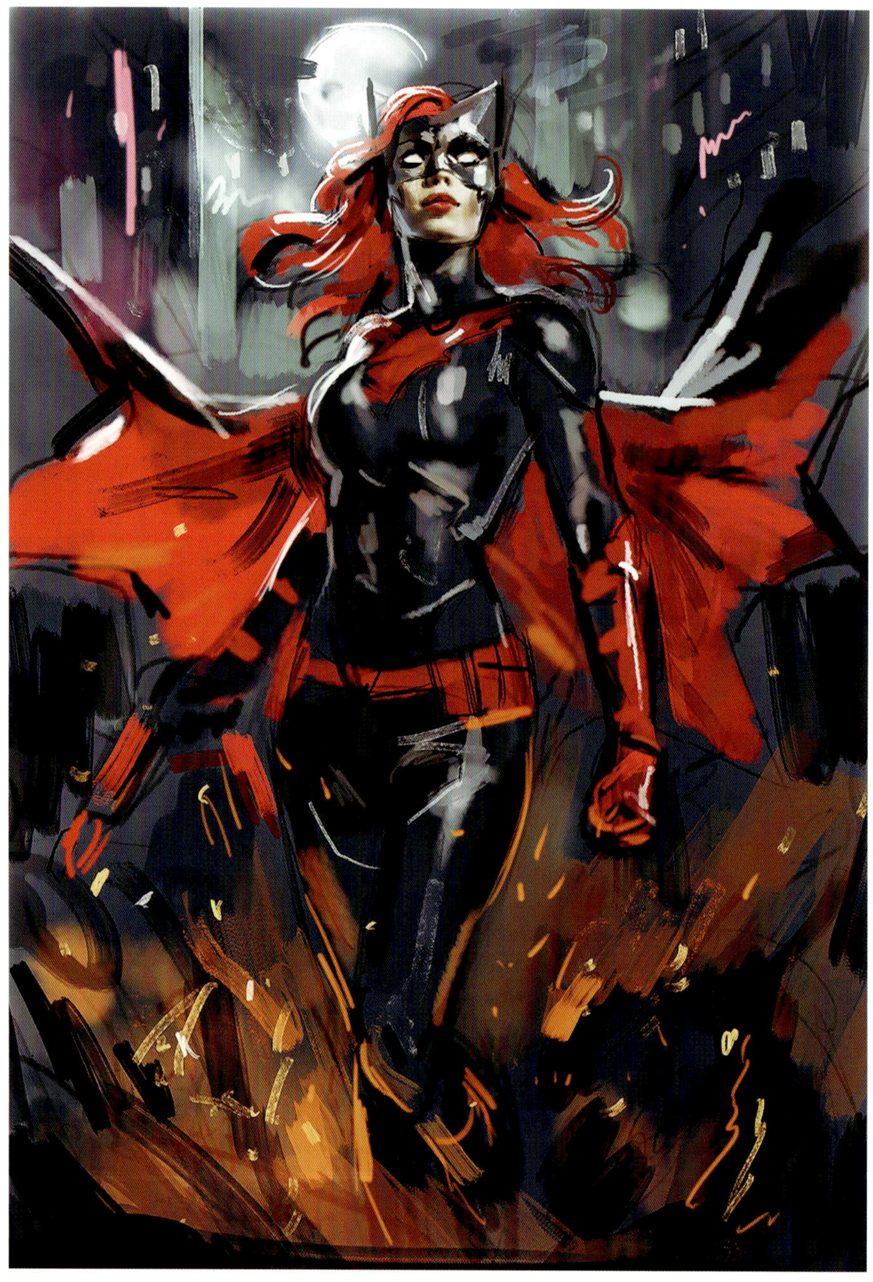

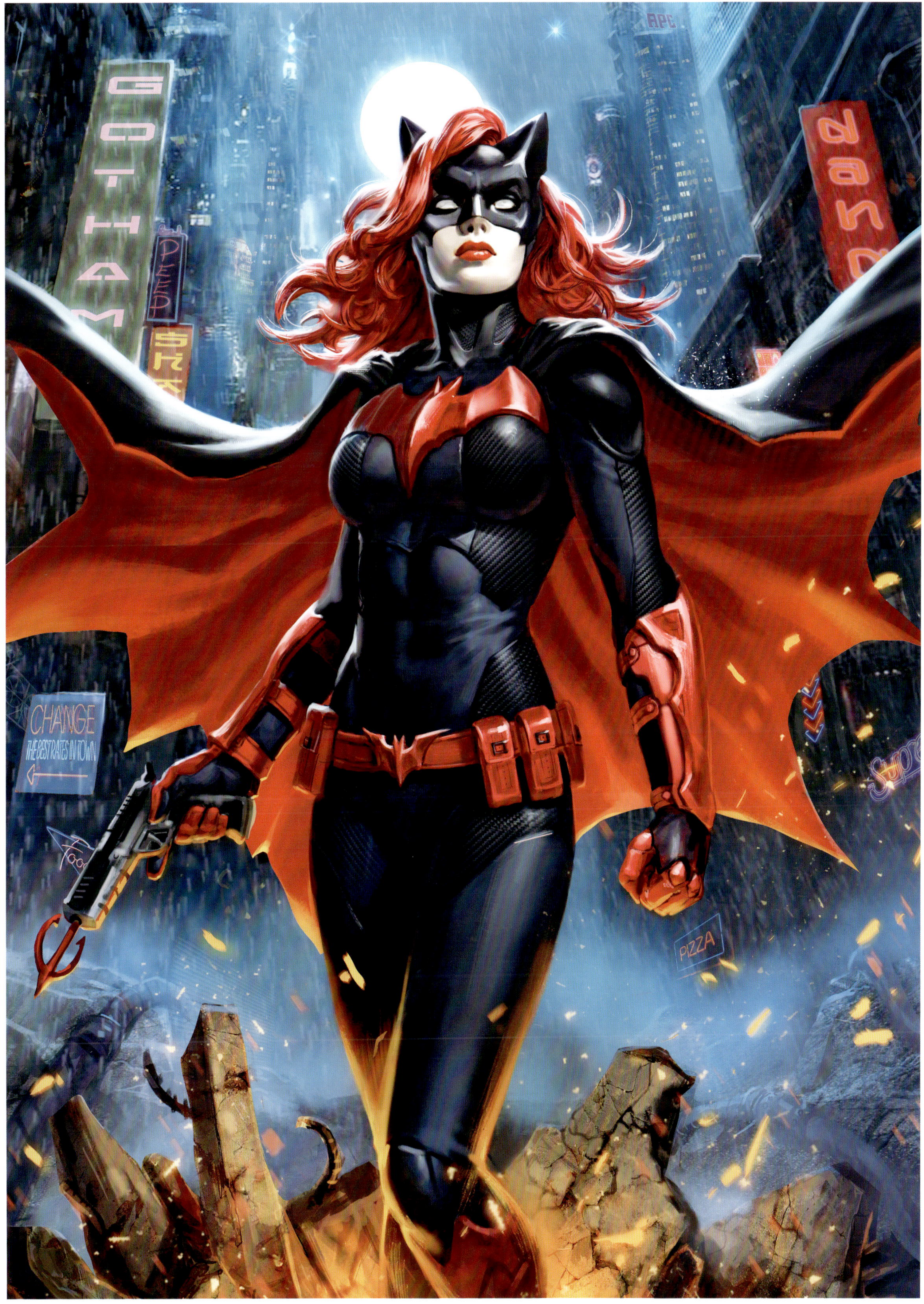
GOTHAM
CHANGE
THE BEST RATES IN TOWN
PIZZA

ASPEN

IAN MACDONALD

Inspired by the work of the late, great Michael Turner, Ian MacDonald's take on the aquatically gifted Aspen Matthews celebrates her beauty and power, and the way she's captured the imaginations of readers everywhere for nearly two decades.

As one of the mystical Blue, the armored Aspen channels her elite talents into manipulating ocean currents and creating sunlit spirals of water to surround her.

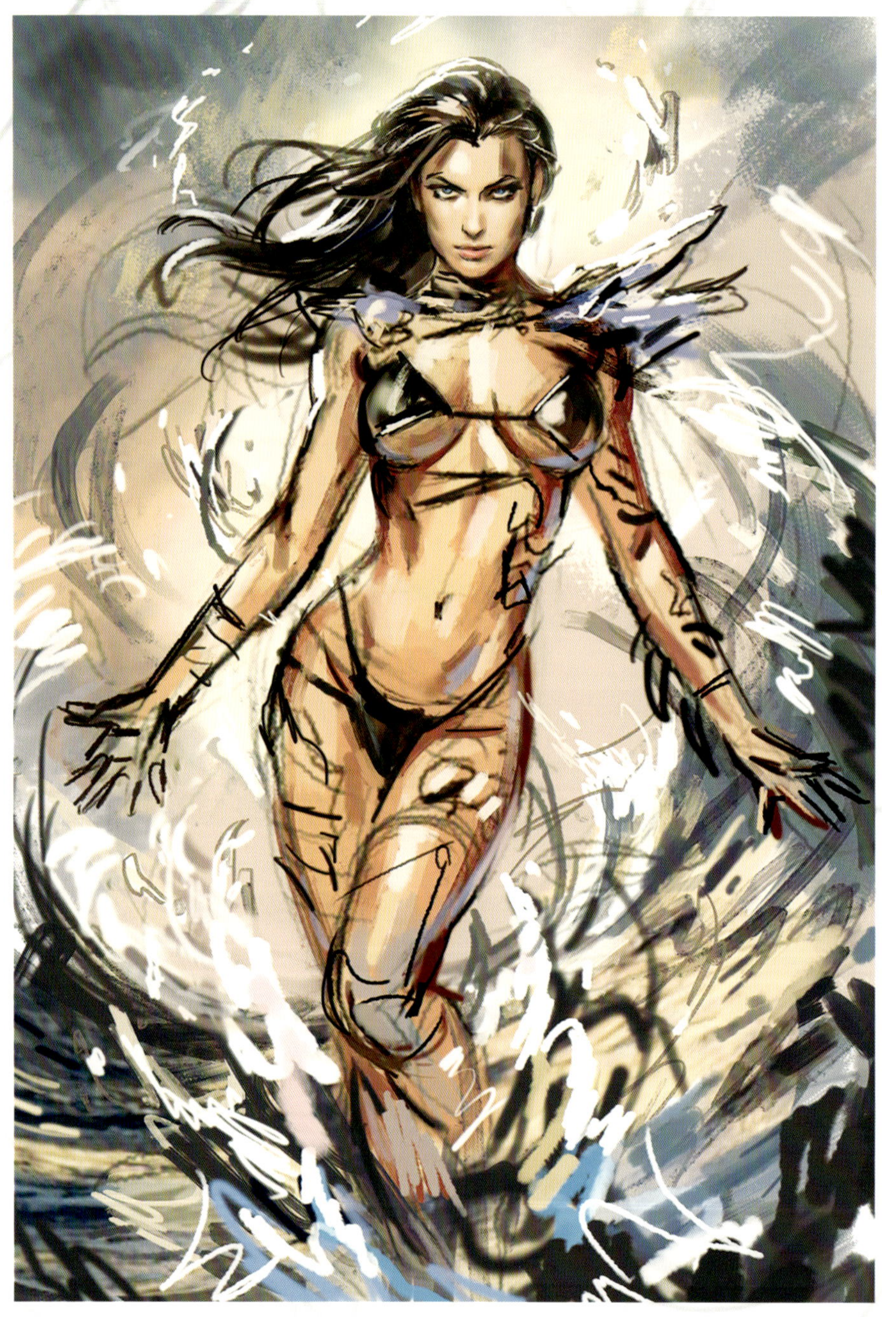

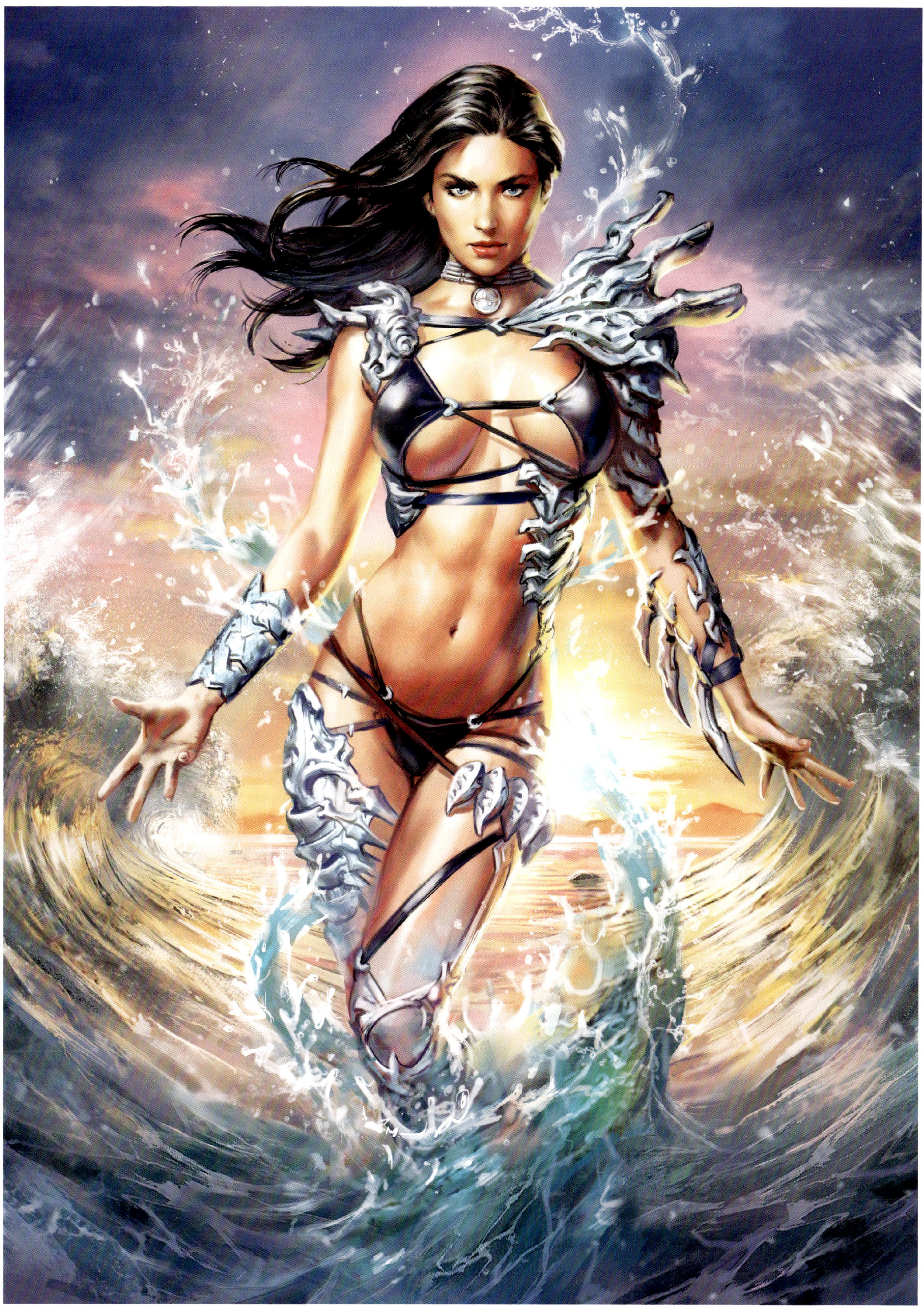

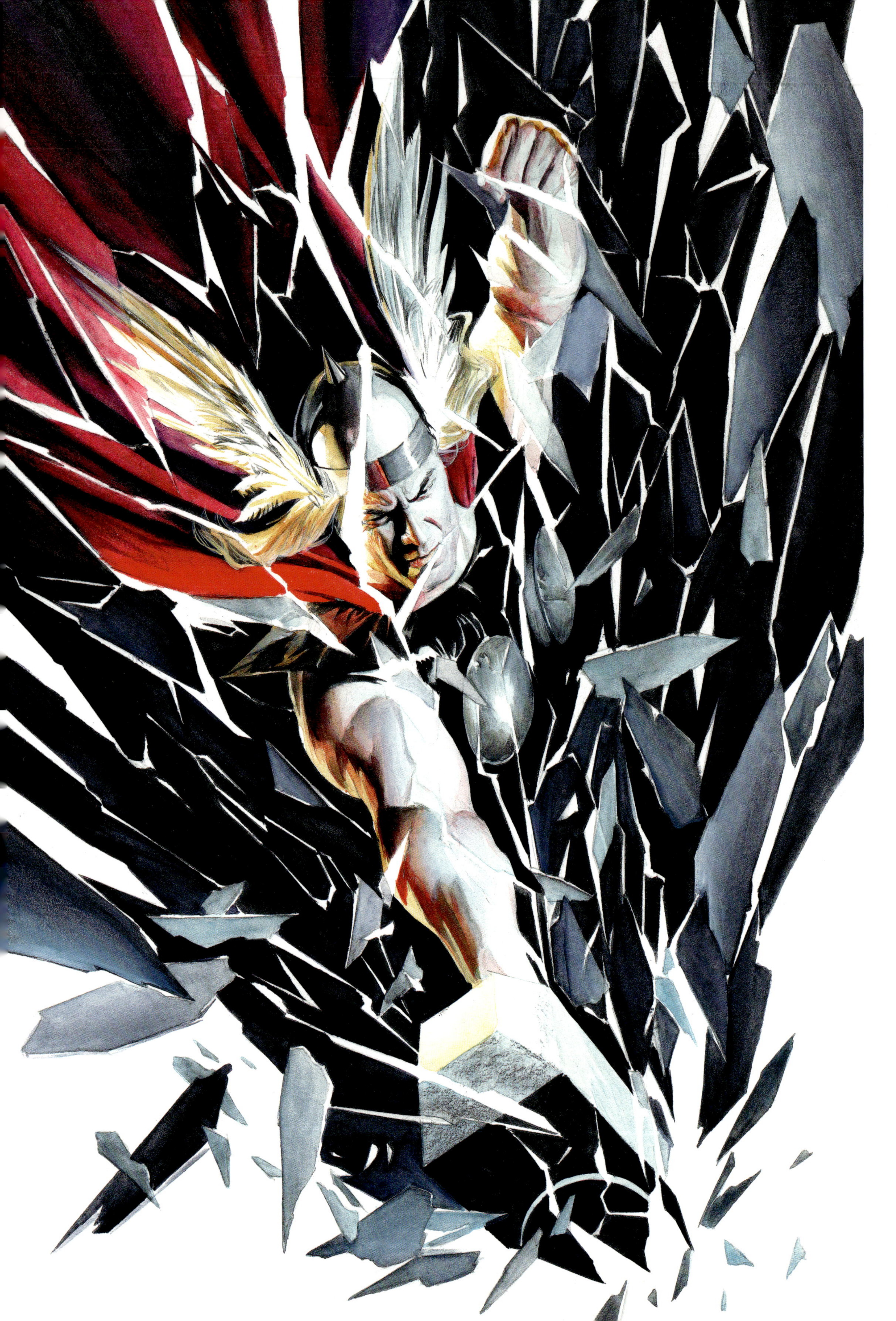

THOR
SHATTERED

ALEX ROSS

Originally created as the cover to a Marvel comic titled *Paradise X: Ragnarok*, this illustration has been specially reproduced for Sideshow as a fine art lithograph in an exclusive limited edition of 300.

The *Thor: Shattered* Fine Art Print features the God of Thunder striking down his hammer in this dynamic display of shards and shapes. Ross's artwork gives a whole new dimension to Thor's legendary strength as Mjolnir's impact resonates throughout the image.

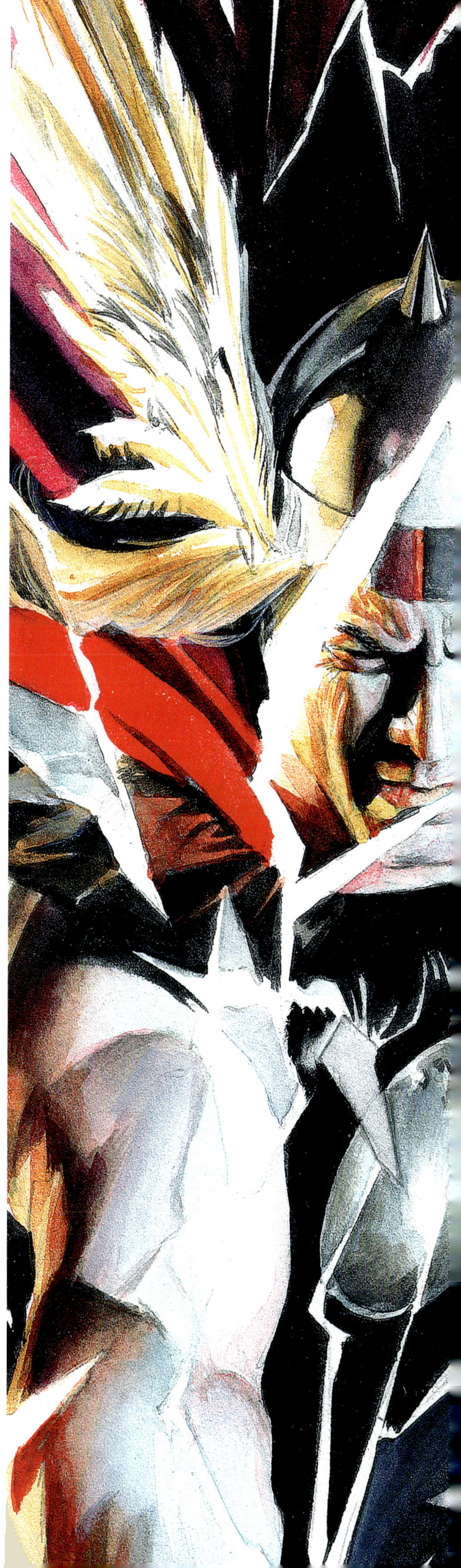

T-REX VS. TRICERATOPS

RJ PALMER

The struggle between the fearsome *Tyrannosaurus rex* and the formidable *Triceratops* is the first print inspired by Sideshow's own Dinosauria collection of statues.

With the dueling dinosaurs surrounded by a lush environment, this print captures the sheer majesty and terrifying strength of two ancient foes locked in a battle for survival.

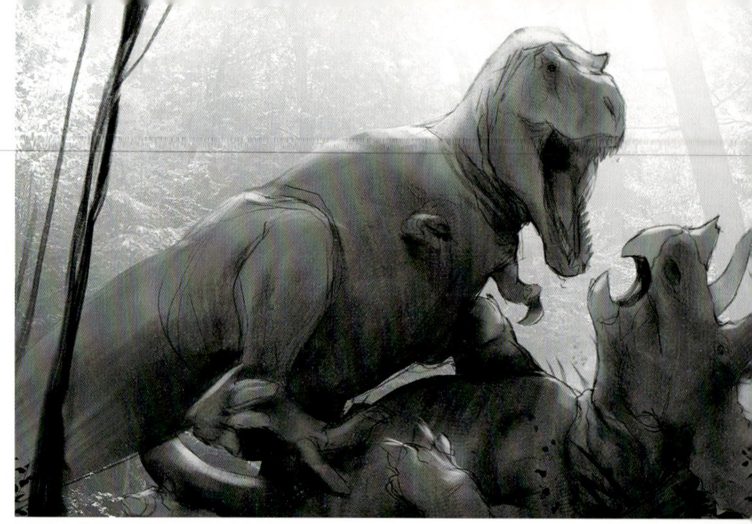

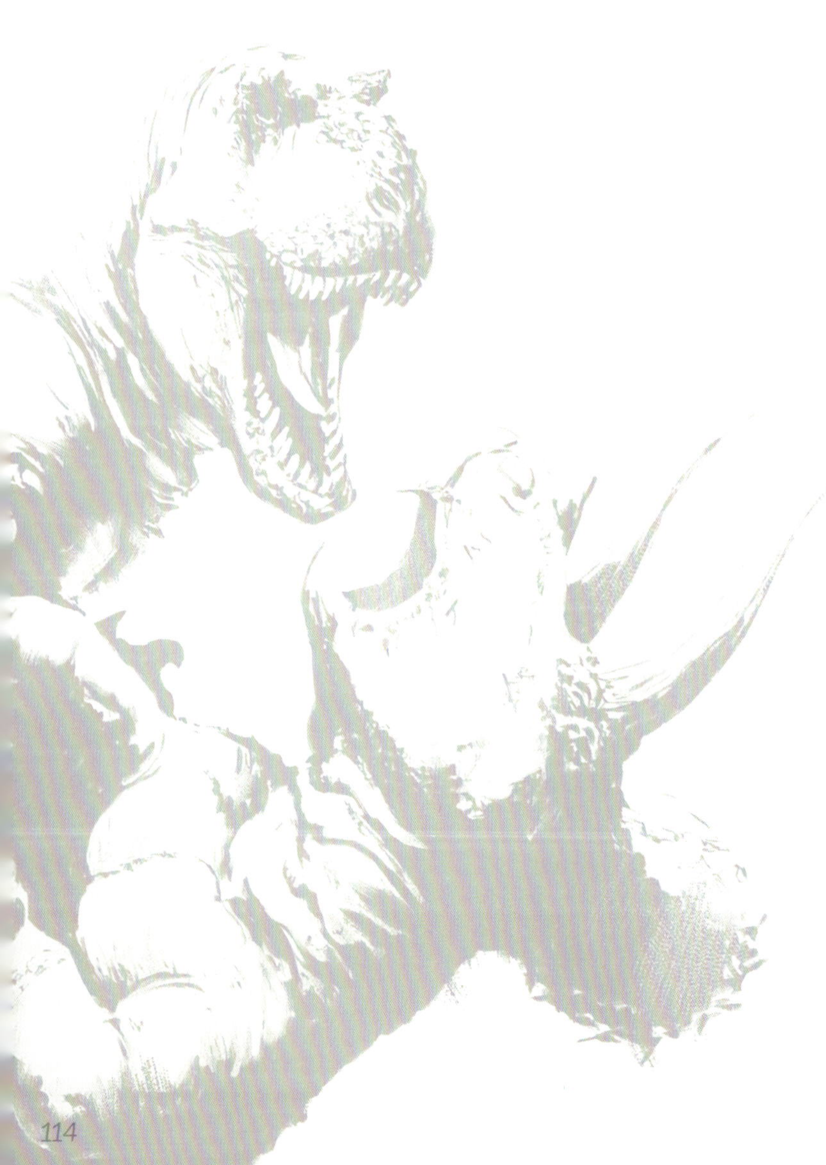

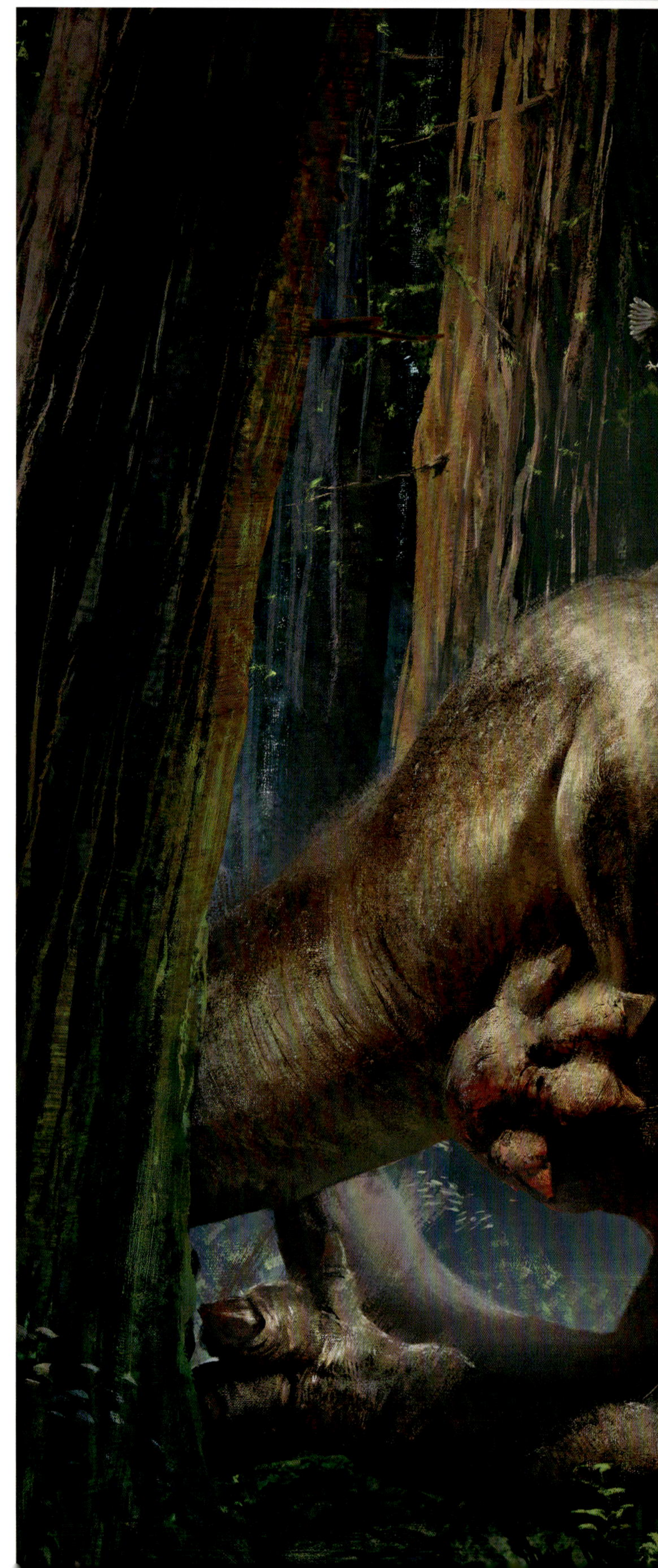

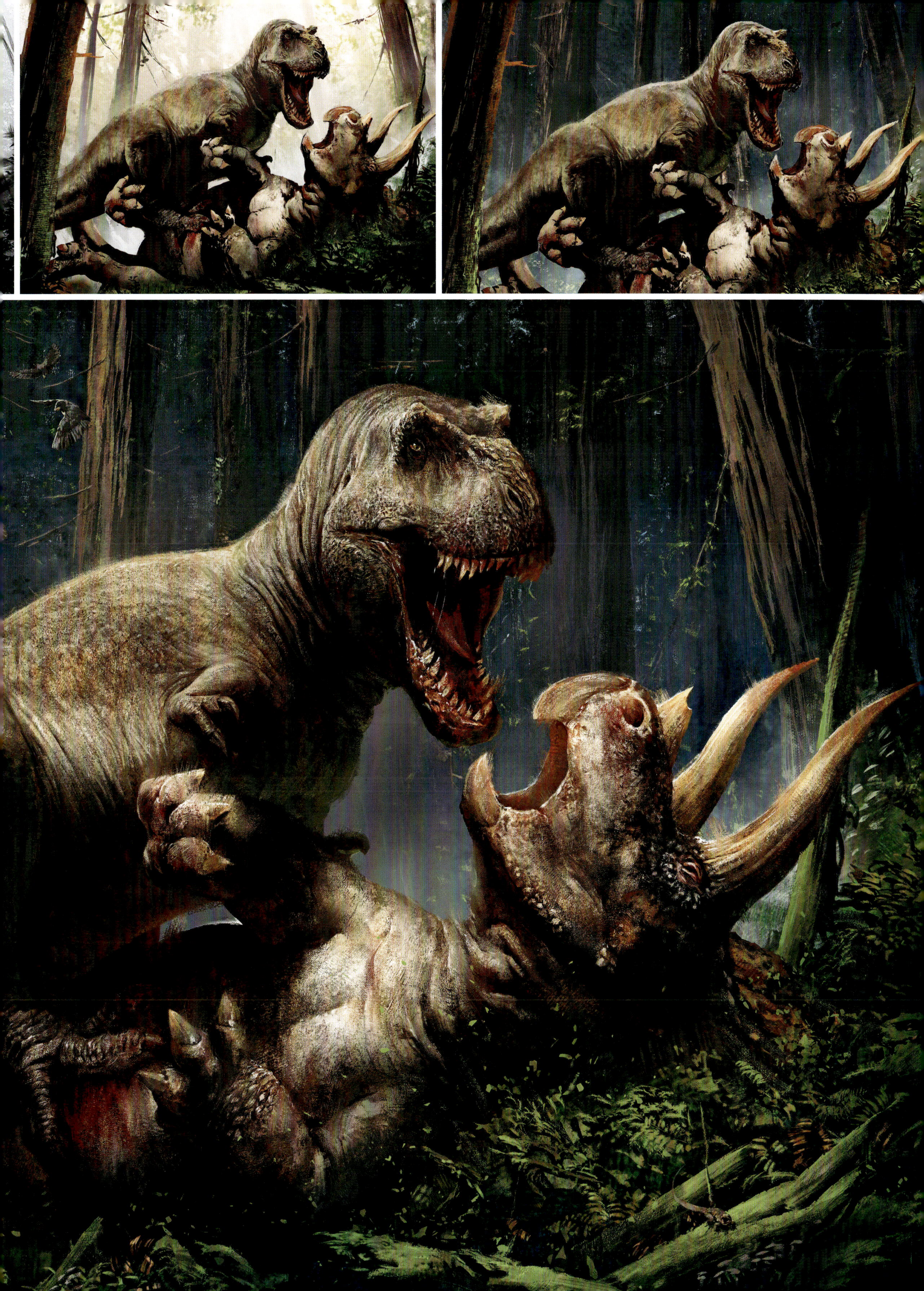

UNIVERSAL MONSTERS

ALEX ROSS

Alex Ross paints seven definitive portraits of the legendary Universal Monsters, depicting the most iconic characters in the history of horror cinema. This classic collection includes renditions of Boris Karloff from *Frankenstein* (1931), Bela Lugosi from *Dracula* (1931), Elsa Lanchester from *The Bride of Frankenstein* (1935), *Creature from the Black Lagoon* (1954), Boris Karloff from *The Mummy* (1932), Lon Chaney Jr. from *The Wolf Man* (1941), and Claude Rains from *The Invisible Man* (1933).

An exclusive eighth print, entitled *The Mash*, depicts all the iconic stars from these "creature features" teamed together in one terrifying tableau.

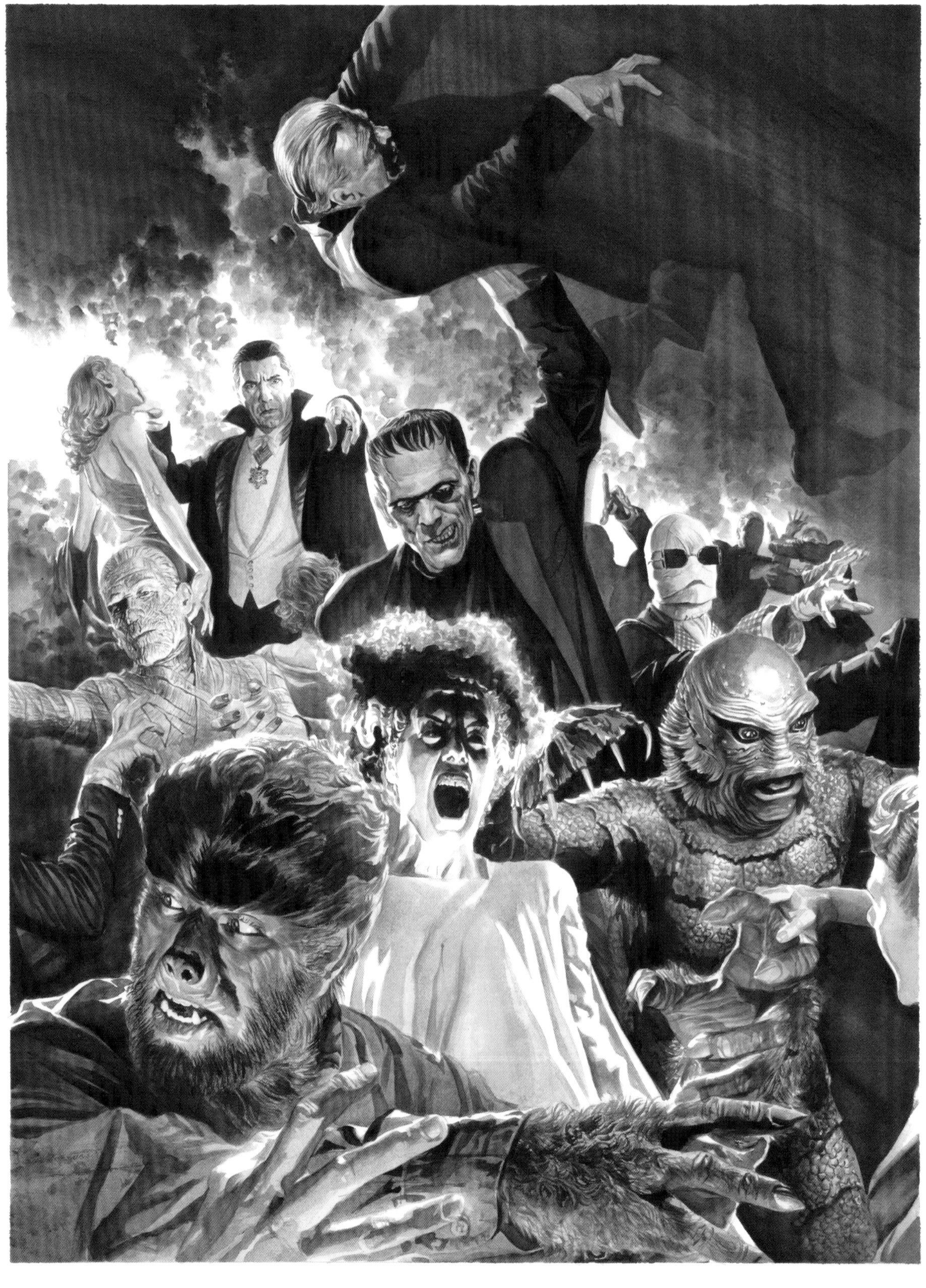

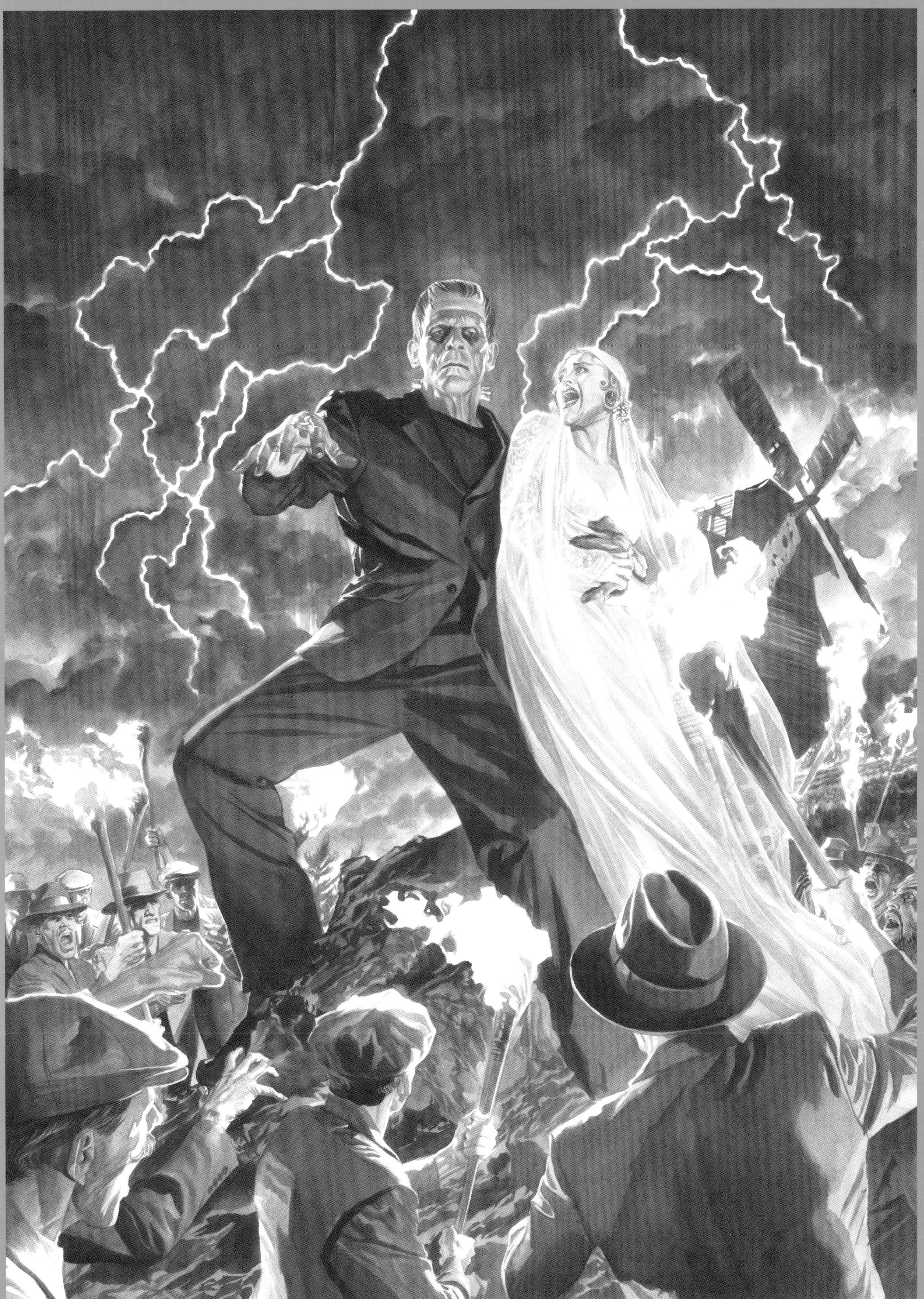

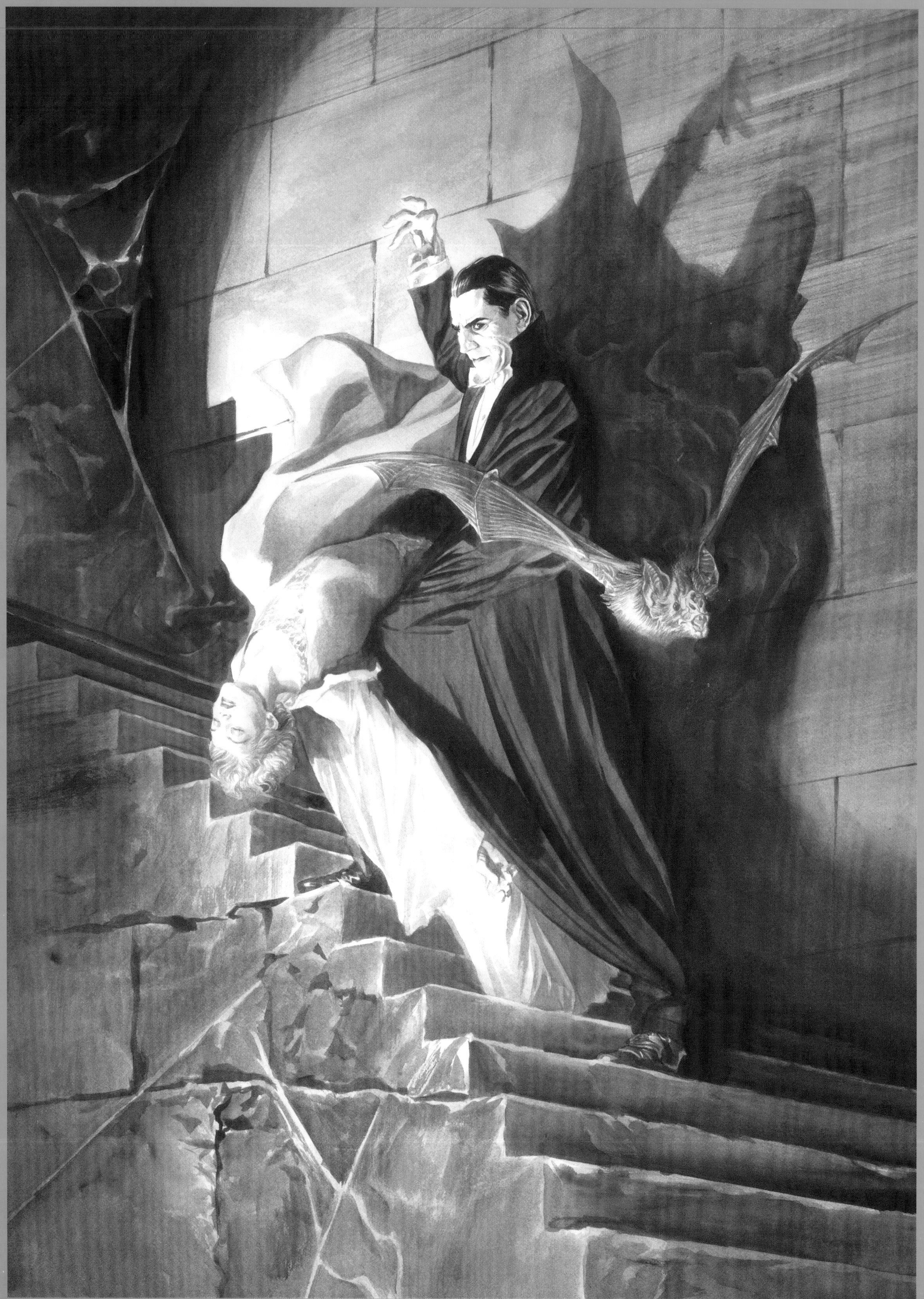

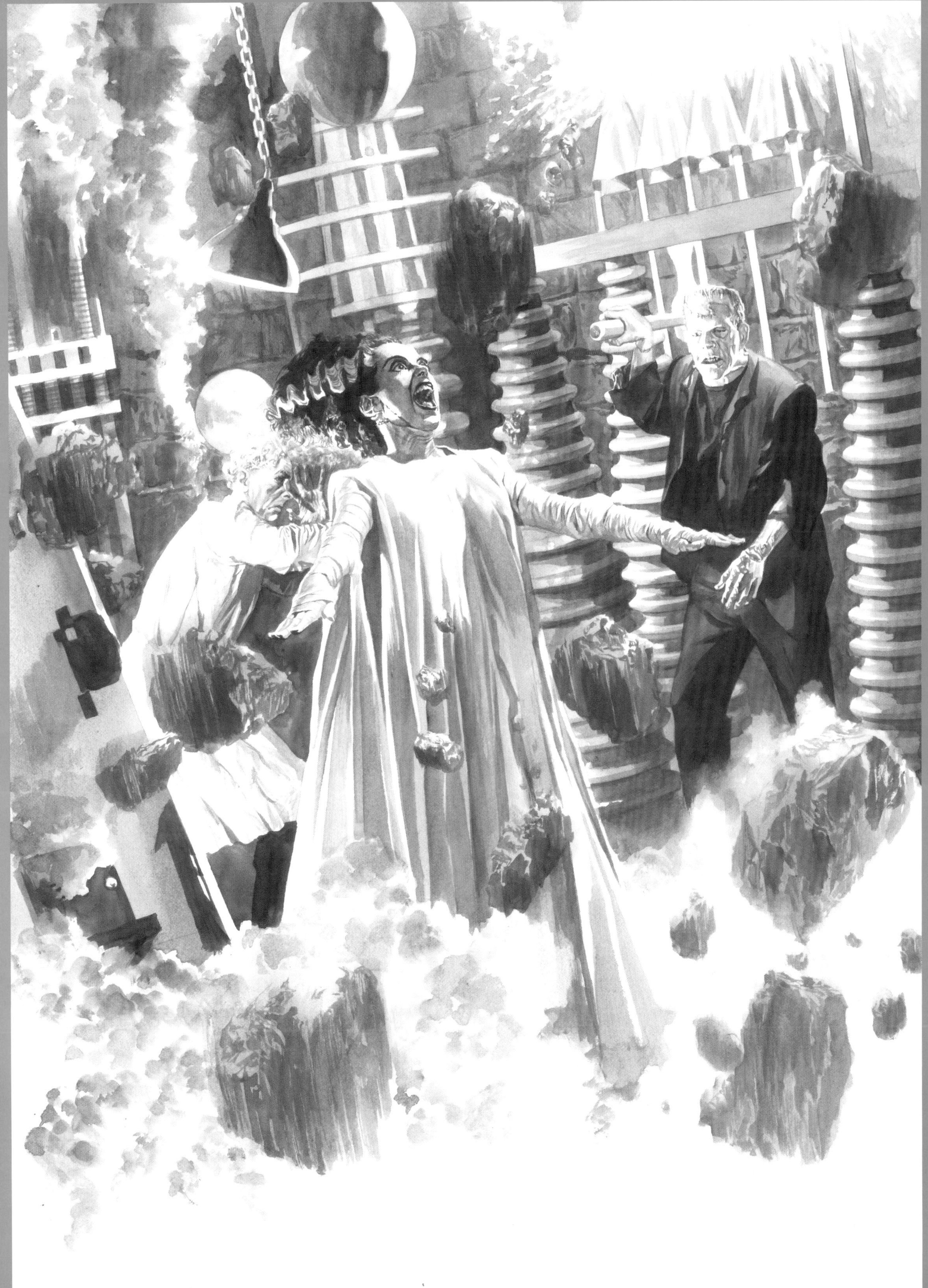

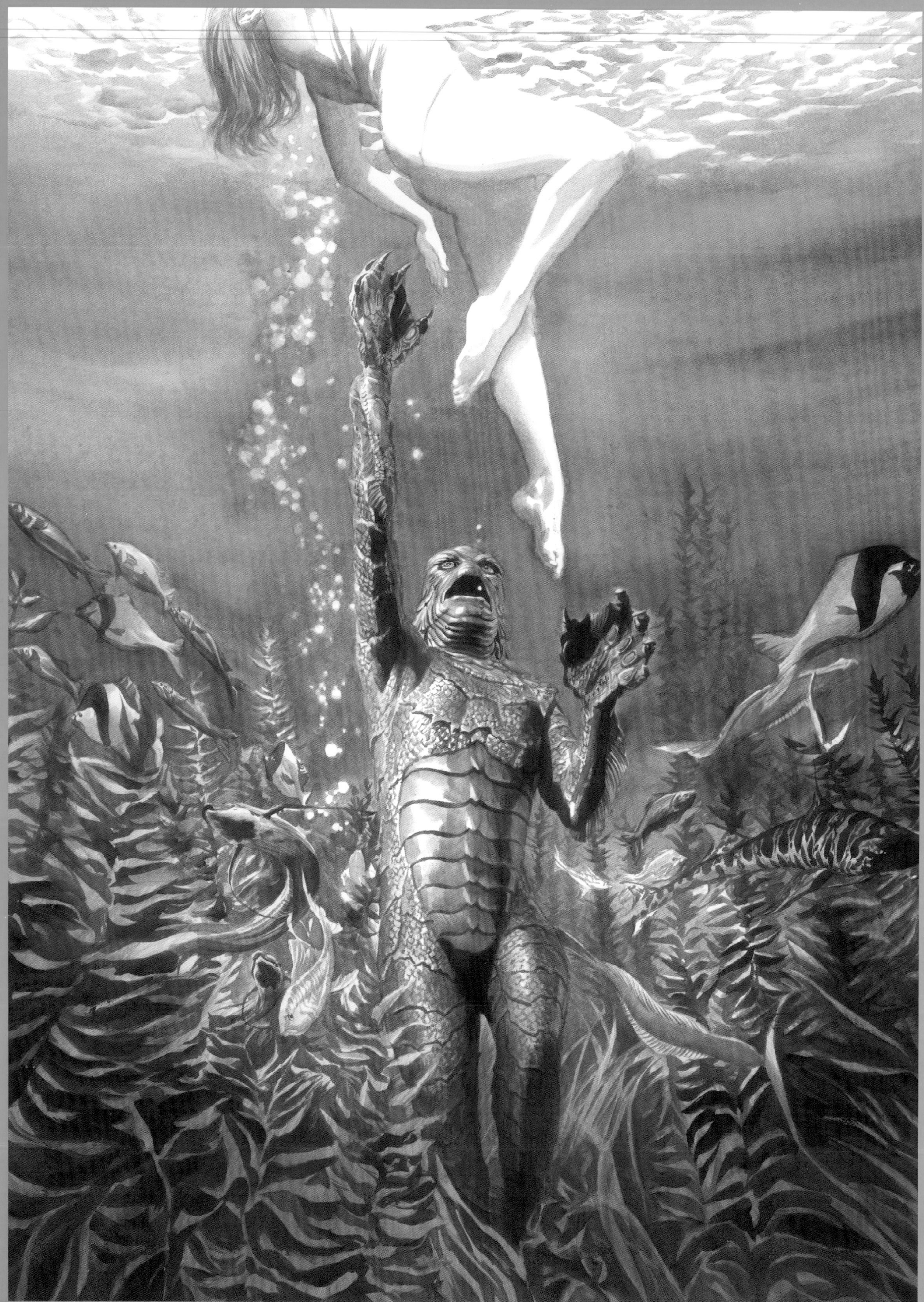

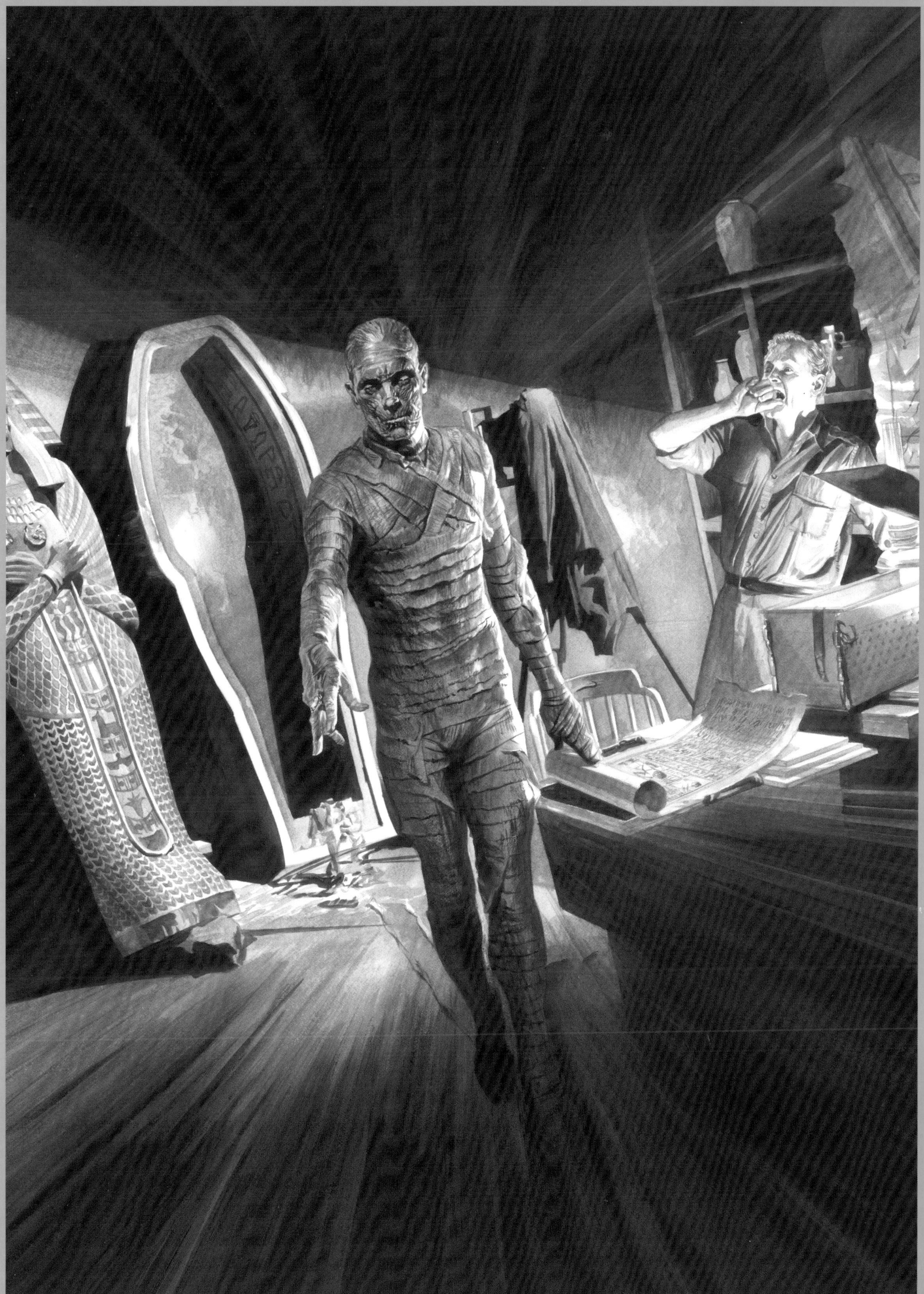

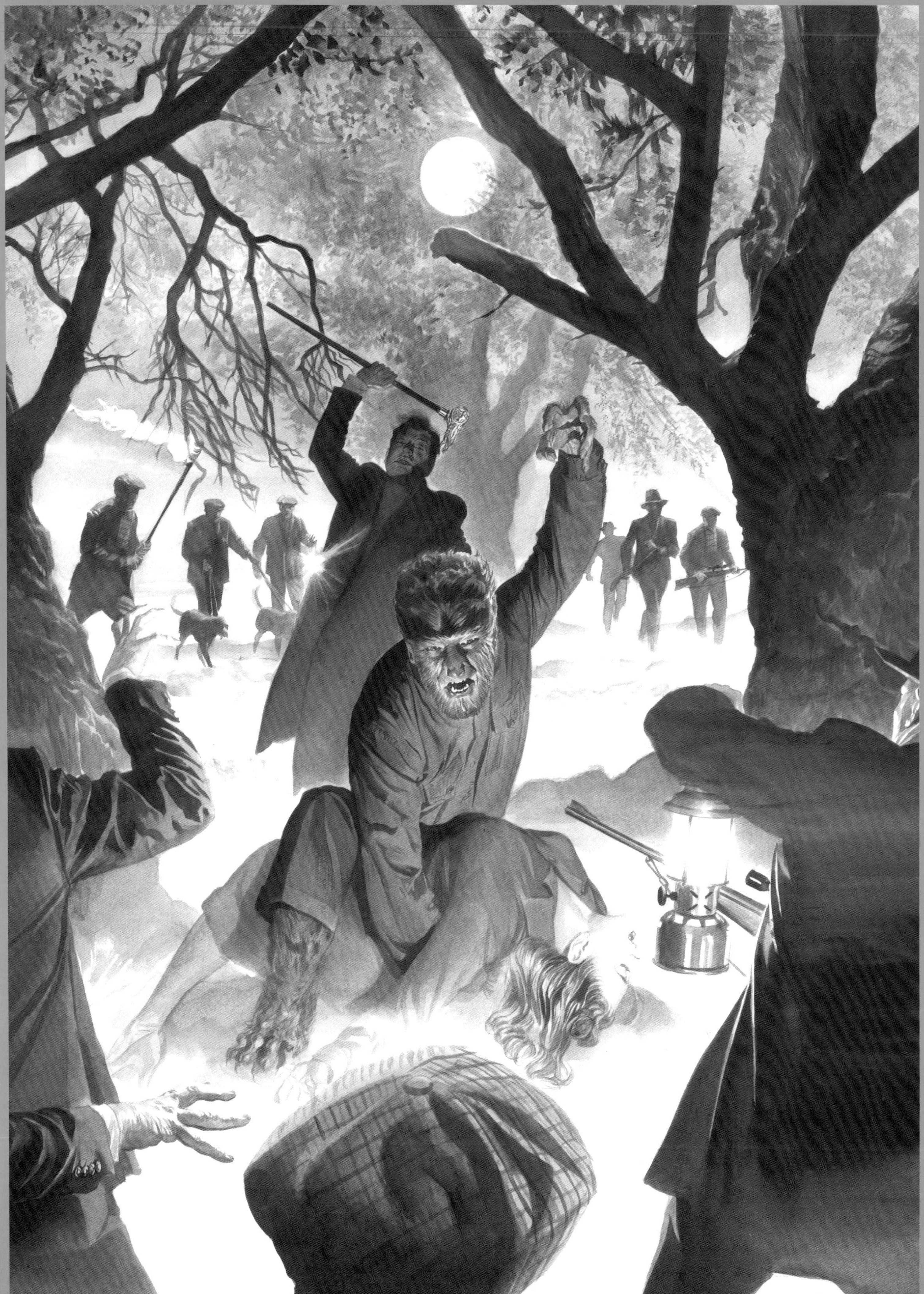

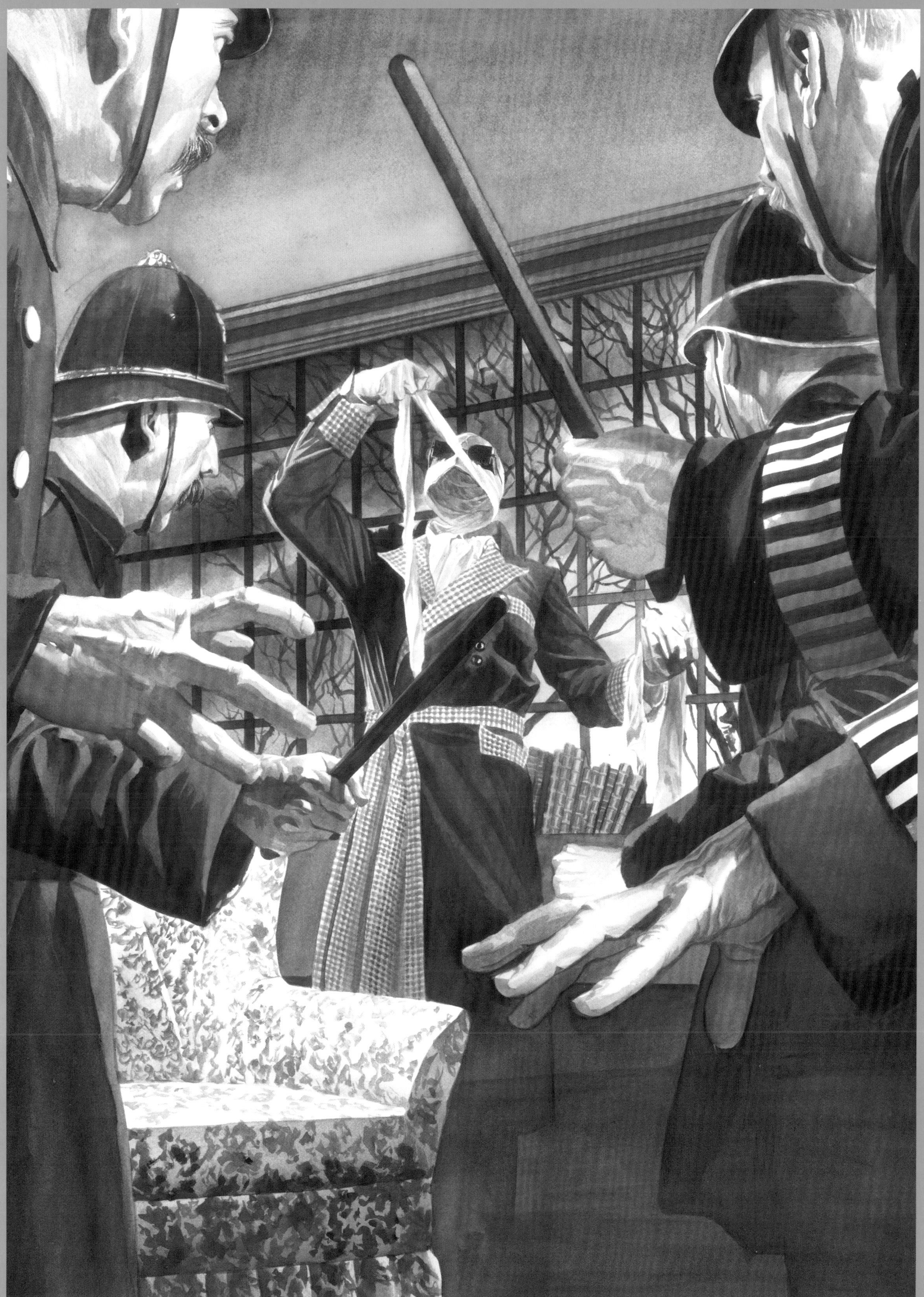

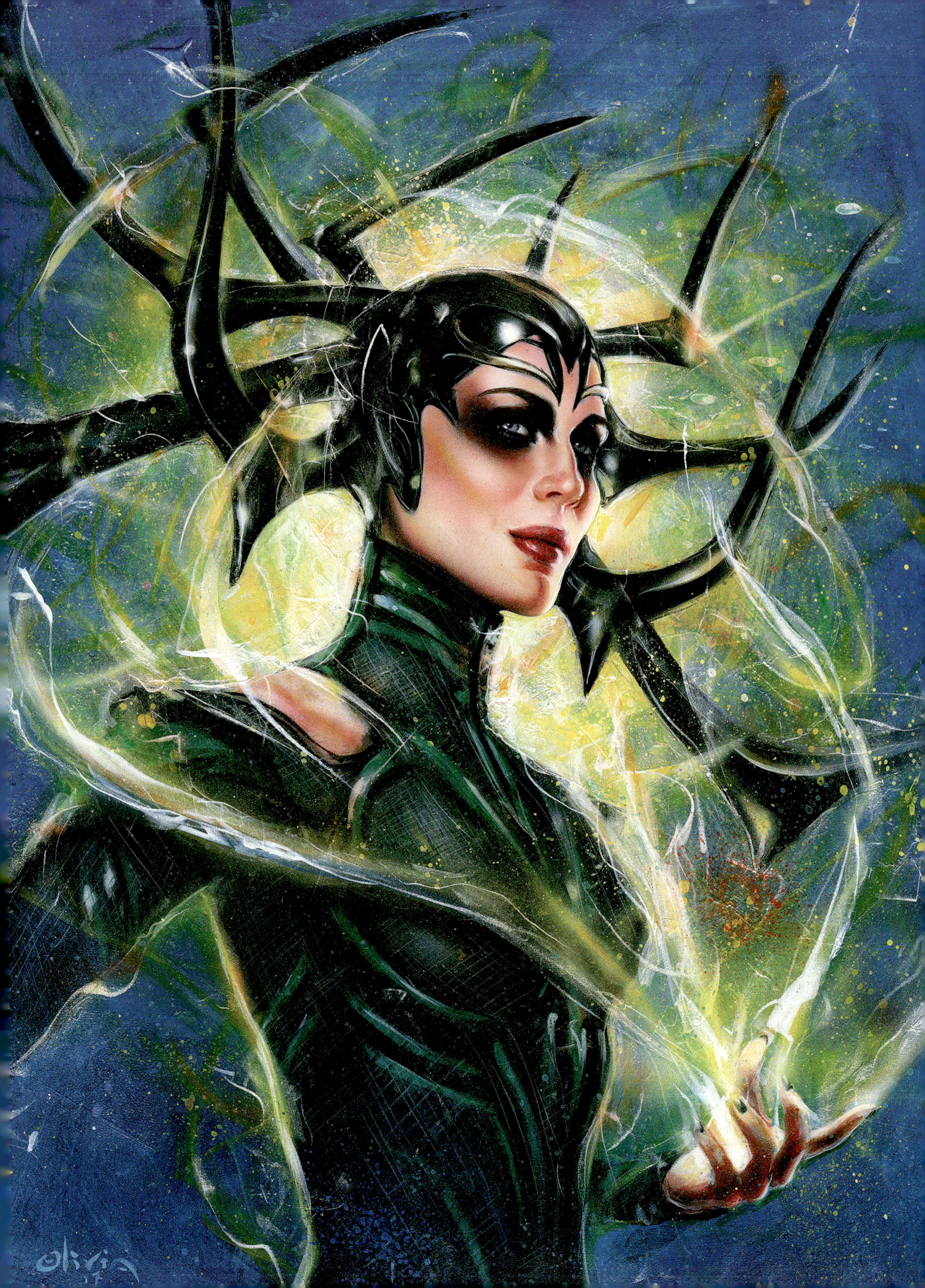

HELA GODDESS OF DEATH

OLIVIA DE BERARDINIS

Based on the likeness of Cate Blanchett in Marvel's *Thor: Ragnarok*, this stunning portrait depicts Hela at the height of her power.

Surrounded by creeping tendrils of magic, the wicked Hela plots to take over Asgard and bring about its ruinous end. Her face is framed by her iconic headdress, and a subtle smirk captures the confidence and ruthlessness of this villainous goddess.

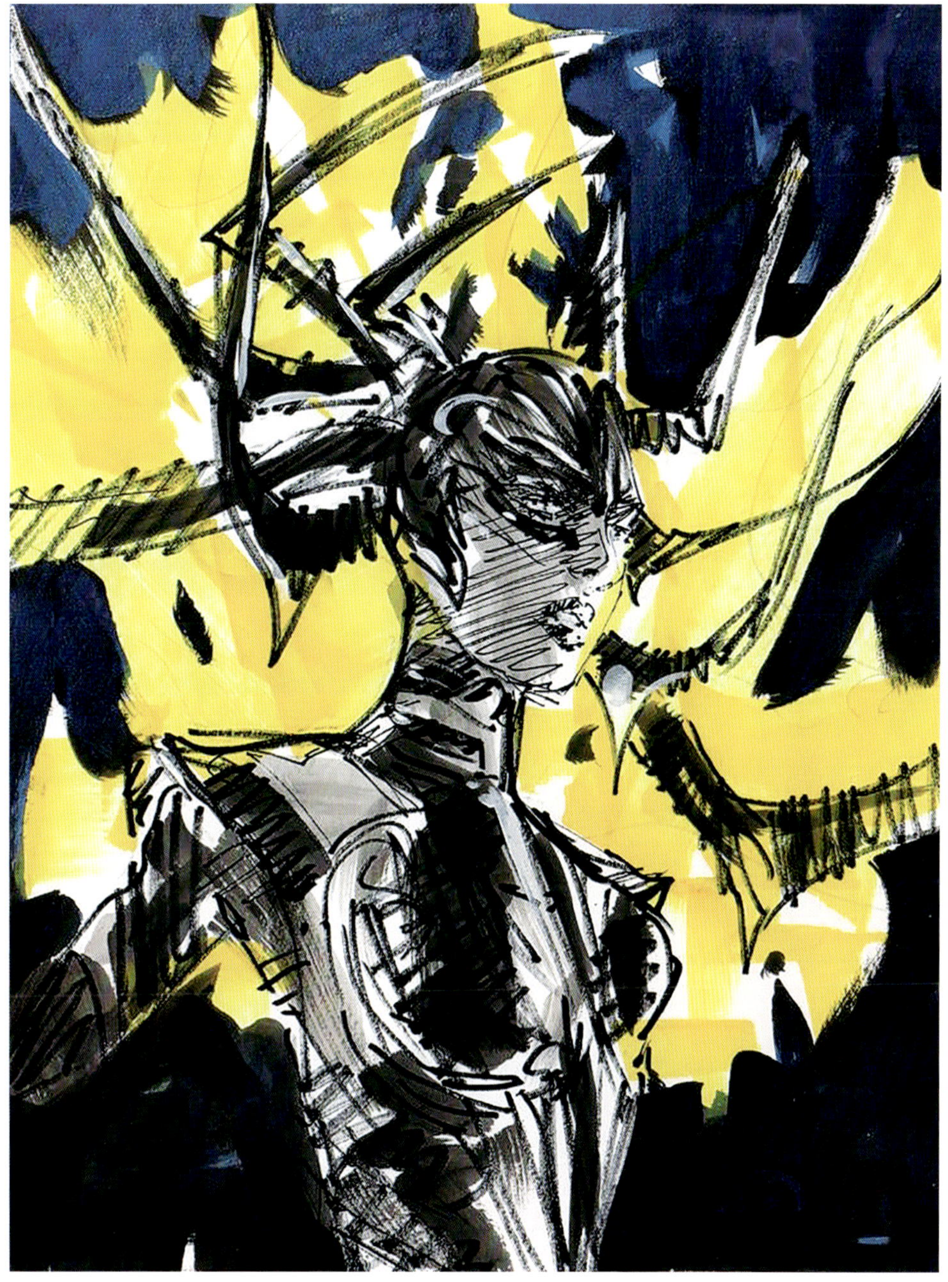

Hela: Goddess of Death © 2017 Olivia De Berardinis

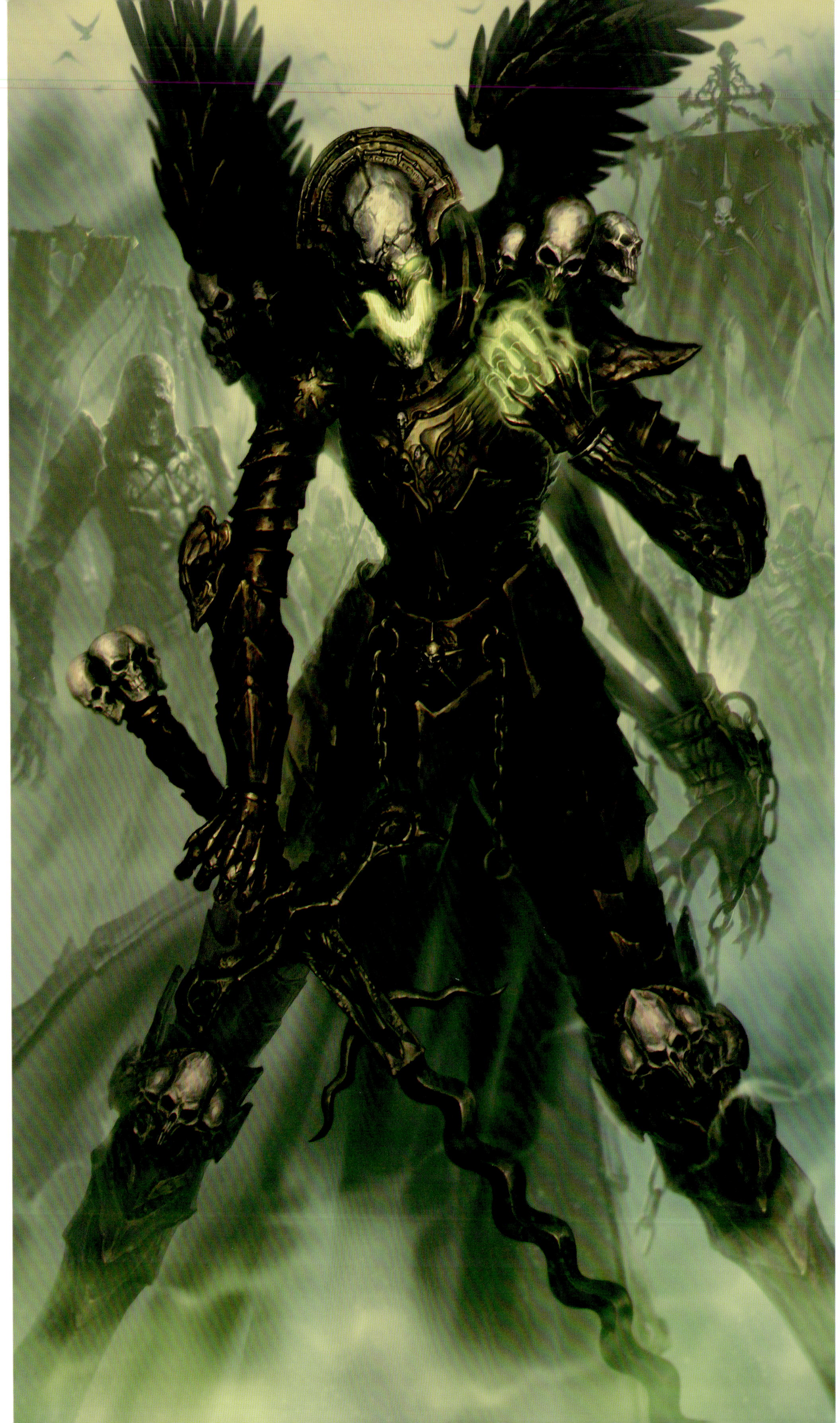

MORTIGHULL
SOLDIER OF CRUEL PURPOSE

JIMMY XU

The Risen Reaper General Mortighull is a scion of the Bone Faction leadership, but he is far from a mirror image of his mentor Demithyle. Forged for the brutal purpose of waging war, Mortighull feels a resolute obligation to end the celestial war. However, he is tempted to revel in the obliteration of his enemies.

An Underworld champion conceived for a noble scheme, yet hammered by its cruel purpose, Mortighull walks the knife's edge of a warrior who must bring about peace through destruction.

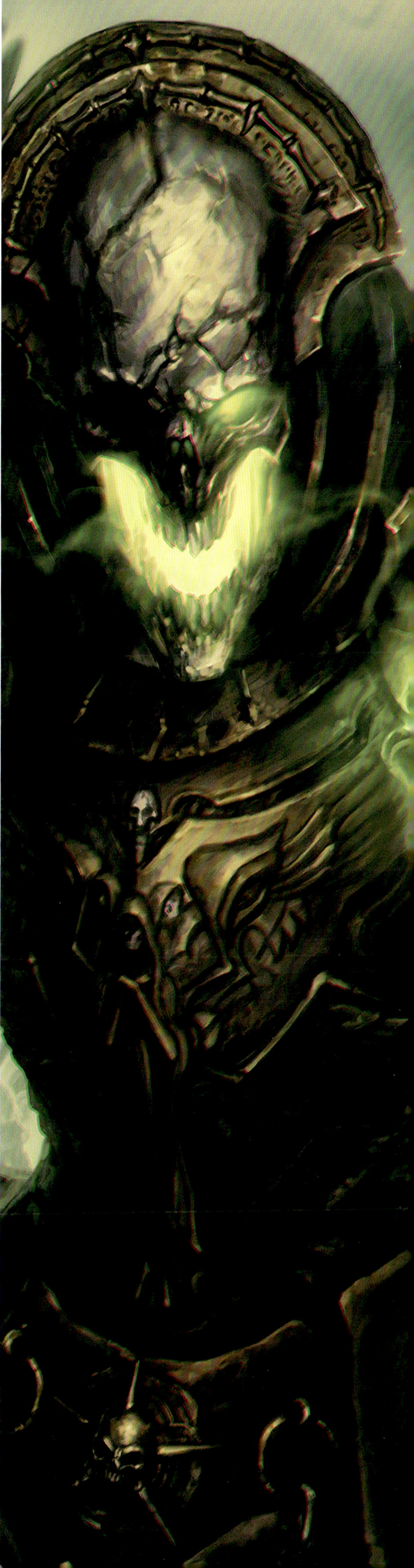

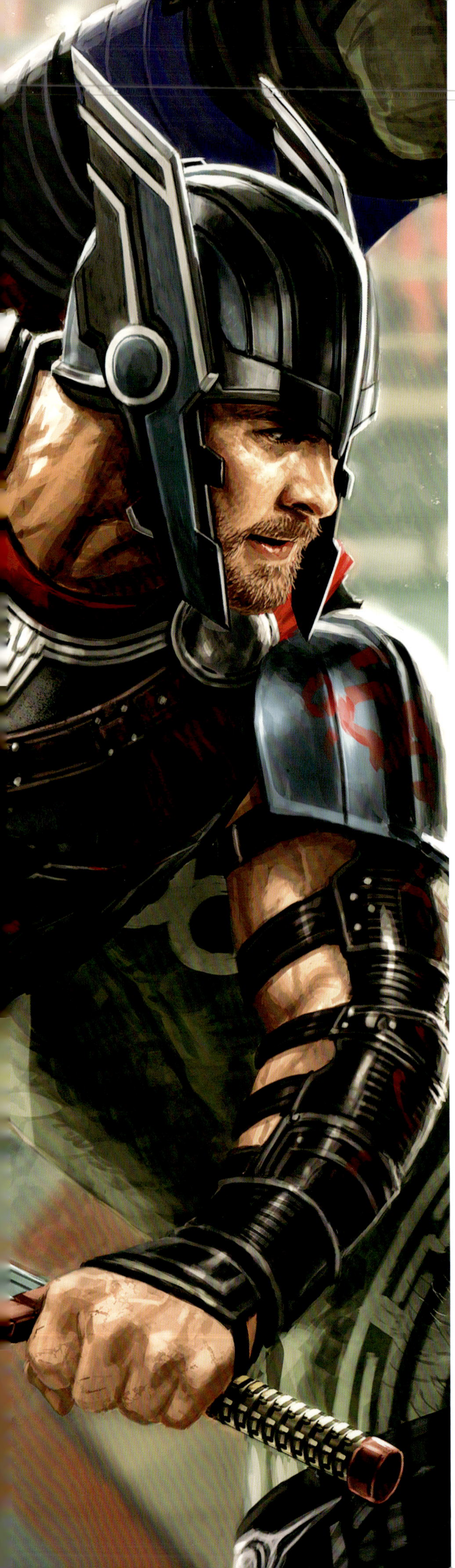

THOR
RAGNAROK

ANDY PARK

The *Thor: Ragnarok* Fine Art Print captures an action-packed scene from the eponymous film, pitting the mighty Thor against the Incredible Hulk in an intense moment of intergalactic gladiatorial combat. As visual development director at Marvel Studios, Andy Park painted keyframe artwork which served to illustrate pivotal story moments, and to help visualize what the finished film could look like during pre-visualization and development stages. This is one of those iconic keyframe moments.

"In this illustration, I wanted to capture this iconic battle in a way that shows off each character in the strongest way," says Park. "It doesn't spell out who actually has the advantage. It's the moment right before the clash. This is the battle between the two strongest Avengers. Who will win?"

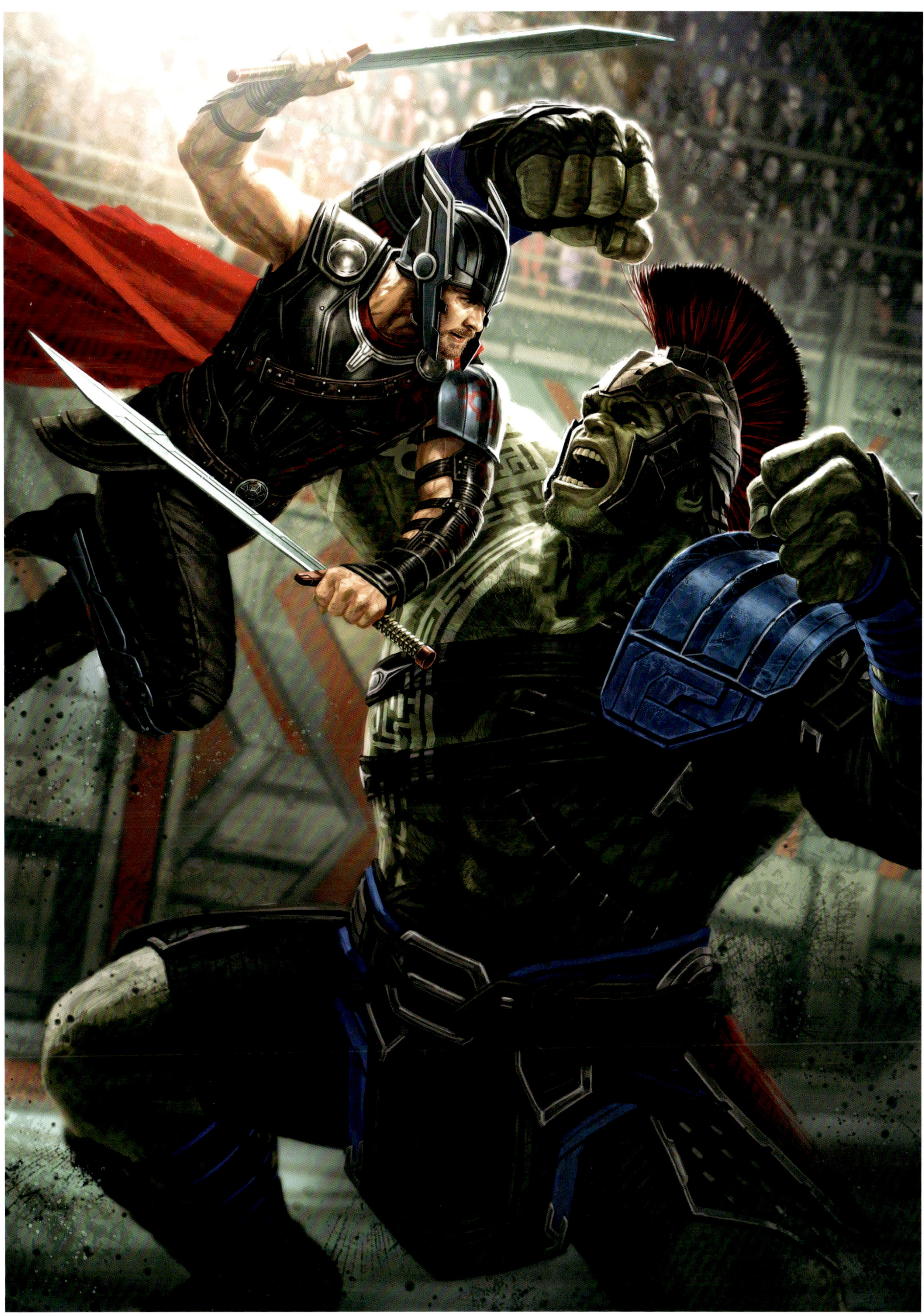

LIBERTY AND JUSTICE

TRINITY

ALEX ROSS

Depicting the famed DC Comics trinity of Batman, Superman, and Wonder Woman, this dynamic art print compiles three illustrations originally created by Alex Ross for the interior of the comic book *JLA: Liberty and Justice.*

The print is limited to an edition size of 300 pieces and features the three heroes soaring into action over crowds, through cities, and on the streets to bring liberty and justice to citizens in need.

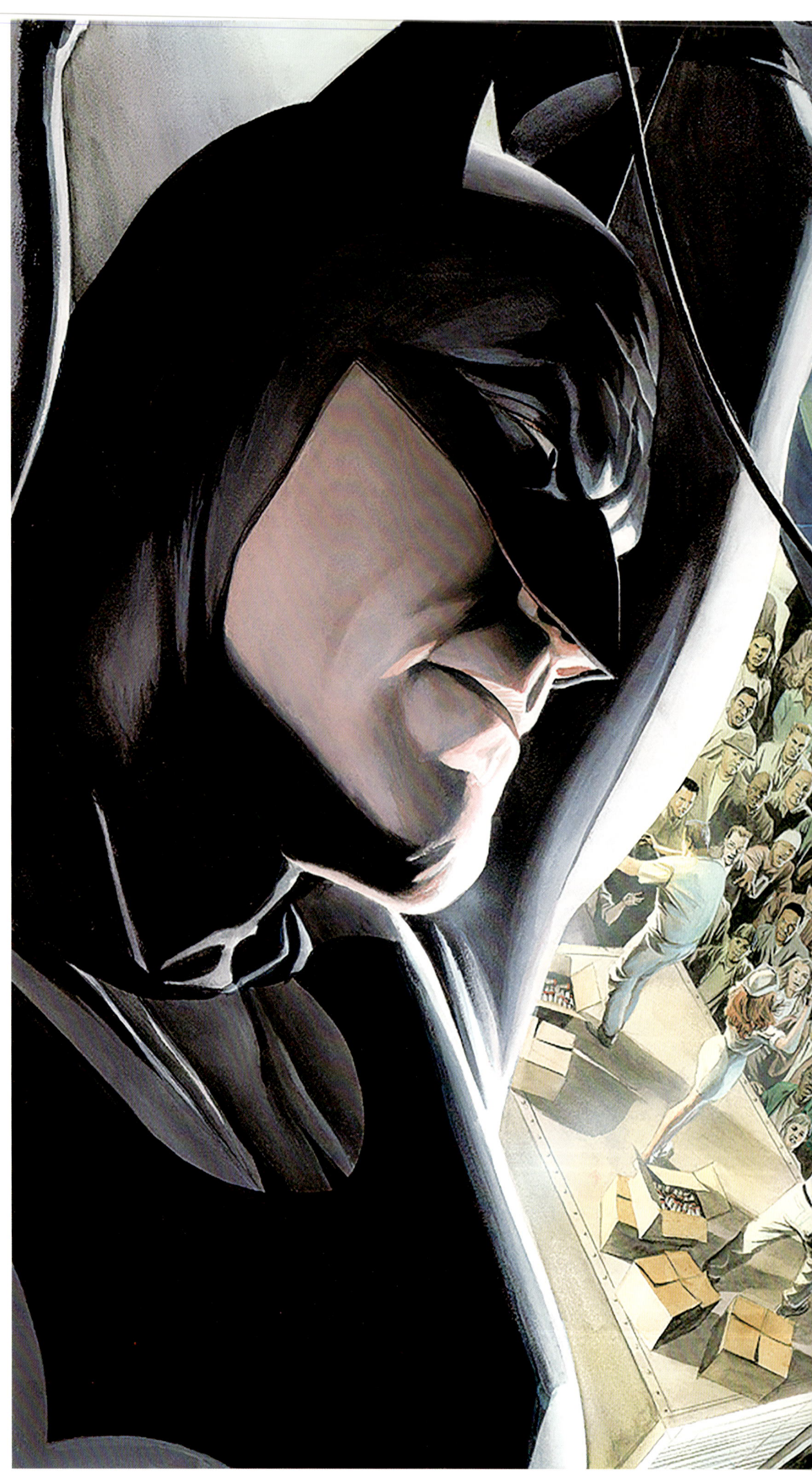

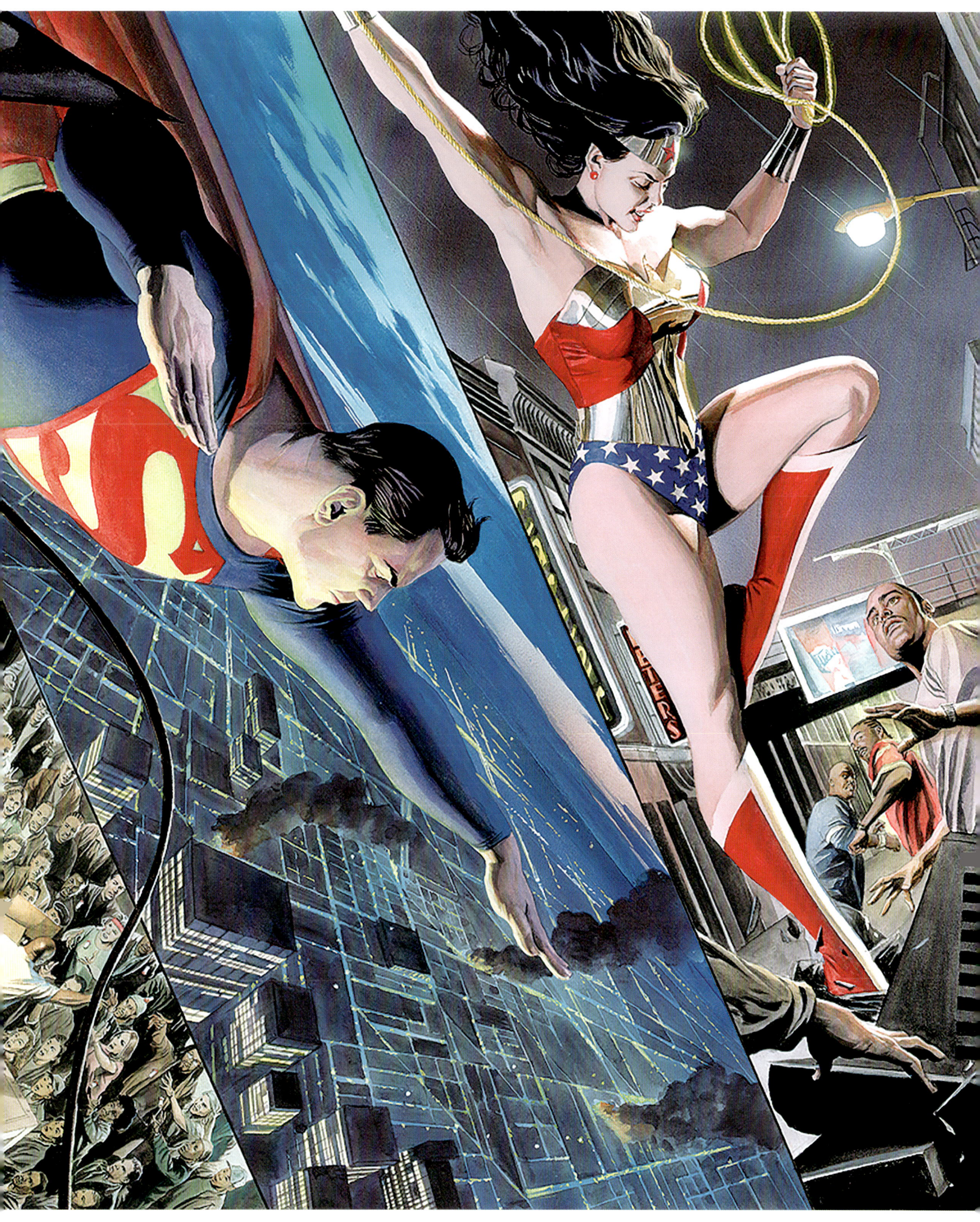

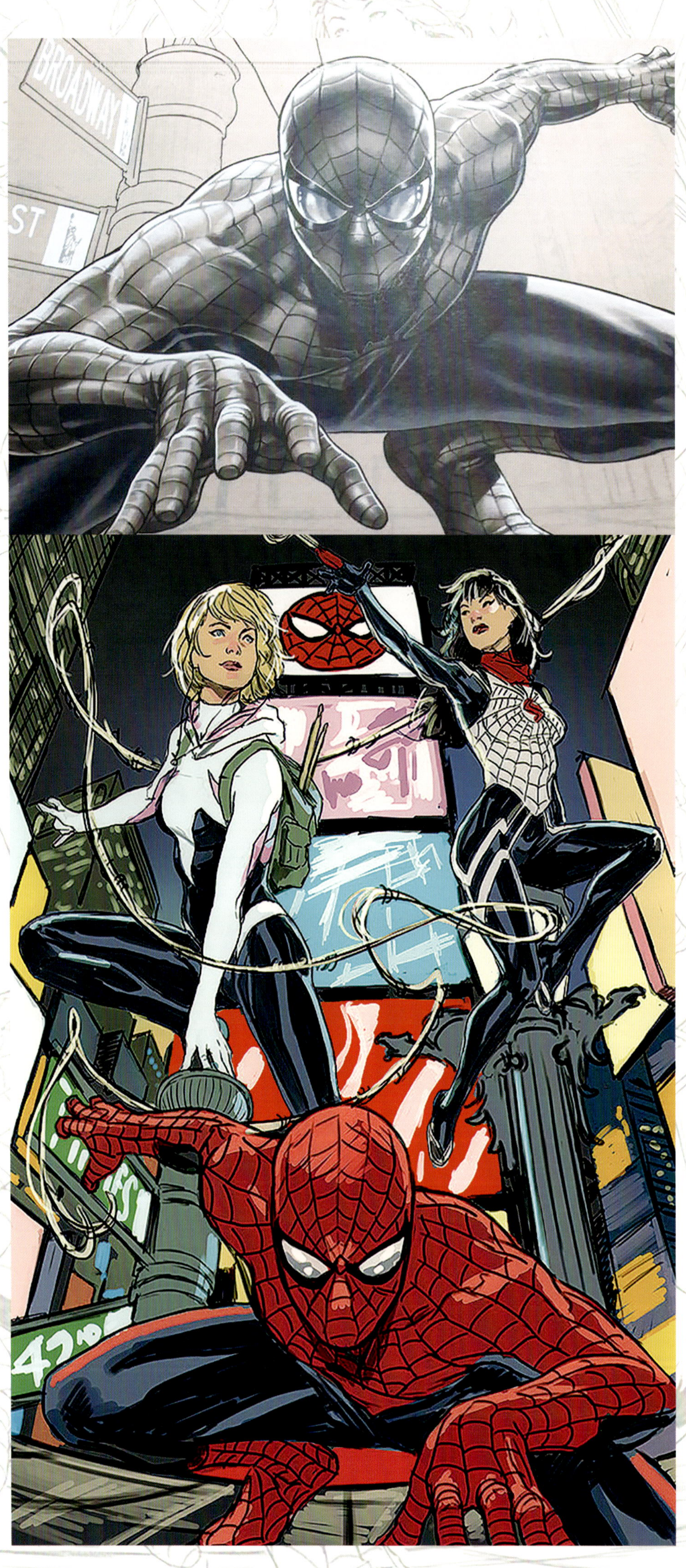

SPIDER-VERSE

MARK BROOKS

From across the Spider-Verse, three powerful web warriors have united to take down crime in every reality! The print features the sensational spider-heroes Spider-Man, Silk, and Spider-Gwen assembled against the vibrant background of Times Square.

Posed on familiar city fixtures while spider-symbols light the New York City skyline behind them, the terrific trio are ready to team up and save the world.

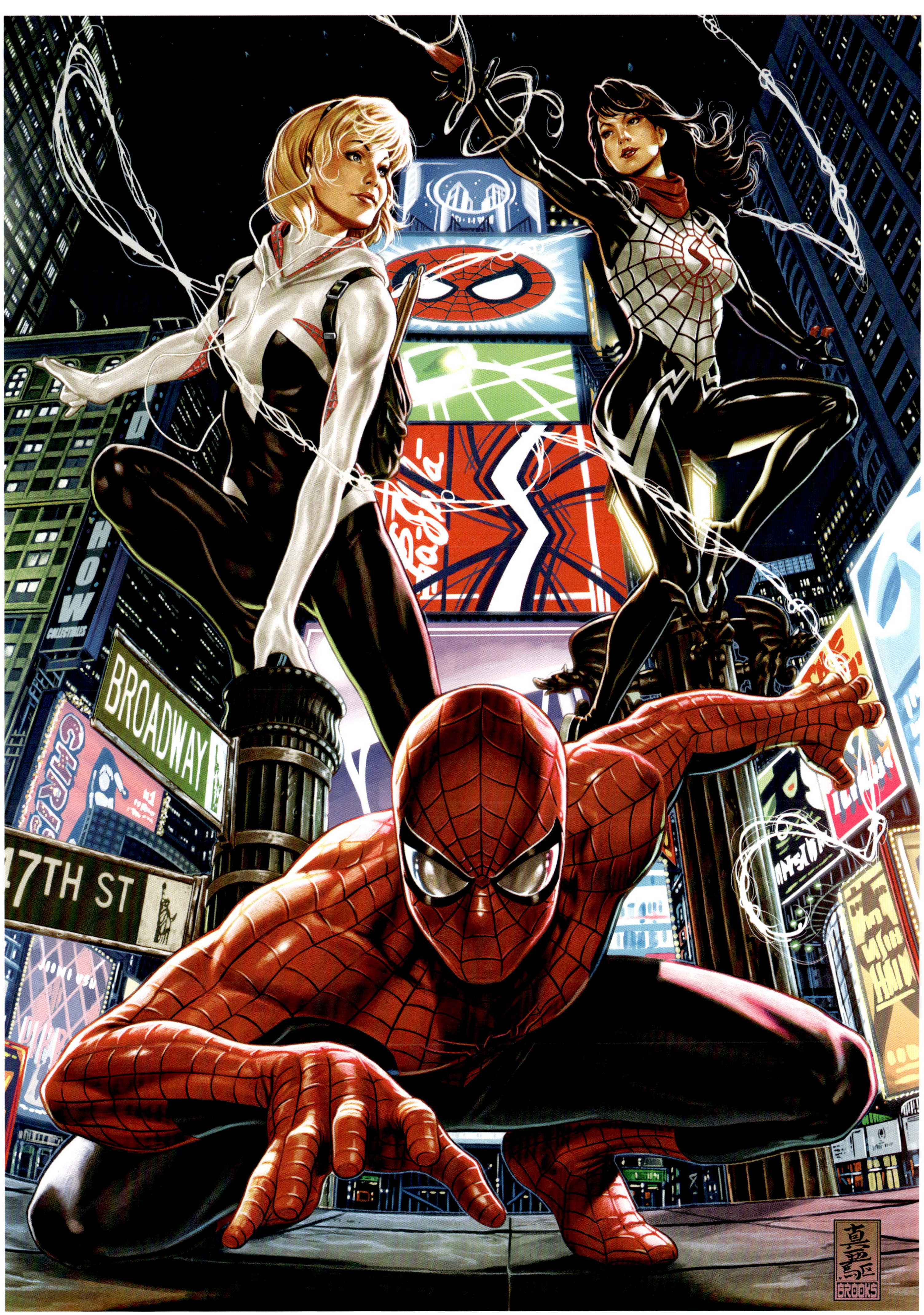
BROADWAY
47TH ST
BROOKS

MARK BROOKS

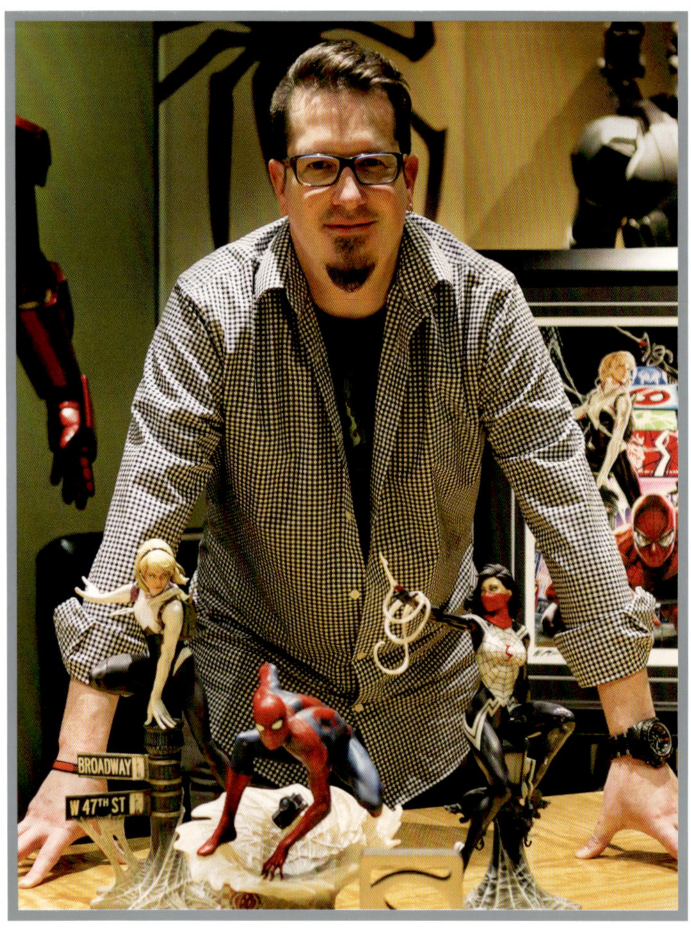

"One of the best things about working with Sideshow has been how collaborative they are with the creators. I always feel heard and that we have the same goals, so it makes it really easy to work together. I want the art prints that represent my work to be of the highest quality in terms of materials and colors. Sideshow understands this and I've always been very impressed by the high quality of the prints they produce."

INSPIRATION

Mark Brooks has been a professional illustrator for nearly twenty years, producing artwork for comics, TV, and video games. For most of that time, he's been drawing for Marvel Comics on titles like *Avengers*, *The Amazing Spider-Man*, *Deadpool*, and *X-Men*. Recently Mark has been drawing for Marvel's hugely popular *Star Wars* line of comics, including providing the art for Marvel's *Han Solo* limited series, which garnered two Eisner nominations. In the last few years, he has also worked with DC Comics on various titles including their flagship Batman book, *Detective Comics*. Mark was also the cover artist for Marvel's big Summer crossover event *Secret Empire*. This is Mark's second stint designing statues for Sideshow, having provided designs for an earlier line that included Dagger, Scarlet Witch, and Psylocke.

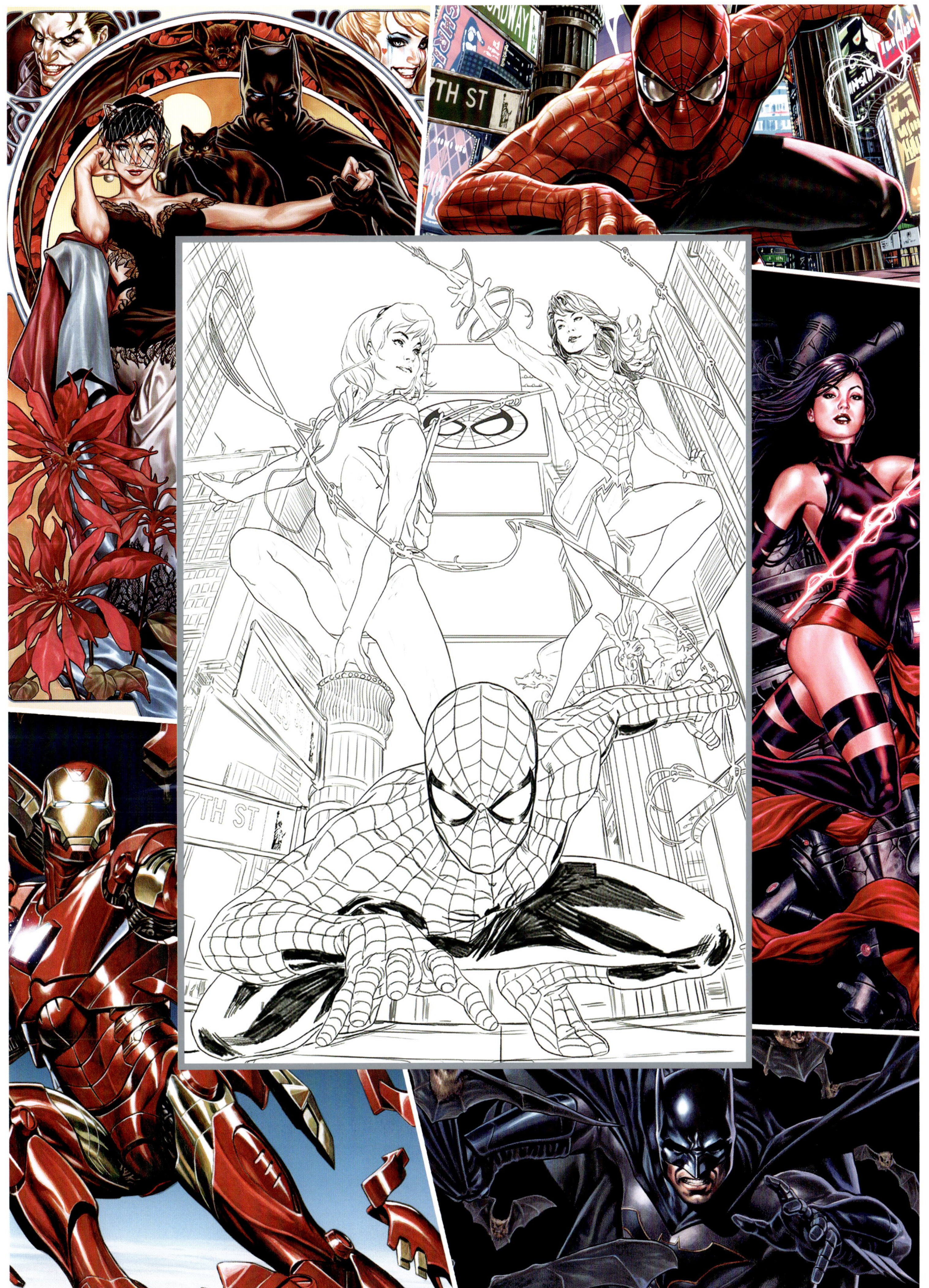

Spider-Verse print and line art. *Tony Stark: Iron Man*, *Psylocke*, *Batman: Detective Comics* #985. Upcoming print release *Batman & Catwoman*.

GREEN LANTERN
DESERTED

DANIEL PICARD

"In brightest day, in blackest night, no evil shall escape my sight!" Sideshow is proud to present the *Green Lantern: Deserted* Premium Art Print by celebrated figure photographer Daniel Picard.

Stranded in the desert in Sector 2814, Hal Jordan needs help to recharge his power ring and return home. This humorous image blends a real-world environment with the Green Lantern Sixth Scale Figure, creating a clever display.

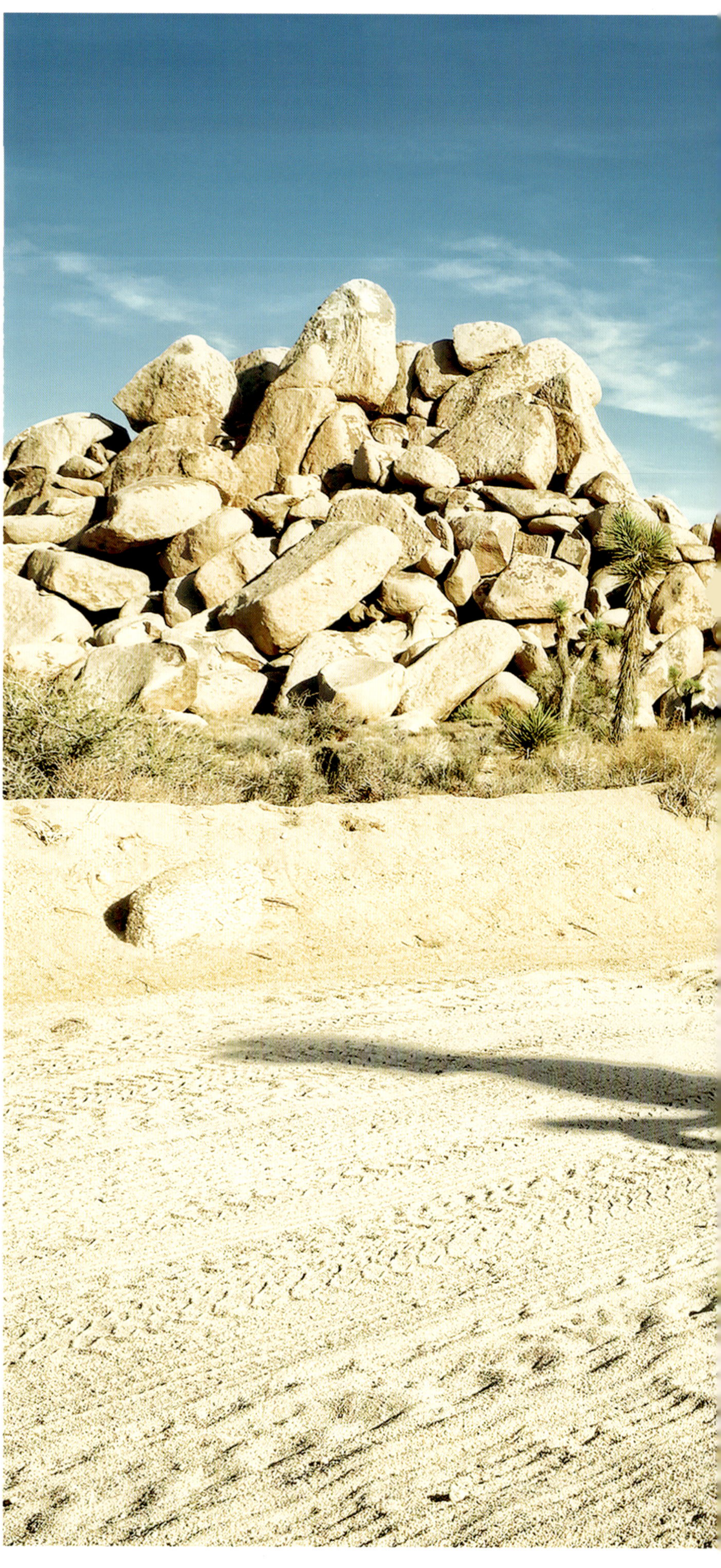

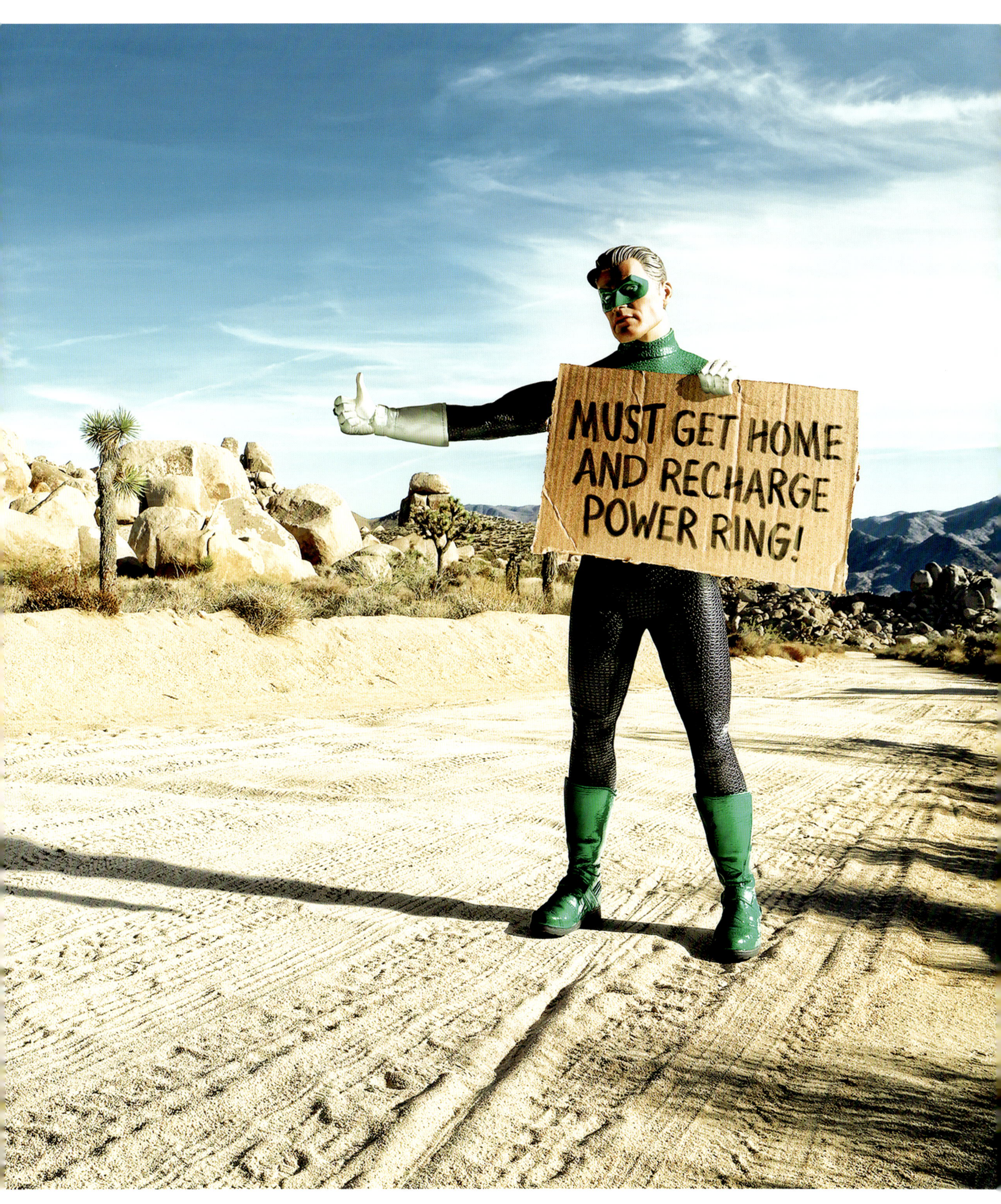
MUST GET HOME
AND RECHARGE
POWER RING!

THANOS ON THRONE
VARIANT

DOO-CHUN & IAN MACDONALD

Witness the destruction of an entire world as a planet explodes behind the near-omnipotent Thanos. With his glaring red eyes and stoic portrait, the Mad Titan looks out over the starways, wielding the power of the Infinity Stones at his fingertips. This crumbling world is a warning to all who may oppose him—the entire universe will fall to its knees before the might of Thanos.

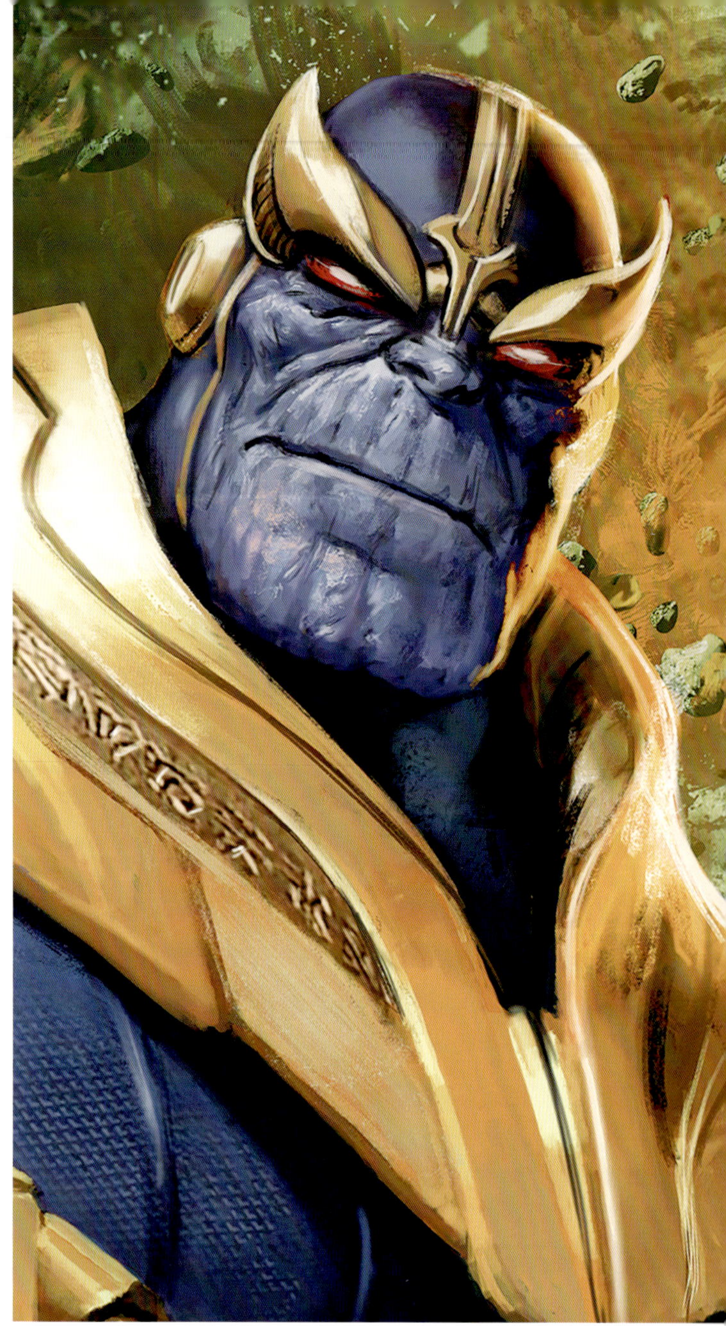

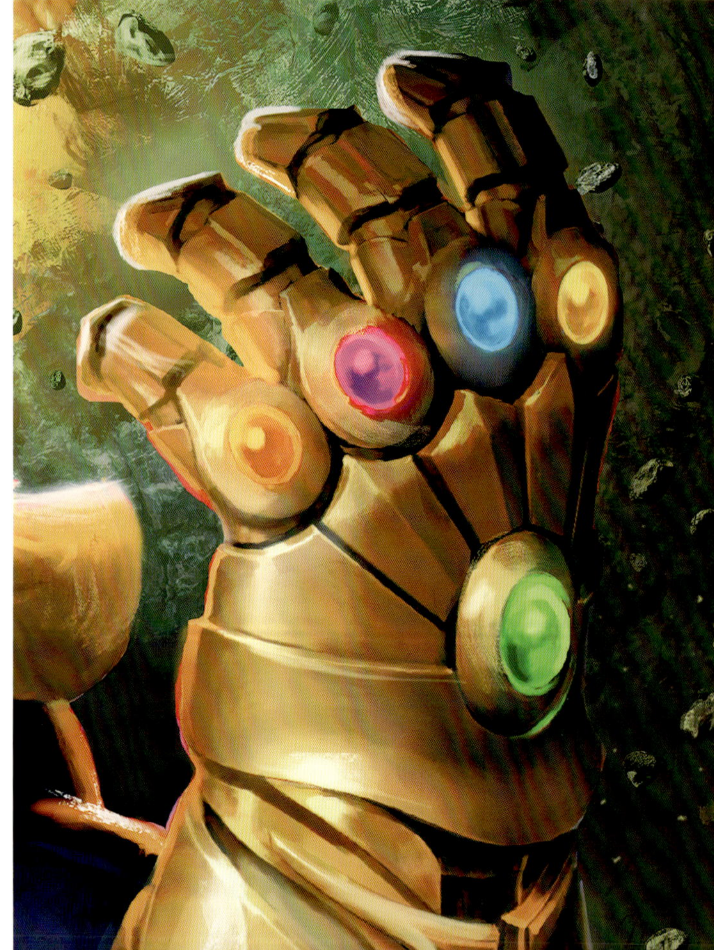

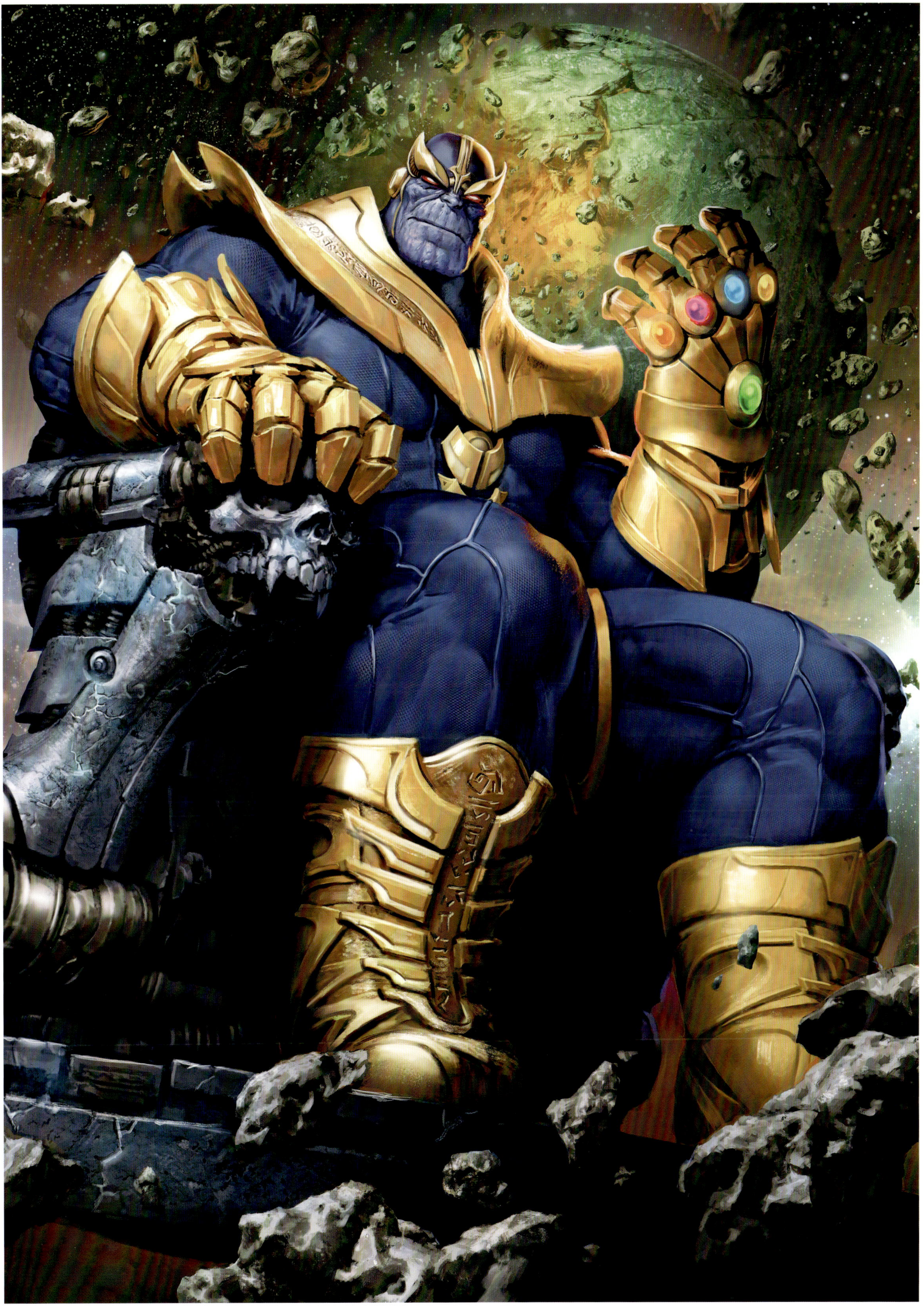

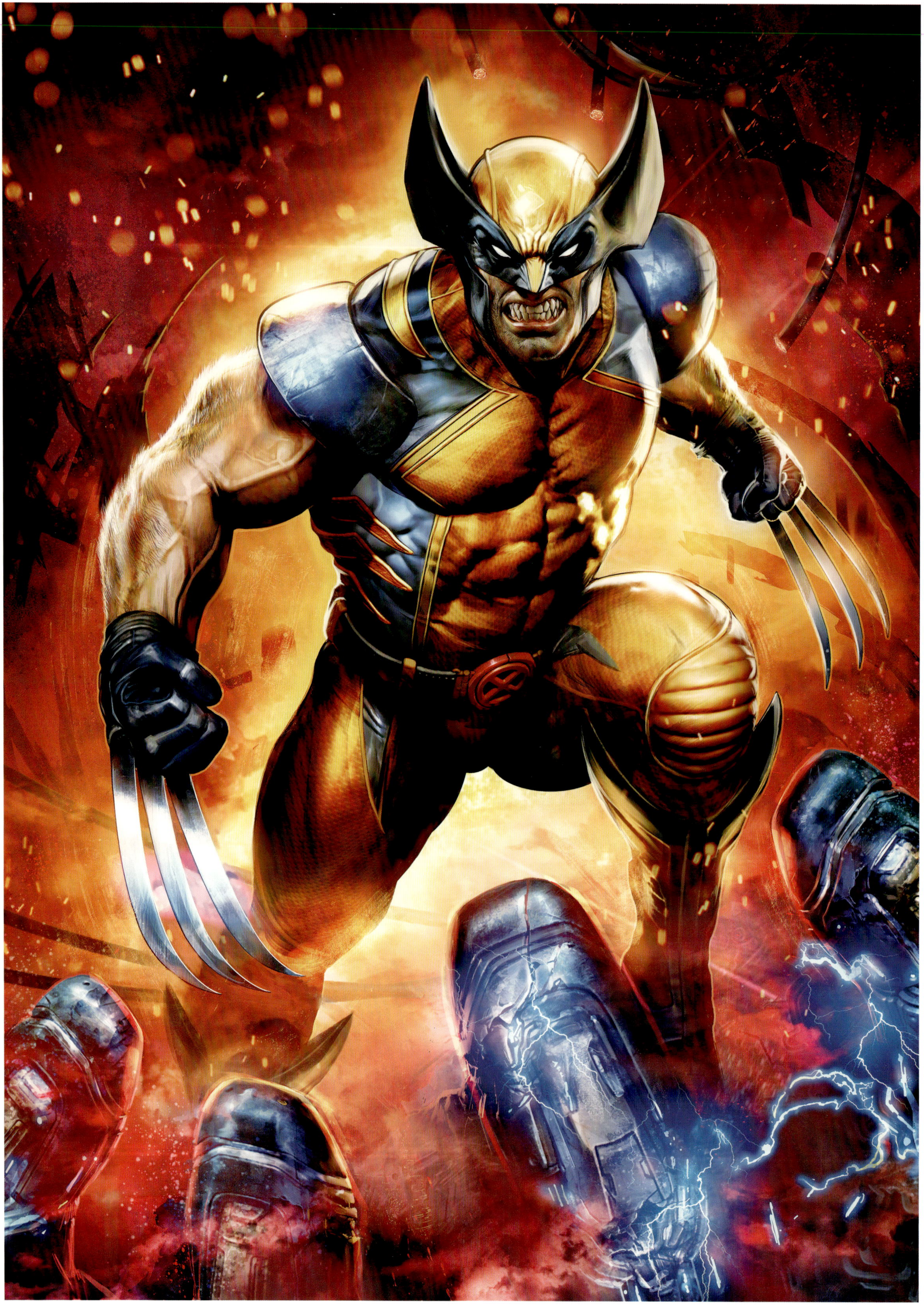

WOLVERINE

DAVE WILKINS

Fighting for the fate of mutantkind, Wolverine stands over the wreckage of a sparking, severed Sentinel hand. He's the best at what he does, destroying his enemies with his signature snarl and a quick *snikt!*

The yellow-and-blue-clad berserker has his formidable adamantium claws unsheathed and ready for action, just in case any other Sentinels want a piece of Wolverine.

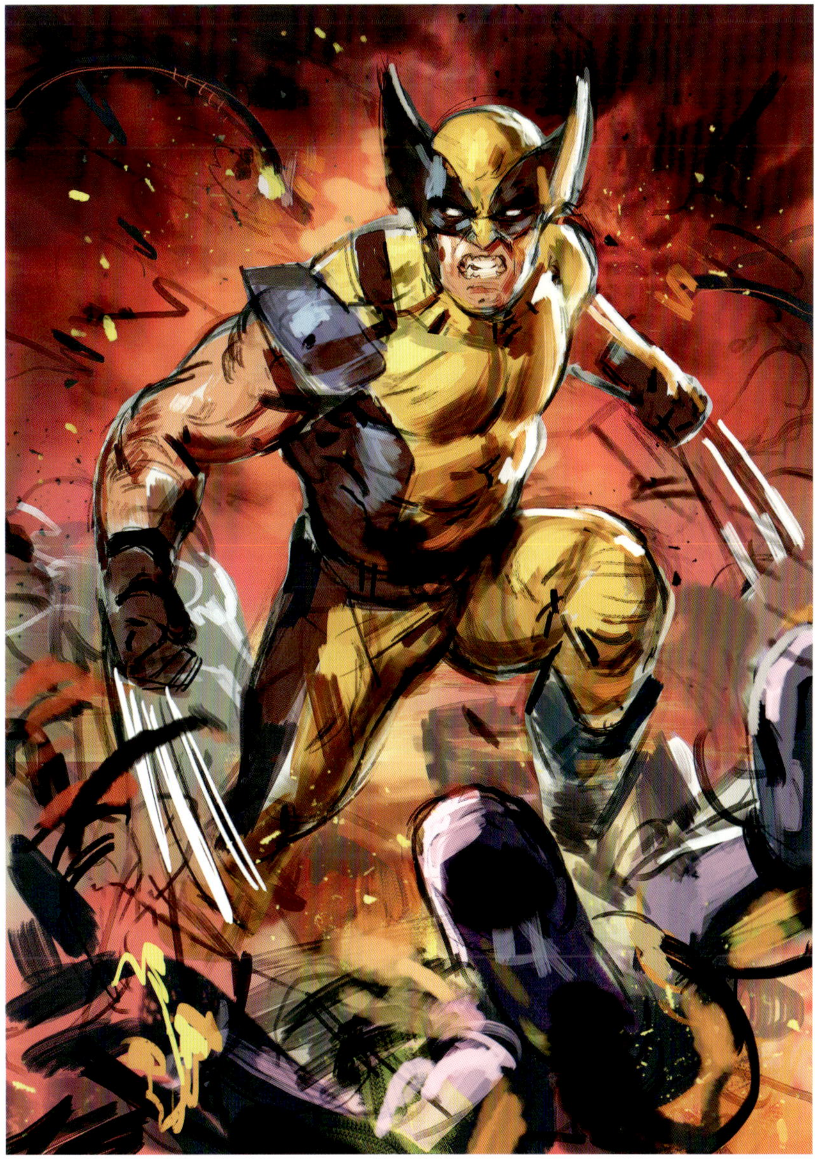

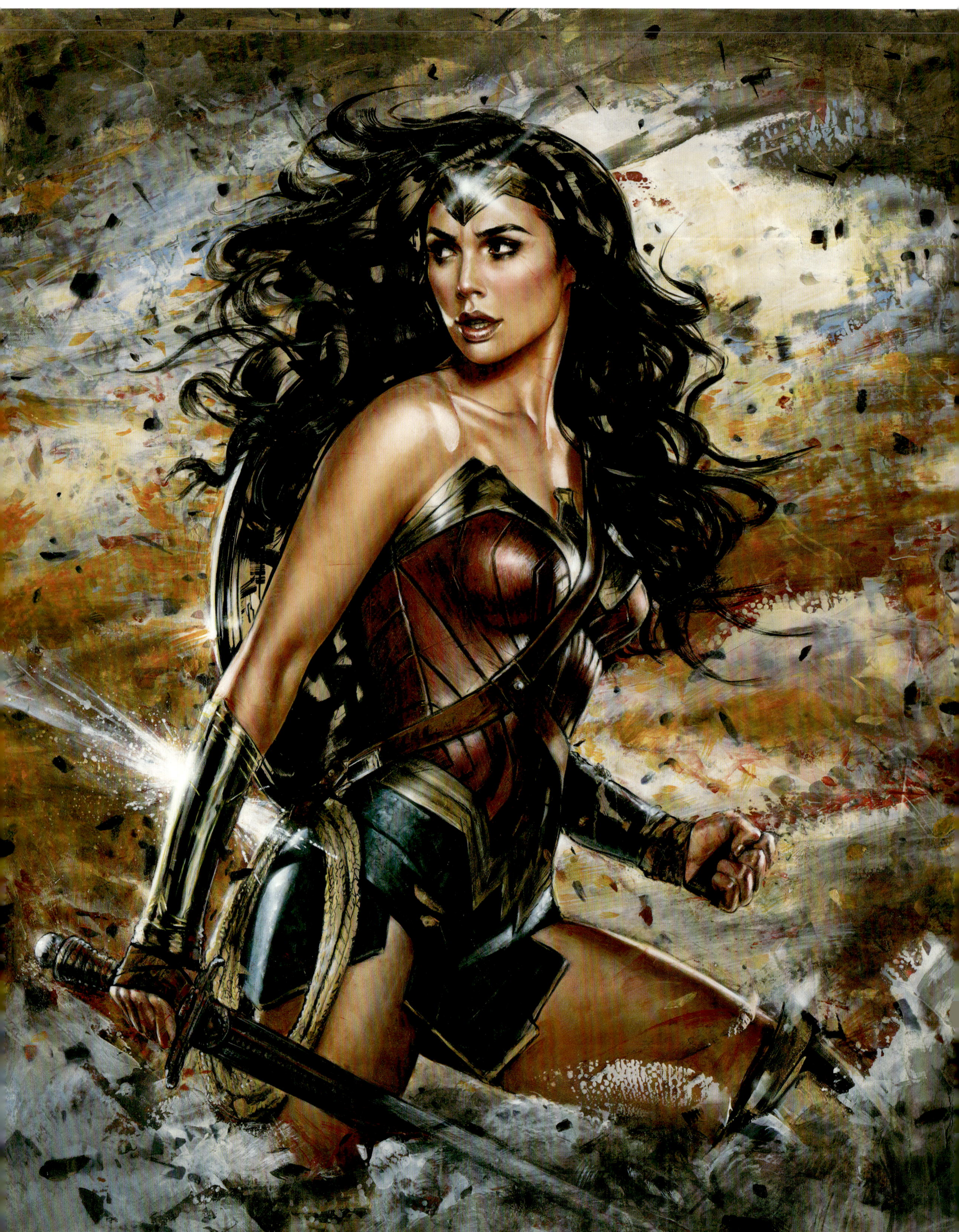

Wonder Woman: Amazon Warrior © 2018 Olivia De Berardinis

WONDER WOMAN
AMAZON WARRIOR

OLIVIA DE BERARDINIS

Based on Gal Gadot's appearance as the iconic heroine Wonder Woman in *Batman v Superman: Dawn of Justice*, this print captures the Amazon in a moment of bravery and strength. In the midst of battle, Wonder Woman shows grace under fire thanks to her incredible warrior upbringing, clutching her sword and fearlessly facing whatever foe may stand in her path. Highlighted against the chaos of the battlefield, this Amazon warrior stands tall as a champion for peace in a tumultuous world.

The *Wonder Woman: Amazon Warrior* Fine Art Print is a faithful reproduction of Olivia De Berardinis's original acrylic-on-wood painting, preserving the incredible detail in a quality display format. Each piece is hand-signed and hand-numbered, including a Certificate of Authenticity signed by De Berardinis as a part of the highly limited edition of 275 pieces.

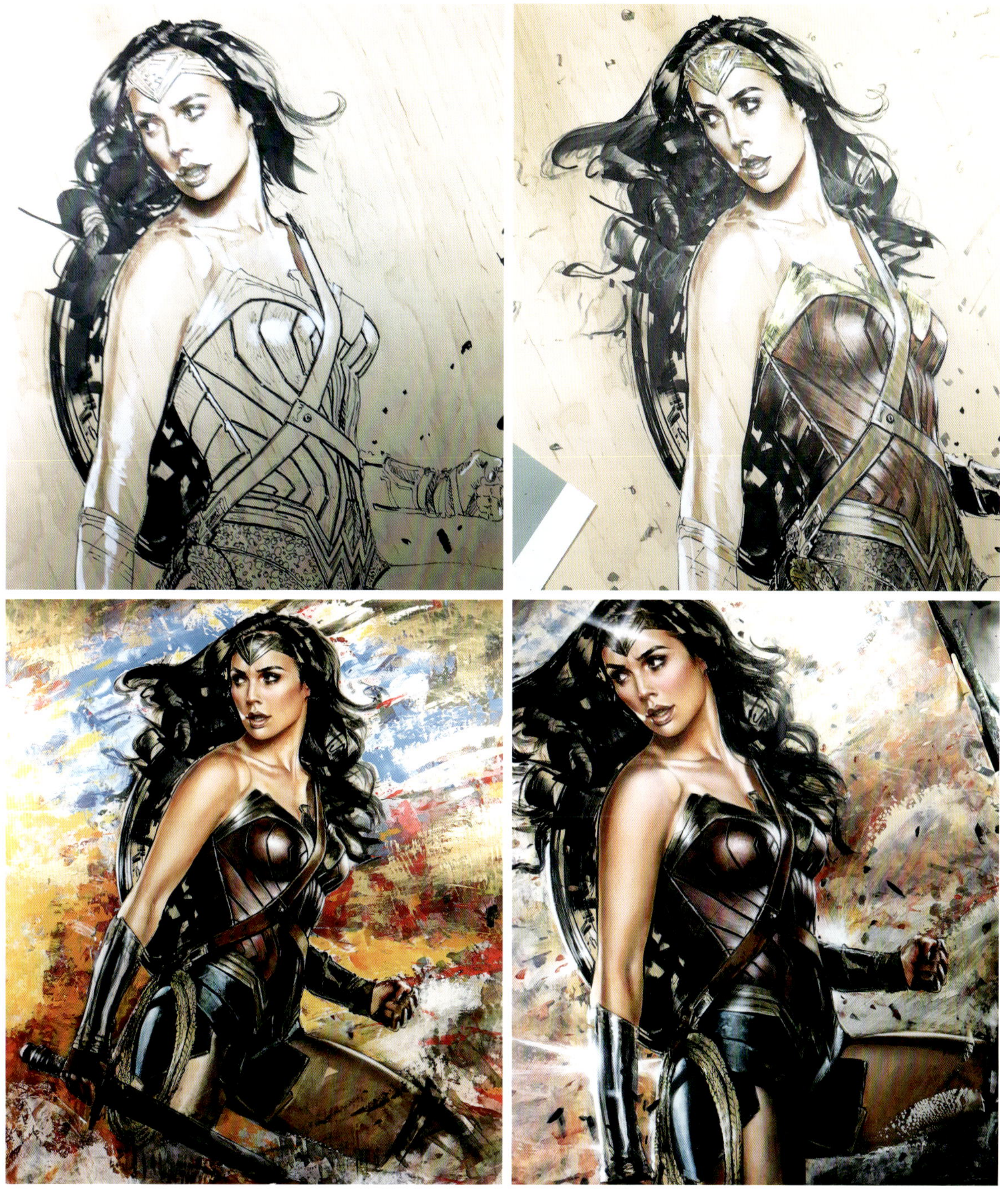

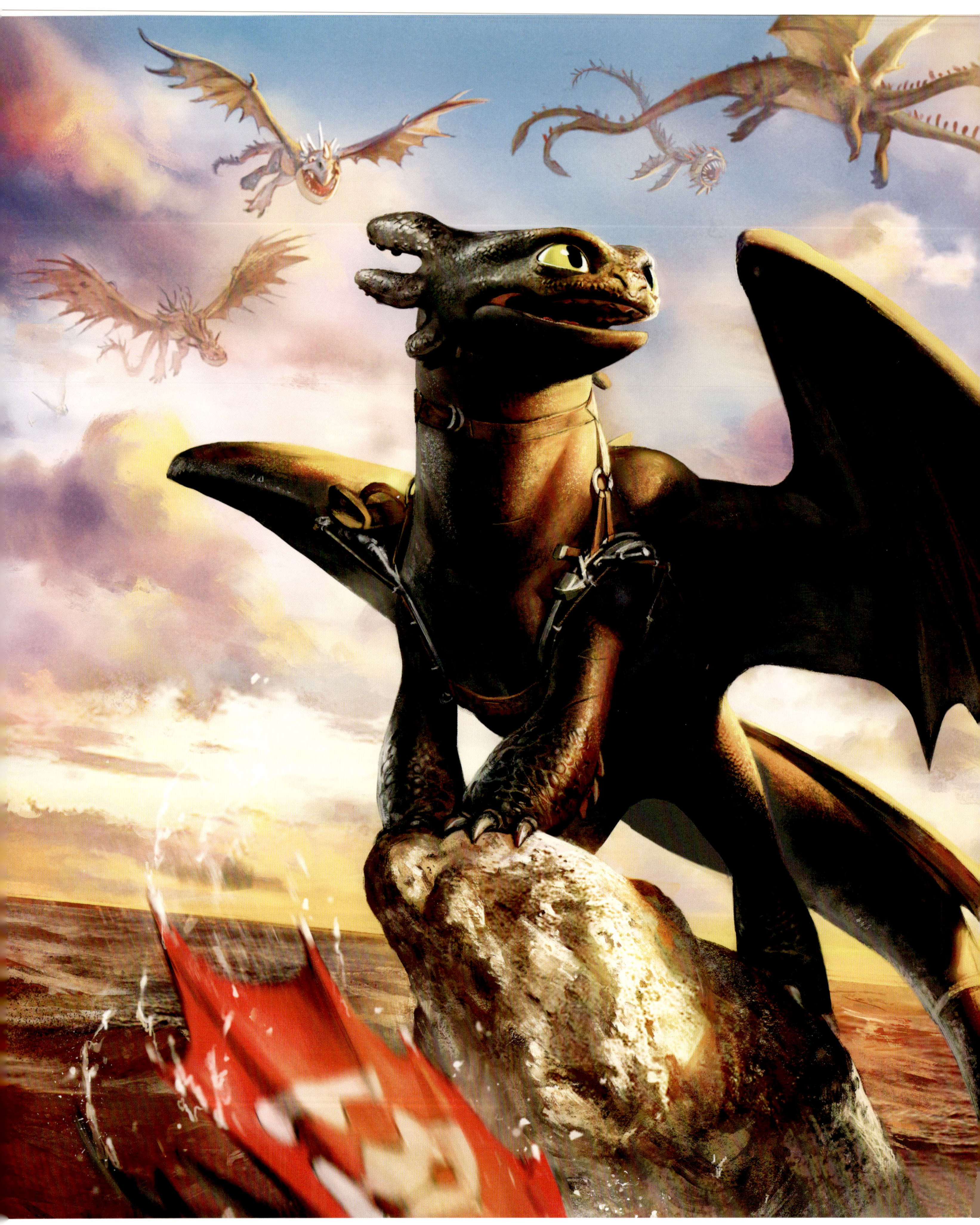

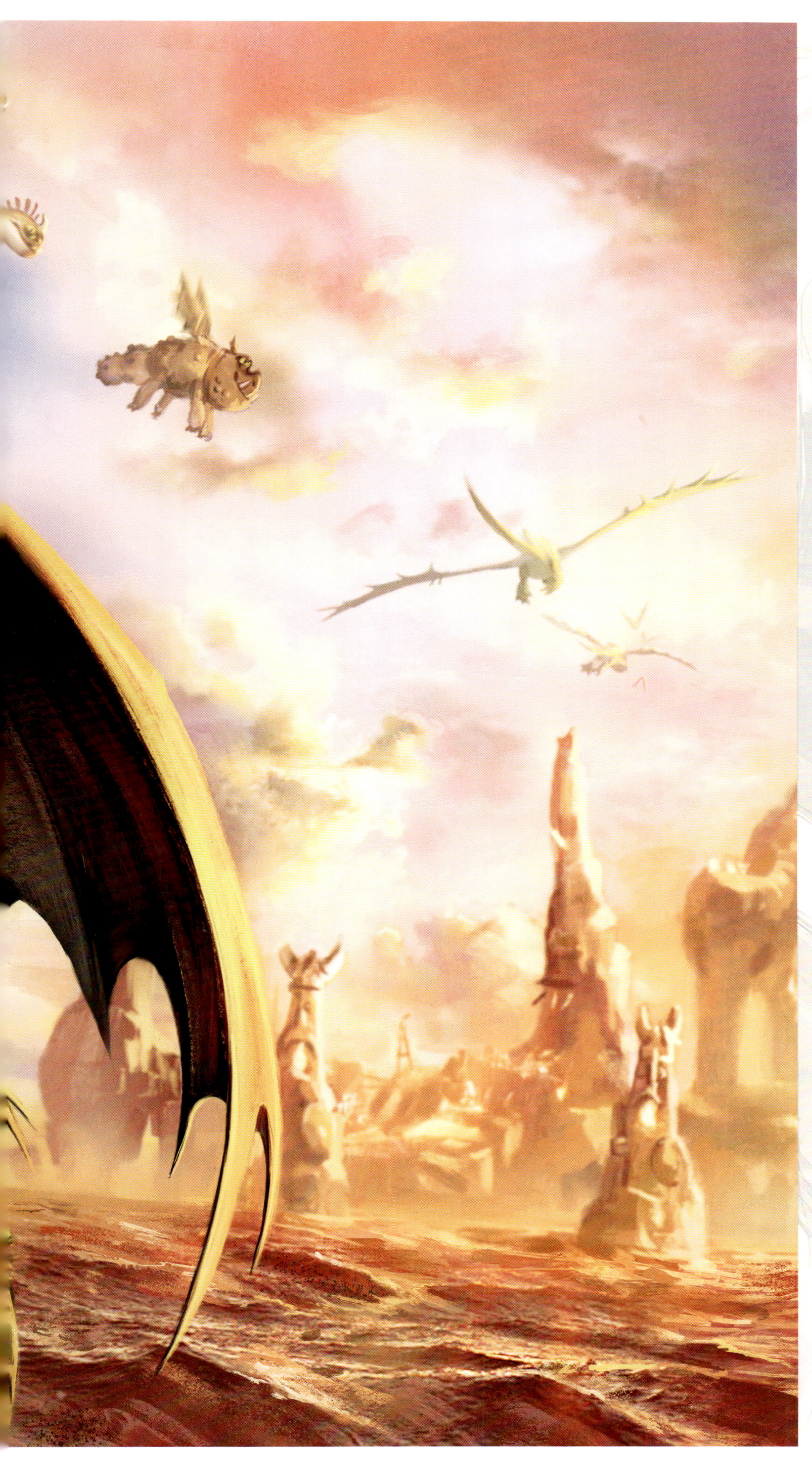

TOOTHLESS & THE DRAGONS OF BERK

IAN MACDONALD

Majestic and monstrous dragons soar high over the seas of Berk in this print inspired by the rich and colorful world of the *How to Train Your Dragon* films.

"I wanted to include some familiar faces in this print, especially since the second film opened up the world and dragon variety significantly," explains artist Ian MacDonald. "I snuck a Whispering Death dragon in the background since I thought it had such a cool mystique surrounding it after being teased in the first film."

The Night Fury Toothless stands on a rocky crag splashed with surf looking out at the horizon as wild dragons like the Deadly Nadder, the Hideous Zippleback, and the Monstrous Nightmare fly through the rocky outcroppings of the isles.

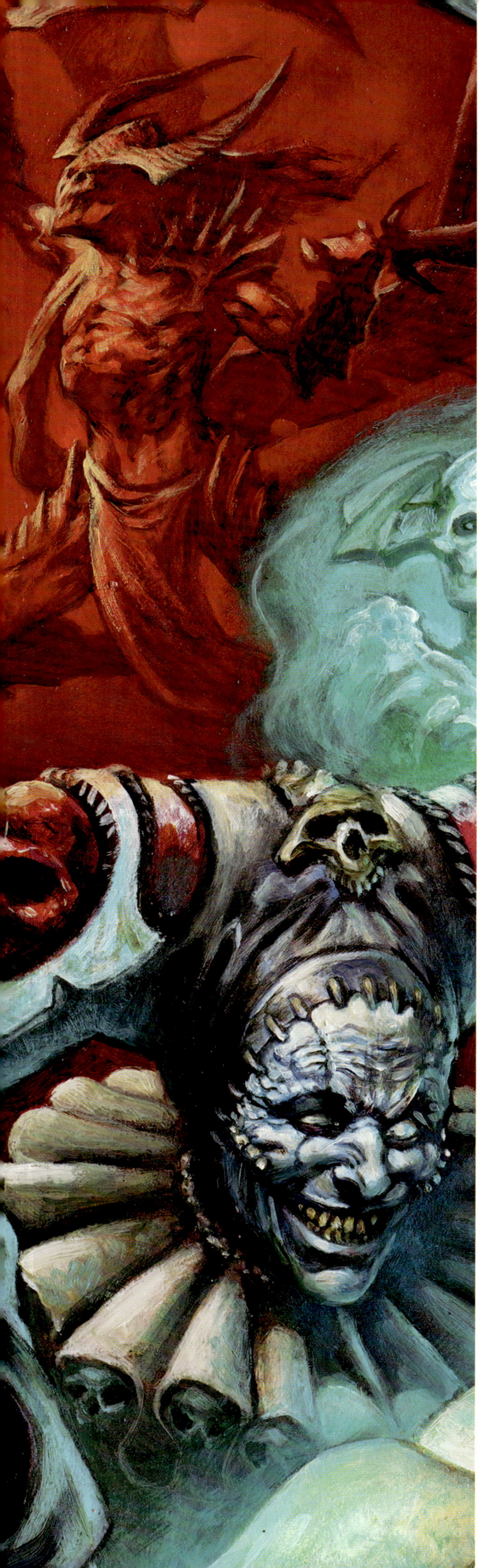

THE UNDERWORLD UNITED

ALEX HORLEY

The *Underworld United* Premium Art Print is a high-end reproduction of an original acrylic and oil painting by world-renowned artist Alex Horley.

This intricate and striking piece captures the dark and twisted conflict faced by Death and his Court of the Dead: All of existence is mired in a battle between the equally vile realms of Heaven and Hell. Death and the Underworld are enslaved to harvest the mortal souls that fuel their war, but they yearn for a more noble purpose—to end the war between Heaven and Hell, and to restore balance to the universe.

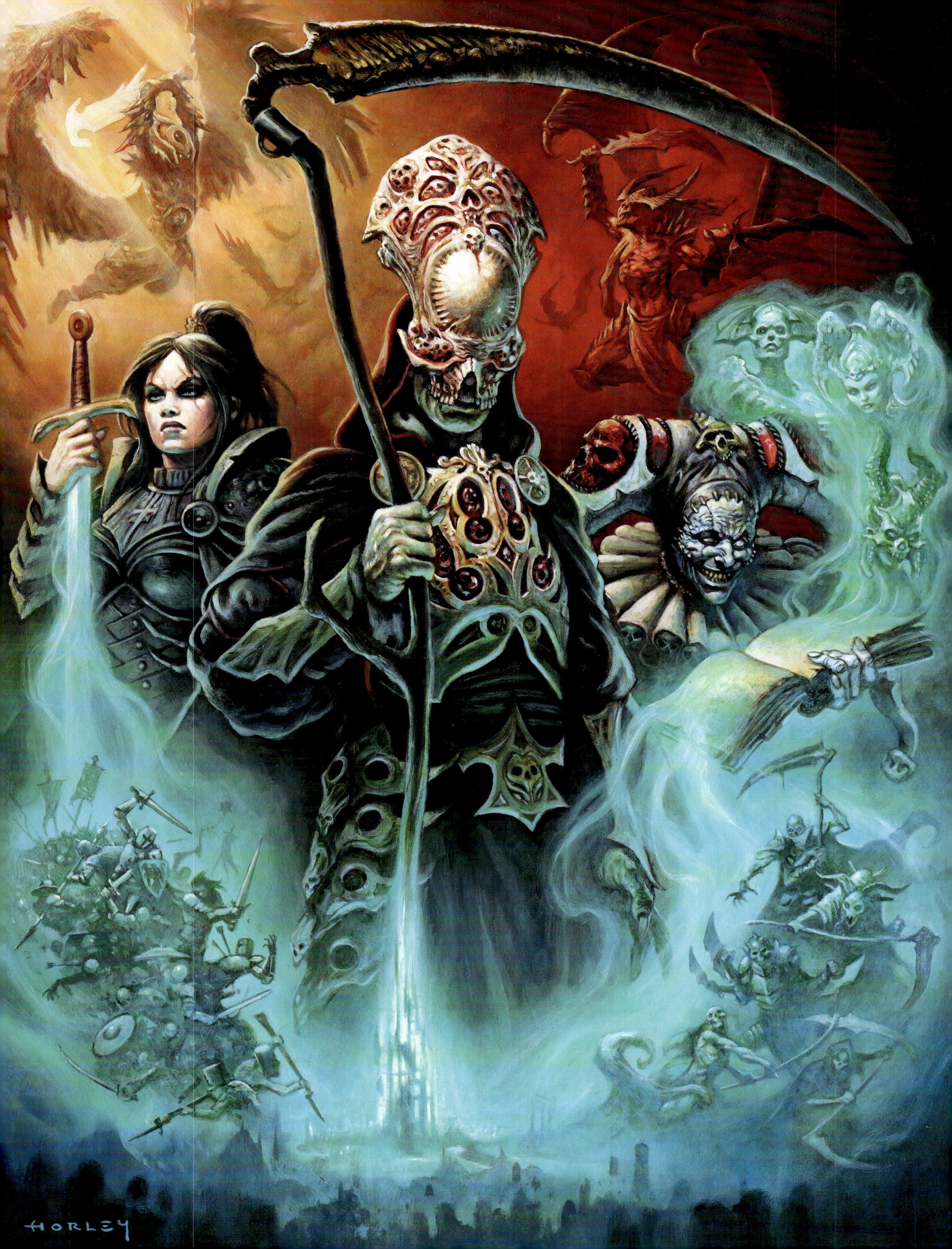
HORLEY

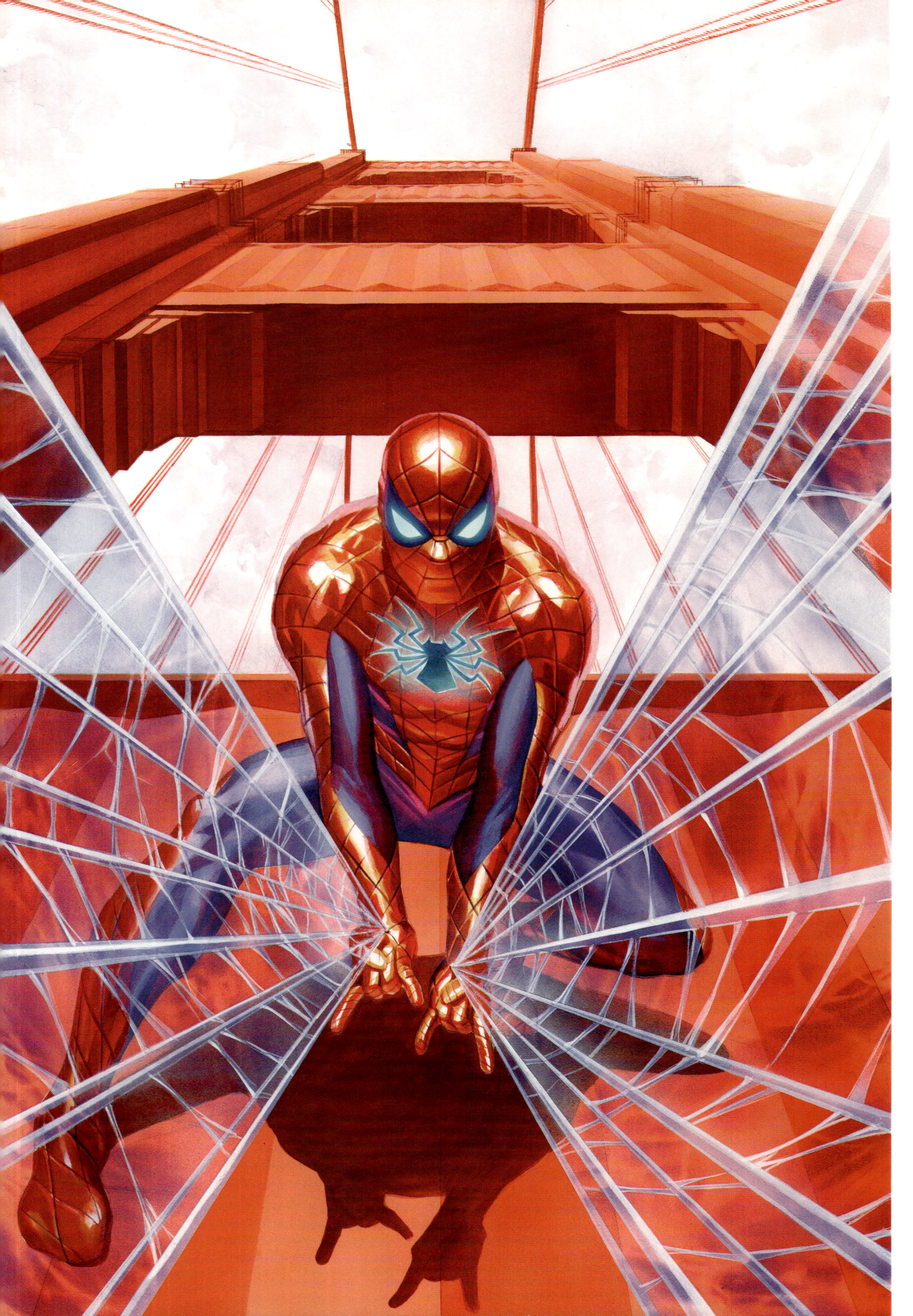

SPIDER-MAN
TROUBLE IN SAN FRANCISCO

ALEX ROSS

Originally created as a cover for an issue of *The Amazing Spider-Man*, Vol. 4, *Spider-Man: Trouble in San Francisco* has been specially reproduced for Sideshow as a fine art lithograph in an exclusive limited edition of 200 pieces.

The print features the wall-crawling hero as he clings to the Golden Gate Bridge, defying gravity with his spider powers. With a quick *thwip*, Spider-Man slings some webs to save the day and stop whatever trouble swings his way.

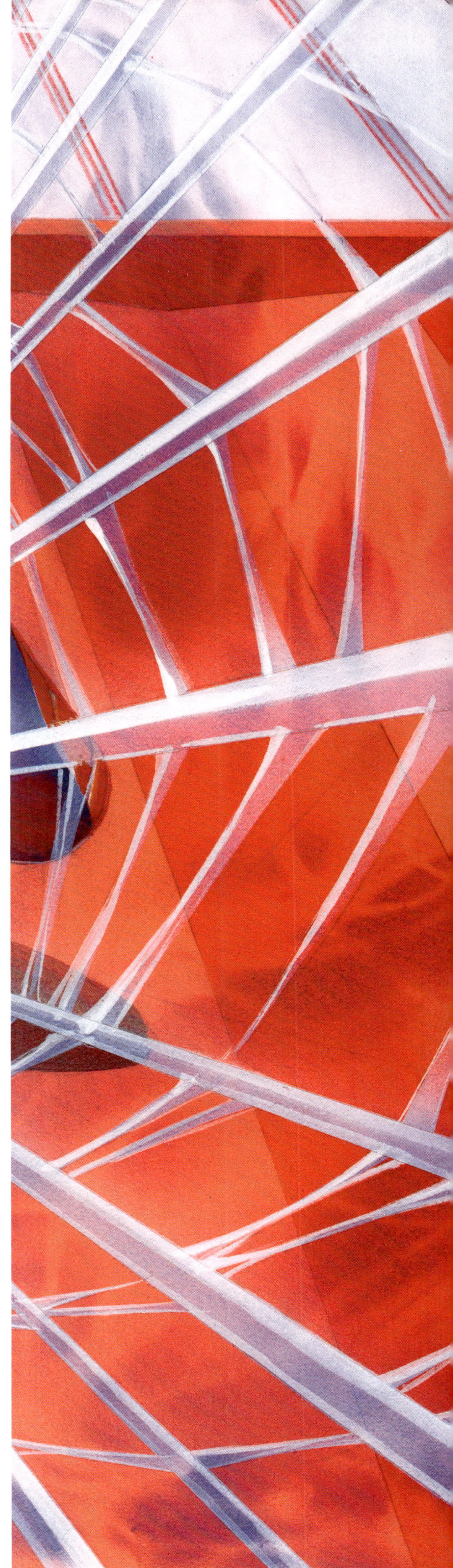

CAPTAIN AMERICA & BLACK WIDOW

ALEX PASCENKO & IAN MACDONALD

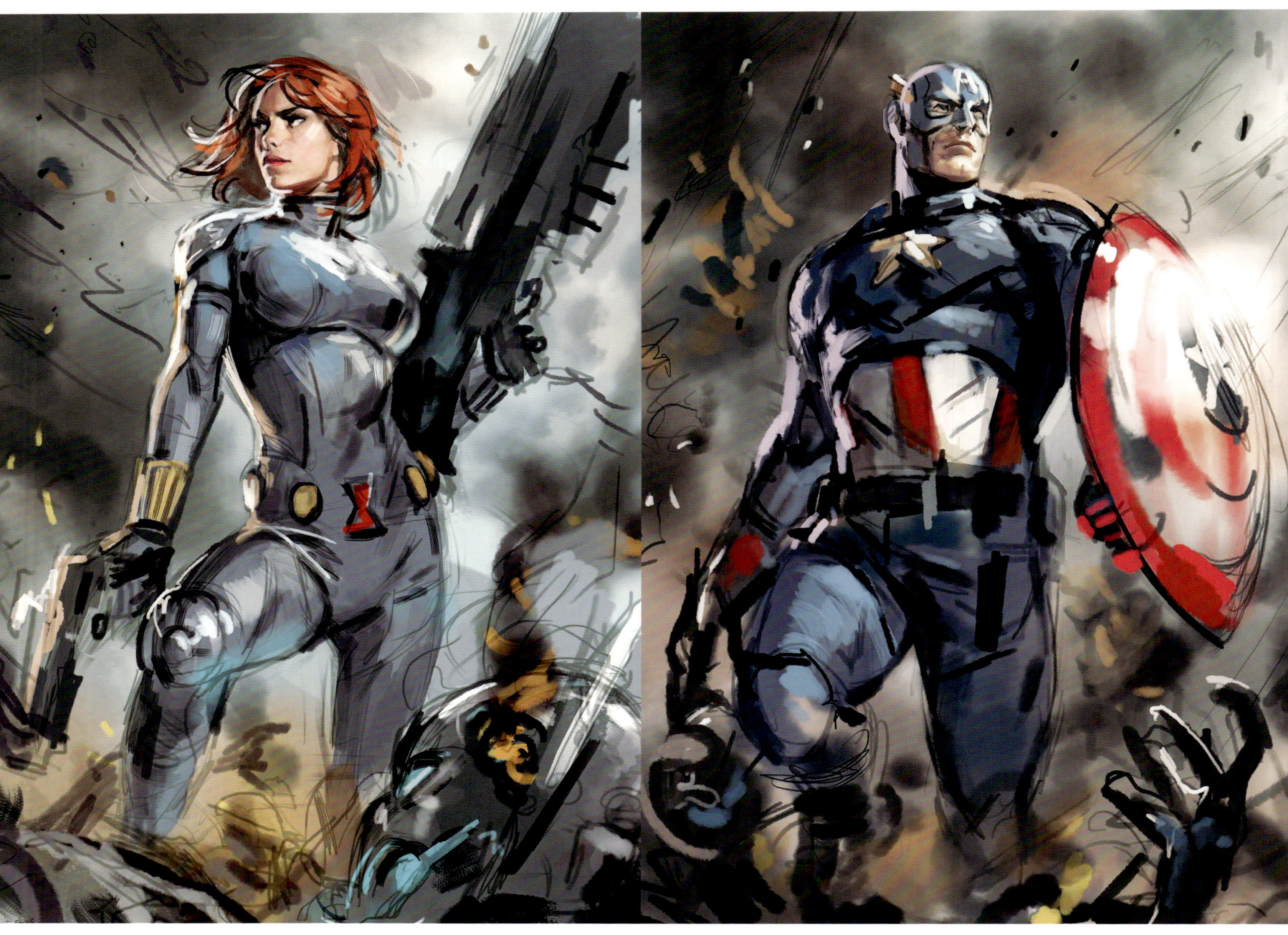

The Captain America & Black Widow Premium Art Print features the two Avengers standing triumphant amidst Ultron's disassembled armies.

The star-spangled super soldier Captain America holds his shield high as the deadly assassin Black Widow stands with guns at the ready. The iconic S.H.I.E.L.D. Helicarrier and a Quinjet fly high in the skies above the heroes, ready to support them in the smoldering battlefield.

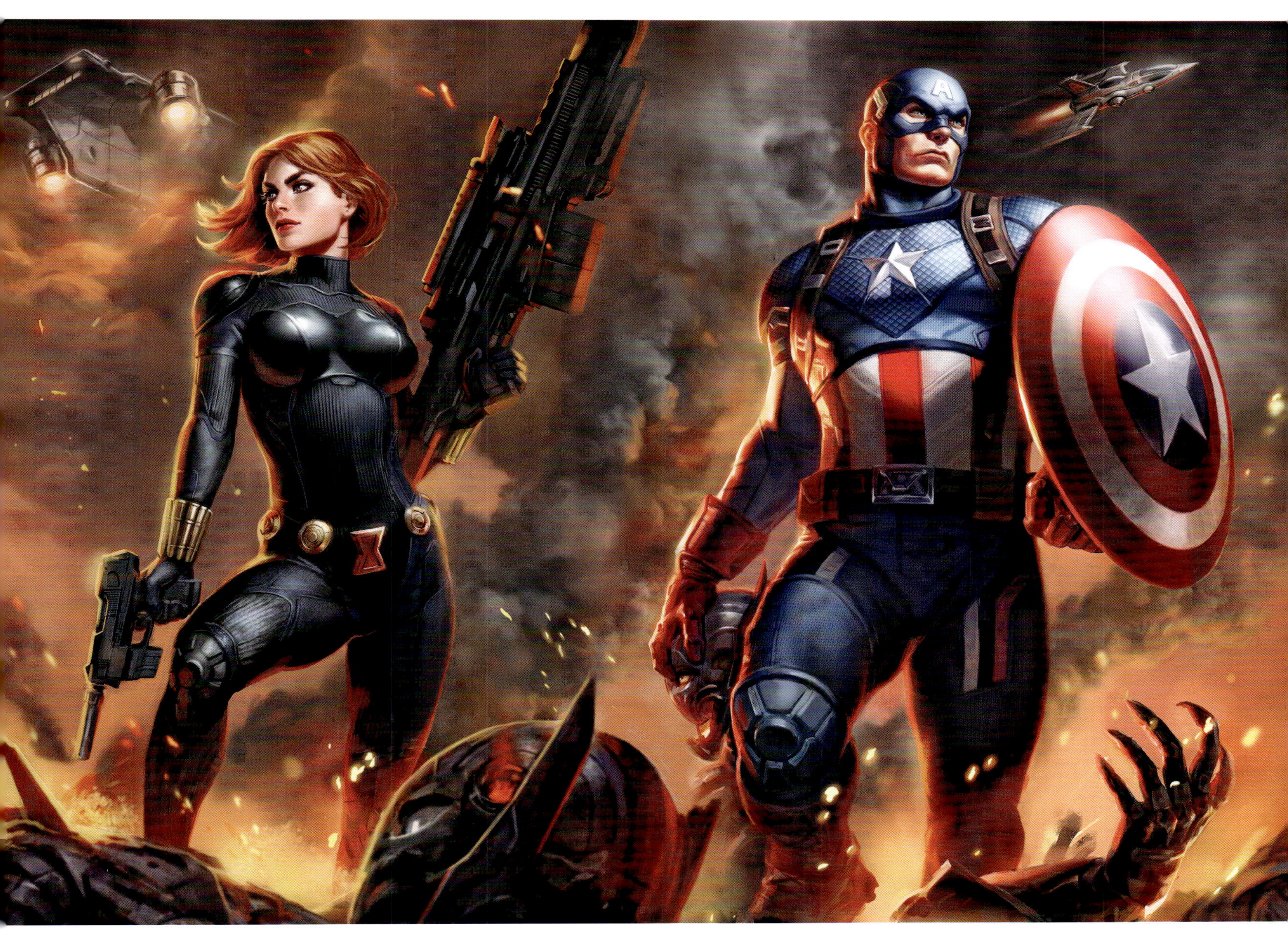

CHAT NOIR

OLIVIA DE BERARDINIS

Based on Michelle Pfeiffer's electrifying performance as Catwoman in Tim Burton's *Batman Returns*, *Chat Noir* embodies all the dangerous allure of the feline femme fatale in one stunning display. Beware the beast behind the beauty!

From her iconic stitched catsuit to her deadly claws, Catwoman's wild style shines through here, captured by her sultry gaze and striking red lips.

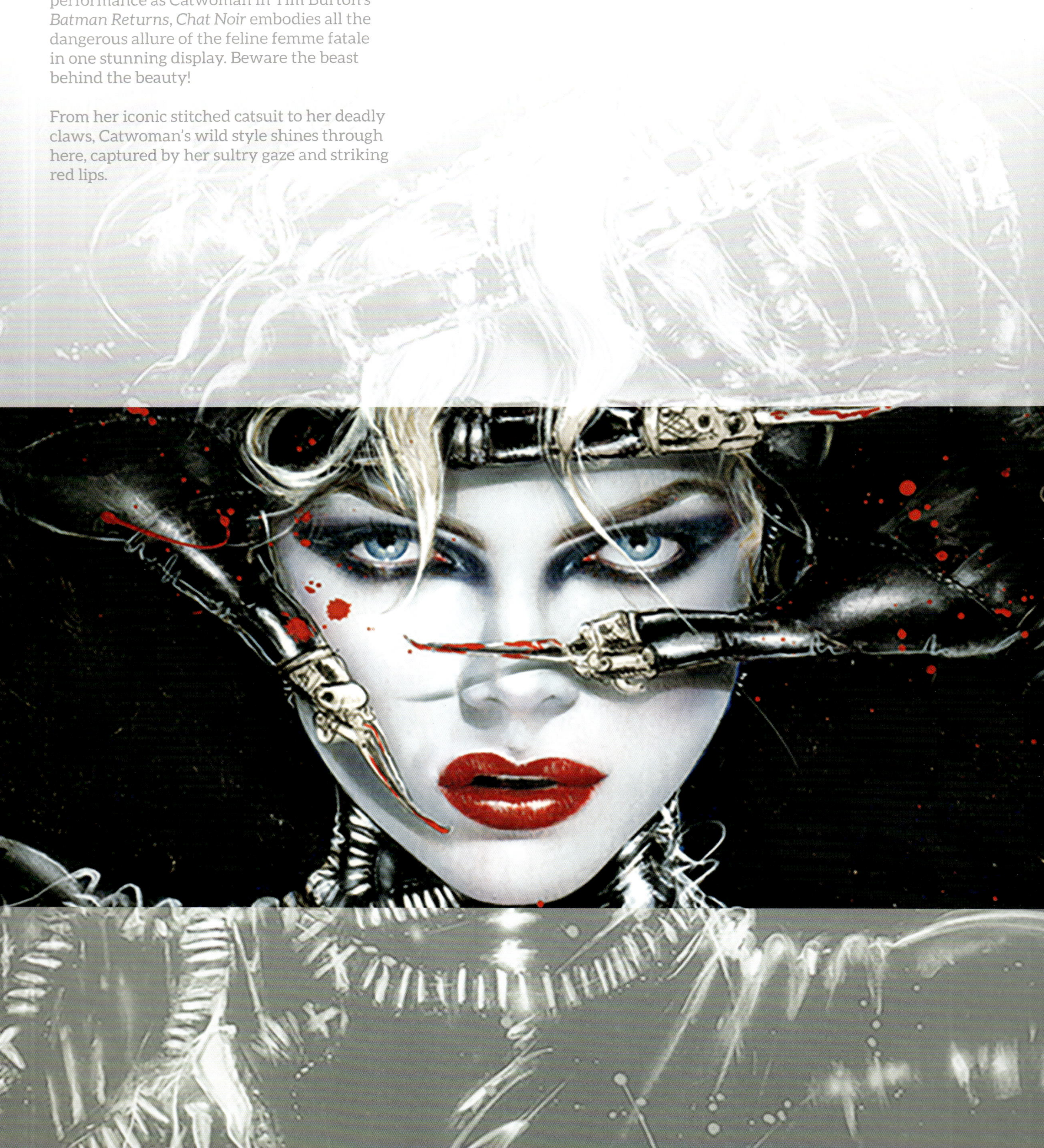

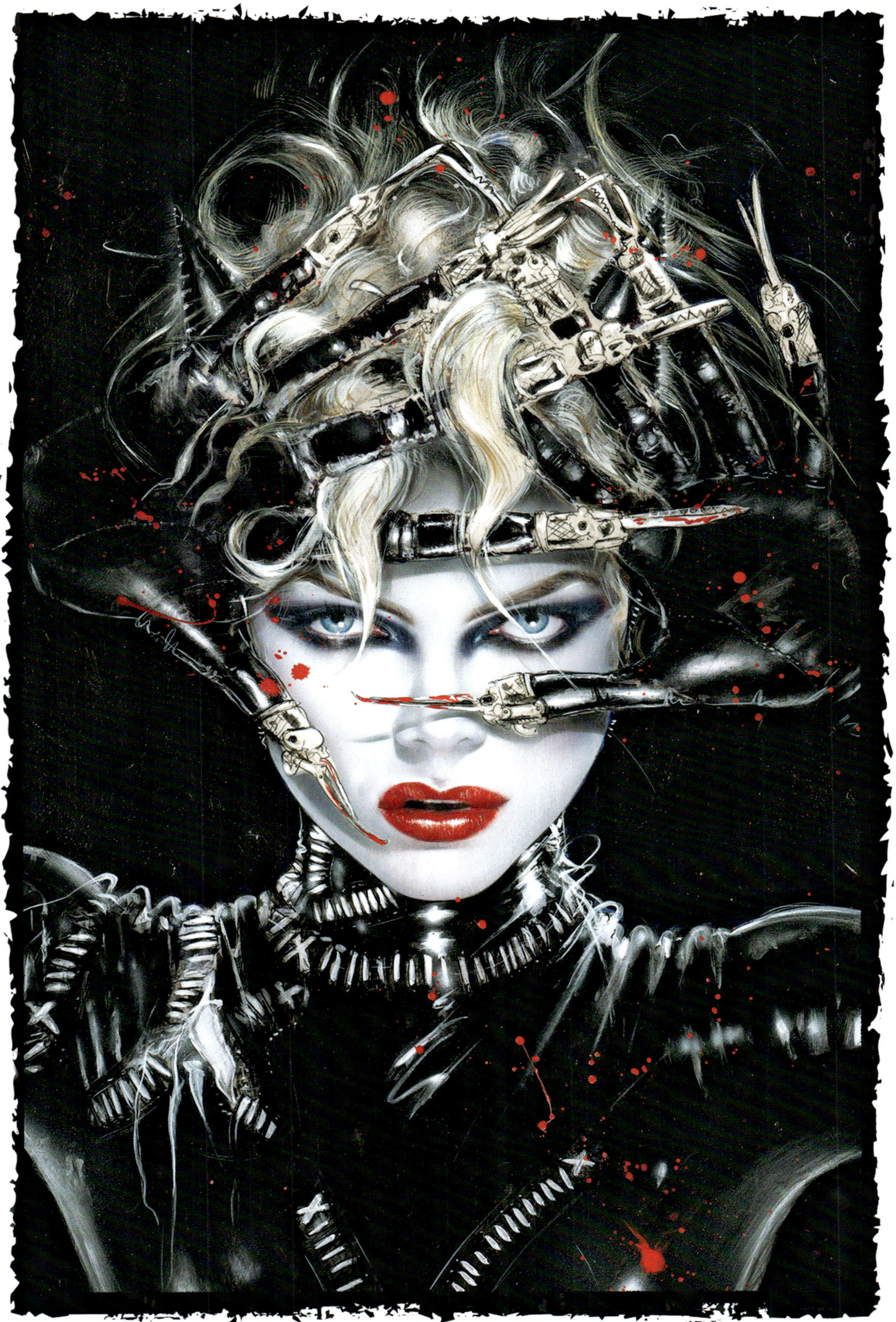

Chat Noir © 2018 Olivia De Berardinis

BLACK PANTHER

RYAN MEINERDING

Black Panther by Ryan Meinerding—part of the Marvel Studios Fine Art Print collection—captures the majesty and energy of the king of Wakanda. Set against the futuristic Wakandan skyline, this character piece features T'Challa alongside his heroic Black Panther persona, highlighted in regal shades of purple. His elite allies, Nakia and Okoye of the Dora Milaje, hold their weapons high while Erik Killmonger stalks the foreground.

As Marvel Studios' head of visual development, Ryan Meinerding notes that the Fine Art Print program is an exceptional celebration of Marvel Studios' art. "Having our concept art celebrated in such a dramatic format is a rare treat that gives fans a chance to see Visual Development's influence on some of their favorite characters and moments."

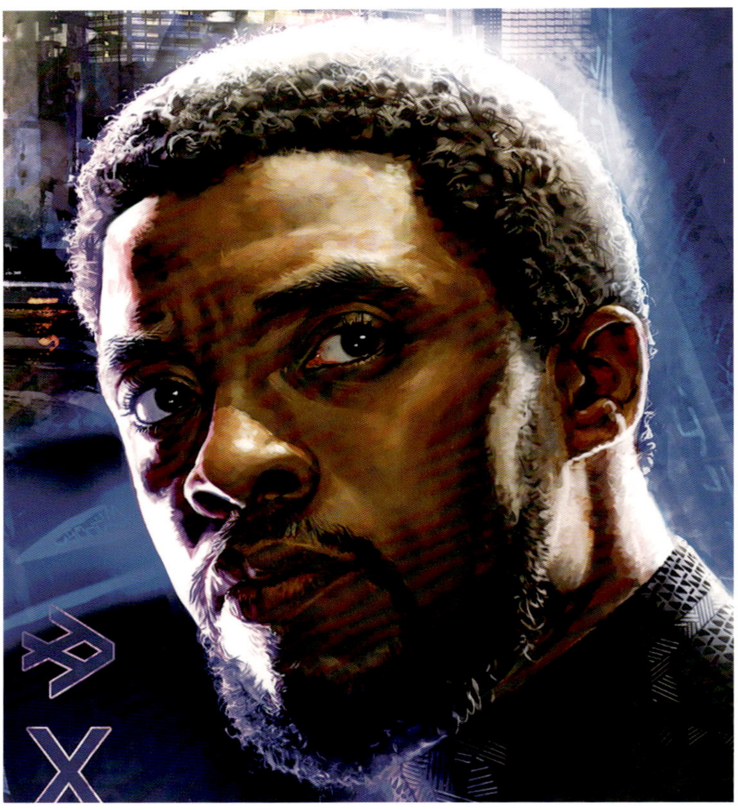

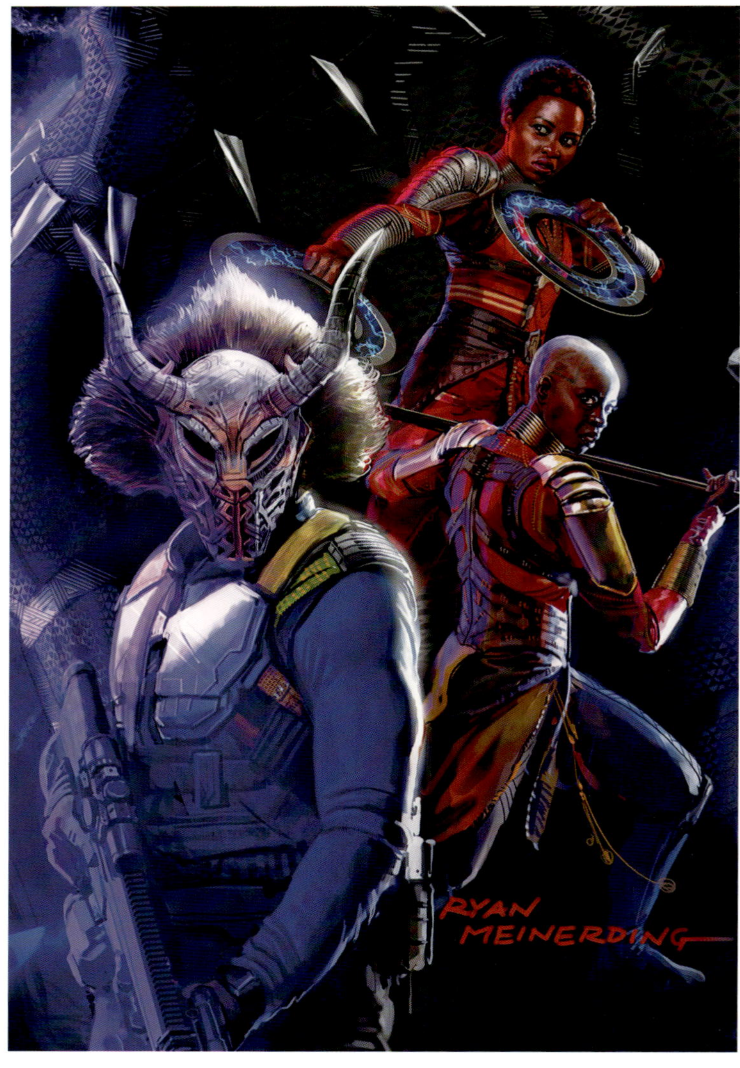

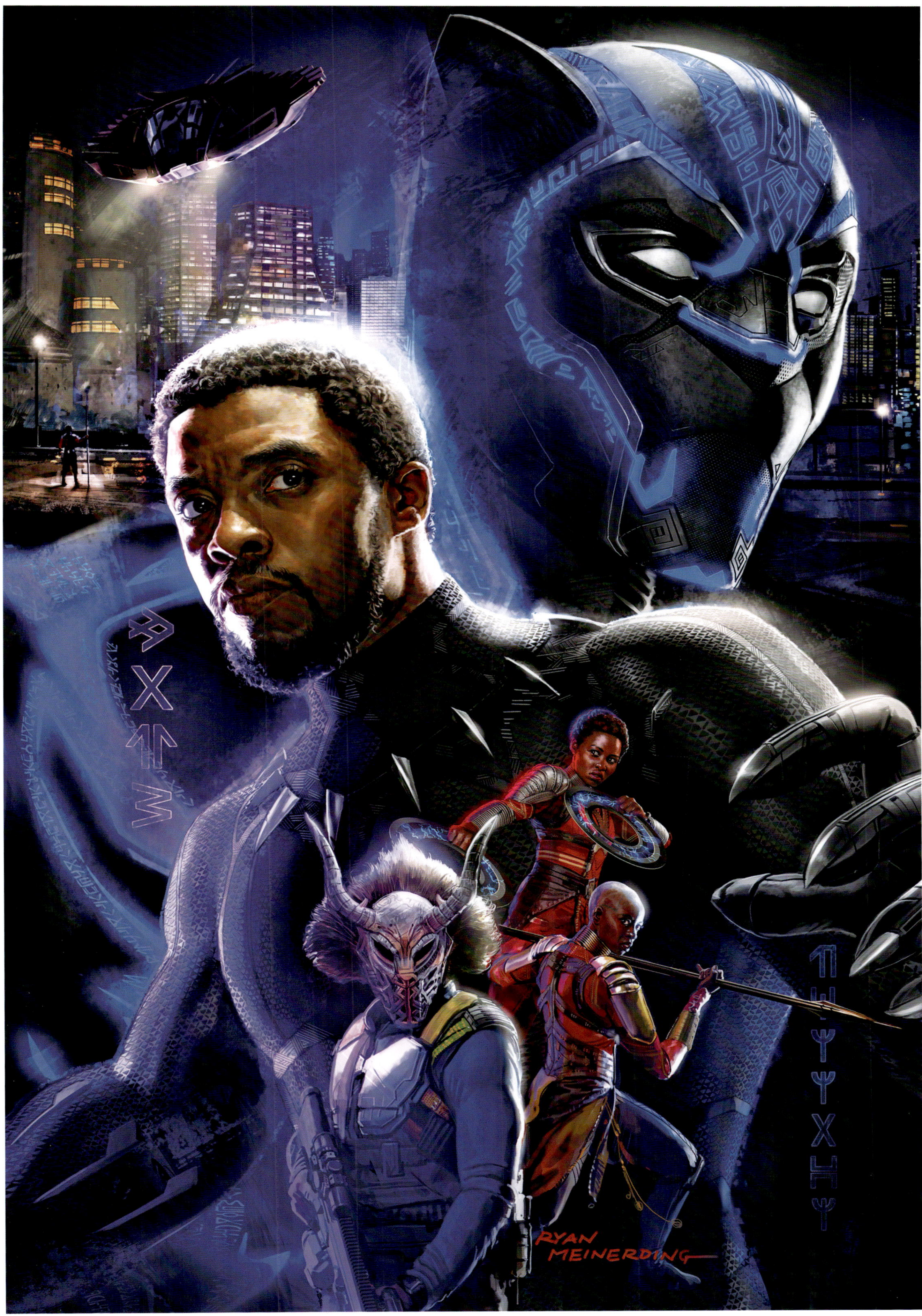
RYAN
MEINERDING

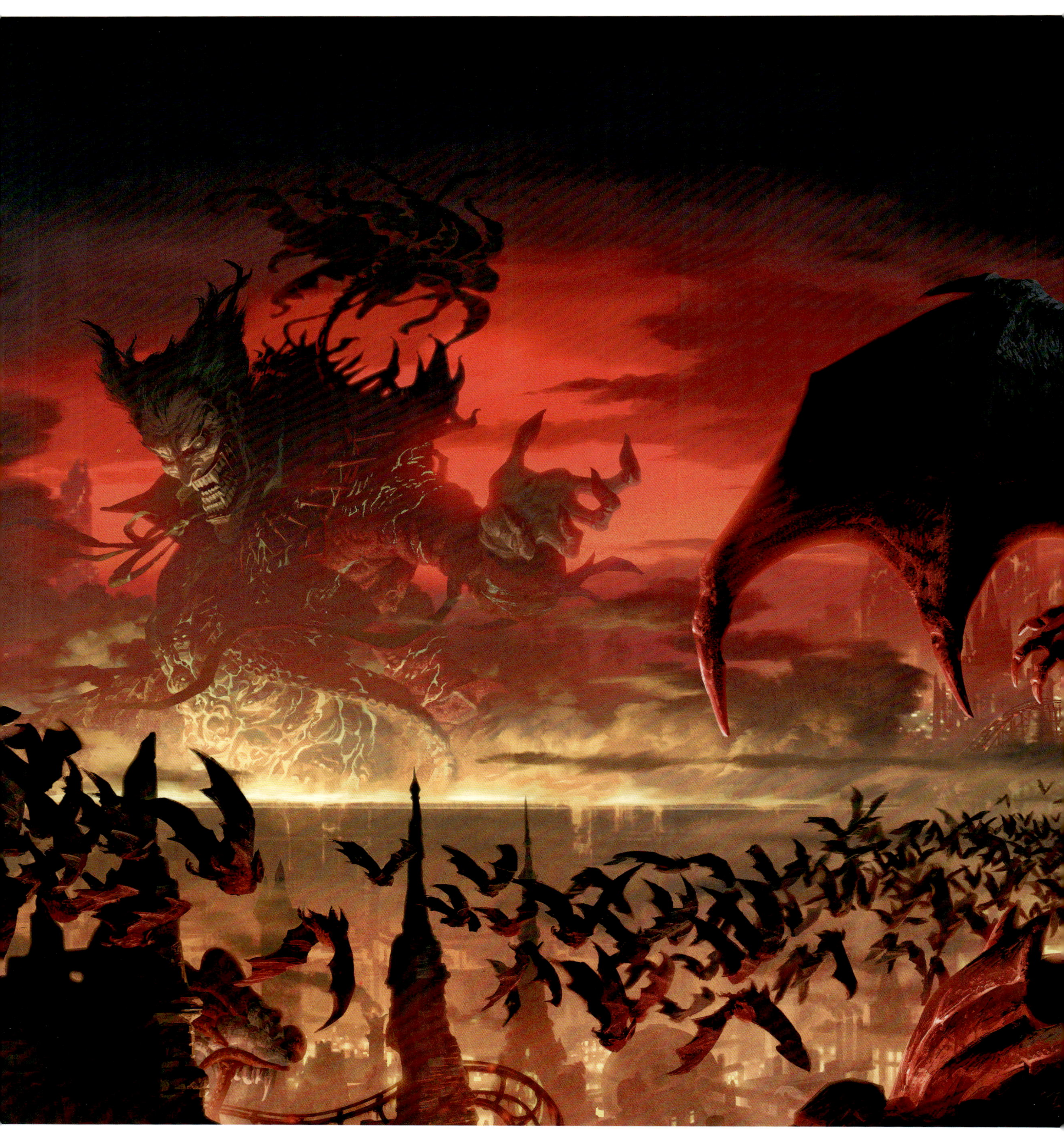

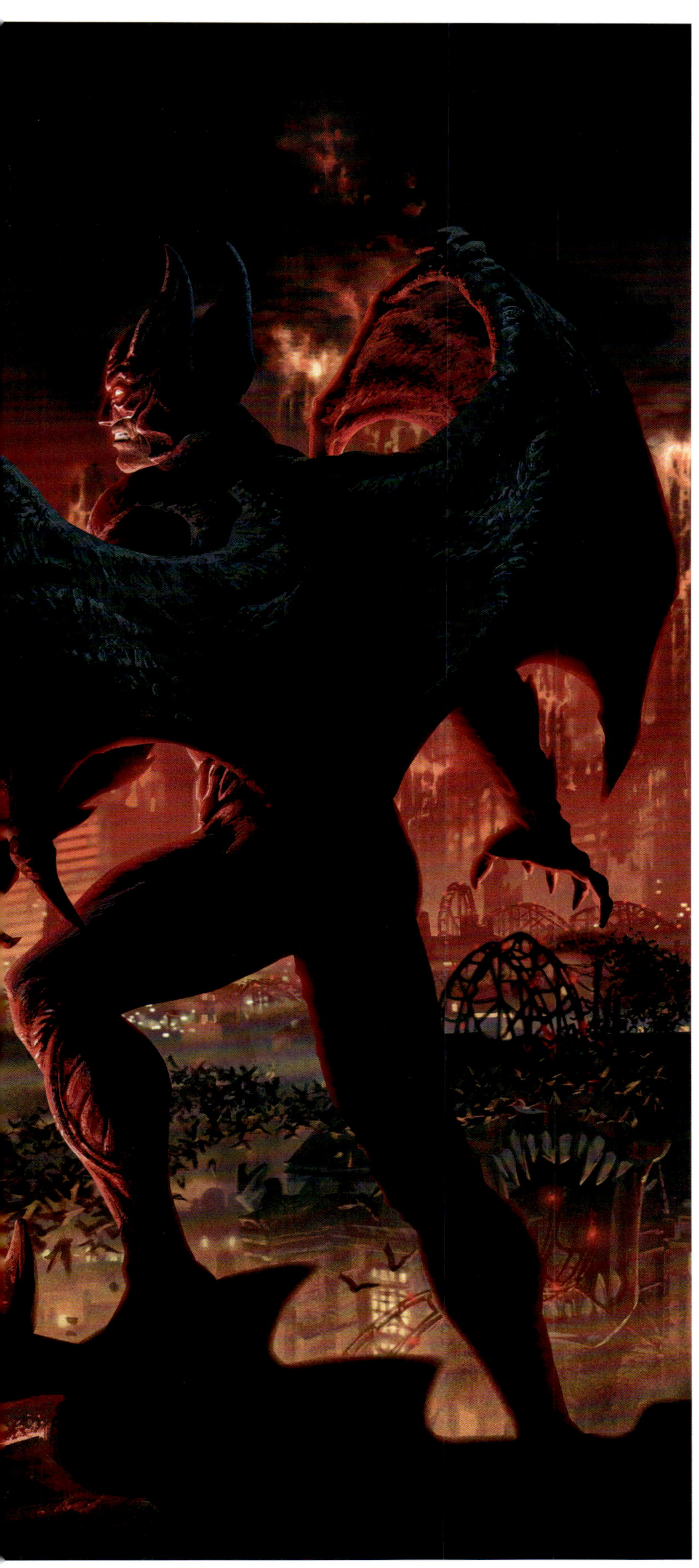

BATMAN GOTHAM CITY NIGHTMARE

FABIAN SCHLAGA

Sideshow's *Batman: Gotham City Nightmare* collection dares to ask, What would the familiar faces of Gotham become when viewed through eyes filled with fear? Fabian Schlaga captures this twisted reality in a hellish landscape featuring a new depiction of the legendary foes Batman and the Joker. Batman, the dark defender of the night, stands on a Gotham gargoyle as bats swarm through the glowing skies.

On the horizon, a warped and wild vision of the Joker looms large over a city filled with the ruins of the villain's crazed carnival. Gotham City itself will be forever changed if the Clown Prince of Crime gets the last laugh.

FABIAN SCHLAGA

"Working with the awesome team at Sideshow has been nothing but a pleasure and inspiration—it's a true haven for creative people. The freedom provided to the individual artists leads to some of the most authentic results, and I consider it an honor to have been able to contribute. Also, any chance to get a glimpse inside the premises should be taken. Those decorated walls are a treat."

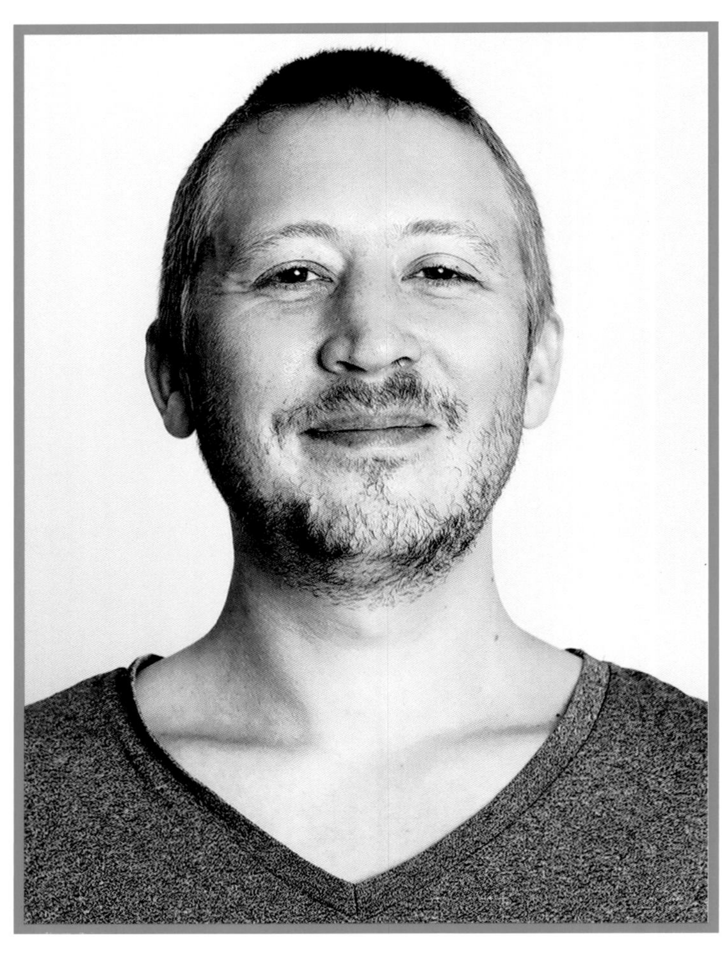

INSPIRATION

Born in 1987, Fabian began his journey into art in 2003, with the arrival of his own PC. Thanks to the internet, he met some like-minded people who never really questioned all the weird stuff he was drawing. Motivated by a creative exchange he had never experienced in real life, he kept going and eventually managed to turn it into a career. He is still daydreaming of being Akira.

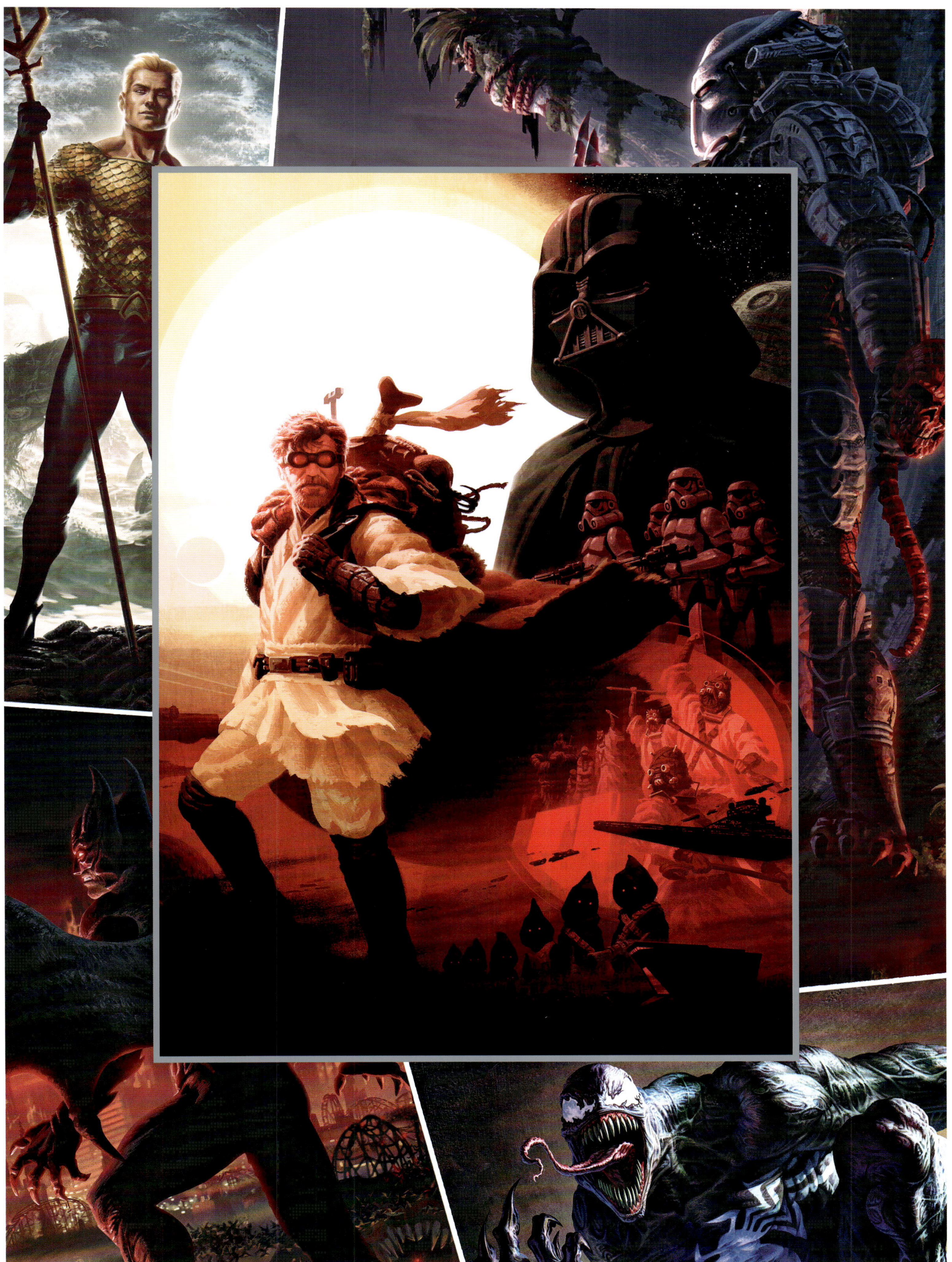

Aquaman, Batman: Gotham City Nightmare, Predator, Venom, and *Obi-Wan Kenobi: Desert Nomad.*

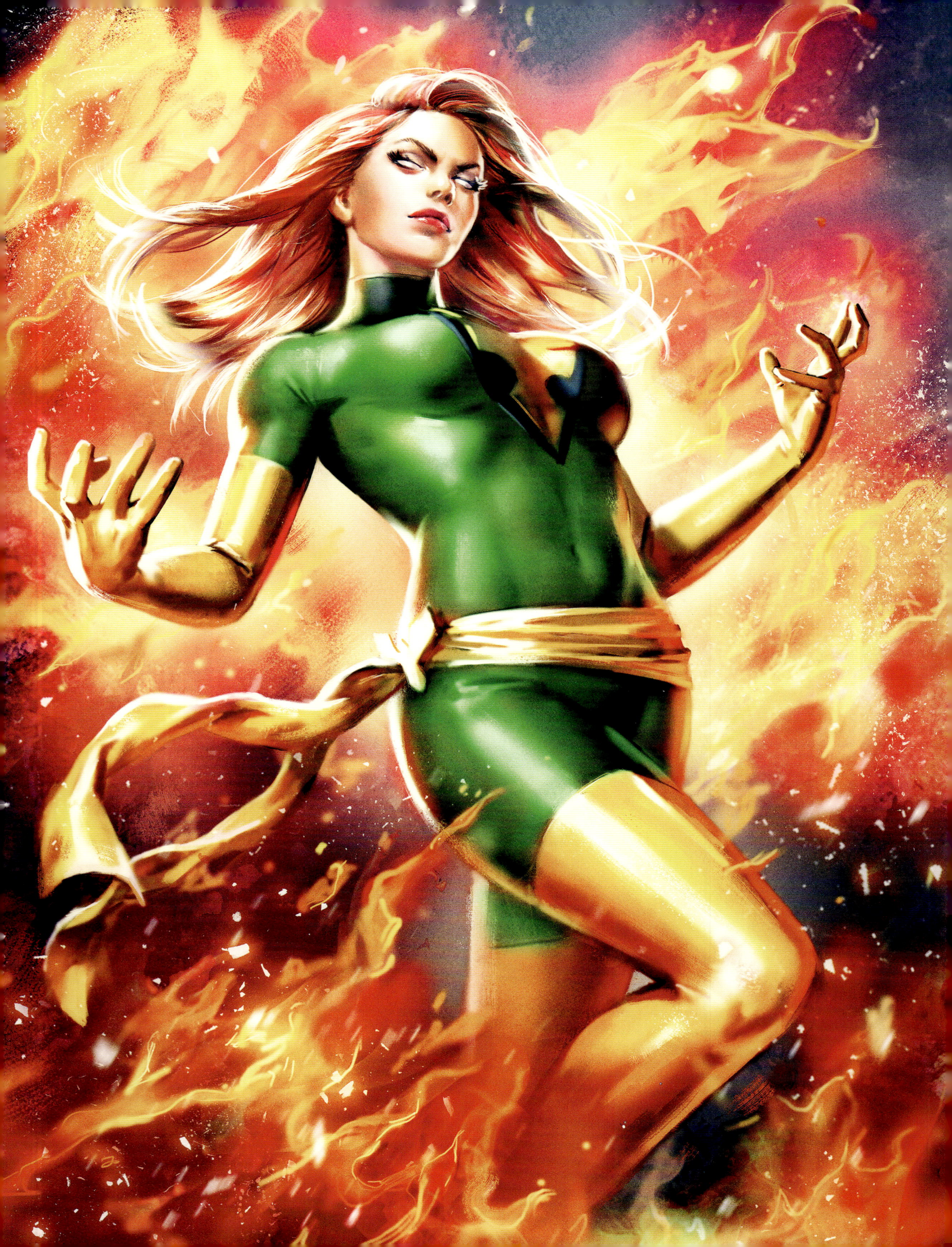

PHOENIX JEAN GREY VARIANT

IAN MACDONALD

The *Phoenix: Jean Grey Variant* Premium Art Print features the captivating mutant Jean Grey clad in her green-and-gold costume and wielding fiery cosmic powers.

Her impressive abilities manifest in the form of the birdlike Phoenix, and her blazing expression captures the dual calm and chaos contained within her mind.

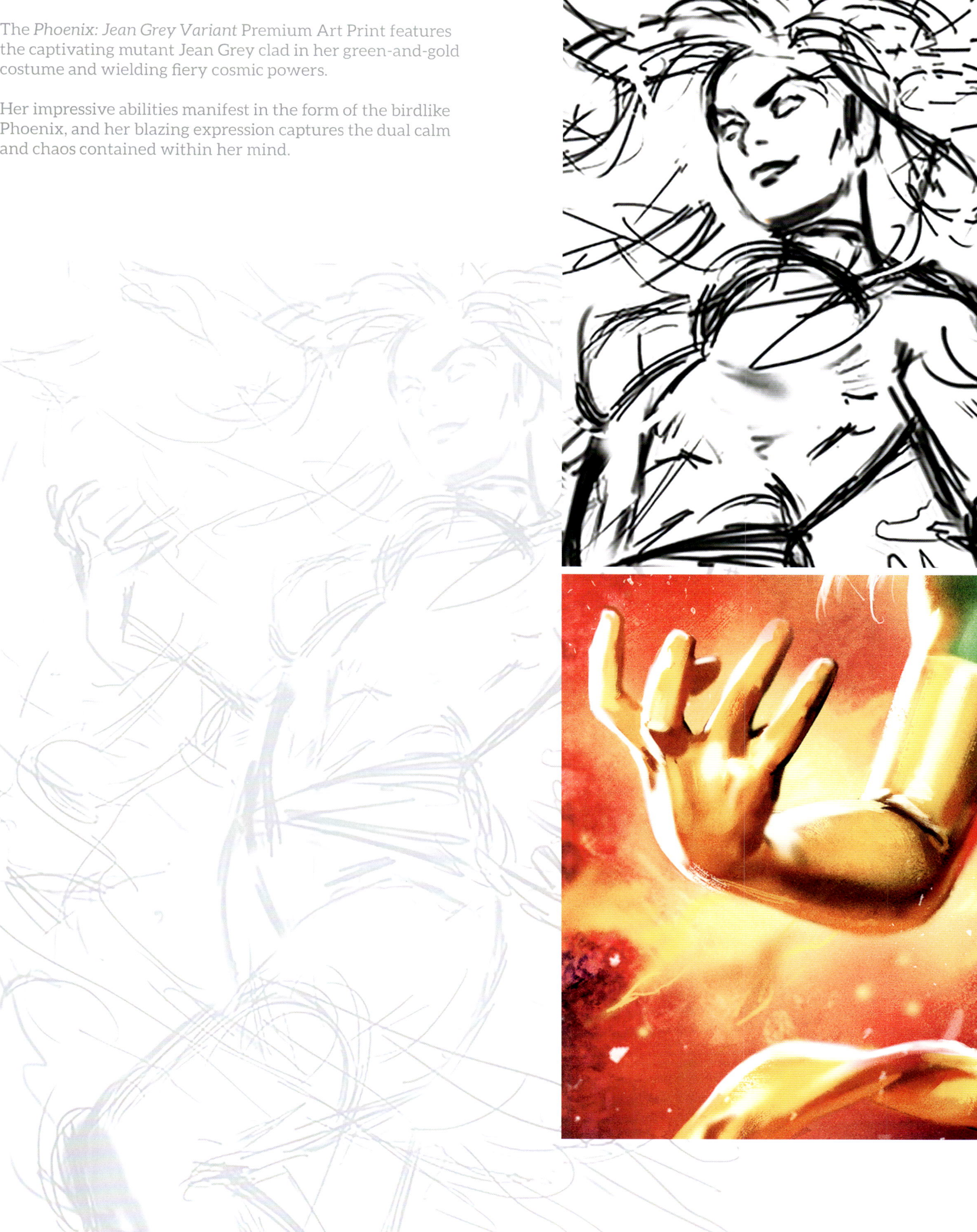

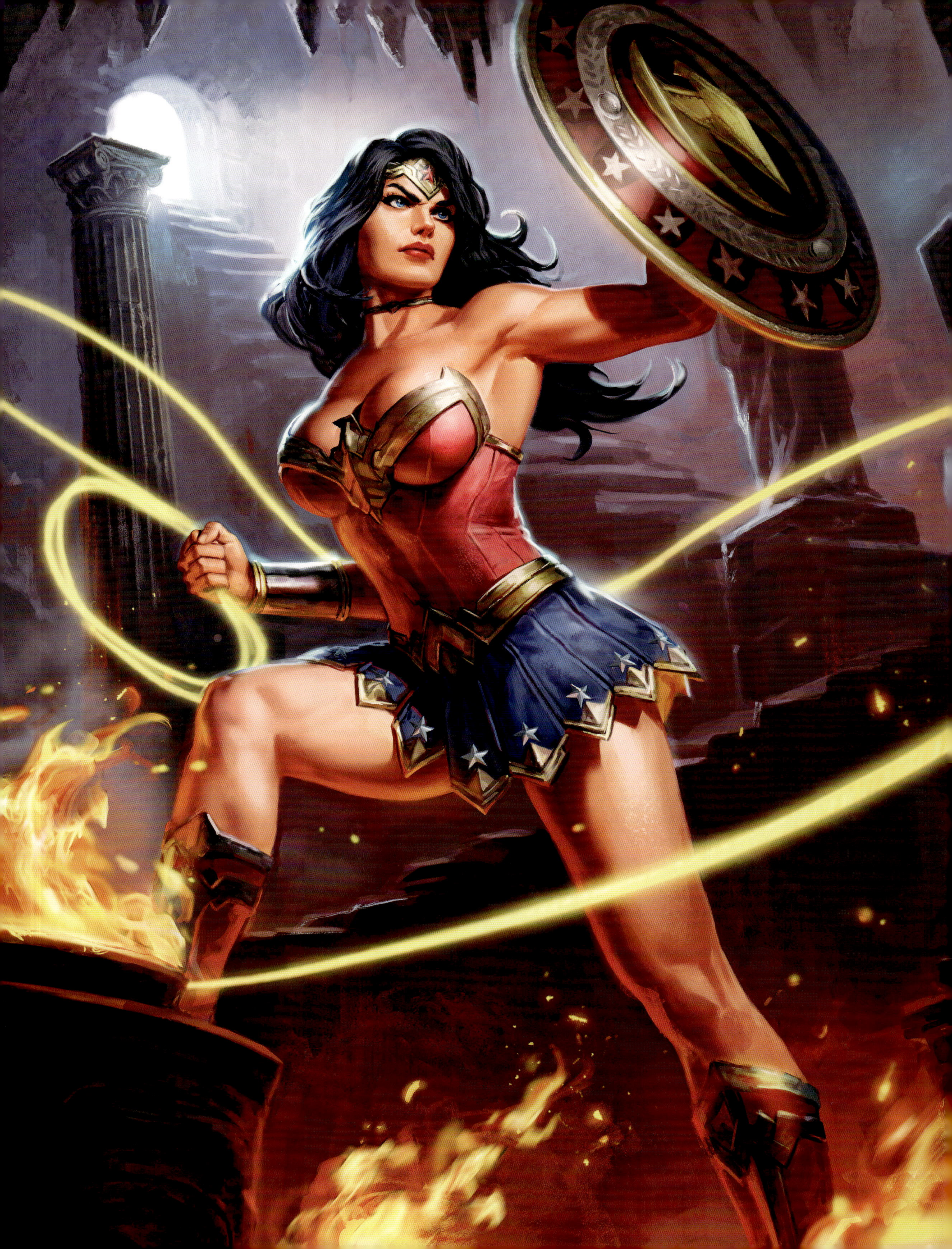

WONDER WOMAN

ALEX PASCENKO & IAN MACDONALD

Descending into the realm of Hades, the Avenging Amazon readies herself for battle against the shades awaiting her in the Underworld.

Ancient fires light Wonder Woman's path as she raises her aegis shield and golden lasso against her dark and dangerous foes.

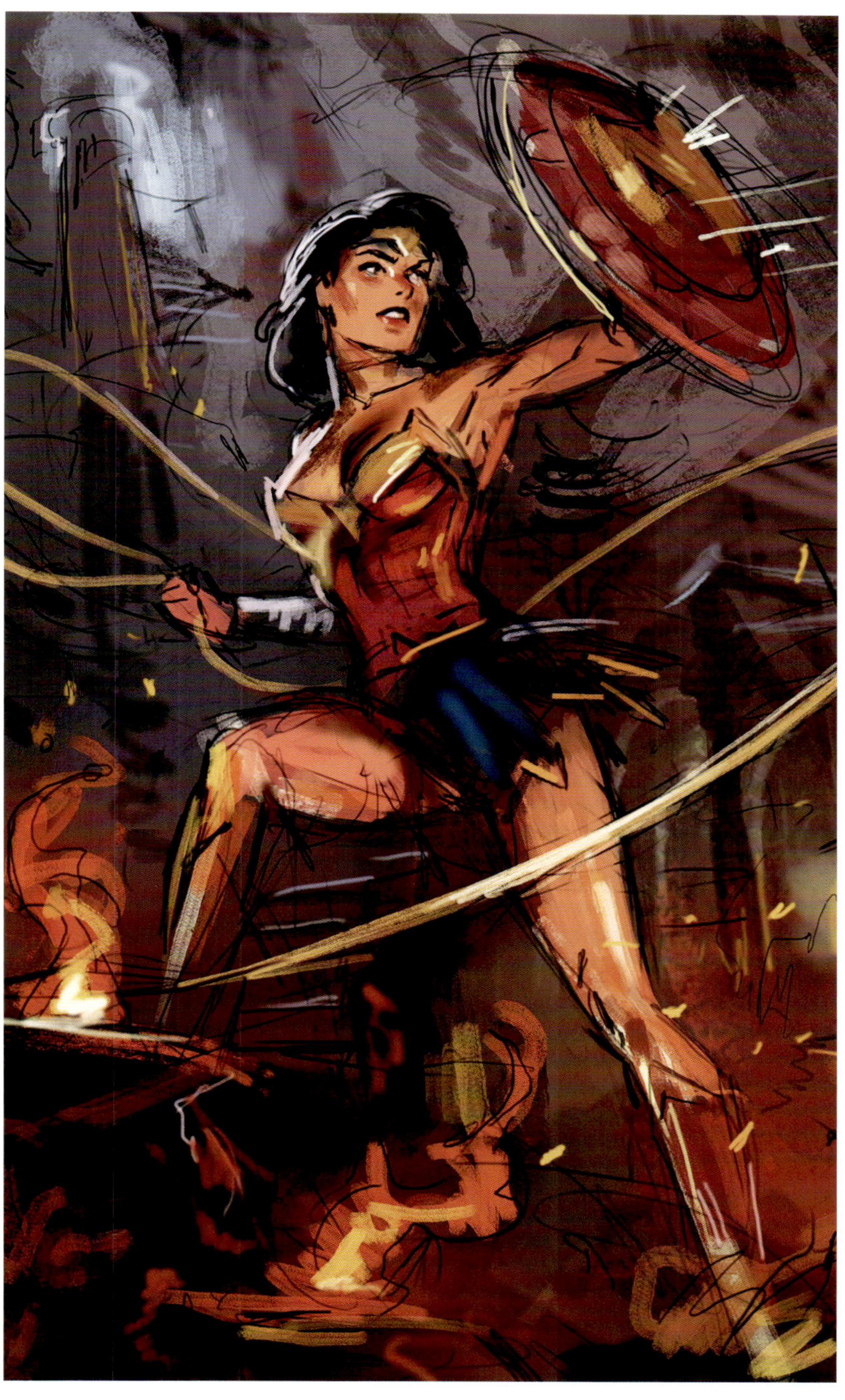

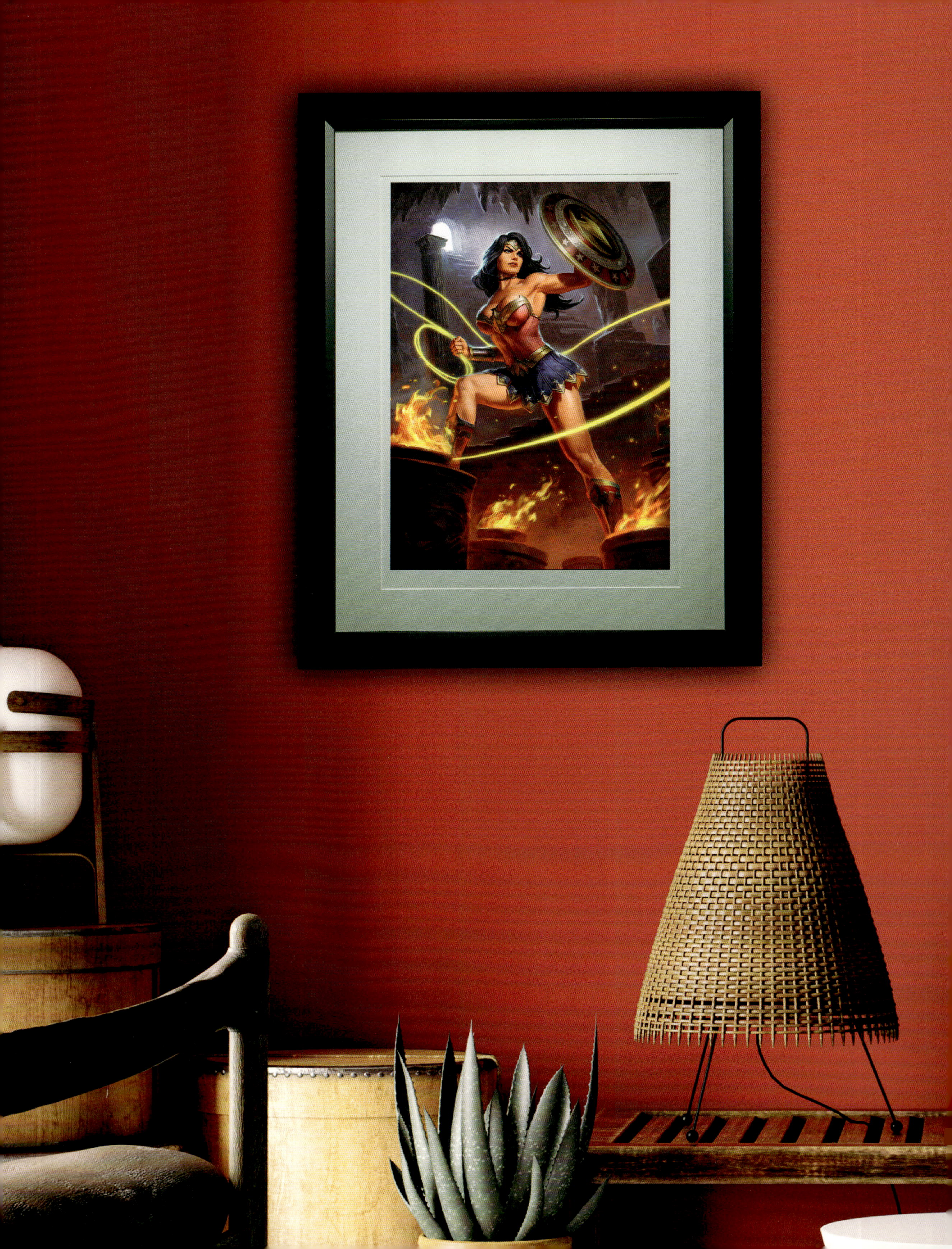

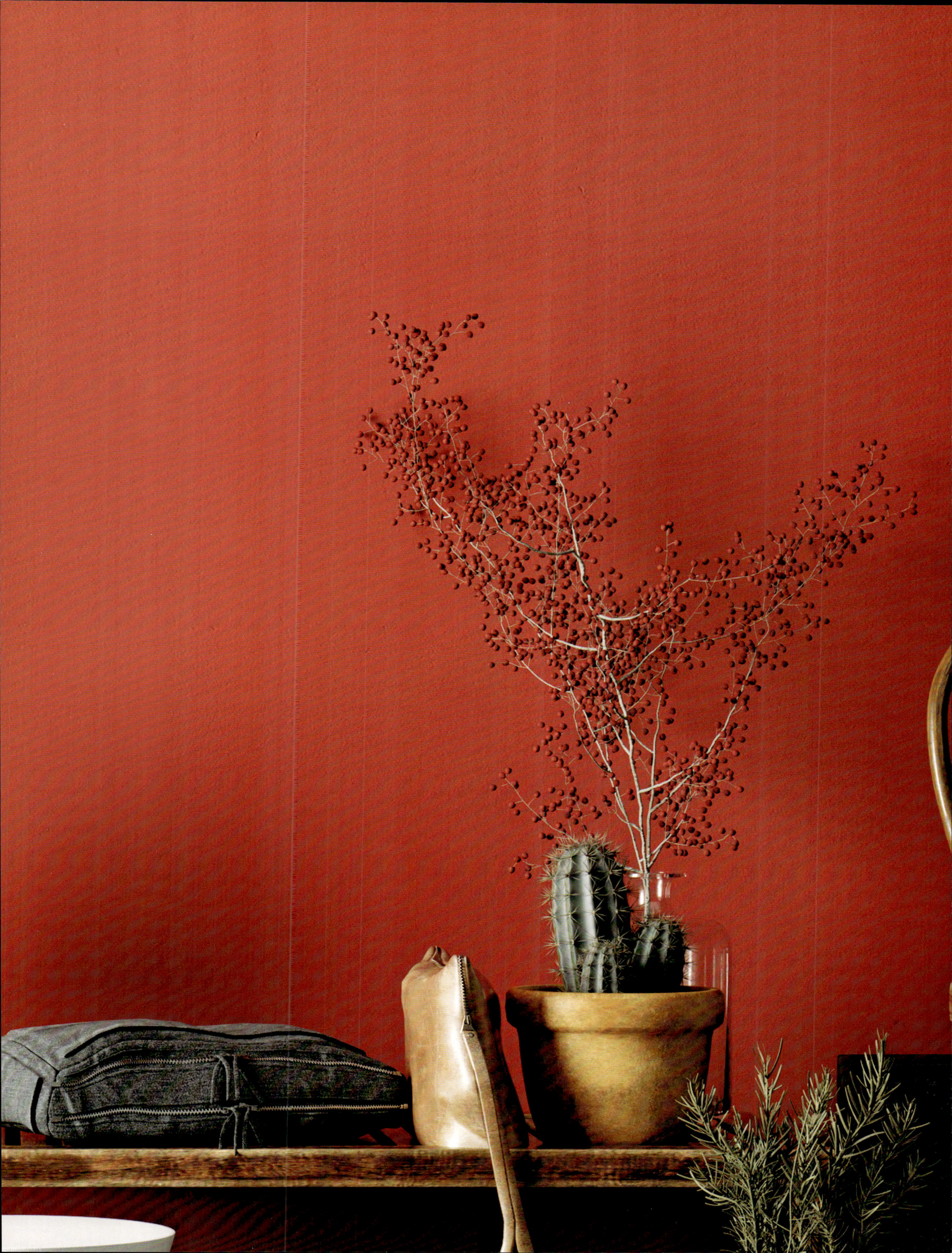

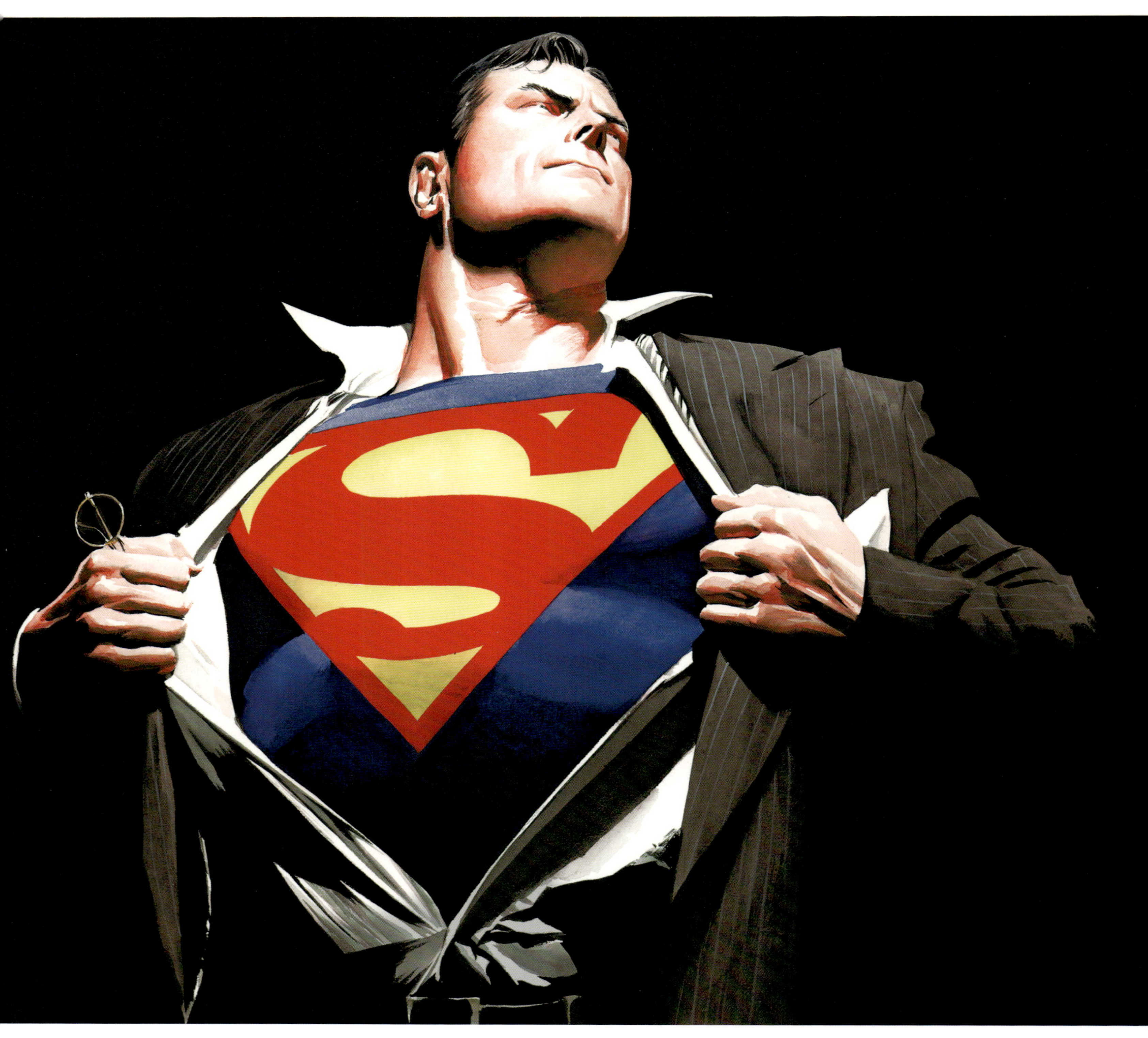

THE MAN OF STEEL

ALEX ROSS

Witness the transformation of the meek Clark Kent into the mighty Superman as he reveals the symbol of the House of El, known to fans worldwide as a bright beacon of hope and heroism.

Originally created as the cover to *Superman Forever* #1, this iconic moment for the Man of Steel has been specially reproduced for Sideshow as a fine art lithograph in an exclusive limited edition of 200 pieces.

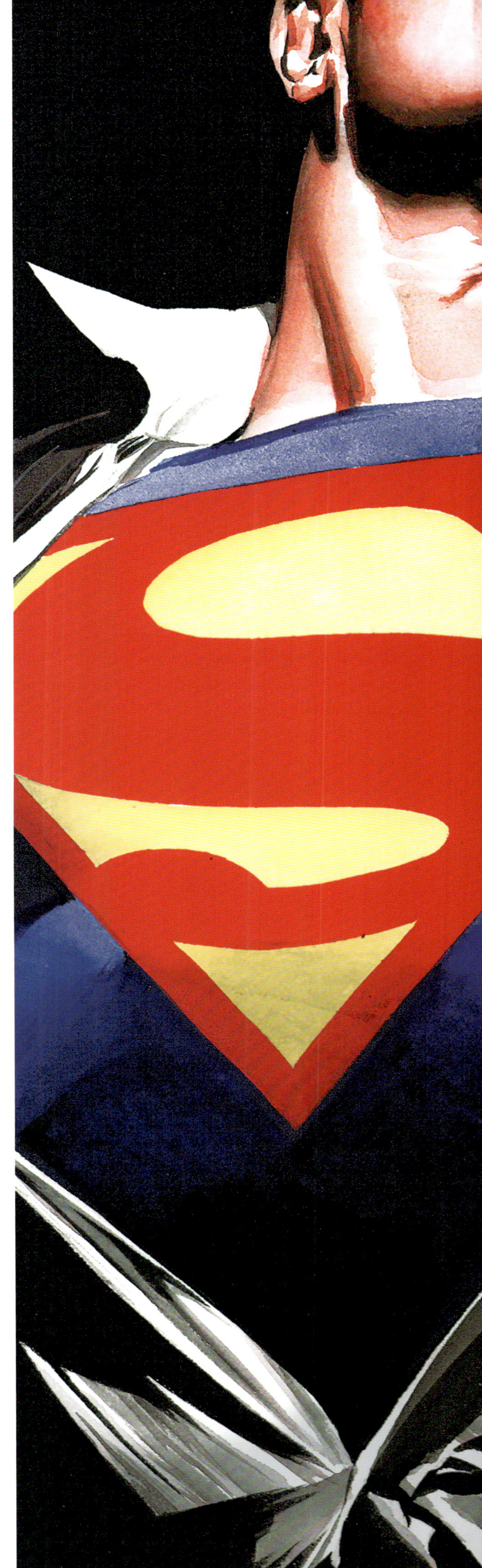

THE IMPERMANENCE OF FLESH

ALEX HORLEY

At the heart of this ornate piece, the Queen of the Dead welcomes you to the Flesh Faction with a wicked, wise, and playful smirk. Flanked by her bodyguards, spies, and assassins, Queen Gethsemoni radiates the dynamic confidence of the Flesh Faction, which she leads. The walking temple of Cryptus Akohr, headquarters for the Flesh Faction, is featured in the upper left corner of the composition.

Flesh is change. Flesh is enigmatic. Flesh is life.

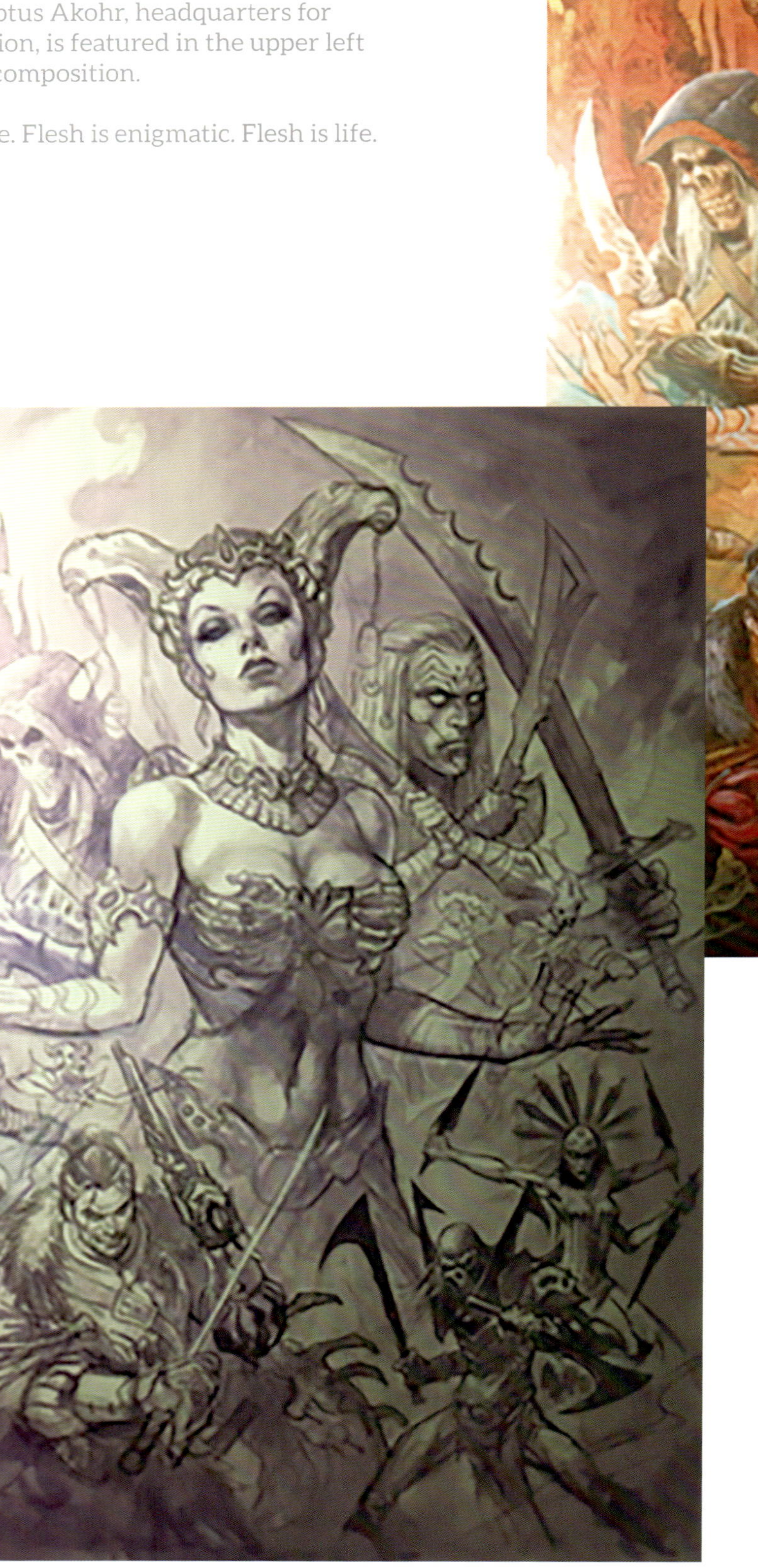

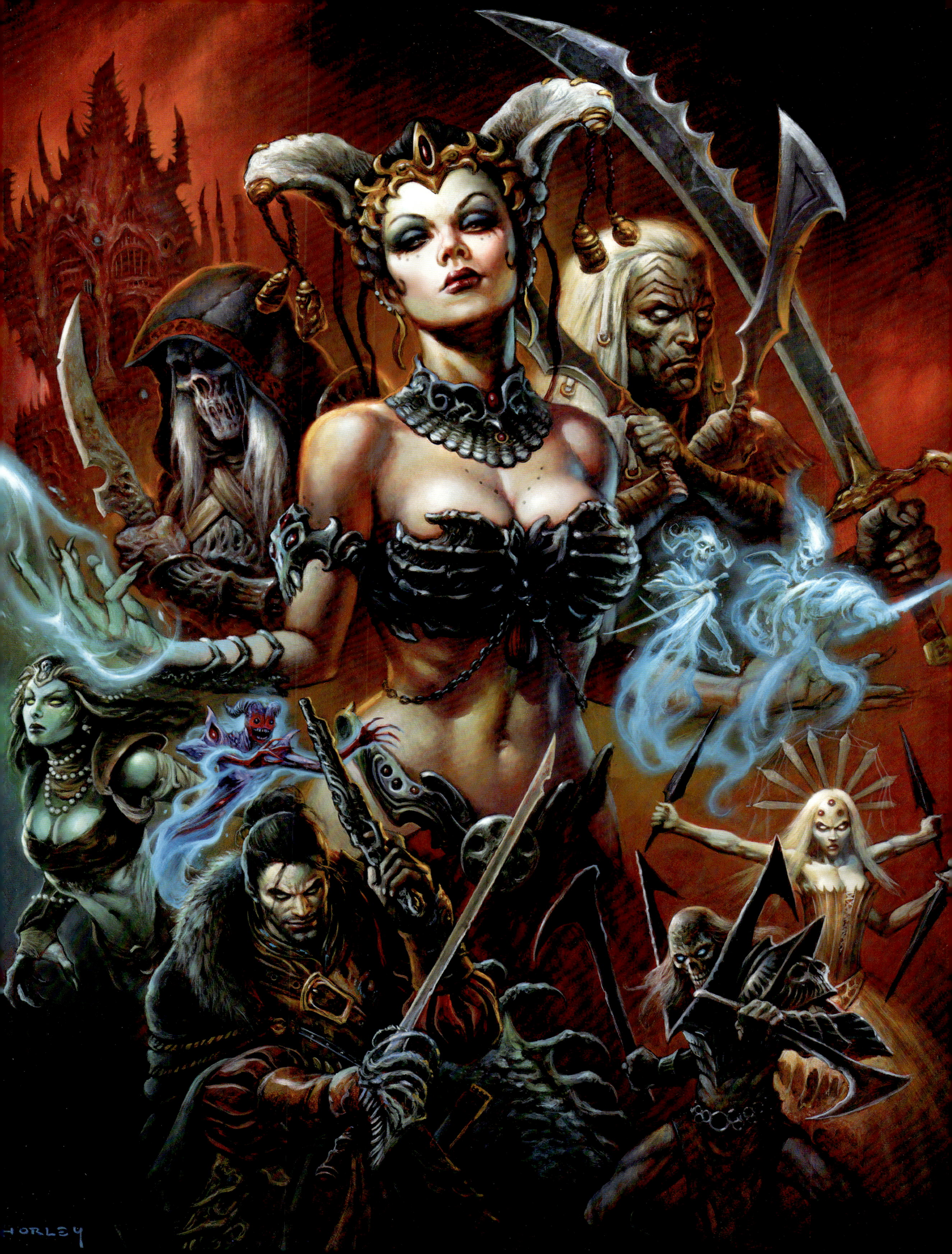
HORLEY

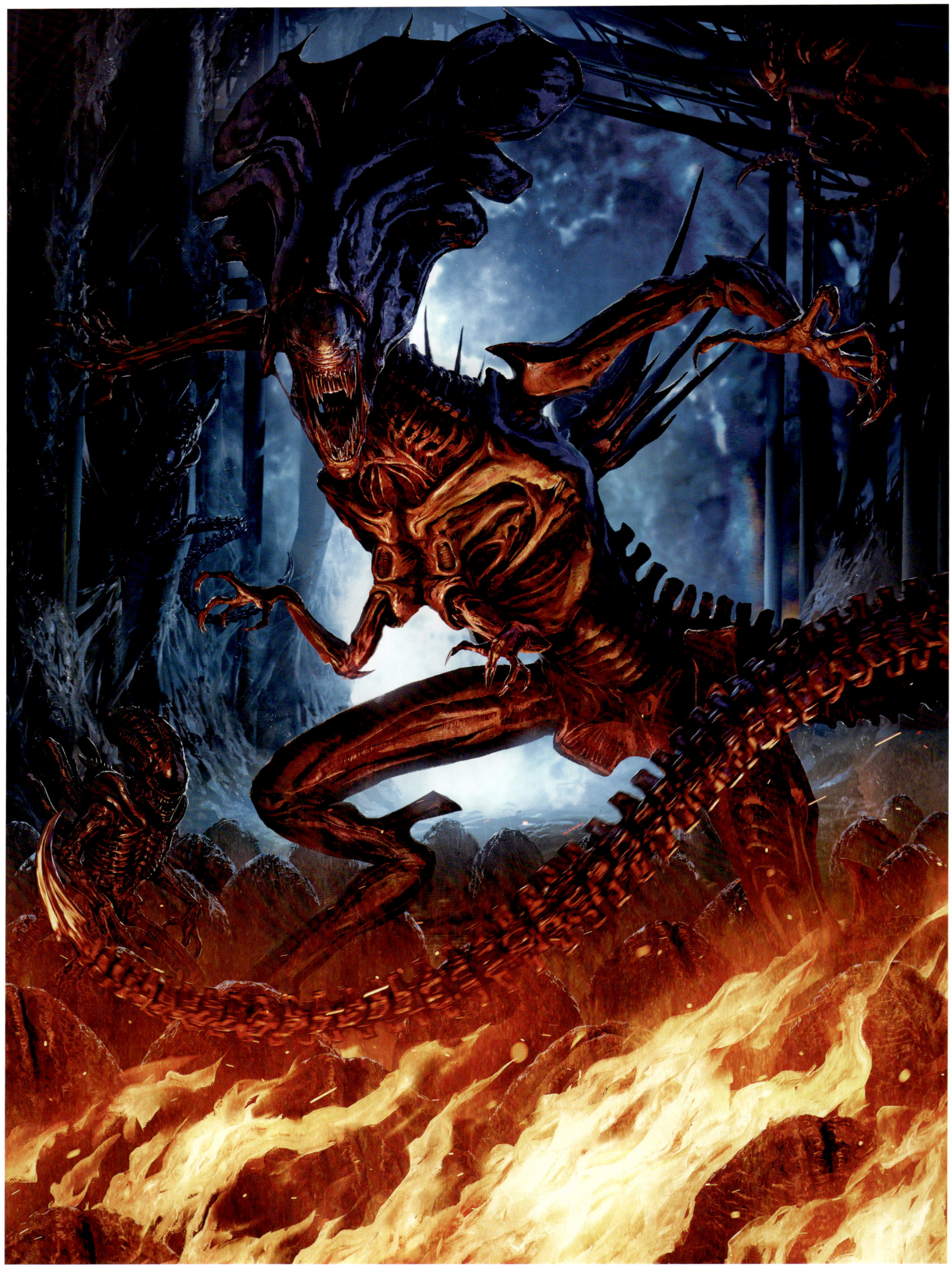

ALIEN QUEEN

RJ PALMER

Based on her otherworldly appearance in *Aliens*, the enraged queen of the xenomorphs stands tall over her blazing brood. The Colonial Marines have fled the scene, trying to destroy the hive while the Alien Queen and her warriors prepare their pursuit.

Violent flames light the egg chamber on LV-426, casting a raging orange glow on the Alien Queen, who is ready to protect her monstrous offspring at all costs.

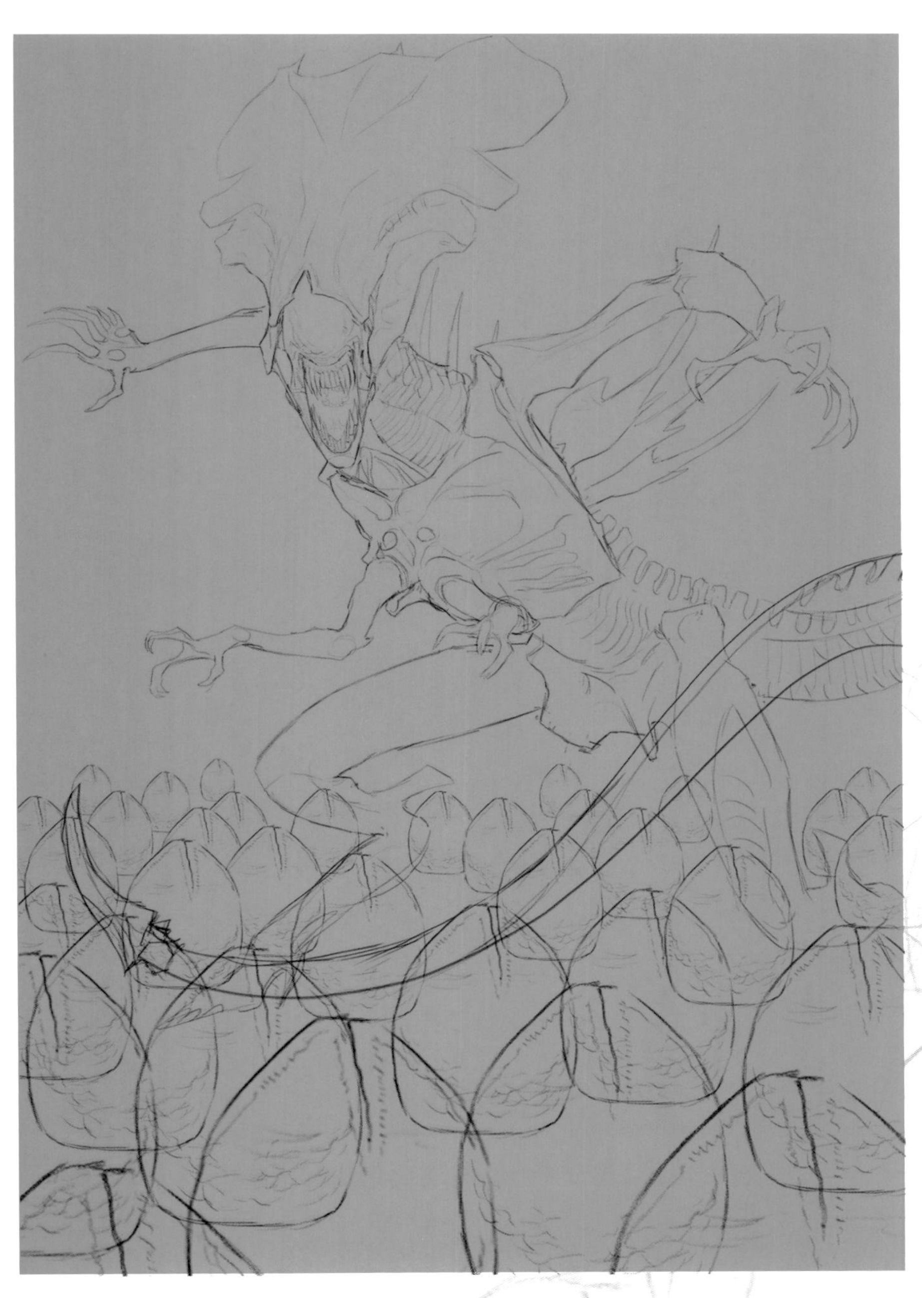

THE DRIFTER

BRIAN ROOD

The Drifter Fine Art Print features Daryl Dixon, the volatile and skilled tracker portrayed by Norman Reedus in *The Walking Dead*. Seen in the foreground with his trusted motorcycle, Daryl rides through a bleak expanse as a lone survivor. The larger portrait of Daryl is framed by his iconic wings against a background of earthy red tones evoking the isolation of the apocalypse.

"I really wanted this art to have a classic, almost desolate, Western feel to it," explains artist Brian Rood. "Daryl is such a great character for this world . . . it's as if the zombie apocalypse has made him a far better person than he would have ever been in normal society."

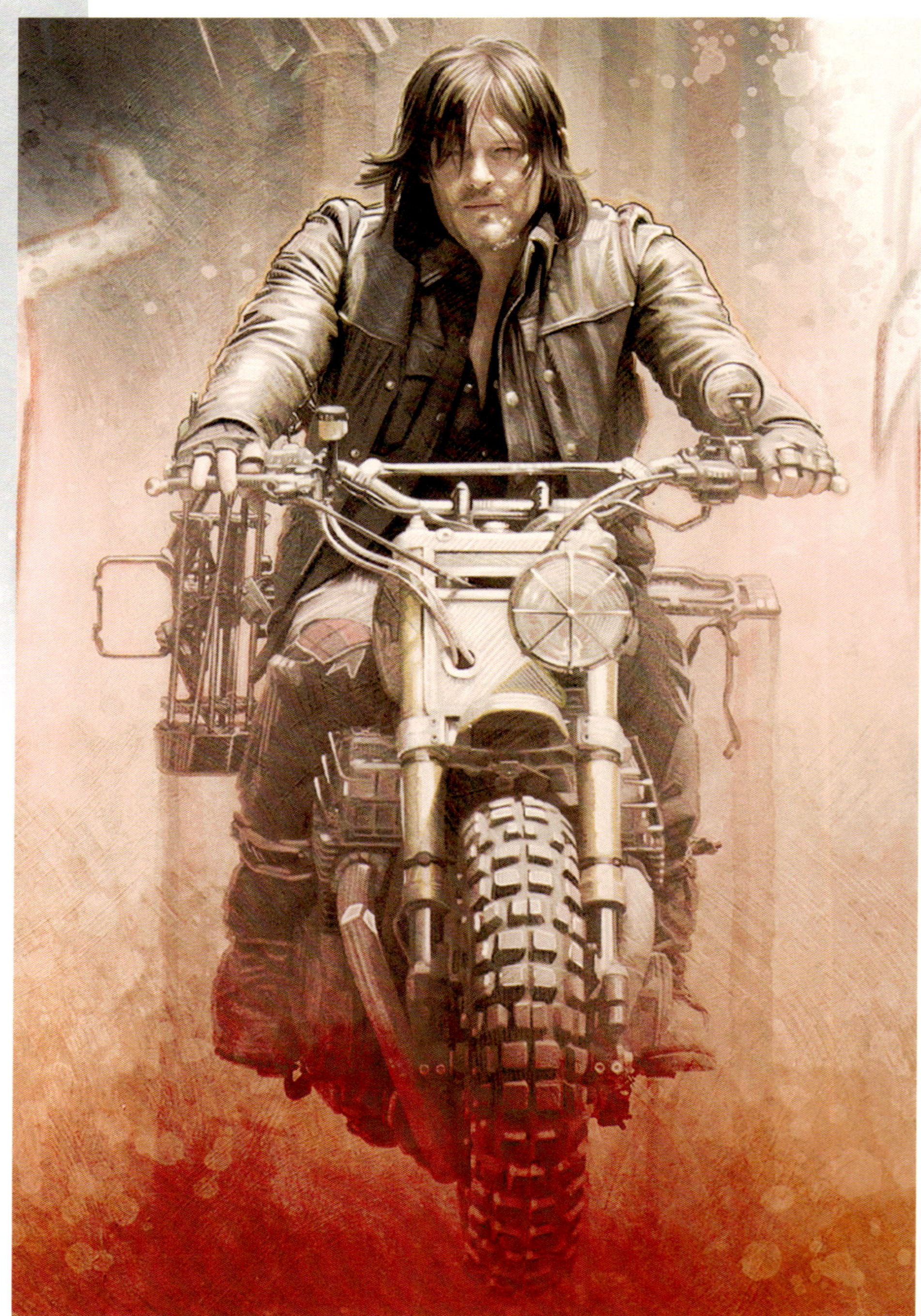

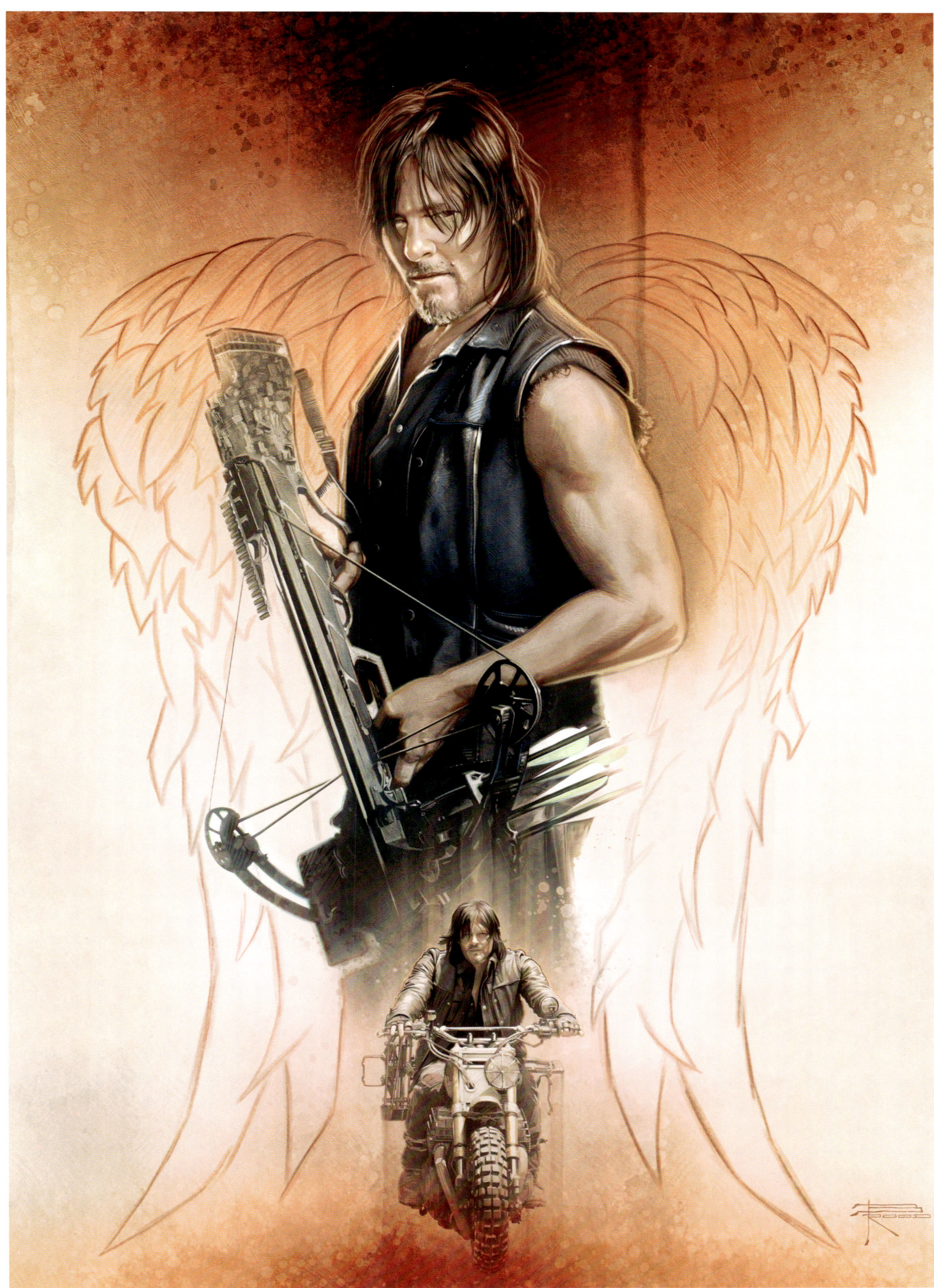

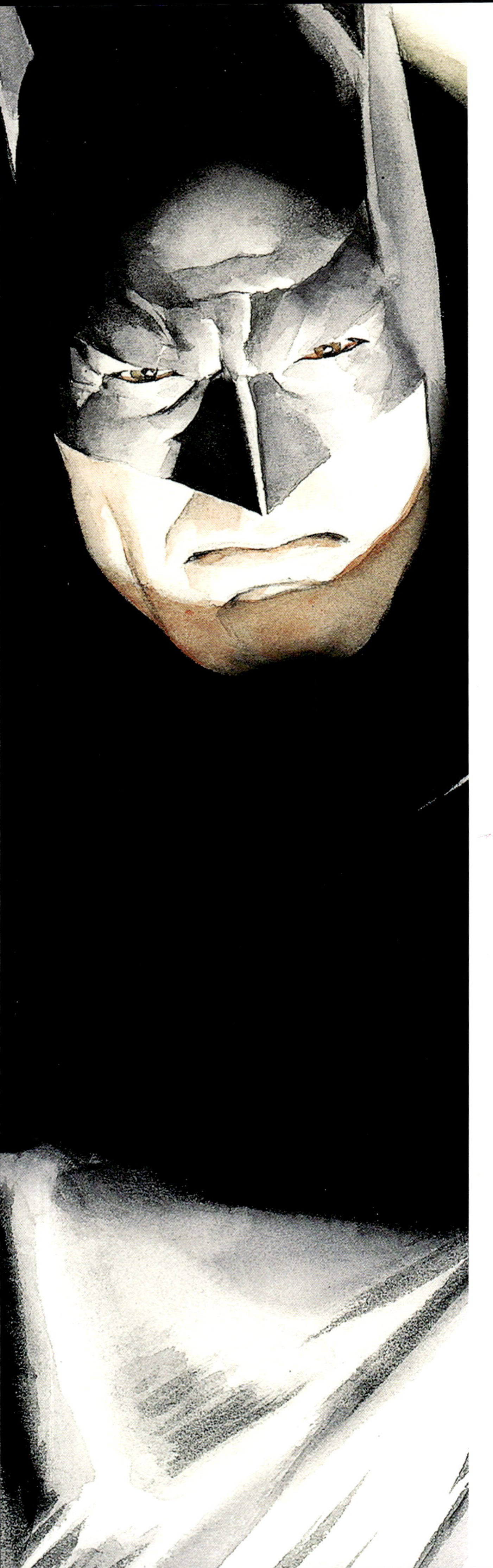

THE BATMAN!

ALEX ROSS

In the darkness, a light shines out and reveals. . . the Batman! Like a beacon of justice in the night, Batman strikes terror into the hearts of even Gotham City's most hardened criminals.

Originally created as the cover for *Batman: No Man's Land* #1, this dramatic portrait of DC's Dark Knight has been specially reproduced for Sideshow as a fine art lithograph in an exclusive limited edition of 200 pieces.

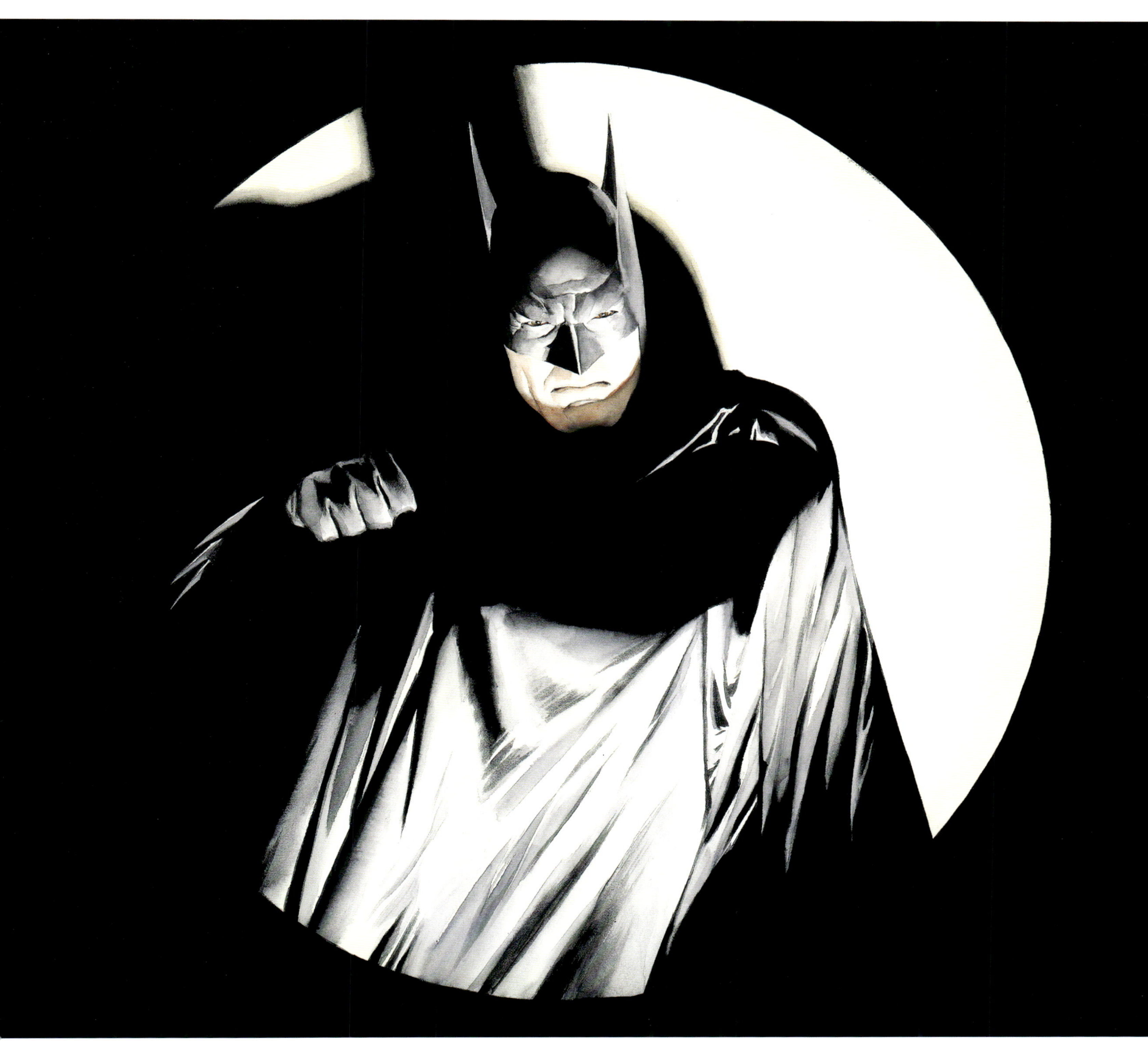

HARLEY QUINN BATTER UP!

OLIVIA DE BERARDINIS

Based on the likeness of Margot Robbie as she appeared in the film *Suicide Squad*, *Harley Quinn: Batter Up!* captures the playful wickedness of Gotham's Maid of Mischief.

Harley stands with her bat aimed like a gun, ready to swing and cause a scene, while bursts of color highlight her electrifying energy.

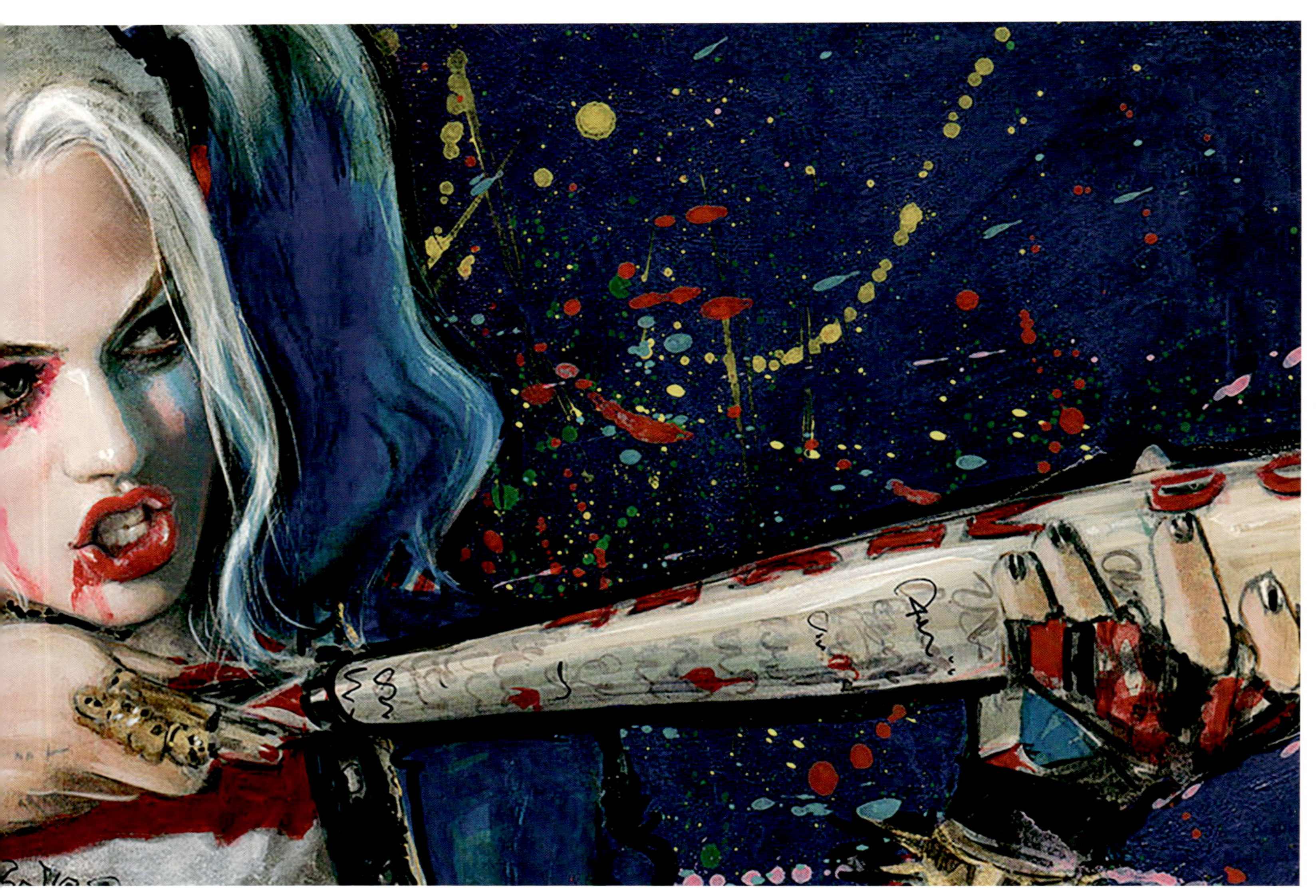

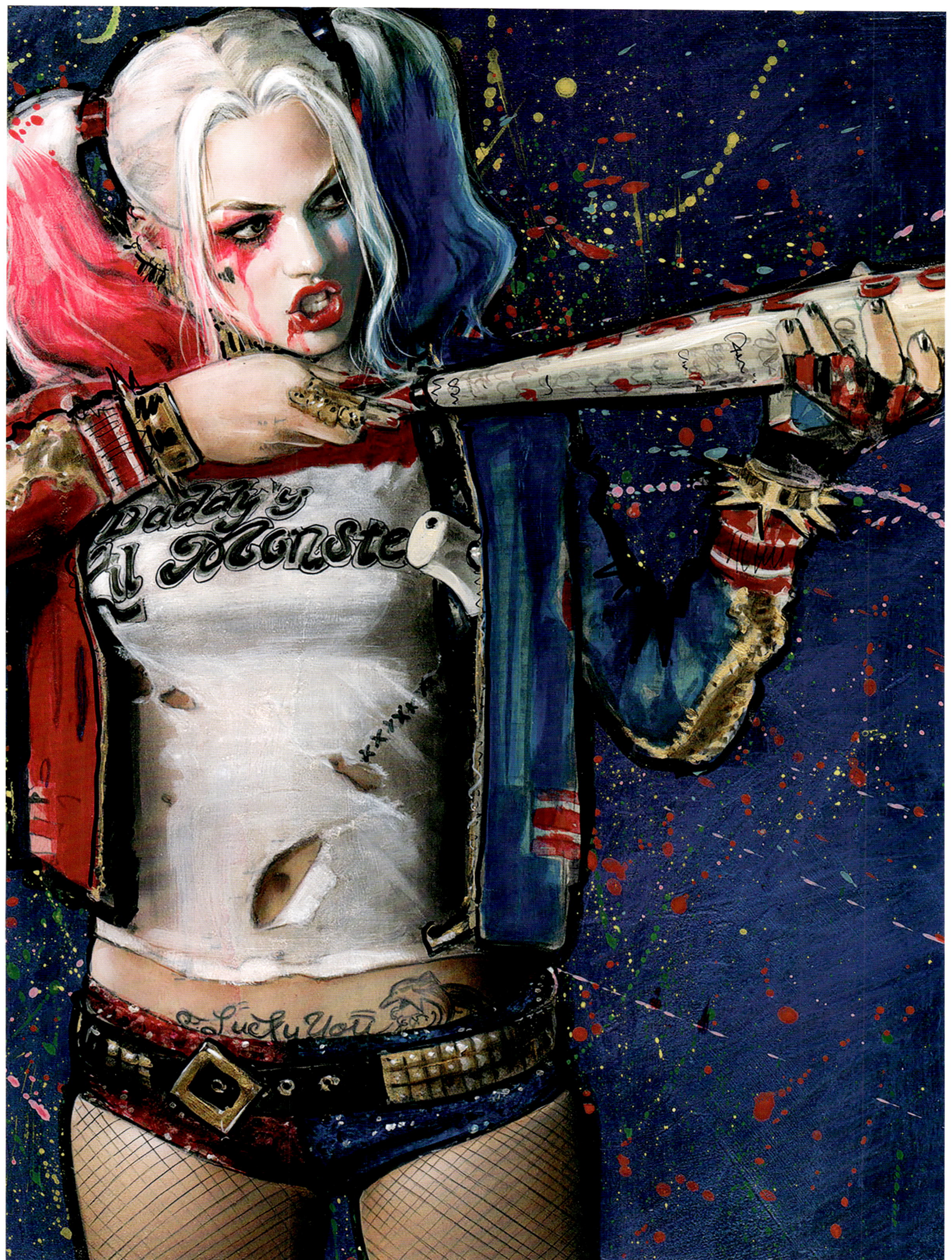

Harley Quinn: Batter Up! © 2018 Olivia De Berardinis

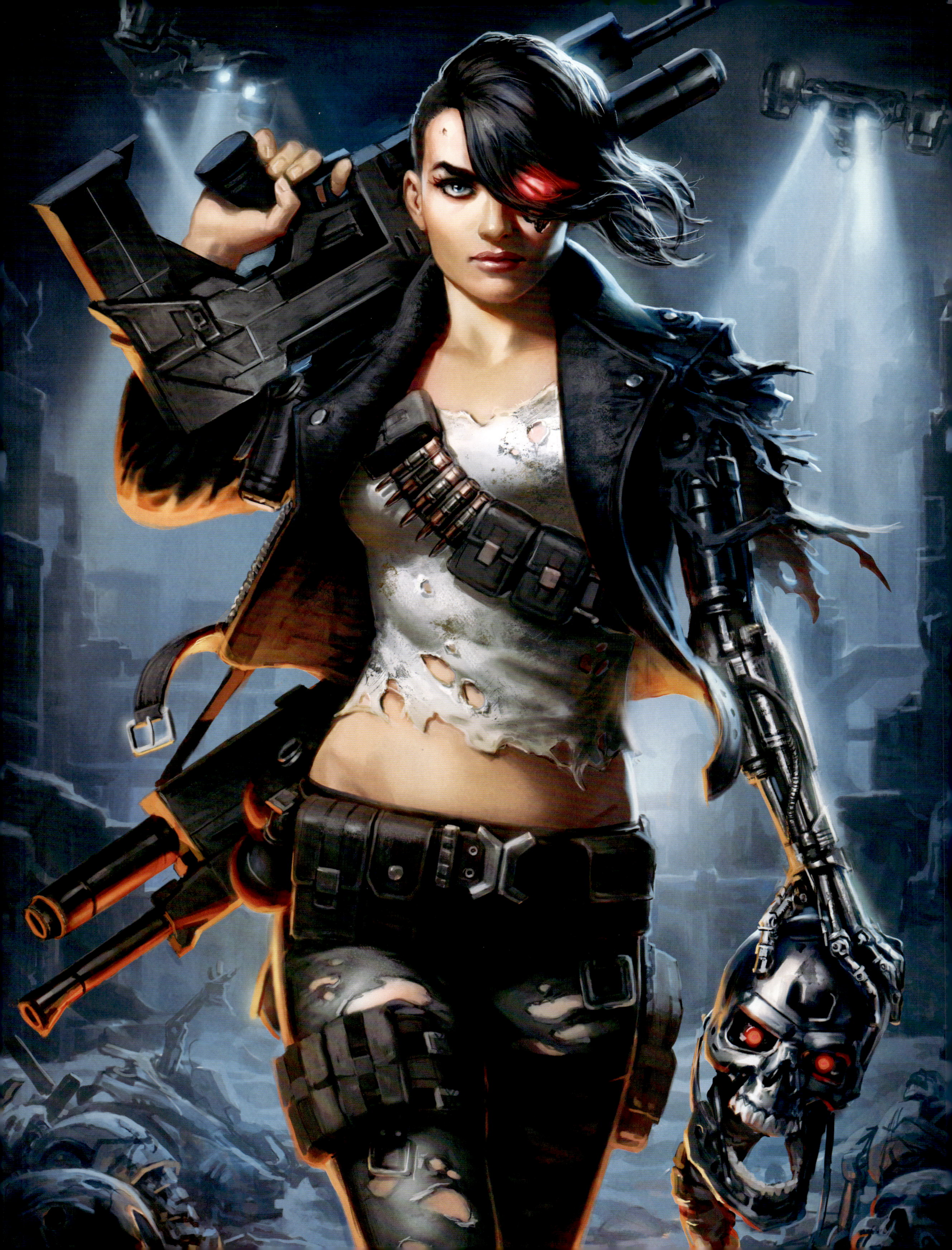

REBEL TERMINATOR

ALEX PASCENKO & IAN MACDONALD

The Rebel Terminator embodies the spirit of technology and humanity, sparking the imagination of fans everywhere, in this entry in Sideshow's Mythos series. Emerging from battle, the Rebel Terminator shows no signs of slowing down as she clutches a severed endo-skull in her mechanical hand.

Prepared to eliminate her next target, the renegade assassin holds a 40-watt plasma rifle triumphantly over her shoulder as the struggle between Skynet and the human resistance rages on in the background.

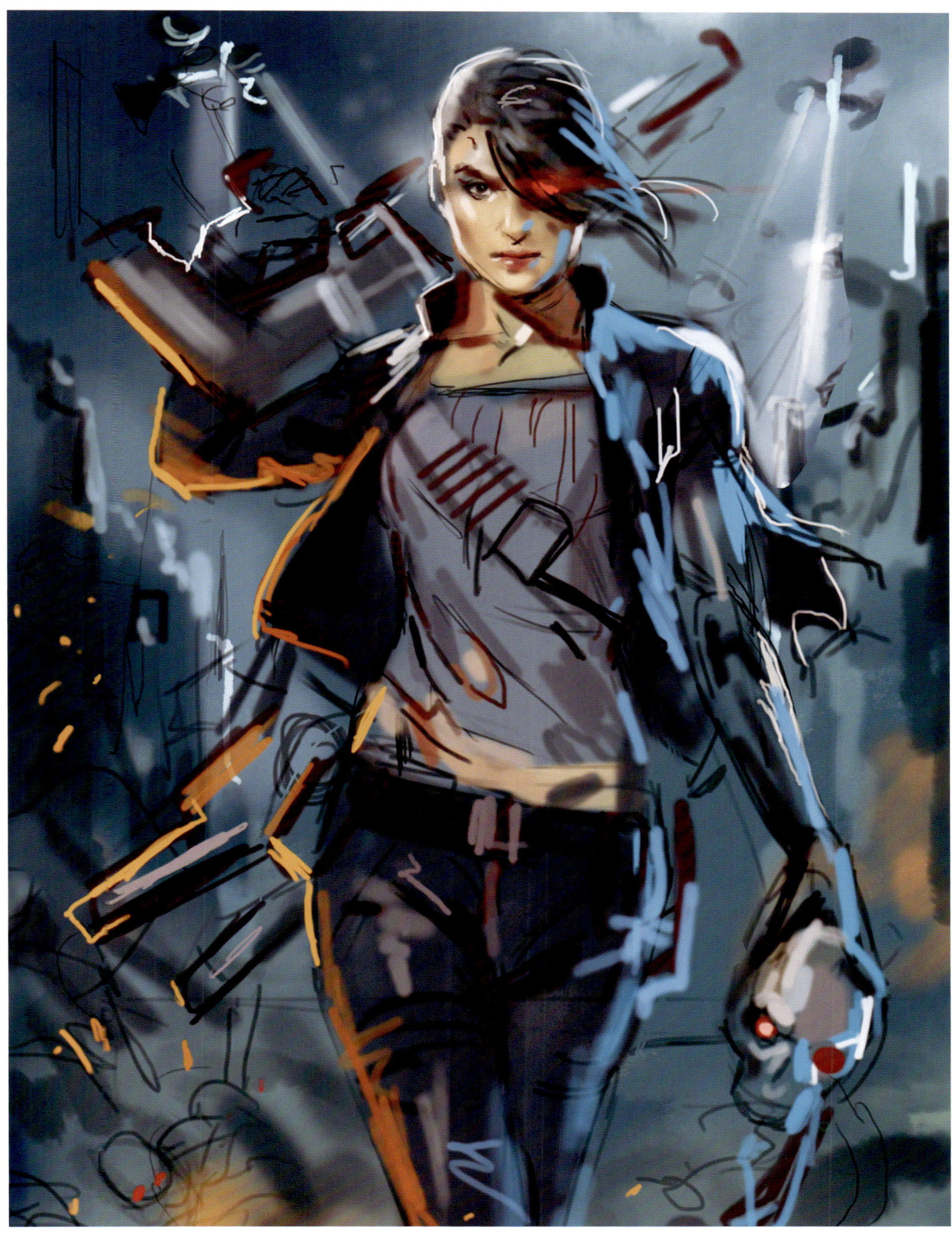

SWAMP THING

DAVE WILKINS

Emerging from murky waters, the mighty Swamp Thing stands to protect the realm of nature from humankind. His ever-changing body is composed of an intricate tangle of vines and roots, balancing humanoid anatomy with growing vegetation.

A moonlit swamp provides the perfect backdrop for this champion of the Green, who is completely in his element surrounded by trees and muddy shores.

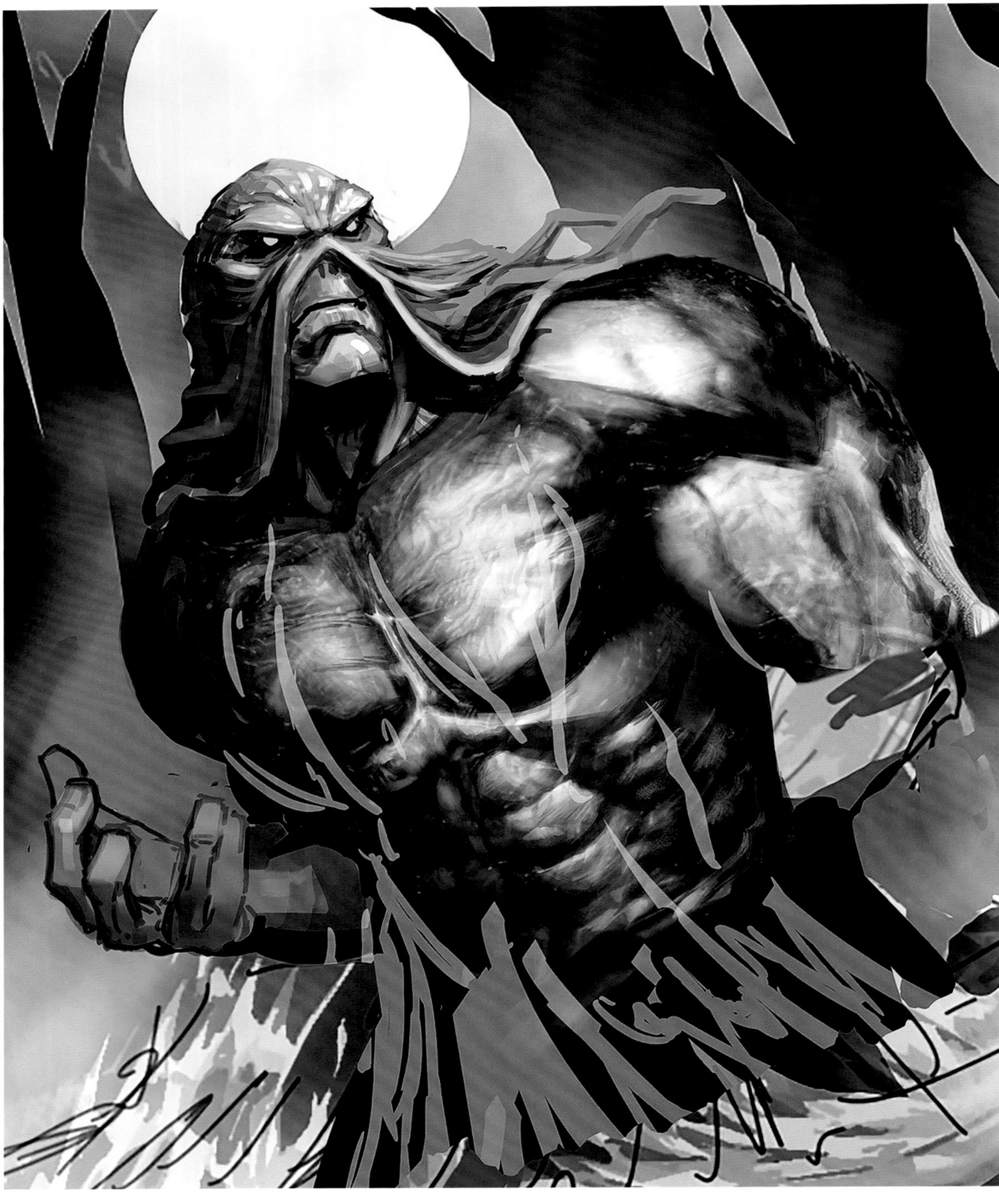

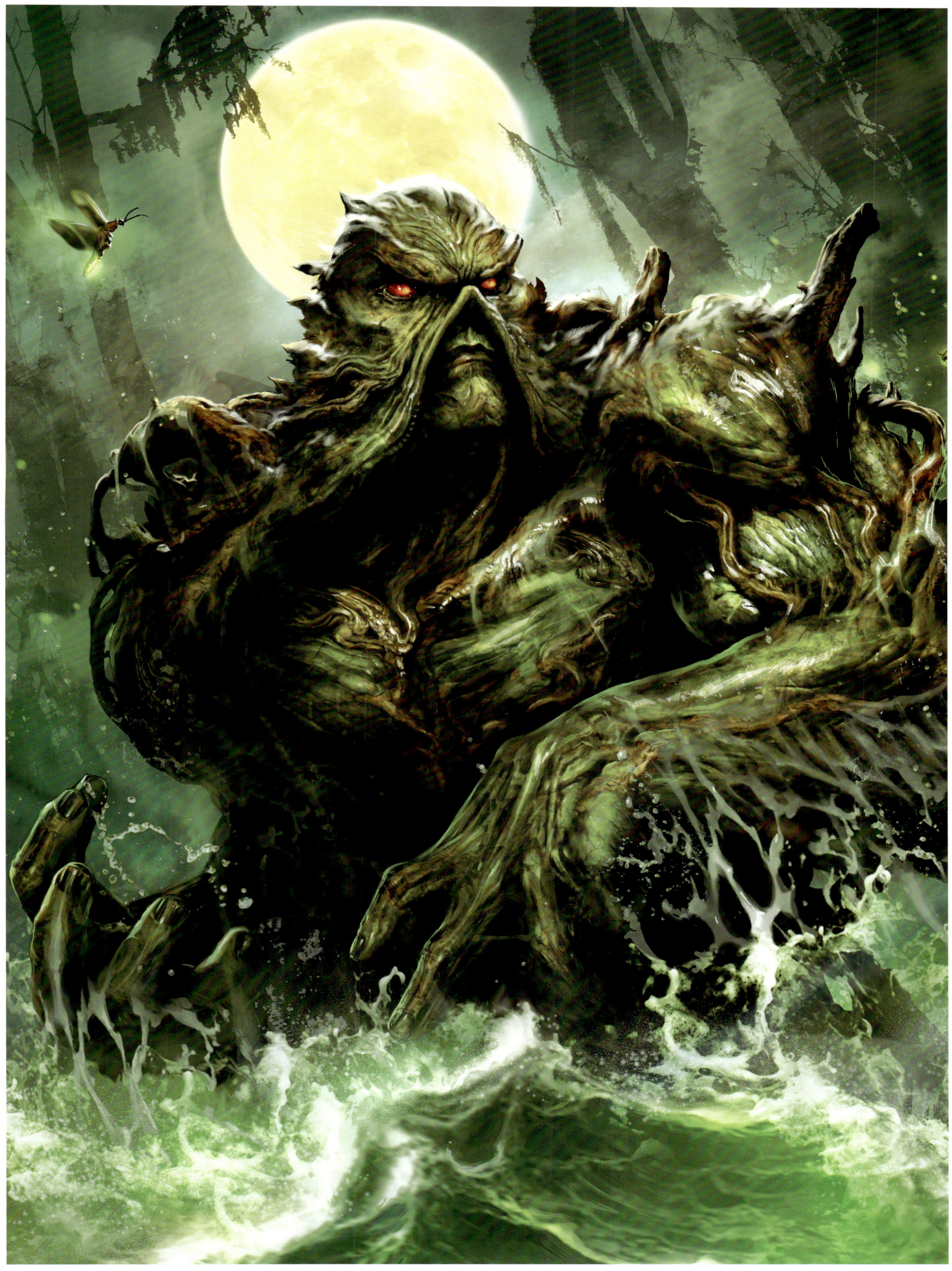

MASTERS OF THE UNIVERSE

ALEX ROSS

Available for the first time ever as a brilliantly rendered full-color illustration, the *Masters of the Universe* fine art lithograph has been specially reproduced for Sideshow in an exclusive limited edition of 100 pieces. A tribute to all that is MOTU, this image assembles the most heroic and villainous warriors in Eternia, as they face off for control of Castle Grayskull.

He-Man and Skeletor are locked in an epic battle, joined by both good and evil allies including Teela, Battle Cat, Evil-Lyn, and Beast Man. Featuring over thirty characters in all, this vibrant and dynamic illustration captures the spirit and strength of the world of *Masters of the Universe.*

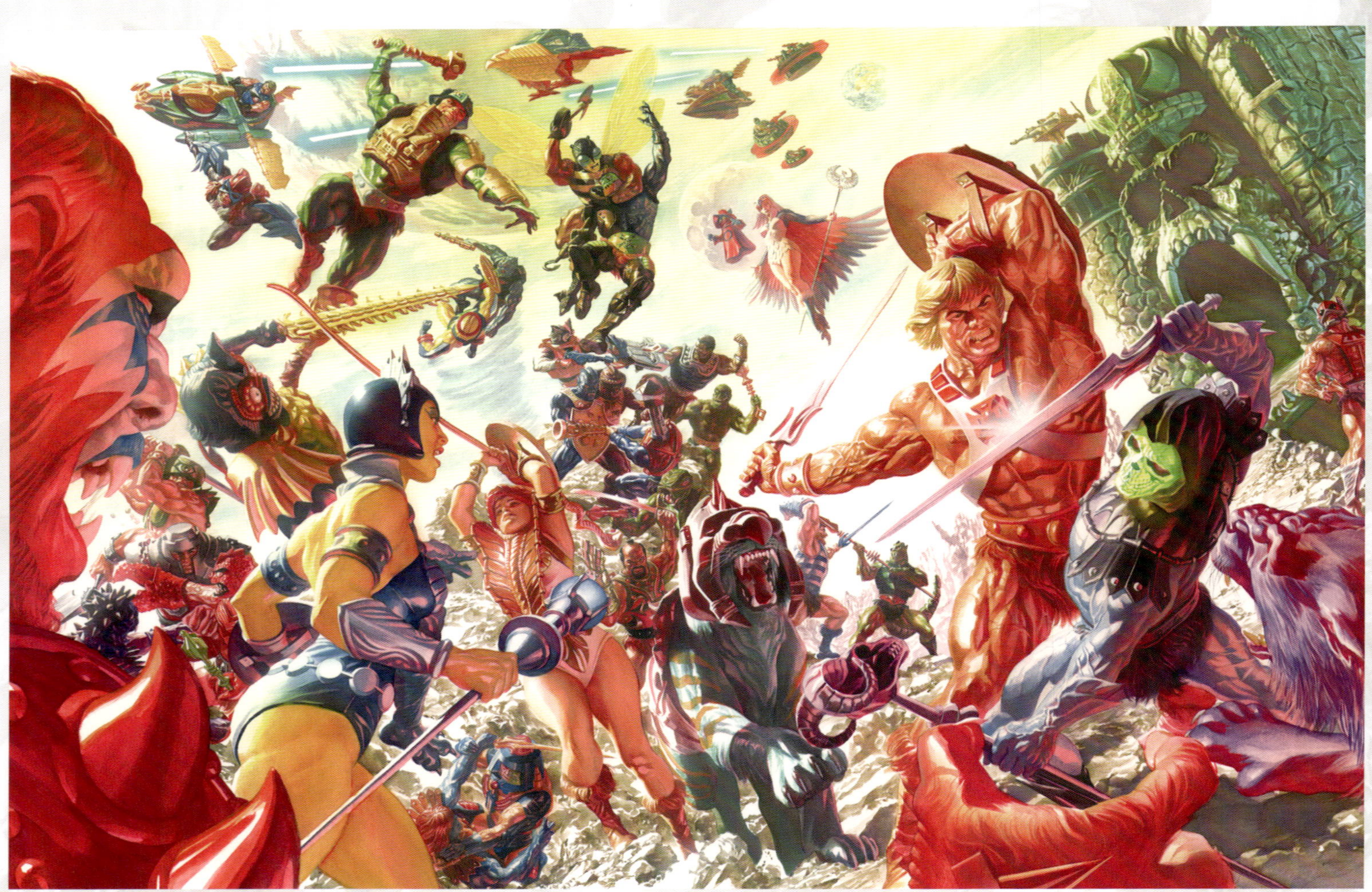

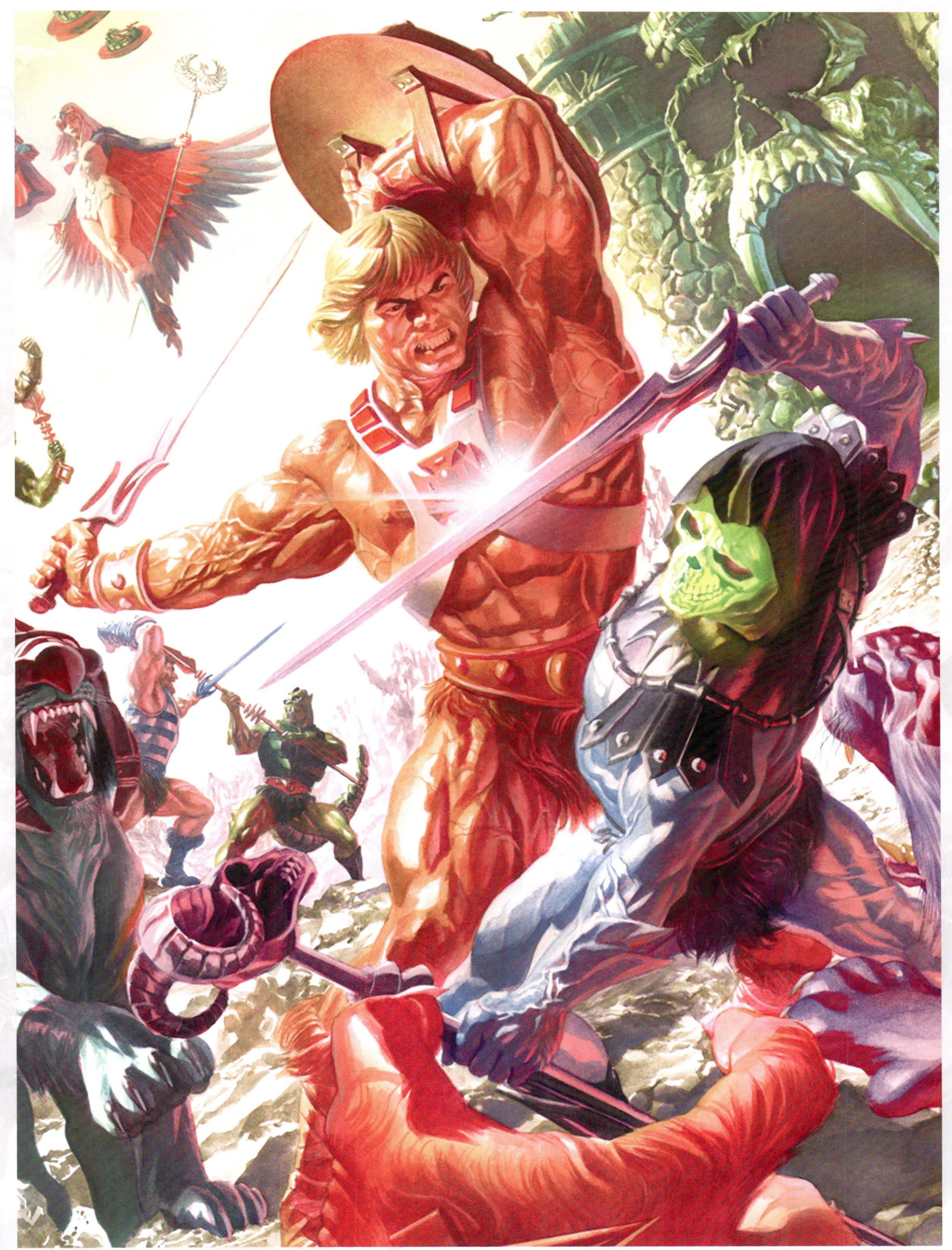

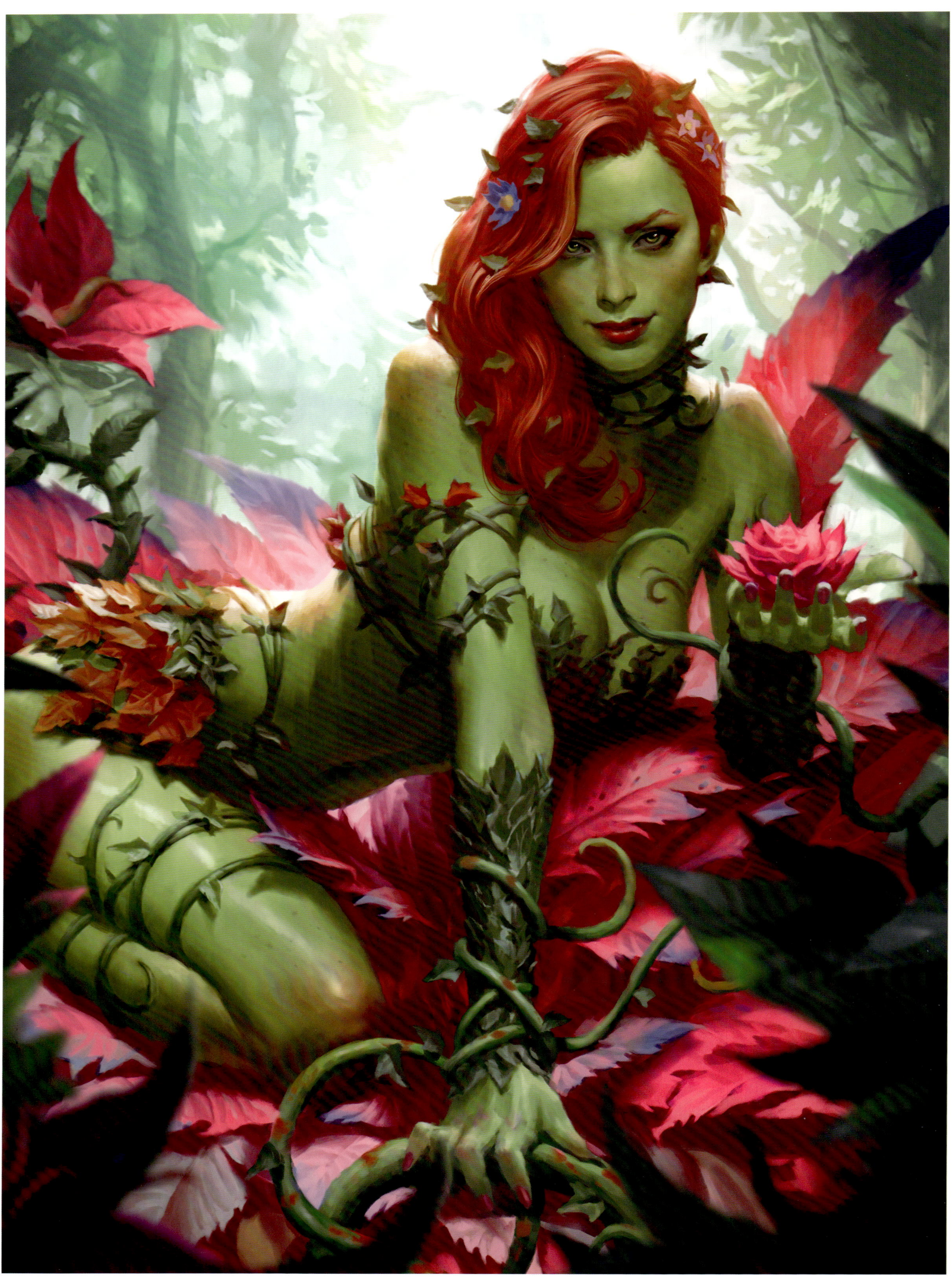

POISON IVY

HEON-HWA CHOE

As lethal as nightshade, Poison Ivy is one with nature as she reclines on a bed of vivid pink plants. Ivy holds a rose in her hand, offering it to her next smitten victim, as dappled vines twist and turn around the villainess.

The scene is filled with flowers in vibrant green, orange, and pink hues—but just remember, even the prettiest plant can hide the deadliest poison.

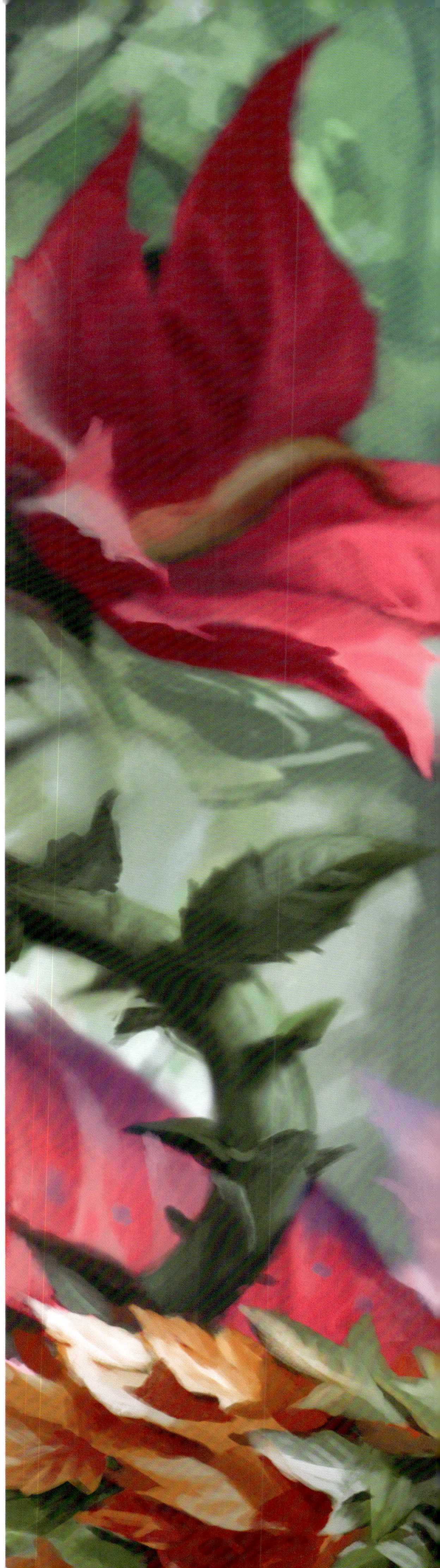

HEON-HWA CHOE

"저는 일러스트레이션 일을 하면서 Sideshow의 아름다운 조각상으로부터 영감을 얻곤 하였습니다. 그러던중 몇 년 전 Sideshow 로부터 연락이 와 당신이 아트 프린트 프로그램에 참여할수 있겠나는 제안을 받고 너무 기뻤습니다. 나의 디지탈 작업이 사이드쇼의 한정판 프린팅으로 만들어진다는 것이 무척 흥미로웠고, 게다가 DC의 매력적인 여성캐릭터들을 그릴수있는 것은 매우 설레는 일이었습니다!"

"I used to get inspiration from the beautiful statues of Sideshow while working on illustrations. Then a few years later, I was thrilled to hear from Sideshow, and to receive an offer to participate in the art print program. It was very exciting to be able to officially draw attractive female characters from DC, and know that my digital work would be produced as limited edition prints!"

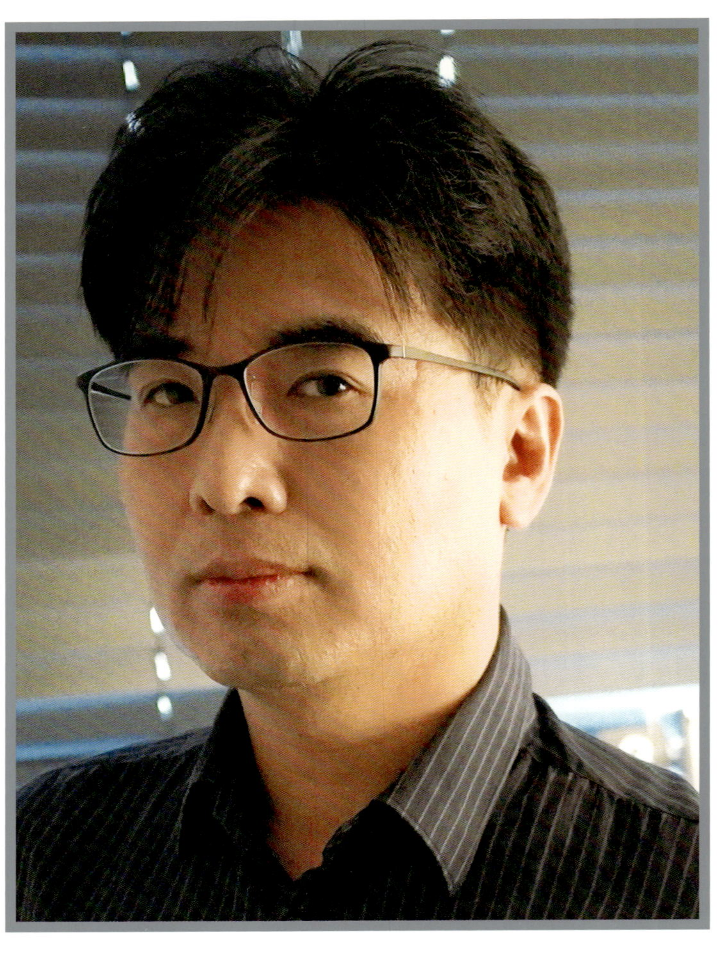

INSPIRATION

Heon-hwa Choe is an illustrator from South Korea. He majored in Visual Design and after graduation, began his career as an animator for a TV 3D animation company. He later worked for NCSoft, a game company, to direct 3D animation for games. Throughout his career, he continued to practice digital painting in his spare time, and gradually found that he preferred painting over working in 3D. So, in 2012, he quit his job and started his career in illustration. His work drew influence from Japanese game art and fantasy worlds, and over time, he gradually developed his own unique style. Since then he has worked as a freelance illustrator for such companies as Riot Games, Valve, and Cygames. Currently he is also doing illustration work for *Magic: The Gathering* with Wizards of the Coast.

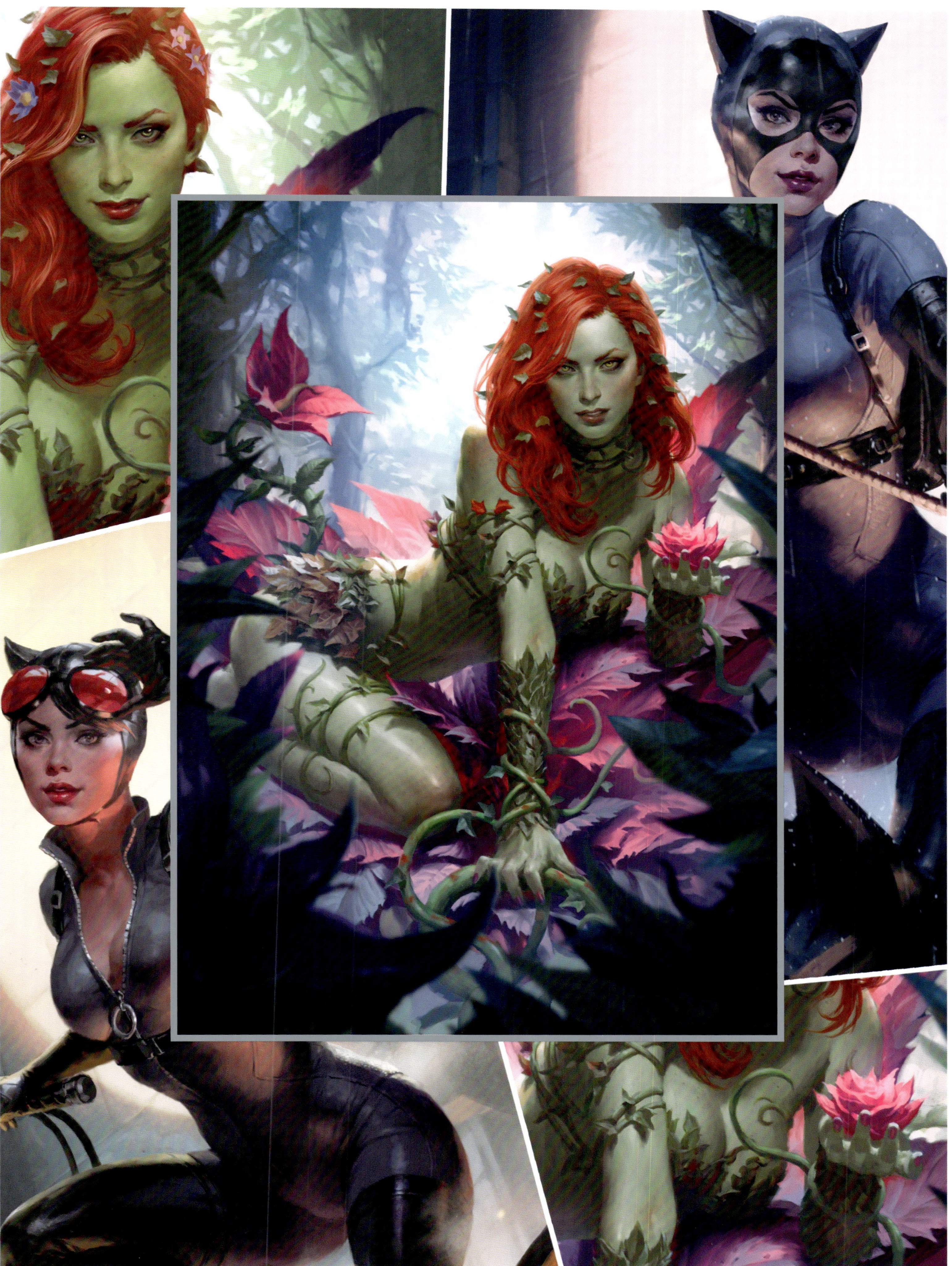

Poison Ivy, Poison Ivy Variant, Catwoman, and Catwoman Variant.

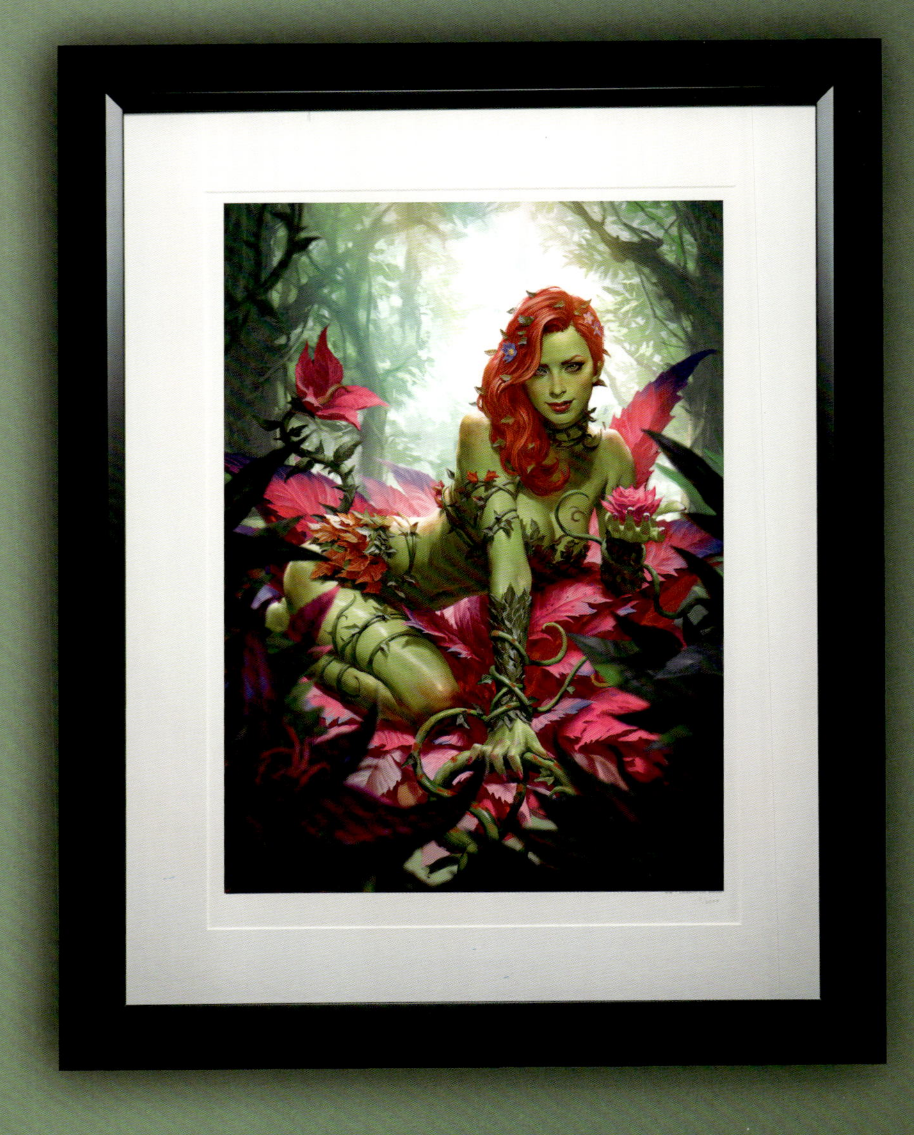

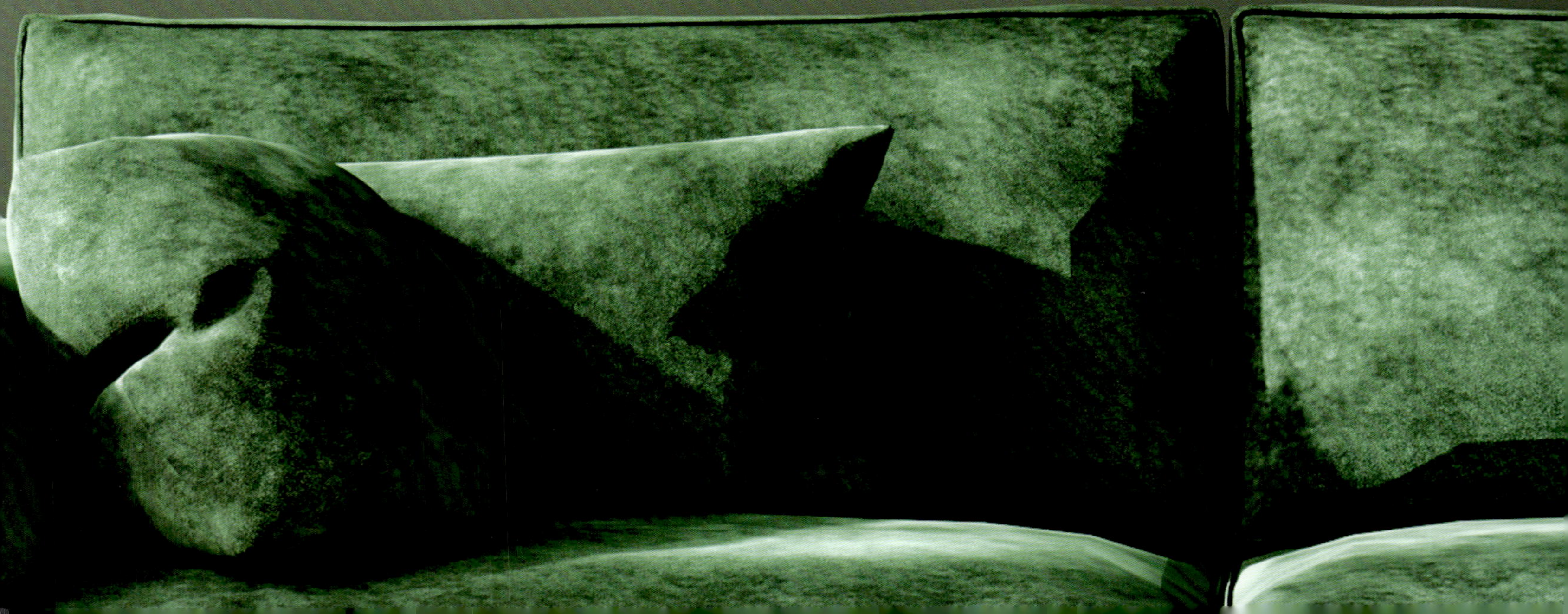

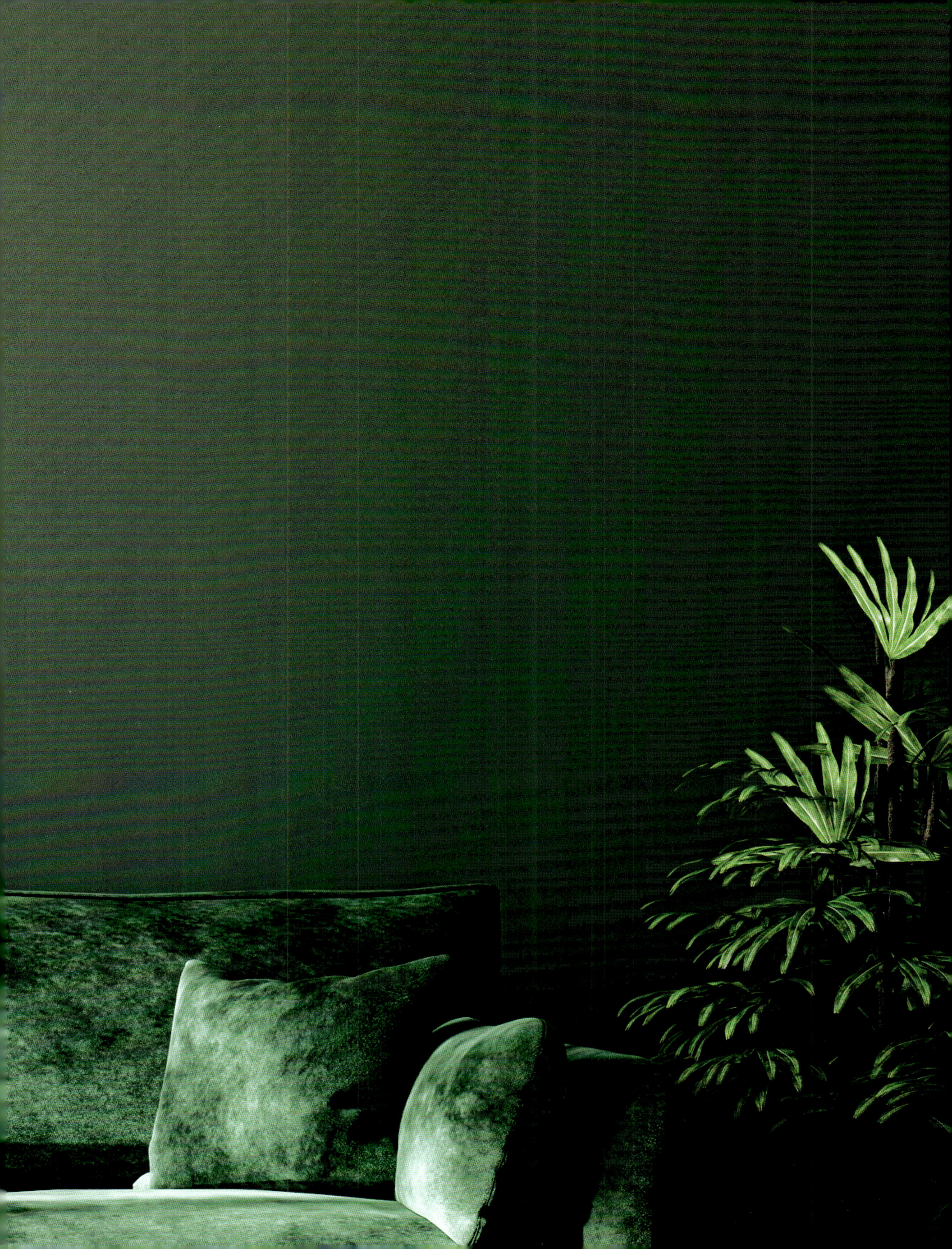

LEIA PRINCESS OF ALDERAAN

OLIVIA DE BERARDINIS

Lovingly rendered in the indelible likeness of Carrie Fisher as Princess Leia, this portrait captures the regal and rebellious face of hope that has inspired an entire galaxy of *Star Wars* fans across generations.

Seen here in her stunning white gown and with her iconic hairstyle from *Star Wars: Episode IV—A New Hope*, this depiction of Princess Leia encapsulates the character's strength, grace, and determination.

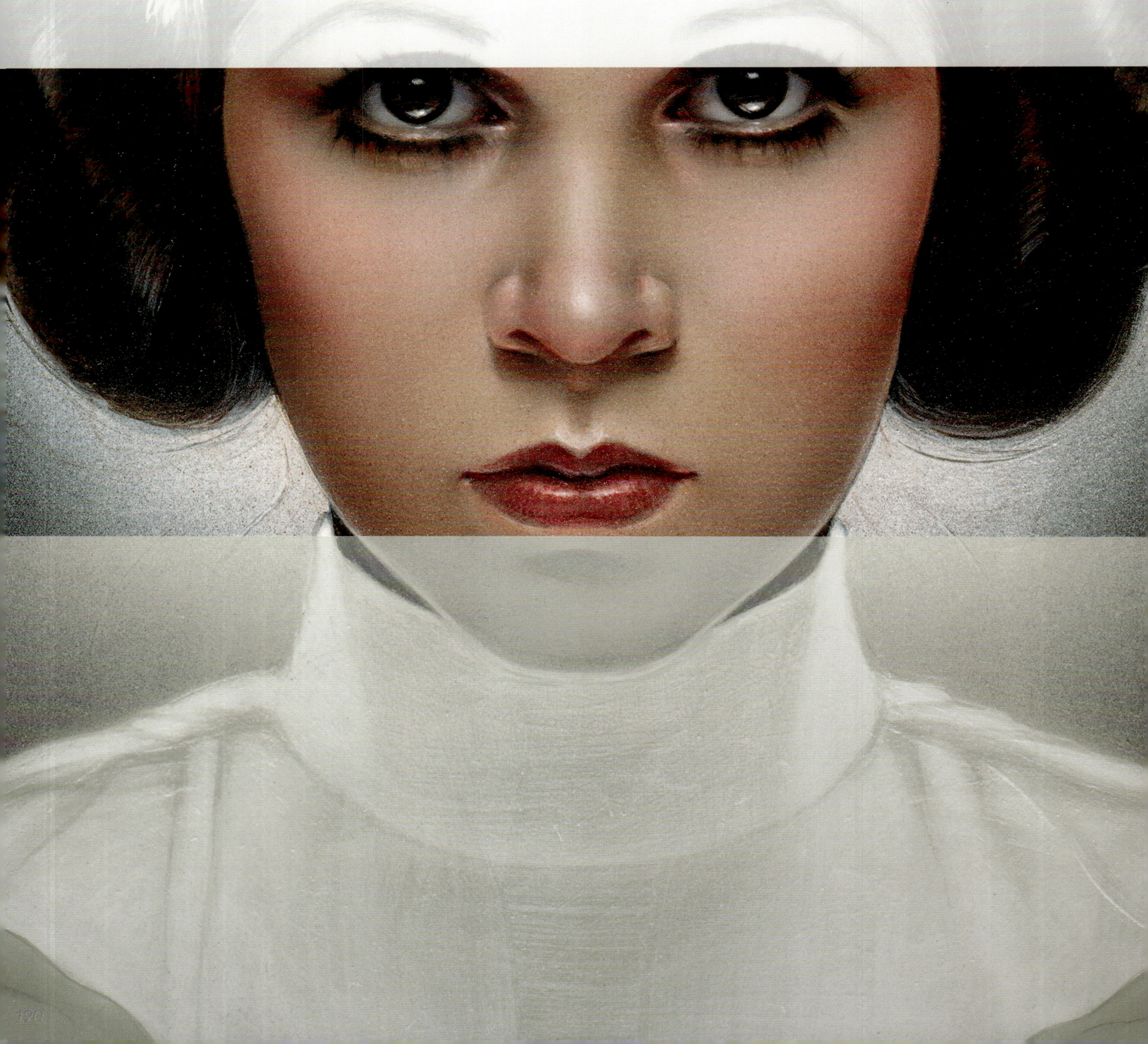

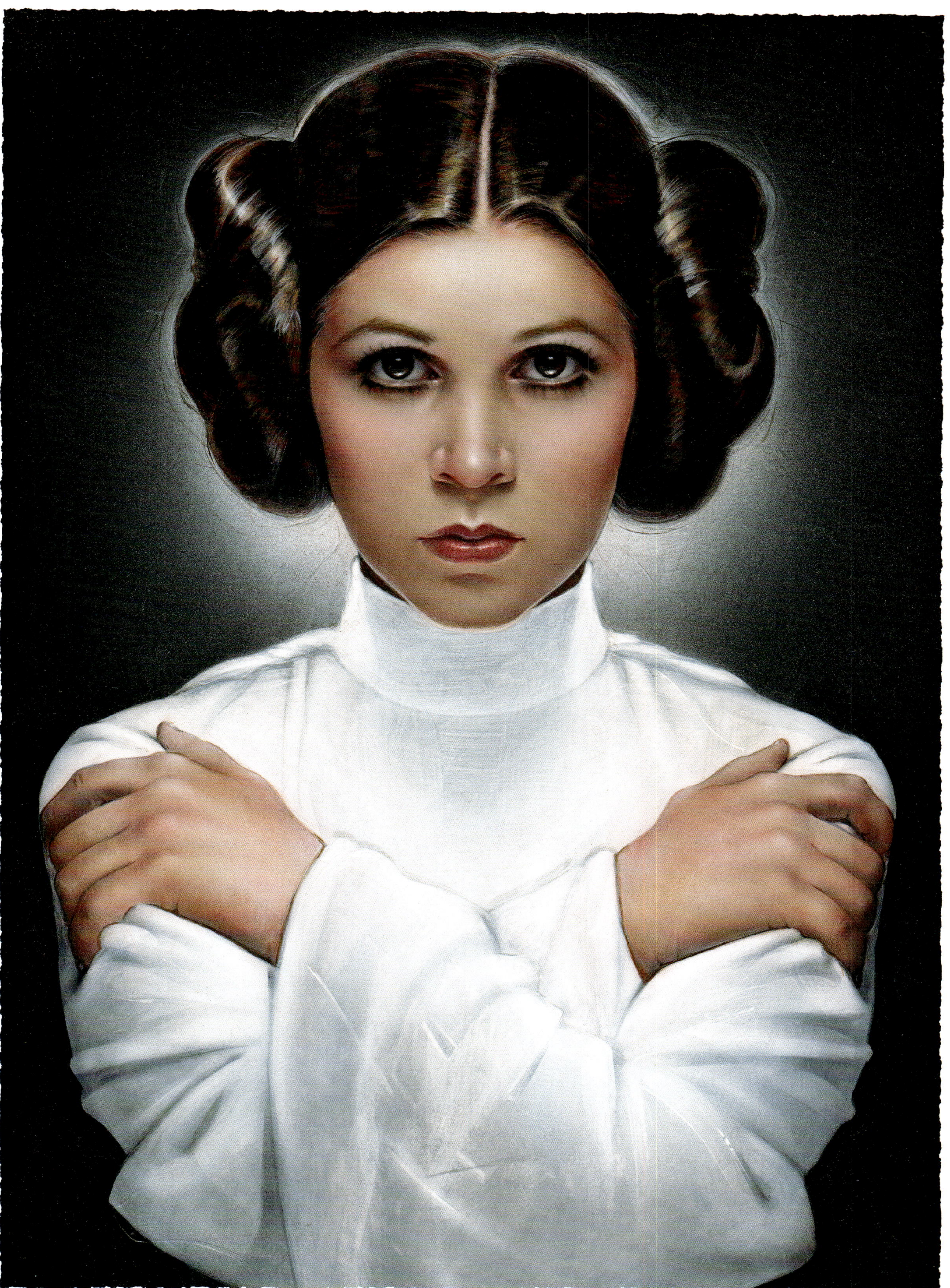

Leia: Princess of Alderaan © 2018 Olivia De Berardinis

THUNDERCATS

ALEX PASCENKO

With the Sword of Omens raised high, Lion-O leads the proud ThunderCats in the fight for Thundera against Mumm-Ra and his mutant allies. Alex Pascenko called on fellow artists Ian MacDonald and Zac Roane to help reimagine this exciting pantheon of characters.

The *ThunderCats* Premium Art Print features thirteen fan-favorite faces in all, assembling the ThunderCats—Panthro, Cheetara, Tygra, Wilykat, Wilykit, and Snarf—in an epic battle against Mumm-Ra and his Mutants.

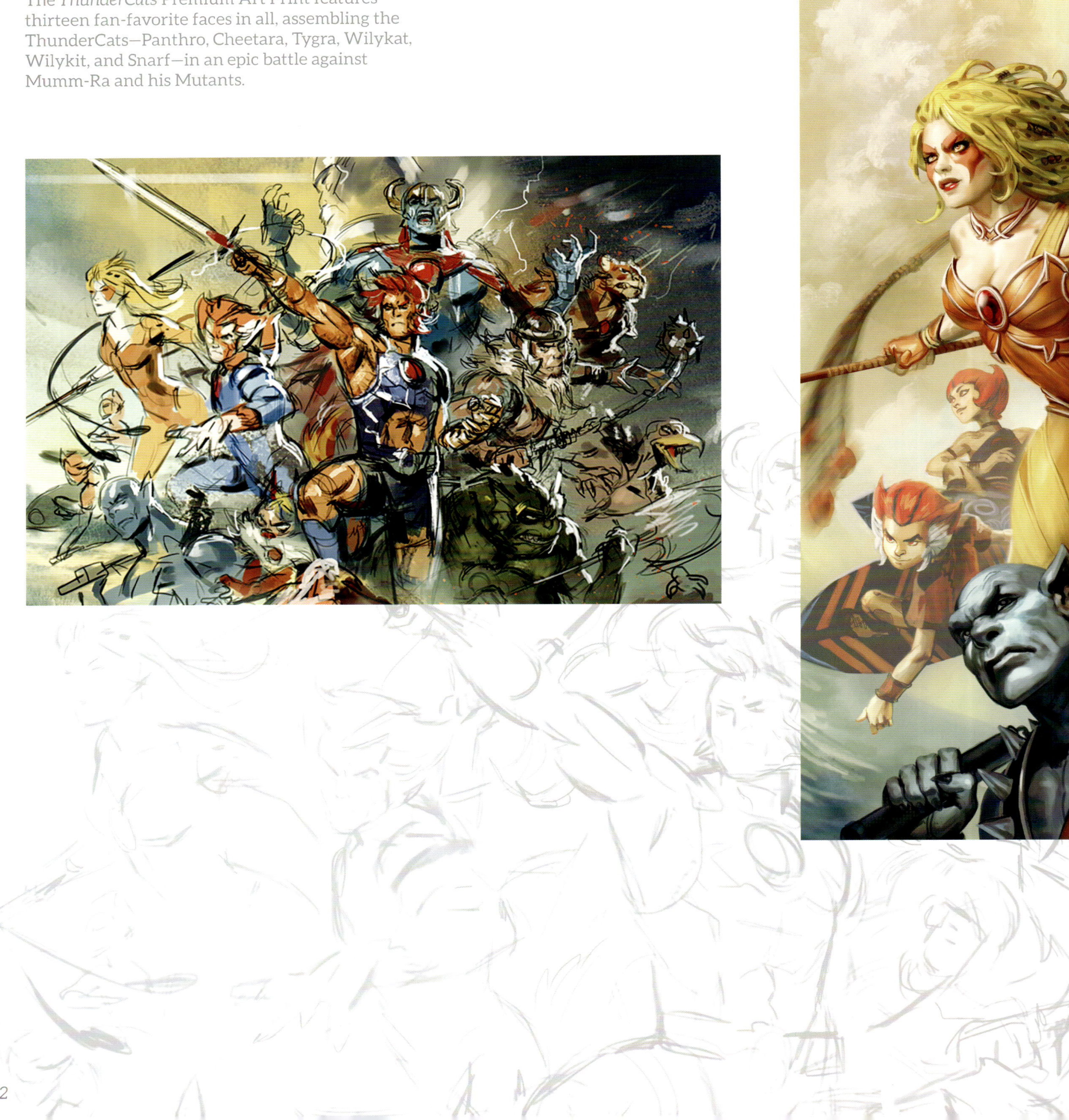

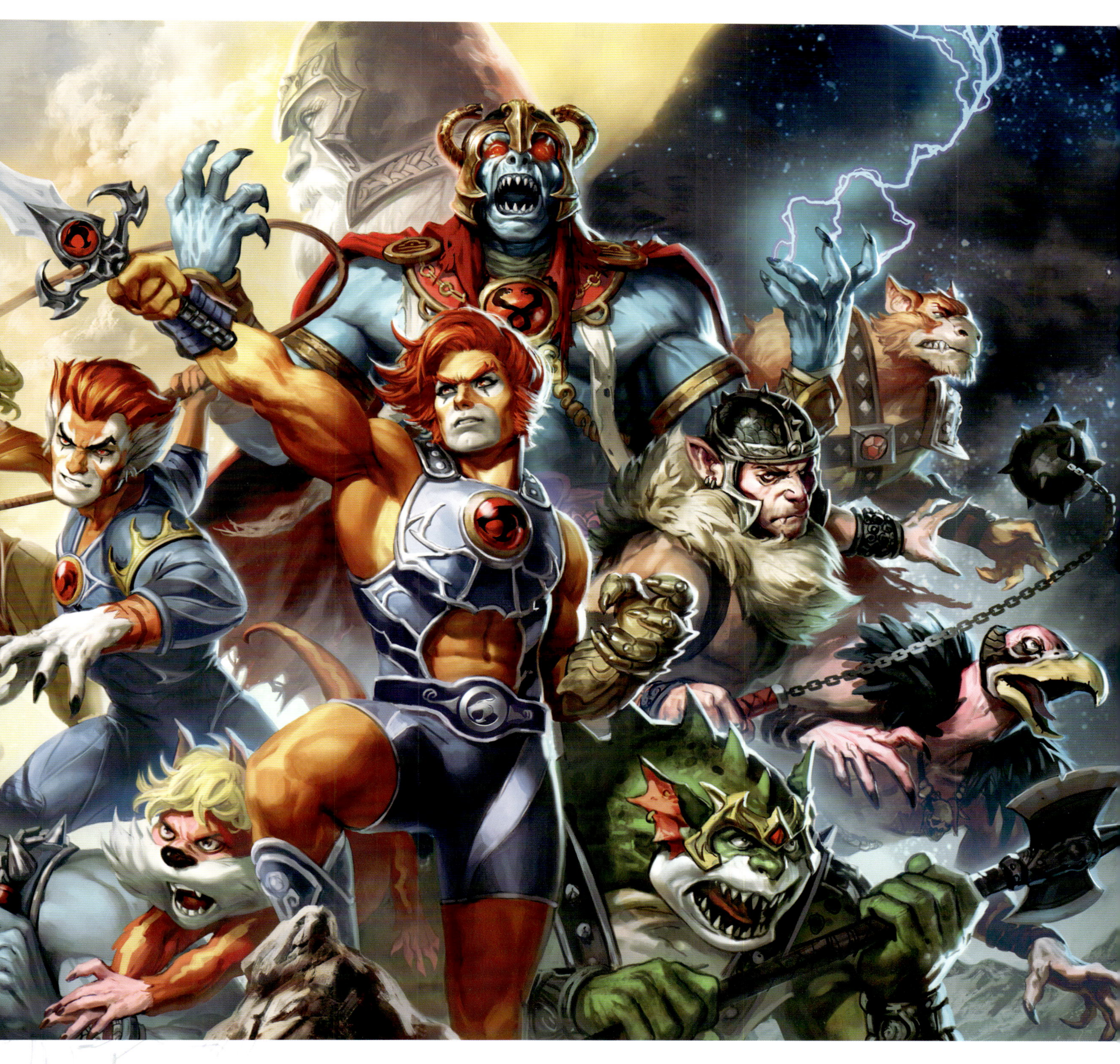

THE DEATH OF WOLVERINE

ALEX ROSS

Originally created as a variant cover in honor of Marvel's 75th anniversary, the *Death of Wolverine* fine art lithograph features iconic moments from the life of this legendary superhero.

All roads must end somewhere, and every hero's story must eventually come to a close. From his battle with the Hulk, to taking his place among the X-Men, this tableau captures the face of Wolverine throughout the ages, in a stylish and fitting tribute to Logan's presence in Marvel history.

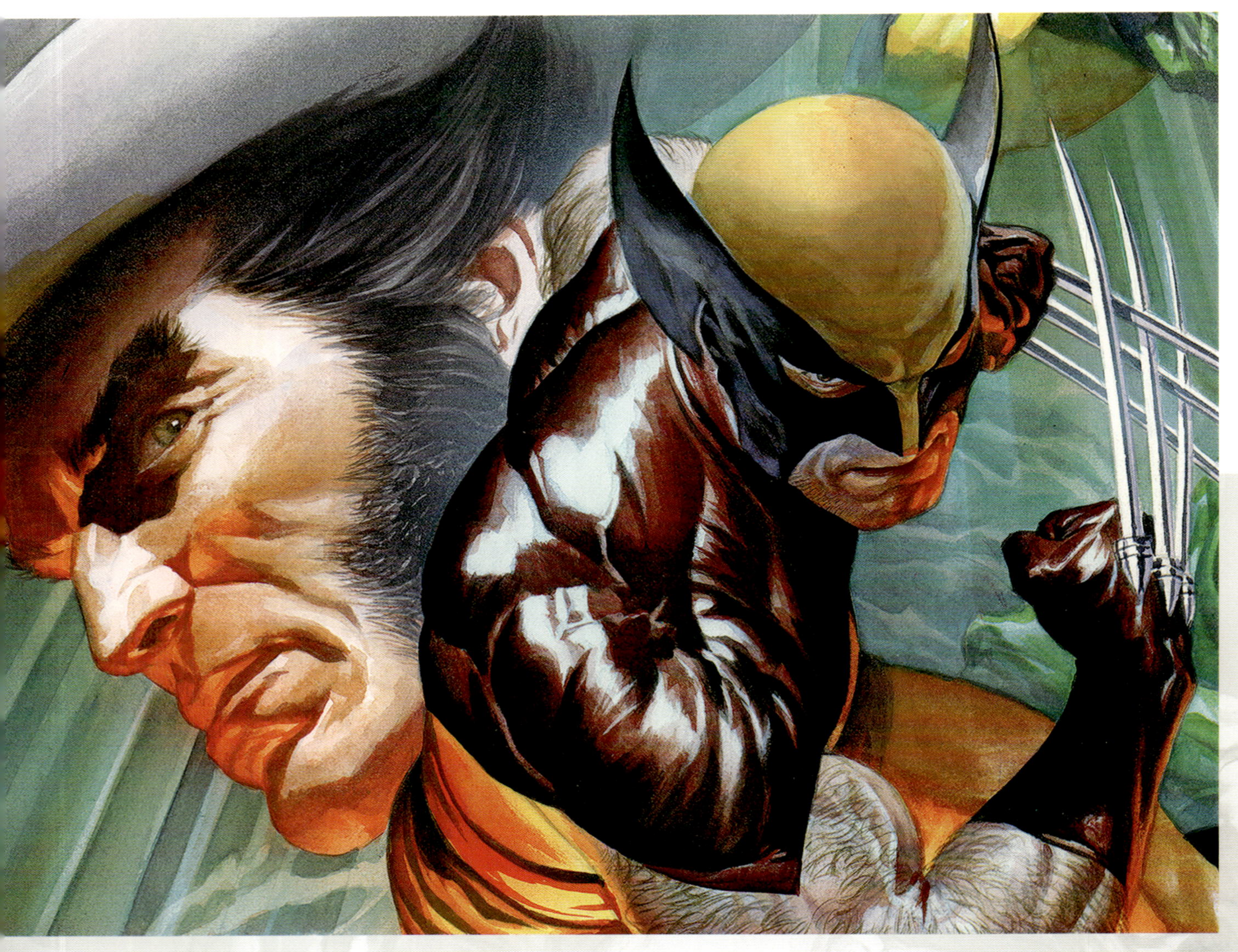

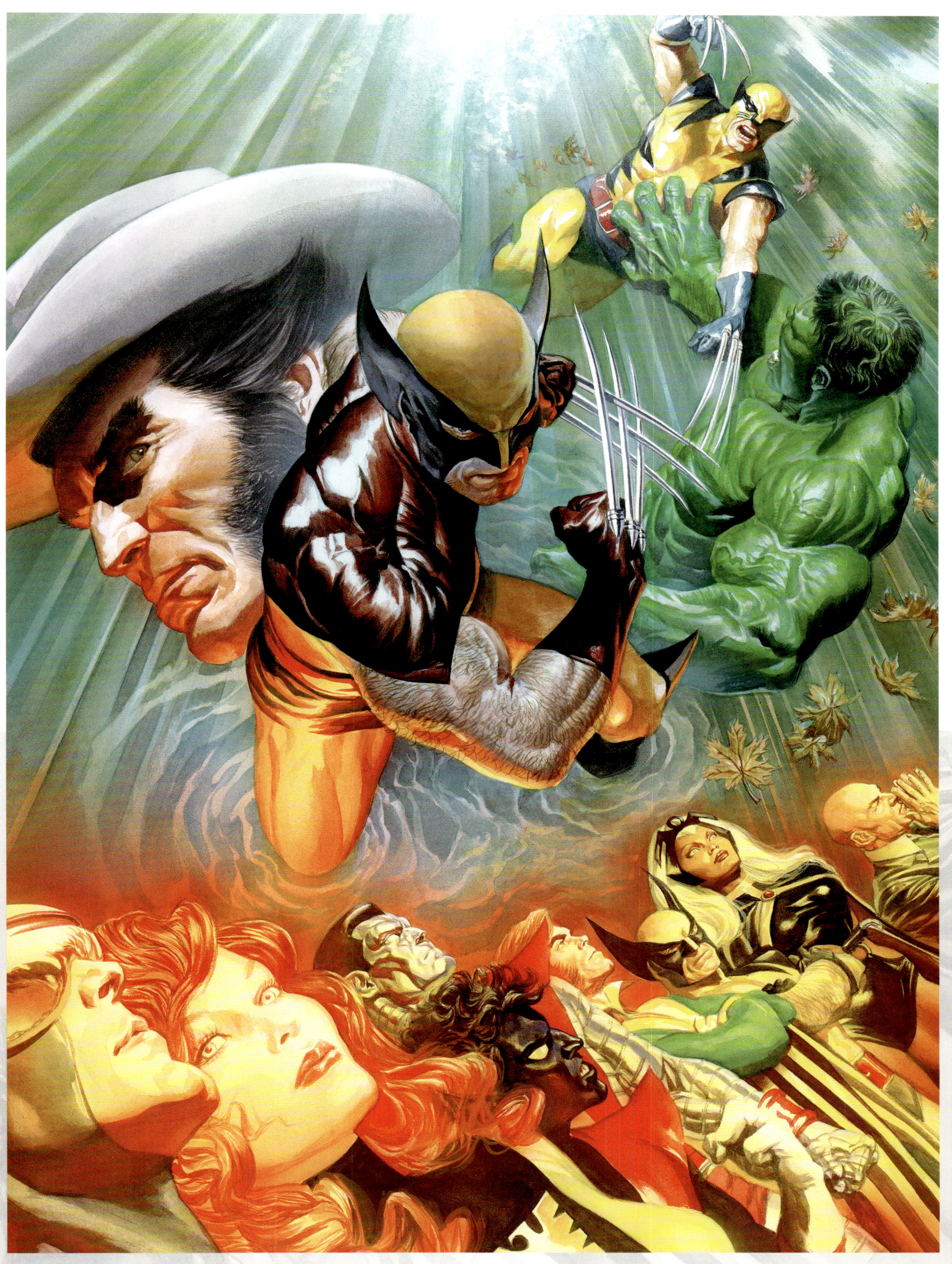

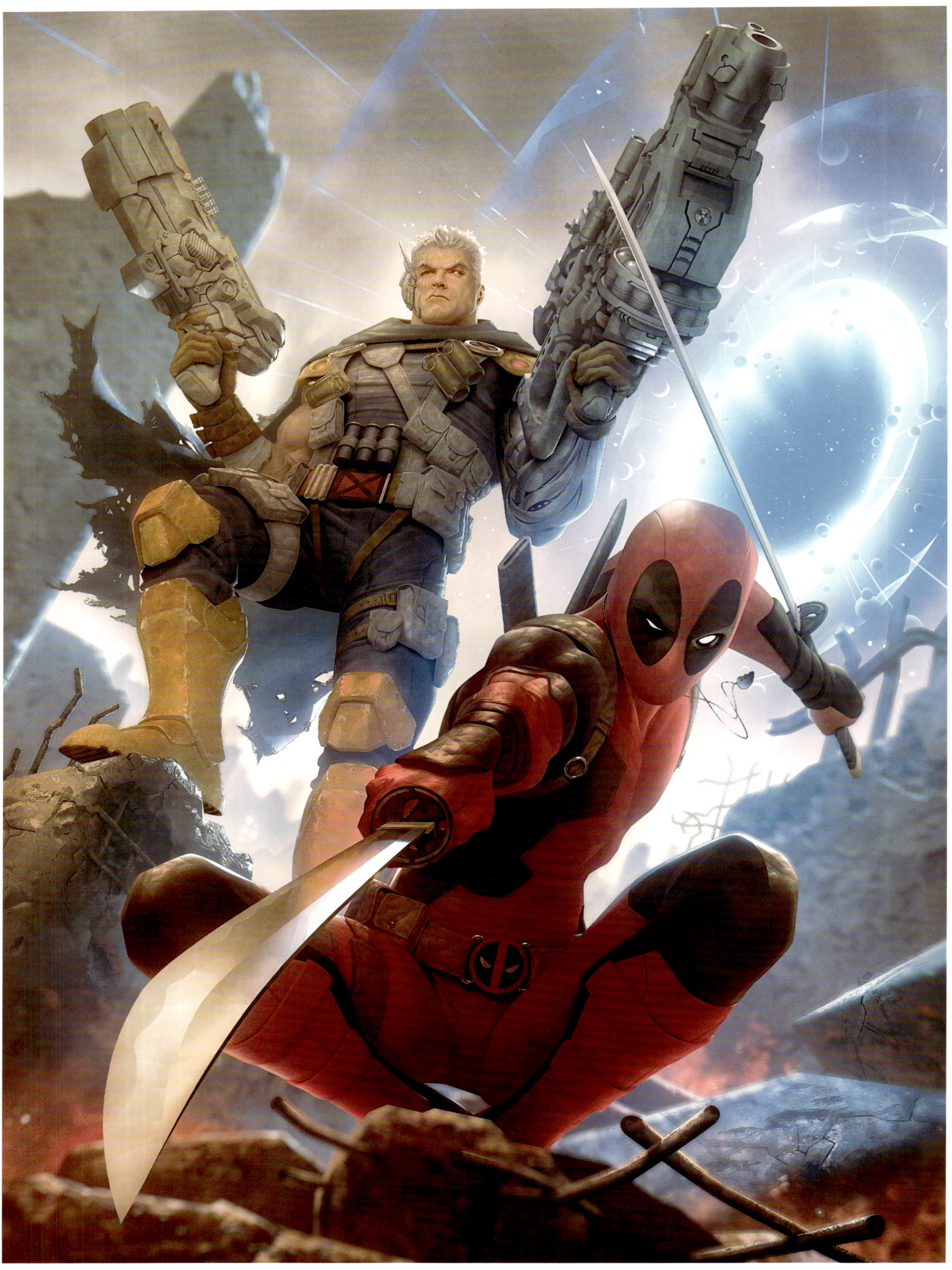

DEADPOOL & CABLE

ALEX GARNER

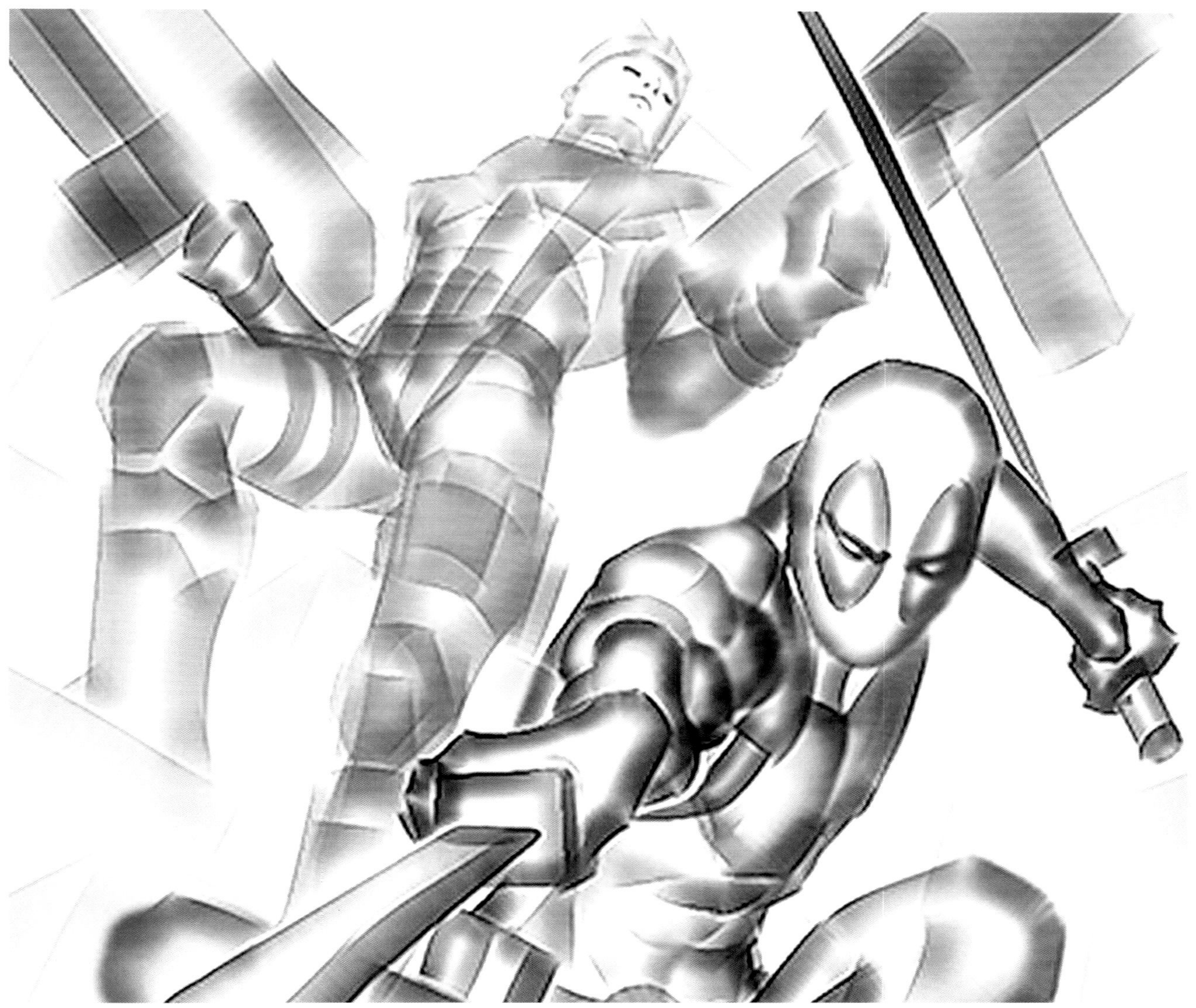

Straight from the pages of *X-Force* comes Marvel's oddest couple, the stoic Cable and the infamous Merc with a Mouth, Deadpool. The two mutant mercenaries come together from various time streams in this celebration of their legendary partnership.

Brandishing his katanas, Deadpool takes point, while Cable brings the big guns, emerging from an interdimensional portal to dispense vengeance on his victims.

BATMAN

ALEX PASCENKO & IAN MACDONALD

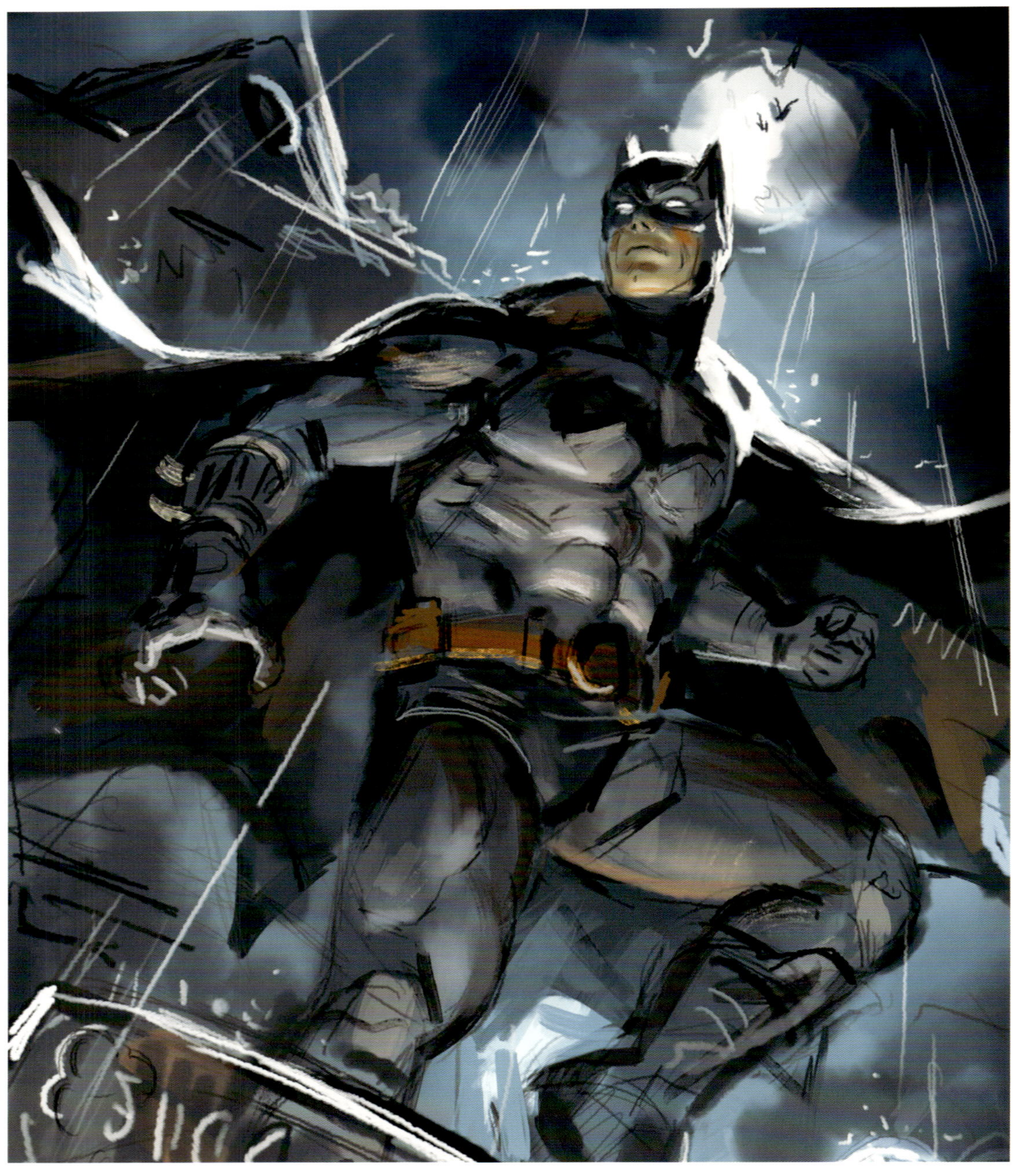

Criminals cower in fear when the Caped Crusader steps out of the shadows. Illuminated by moonlight during a stormy night, Batman prepares for action, standing in the midst of the Arkham Asylum cemetery. The gravestones bear markings of madness from an inmate of the infamous asylum, as bats take wing in the night.

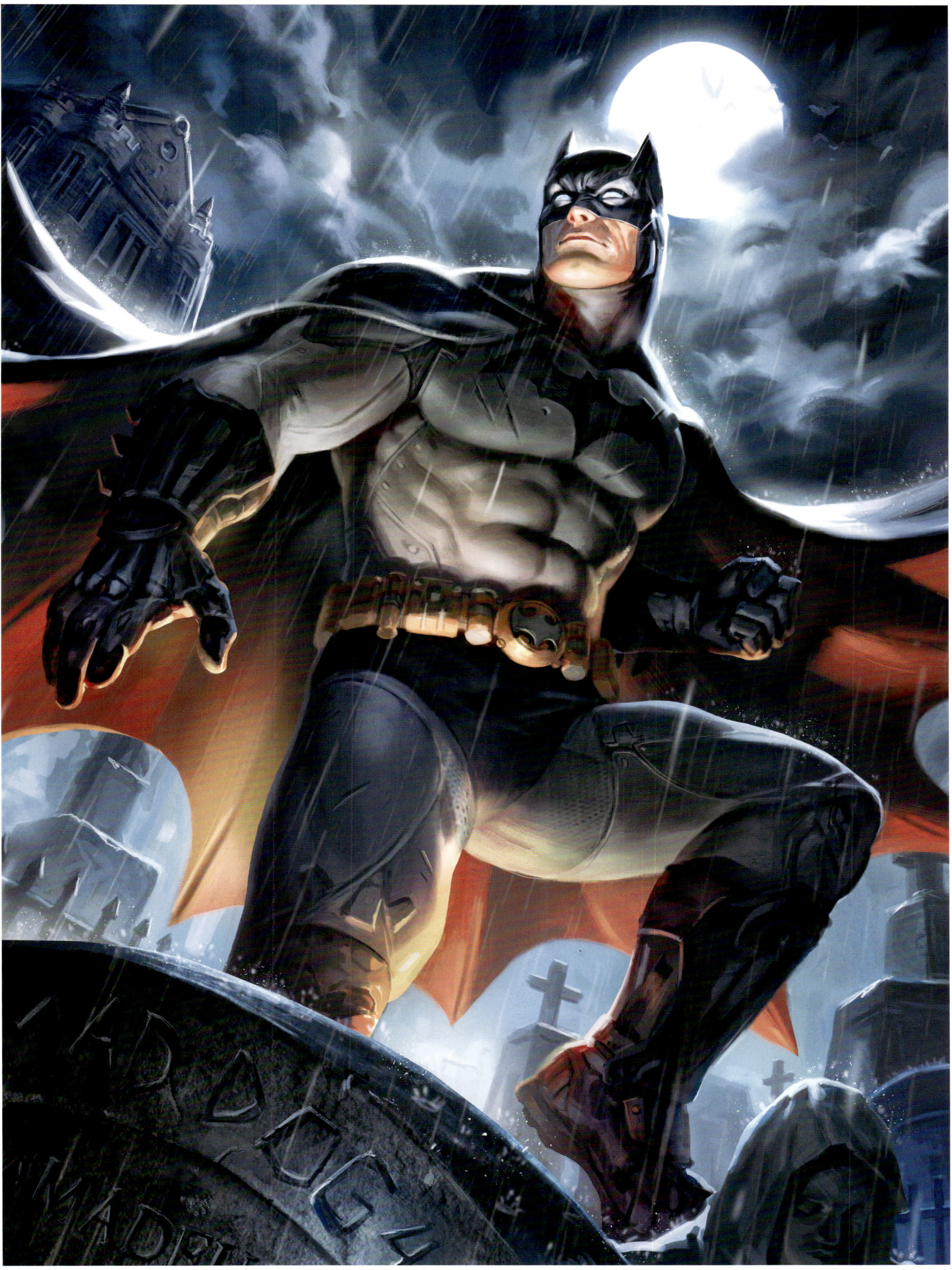

PREDATOR JUNGLE HUNTER

FABIAN SCHLAGA

Standing high above the tropics of Val Verde, the Predator scouts for his prey from the treetops. He is surrounded by an array of flayed skeletal trophies, clutching his latest spoils—a skull and severed spinal cord.

The Jungle Hunter's wrist blades are sharpened and ready for action as a distant helicopter flies along the horizon.

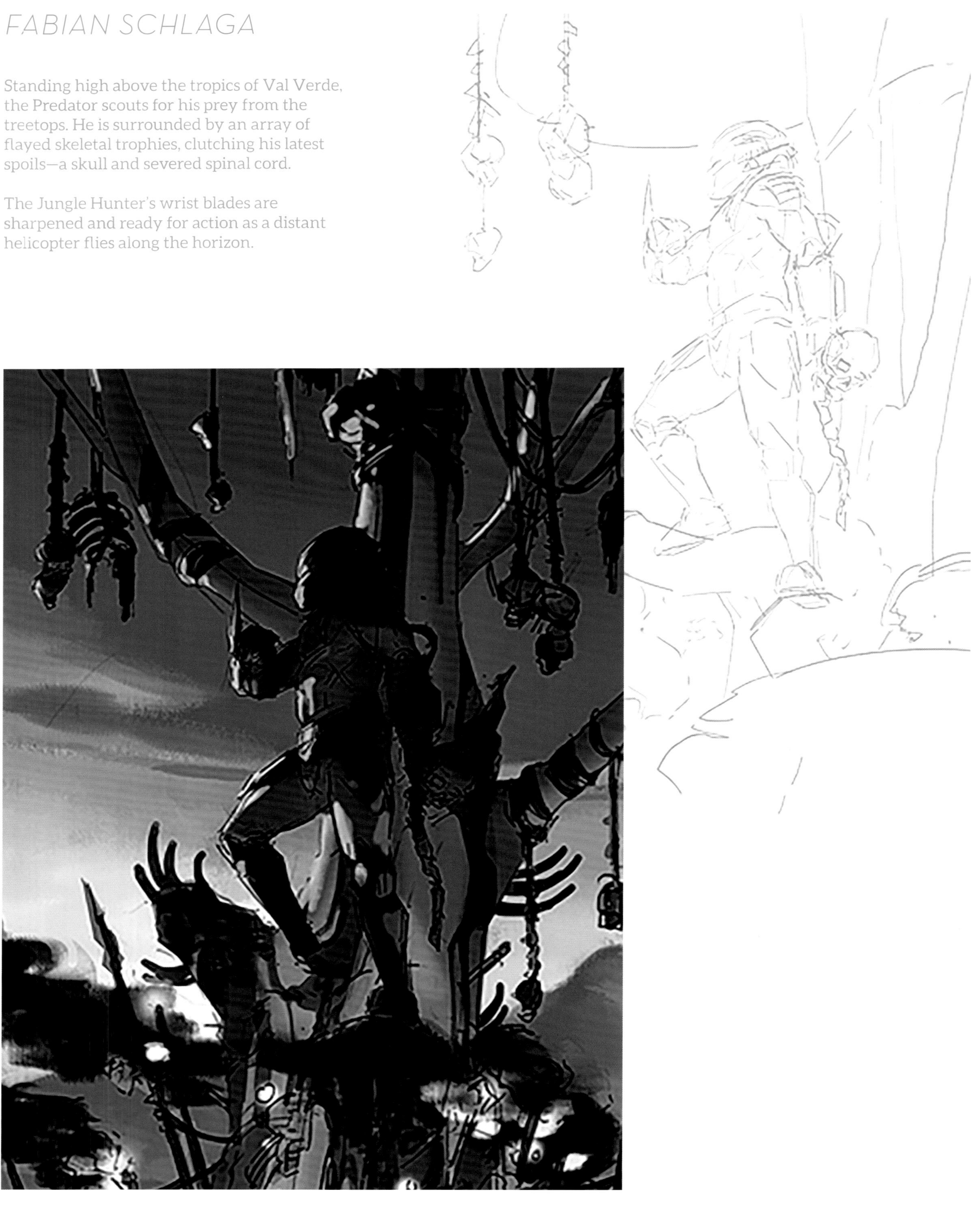

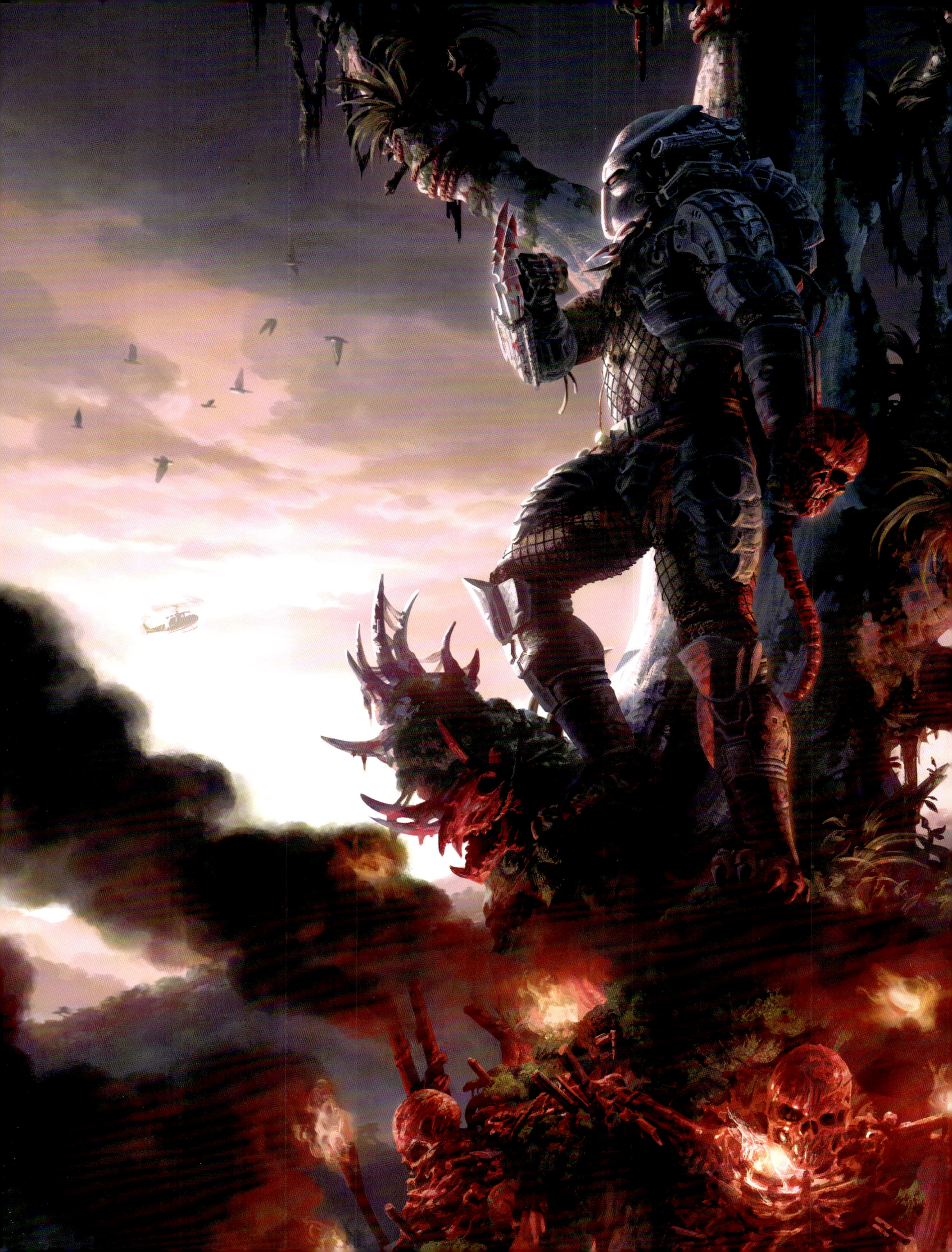

THE JOKER
PORTRAITS OF VILLAINY
ALEX ROSS

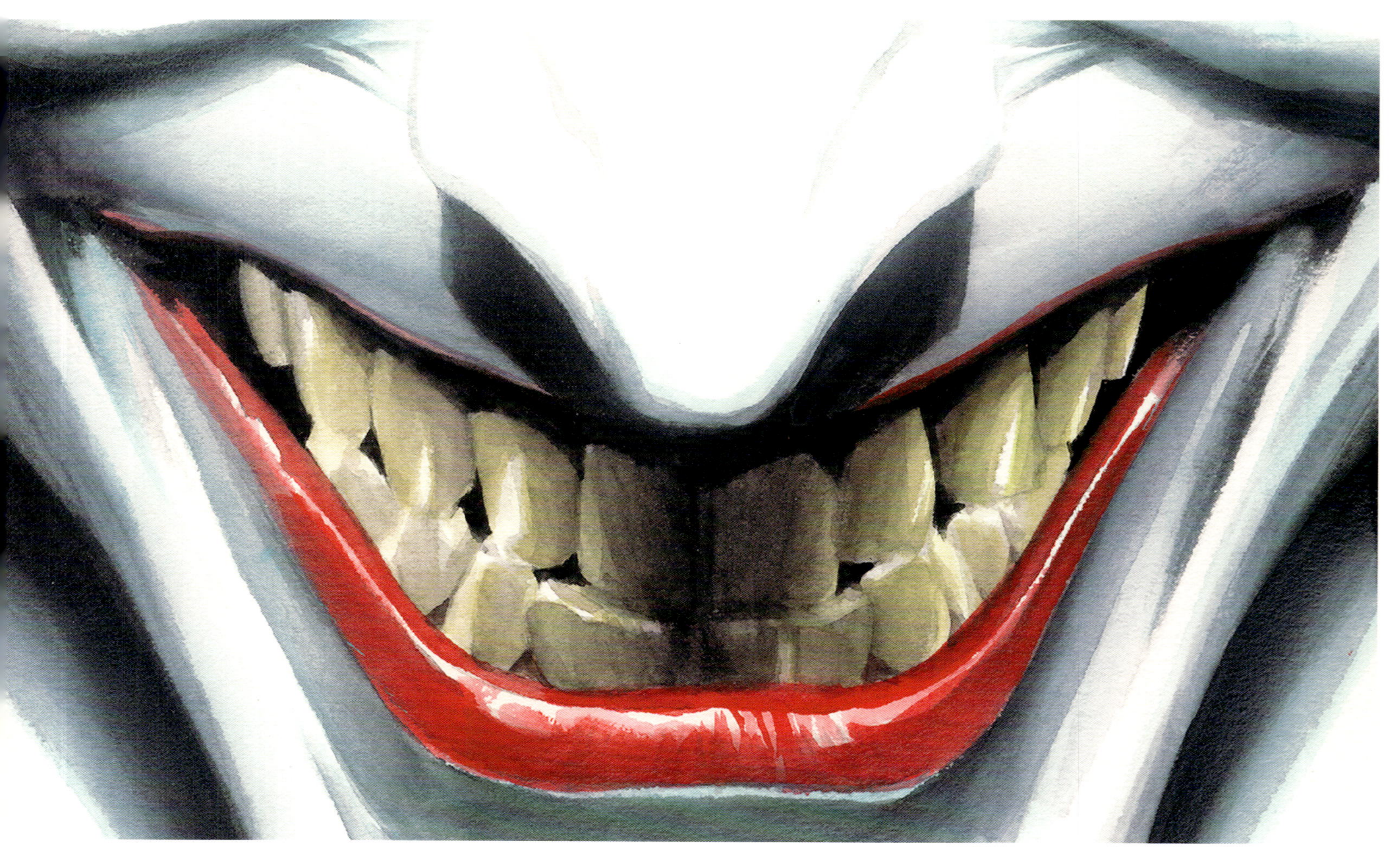

Available in print for the first time, *The Joker: Portraits of Villainy* by Alex Ross captures the derangement and delight of Gotham's Clown Prince of Crime. This expertly rendered portrait of the Joker with his sinister smile is a chilling look into the insanity of Batman's greatest foe.

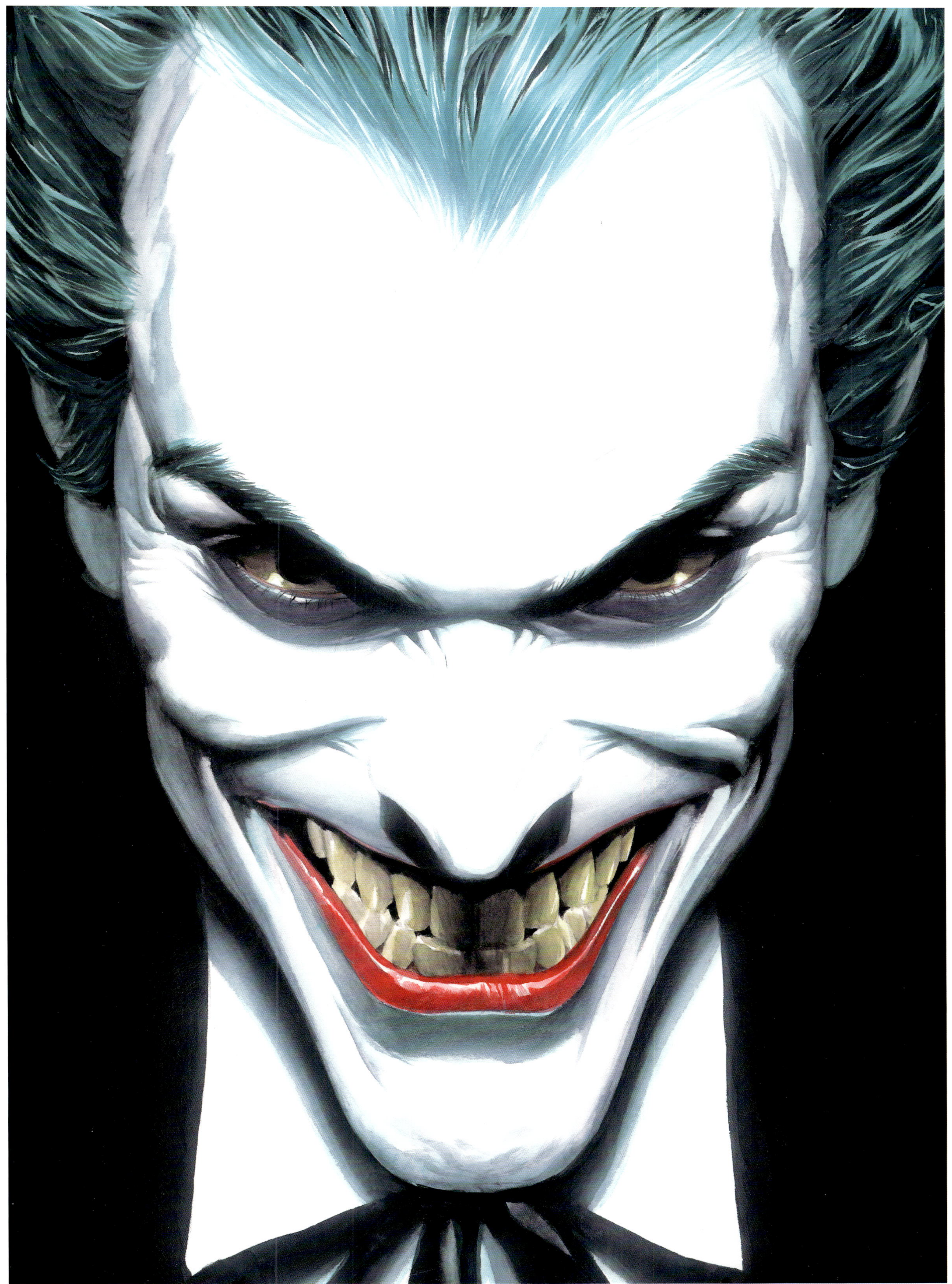

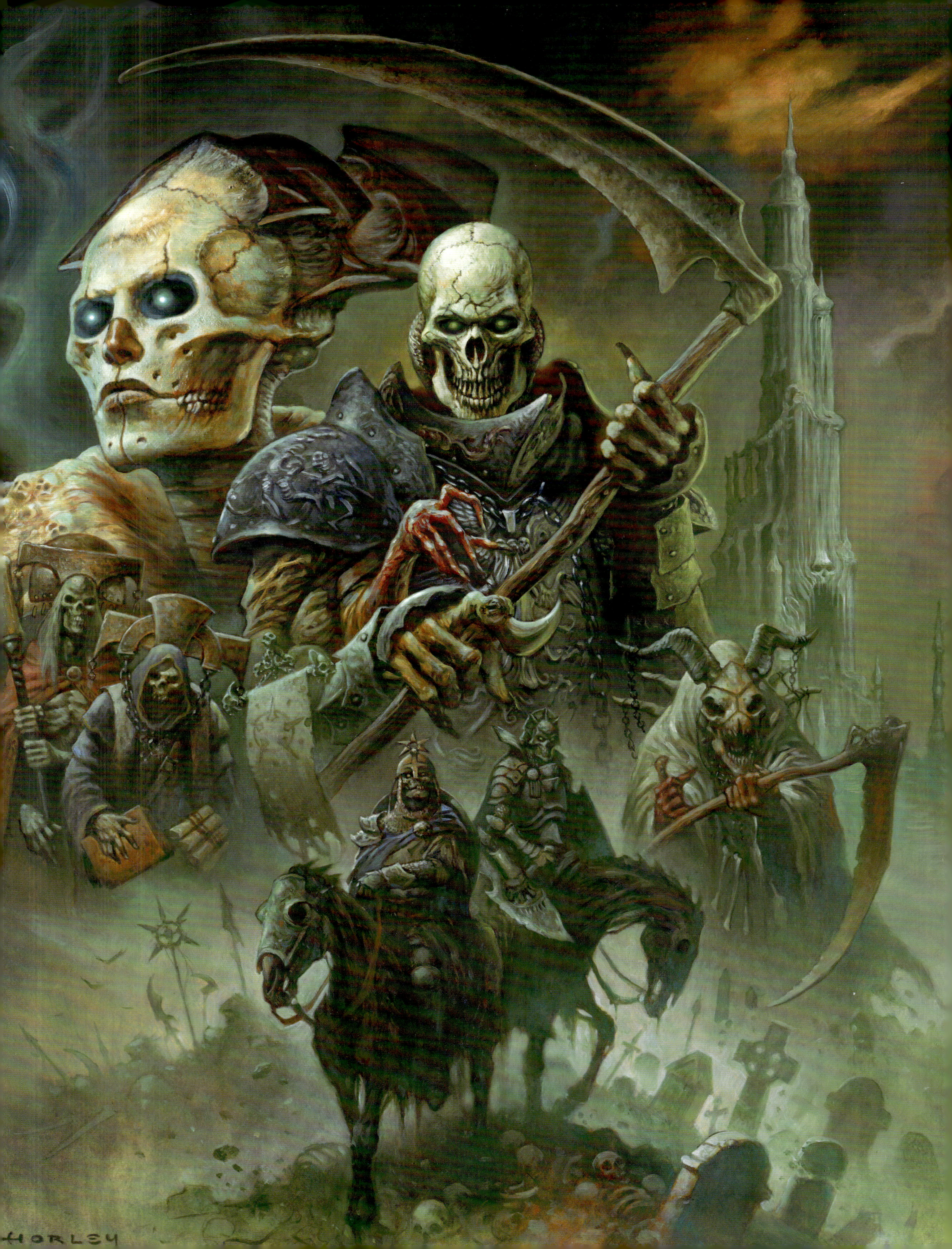
HORLEY

THE STRENGTH OF BONE

ALEX HORLEY

The Strength of Bone Premium Art Print is a high-end reproduction of an original acrylic and oil painting by world-renowned artist Alex Horley. This striking piece features the Reaper General Demithyle, who beckons the viewer to join the Underworld forces. Over his shoulder, Bone Faction leader Xiall, the Great Osteomancer, looks to the future rebellion with her burning etherea-blue eyes.

Their stoic and ghastly leadership is underpinned by the ghoulish Council of Osteomancy, the fearless adventurer Relic Ravlatch, the haunting beacon Shieve, and the vast and varied host of the reaper army. Without the Bone Faction to uphold its principles and law, the Underworld would crumble.

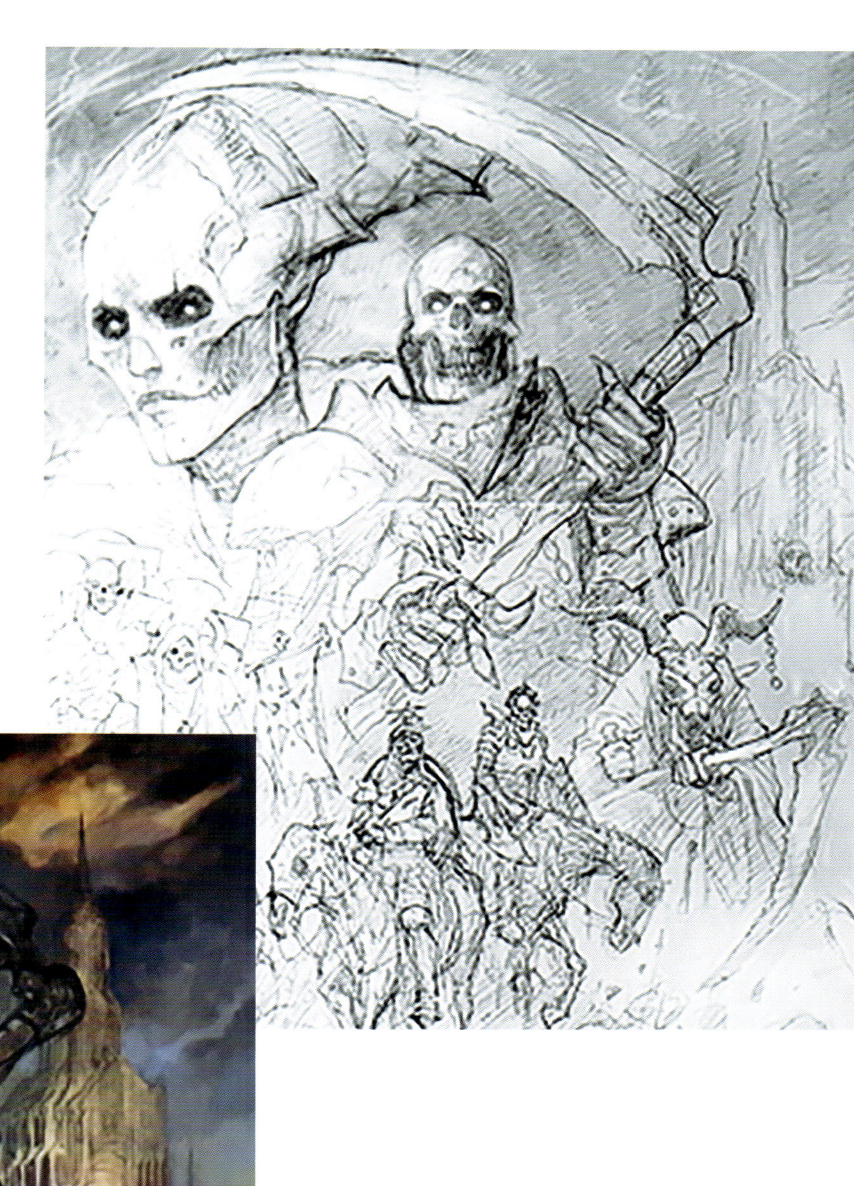

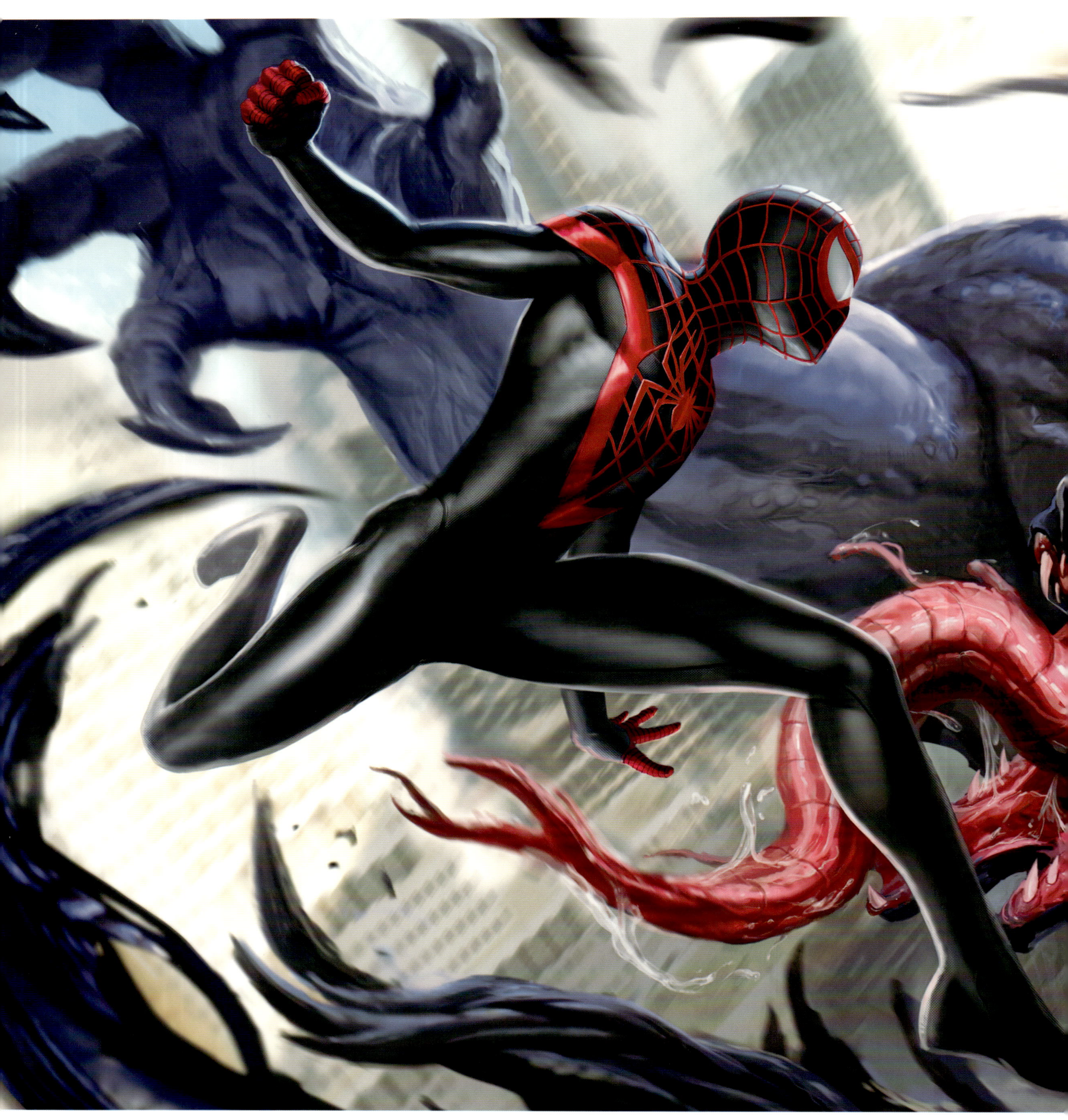

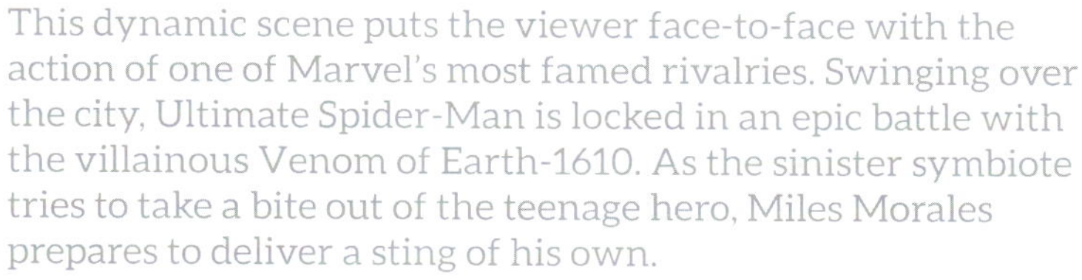

SPIDER-MAN MILES MORALES

ANTHONY FRANCISCO

This dynamic scene puts the viewer face-to-face with the action of one of Marvel's most famed rivalries. Swinging over the city, Ultimate Spider-Man is locked in an epic battle with the villainous Venom of Earth-1610. As the sinister symbiote tries to take a bite out of the teenage hero, Miles Morales prepares to deliver a sting of his own.

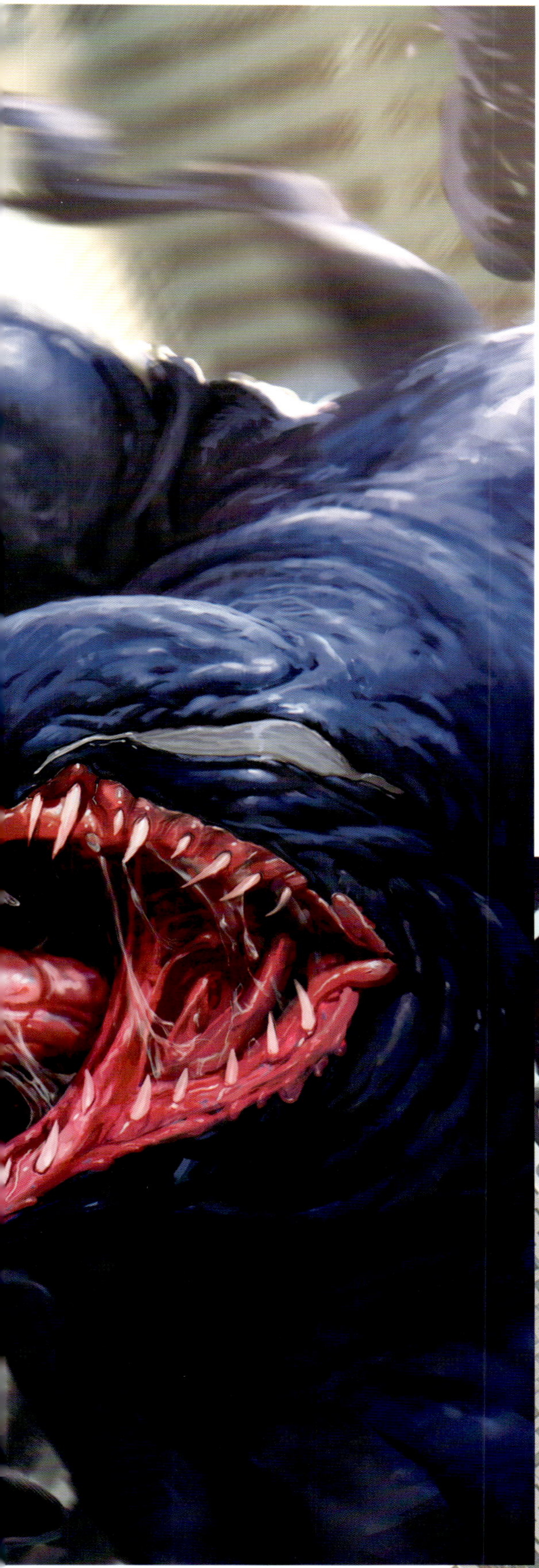

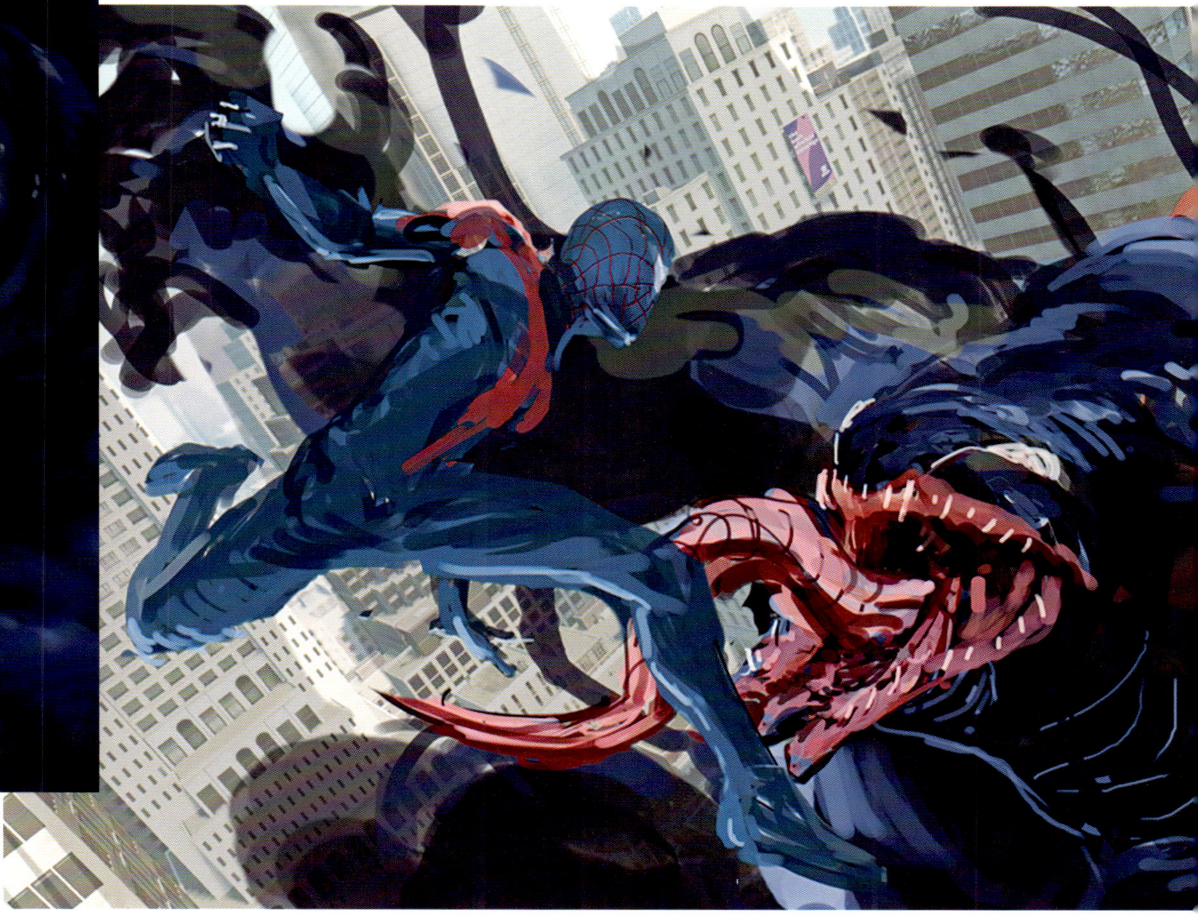

ANTHONY FRANCISCO

"Collaborating on the X-Men Gold and Blue team print with the Sideshow team was a dream come true! I had so much fun creating the composition and design. Unfortunately, at the time we were working on it, I suffered a very emotional loss in my family. But now whenever I look at it, this image brings back a lot of warm memories of someone I loved so dearly."

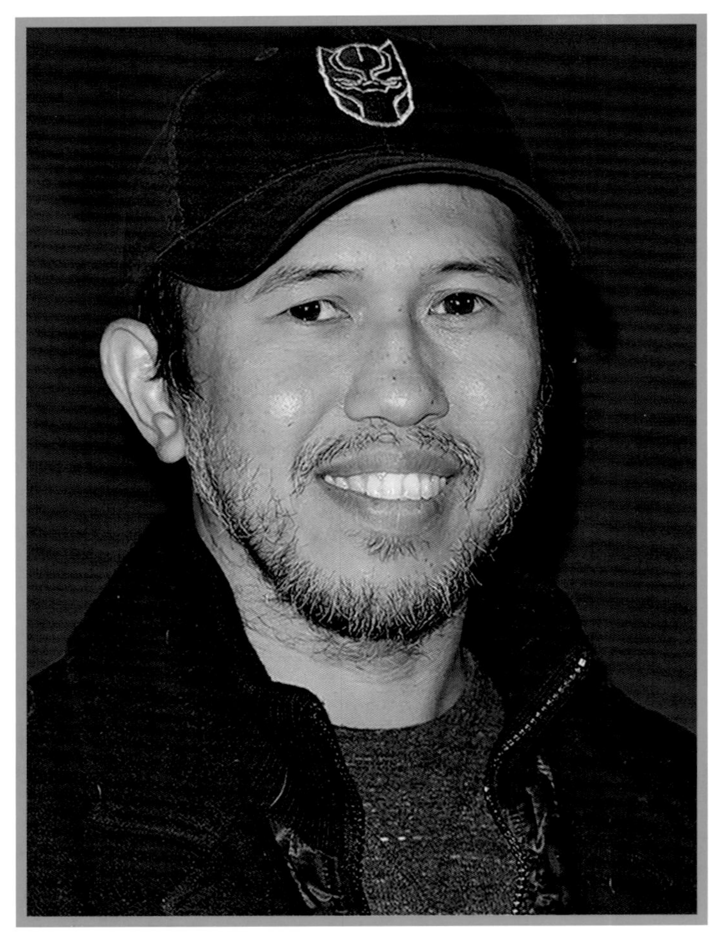

INSPIRATION

Anthony Francisco is a senior staff member in the Marvel Studios Visual Development Department, where he helps with designing the Heroes and Villains of the Marvel Cinematic Universe. Dubbed the "visual father of Baby Groot," he has also designed iconic characters like the Dora Milaje, Okoye and Nakia, Loki for *Thor: Ragnarok*, Tazerface and Teen Groot, to name a few. Additionally, he helped shape scenes in movies, such as *Avengers: Infinity War*, for which he suggested the idea of dropping the moon on Doctor Strange during his battle with Thanos. Other Marvel films and series he has contributed to include *Guardians of the Galaxy Vol. 1, 2,* and *3*; *Ant-Man, Ant-Man and the Wasp*, and *Ant-Man and the Wasp: Quantumania*; *Black Panther 1* and *2*; *Captain Marvel 1* and *2*; *Doctor Strange*; *Avengers: Endgame*; *WandaVision*; *Thor: Love and Thunder*; *Black Widow*; and *Shang-Chi and the Legend of the Ten Rings*.

In the beginning of his twenty-year career as a concept artist, he worked for FX houses like Stan Winston Studios, Rick Baker, ADI, Harlow FX, Steve Johnson, and Captive Audience, which gave Anthony the opportunity to work on movies like *Superman Returns*, *A.I.*, *Men in Black 2*, *Sam Raimi's Spider-Man*, *Alien vs. Predator*, *Species III*, *The Passion of the Christ*, and *The Chronicles of Riddick*. From 2004 to 2006 he worked as a concept artist at NCsoft Santa Monica on the *Guild Wars* and *Tabula Rasa* MMO titles. After his time at NCsoft, Anthony joined the team at Offset Software as the lead concept/story artist to work on a fantasy-based first-person shooter game. In 2011 he worked at Rhythm & Hues on *Hunger Games*, *RIPD* and *Seventh Son*. Anthony also did illustration work for Magic: The Gathering and has been an instructor at Gnomon School for Visual Effects, ArtCenter College of Design in Pasadena, Concept Design Academy and CGMW online.

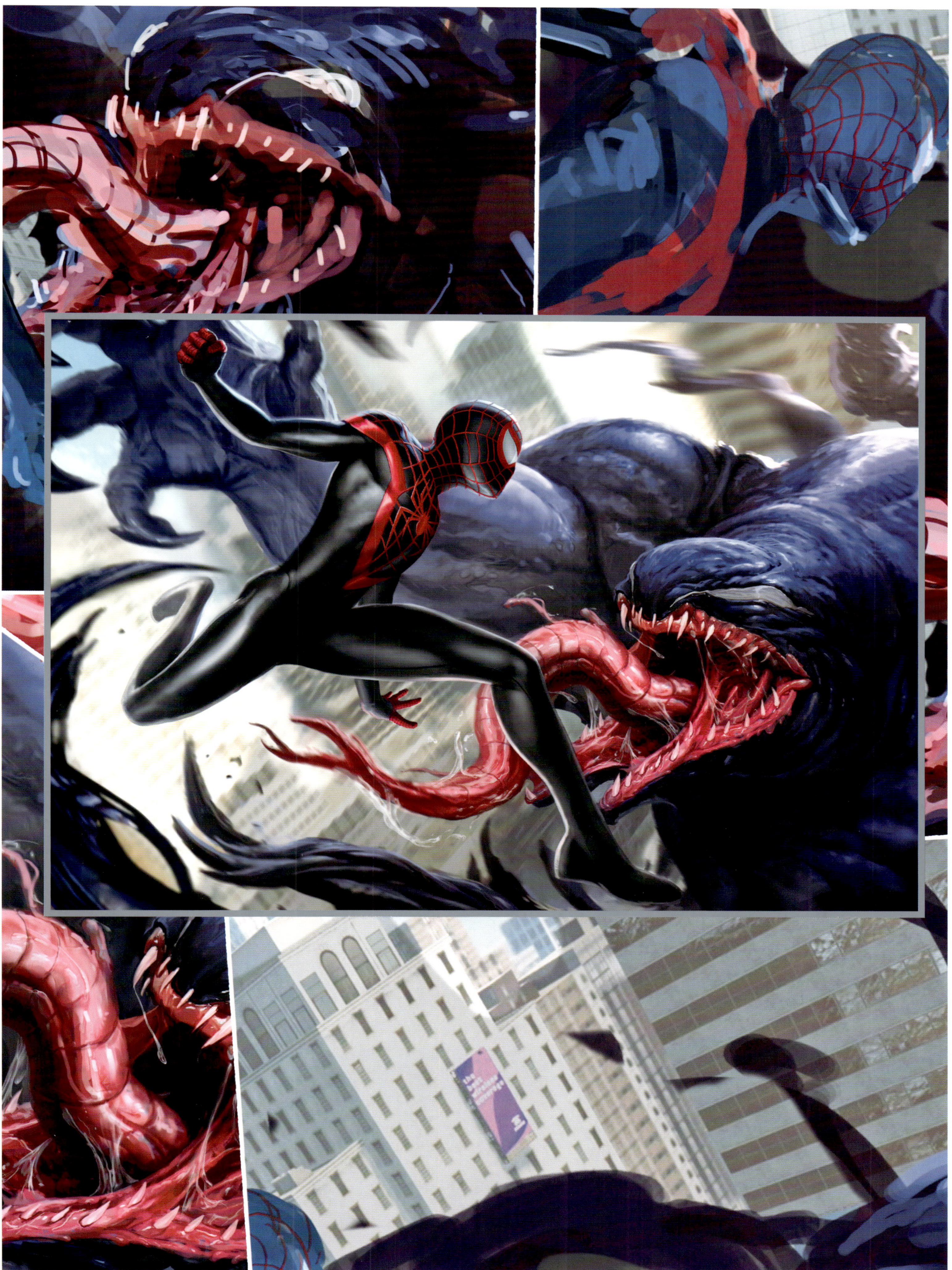

Spider-Man Miles Morales and concept art.

BLACK PANTHER VS. ERIK KILLMONGER

ADI GRANOV

A thrilling entry in the Marvel Studios Fine Art Print collection, this piece by Adi Granov pits two fierce fighters against each other in a struggle for the fate of Wakanda. Who will triumph in this battle of might and morals?

Capturing the energy and skill of both Black Panther and Erik Killmonger, this Fine Art Print highlights their climactic battle with the blue-and-green tones of Wakanda's vibranium mines.

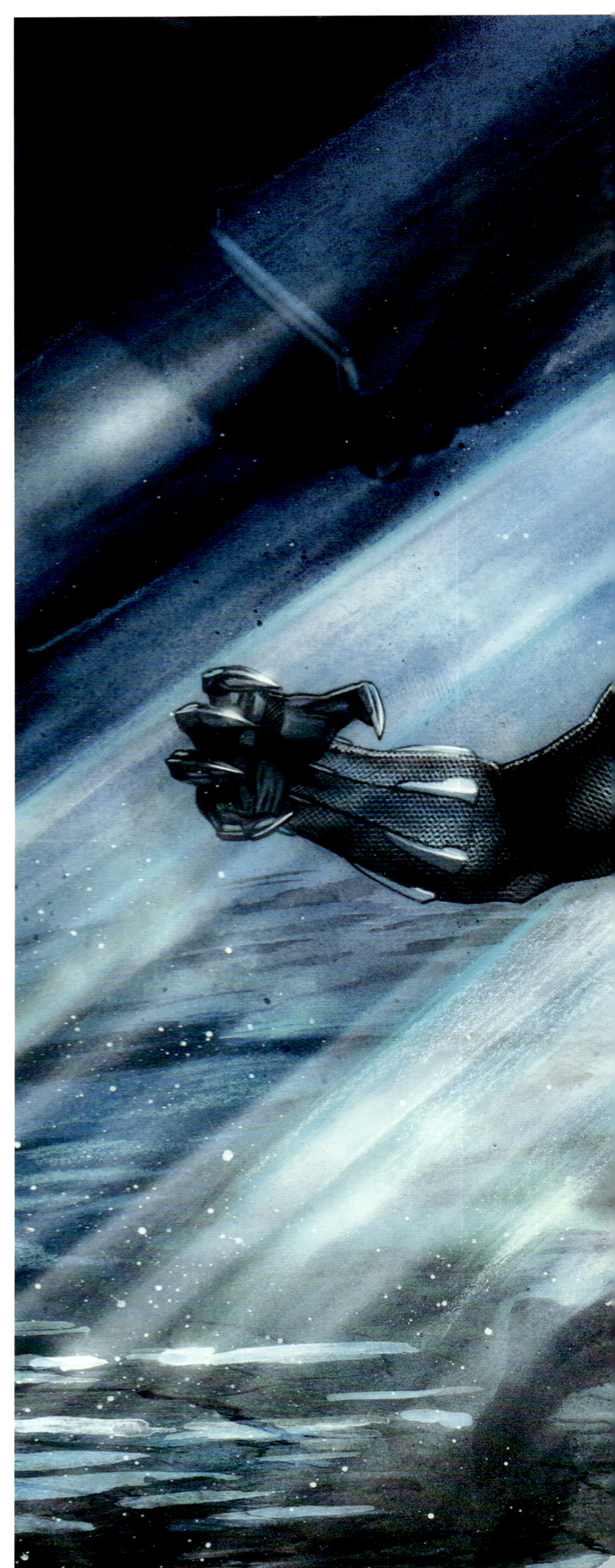

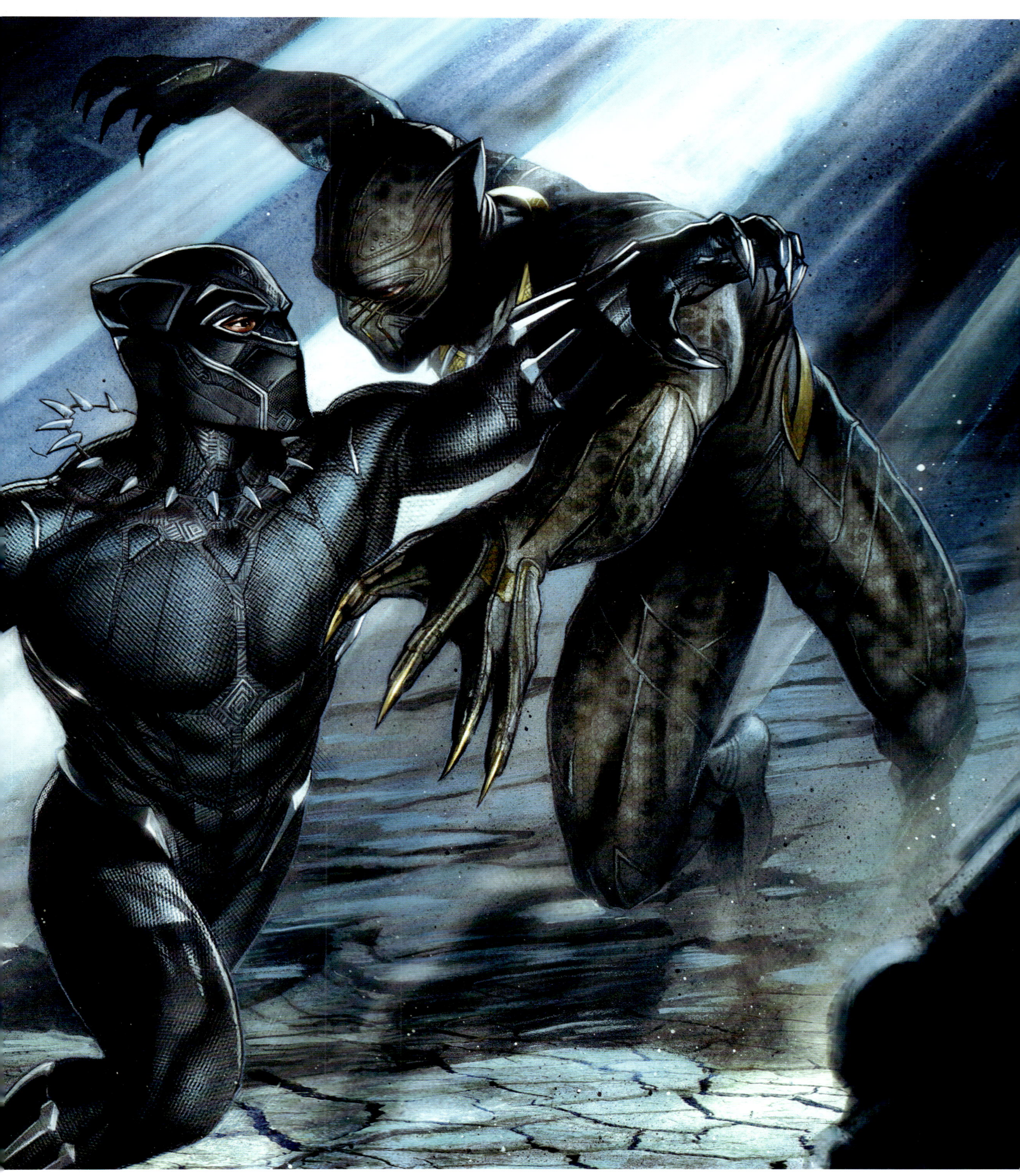

SUPERMAN

ALEX PASCENKO & IAN MACDONALD

The Last Son of Krypton bravely stands between Earth and his nemesis Brainiac. As a symbol of hope to all, the determined Superman will not bow to the Coluan conqueror.

In this colorful scene, Superman flies out of the clutches of Brainiac's tentacled skull ship, which serves as an extension of the villain's own mind and body.

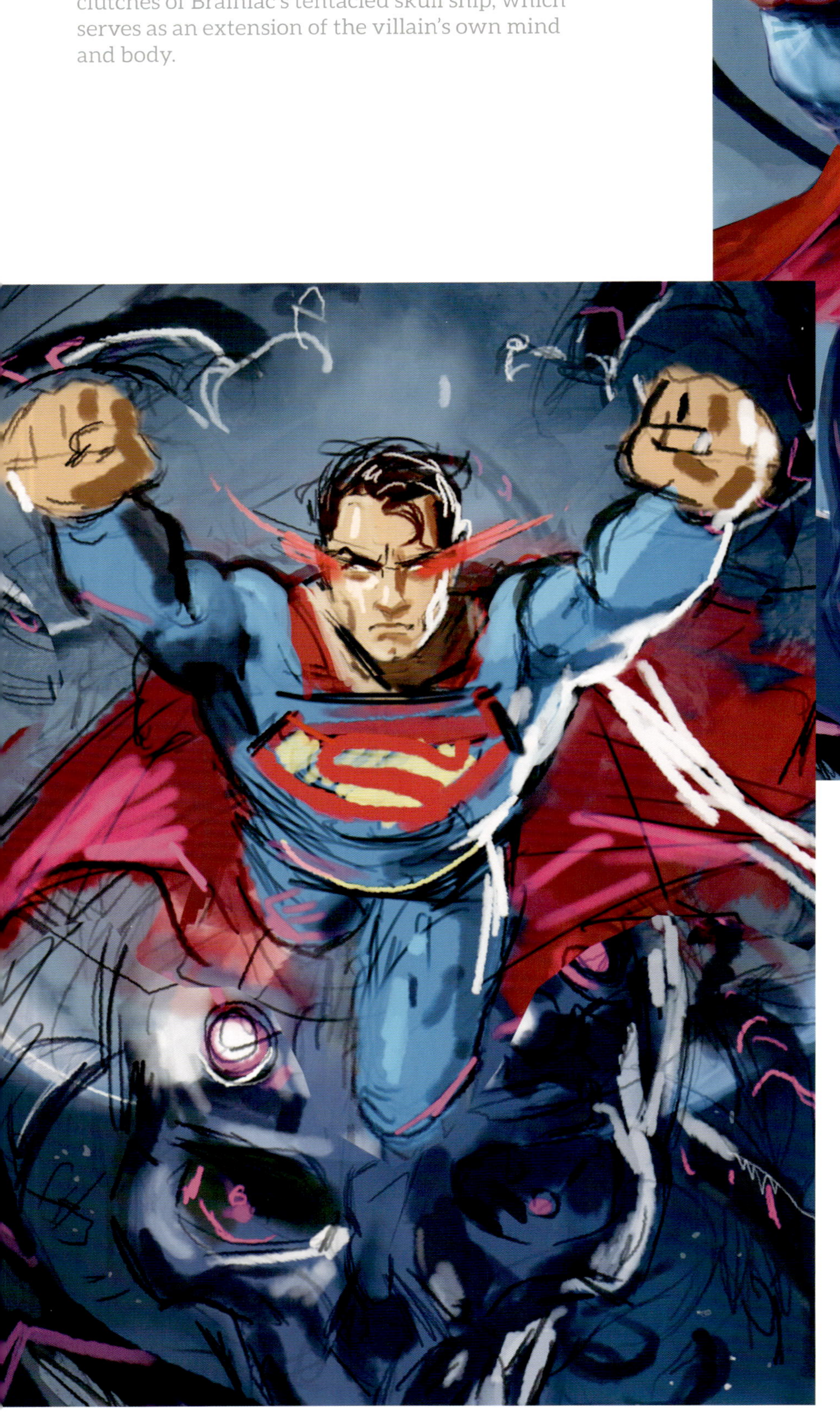

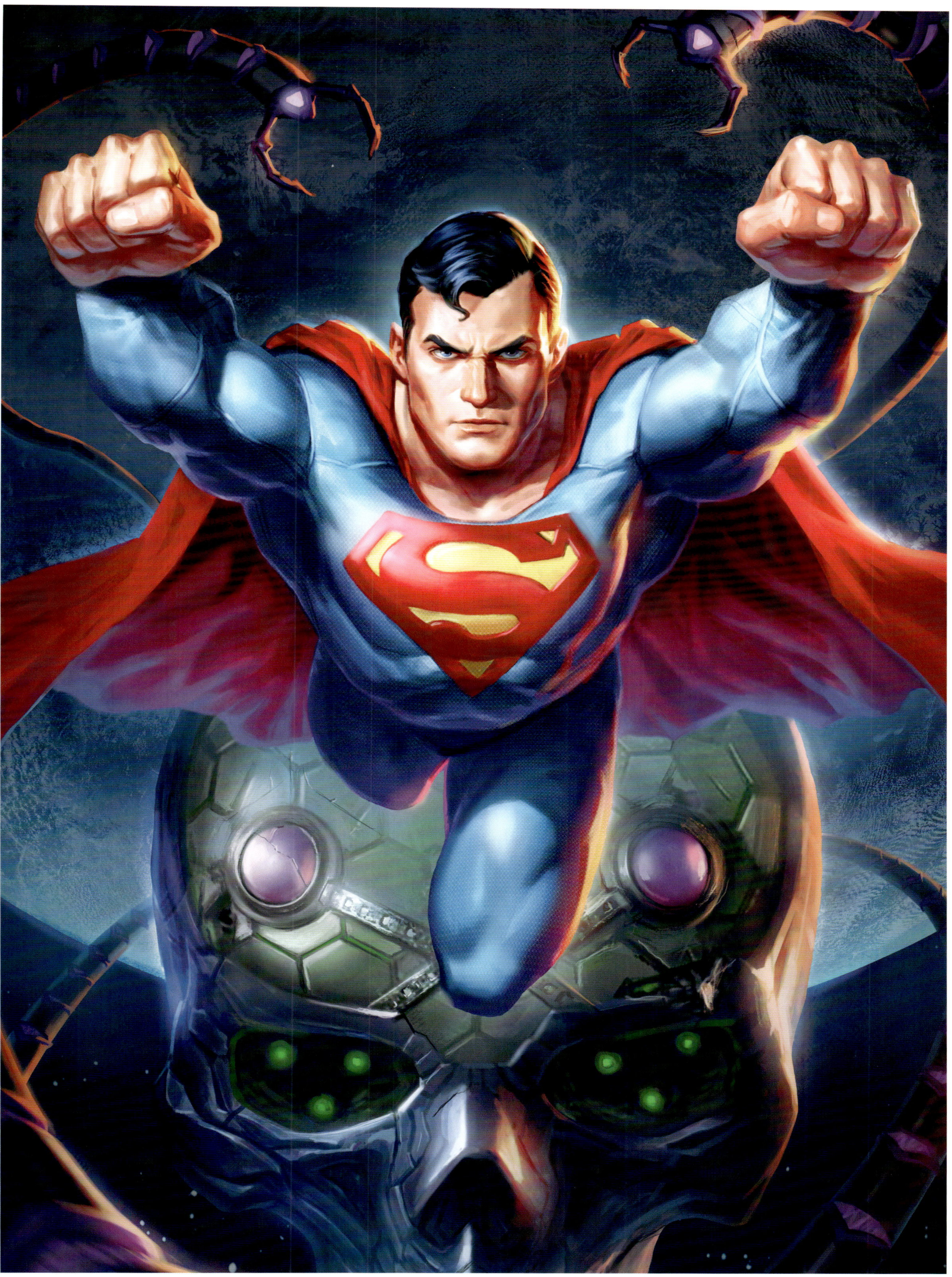

GALLEVARBE EVISCERATOR

OLIVIA DE BERARDINIS

In delightfully bright and aggressive hues, Olivia De Berardinis depicts the vicious mortal soul hunter Gallevarbe delivering savage justice. Court of the Dead creator Tom Gilliland helped guide and inspire Berardinis in the creation of this masterpiece.

"Olivia has captured the explosive nature of Gallevarbe, a mortal scorned, who is now taking her revenge from beyond the grave," explains Gilliland. "Gallevarbe takes no prisoners and eviscerates all those who oppose her." As a member of the Faction of Flesh, Gallevarbe is freed from the constraints of human form and can shapeshift at will. She is pictured here in a unique transformation, acting as judge, jury, and executioner, and carrying out her sentence in one fell swoop.

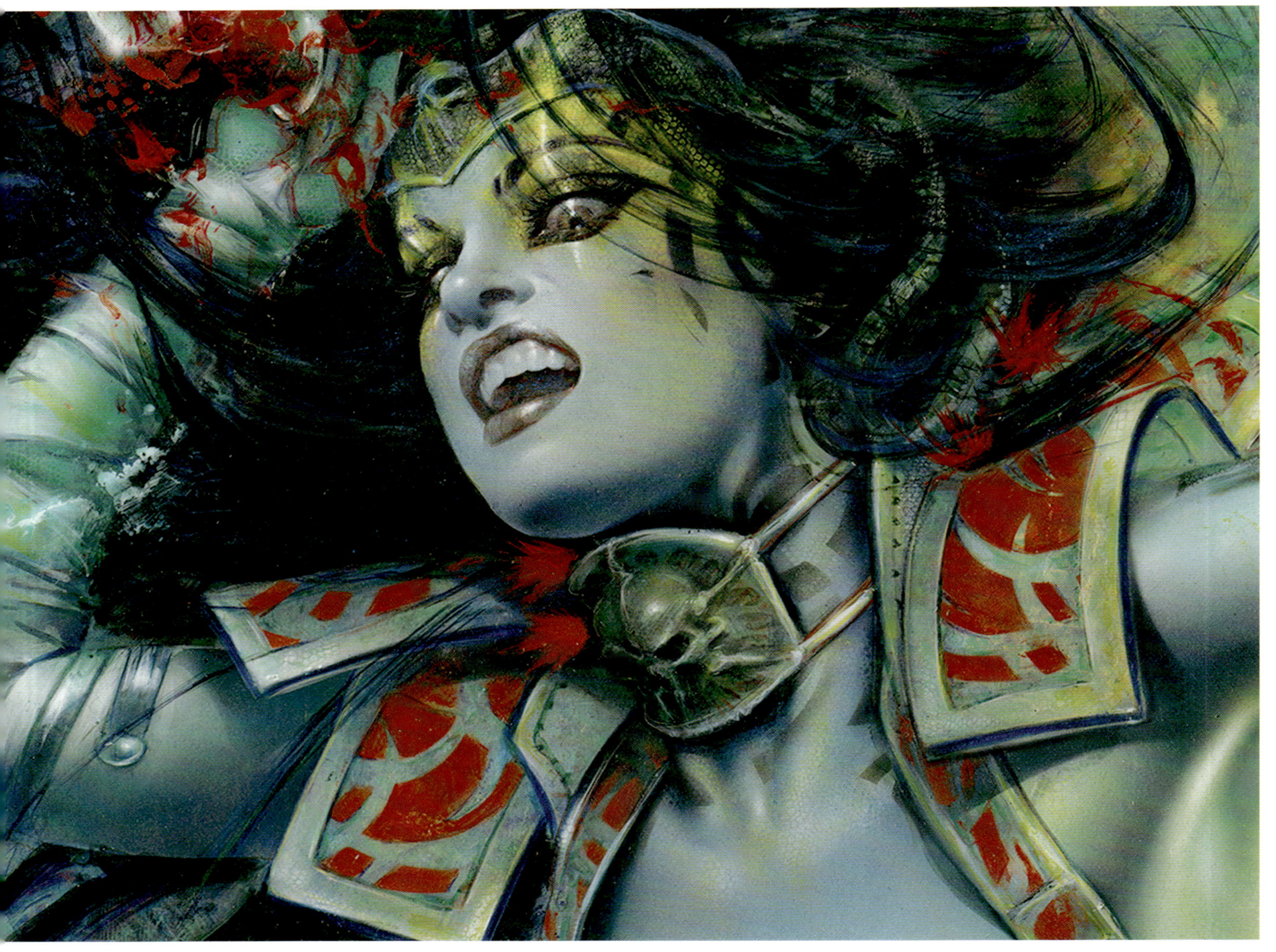

Gallervarbe: Eviscerator © 2018 Olivia De Berardinis

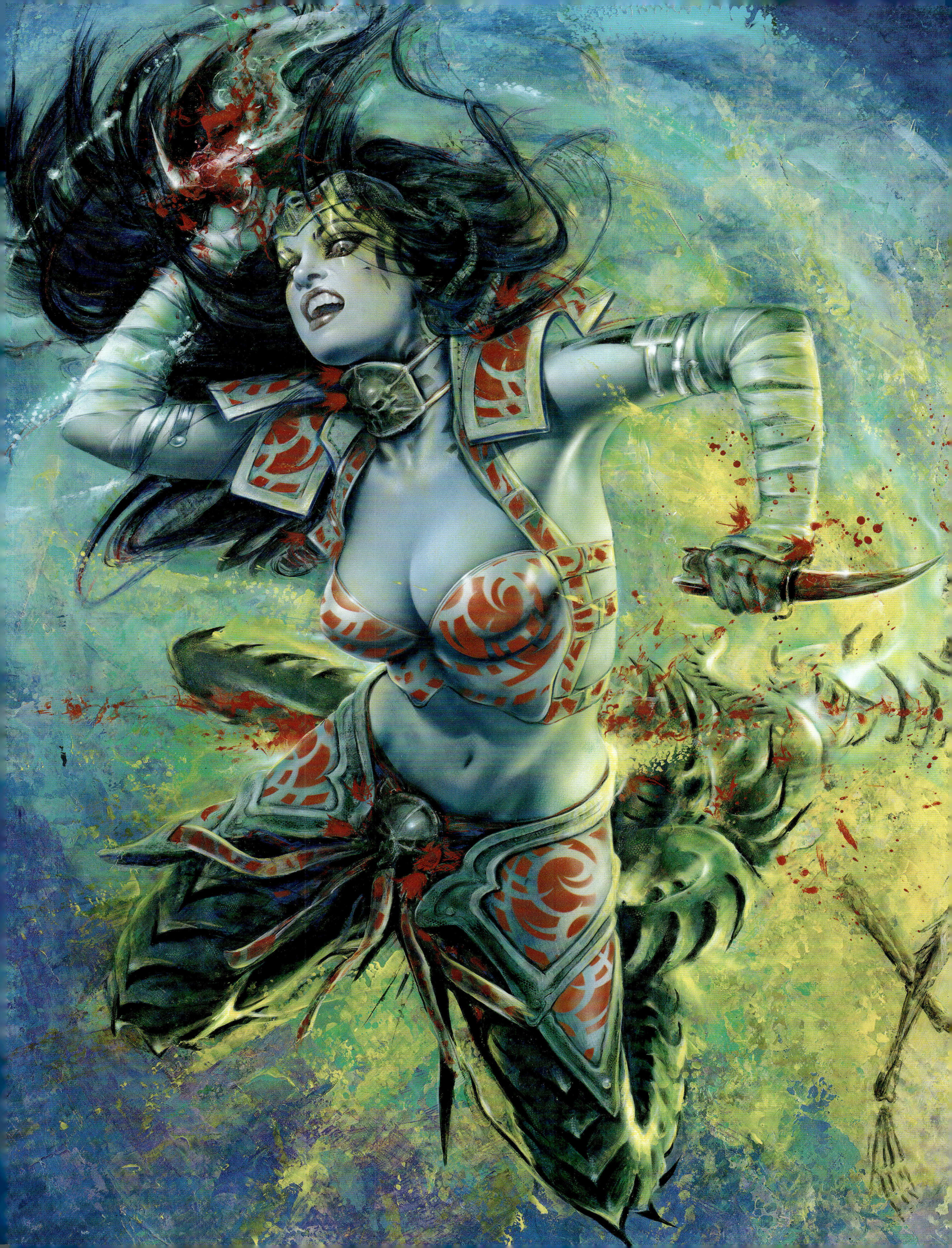

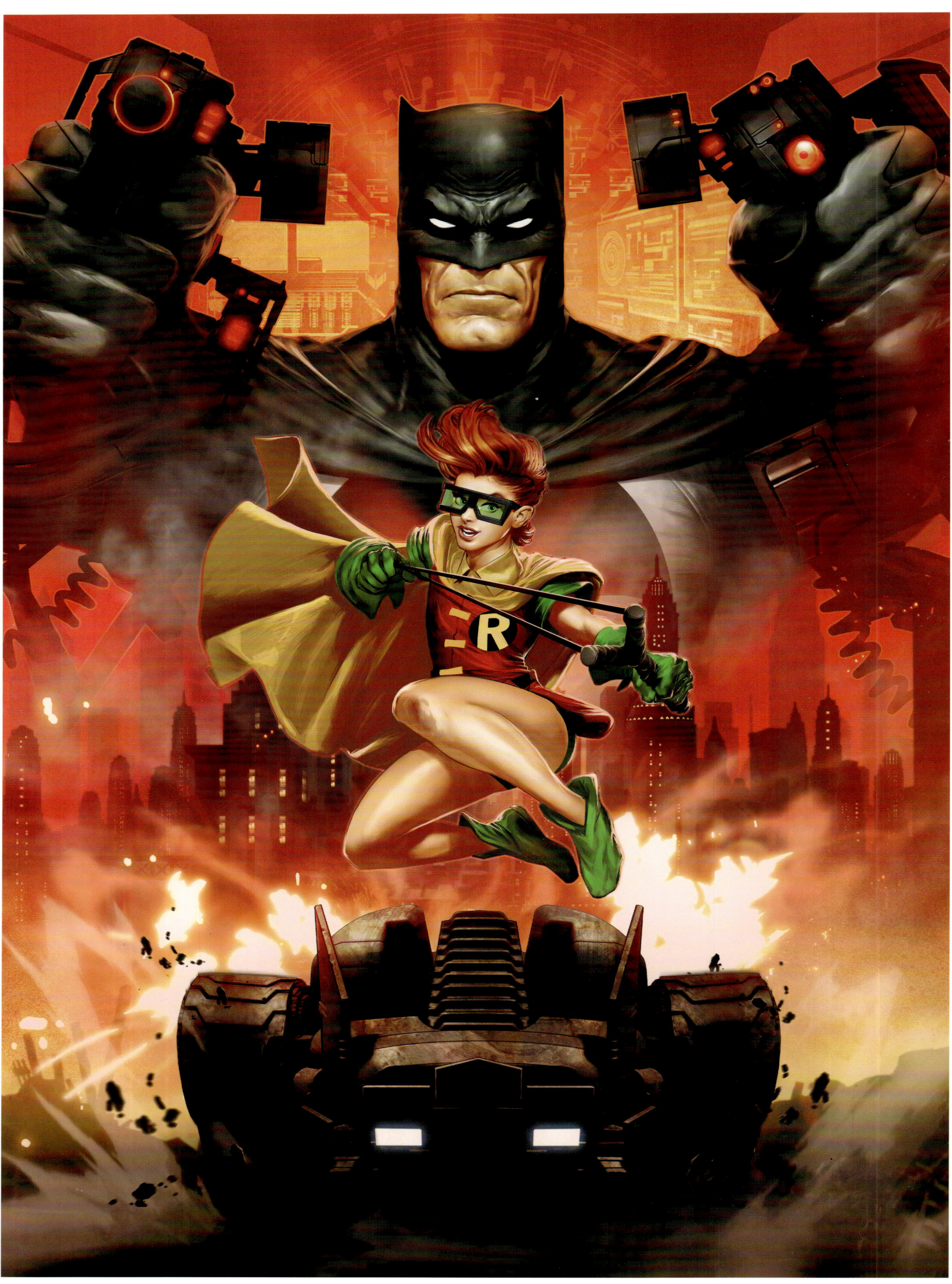

BATMAN

THE DARK KNIGHT RETURNS

DAVE WILKINS

Inspired by the seminal DC Comics miniseries, the *Batman: The Dark Knight Returns* Premium Art Print features the dynamic dystopian duo of Batman and Robin as they launch into action to protect Gotham City.

The Batmobile races into the foreground, with Bruce Wayne piloting his armored vehicle, surrounded by orange grids and display panels. Meanwhile, Carrie Kelley aims her slingshot, leaping into the fray.

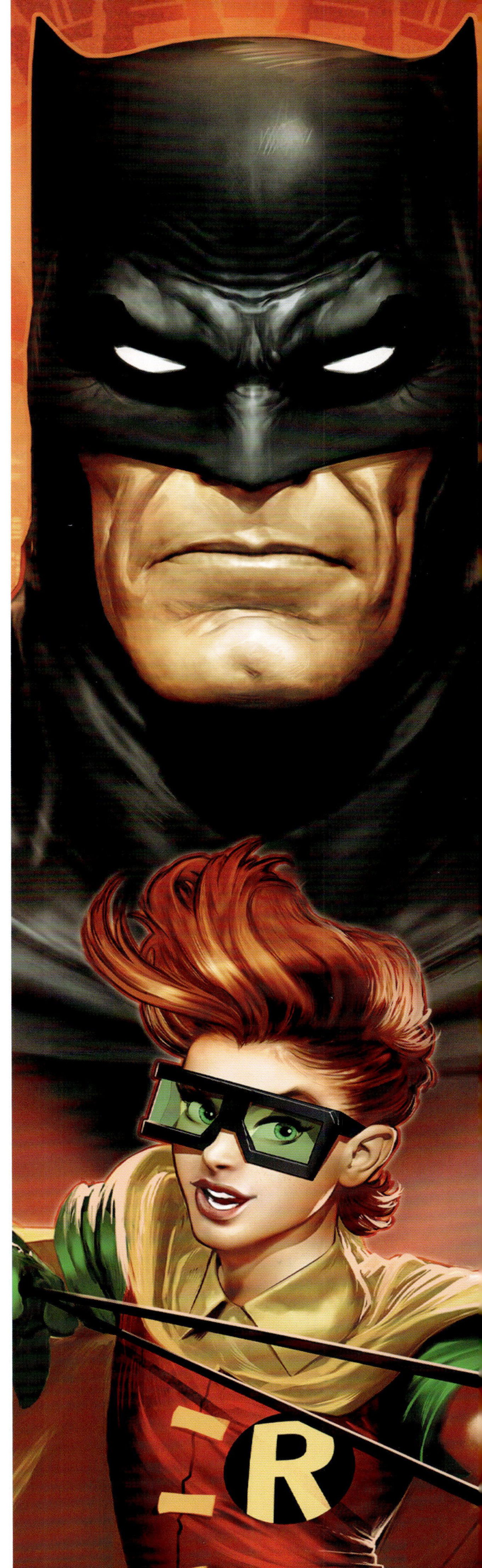

DOCTOR STRANGE OMNIBUS

ALEX ROSS

Dr. Stephen Strange projects his ghostly astral form in a dazzling display of his true magical might, channeling his immense mystic powers through the Eye of Agamotto.

This supernatural rendition of the iconic Marvel superhero was originally created as a book cover for a compilation of classic Doctor Strange comics and has been specially reproduced by Sideshow as a limited edition Fine Art Print.

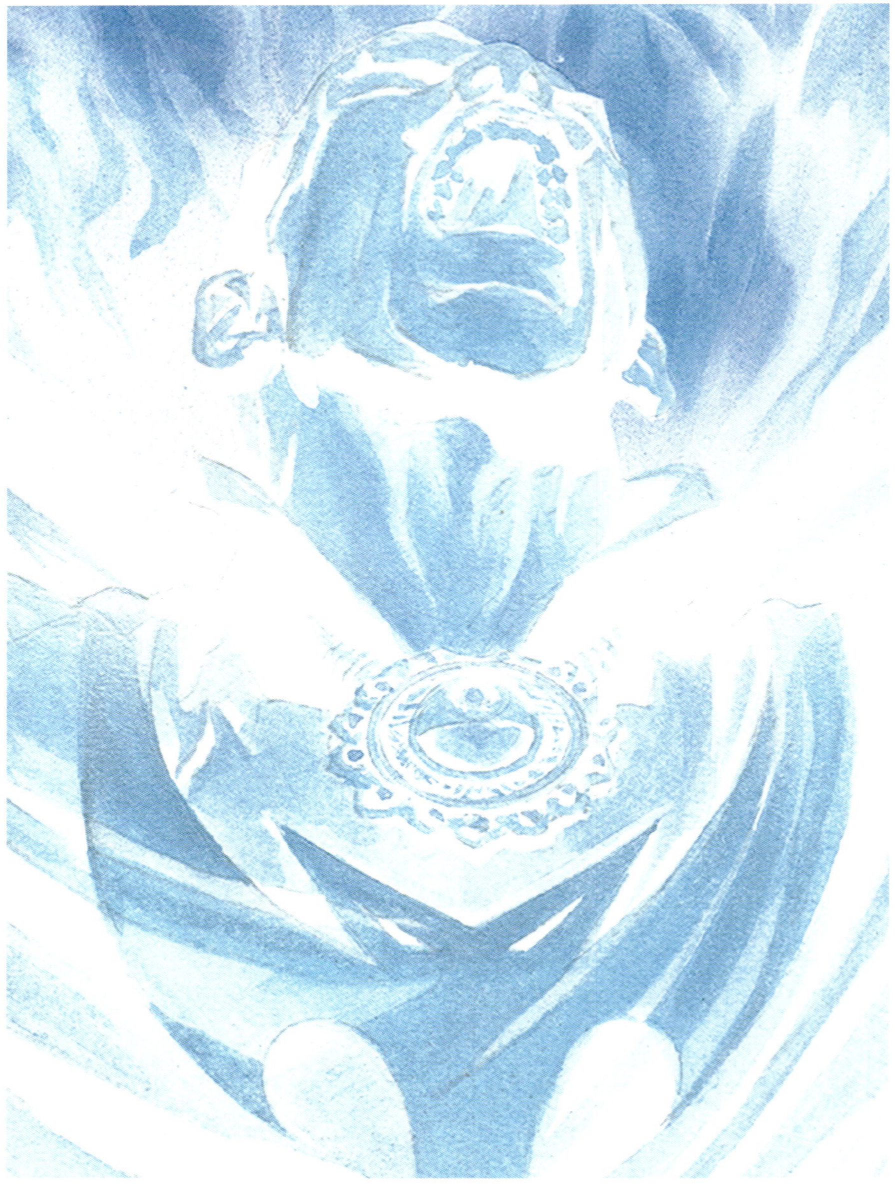

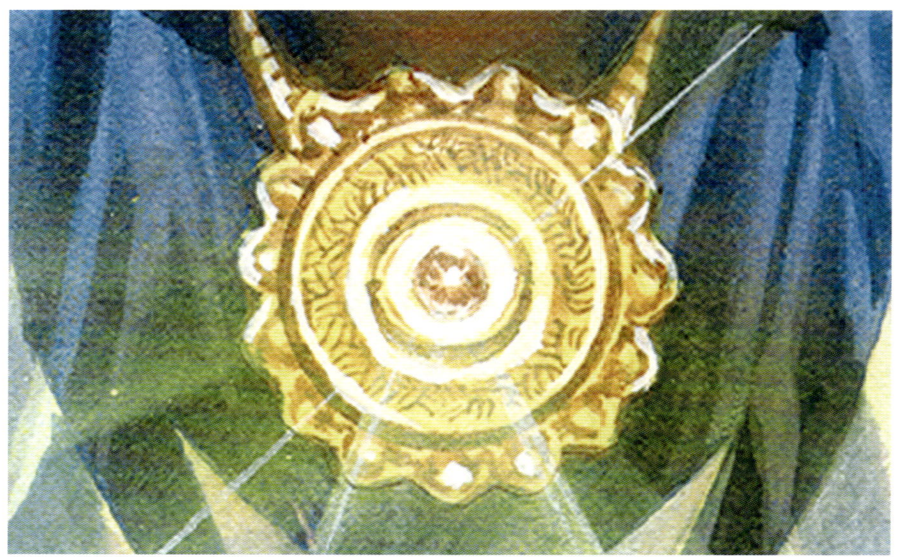

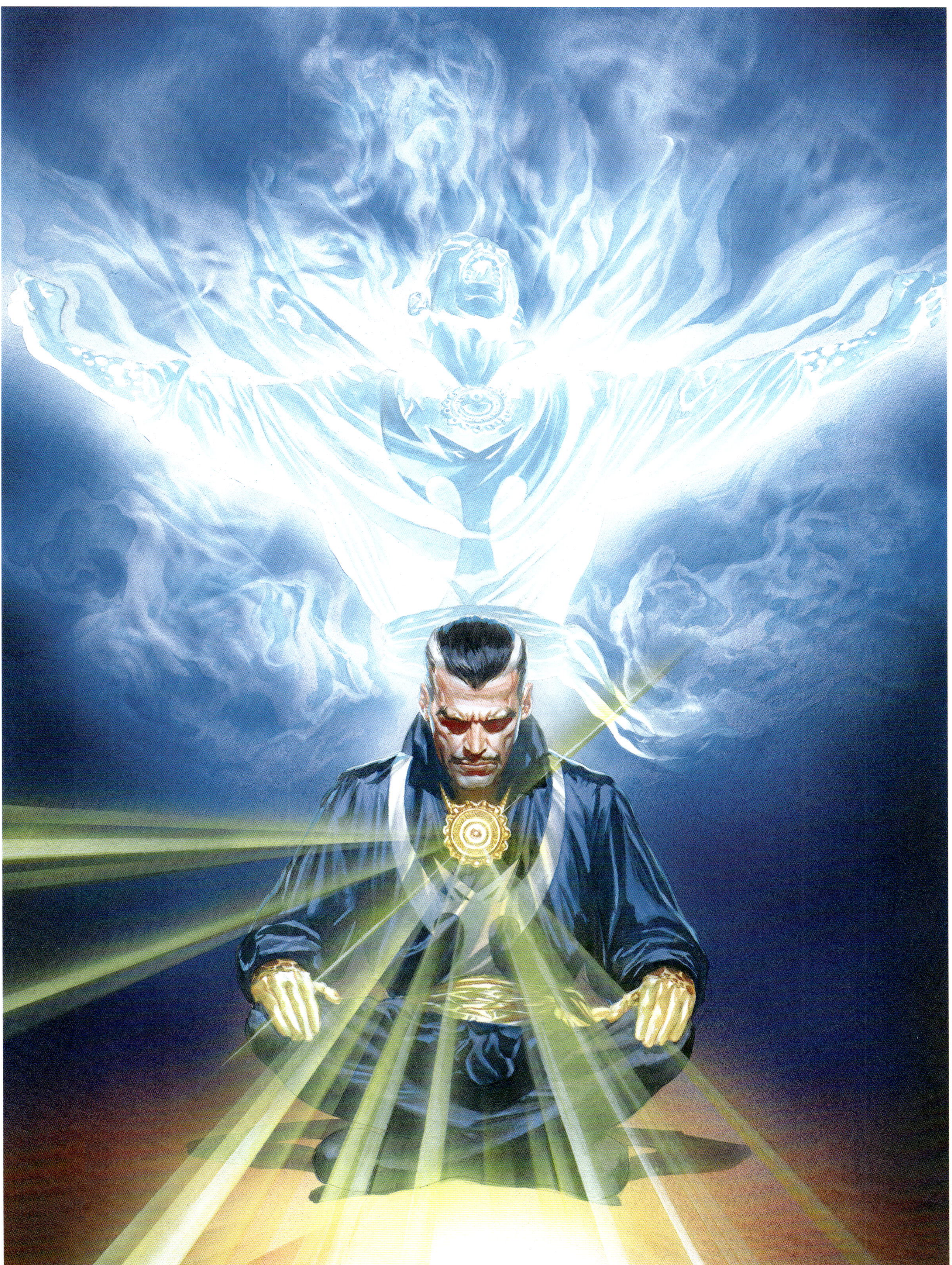

EMMA FROST

IAN MACDONALD

The talented mutant telepath Emma Frost demonstrates the sheer strength of her mental abilities as she takes a stand in the X-Men's Cerebro room. Tough as diamonds, she focuses her psionic energies as the debris of battle hovers around her, levitated by her immense power.

Dressed in her iconic white costume, Emma Frost is ready to wield her mind against any threat foolish enough to face her.

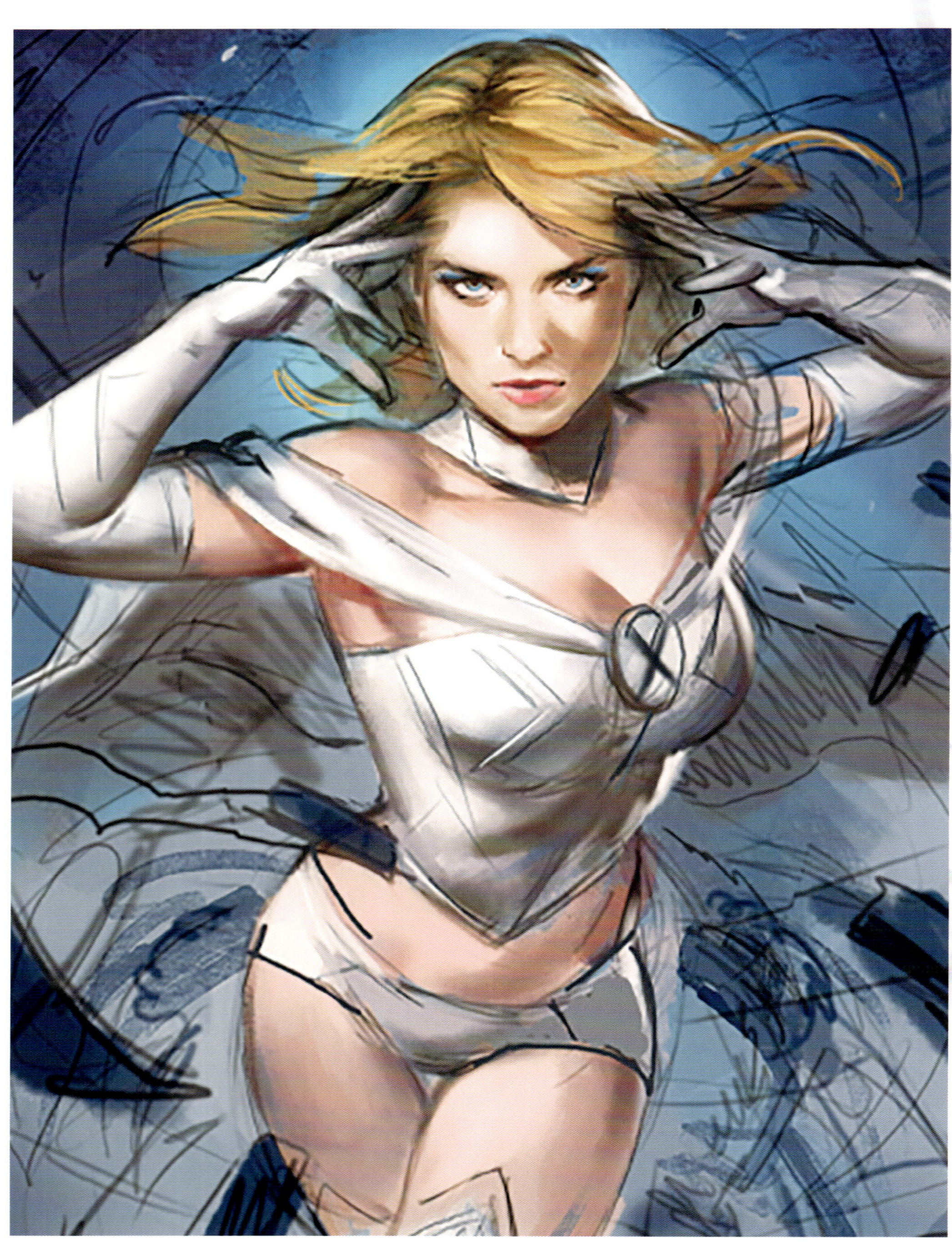

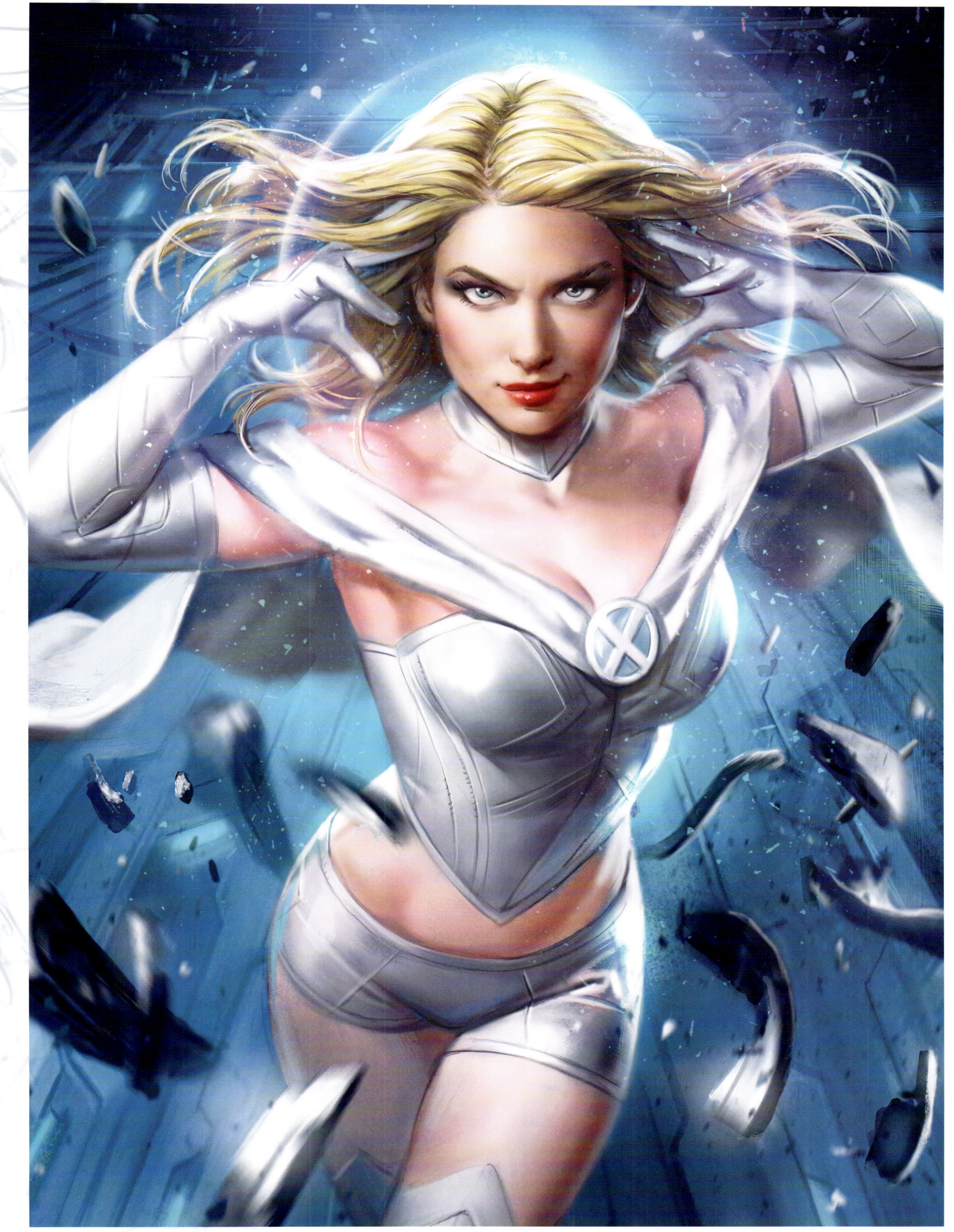

MARVEL GENERATIONS

ALEX ROSS

Originally created for the *Marvel Generations* series, this deluxe lithograph celebrates the legacy of Marvel's heroes with classic and modern incarnations of beloved characters.

The *Marvel Generations* fine art lithograph features dynamic pairings of heroes from the dawn of the Marvel Universe to today, including Iron Man and Ironheart, Captain Marvel and Ms. Marvel, and the two Spider-Men, Peter Parker and Miles Morales.

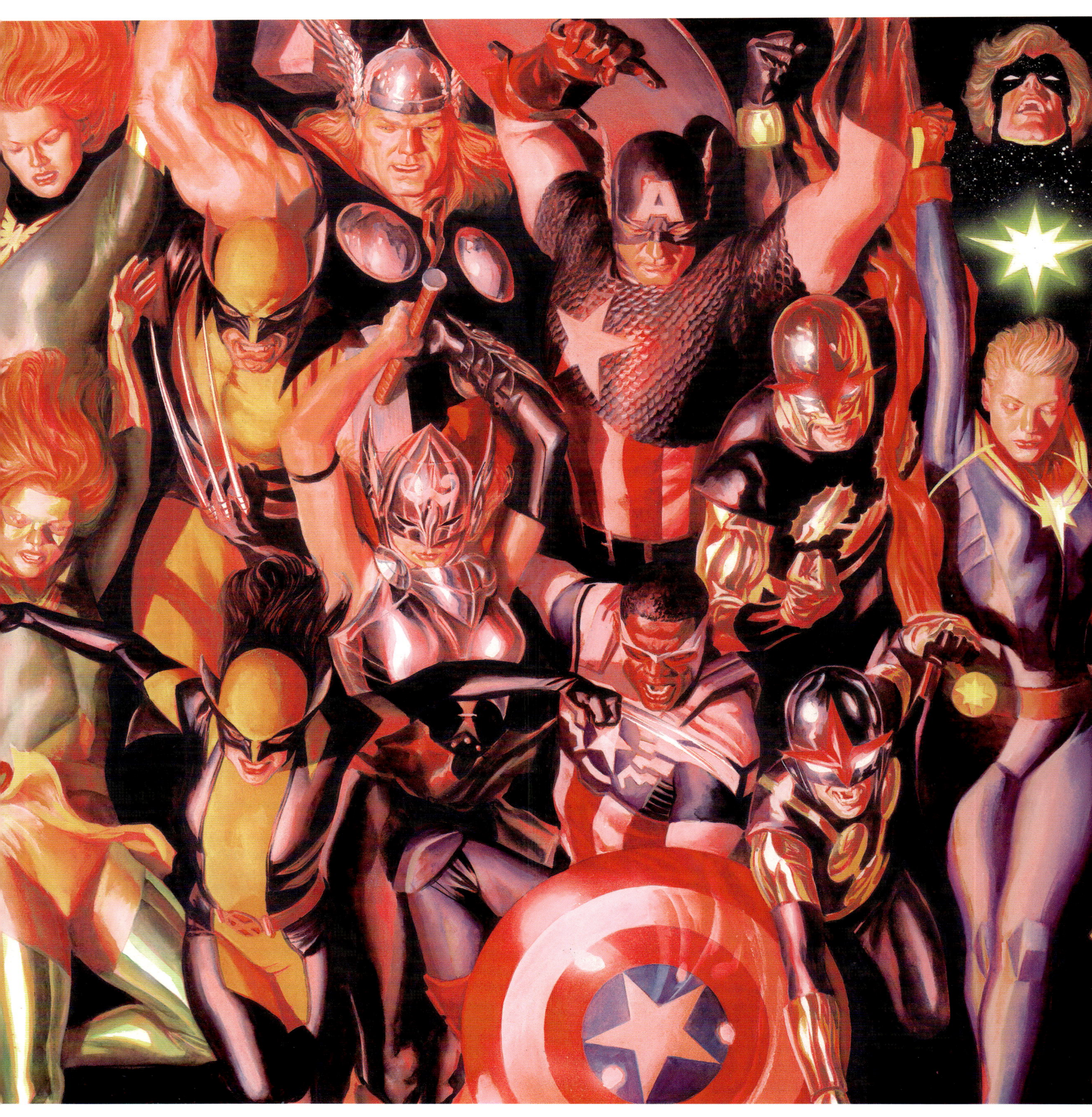

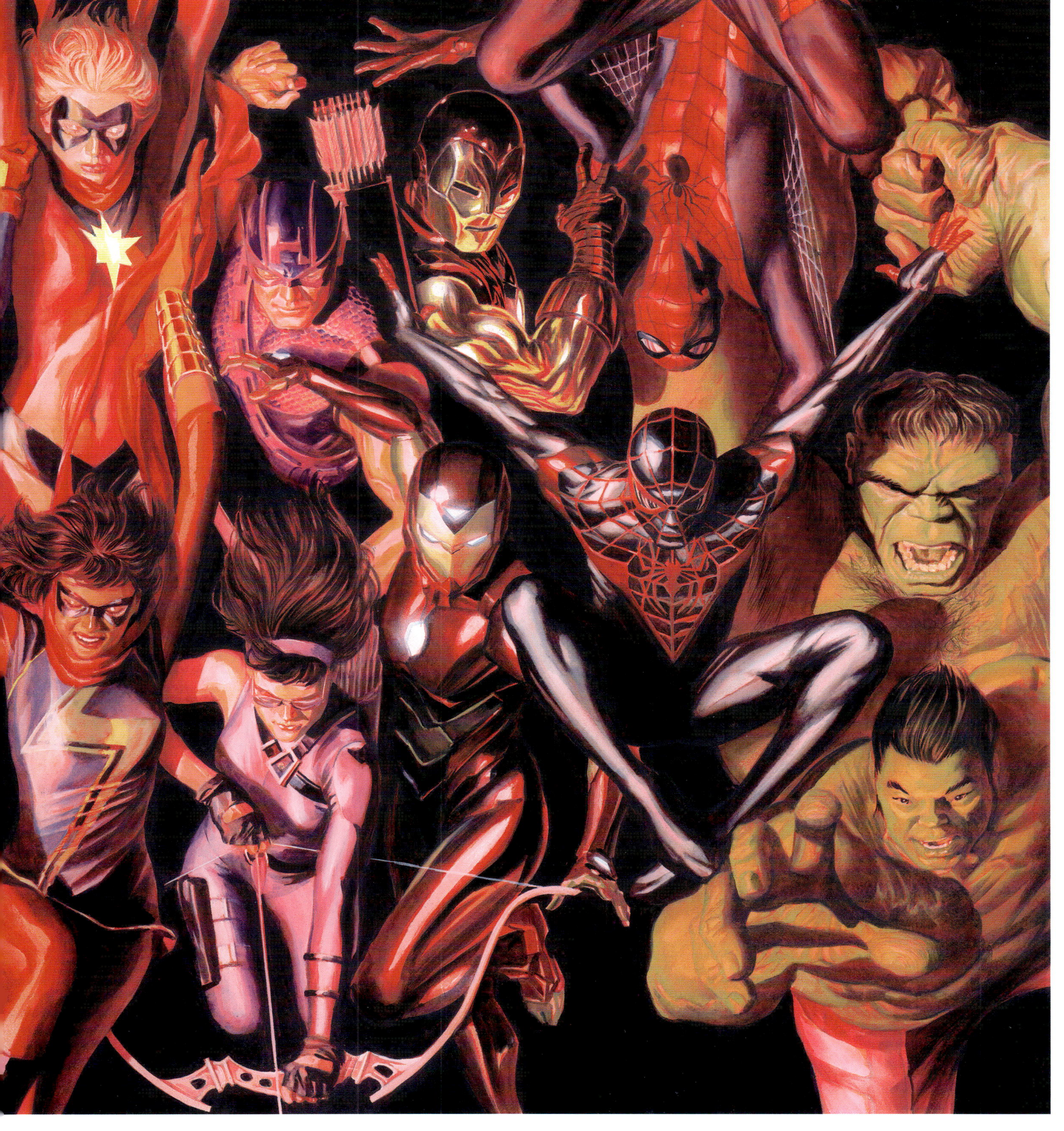

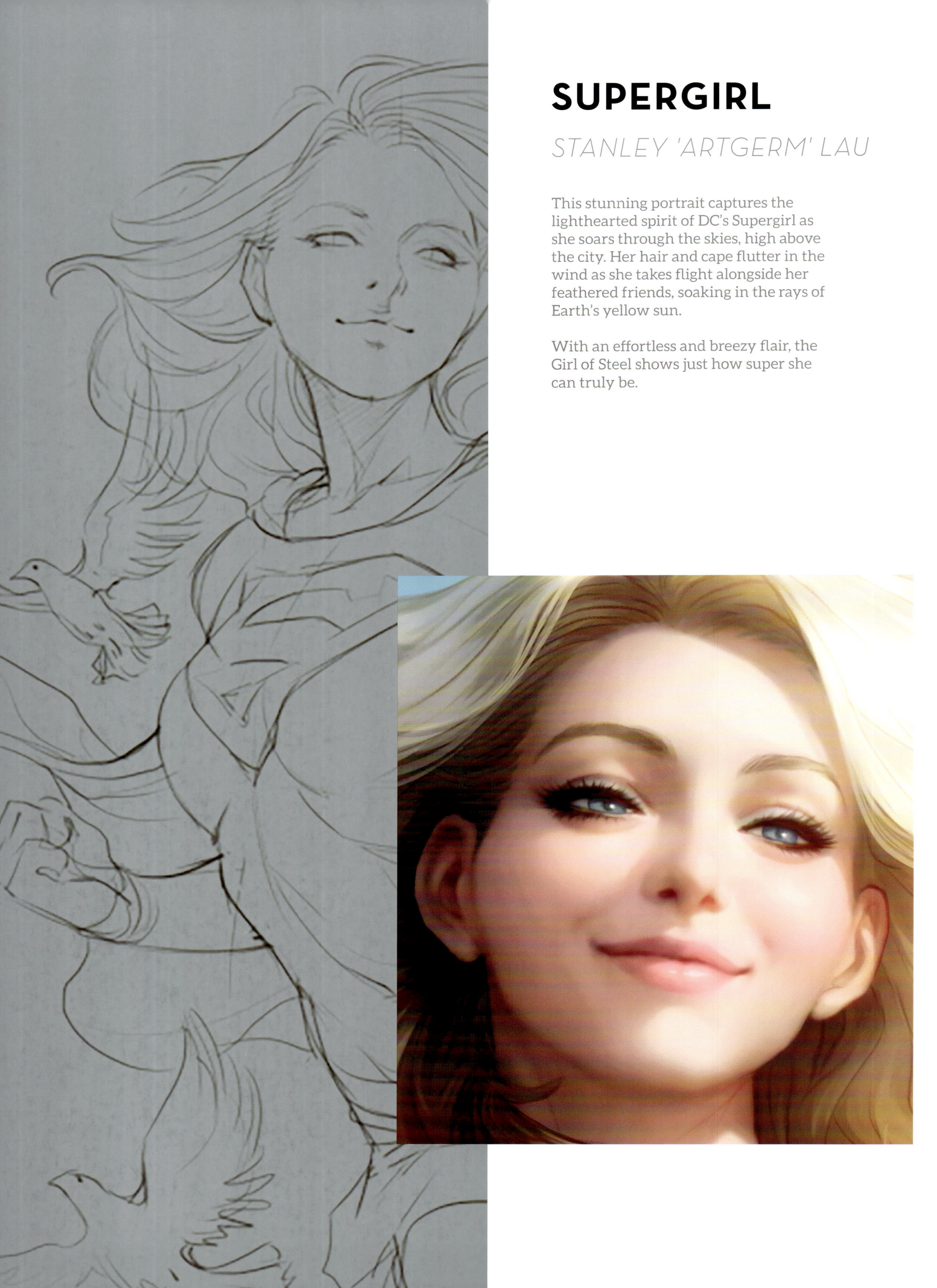

SUPERGIRL

STANLEY 'ARTGERM' LAU

This stunning portrait captures the lighthearted spirit of DC's Supergirl as she soars through the skies, high above the city. Her hair and cape flutter in the wind as she takes flight alongside her feathered friends, soaking in the rays of Earth's yellow sun.

With an effortless and breezy flair, the Girl of Steel shows just how super she can truly be.

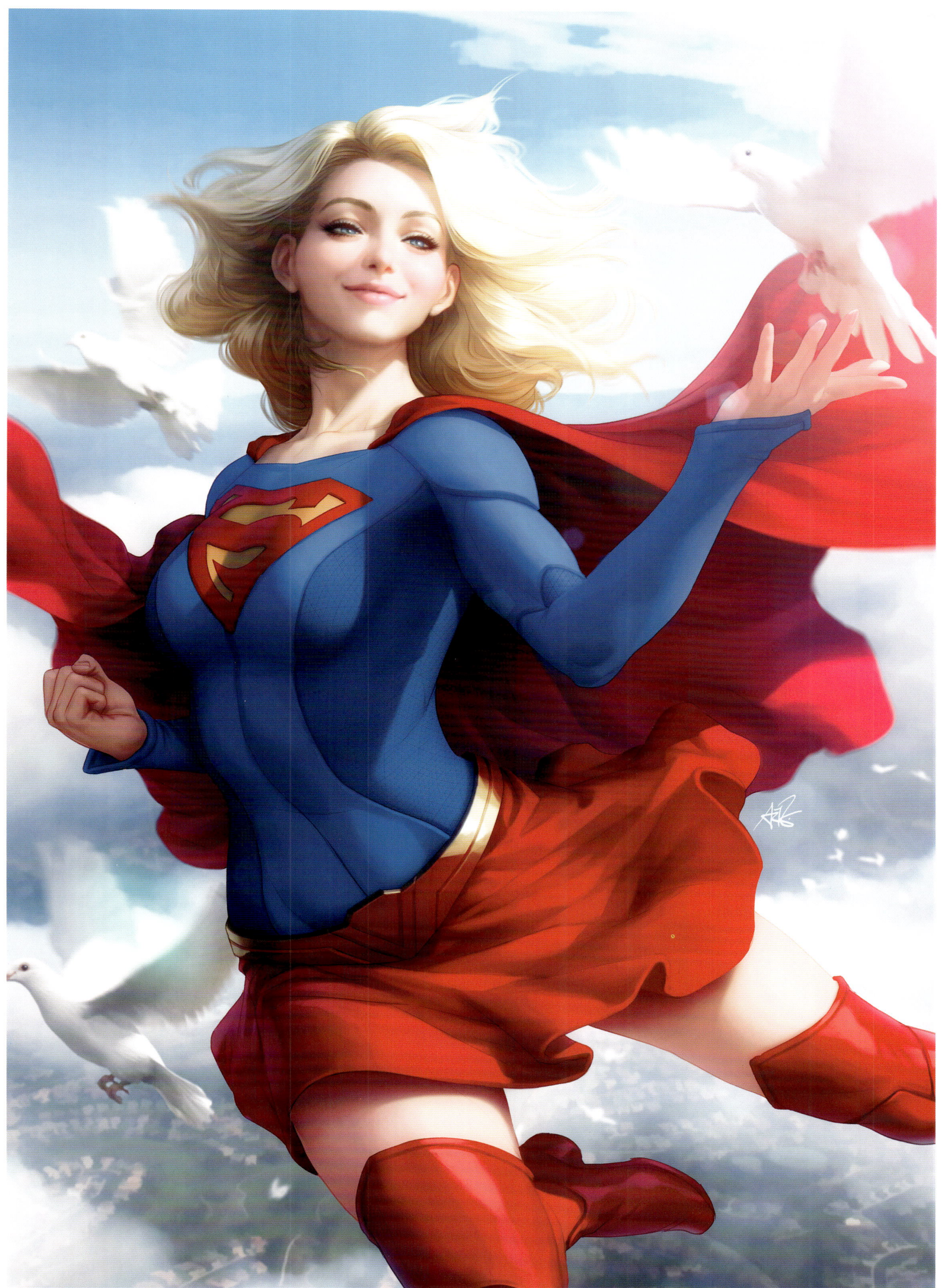

IRON MAN MARK III

ADI GRANOV

Part of the Marvel Studios Fine Art Print collection, this piece by Adi Granov conceptualizes an iconic action sequence from the original Iron Man film. "The flying Iron Man image came about from a conversation Jon [Favreau , the film's director] and I had after he saw a comic cover I did of Iron Man flying with military jets," explains Granov. "There was no script at the time, so I just painted a nice shot of Iron Man, and then the whole sequence in the film was written around that."

Flanked by military jets, Tony Stark must put his red-and-gold Mark III suit to the test as he narrowly avoids being shot out of the sky. This keyframe moment captures the high-octane energy of Iron Man in flight, ready to take on the world and prove himself an invincible hero.

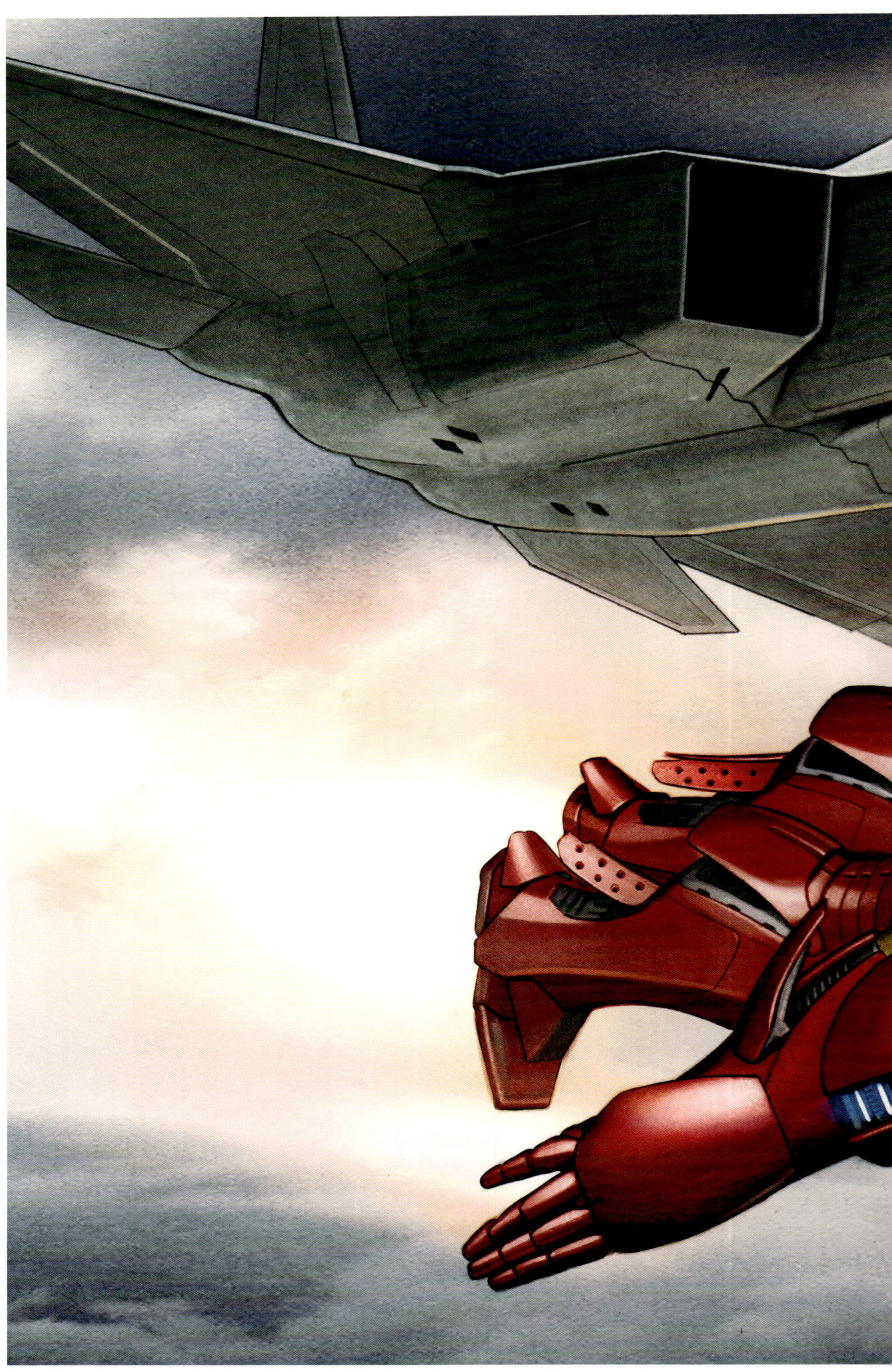

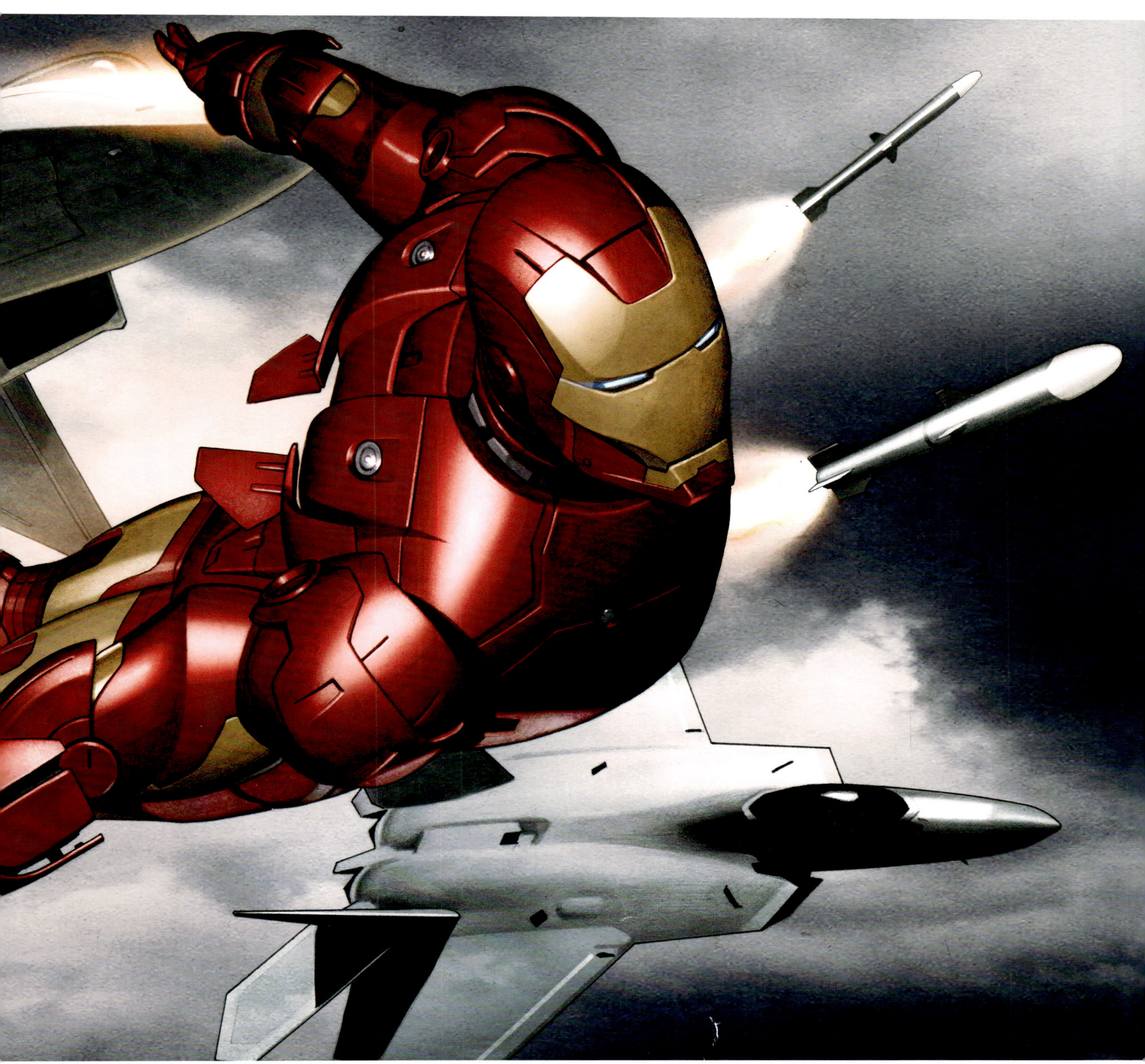

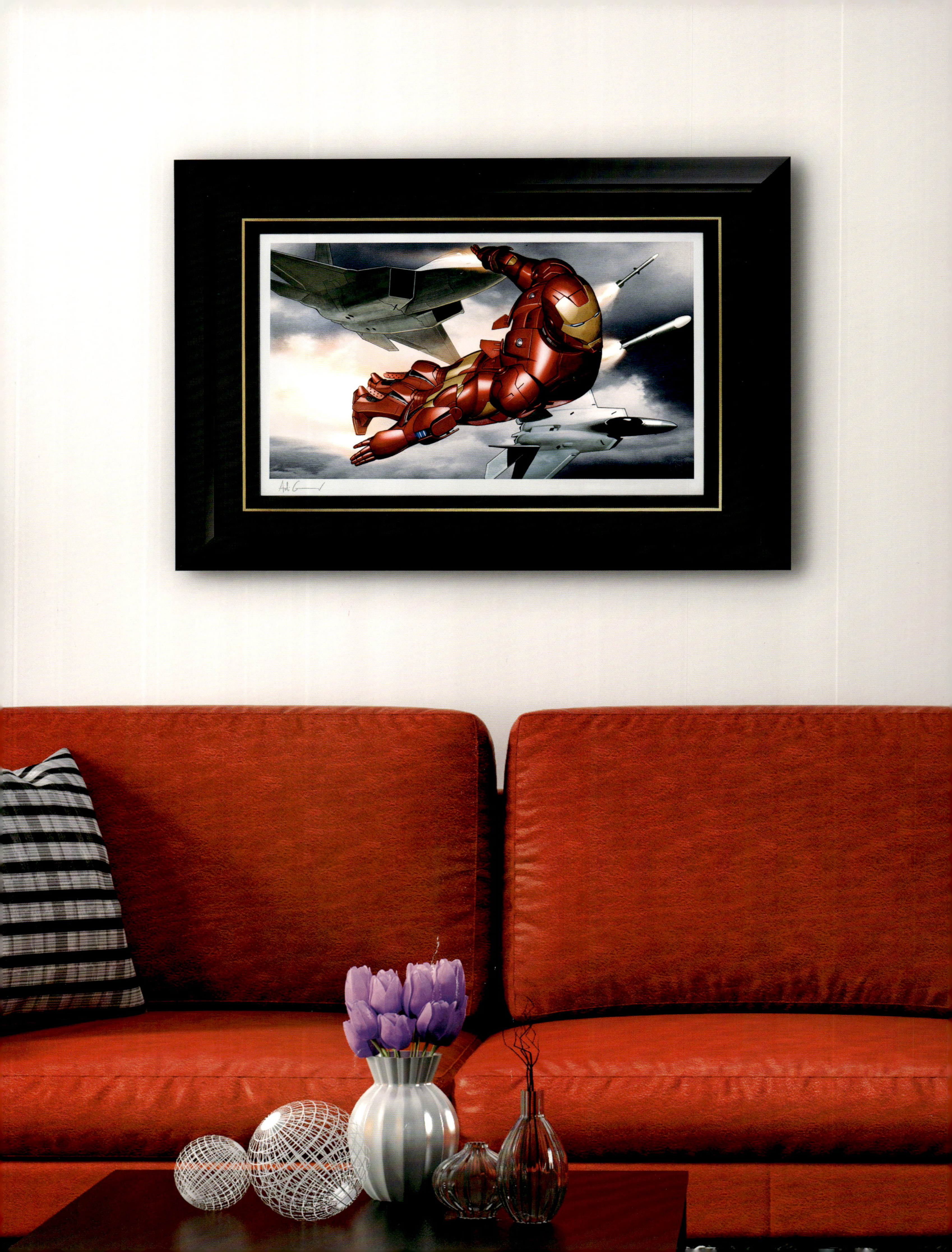

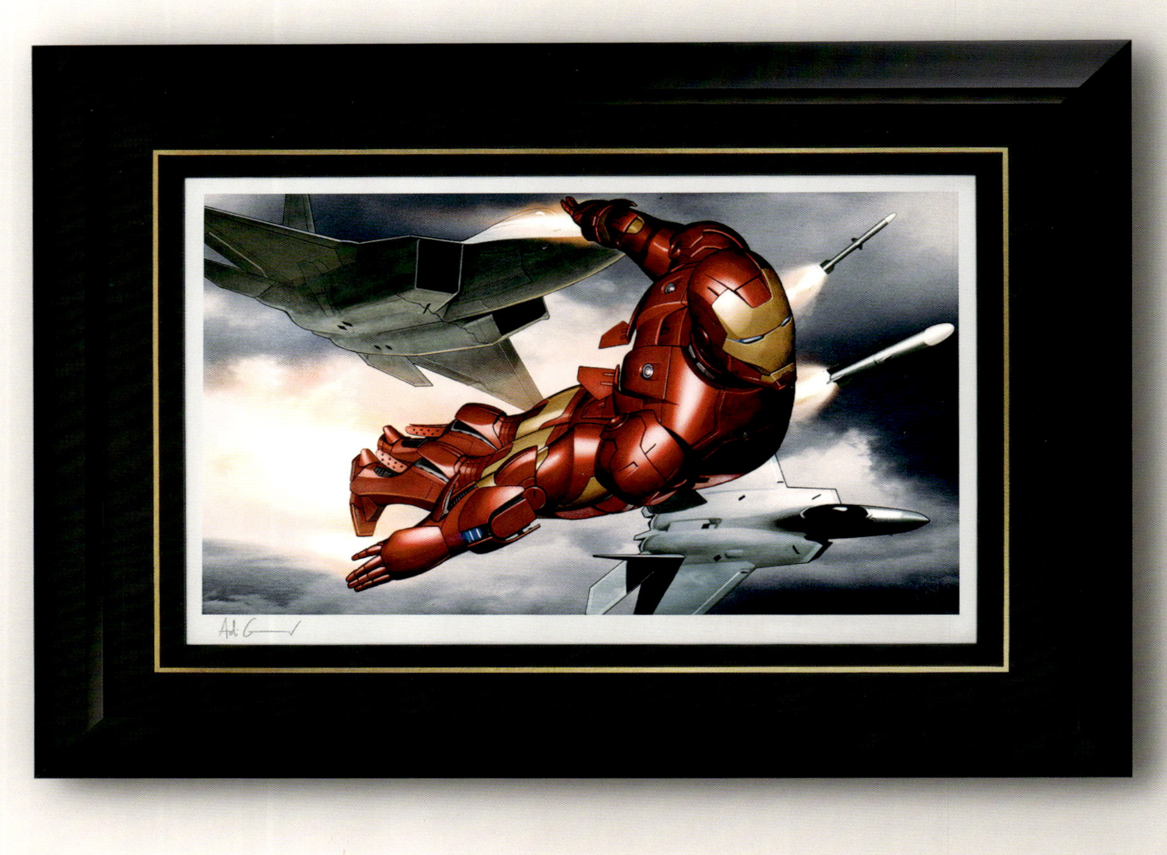

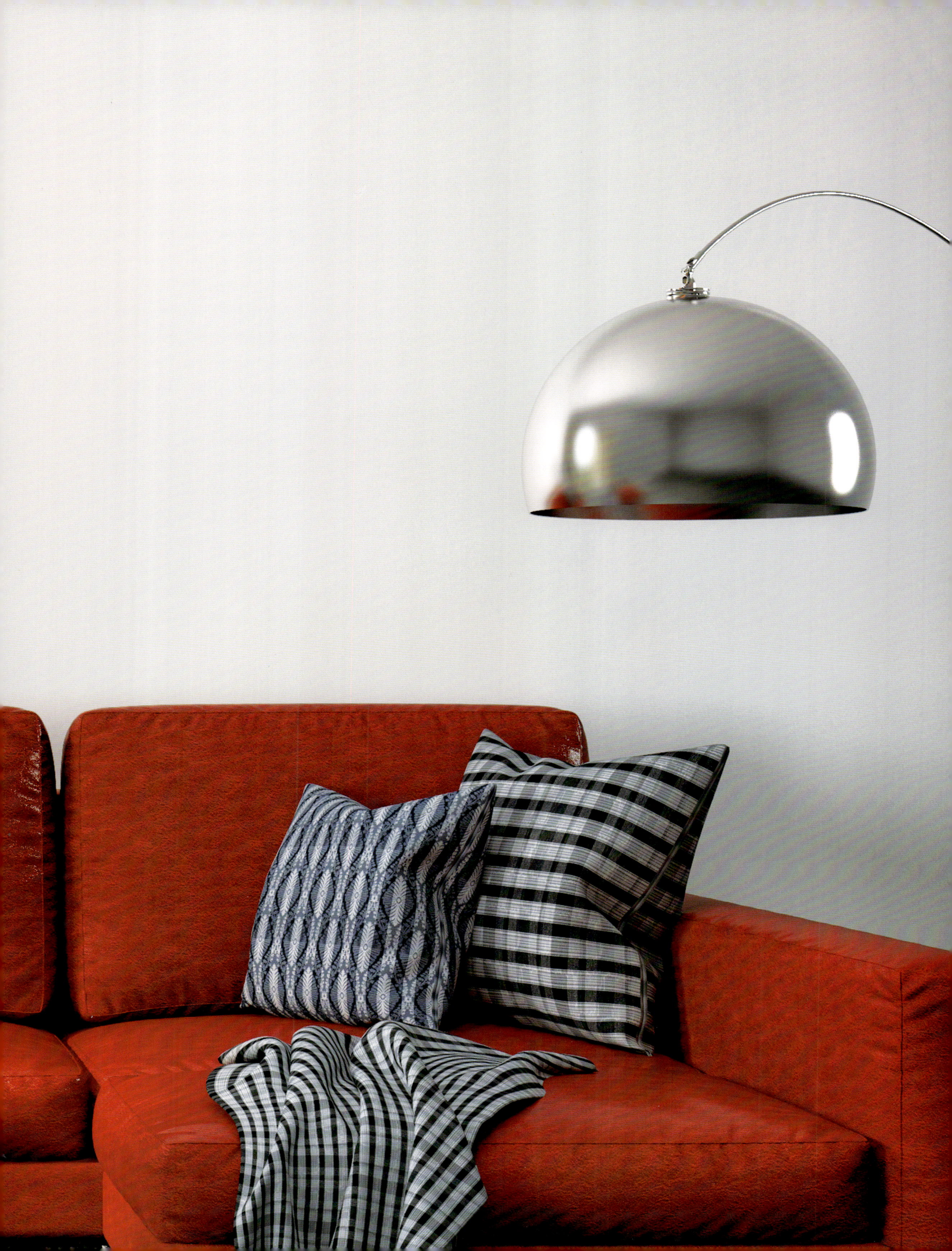

BATMAN THE DARK KNIGHT

BRIAN ROOD

Inspired by Christopher Nolan's acclaimed film *The Dark Knight*, this Fine Art Print features some of Gotham's most notable faces.

Brian Rood captures the duality of Harvey Dent, the delirium of the Joker, and the determination of Batman in this engaging composition that pays tribute to an iconic DC film. In the foreground, the Dark Knight drives the Batpod through the streets of Gotham while his greatest foe stands in wait, prepared to execute his next sickening scheme.

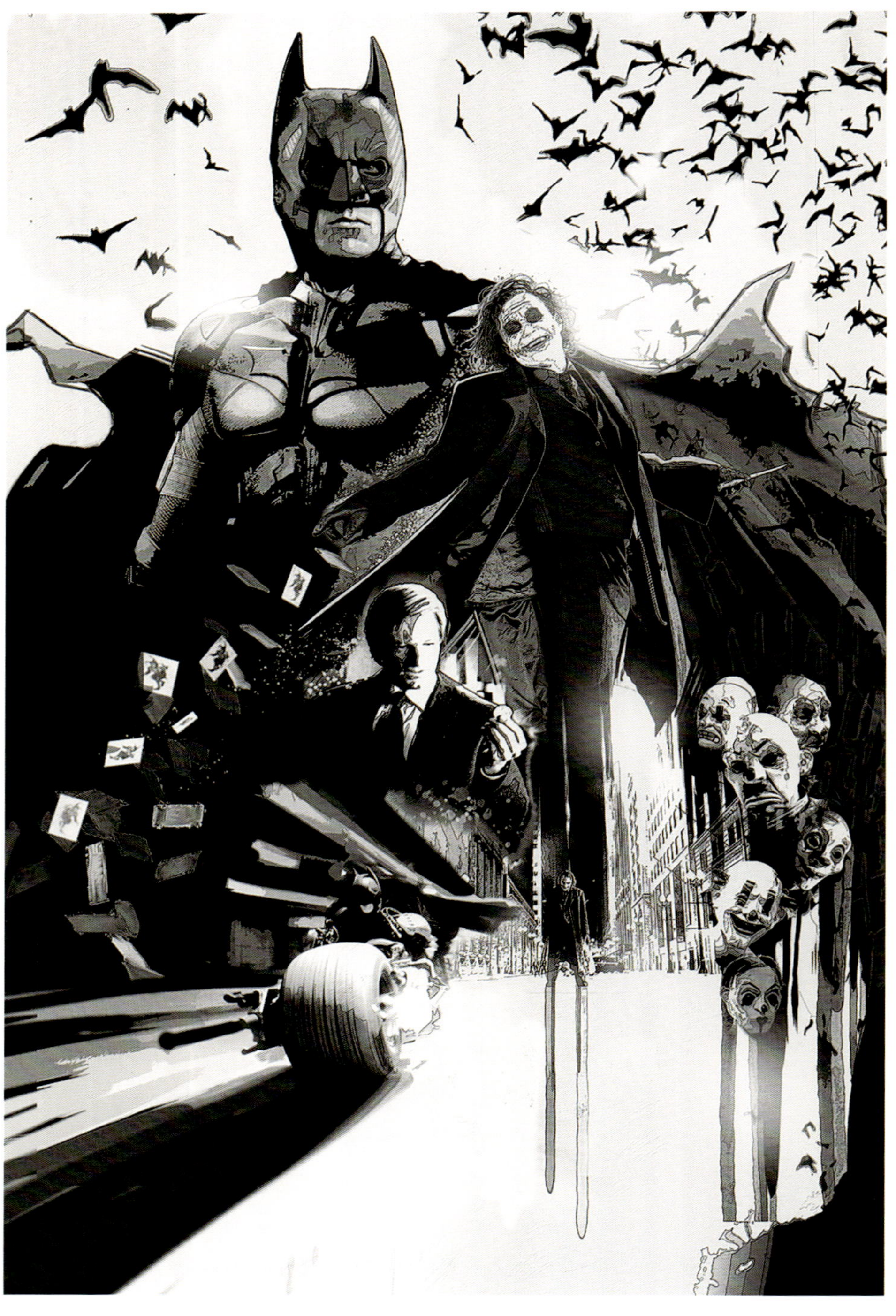

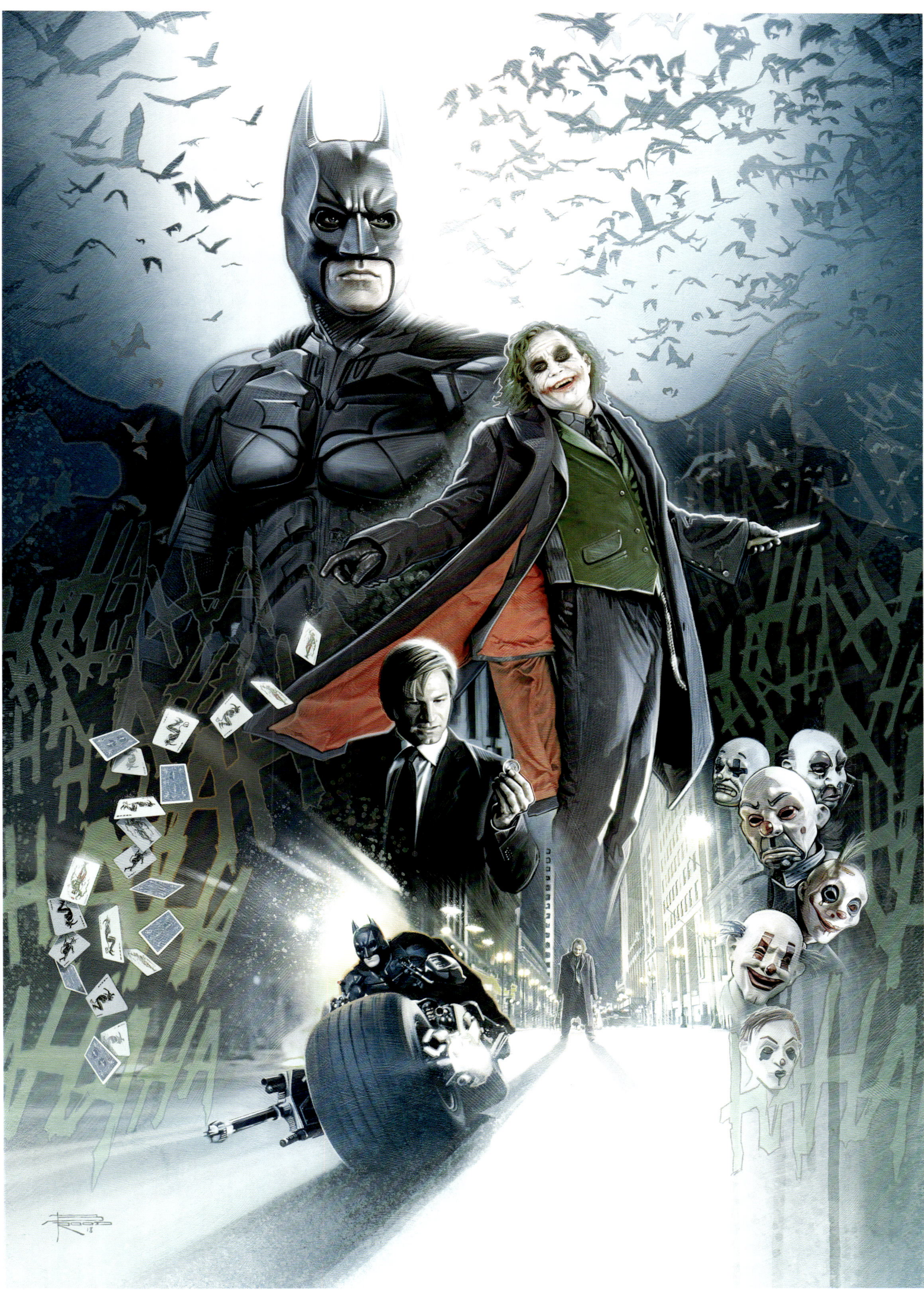

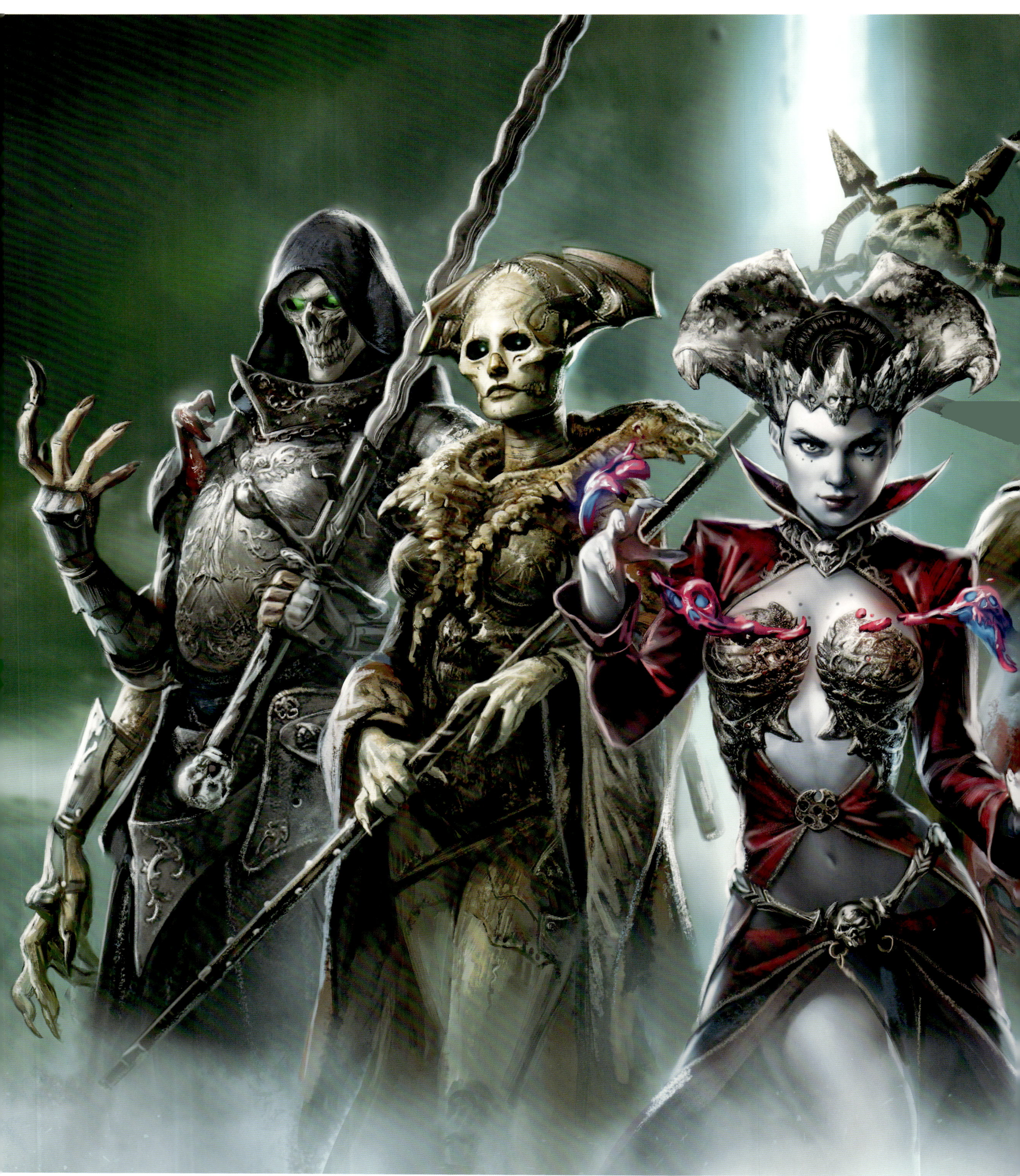

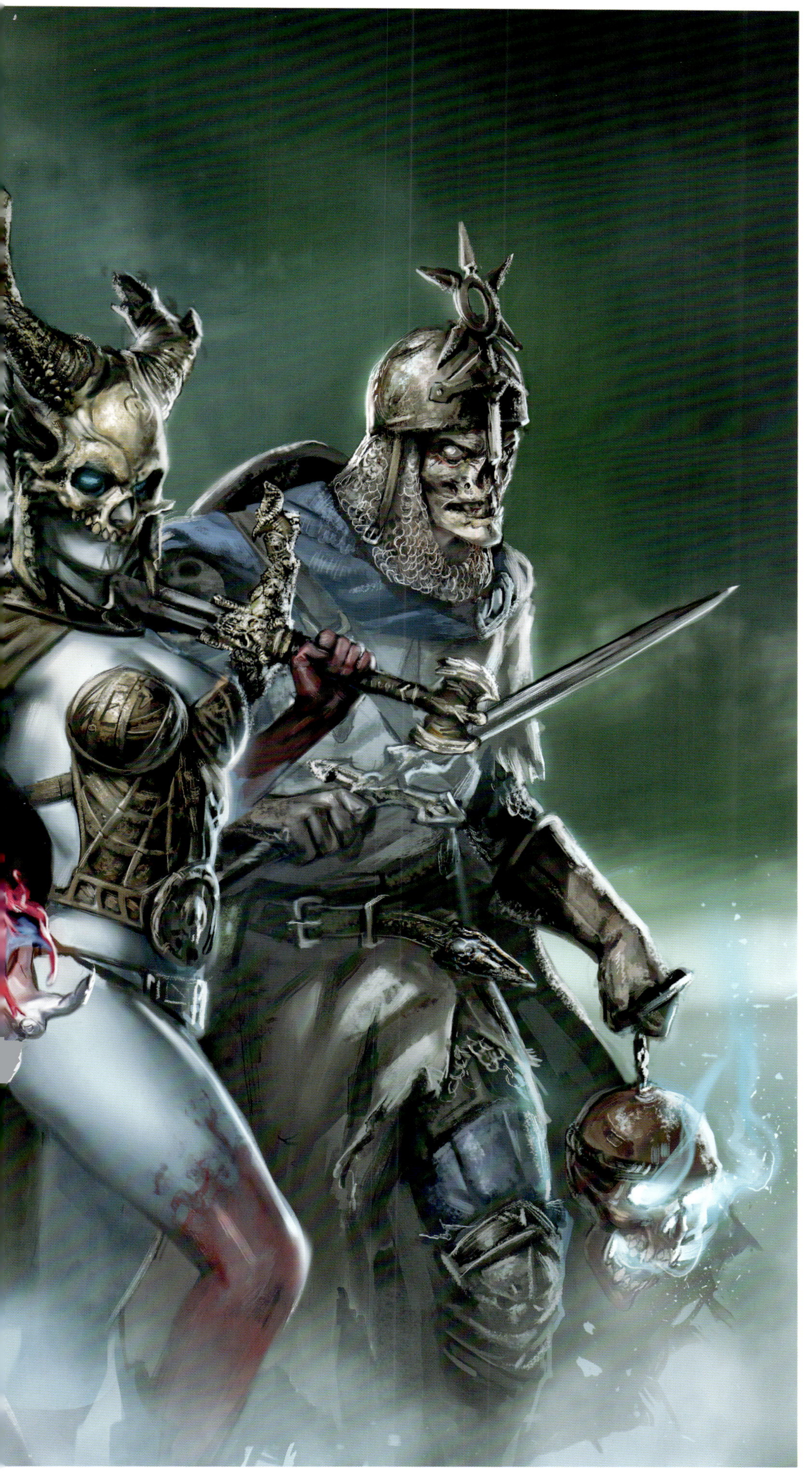

PILLARS OF REBELLION

IAN MACDONALD

The *Pillars of Rebellion* Fine Art Print is a high-end reproduction of Sideshow's 2018 San Diego Comic-Con banner—a twenty-foot-tall display that hung behind the environmental Underworld booth featuring Sideshow's *Court of the Dead* collection.

Pillars of Rebellion was digitally painted by Sideshow artist and *Court of the Dead* designer Ian MacDonald. Any corrupt angel, demon, or dreadsgripped raker would shiver in terror at the sight of this powerful league of Underworld heroes.

"This print features five of the most popular and important *Court of the Dead* characters: Gethsemoni, Demithyle, Xiall, Kier, and—my favorite and that of many others—Relic Ravlatch, aka Bobby," says Senior Brand Manager Ricky Lovas. "These are Death's most triumphant and loyal warriors, in what represents a good glimpse at what the celestial forces have waiting for them on the other side of the veil."

DARTH MAUL
DARK DISCIPLE

WALTER O'NEAL

The *Darth Maul: Dark Disciple* Fine Art Print by Walter O'Neal captures the powerful Sith in a tableau of rage, discipline, and darkness. See the strength of the fearsome Dathomirian warrior as he wields his iconic dual-edged lightsaber, prepared to strike at any foe. At the forefront, Darth Maul pauses in a moment of intense concentration, gathering his dark and dangerous energy to bring the galaxy to its knees.

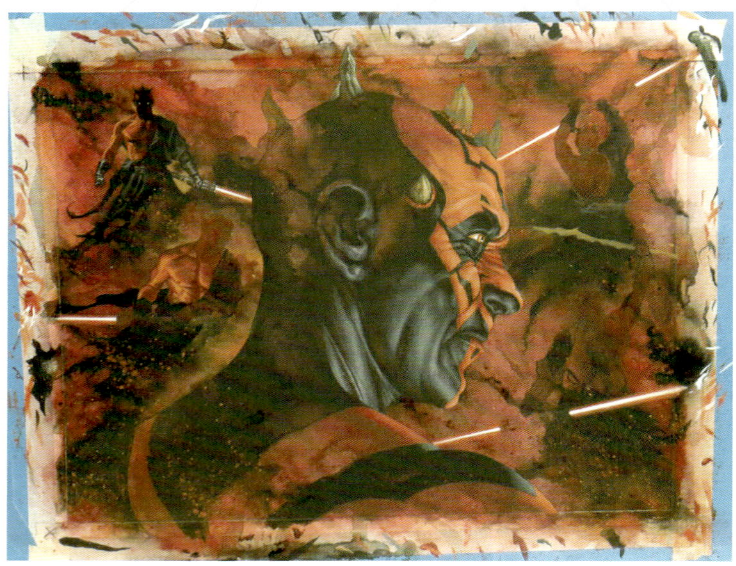

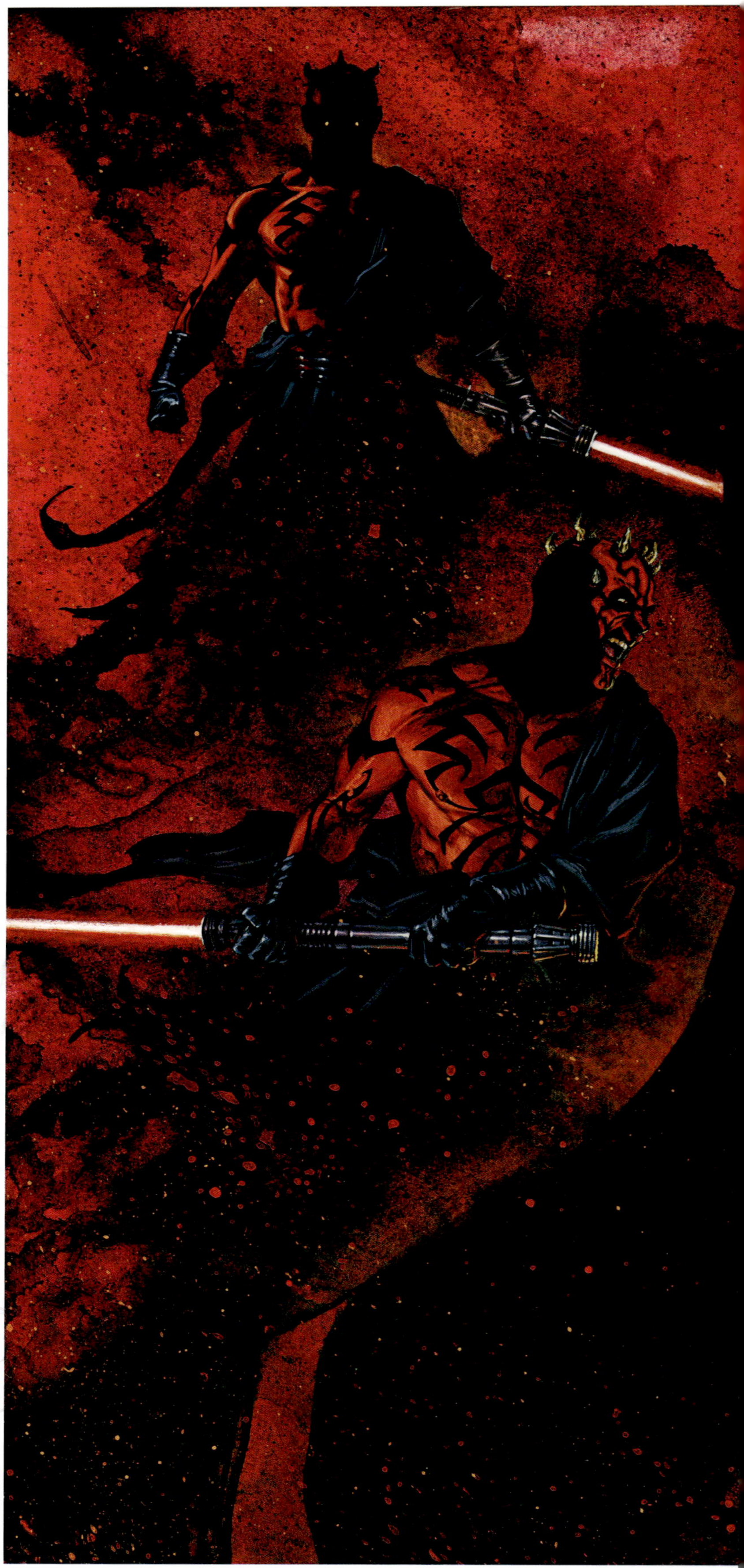

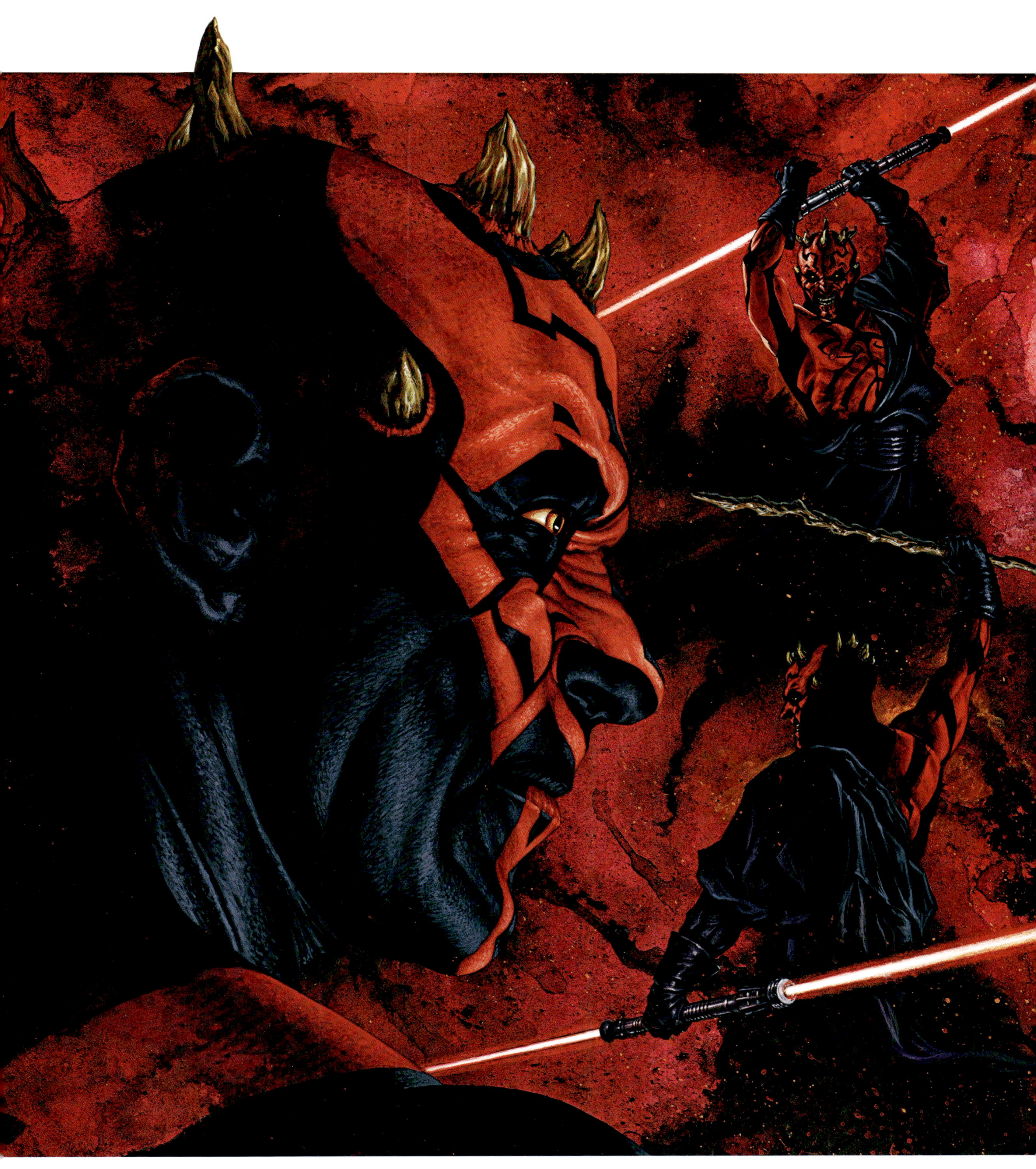

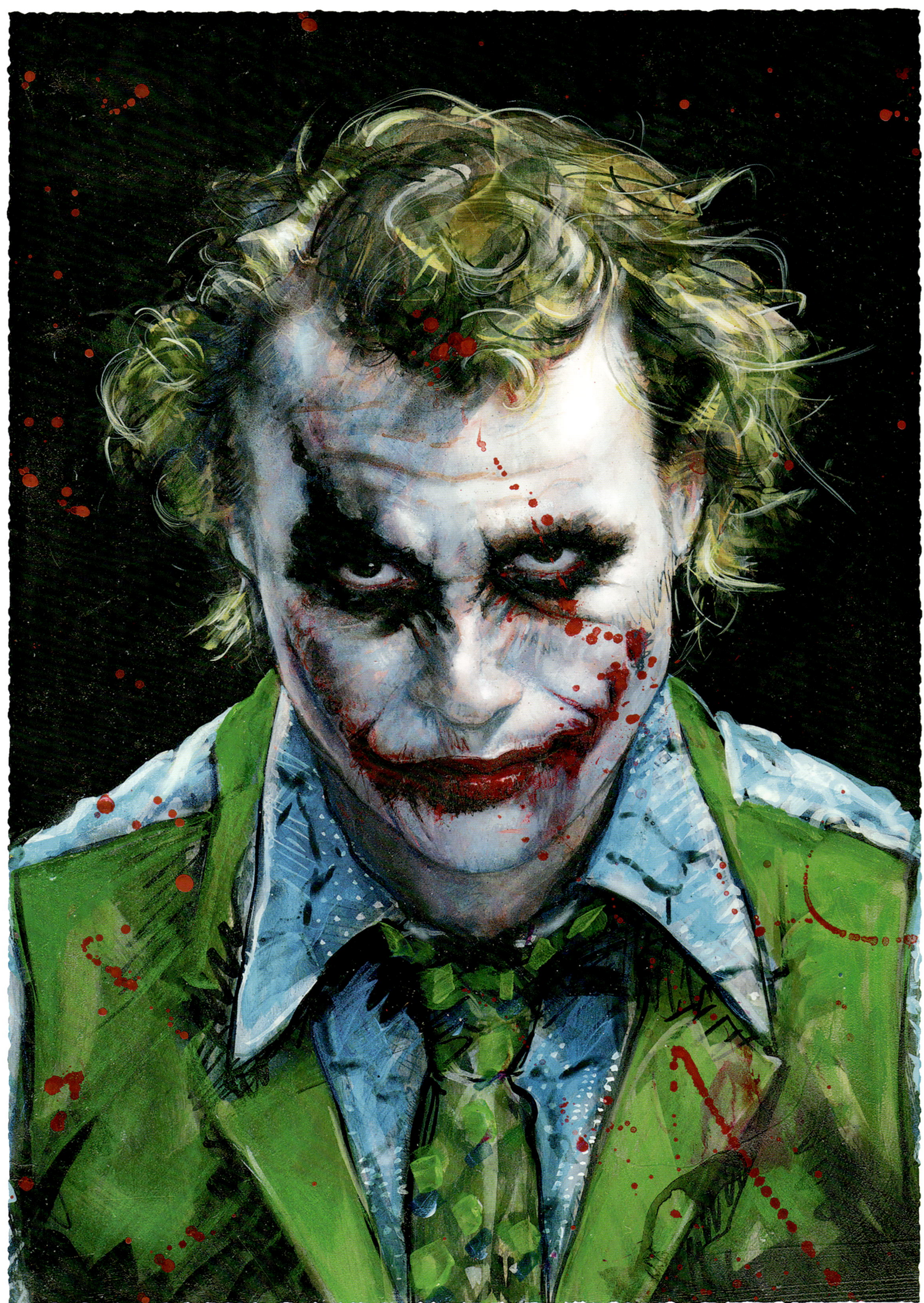

Why So Serious? © 2018 Olivia De Berardinis

WHY SO SERIOUS?

OLIVIA DE BERARDINIS

Based on Heath Ledger's iconic portrayal of the Joker in *The Dark Knight*, this print captures the sadistic madness of Batman's most legendary foe.

This chilling portrait of the Joker features his twisted red grin and haunting dark eyes, while bold red splatters punctuate the image, and reveal the villain's murderous intentions.

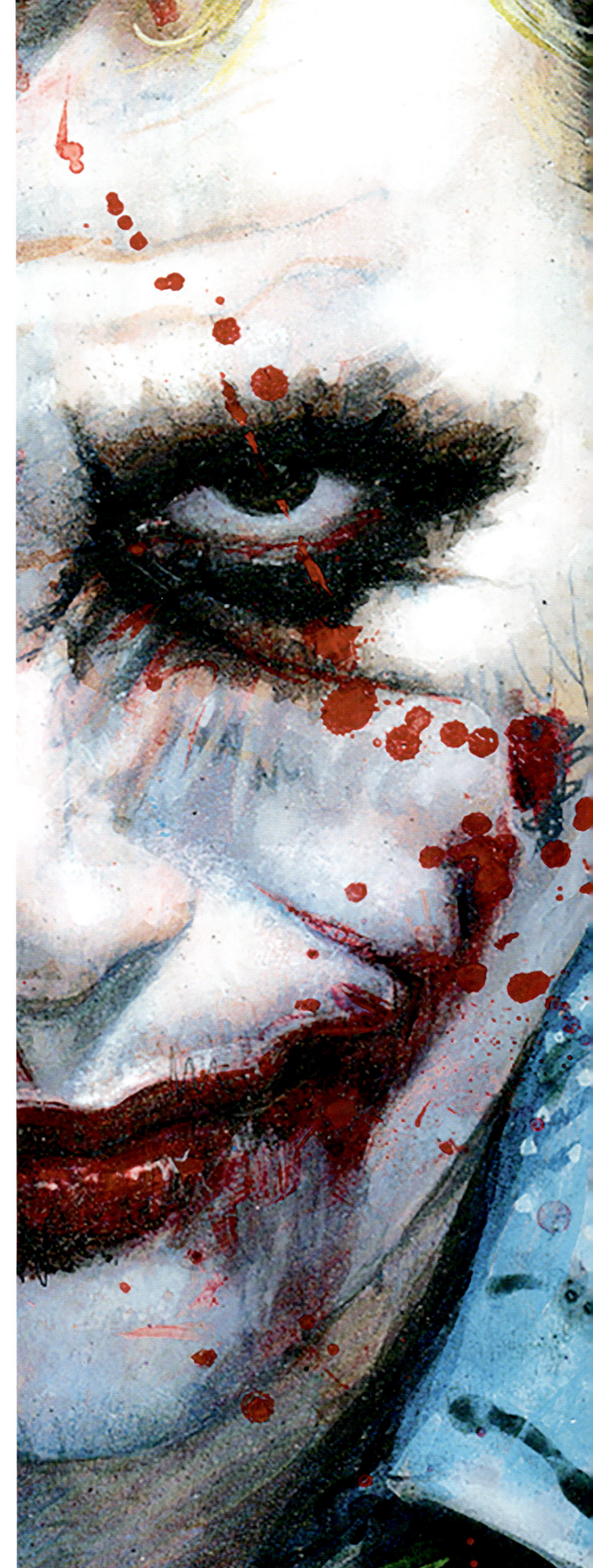

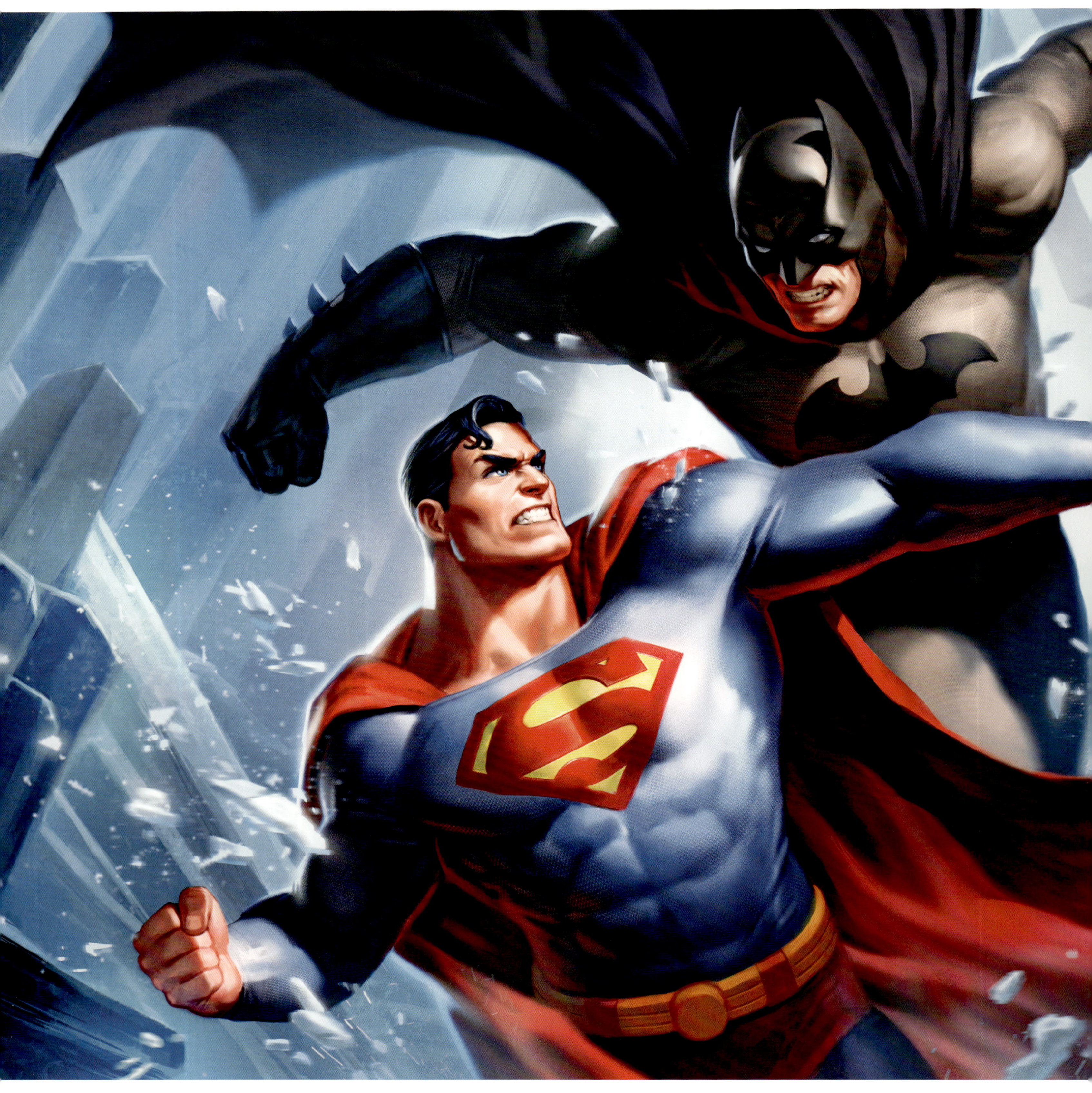

BATMAN VS. SUPERMAN

IAN MACDONALD & ALEX PASCENKO

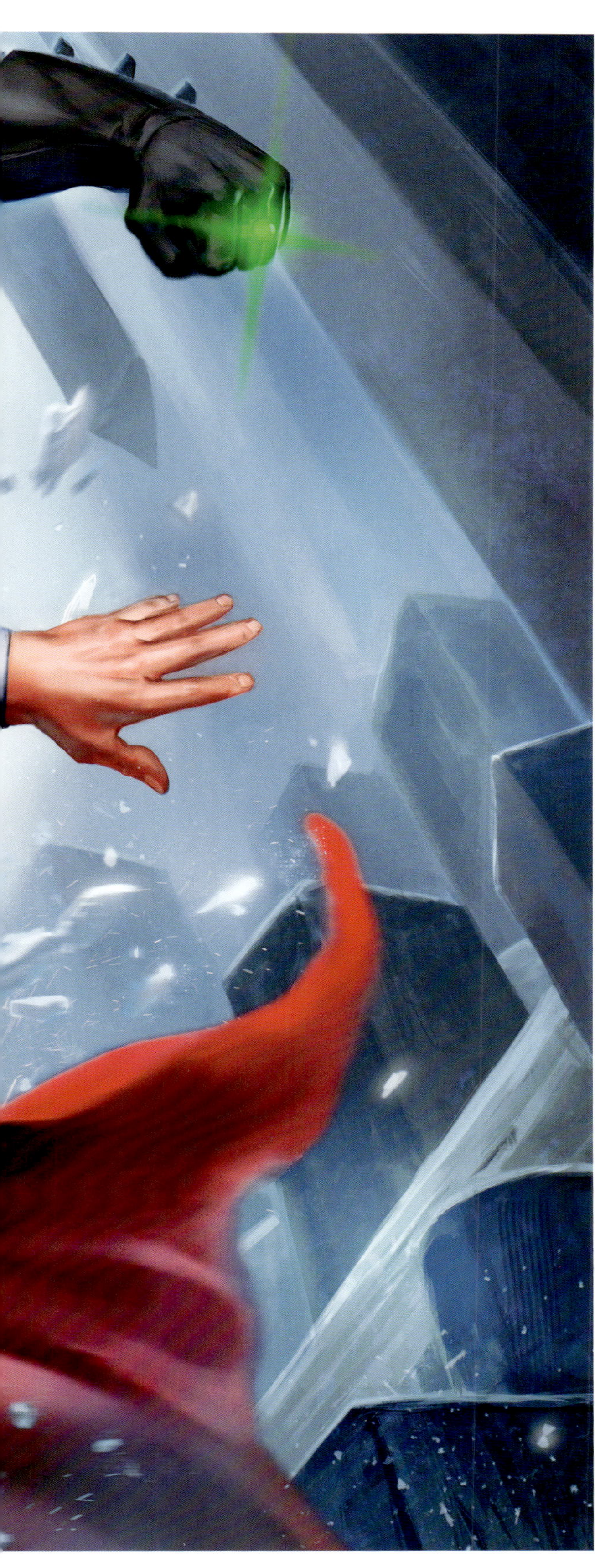

The Man of Steel battles the Dark Knight in the Fortress of Solitude, as the heavens tremble. The *Batman vs. Superman* Fine Art Print captures the classic comic book essence of these two legendary heroes, locked in their own rivalry over the proper path to justice.

The crystalline hideout erupts into chaos as Batman descends wearing a Kryptonite ring, prepared to deal a devastating blow to Superman. Kal-El acts quickly to defend himself, winding up a super punch of his own to stop the Bat in his tracks.

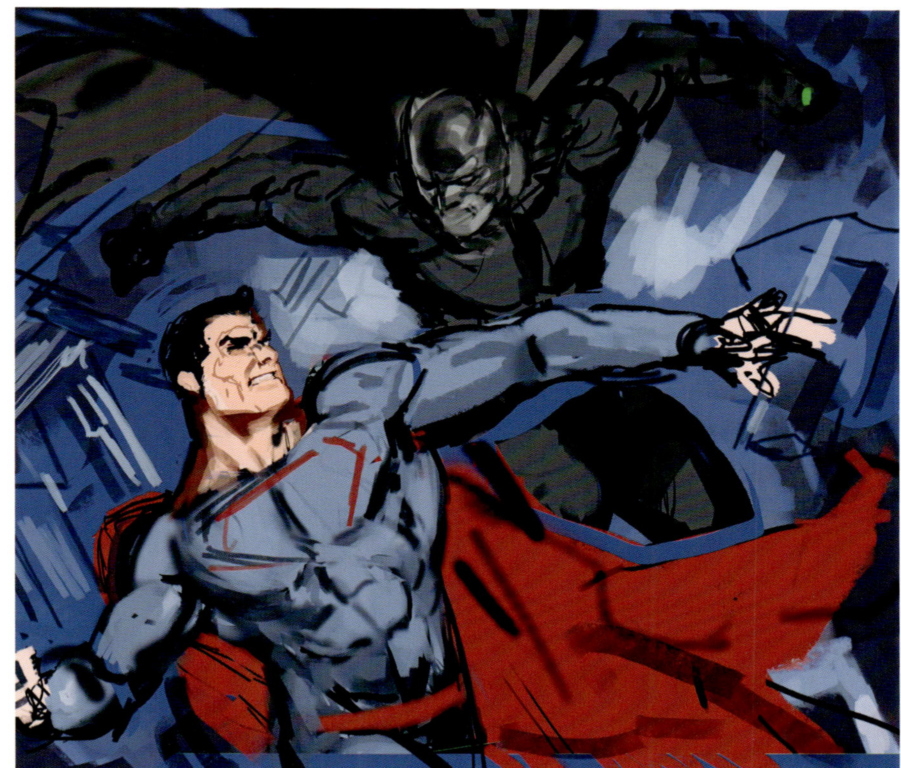

DAREDEVIL & ELEKTRA

HOI MUN THAM

Hell's Kitchen is bathed in red as Daredevil and Elektra stand guard on the rooftops. The Man Without Fear looms large, listening to the telltale sounds of crime in the city as Elektra, the deadly assassin, holds her twin sai at the ready.

This print features a unique glow in the dark element, which illuminates the heroes' weapons, Daredevil's eyes, and the logo on his chest.

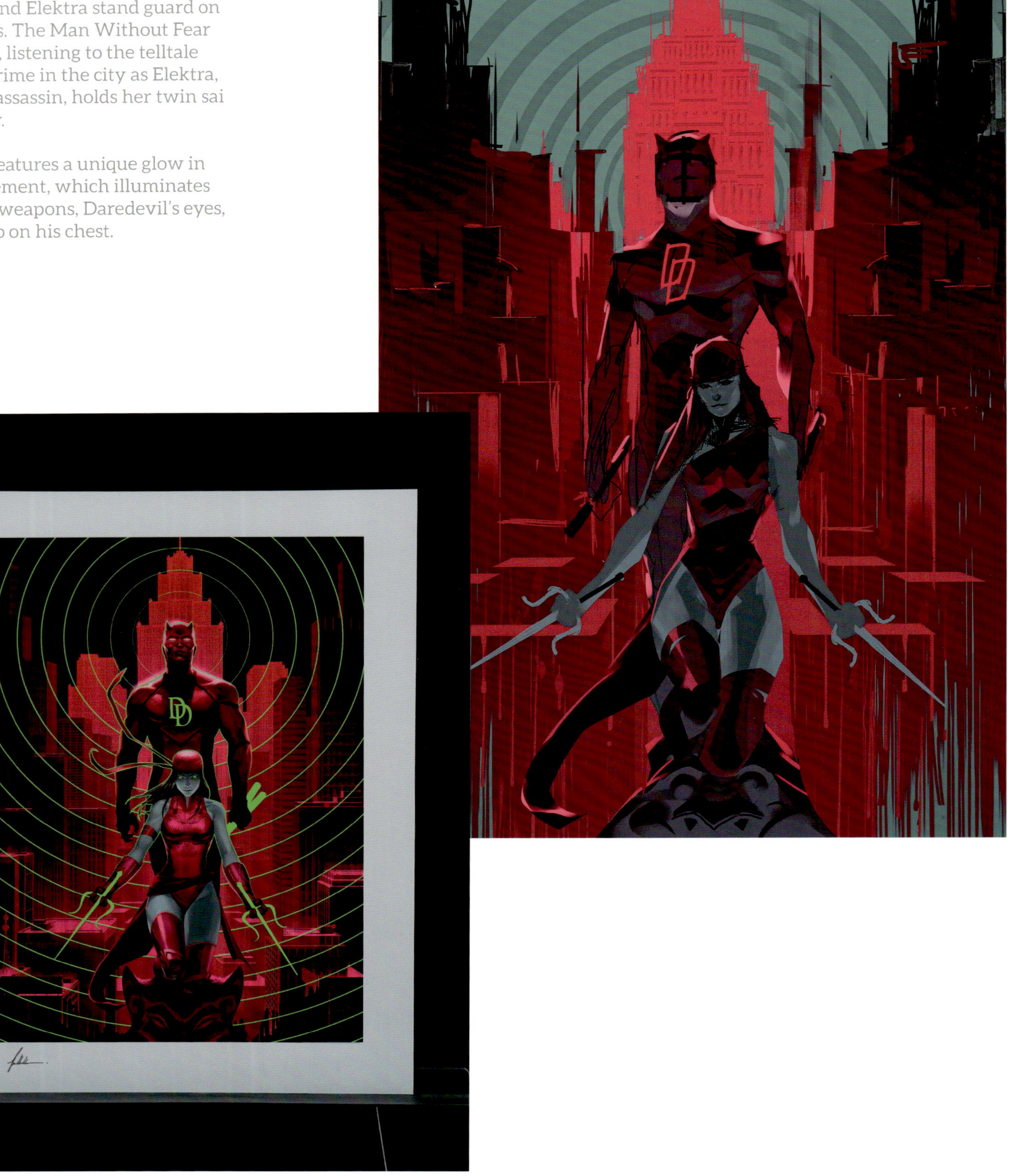

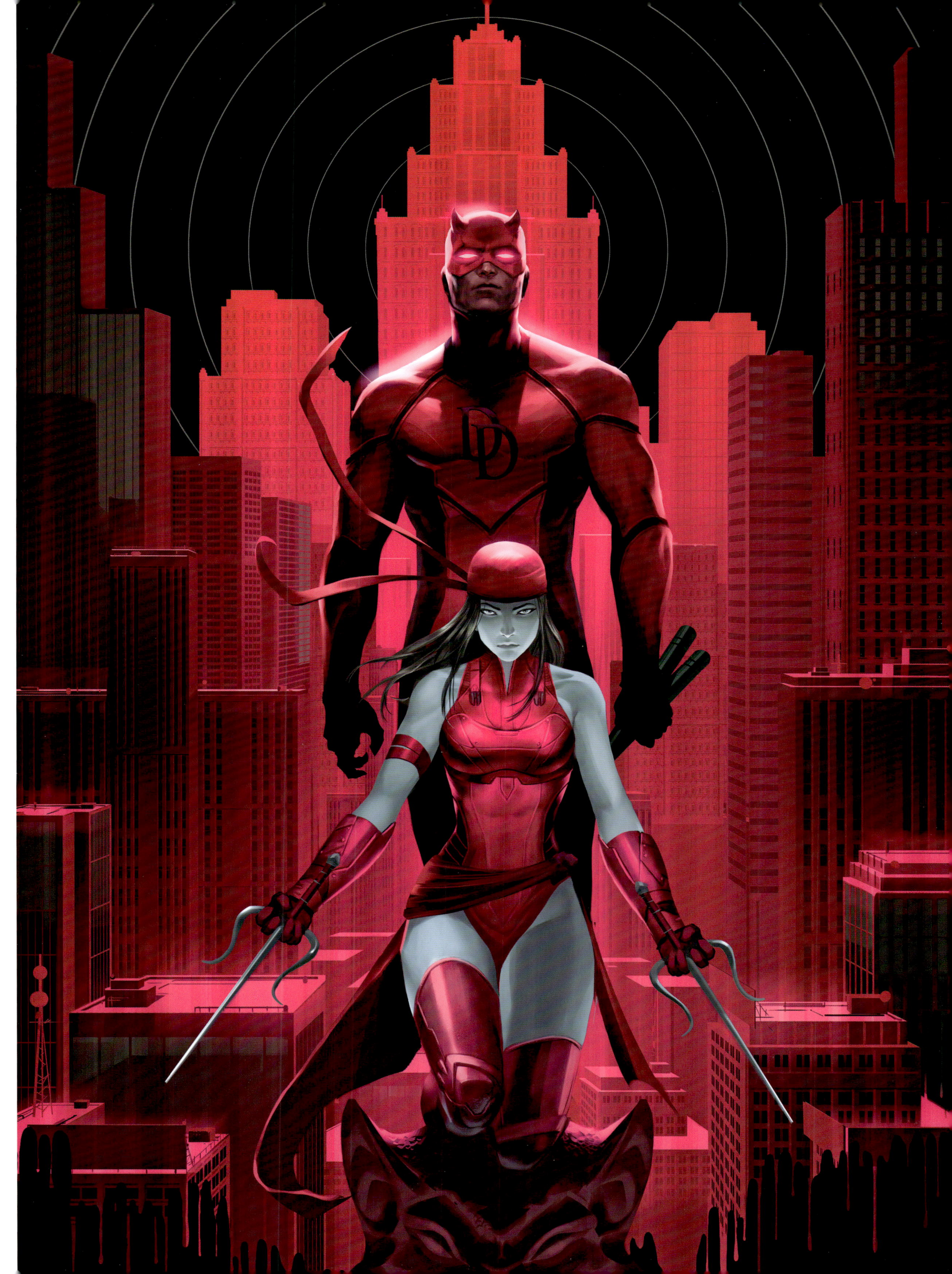

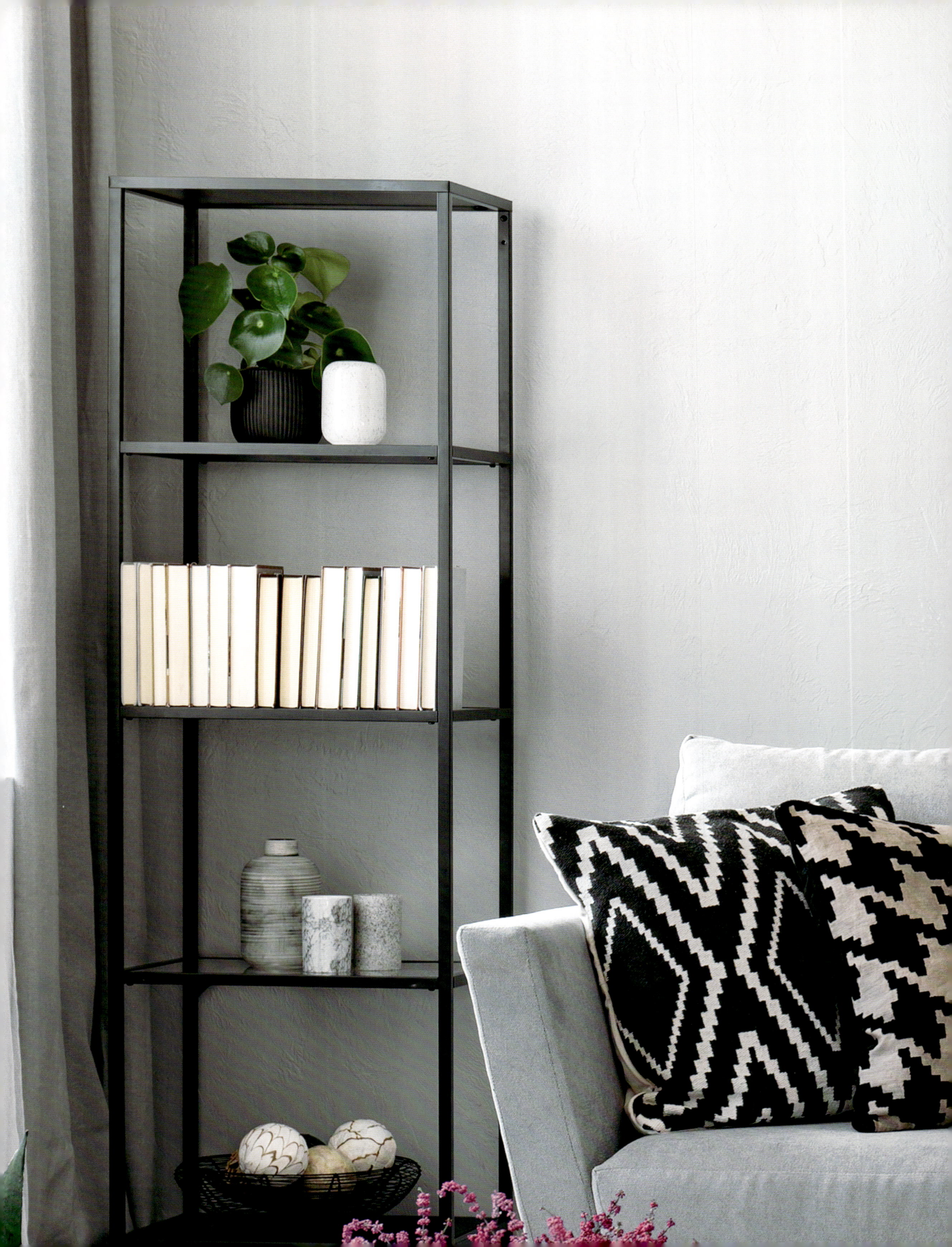

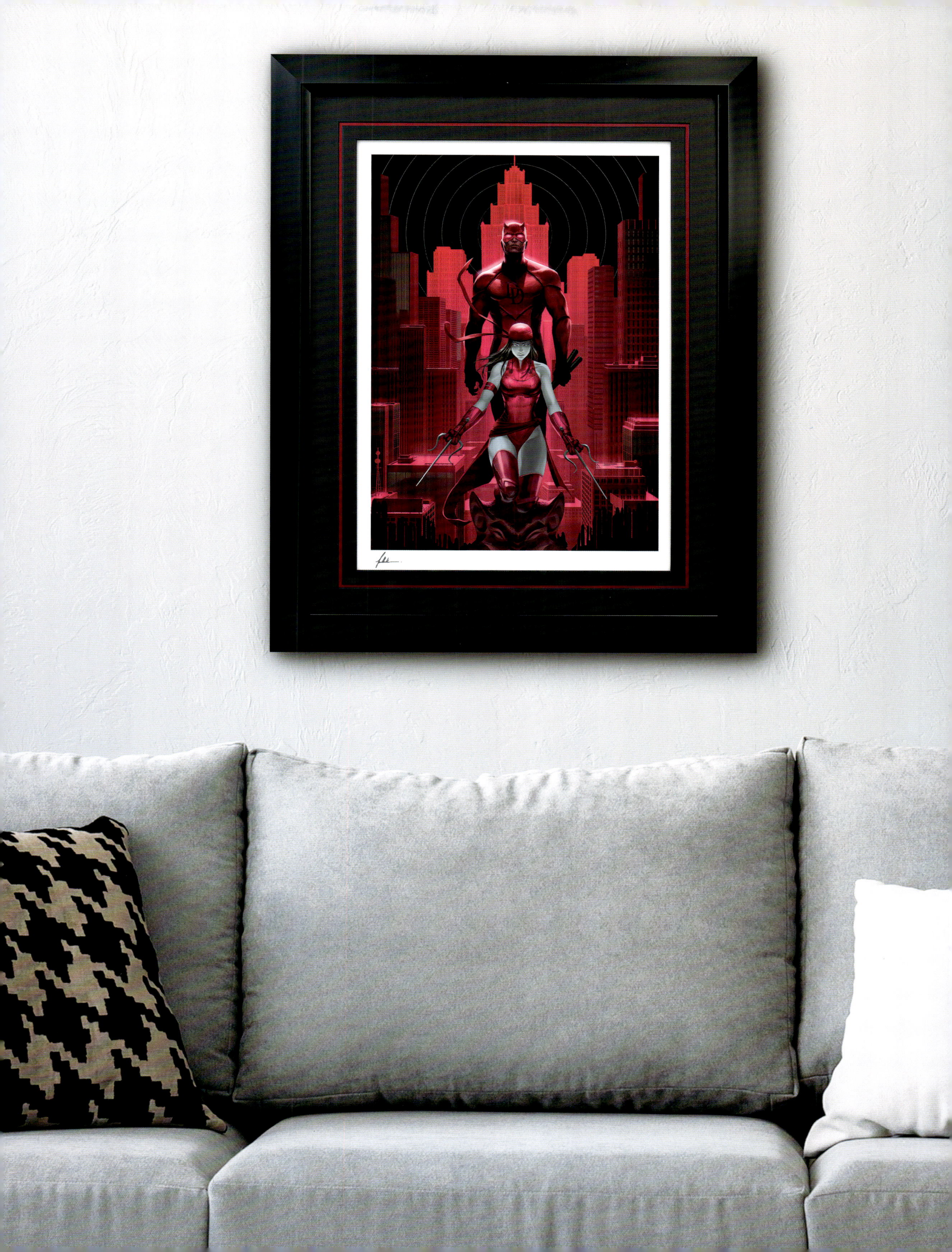

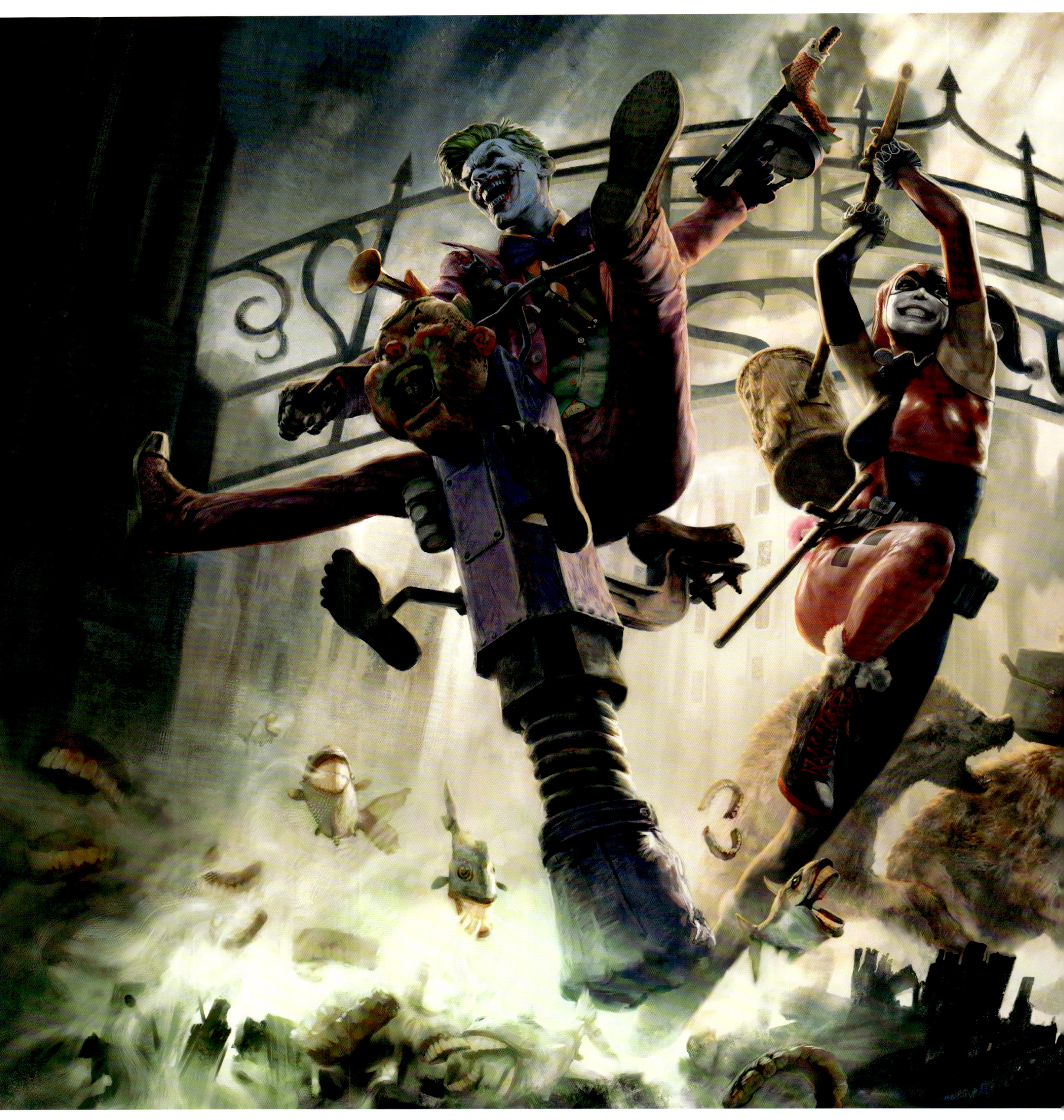

THE JOKER & HARLEY QUINN

ARKHAM ASYLUM BREAKOUT

JON FOSTER

The Joker and Harley Quinn make a mad break for it as the gates of Arkham Asylum are blown wide open in this explosive composition. The Clown Prince of Crime rides tall atop a pogo-fist, while Joker Fish and snapping teeth go flying in his wake. The Maid of Mischief has her hammer raised high, ready to crack some jokes and some skulls on her next big crime spree.

Behind Harley, her faithful hyenas Bud and Lou take a bite out of a Bat-in-the-box, spelling certain doom for Gotham's Dark Knight if he dares try to stop these crazy criminals.

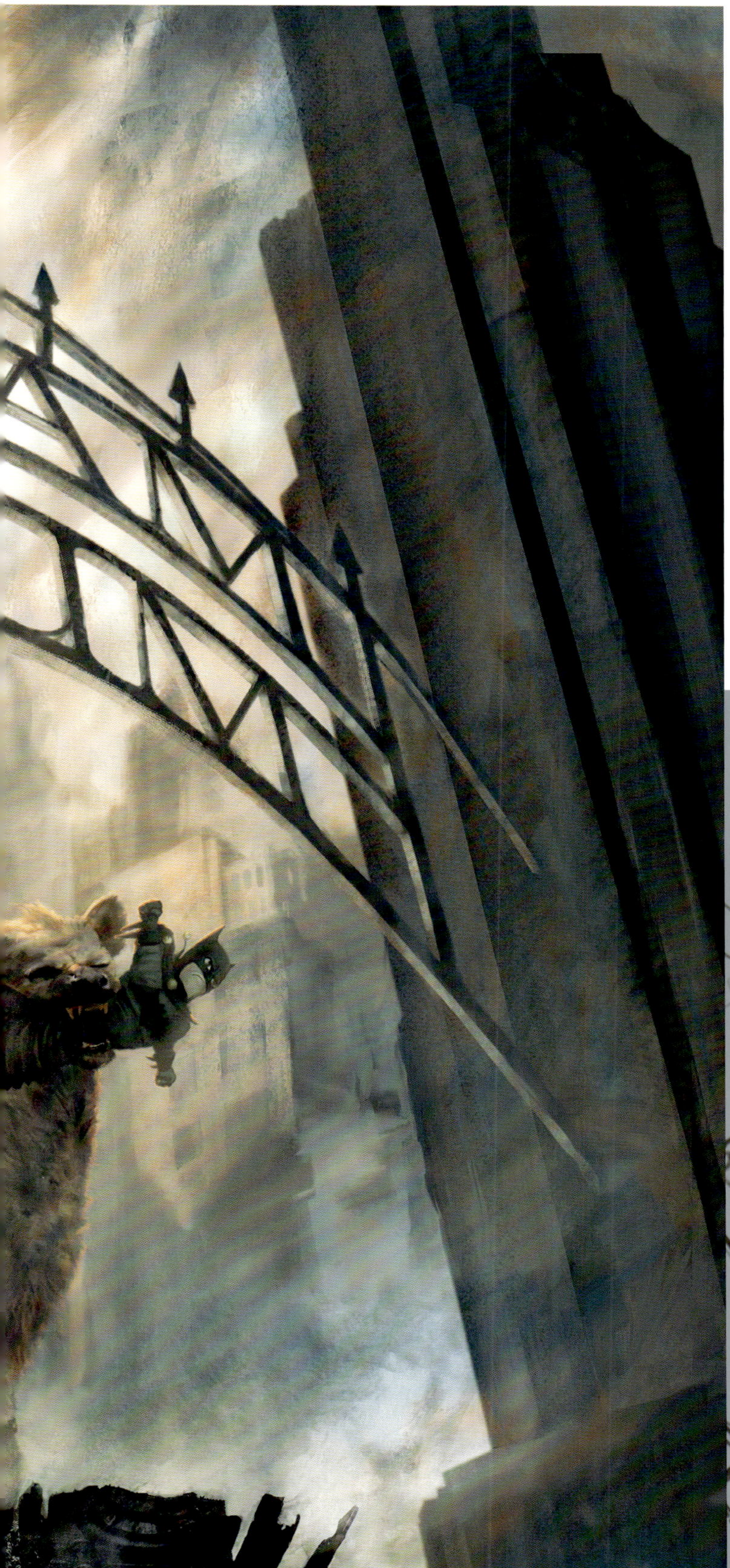

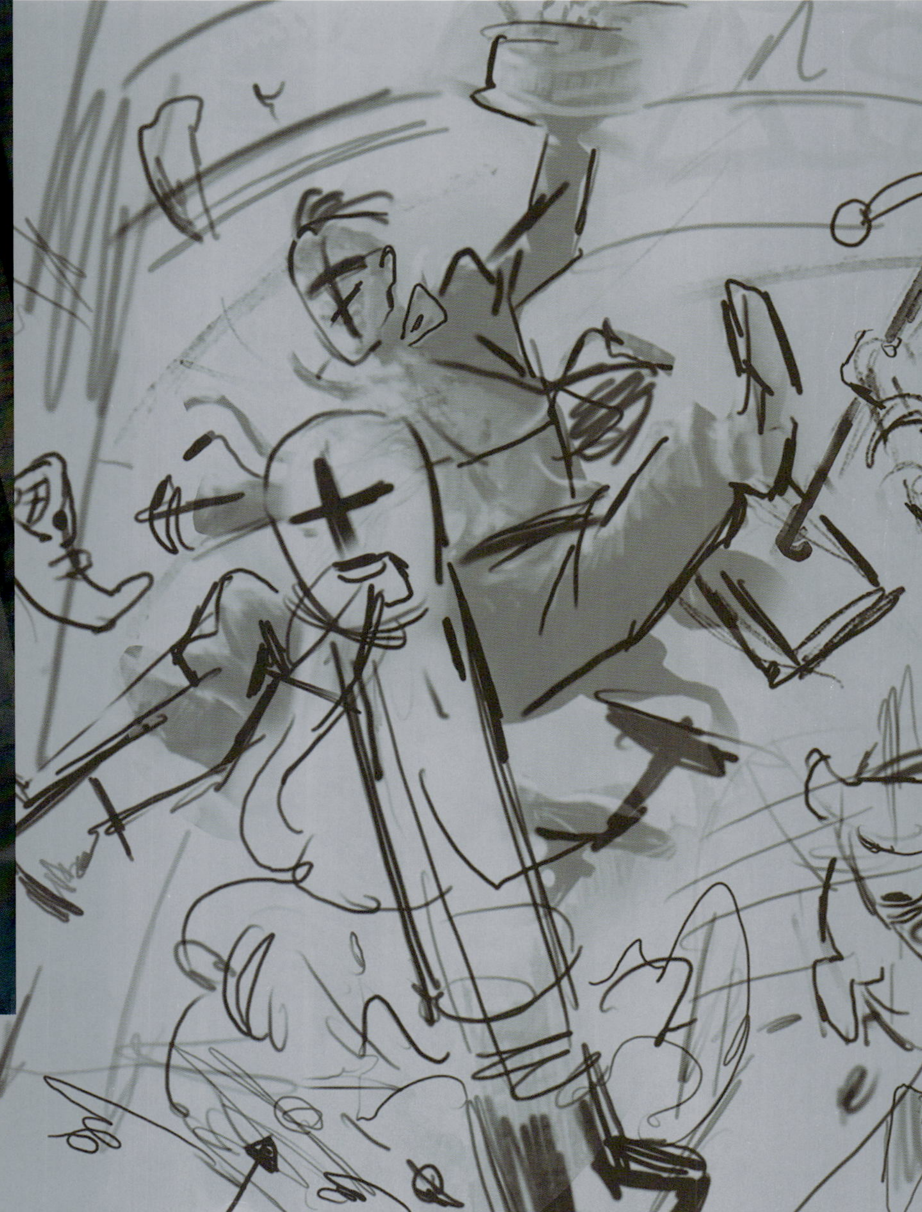

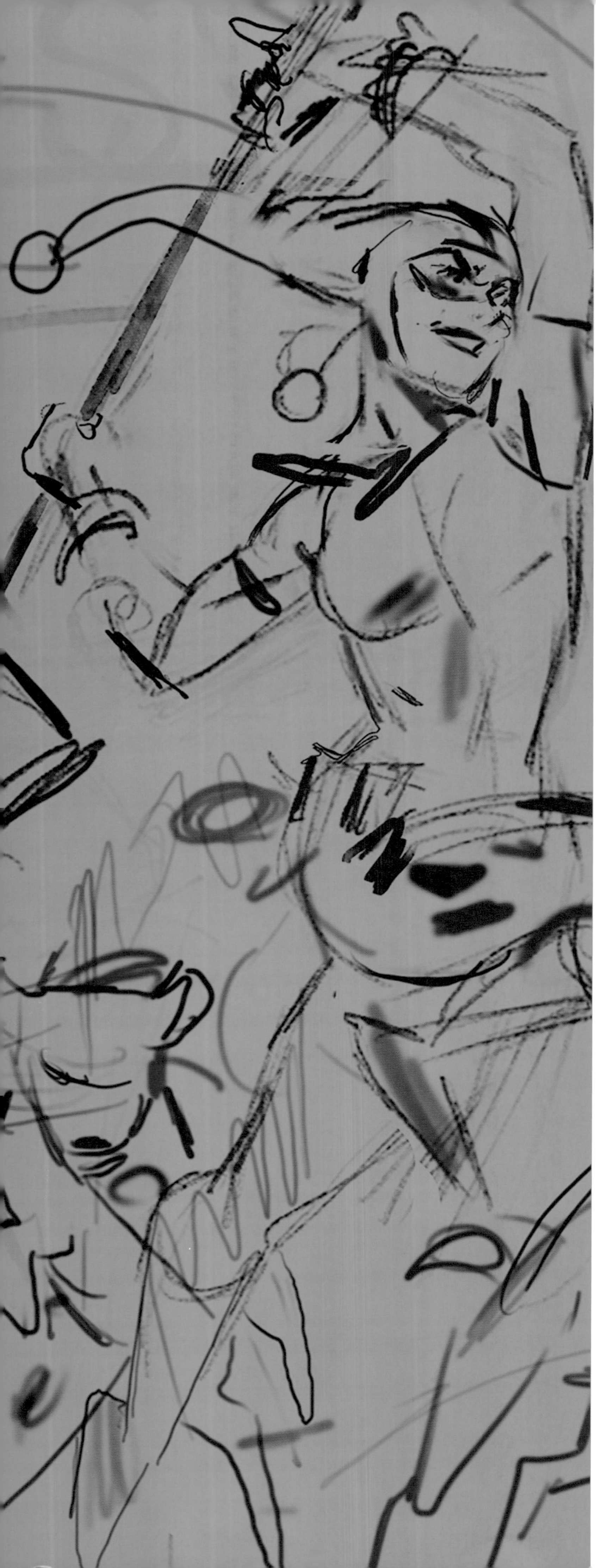

JON FOSTER

INSPIRATION

Jon Foster graduated from Rhode Island School of Design in 1989 with a BFA in illustration. His works have appeared in periodicals such as *National Geographic* and the *Boston Globe*, and in publications from Universal Orlando; Dark Horse Comics; DC Comics; Tor Books; Simon & Schuster; Harry N. Abrams; Underwood Books; Knopf; Delacorte Press; Del Rey Books; Scholastic; Fox Atomic; Little, Brown and Company; Night Shade Books; and Subterranean Press.

In addition to his inclusion in the Society of Illustrators annual publication, he has received two silver and three gold awards from *Spectrum: The Best in Contemporary Fantastic Art*. Jon also was awarded the David P. Usher/Greenwich Workshop Memorial Award by the Society of Illustrators: Annual 43, has been nominated twice for the Chesley Awards, and was winner of the 2008 Dark Scribe Quill Award for Best Cover.

Jon frequently travels to lecture at various schools around the country, and is also a member of The Illustration Academy faculty.

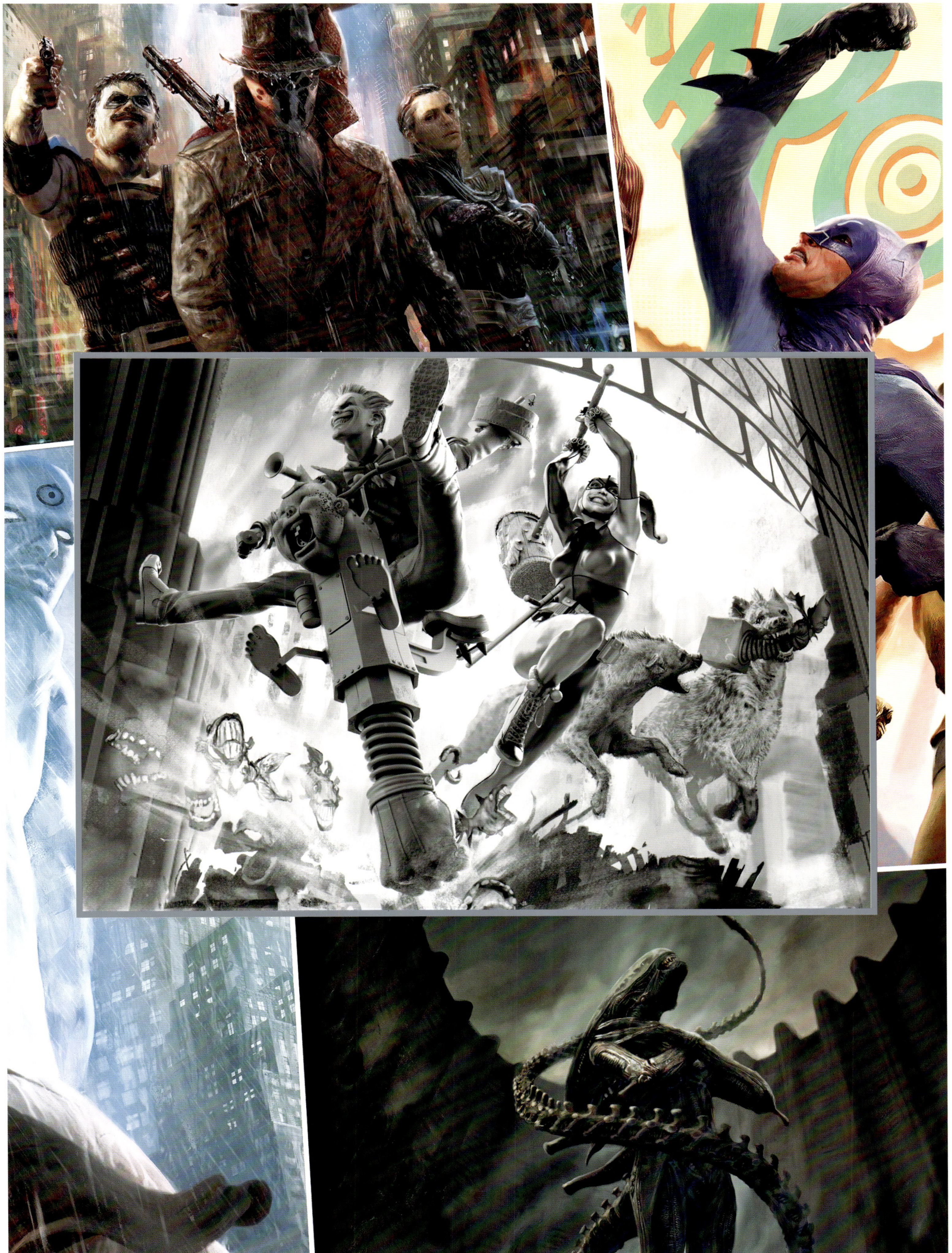

Who Watches the Watchmen, *Alien Internecivus Raptus*, *Batman Robin: The Dynamic Duo* and concept art for *The Joker and Harley Quinn Arkham Asylum Breakout*.

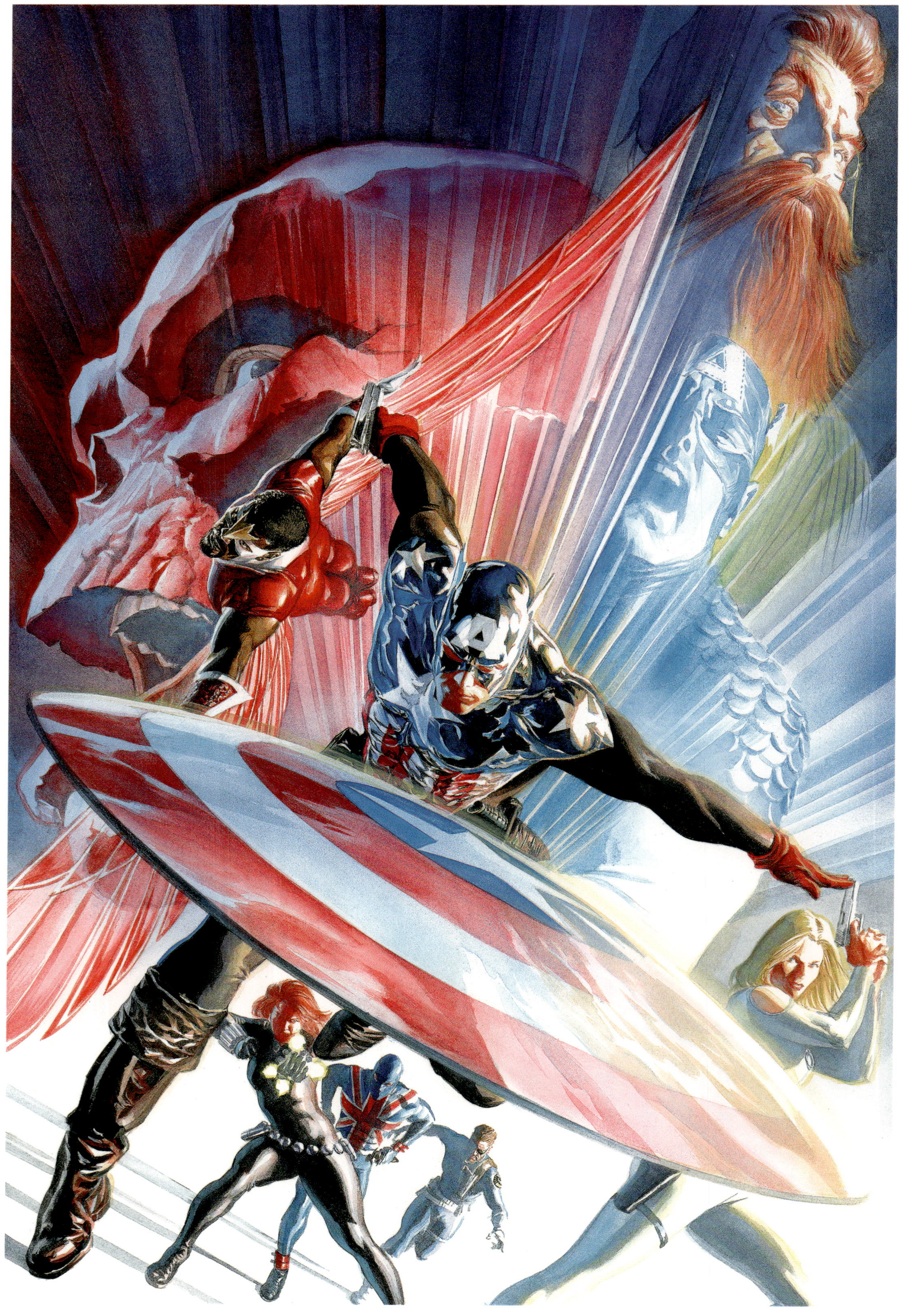

CAPTAIN AMERICA 600

ALEX ROSS

Originally created as a limited variant cover for Marvel's *Captain America* #600, this fine art lithograph commemorates a major milestone in the legacy of this iconic character. In the wake of Steve Rogers's death, Bucky Barnes dons the iconic Captain America suit, while allies Falcon and Sharon Carter flank him as they charge into battle. Black Widow, Union Jack, and Nick Fury follow closely behind, while the portraits of Captain America, Doctor Faustus, and Red Skull loom large in the background of this dynamic and engaging composition.

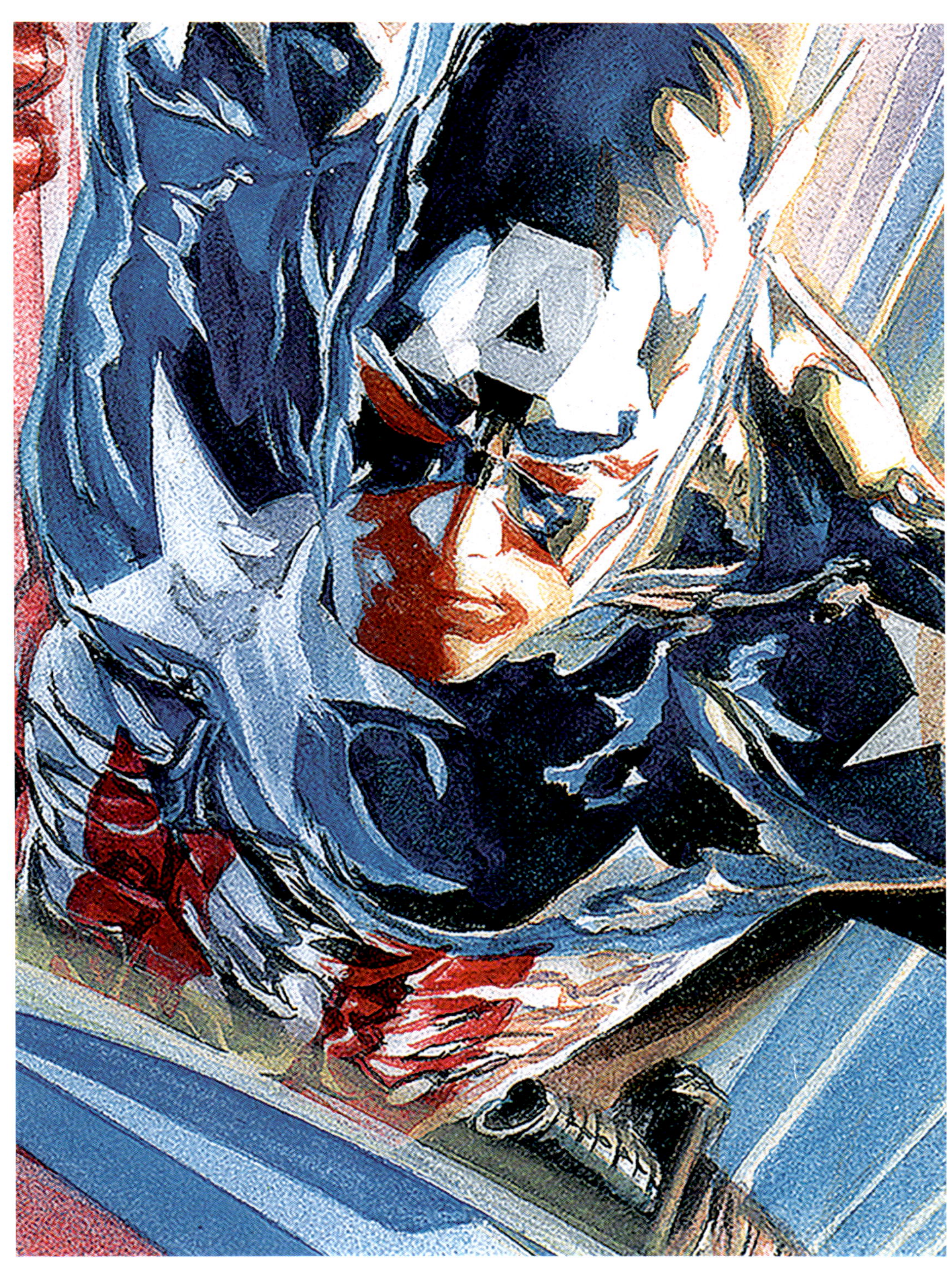

THE TRANSCENDENCE OF SPIRIT

ALEX HORLEY

Death's Valkyrie, Kier, confidently leads this beautiful panoply of the Underworld's most notable Spirit Faction beings. Though Kier may be the de facto leader of the Spirit Faction, her anchor and the true heart of the faction, Ellianastis, looks after her with her ghostly gaze from above.

Some of the most notoriously monstrous members of the faction—Avarkus and Oglavaeil—flank Kier in action-ready poses. The Spirit Faction brings balance and peace, sometimes through brutal truths.

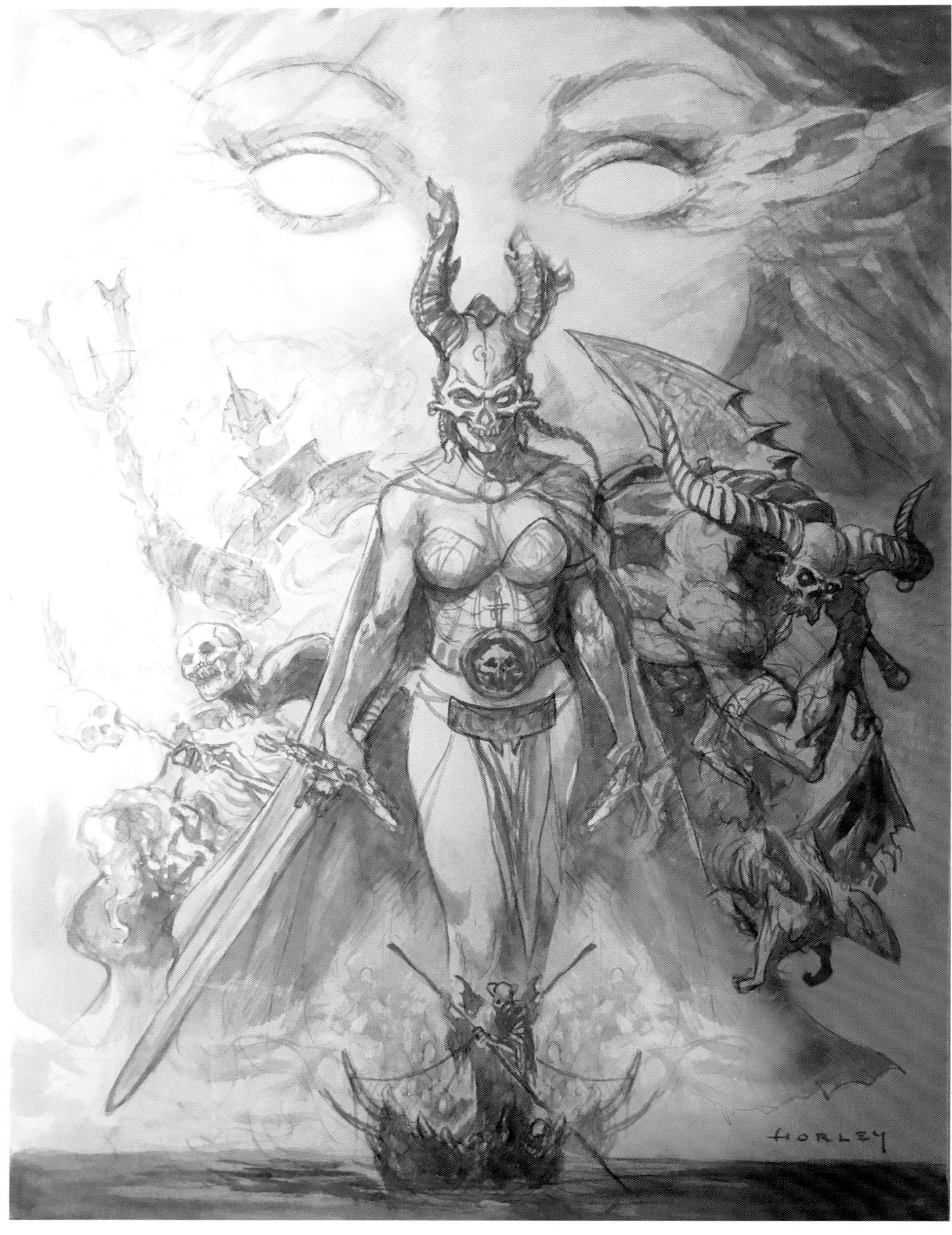

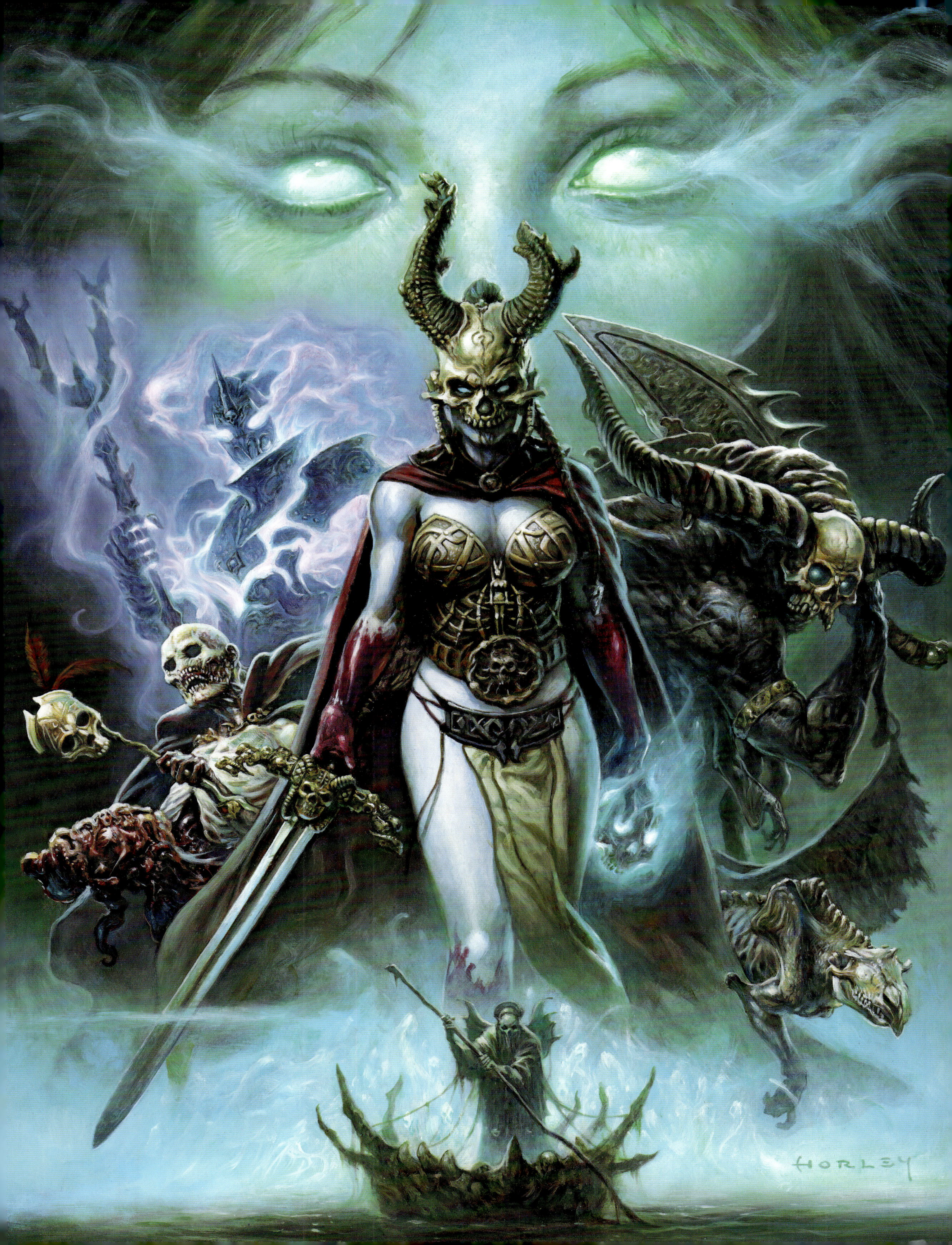
HORLEY

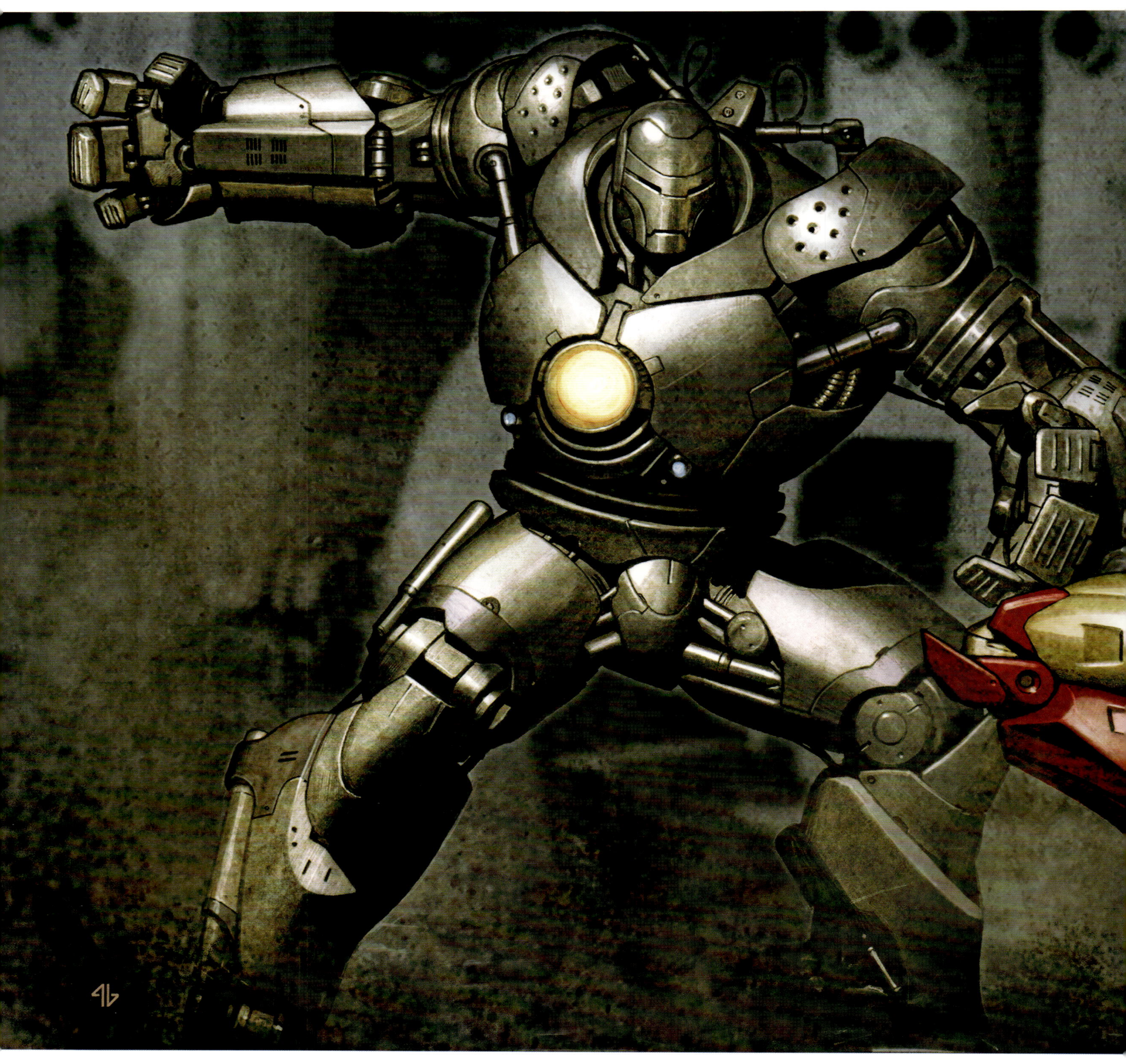

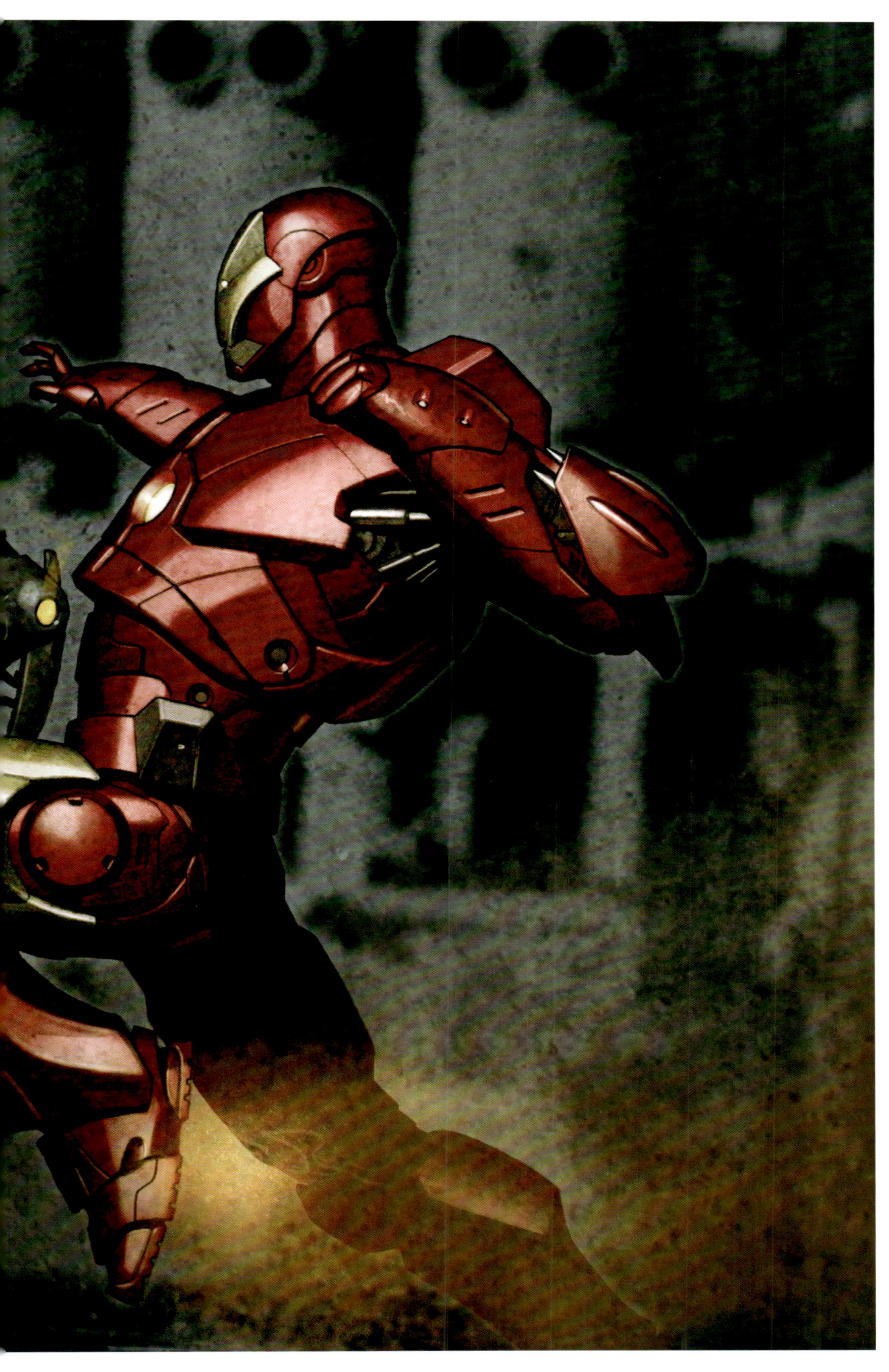

IRON MAN VS. IRON MONGER

ADI GRANOV

A piece of concept art created during the pre-production phase of *Iron Man*, this piece by Adi Granov proved to be foundational for the film. "The *Iron Man vs. Iron Monger* piece was important, because it set the tone for the entire production. When [*Iron Man* director] Jon Favreau saw that painting, it became the image he really centered on," explains Granov. "It was the first time the finalized Iron Monger was painted in a scene."

The *Iron Man vs. Iron Monger* Fine Art Print by Adi Granov pits tech titans Tony Stark and Obadiah Stane against each other in an iconic Marvel Cinematic Universe battle. The red-and-gold Iron Man faces off against the hulking silver Iron Monger in a rivalry that encompasses more than just the physical brawl. This concept artwork captures the intensity and intricacy of everything that Tony Stark has worked to create—from his past as a weapons manufacturer to his future as a superhero.

MY BROTHER'S KEEPER

BRIAN ROOD

My Brother's Keeper captures the struggle to live another day in the hellish world of *The Walking Dead*.

The print features key survivors such as Michonne, Rick Grimes, and Negan standing against an endless tide of the savage walkers. Armed with his infamous baseball bat, Lucille, Negan looms large against the zombie horde, while even more decaying creatures shamble and swarm in the foreground, surrounding the survivors from all sides.

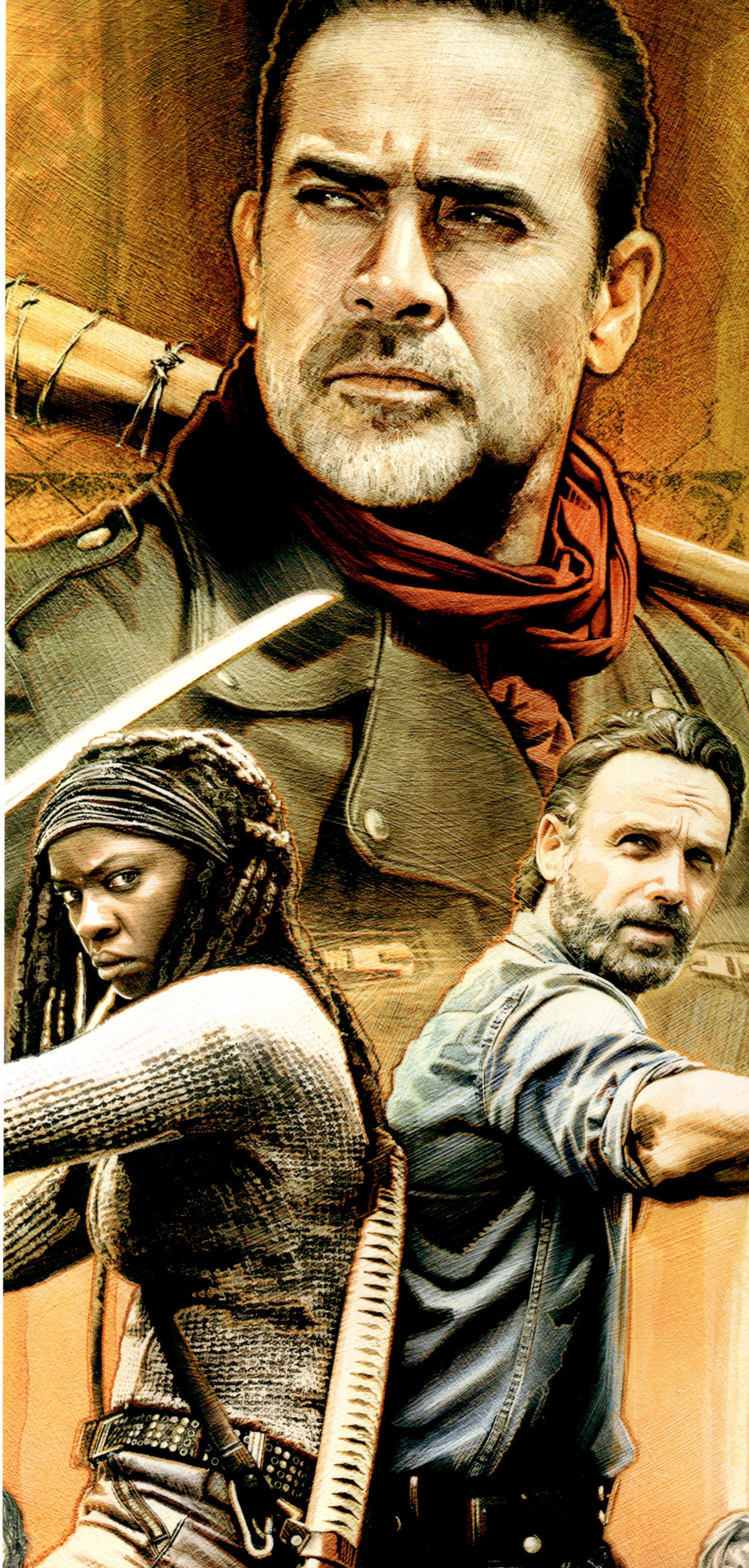

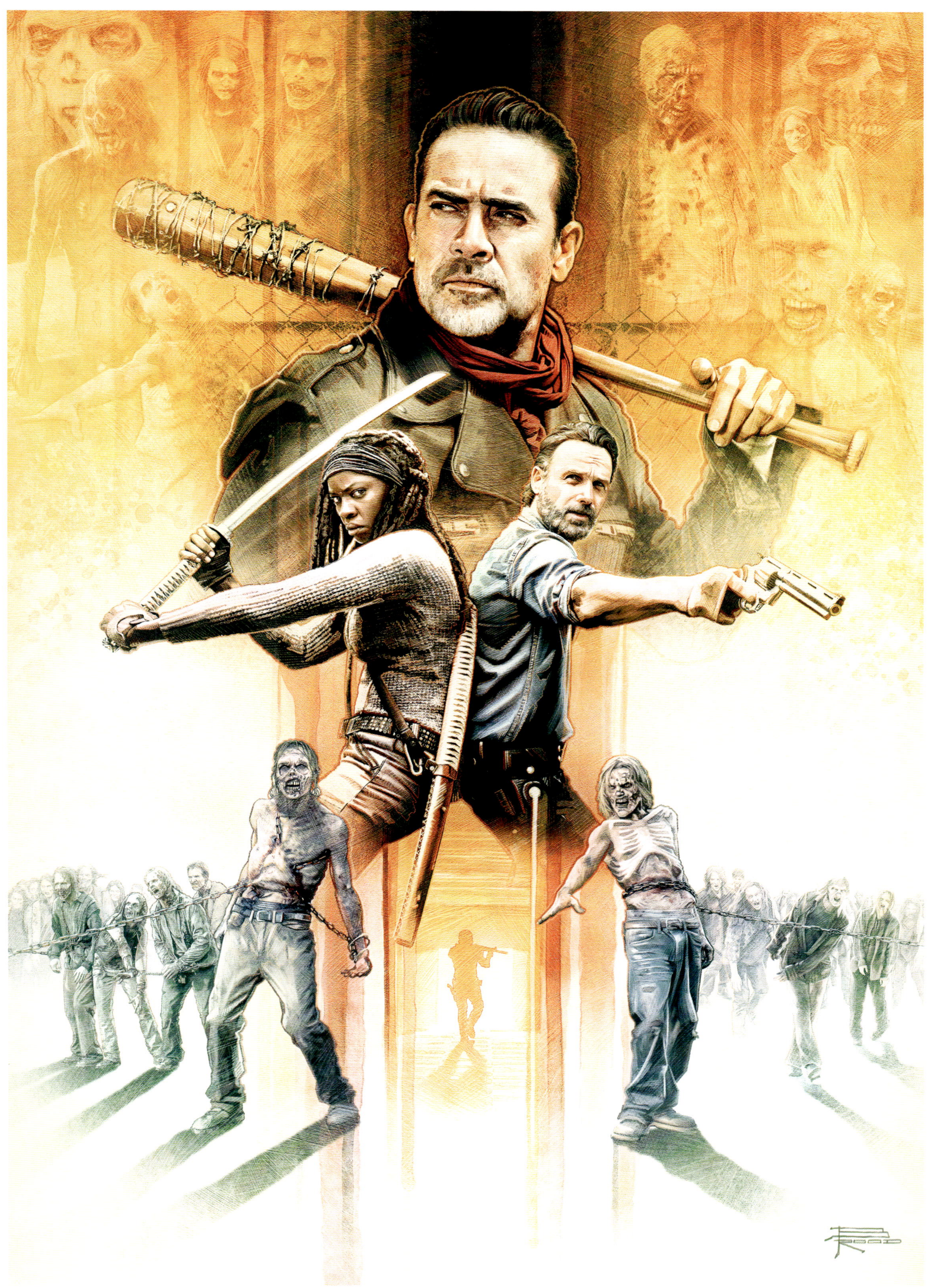

GUARDIANS OF THE GALAXY VOL. 2

ANDY PARK

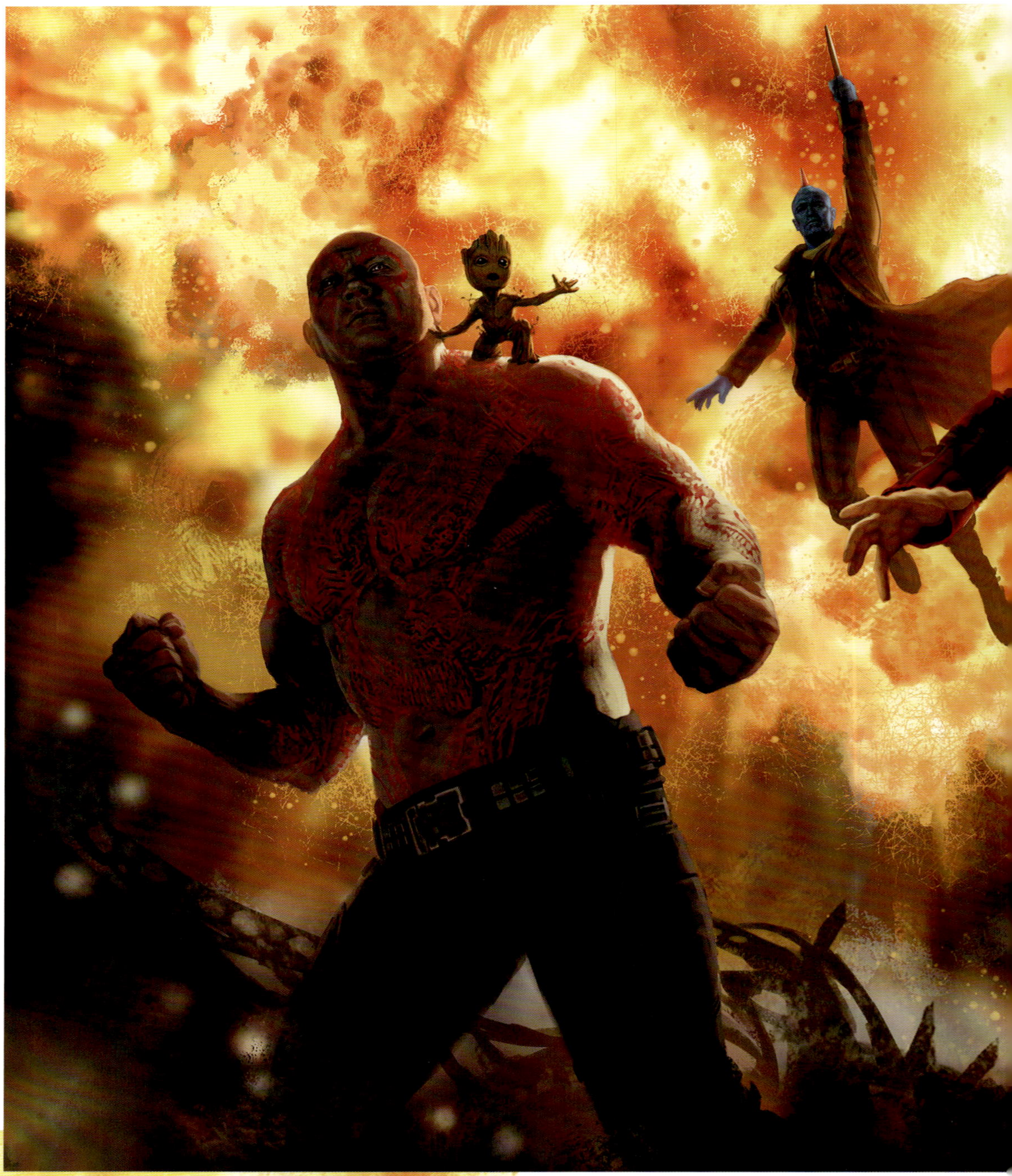

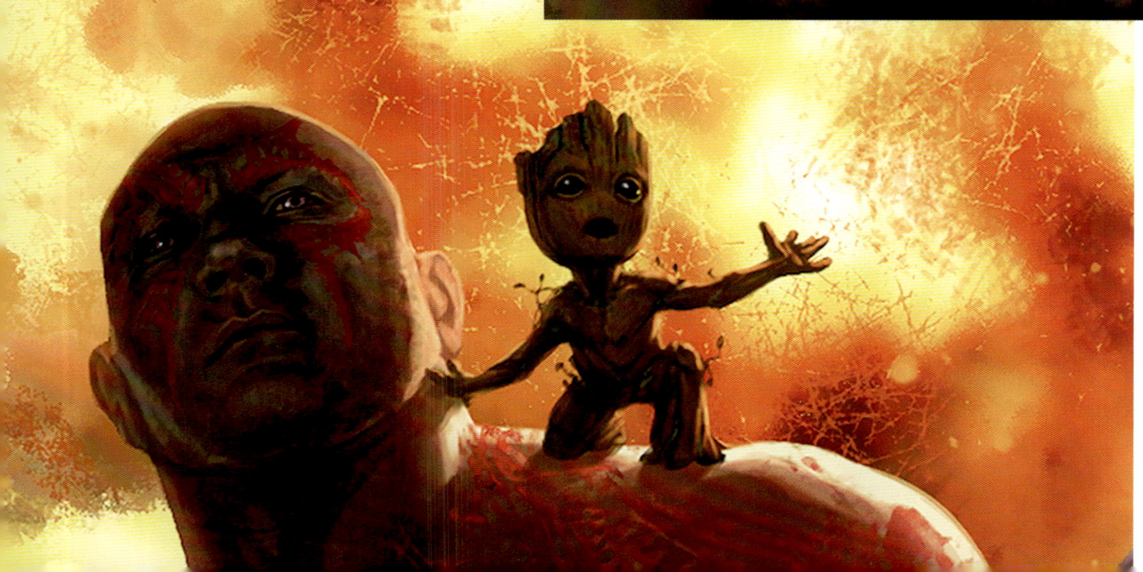

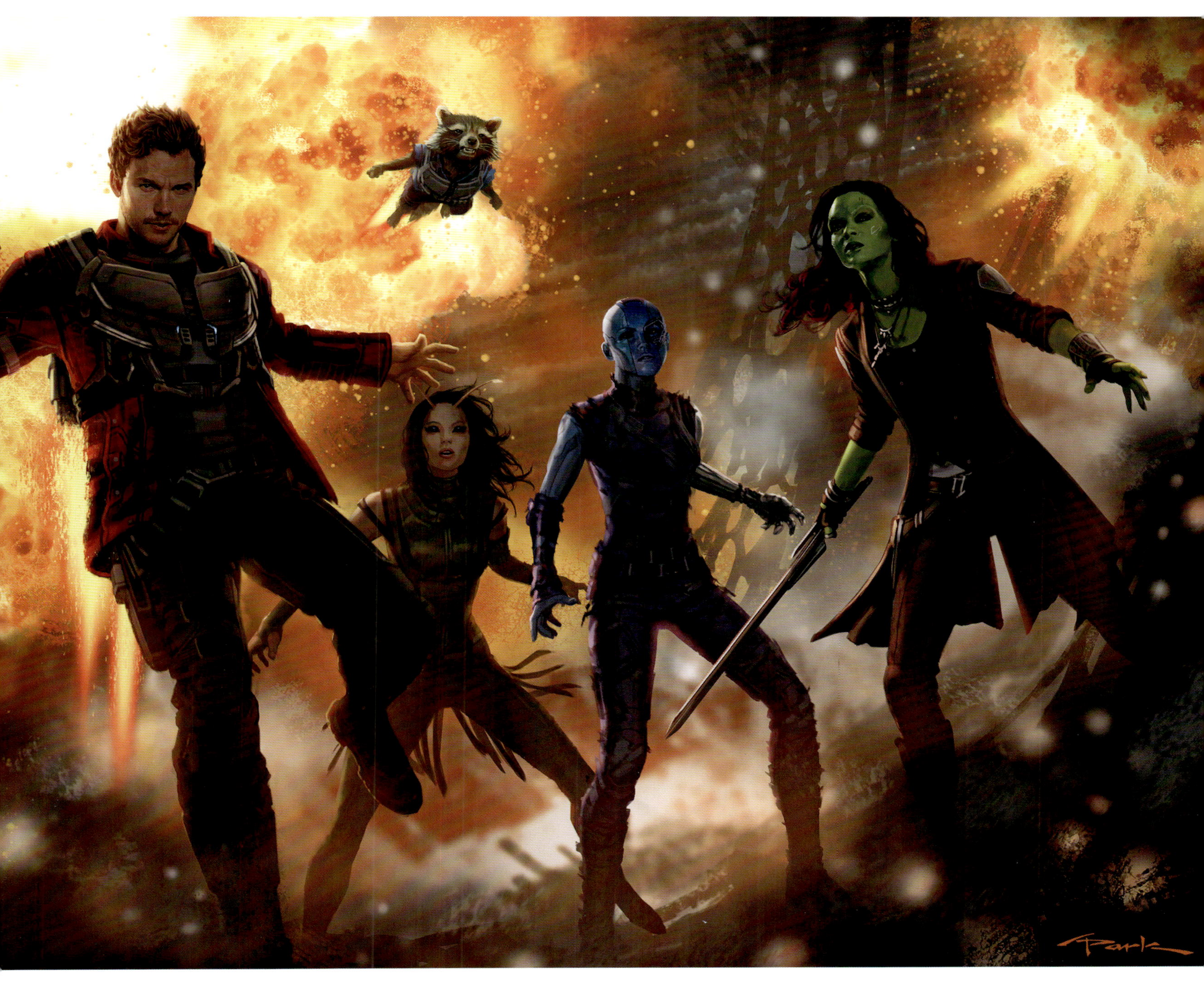

The Marvel Studios Fine Art Print collection celebrates the legacy of the Marvel Cinematic Universe, showcasing official concept art and illustrated keyframes created by celebrated artists who are responsible for designing the entire look and feel of Marvel's immensely popular films.

The *Guardians of the Galaxy Vol. 2* Fine Art Print is an awesome mix of roguish heroes in one explosive scene. The original cast of galactic A-holes from the first film appear with antagonists-turned-allies like Nebula and Yondu, as well as the latest addition to the team, Mantis. In the center of the action, the fearless Star-Lord leads the charge as the Guardians set off to do something good, something bad, or maybe a bit of both.

HISTORY OF THE DC UNIVERSE

ALEX ROSS

Originally illustrated as a book cover for the expansive *History of the DC Universe* guidebook, this dramatic composition pays heroic homage to the origins of DC's most beloved characters.

This print captures the evolving scope of the DC Universe, from the destruction of Krypton to the death of the Waynes and the foundation of heroic organizations such as the Green Lantern Corps, the Legion of Super-Heroes, and the Justice League. The dynamic illustration honors DC heroes Wonder Woman, Batman, Shazam, Superman, and more while the villainous visage of Darkseid and the planet Apokolips signal a darker horizon to this expansive universe.

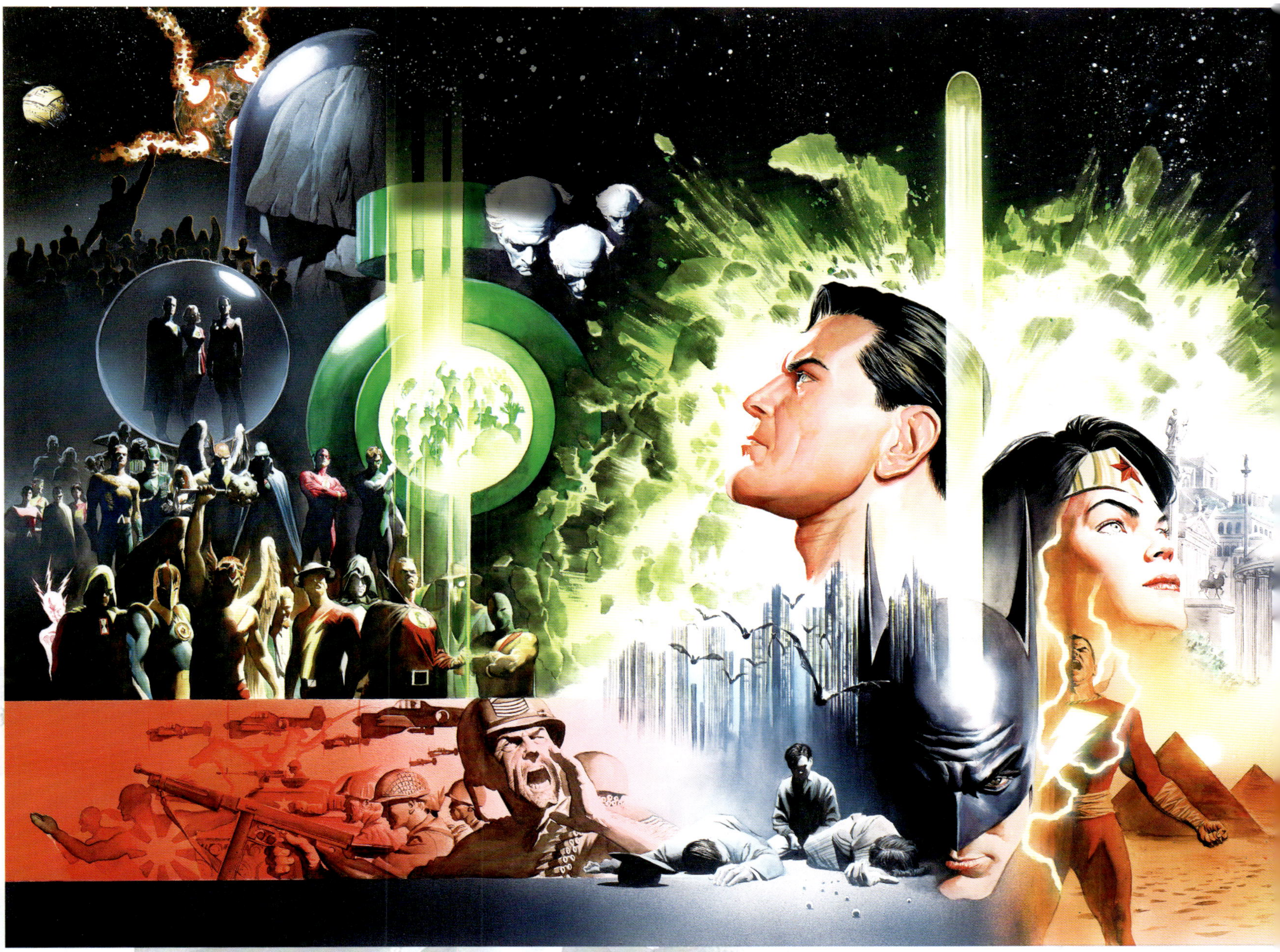

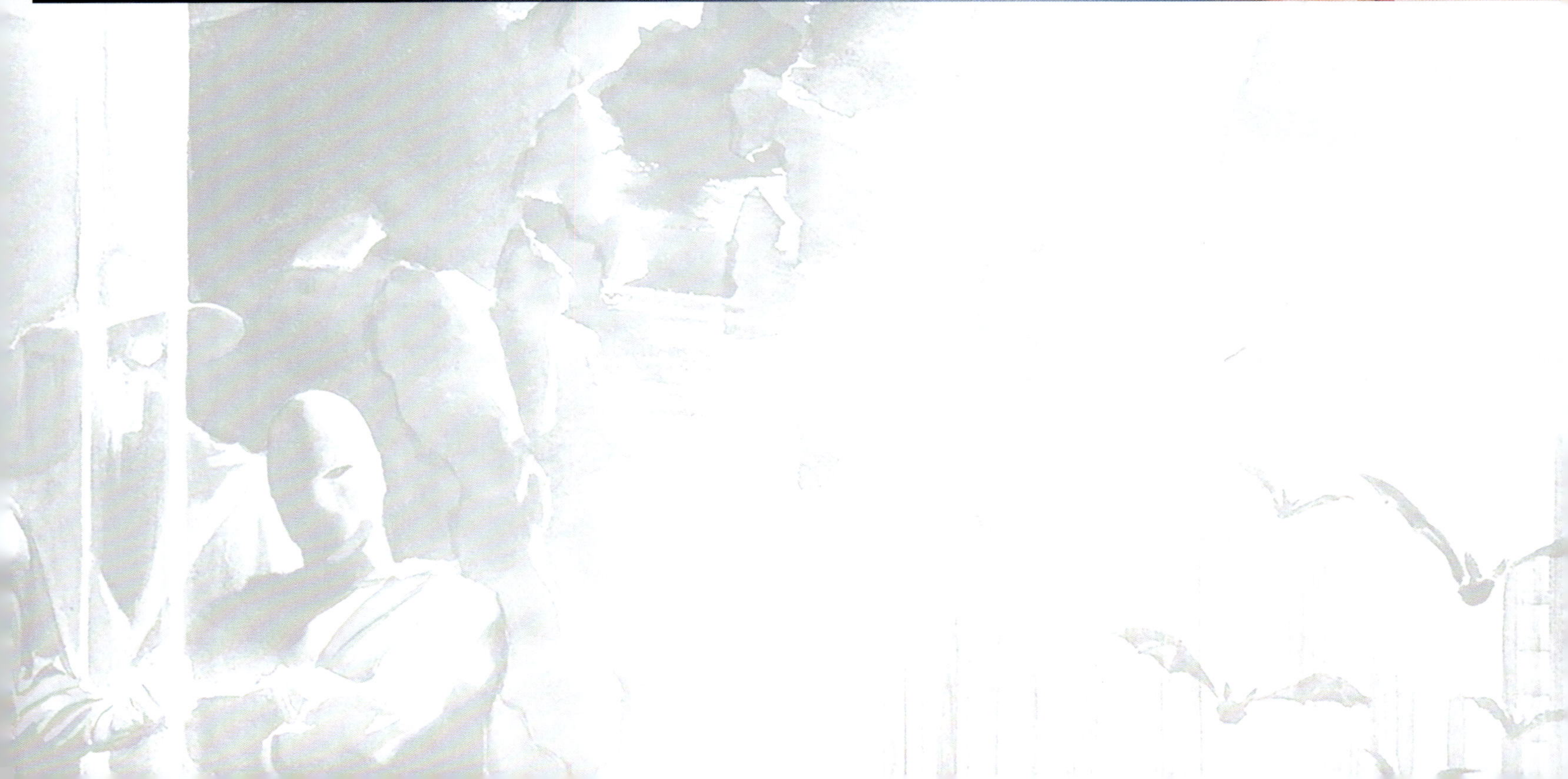

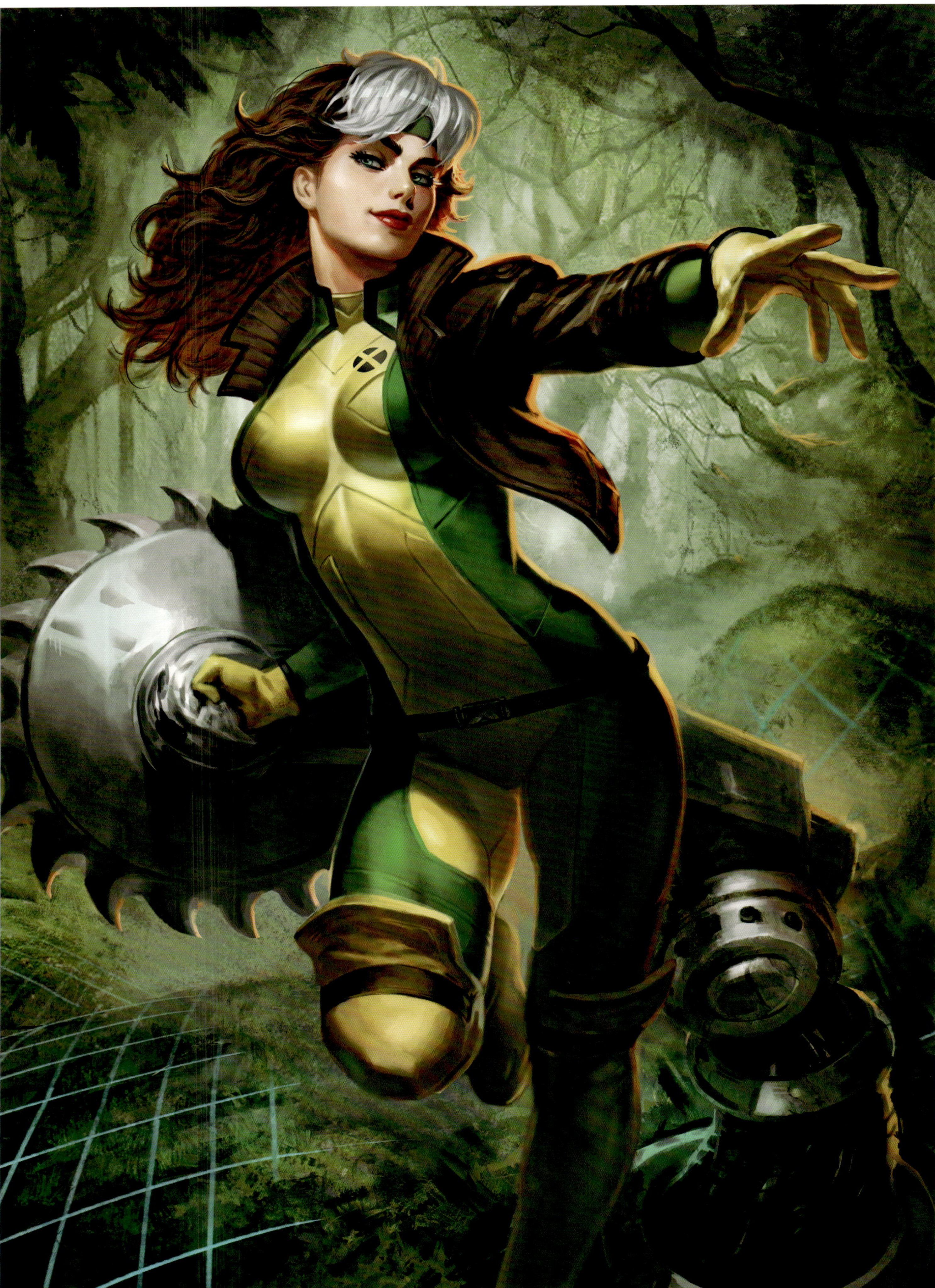

1

ROGUE

IAN MACDONALD & ALEX PASCENKO

When things are going south for the X-Men, that's when Rogue is ready to shine! Using her marvelous absorbed powers, the heroine wrenches a mechanical buzz-saw arm from the floor of the Danger Room facility, which is projecting a lush and overgrown forest simulation to test her mutant might.

Rogue is clad in her classic '90s-era green-and-yellow costume, complete with her stylish bomber jacket and wild hairstyle, ready to take out any unwelcome X-Mansion guests with her strength and Southern charm.

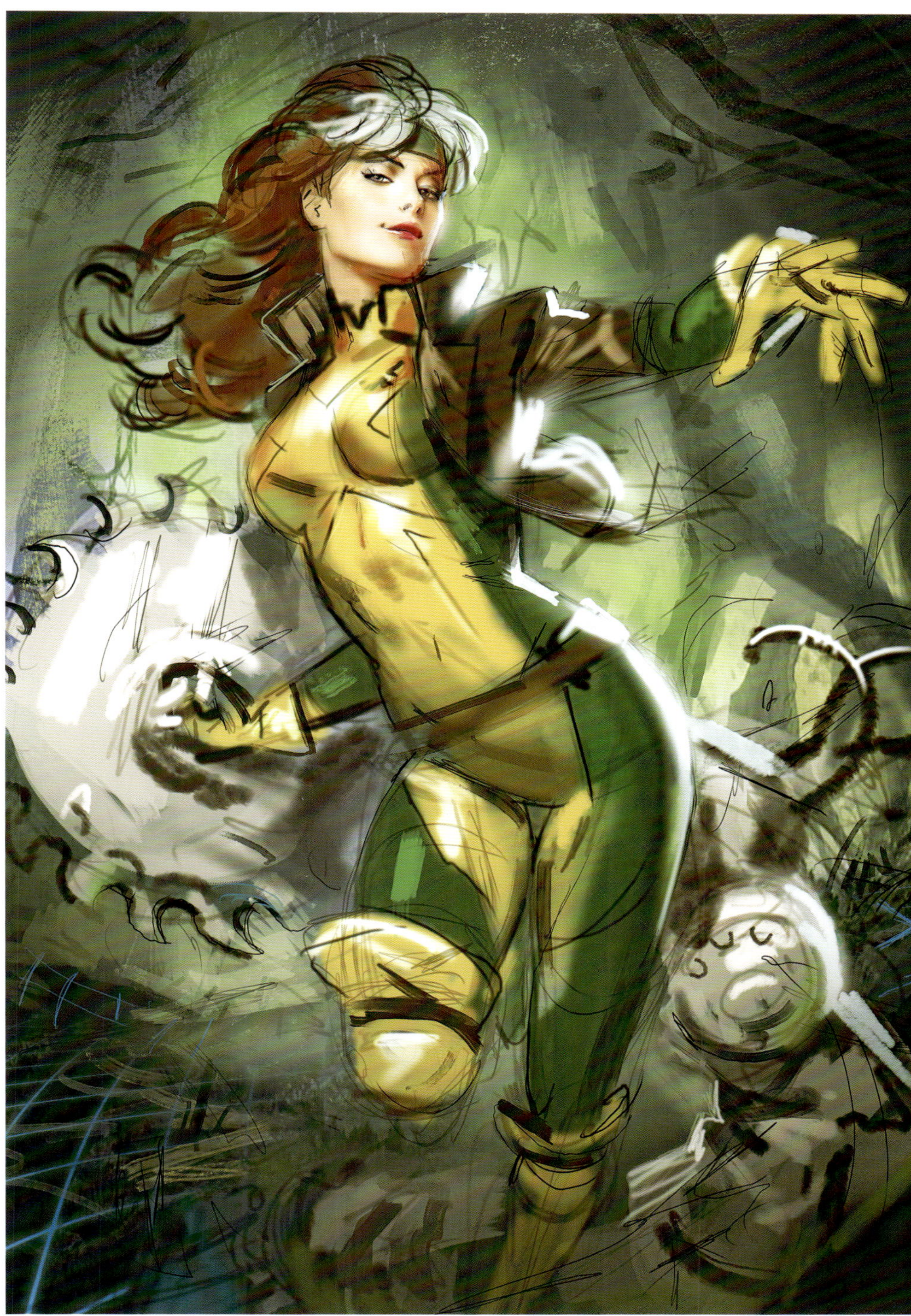

CLAWSPLAY

OLIVIA DE BERARDINIS

Clawsplay captures Michelle Pfeiffer's sultry and sensational performance as the feline femme fatale Catwoman in Tim Burton's *Batman Returns*. Wearing her iconic catsuit, Selina Kyle gives herself a quick cleaning after a busy day of getting the better of Batman, enticing the viewer with her antagonistic allure. She is surrounded by a gathering of black cats reclining on and around a luxurious bed, each with its own distinct personality.

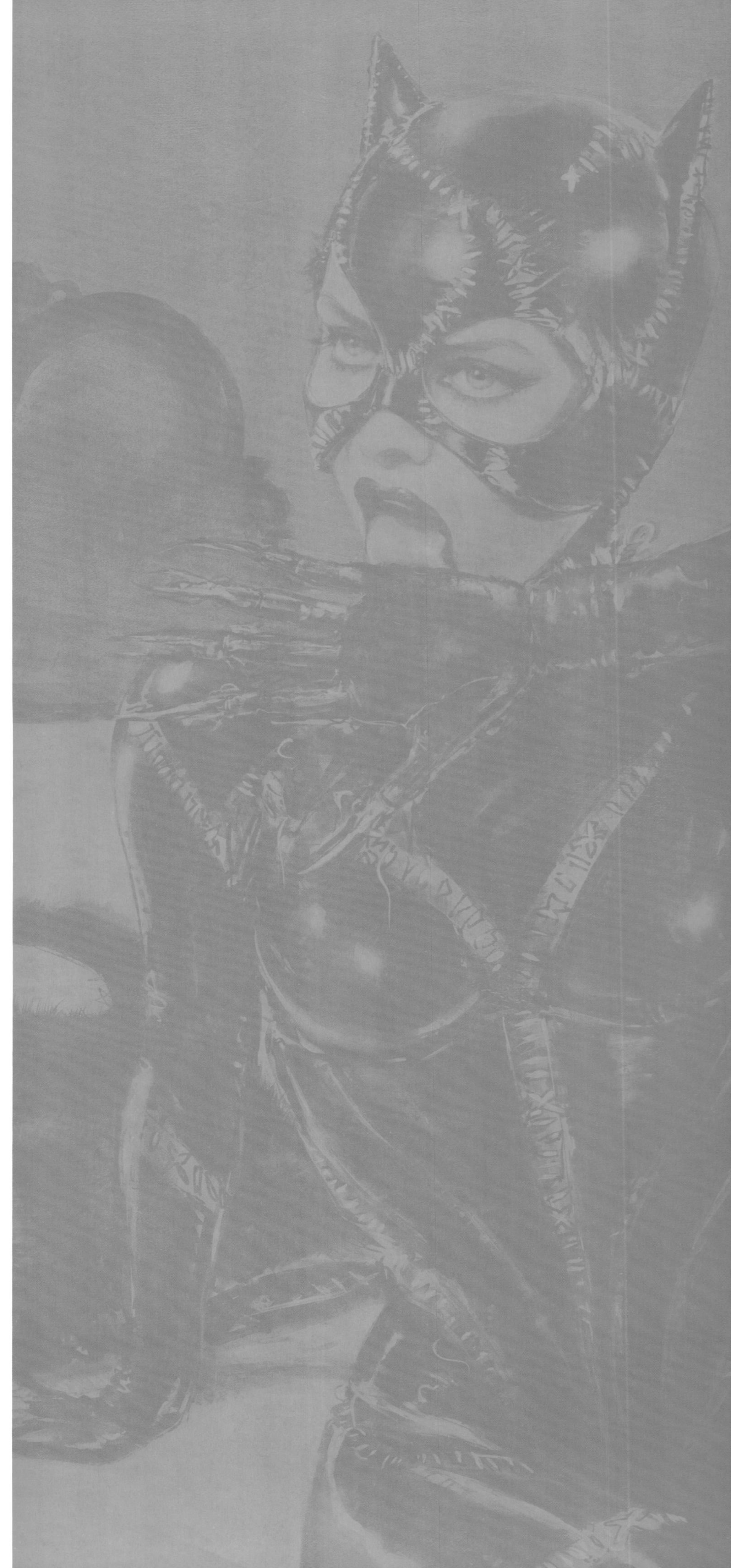

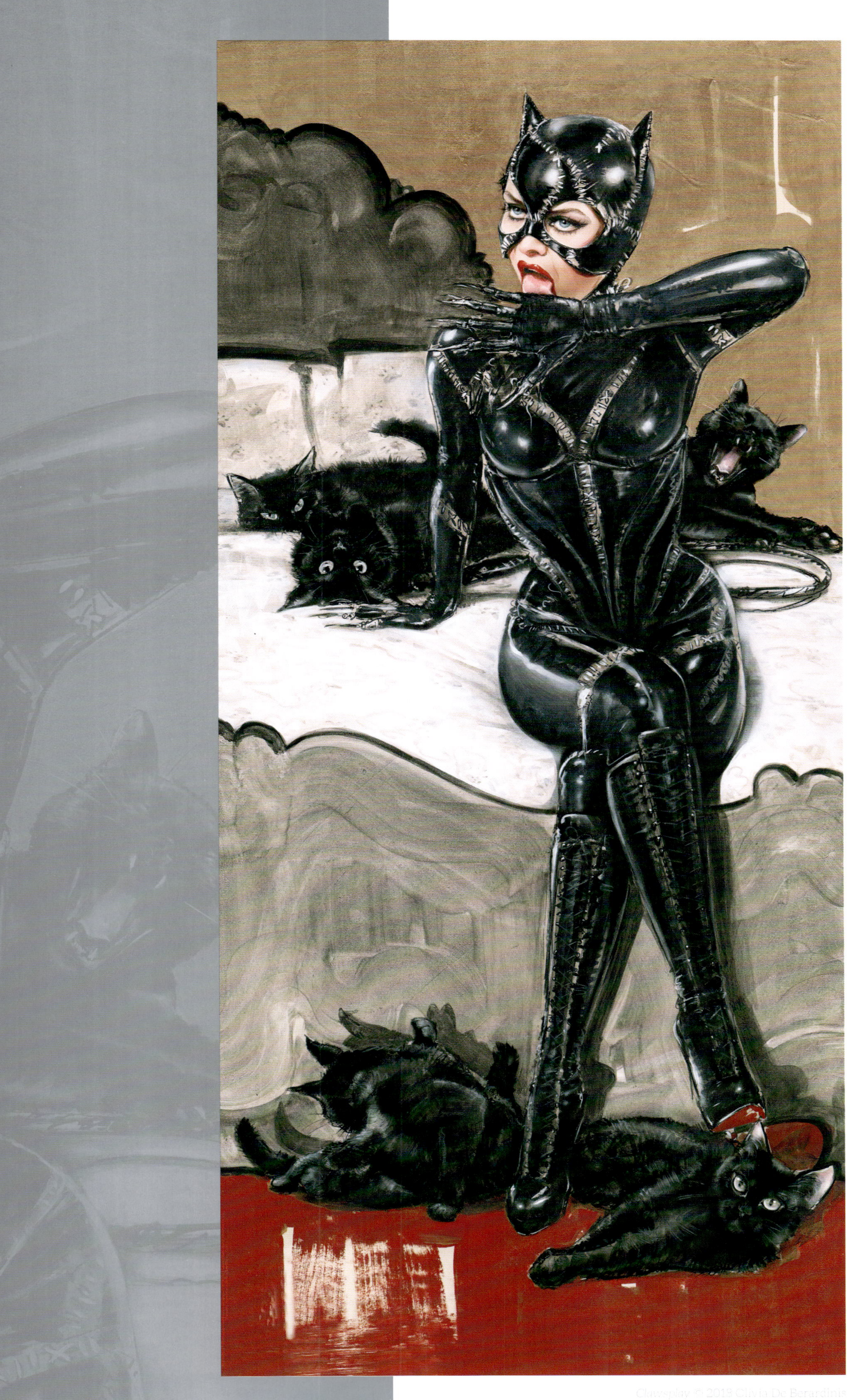

Clawsplay © 2019 Olivia De Berardinis

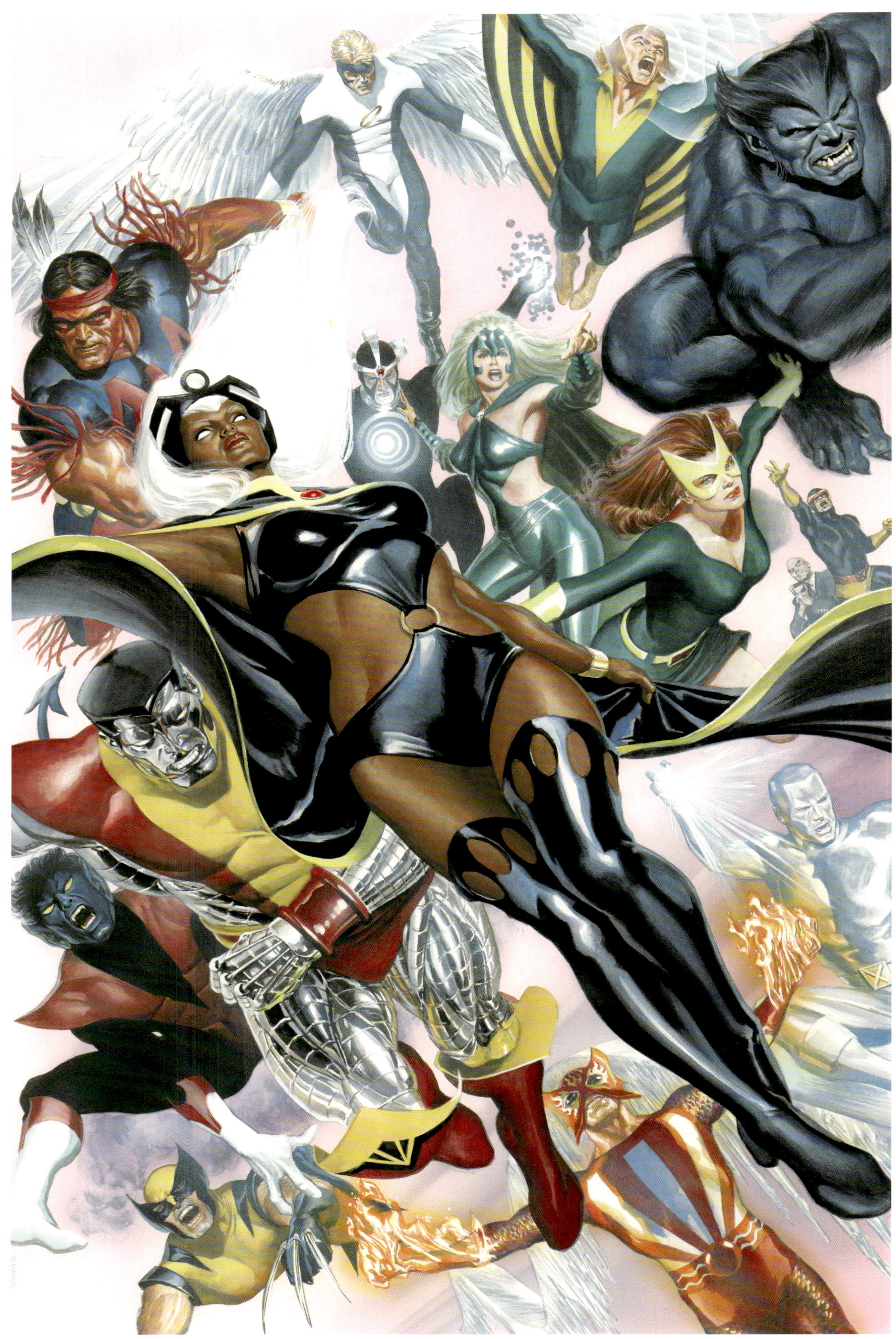

UNCANNY X-MEN

ALEX ROSS

Commissioned as a limited variant cover in celebration of Marvel's 75th anniversary, the *Uncanny X-Men* fine art lithograph unites some of Marvel's most notable mutants into one dynamic composition.

The *Uncanny X-Men* fine art lithograph pays tribute to these beloved heroes, fighting for peaceful coexistence between mutants and mankind. The image features an exciting lineup of X-Men in their iconic uniforms, with Storm leading the charge, while teammates Colossus, Nightcrawler, Wolverine, Beast, Thunderbird, and more follow behind. This exciting display of mutant heroes assembles fifteen X-Men in all, as the stoic leader Charles Xavier guides his chosen family from afar.

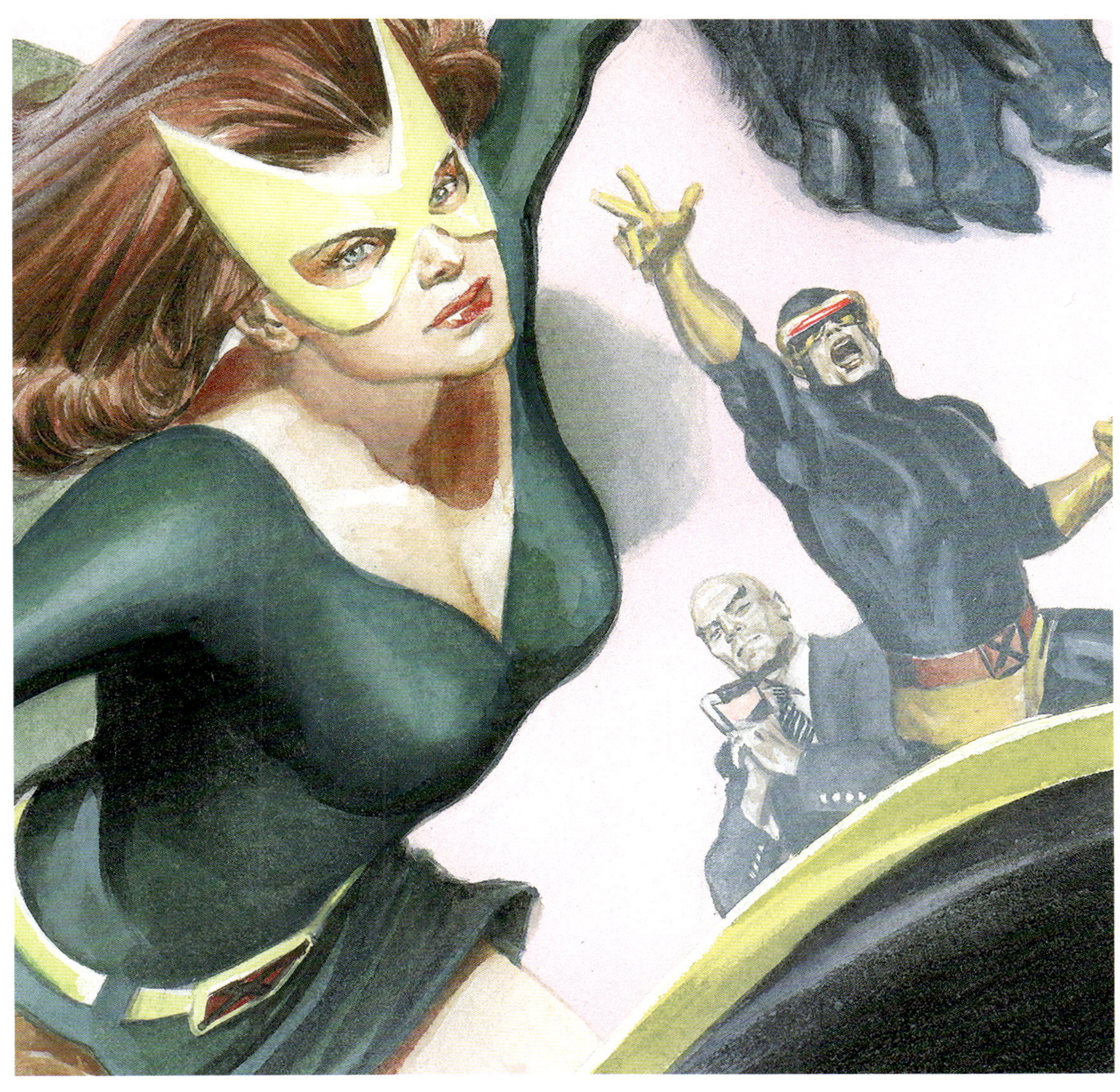

JUSTICE LEAGUE

PAOLO RIVERA

This awe-inspiring artwork unites some of the greatest heroes in DC Comics as the iconic trinity of Superman, Batman, and Wonder Woman lead the Justice League in their fight to protect the world.

Featuring classic team members as well as modern recruits, the *Justice League* Fine Art Print brings together twelve iconic superheroes in all. The Flash, Cyborg, Aquaman, and Power Girl join the Trinity standing atop the Hall of Justice, while Zatanna, Hawkgirl, Red Tornado, Martian Manhunter, and Green Lantern John Stewart lend support from the skies above.

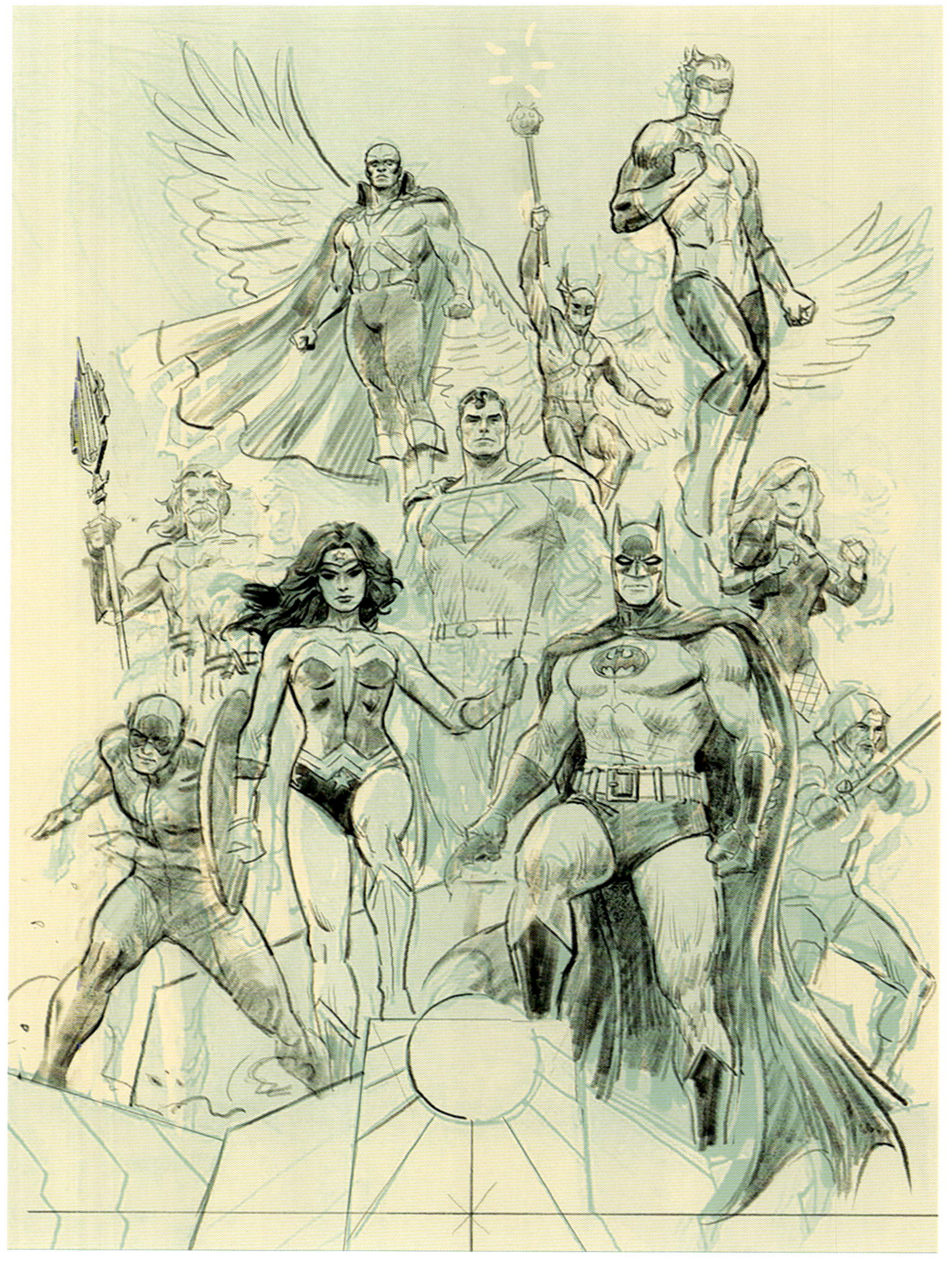

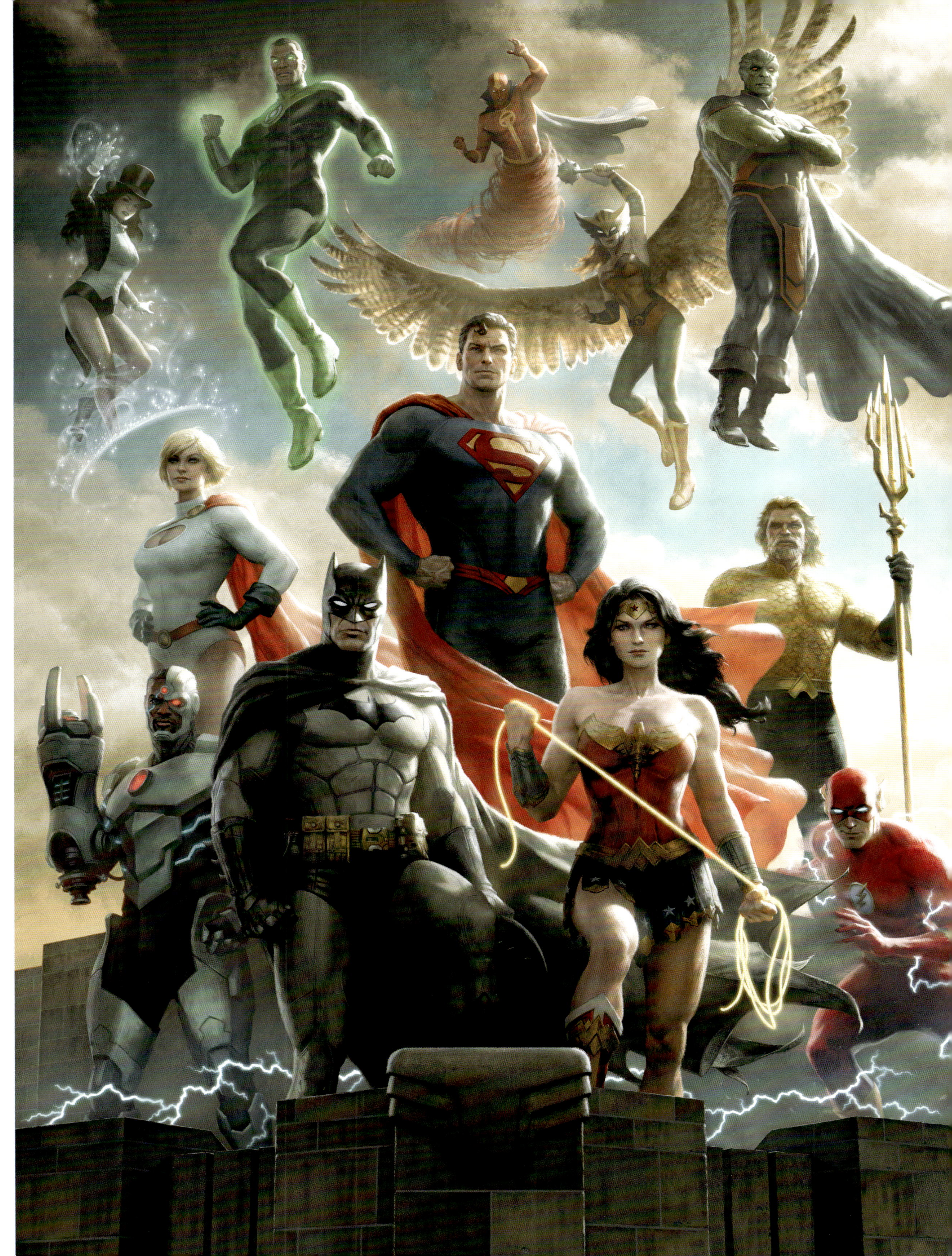

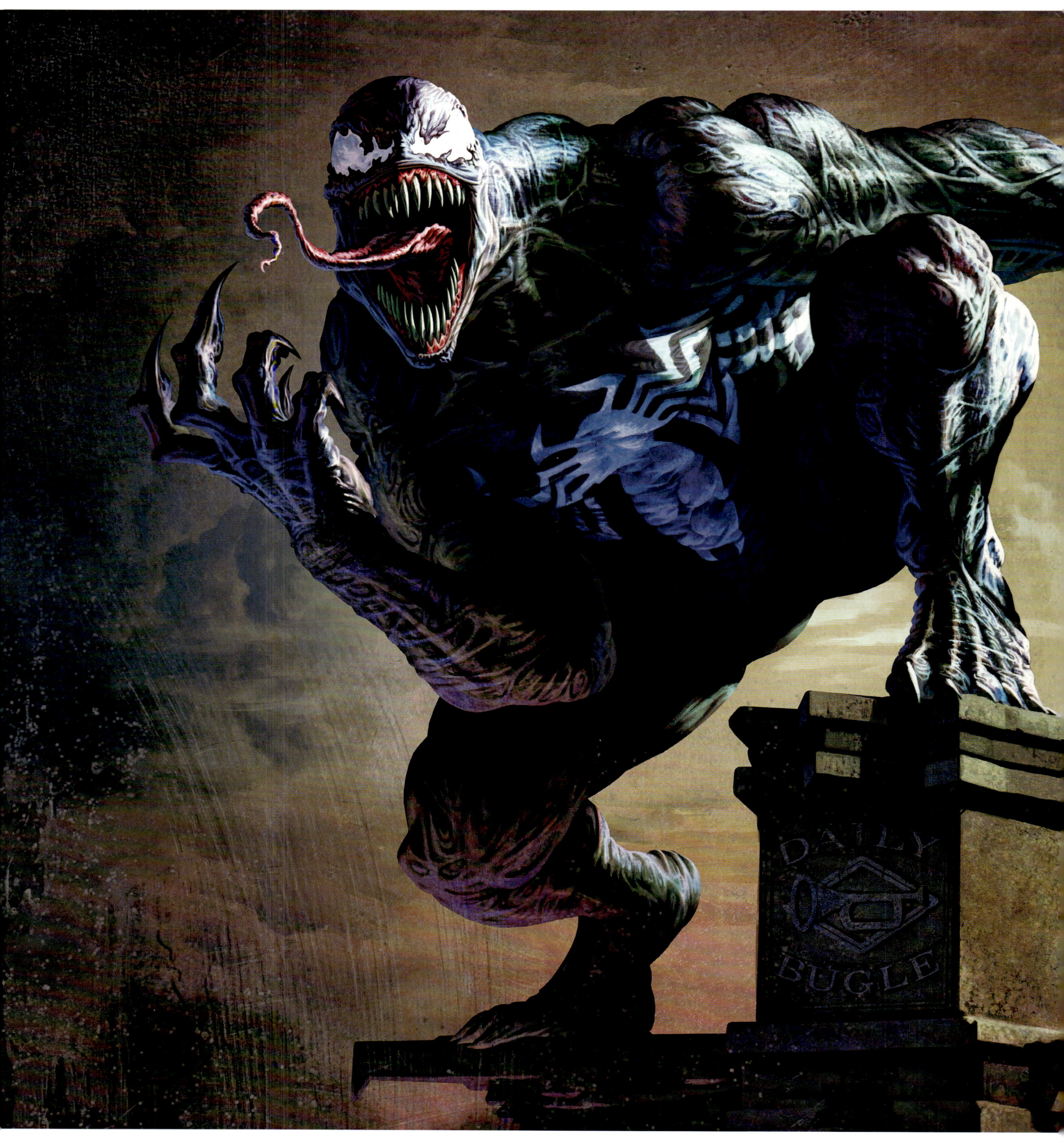
DAILY
BUGLE

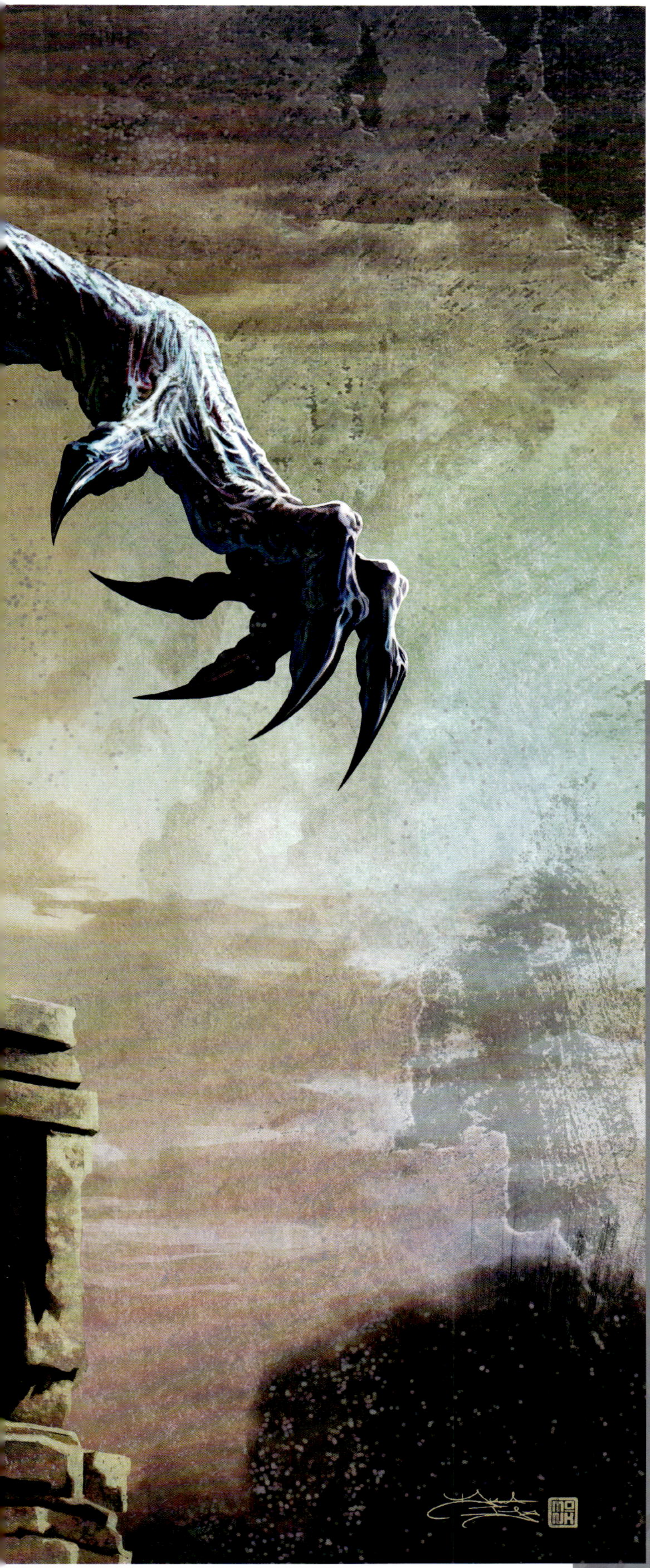

VENOM

DAVID IGO & FABIAN SCHLAGA

Fear the sinister symbiote Venom as he menaces the Marvel Universe with his lethal brand of vigilantism, captured in a collectible fine art format.

Venom is crouched atop the *Daily Bugle* building, bonded with Eddie Brock to create the monstrous antihero known for his razor-sharp teeth and terrifying tongue. His sinewy muscles are highlighted with bold teals, purples, and blues, giving the symbiote a unique and vibrant visual texture.

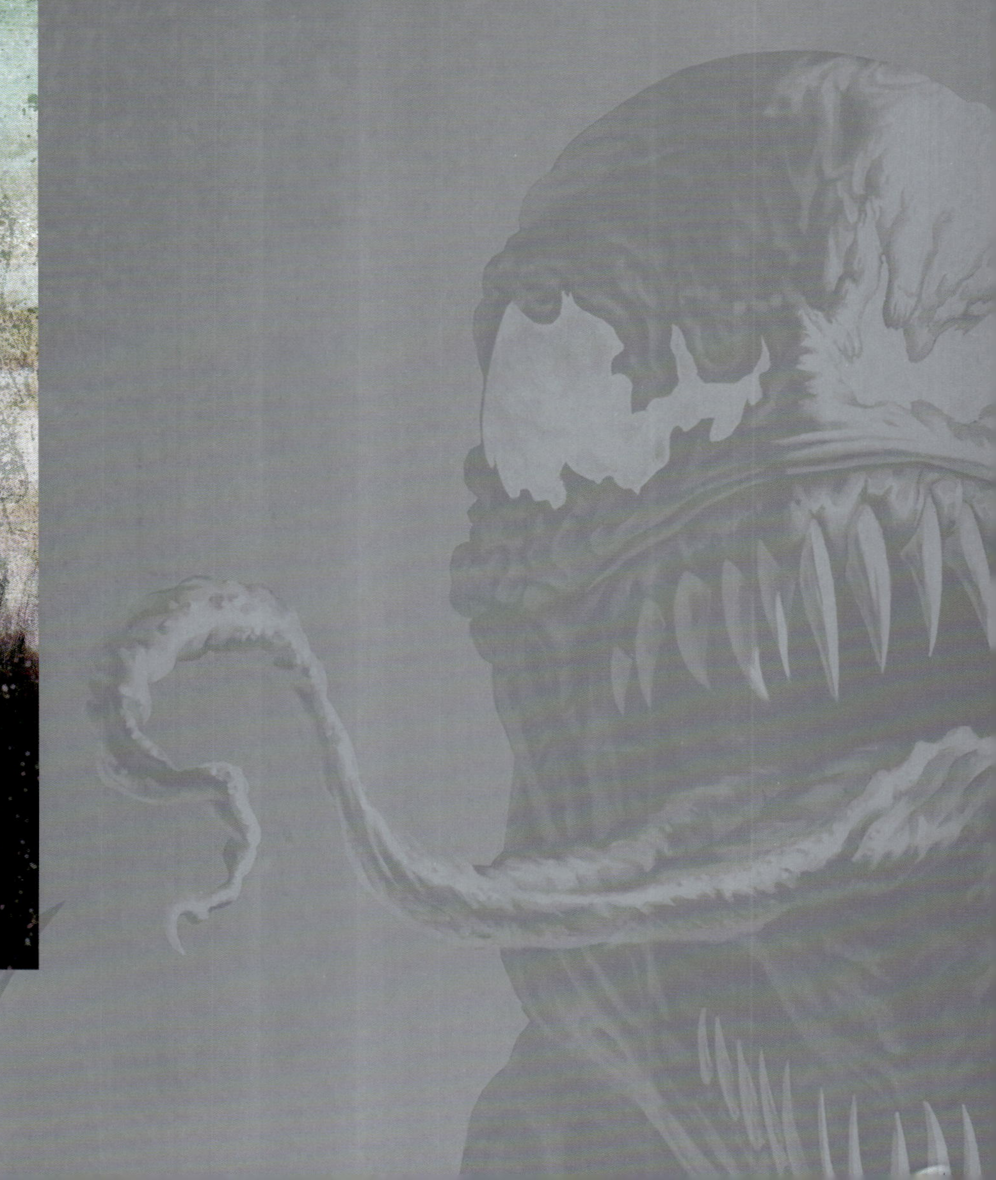

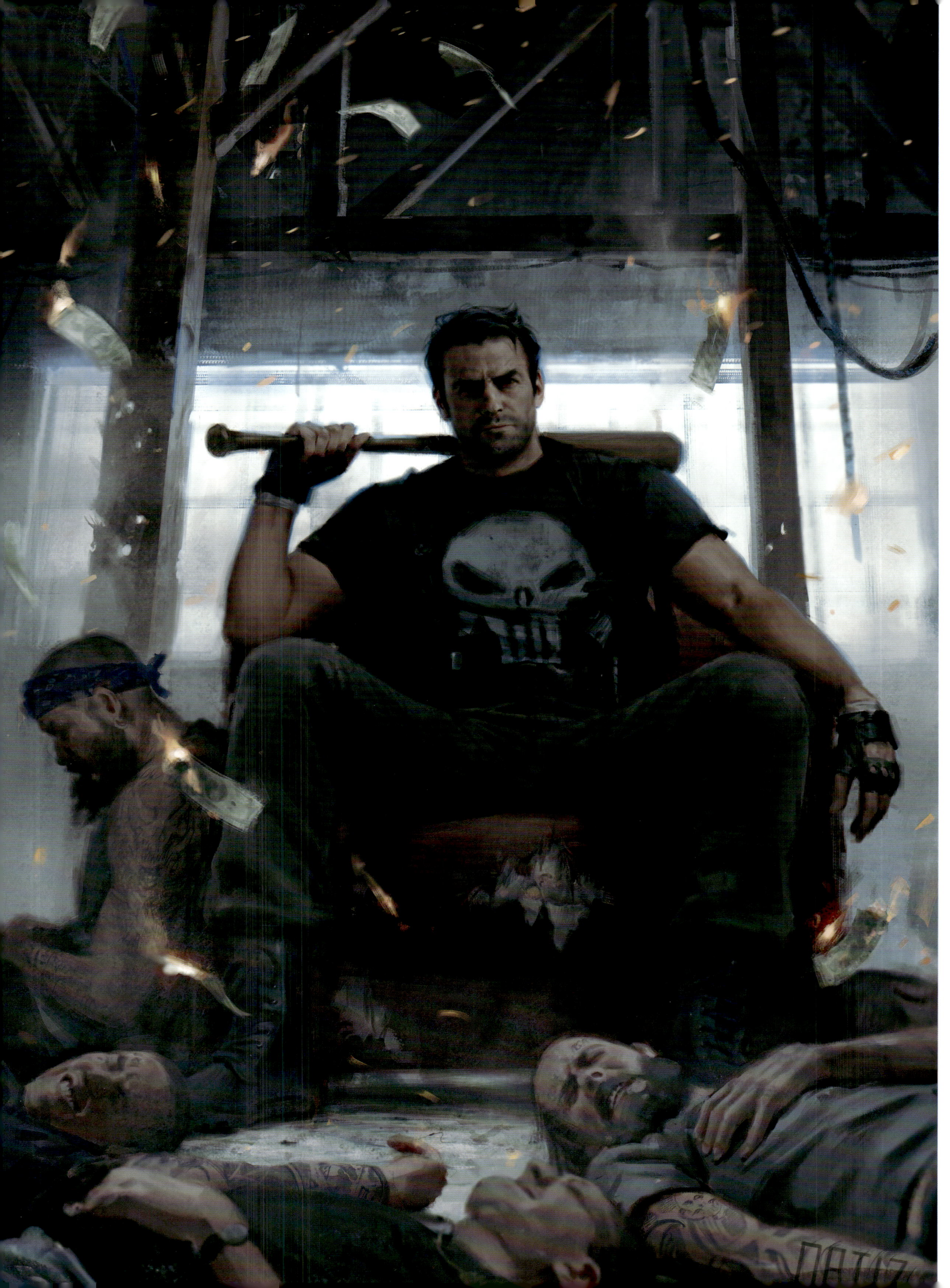

PUNISHER ON THRONE

KARLA ORTIZ

Frank is king of the castle in this gritty illustration that captures the Punisher in a moment of victory and vengeance against the scum of the Marvel Universe.

The Punisher has tactically busted a Mafia safe house using only a baseball bat, doling out punishment to the battered criminals surrounding him. Ashes scatter from burning dollar bills as this criminal operation goes up in flames, courtesy of Frank Castle's twisted sense of justice.

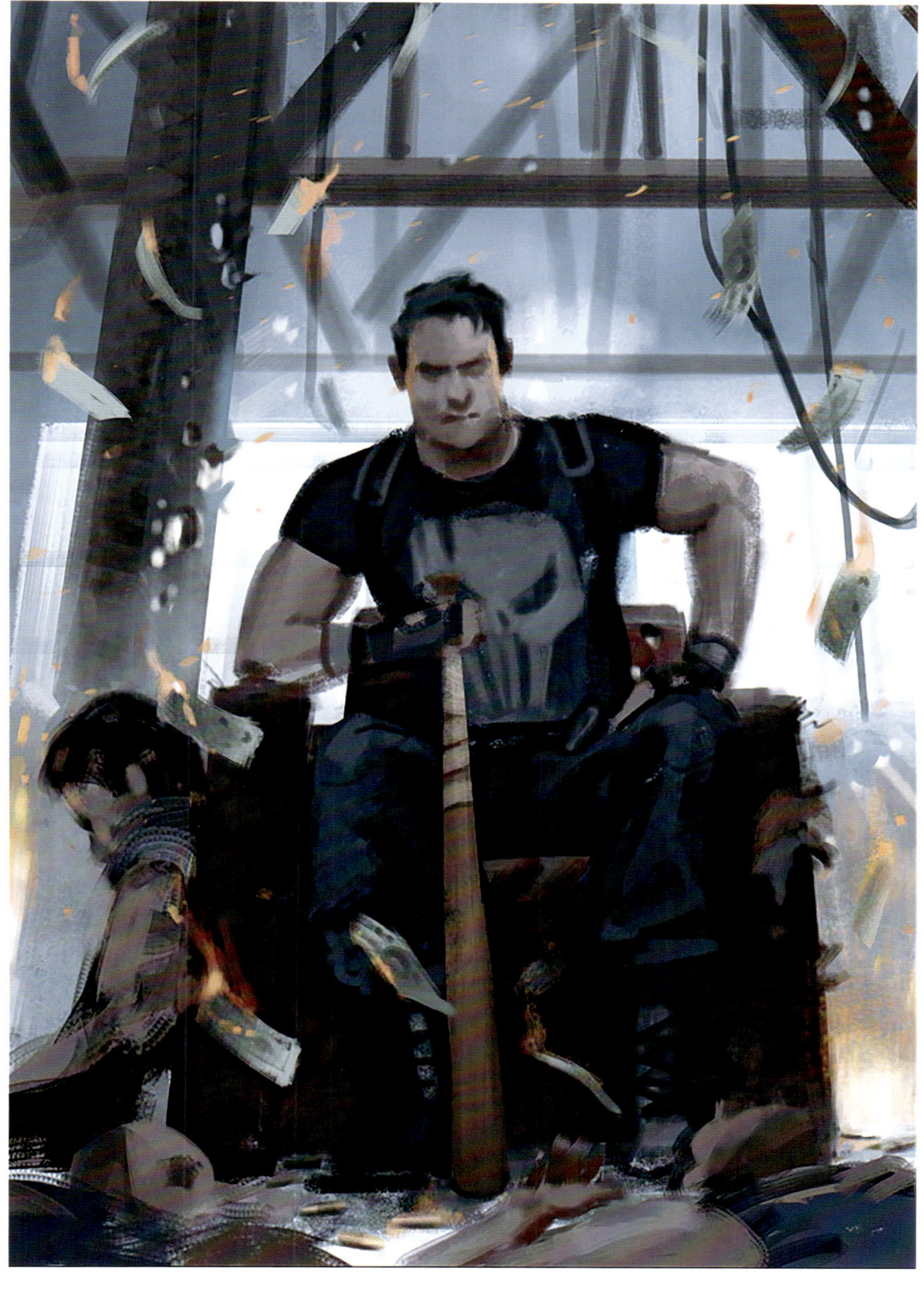

SUPERGIRL & POWER GIRL

ALEX GARNER

Worlds collide in this high-flying tableau featuring Supergirl of Earth-1 and Power Girl of Earth-2. From across the multiverse, these two Kryptonian counterparts have taken to the skies to make their world a better place while they're powered by Earth's yellow sun.

Soaring above the sunlit clouds, Supergirl and Power Girl share the strength and compassion to be heroes in every reality.

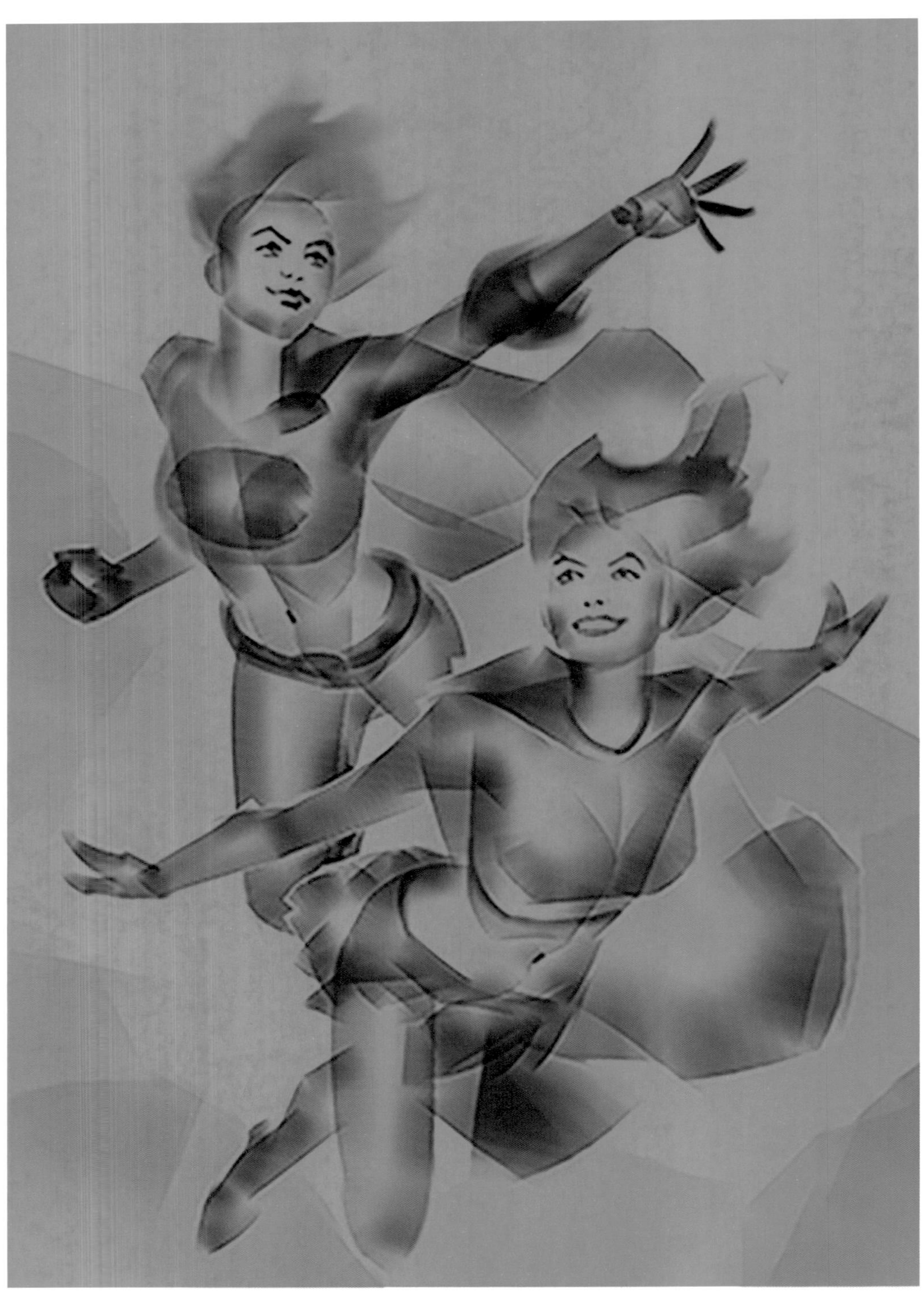

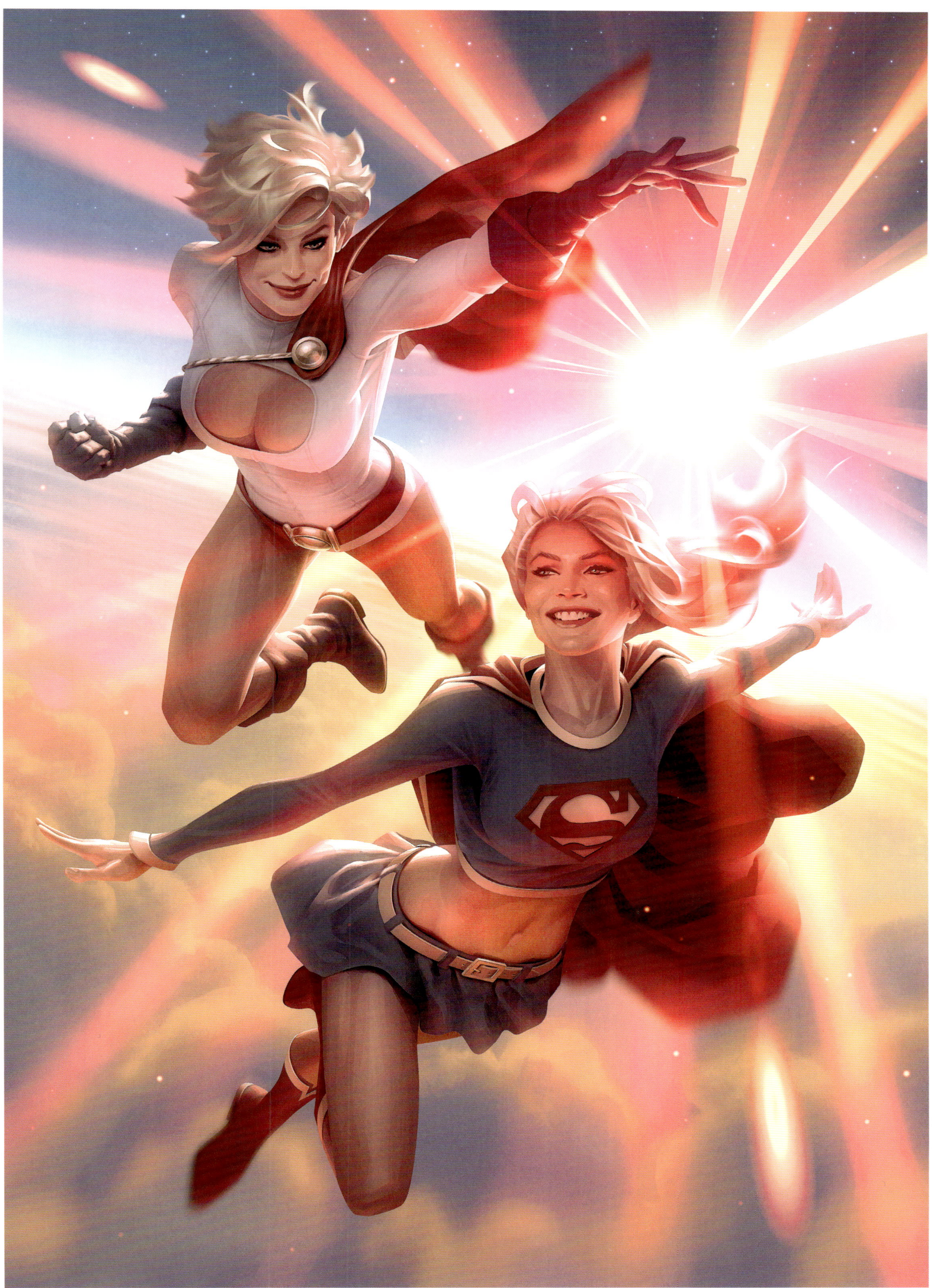

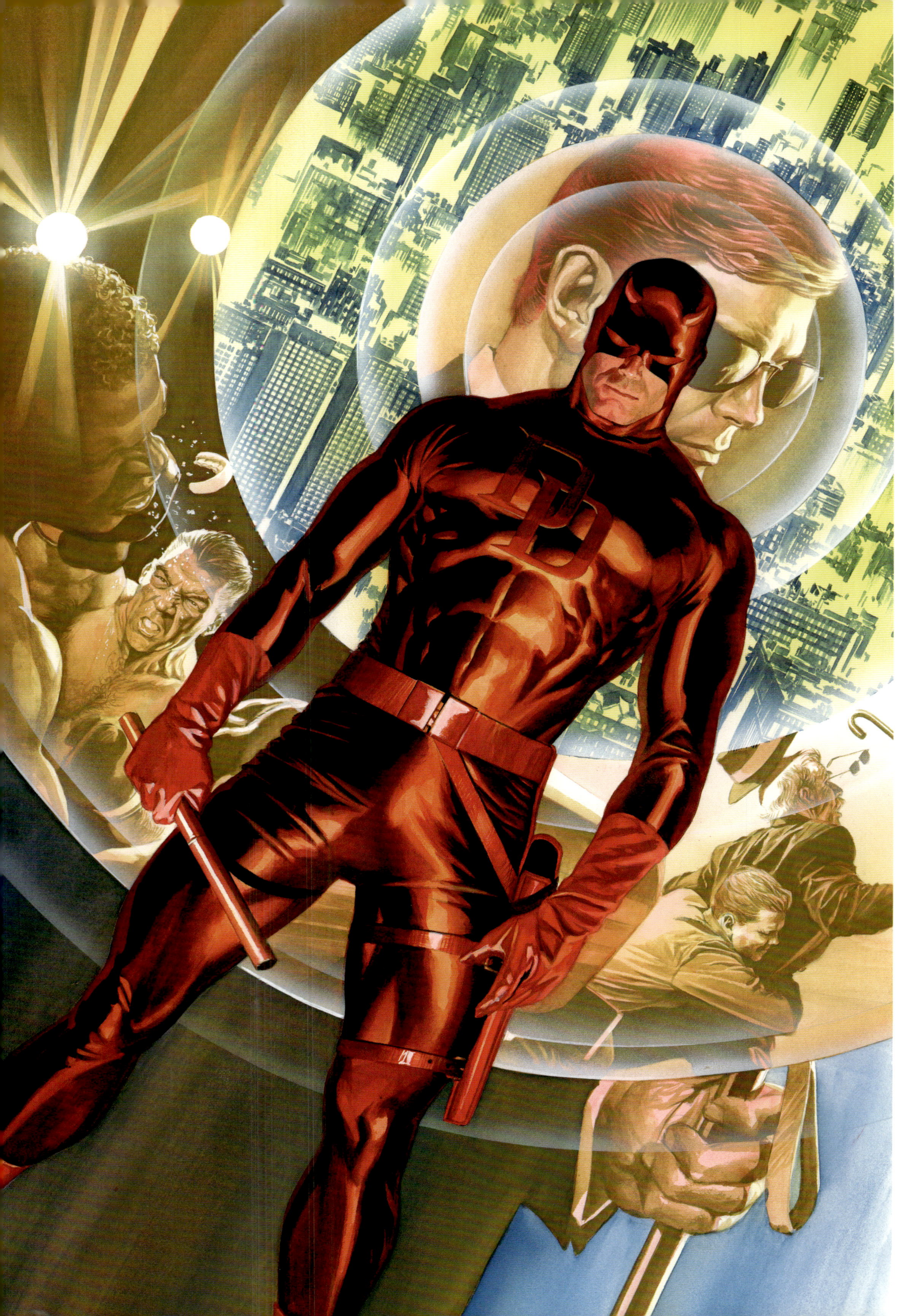

DAREDEVIL THE MAN WITHOUT FEAR

ALEX ROSS

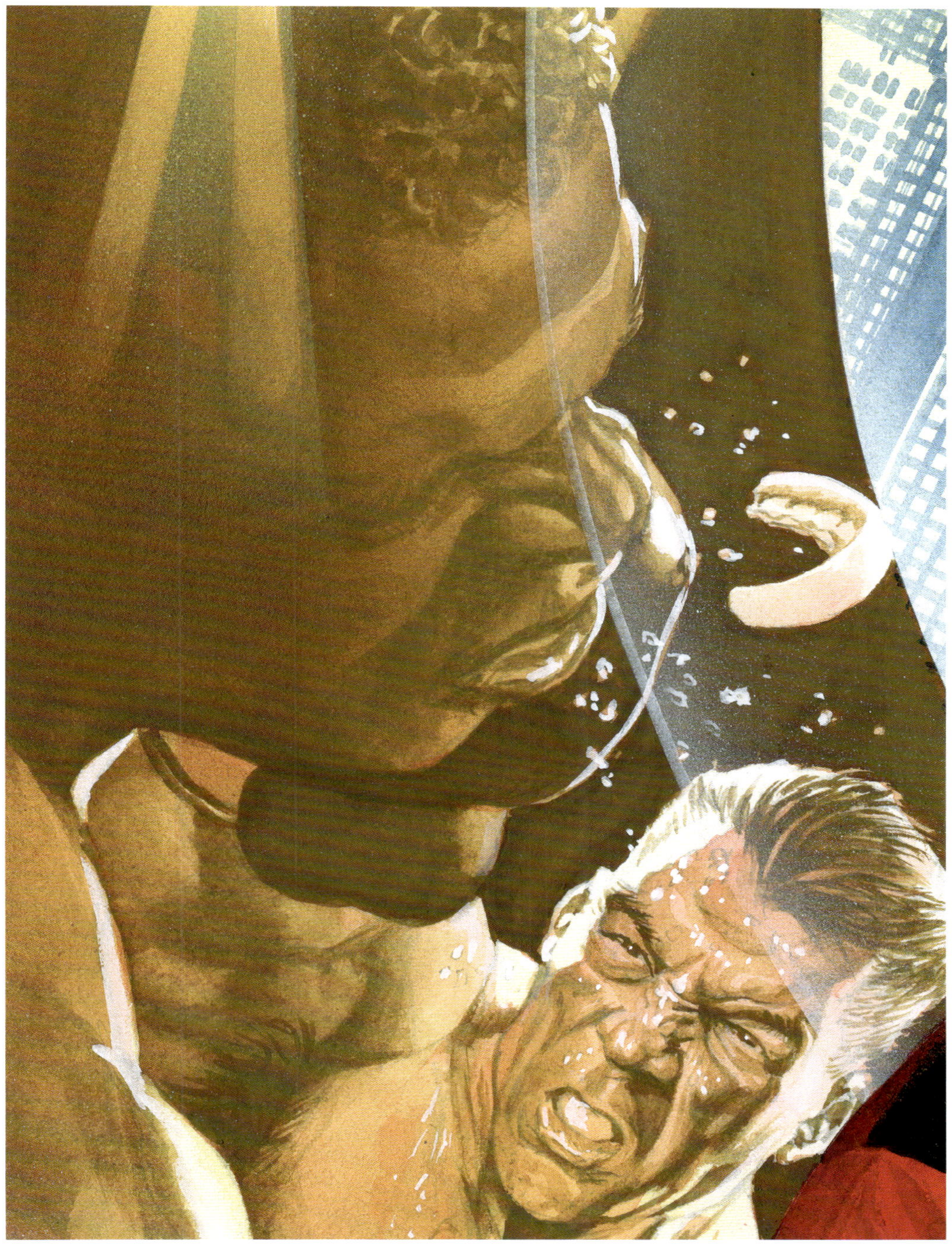

The Devil of Hell's Kitchen stands tall in the center of the image, as his radar sense reveals a glimpse of the man behind the mask. Important scenes from Matt Murdock's life play out behind Daredevil, from memories of his father, Battlin' Jack Murdock, to the moment when the young boy lost his sight forever.

Originally created as a variant cover in honor of Marvel's 75th anniversary, the *Daredevil: The Man Without Fear* fine art lithograph has been specially reproduced for collectors in a Sideshow exclusive limited edition.

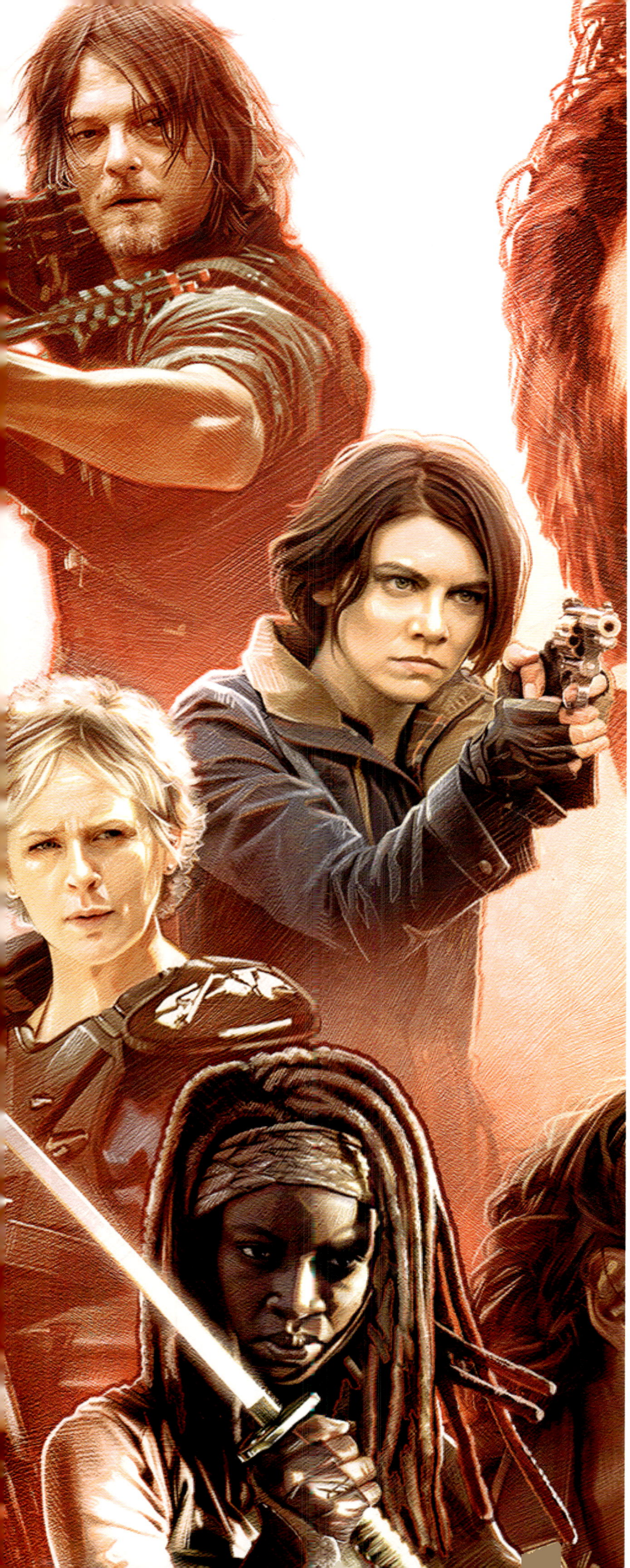

THE LAST STAND

BRIAN ROOD

Inspired by Season 8 of *The Walking Dead*, this dynamic collage of fan-favorite characters features Rick Grimes and his fellow survivors standing armed against the unending tide of undead and human enemies.

Black and red accents bring together this assemblage of *The Walking Dead*'s most famous faces as they prepare for an all-out war between Alexandria, the Hilltop, and the Kingdom. A grim portrait of Negan, leader of the Saviors, looks down while Michonne, Rick, Carol, Maggie, and Daryl take up arms and make their last stand against the terrors of the postapocalyptic landscape.

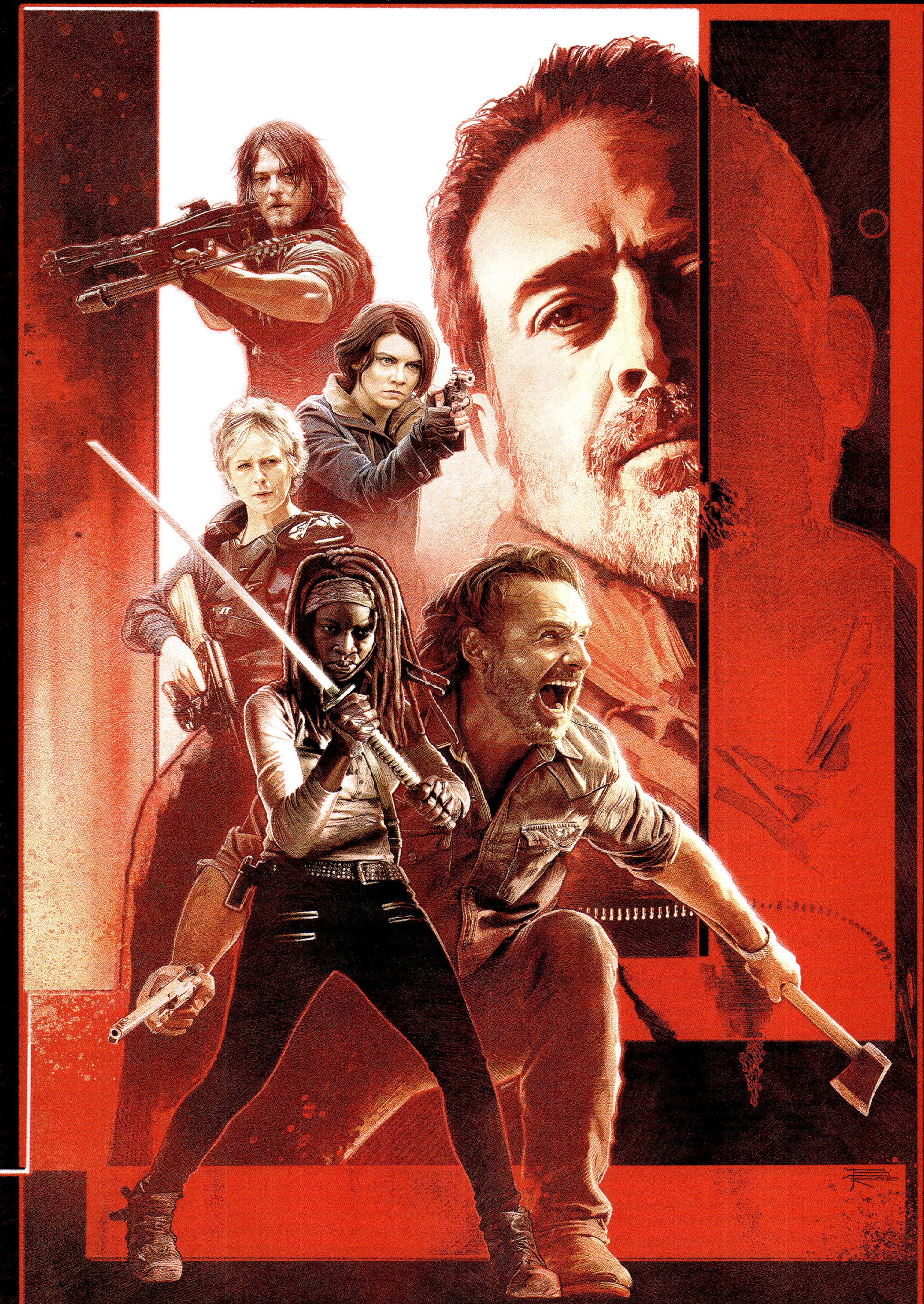

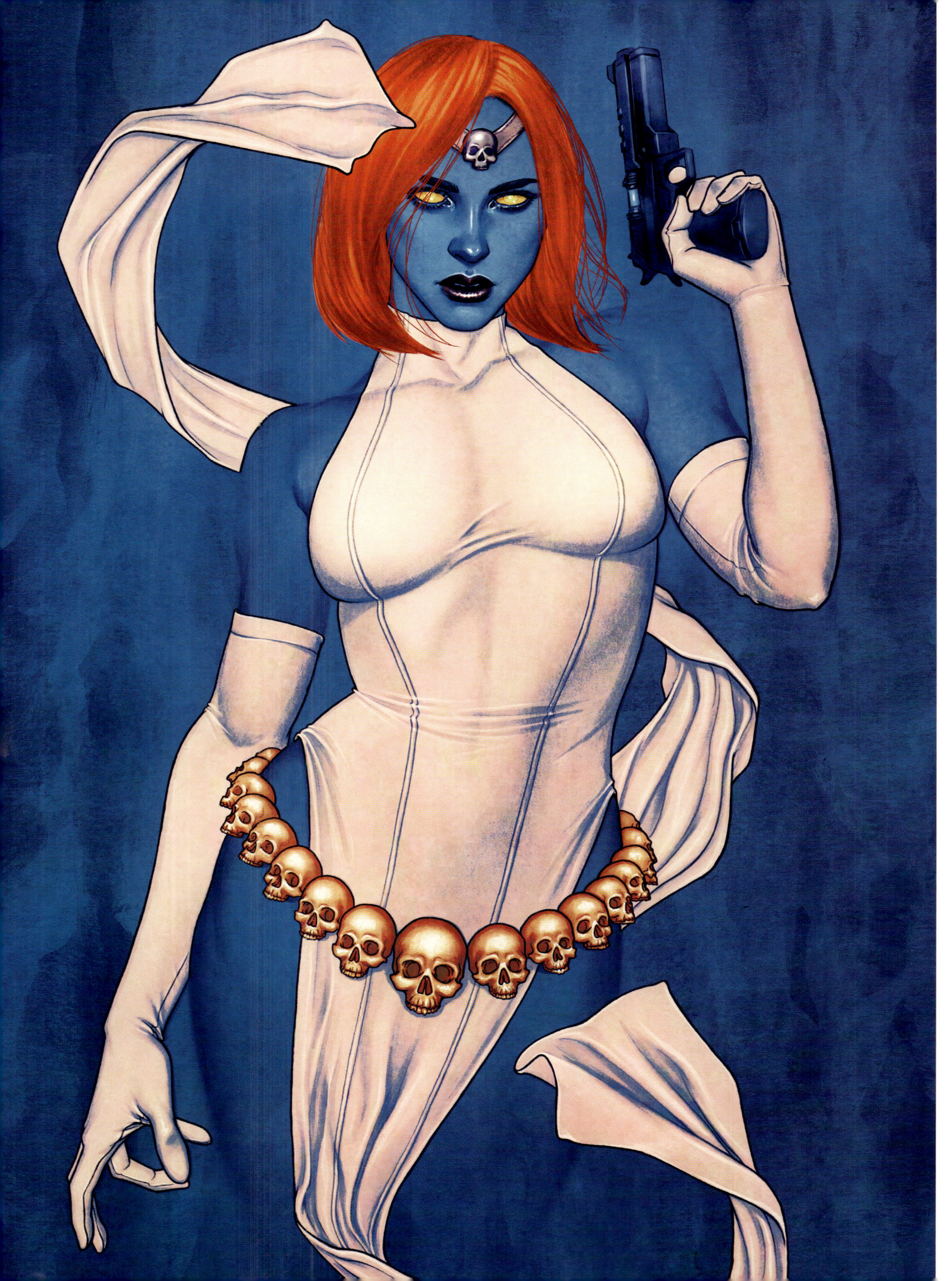

MYSTIQUE

JENNY FRISON

The sly shapeshifter Mystique shows her true face in this Marvel fine art collectible, depicting the iconic character in her classic white costume, complete with a skull belt and diadem. This mysterious mutant has bright red hair and piercing yellow eyes, while her signature blue skin blends with the backdrop to further heighten her elusiveness.

Whether she's teamed with Magneto's Brotherhood of Mutants or only out for herself, Mystique is a dangerous and dynamic force to be reckoned with.

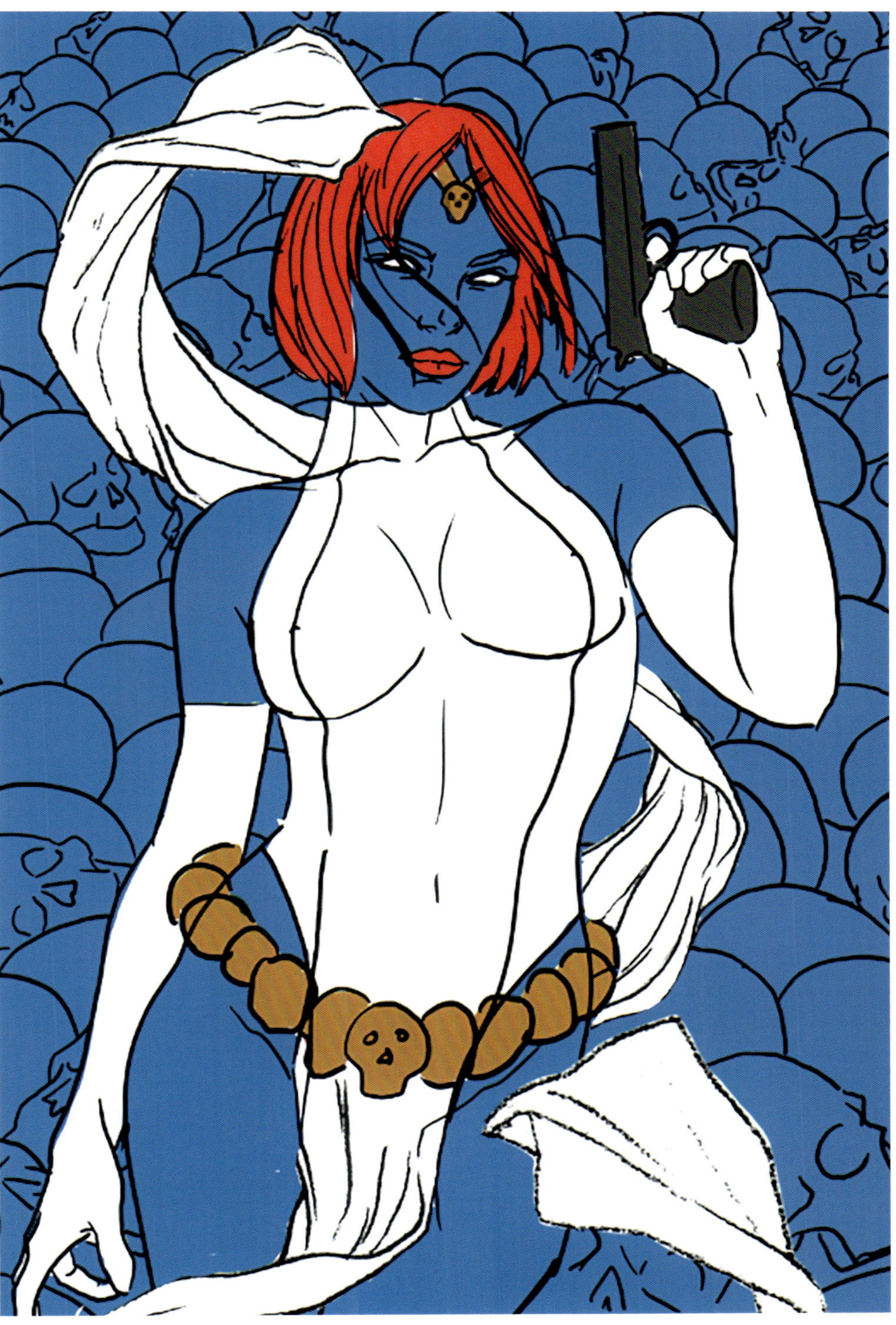

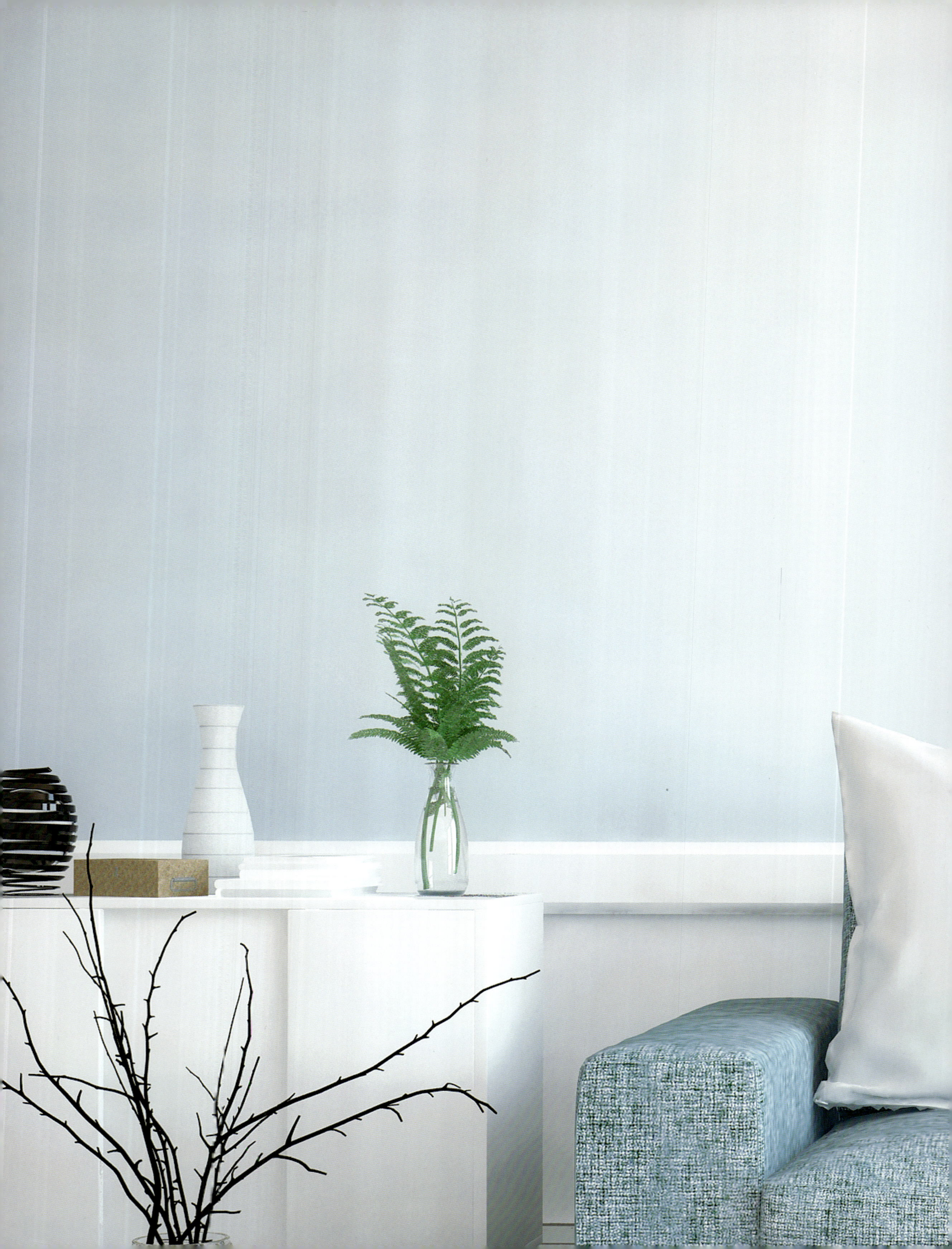

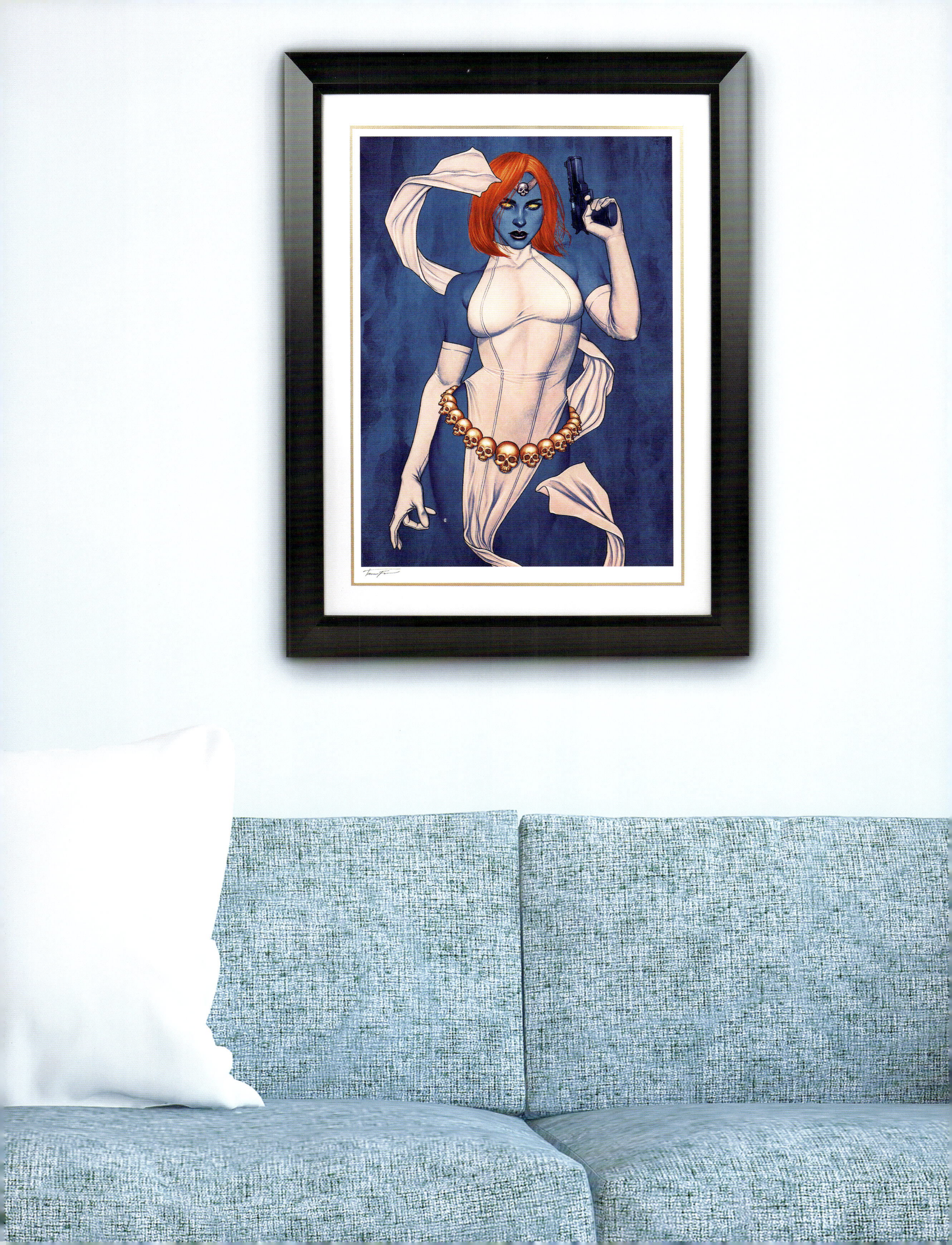

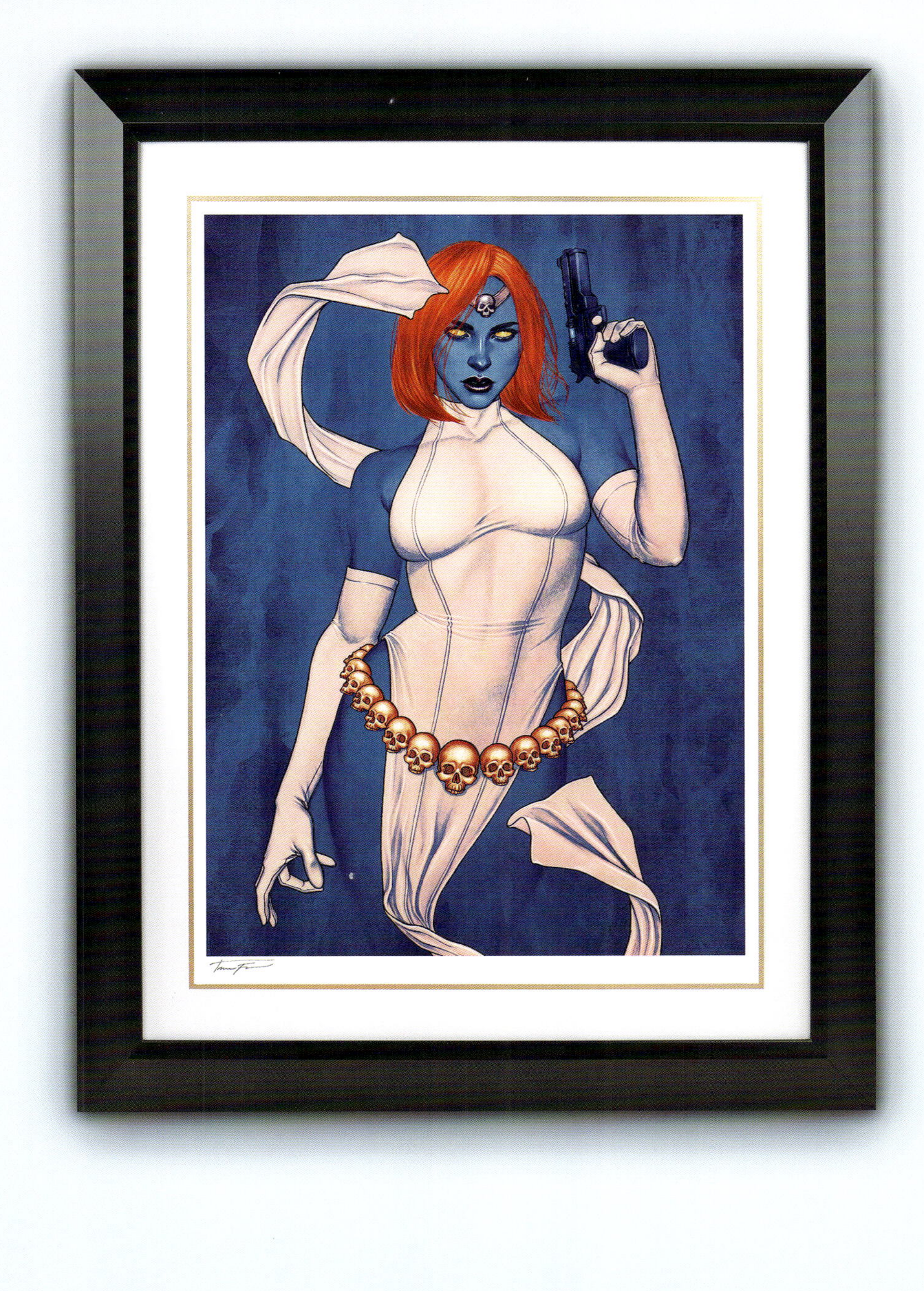

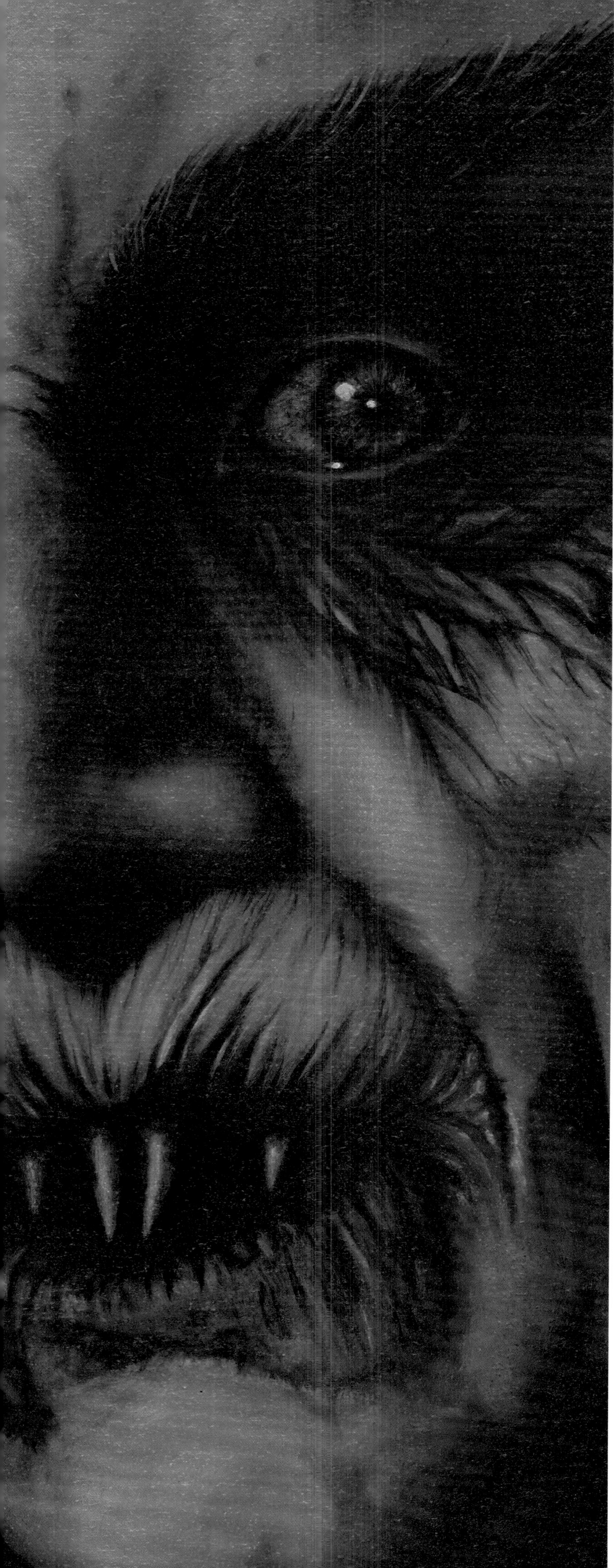

NOSFERATU

DAN COLONNA

Replicated from an original oil-on-canvas painting, Dan Colonna's *Nosferatu* Fine Art Print captures the haunting countenance of one of the most iconic vampires of the silver screen, rendered in astonishing and terrifying detail.

Partially inspired by a design for the Timeless Terrors series by Quarantine Studio, this fine art collectible depicts the dreaded vampire count with glistening, bloodshot eyes, yellowed fangs, and wrinkled, sallow skin.

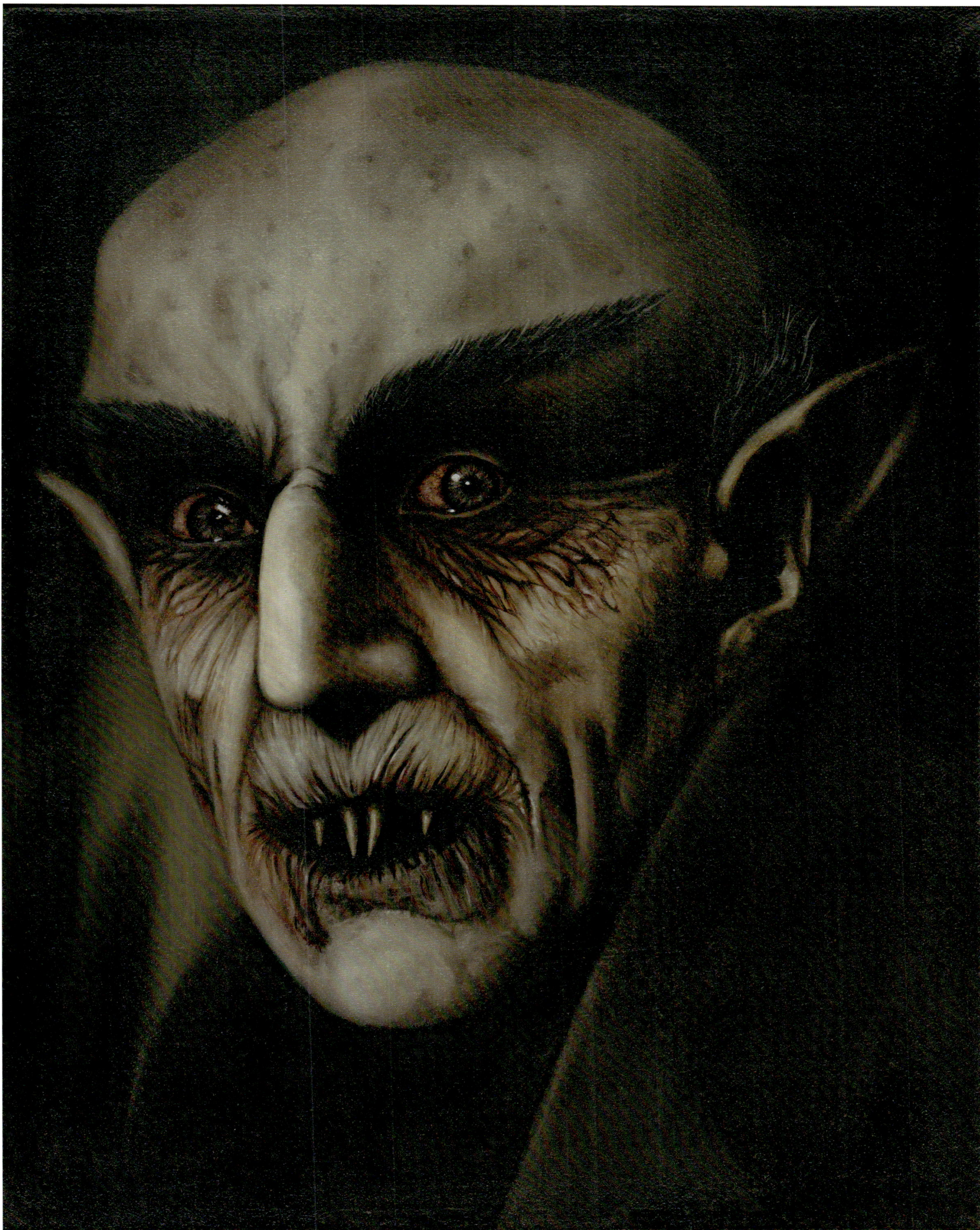

OBI-WAN KENOBI DESERT NOMAD

FABIAN SCHLAGA

Set after the fall of the Jedi Order, the *Obi-Wan Kenobi: Desert Nomad* Fine Art Print imagines the legendary hero as a mysterious wanderer.

Kenobi has witnessed the destruction of the Jedi Order at the hands of the Galactic Empire, carrying the memories of his noble past on his back as he roams the wastelands of Tatooine. Keeping a distant but watchful eye over the young Luke Skywalker, the nomadic Jedi climbs the harsh dunes while scenes of danger loom on the horizon—from the rise of Darth Vader and the Death Star, to the everyday realities of hardy Tusken Raiders and scavenging Jawas in the shifting sands. Fabian Schlaga evokes the colors of the binary sunset throughout the composition, as Obi-Wan searches tirelessly for a way to introduce a new hope to the galaxy.

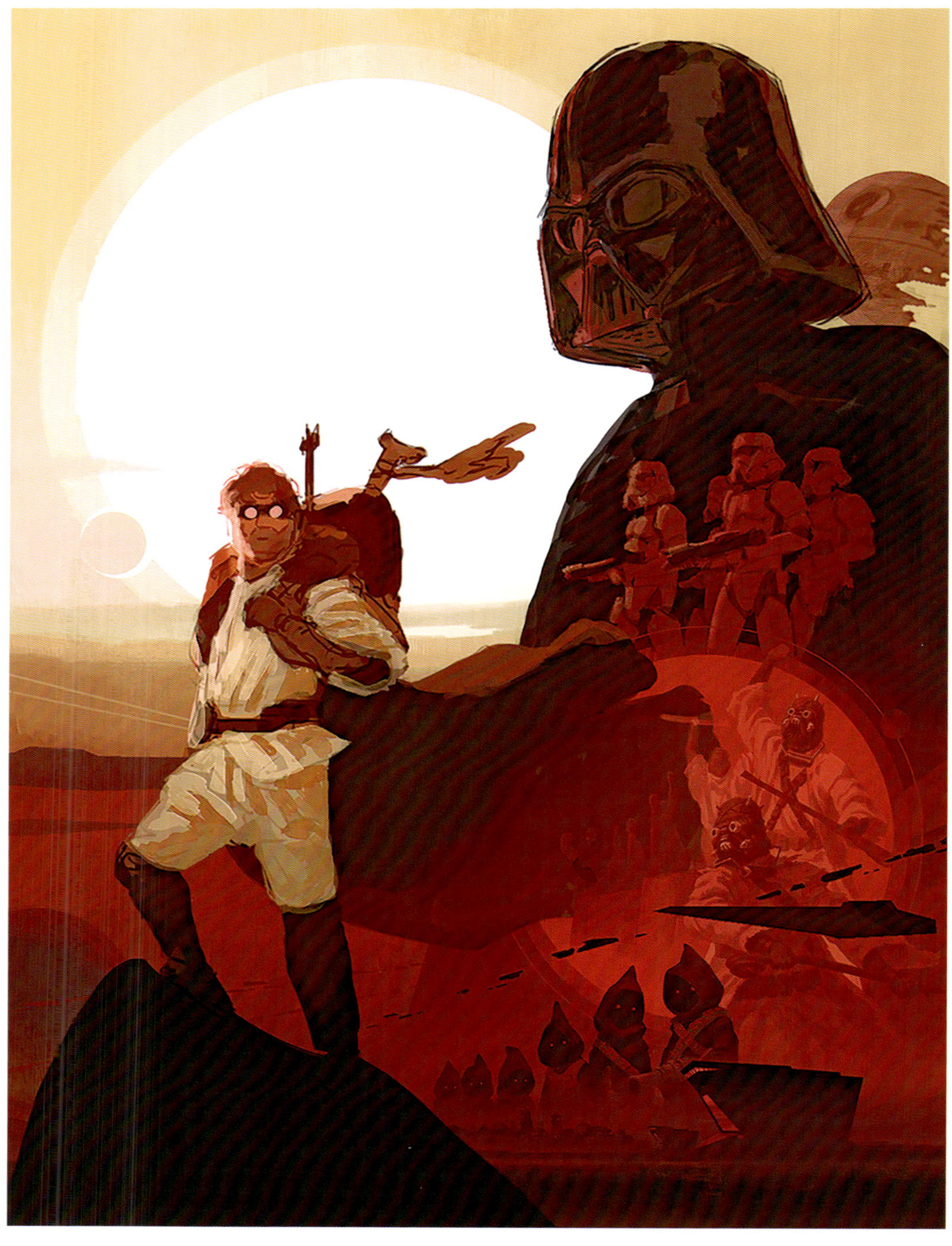

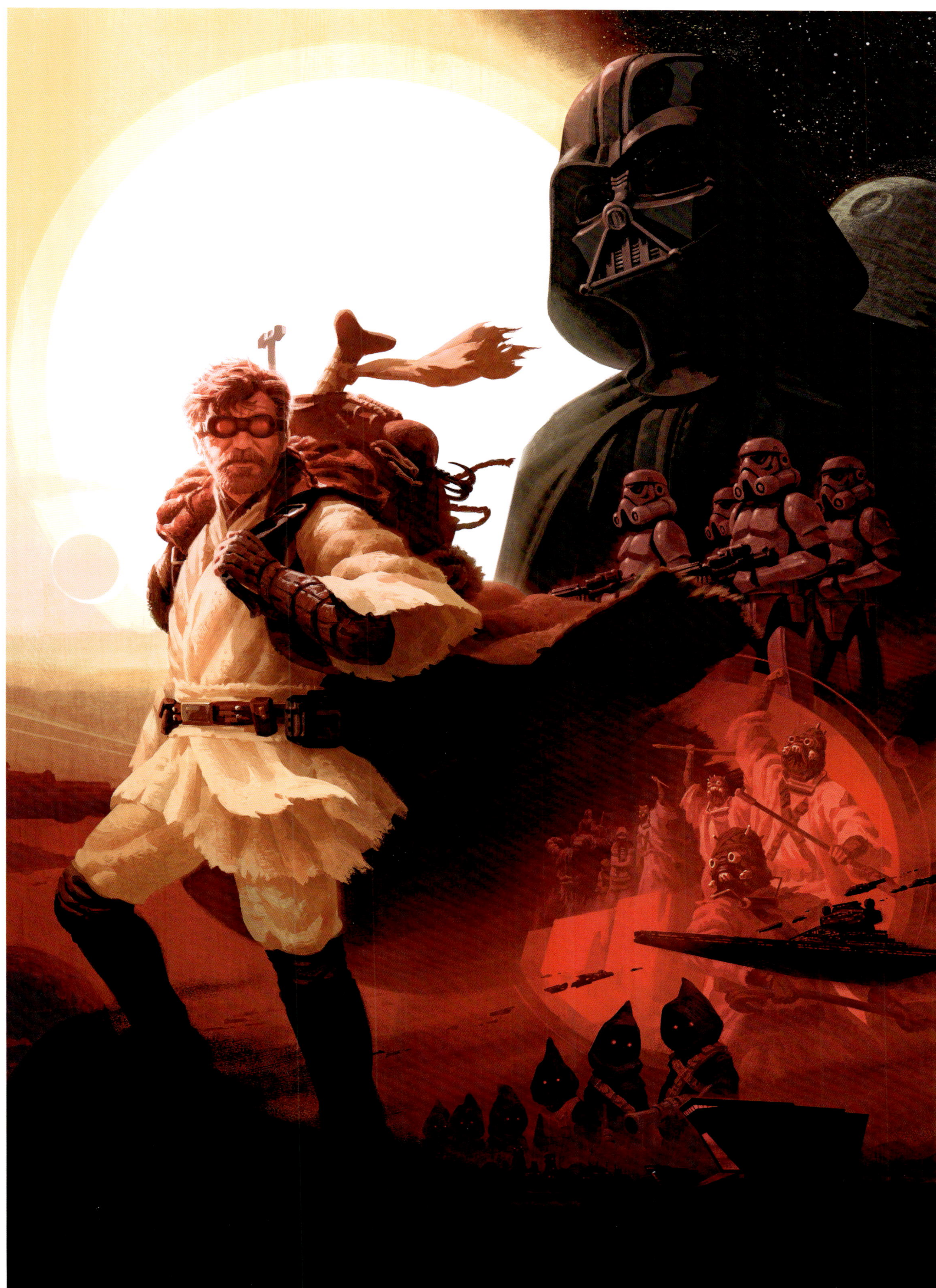

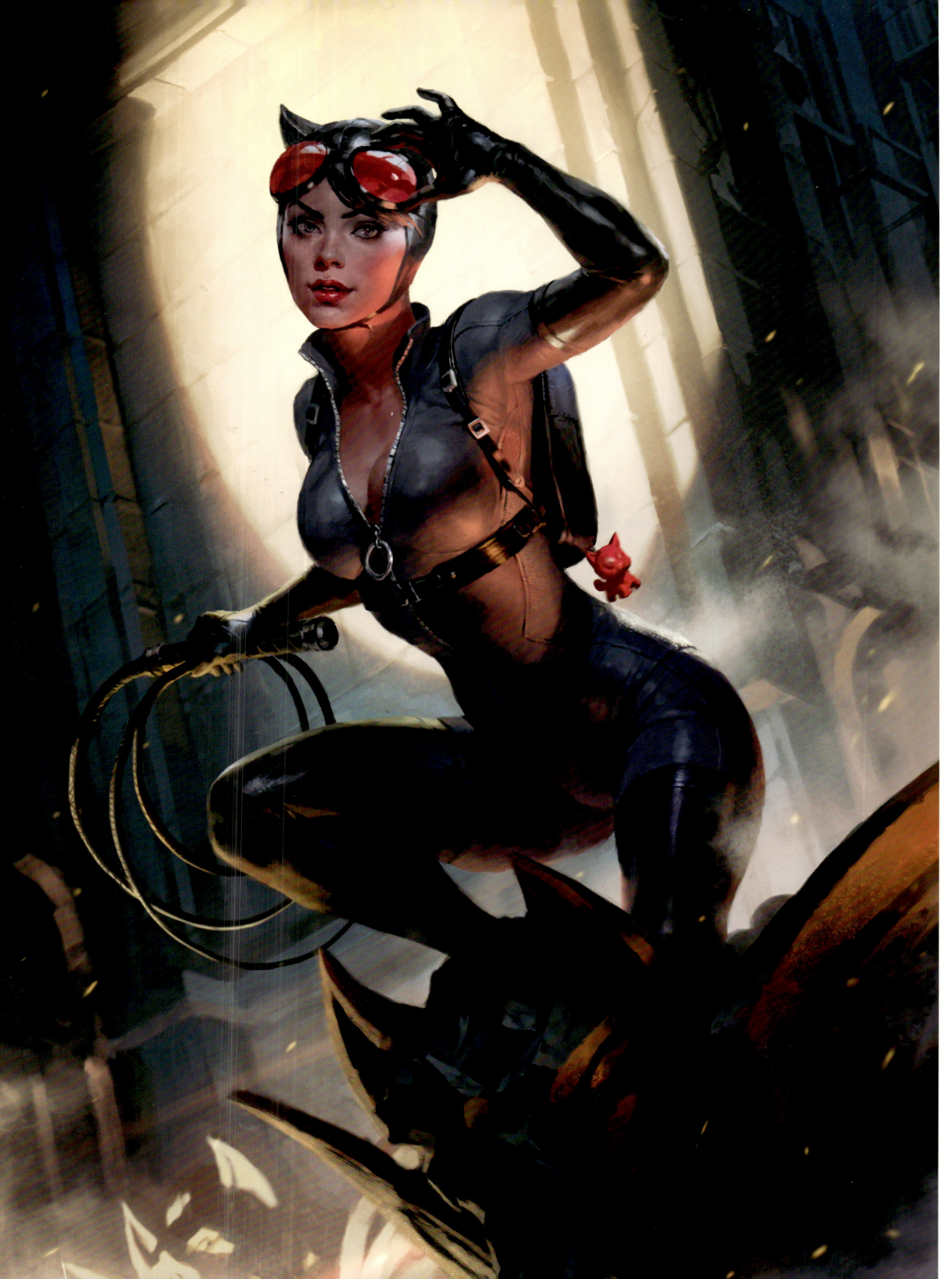

CATWOMAN

HEON-HWA CHOE

All of Gotham is on the lookout for the city's craftiest cat burglar as she prepares to make her next steal. Holding her signature bullwhip and decked out in her classic gray-and-black catsuit, the elusive Catwoman crouches atop a bat-like gargoyle in the shadows as she avoids the spotlight—and the searchlight.

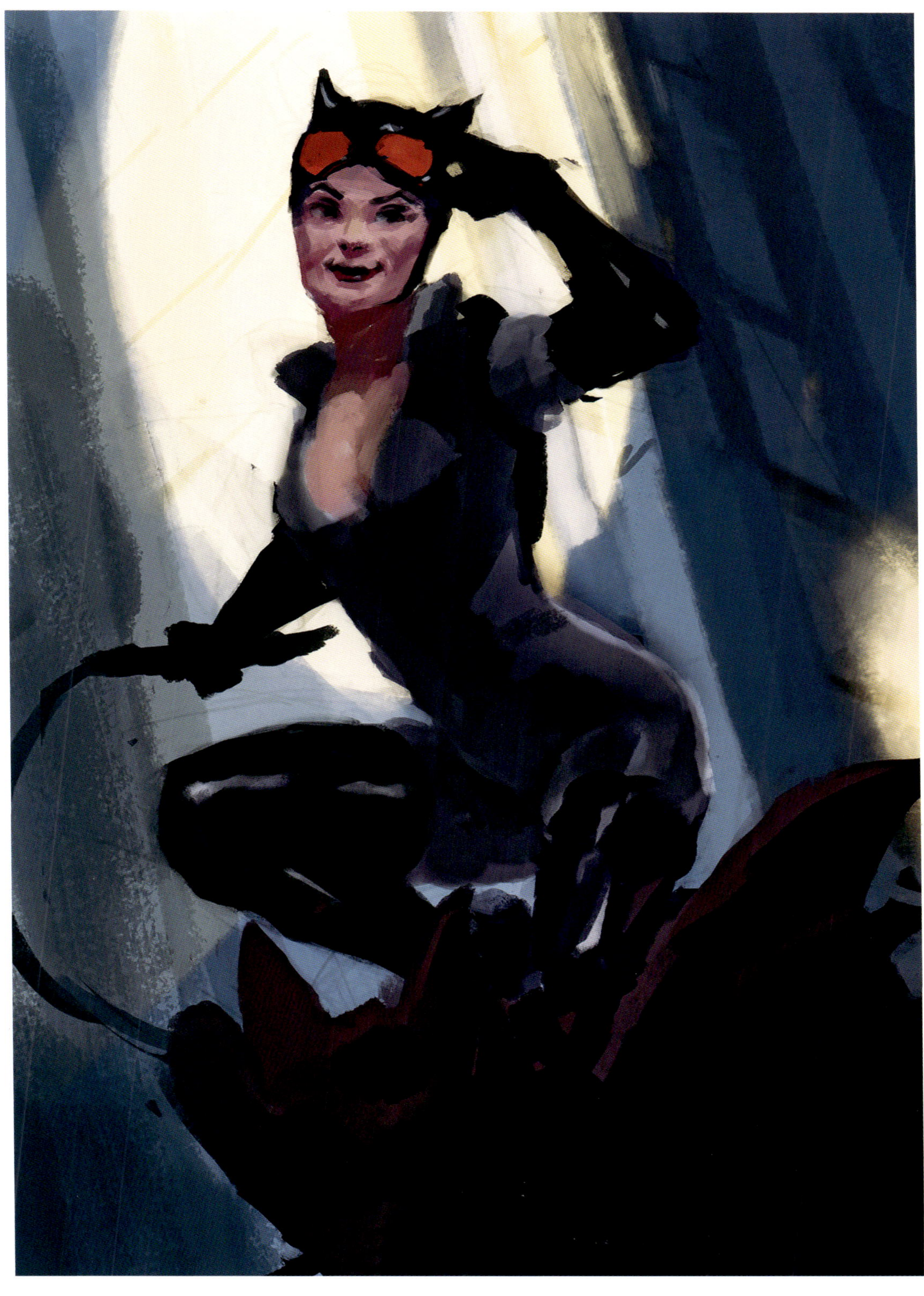

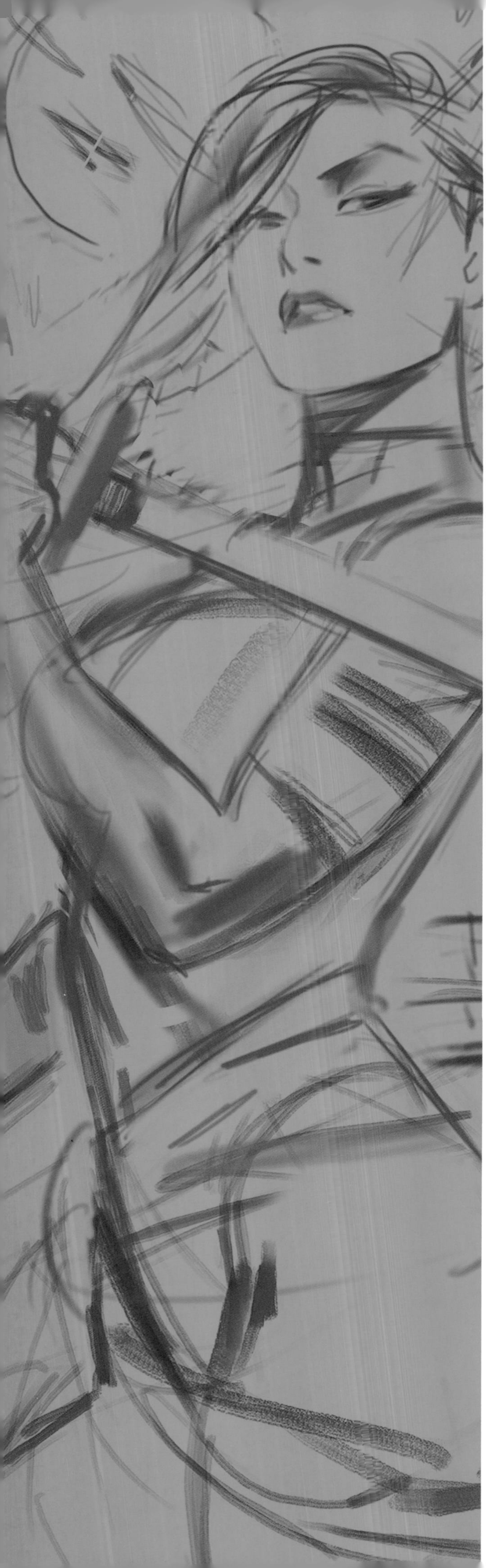

PSYLOCKE

IAN MACDONALD

This striking Marvel art collectible captures the psychic mutant Psylocke with her psionic abilities on display.

Dressed in her iconic blue bodysuit and red sash, Psylocke stands against a moonlit background as buildings blaze behind her. Her intense gaze emphasizes the deadly strength and precision of this skilled fighter—whether she wields a psi-blade or a sword, Psylocke is a force to be reckoned with.

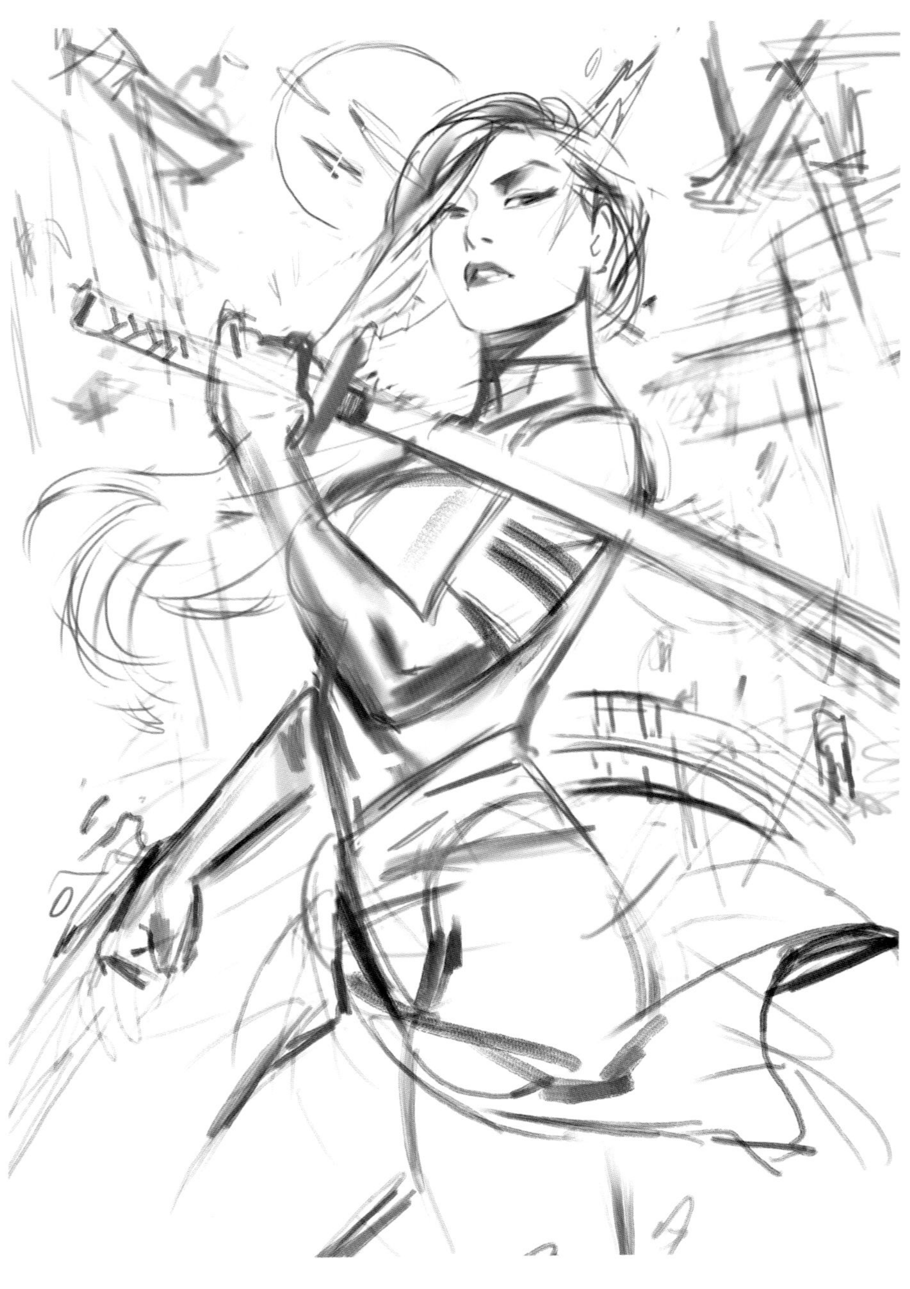

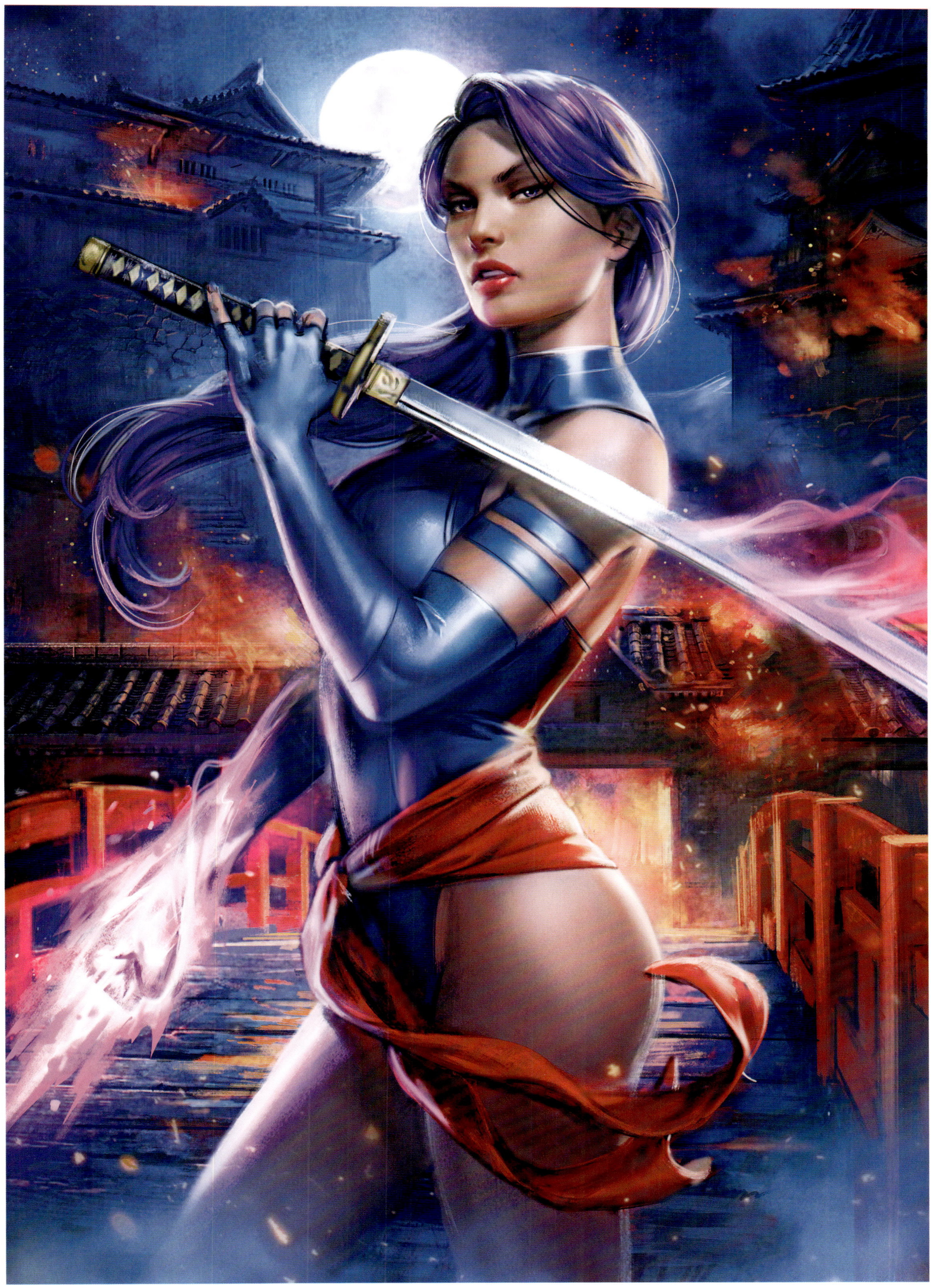

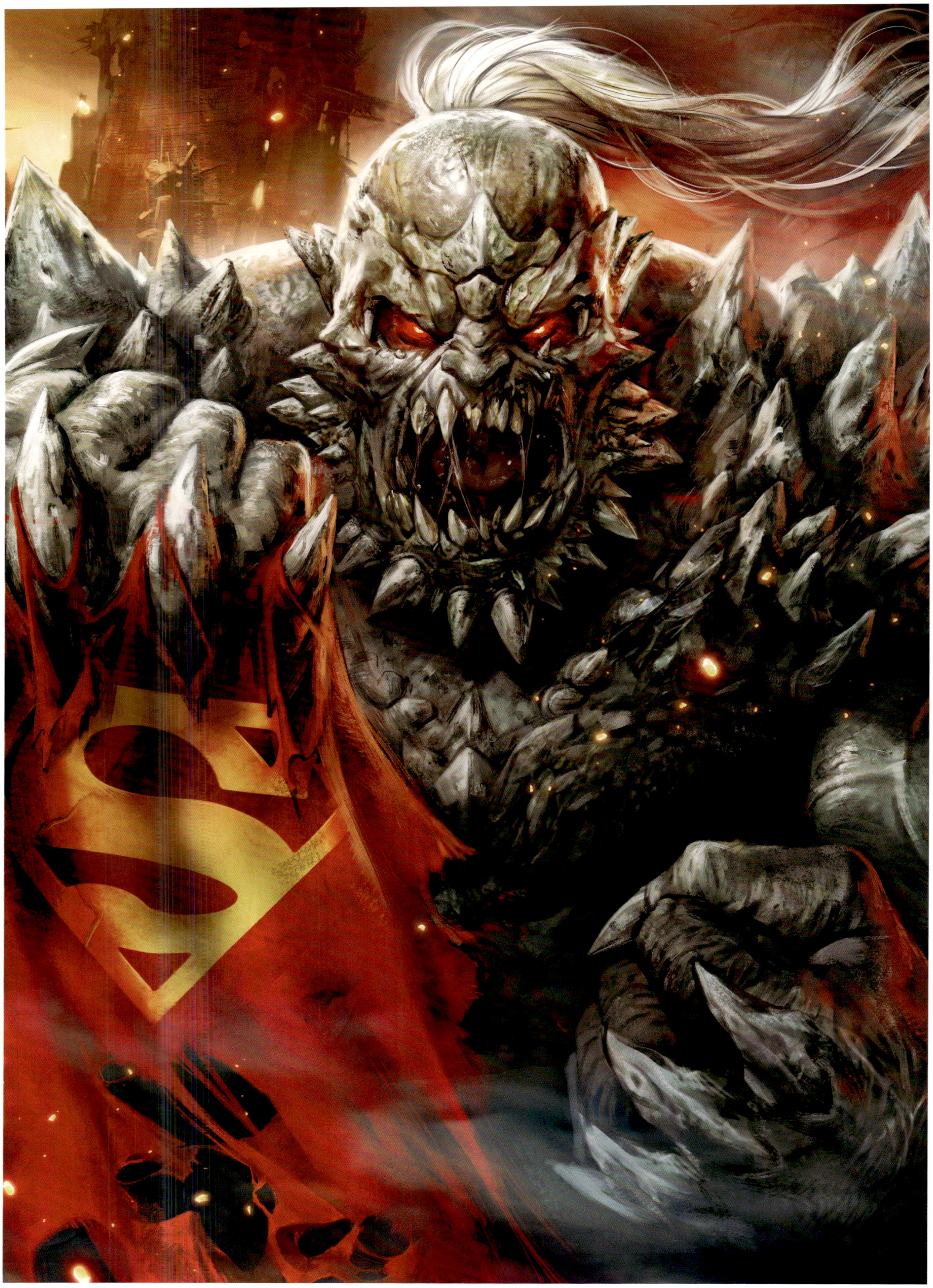

DOOMSDAY

DAVE WILKINS & IAN MACDONALD

Death comes for the DC Universe in the *Doomsday* Fine Art Print, featuring the nigh-unstoppable monster spawned from the primordial wastes of prehistoric Krypton.

The ultimate fearsome foe, Doomsday will not rest until he has brought total devastation to everything that the Justice League holds dear. Clutching Superman's tattered cape, the beastly villain gives a mighty roar as ashes and destruction settle in the wake of his devastating attacks.

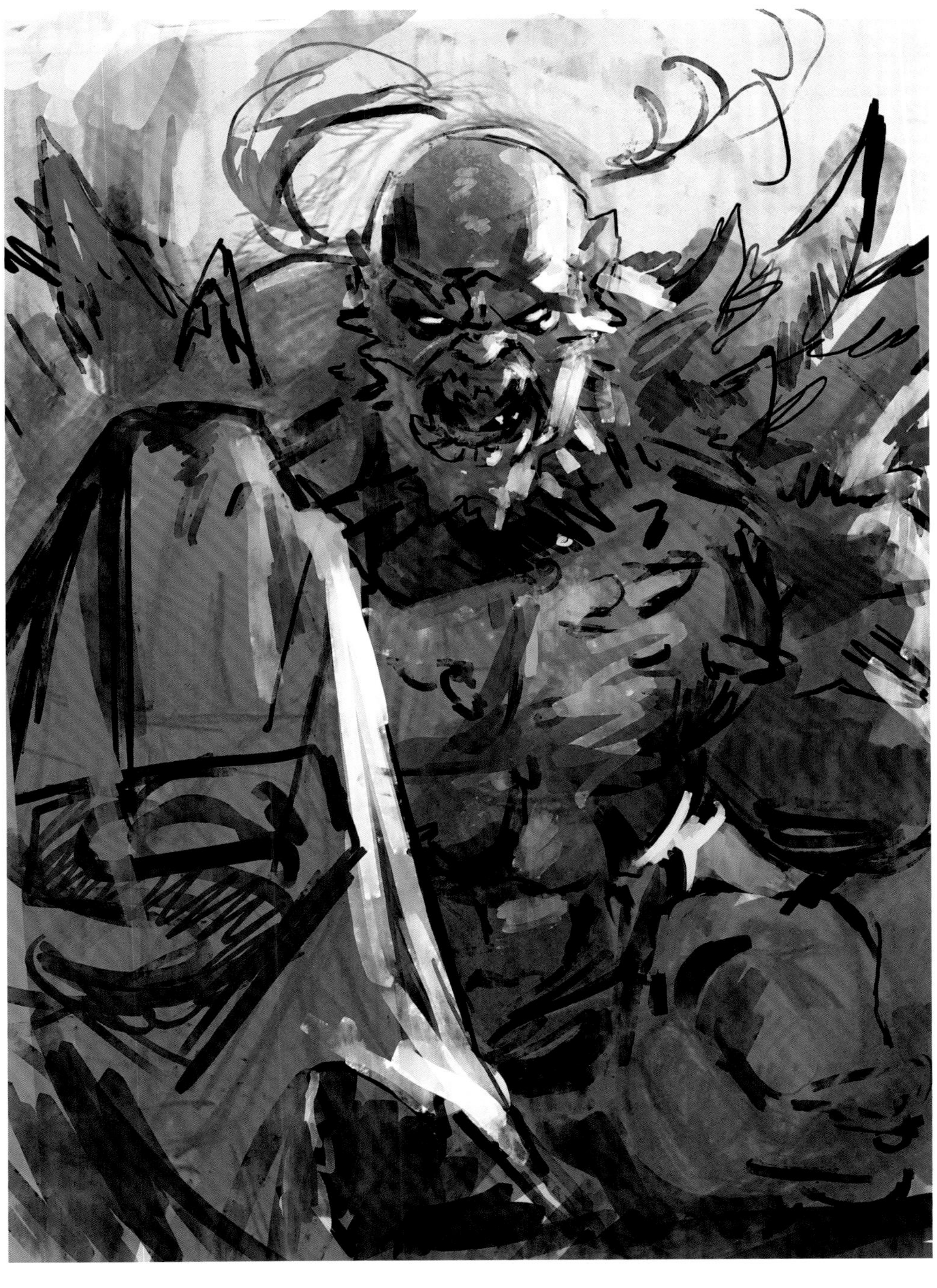

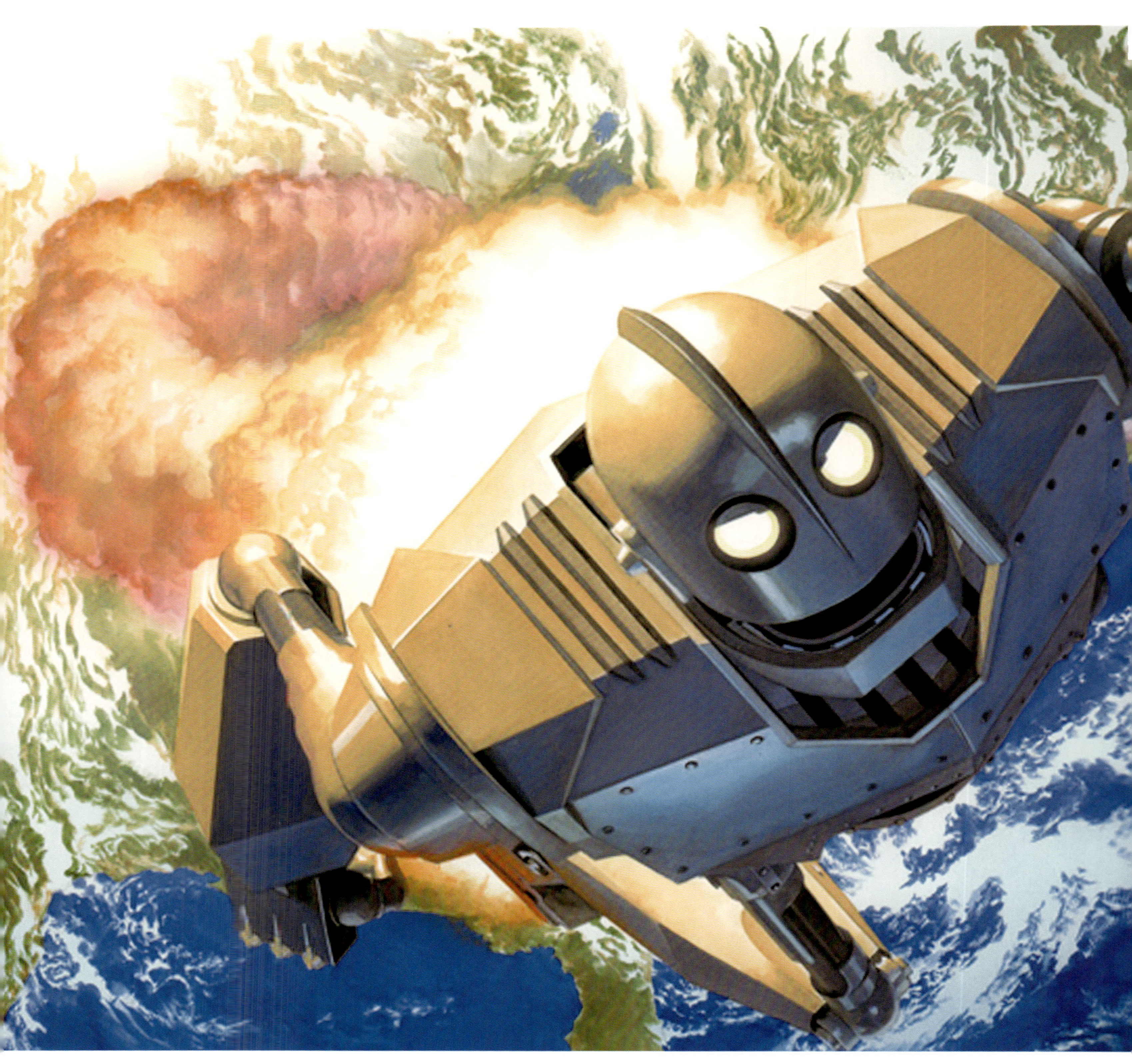

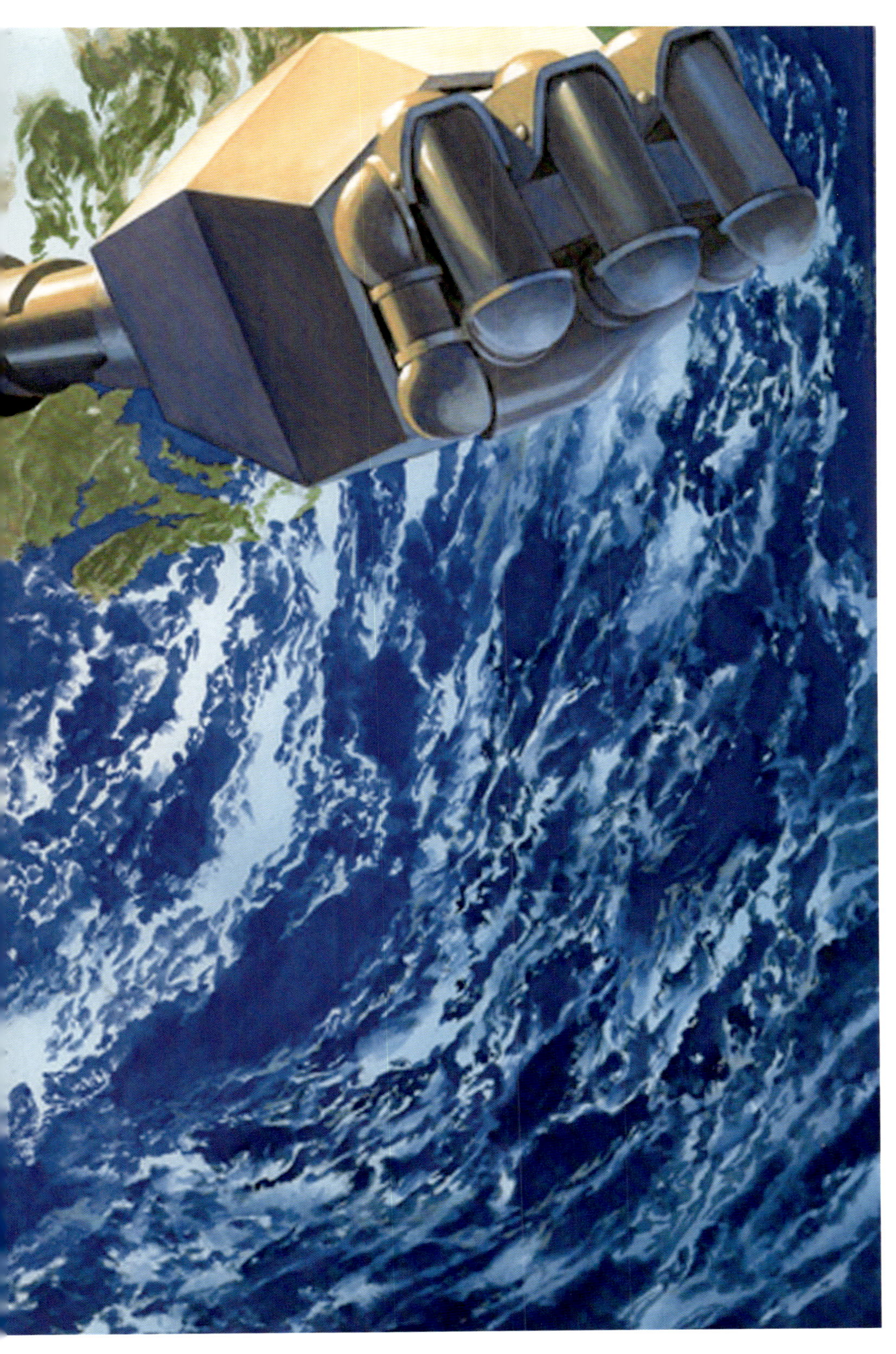

IRON GIANT
"NO ATOMO, I SUPERMAN"

ALEX ROSS

This fine art lithograph captures the action, emotion, and epic scale of the beloved animated classic *The Iron Giant*. Alex Ross's dramatic illustration features the misunderstood machine taking flight into space. High above Earth's atmosphere, the Iron Giant chooses to save the planet he was created to destroy.

Through the cold shadows of space and the bright light of rocket flames, Ross brings the Iron Giant to life with stunning detail and proves that this machine has the soul of a hero.

BOBA FETT A FORCE TO BE RECKONED WITH

DARREN TAN

Sideshow's Mythos series of fine art collectibles allows fans to imagine what could have been, but maybe never was. The *Boba Fett: A Force to Be Reckoned With* Fine Art Print powerfully captures the legend of this feared bounty hunter.

Within every sprawling galactic metropolis lies a seedy underbelly of criminal activity where Boba Fett is primed to make his next capture. This fine art collectible depicts the indomitable Mandalorian warrior making his latest acquisition, taking on a new trophy as the bustling urban skyline glows above him.

No matter the target, Boba Fett is prepared to track even the most elusive target to the farthest reaches of the galaxy, all while armed with an arsenal of dangerous weaponry.

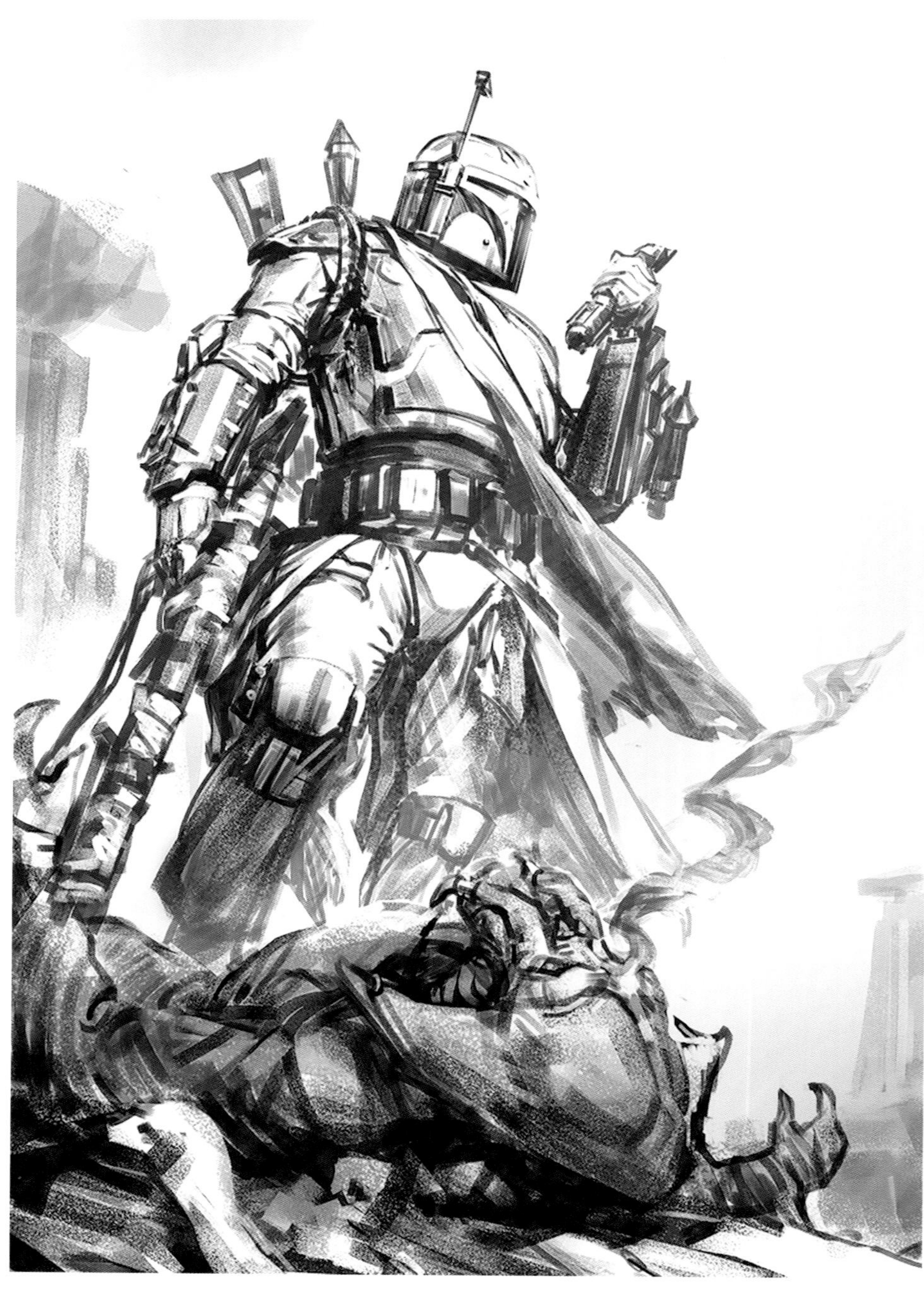

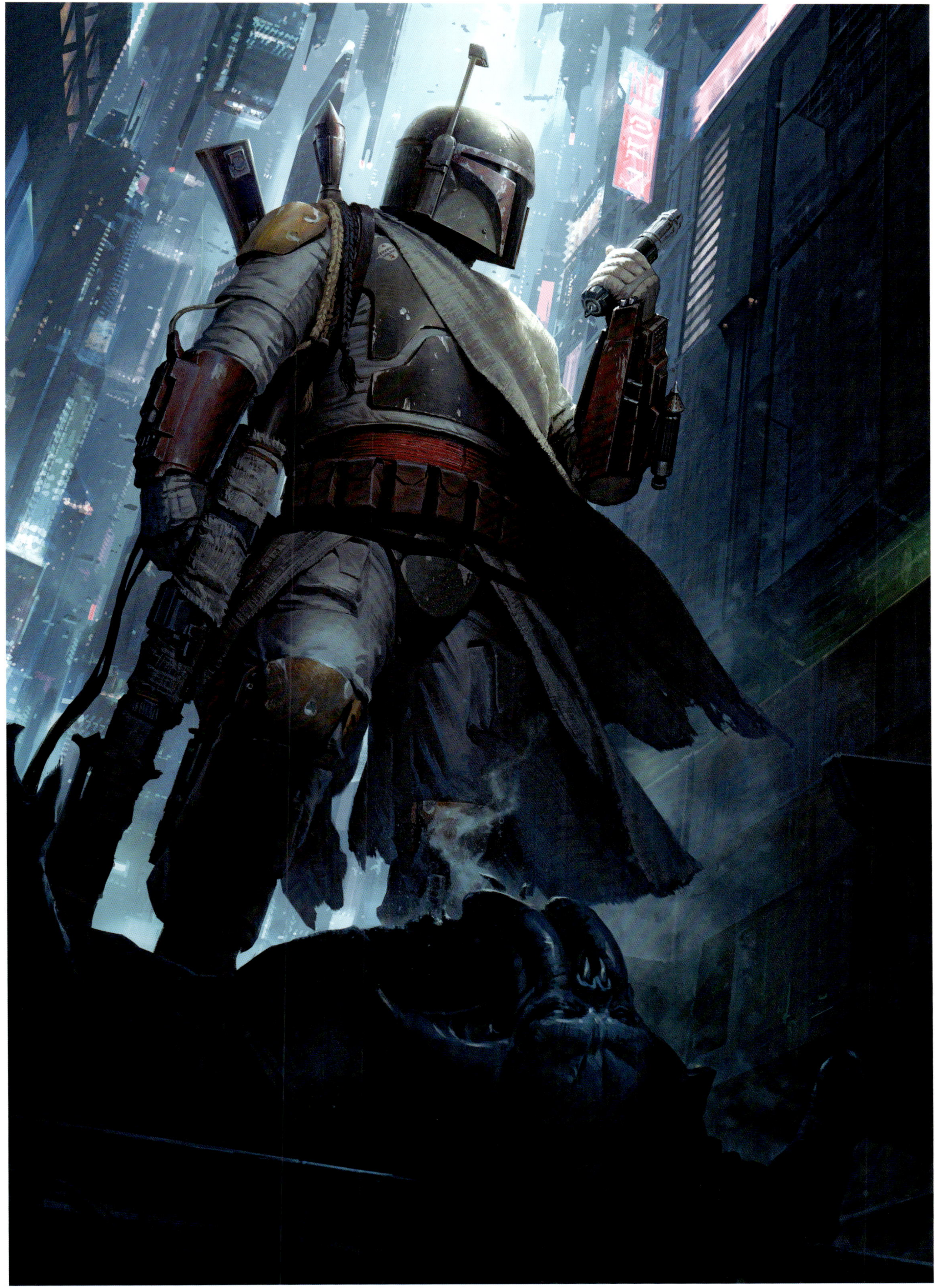

ULTIMATE SPIDER-MAN MILES MORALES

DERRICK CHEW

Swinging in from the Ultimate Marvel Universe, this thrilling Fine Art Print features the teenage hero Miles Morales web-slinging his way through New York City as Venom rampages close behind. Earth-1610 is rocked by this classic rivalry, as the monstrous symbiote villain tears apart the city that Spider-Man is sworn to protect.

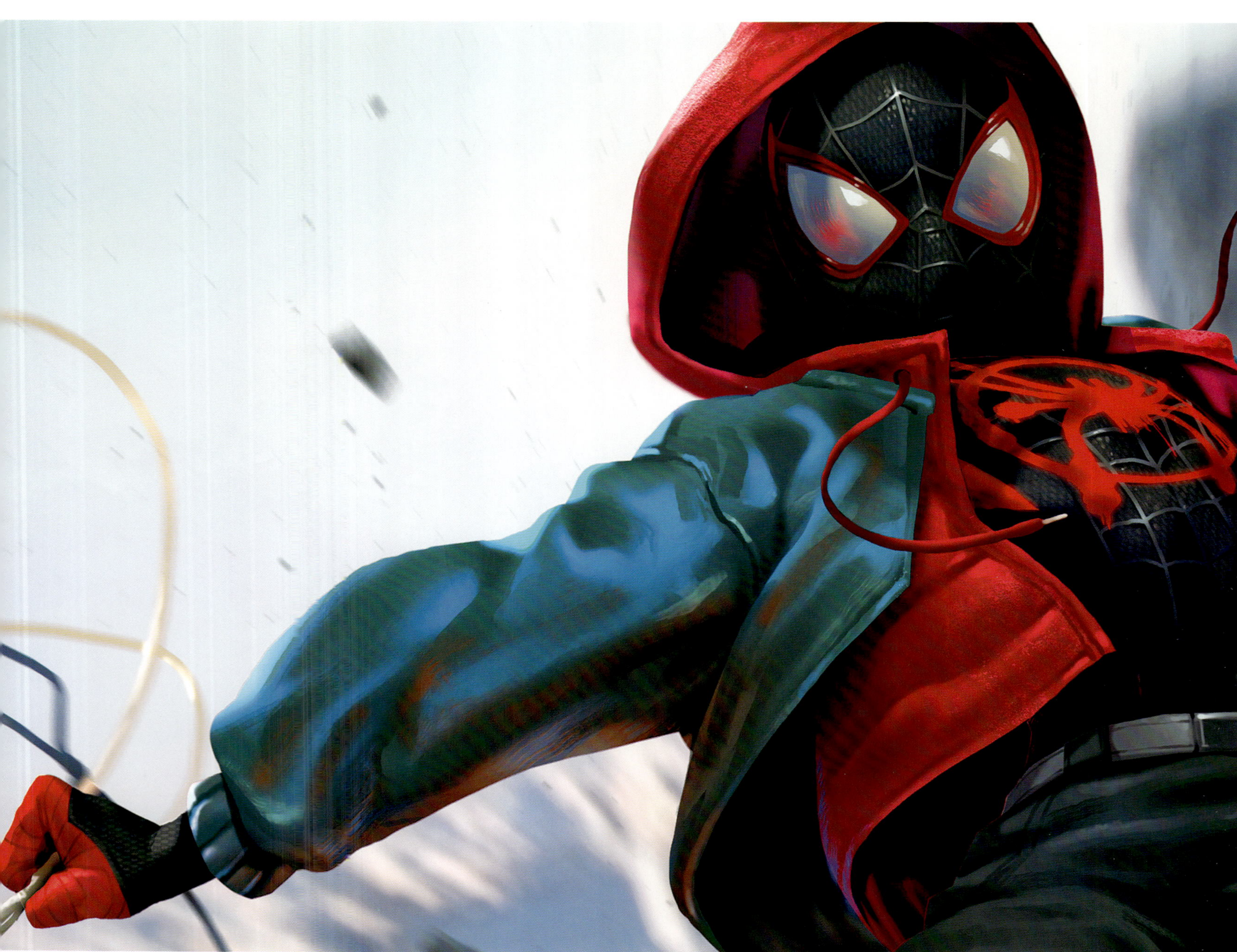

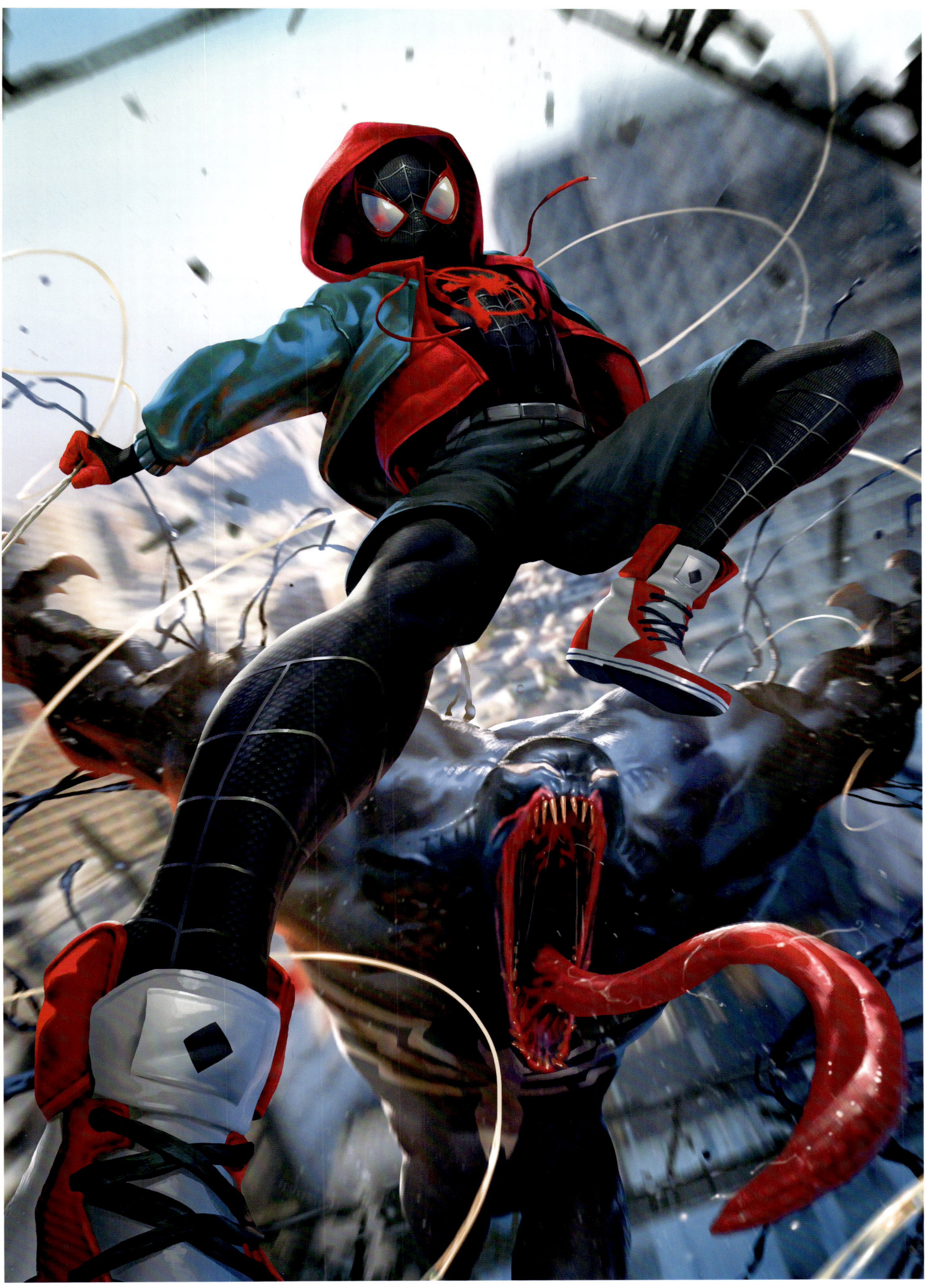

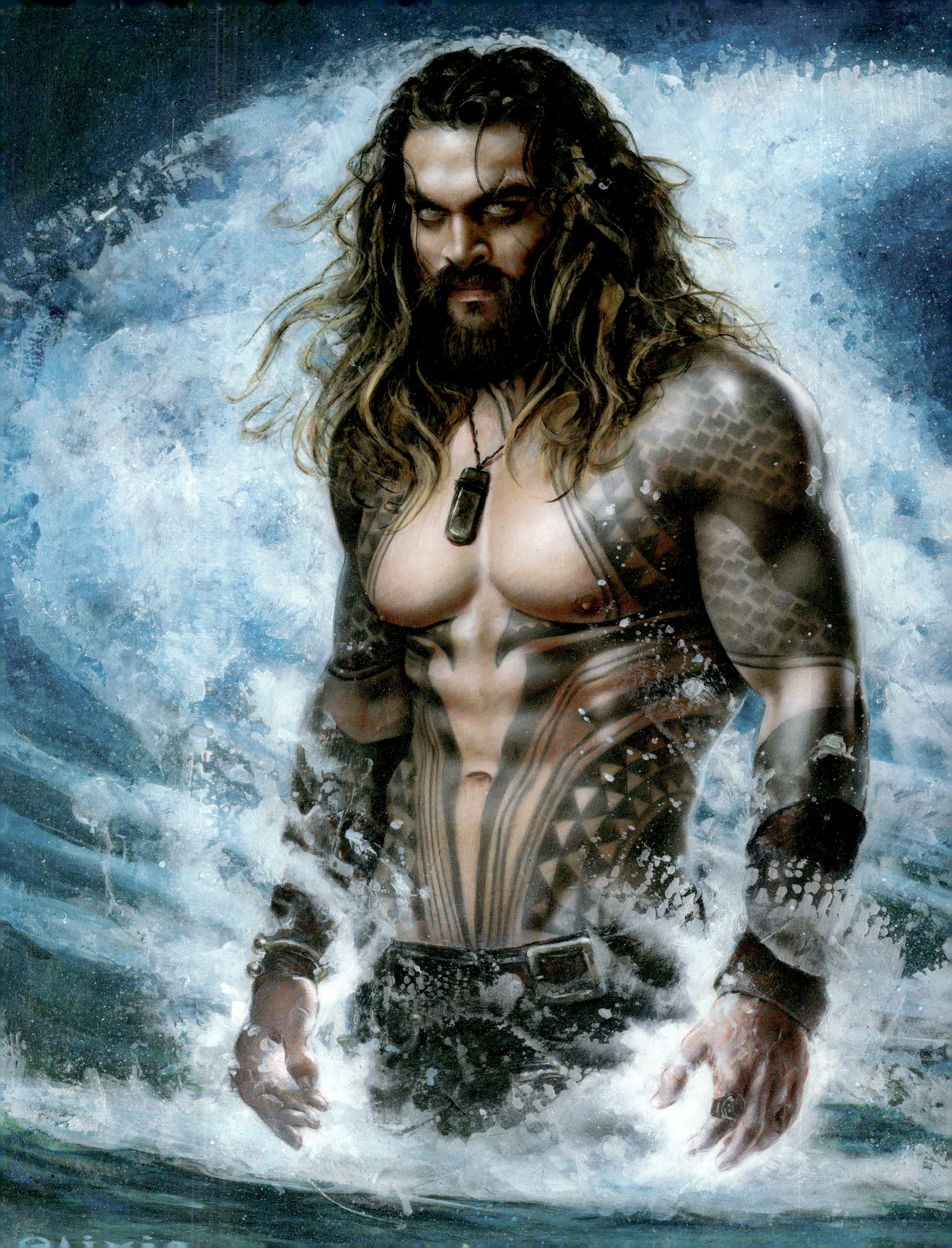

AQUAMAN PERMISSION TO COME ABOARD

OLIVIA DE BERARDINIS

Based on Jason Momoa's appearance as Aquaman, this fine art collectible captures a rugged, handsome, and cinematic take on a classic DC Comics hero. Aquaman emerges from the waves, surrounded by a spray of surf as he confronts anyone who would challenge the peace between the land above and the seas below.

Inspired by James Wan's epic cinematic vision for Aquaman, the powerful Atlantean hero's muscular physique features detailed tattoos, arm gauntlets, and jewelry—all framed by the aquatic blues of his ocean dominion.

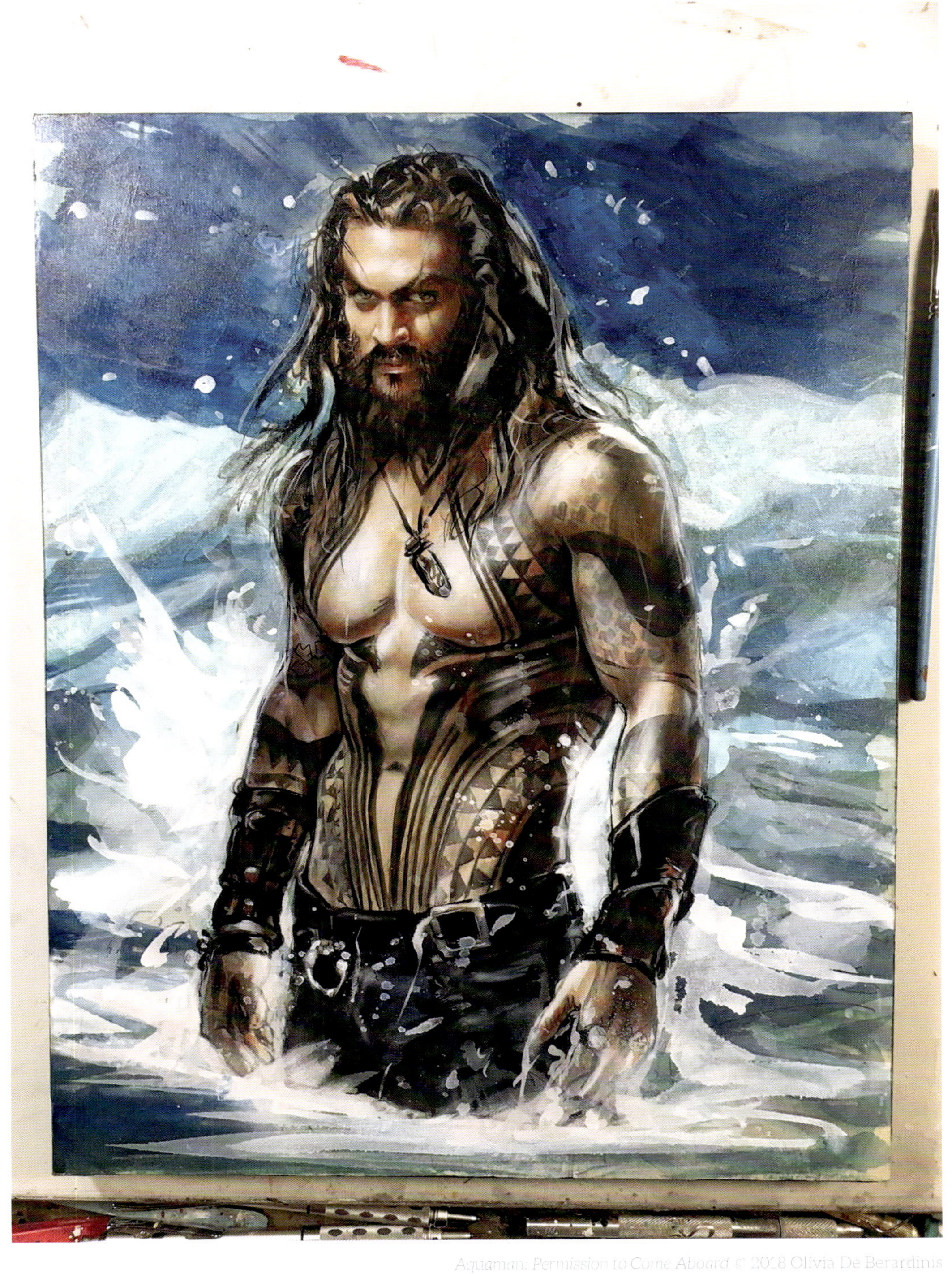

Aquaman: Permission to Come Aboard © 2018 Olivia De Berardinis

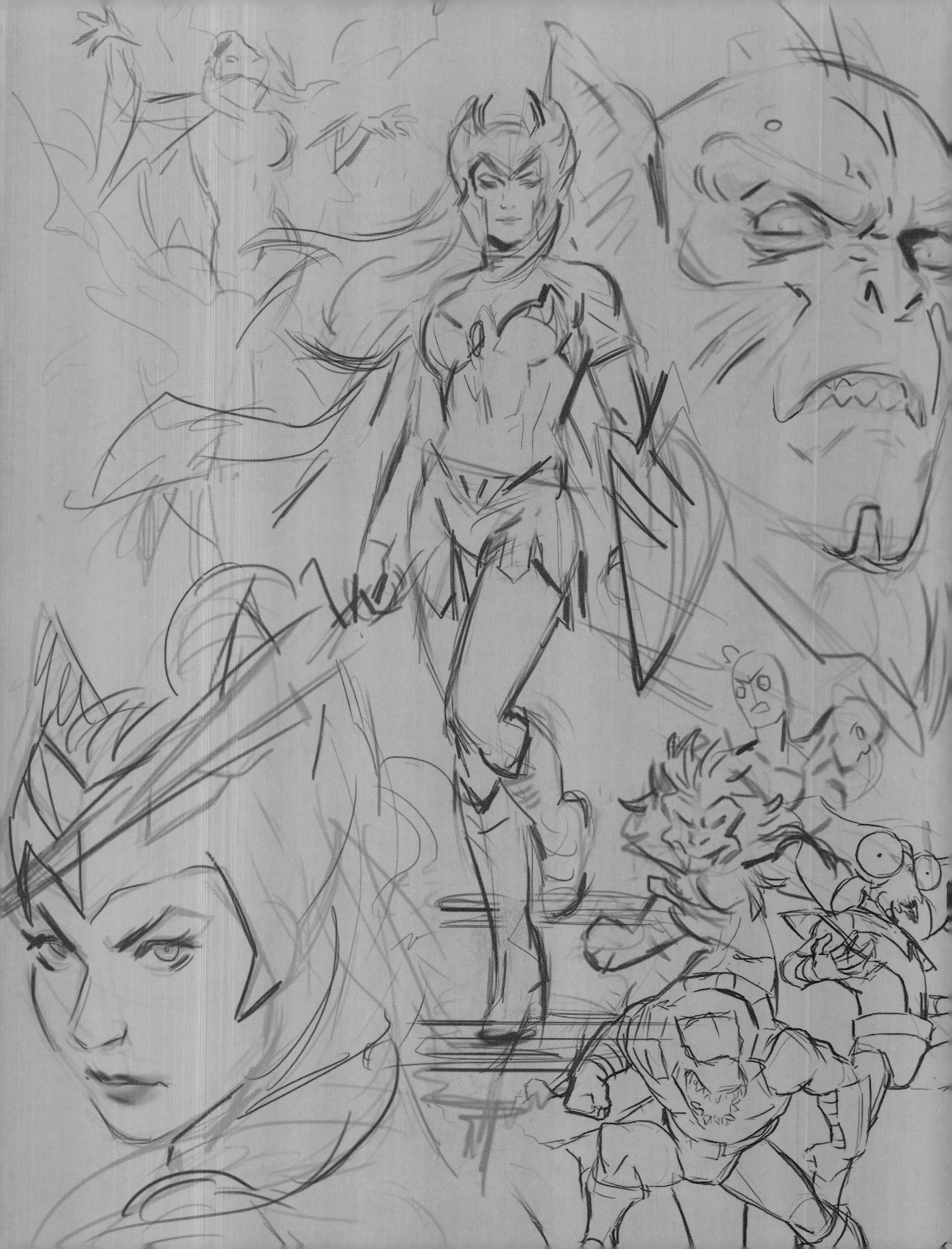

INDEX

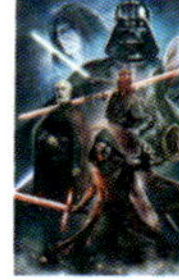

PAGE 10 | *Force of Darkness*
PROPERTY | *Star Wars*, Lucasfilm Ltd.
ARTIST | Ian MacDonald
PRINT SIZE | 18" x 24"
EDITION SIZE | 300
RELEASE DATE | January 2017
MEDIUM | Digital Mixed Media
PRINT | Fine art giclée
Produced in collaboration with ACME Archives. © & ™ Lucasfilm Ltd.

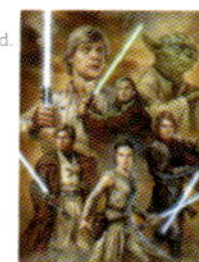

PAGE 12 | *Force of Hope*
PROPERTY | *Star Wars*, Lucasfilm Ltd.
ARTIST | Ian MacDonald
PRINT SIZE | 18" x 24"
EDITION SIZE | 300
RELEASE DATE | January 2017
MEDIUM | Digital Mixed Media
PRINT | Fine art giclée
Produced in collaboration with ACME Archives. © & ™ Lucasfilm Ltd.

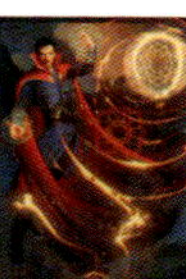

PAGE 14 | *Doctor Strange*
PROPERTY | *Doctor Strange*, Marvel Studios
ARTIST | Allen Williams
PRINT SIZE | 18" x 24"
EDITION SIZE | 200
RELEASE DATE | January 2017
MEDIUM | Digital Mixed Media
PRINT | Fine art giclée
© Marvel

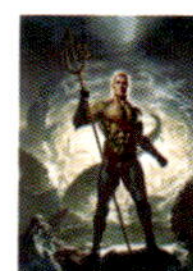

PAGE 18 | *Aquaman*
PROPERTY | DC Comics
ARTIST | Fabian Schlaga
PRINT SIZE | 18" x 24"
EDITION SIZE | 200
RELEASE DATE | January 2017
MEDIUM | Digital Mixed Media
PRINT | Fine art giclée
AQUAMAN and all related characters and elements (c) & (TM) DC Comics (s17)

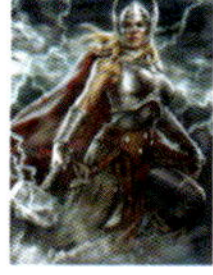

PAGE 20 | *Thor: Jane Foster*
PROPERTY | Marvel
ARTIST | Ian MacDonald
PRINT SIZE | 18" x 24"
EDITION SIZE | 225
RELEASE DATE | February 2017
MEDIUM | Digital Mixed Media
PRINT | Fine art giclée
© Marvel

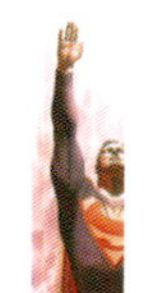

PAGE 22 | *Superman: Immortal*
PROPERTY | DC Comics
ARTIST | Alex Ross
PRINT SIZE | 13" x 36"
EDITION SIZE | 200
RELEASE DATE | February 2017
MEDIUM | Gouache
PRINT | Fine art lithograph
Produced in collaboration with Alex Ross Art. SUPERMAN and all related characters and elements (c) & (TM) DC Comics (s17)

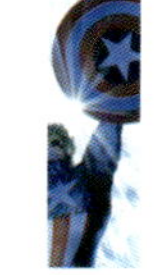

PAGE 24 | *Captain America: Triumphant*
PROPERTY | Marvel
ARTIST | Alex Ross
PRINT SIZE | 13" x 36"
EDITION SIZE | 200
RELEASE DATE | February 2017
MEDIUM | Gouache
PRINT | Fine art lithograph
Produced in collaboration with Alex Ross Art. © Marvel

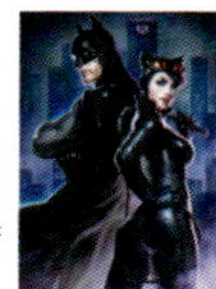

PAGE 28 | *Batman & Catwoman*
PROPERTY | DC Comics
ARTIST | Alex Pascenko
PRINT SIZE | 18" x 24"
EDITION SIZE | 300
RELEASE DATE | February 2017
MEDIUM | Digital Mixed Media
PRINT | Fine art giclée
BATMAN and all related characters and elements (c) & (TM) DC Comics (s17)

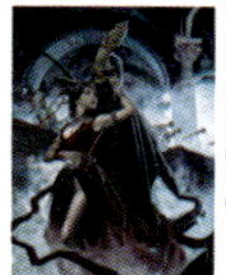

PAGE 30 | *Love You to Death*
PROPERTY | *Court of the Dead*
PRINT SIZE | 18" x 24"
EDITION SIZE | 150
RELEASE DATE | February 2017
MEDIUM | Digital Mixed Media
PRINT | Fine art giclée
(c) 2017 Sideshow Inc.

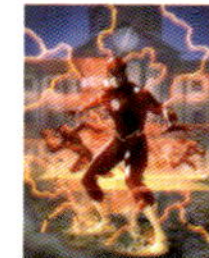

PAGE 32 | *The Flash*
PROPERTY | DC Comics
ARTIST | Alex Garner
PRINT SIZE | 18" x 24"
EDITION SIZE | 200
RELEASE DATE | March 2017
MEDIUM | Digital Mixed Media
PRINT | Fine art giclée
THE FLASH and all related characters and elements (c) & (TM) DC Comics (s17)

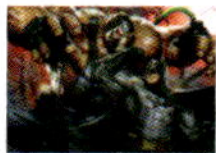

PAGE 36 | *Batman vs. Bane*
PROPERTY | DC Comics
ARTIST | Dave Wilkins
PRINT SIZE | 18" x 24"
EDITION SIZE | 225
RELEASE DATE | March 2017
MEDIUM | Digital Mixed Media
PRINT | Fine art giclée
BATMAN and all related characters and elements (c) & (TM) DC Comics (s17)

PAGE 38 | *The Thin Dead Line*
PROPERTY | Court of the Dead
ARTIST | Stephen Schirle
PRINT SIZE | 24" x 18"
EDITION SIZE | 125
RELEASE DATE | March 2017
MEDIUM | Digital Mixed Media
PRINT | Fine art giclée
(c) 2017 Sideshow Inc.

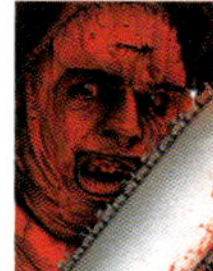

PAGE 40 | *Leatherface*
PROPERTY | *Texas Chainsaw Massacre*
ARTIST | Matt Ryan Tobin
PRINT SIZE | 18" x 24"
EDITION SIZE | 125
RELEASE DATE | January 2017
MEDIUM | Digital Mixed Media
PRINT | Full bleed four-color screen print with metallic silver inks. Printed by VGKIDS. The Texas Chainsaw Massacre ©1974 Vortex, Inc./Kim Henkel/Tobe Hooper. All Rights Reserved.

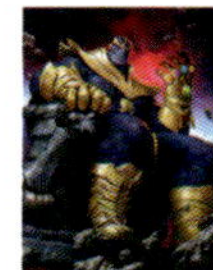

PAGE 42 | *Thanos on Throne*
PROPERTY | Marvel
ARTIST | Doo-chun & Ian MacDonald
PRINT SIZE | 18" x 24"
EDITION SIZE | 200
RELEASE DATE | March 2017
MEDIUM | Digital Mixed Media
PRINT | Fine art giclée
© Marvel

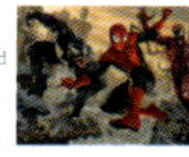

PAGE 44 | *Spider-Man vs. Venom and Carnage*
PROPERTY | Marvel
ARTIST | Paolo Rivera
PRINT SIZE | 24" x 18"
EDITION SIZE | 350
RELEASE DATE | April 2017
MEDIUM | Gouache
PRINT | Fine art giclée
© Marvel

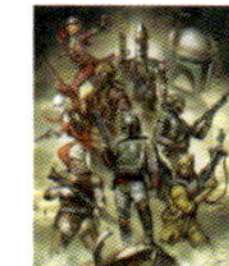

PAGE 46 | *Scum & Villainy*
PROPERTY | *Star Wars*, Lucasfilm Ltd.
ARTIST | Ian MacDonald
PRINT SIZE | 18" x 24"
EDITION SIZE | 400
RELEASE DATE | April 2017
MEDIUM | Digital Mixed Media
PRINT | Fine art giclée
Produced in collaboration with ACME Archives. © & ™ Lucasfilm Ltd.

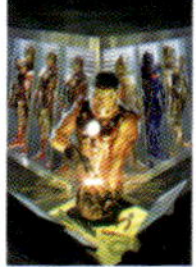

PAGE 48 | *Iron Man: The Golden Avenger*
PROPERTY | Marvel
ARTIST | Alex Ross
PRINT SIZE | 18" x 24"
EDITION SIZE | 250
RELEASE DATE | April 2017
MEDIUM | Gouache
PRINT | Fine art lithograph
Produced in collaboration with Alex Ross Art. © Marvel

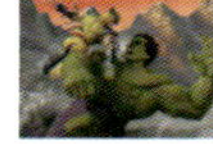

PAGE 50 | *Hulk and Wolverine First Appearance Variant*
PROPERTY | Marvel
ARTIST | Paolo Rivera
PRINT SIZE | 24" x 18"
EDITION SIZE | 350
RELEASE DATE | April 2017
MEDIUM | Gouache and digital mixed media
PRINT | Fine art giclée
© Marvel

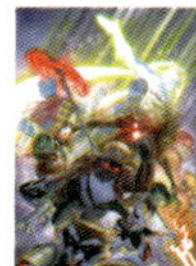

PAGE 52 | *Guardians of The Galaxy*
PROPERTY | Marvel
ARTIST | Alex Ross
PRINT SIZE | 18" x 24"
EDITION SIZE | 250
RELEASE DATE | May 2017
MEDIUM | Gouache
PRINT | Fine art lithograph
© Marvel

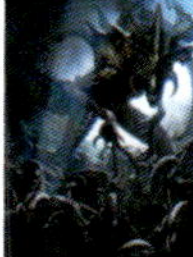

PAGE 54 | *Alien King*
PROPERTY | *Alien*, Twentieth Century Fox
ARTIST | RJ Palmer
PRINT SIZE | 18" x 24"
EDITION SIZE | 150
RELEASE DATE | May 2017
MEDIUM | Digital Mixed Media
PRINT | Fine art giclée
Alien TM & © 2017 Twentieth Century Fox Film Corporation. All Rights Reserved.

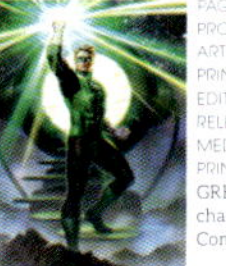

PAGE 56 | *Green Lantern*
PROPERTY | DC Comics
ARTIST | Alex Pascenko
PRINT SIZE | 18" x 24"
EDITION SIZE | 200
RELEASE DATE | May 2017
MEDIUM | Digital Mixed Media
PRINT | Fine art giclée
GREEN LANTERN and all related characters and elements © & ™ DC Comics. (s17)

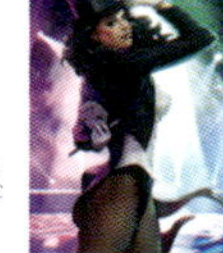

PAGE 58 | *Zatanna*
PROPERTY | DC Comics
ARTIST | Stanley 'Artgerm' Lau
PRINT SIZE | 18" x 24"
EDITION SIZE | 350
RELEASE DATE | May 2017
MEDIUM | Digital Mixed Media
PRINT | Fine art giclée
JUSTICE LEAGUE and all related characters and elements © & ™ DC Comics. (s17)

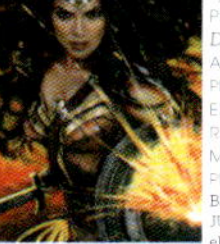

PAGE 60 | *Wonder Woman: Diana of Themyscira*
PROPERTY | *Batman v Superman: Dawn of Justice*, Warner Bros.
ARTIST | Olivia De Berardinis
PRINT SIZE | 18" x 24"
EDITION SIZE | 275
RELEASE DATE | June 2017
MEDIUM | Acrylic
PRINT | Fine art giclée
BATMAN V SUPERMAN: DAWN OF JUSTICE and all related characters and elements (c) & (TM) DC Comics and Warner Bros. Entertainment Inc. WB SHIELD: TM & (c) WBEI. (s17)

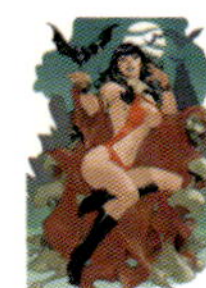

PAGE 62 | *Vampirella: A Scarlet Thirst*
PROPERTY | Vampirella, Dynamite
ARTIST | Terry & Rachel Dodson
PRINT SIZE | 18" x 24"
EDITION SIZE | 250
RELEASE DATE | June 2017
MEDIUM | Mixed Media
PRINT | Fine art giclée
Dynamite logo & Vampirella is ® and © 2017 Dynamite. All Rights Reserved.

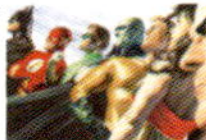

PAGE 64 | *Liberty and Justice: JLA*
PROPERTY | DC Comics
ARTIST | Alex Ross
PRINT SIZE | 18" x 24"
EDITION SIZE | 300
RELEASE DATE | June 2017
MEDIUM | Gouache
PRINT | Fine art lithograph
Produced in collaboration with Alex Ross Art. JUSTICE LEAGUE and all related characters and elements © & ™ DC Comics. (s17)

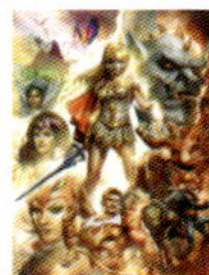

PAGE 68, 300 | *She-Ra: Princess of Power*
PROPERTY | *Masters of the Universe*, Mattel
ARTIST | Dave Wilkins
PRINT SIZE | 18" x 24"
EDITION SIZE | 300
RELEASE DATE | June 2017
MEDIUM | Digital Mixed Media
PRINT | Fine art giclée
TM & © Mattel, Inc. All rights reserved. Under license to Classic Media.

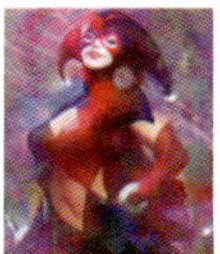

PAGE 71 | *Gotham Sirens Artist Series Portfolio*
PROPERTY | DC Comics
ARTIST | Stanley 'Artgerm' Lau
PRINT SIZE | 11" x 14"
EDITION SIZE | 250
RELEASE DATE | June 2017
MEDIUM | Digital Mixed Media
PRINT | Fine art giclée
BATMAN and all related characters and elements (c) & (TM) DC Comics (s17)

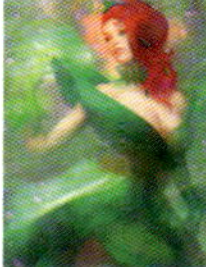

PAGE 72 | *Gotham Sirens Artist Series Portfolio*
PROPERTY | DC Comics
ARTIST | Stanley 'Artgerm' Lau
PRINT SIZE | 11" x 14"
EDITION SIZE | 250
RELEASE DATE | June 2017
MEDIUM | Digital Mixed Media
PRINT | Fine art giclée
BATMAN and all related characters and elements (c) & (TM) DC Comics (s17)

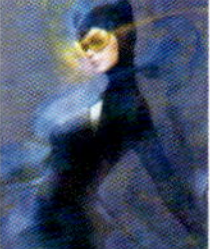

PAGE 73 | *Gotham Sirens Artist Series Portfolio*
PROPERTY | DC Comics
ARTIST | Stanley 'Artgerm' Lau
PRINT SIZE | 11" x 14"
EDITION SIZE | 250
RELEASE DATE | June 2017
MEDIUM | Digital Mixed Media
PRINT | Fine art giclée
BATMAN and all related characters and elements (c) & (TM) DC Comics (s17)

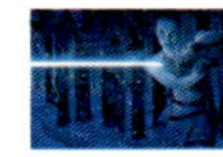

PAGE 74 | *In a Galaxy Far Far Away*
PROPERTY | *Star Wars*, Lucasfilm Ltd.
ARTIST | Adam Hughes
PRINT SIZE | 24" x 18"
EDITION SIZE | 500
RELEASE DATE | July 2017
MEDIUM | Mixed Media
PRINT | Fine art giclée
Produced in collaboration with ACME Archives. © & ™ Lucasfilm Ltd.

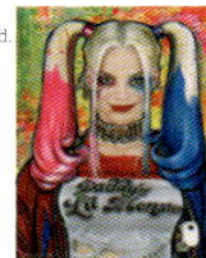

PAGE 78 | *Harley Quinn: Daddy's Lil Monster*
PROPERTY | *Suicide Squad*, Warner Bros.
ARTIST | Olivia De Berardinis
PRINT SIZE | 18.5" x 23"
EDITION SIZE | 400
RELEASE DATE | July 2017
MEDIUM | Acrylic
PRINT | Fine art giclée
SUICIDE SQUAD and all related characters and elements (c) & (TM) DC Comics and Warner Bros. Entertainment Inc. (s17)

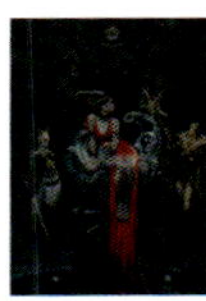

PAGE 80 | *Divided We Stand*
PROPERTY | *Court of the Dead*
ARTIST | Allen Williams
PRINT SIZE | 18" x 24"
EDITION SIZE | 150
RELEASE DATE | July 2017
MEDIUM | Mixed Media
PRINT | Fine art giclée
© & ™ Lucasfilm Ltd.

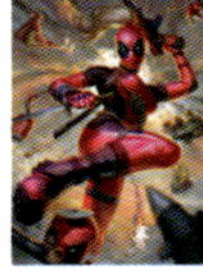

PAGE 82 | *Lady Deadpool*
PROPERTY | Marvel
ARTIST | Alex Pascenko
PRINT SIZE | 18" x 24"
EDITION SIZE | 225
RELEASE DATE | July 2017
MEDIUM | Digital Mixed Media
PRINT | Fine art giclée
© Marvel

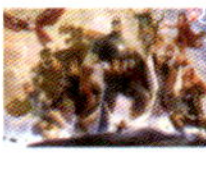

PAGE 84 | *Avengers: Team Cap*
PROPERTY | Marvel
ARTIST | Alex Garner
PRINT SIZE | 24" x 18"
EDITION SIZE | 300
RELEASE DATE | July 2017
MEDIUM | Digital Mixed Media
PRINT | Fine art giclée
© Marvel

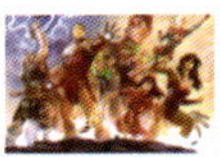

PAGE 86 | *Avengers: Team Iron Man*
PROPERTY | Marvel
ARTIST | Alex Garner
PRINT SIZE | 24" x 18"
EDITION SIZE | 300
RELEASE DATE | July 2017
MEDIUM | Digital Mixed Media
PRINT | Fine art giclée
© Marvel

PAGE 88 | *Avengers Assemble*
PROPERTY | Marvel
ARTIST | Alex Garner
PRINT SIZE | 42" x 18"
EDITION SIZE | 300
RELEASE DATE | July 2017
MEDIUM | Digital Mixed Media
PRINT | Fine art giclée
© Marvel

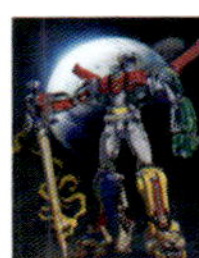

PAGE 90 | *Voltron, Defender of the Universe Variant*
PROPERTY | Voltron, Dreamworks Animation
ARTIST | Tom Jilesen & Josh Nizzi
PRINT SIZE | 18" x 24"
EDITION SIZE | 250
RELEASE DATE | August 2017
MEDIUM | Digital Mixed Media
PRINT | Fine art giclée
TM & © World Events Productions, LLC. Under license to Classic Media, LLC.

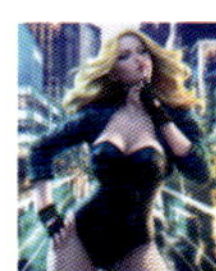

PAGE 92 | *Black Canary: Birds of Prey*
PROPERTY | DC Comics
ARTIST | Stanley 'Artgerm' Lau
PRINT SIZE | 18" x 24"
EDITION SIZE | 500
RELEASE DATE | August 2017
MEDIUM | Digital Mixed Media
PRINT | Fine art giclée
BLACK CANARY and all related characters and elements © & ™ DC Comics. (s17)

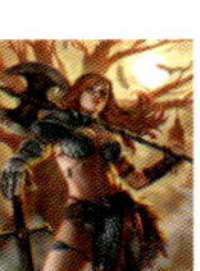

PAGE 94 | *Red Sonja: Queen of Scavengers*
PROPERTY | Red Sonja, Dynamite
ARTIST | Alex Pascenko
PRINT SIZE | 18" x 24"
EDITION SIZE | 300
RELEASE DATE | August 2017
MEDIUM | Digital Mixed Media
PRINT | Fine art giclée
Red Sonja ® & © 2017 Red Sonja, LLC. Dynamite ® 2017 Dynamite. All Rights Reserved.

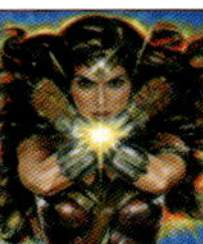

PAGE 96 | *Wonder Woman: Hell Hath No Fury*
PROPERTY | *Batman v Superman: Dawn of Justice*, Warner Bros.
ARTIST | Olivia De Berardinis
PRINT SIZE | 118.5" x 22.5"
EDITION SIZE | 400
RELEASE DATE | January 2017
MEDIUM | Acrylic
PRINT | Fine art giclée
BATMAN V SUPERMAN: DAWN OF JUSTICE and all related characters and elements (c) & (TM) DC Comics and Warner Bros. Entertainment Inc. WB SHIELD: TM & (c) WBEI. (s17)

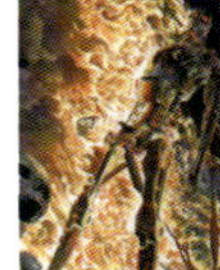

PAGE 98 | *Terminator: The Burning Earth*
PROPERTY | Terminator, Dark Horse Comics
ARTIST | Alex Ross
PRINT SIZE | 18" x 24"
EDITION SIZE | 225
RELEASE DATE | August 2017
MEDIUM | Digital Mixed Media Gouache
PRINT | Fine art lithograph
Produced in collaboration with Alex Ross Art. (c) 2017 Studiocanal S.A. "TM" designates a trademark of Studiocanal S.A. All Rights Reserved.

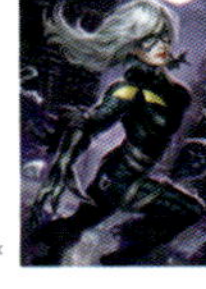

PAGE 4, 100 | *Black Cat*
PROPERTY | Marvel
ARTIST | Alex Pascenko
PRINT SIZE | 18" x 24"
EDITION SIZE | 300
RELEASE DATE | August 2017
MEDIUM | Digital Mixed Media
PRINT | Fine art giclée
© Marvel

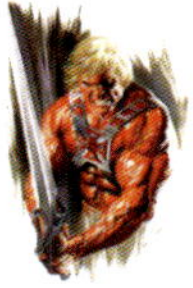

PAGE 102 | *He-Man*
PROPERTY | *Masters of the Universe*, Mattel
ARTIST | Alex Ross
PRINT SIZE | 16" x 20"
EDITION SIZE | 125
RELEASE DATE | September 2017
MEDIUM | Gouache
PRINT | Fine art lithograph
Produced in collaboration with Alex Ross Art. MASTERS OF THE UNIVERSE and associated trademarks are owned by and used under license from Mattel, Inc. (c) 2017 Mattel, Inc. All Rights Reserved. Under license to Classic Media.

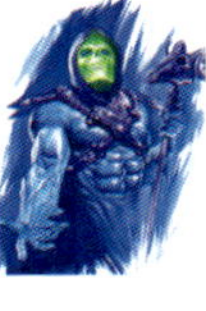

PAGE 103 | *Skeletor*
PROPERTY | *Masters of the Universe*, Mattel
ARTIST | Alex Ross
PRINT SIZE | 16" x 20"
EDITION SIZE | 125
RELEASE DATE | September 2017
MEDIUM | Gouache
PRINT | Fine art lithograph
Produced in collaboration with Alex Ross Art. MASTERS OF THE UNIVERSE and associated trademarks are owned by and used under license from Mattel, Inc. (c) 2017 Mattel, Inc. All Rights Reserved. Under license to Classic Media.

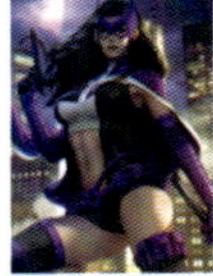

PAGE 104 | *Huntress: Birds of Prey*
PROPERTY | DC Comics
ARTIST | Stanley 'Artgerm' Lau
PRINT SIZE | 18" x 24"
EDITION SIZE | 500
RELEASE DATE | September 2017
MEDIUM | Digital Mixed Media
PRINT | Fine art giclée
BATMAN and all related characters and elements © & ™ DC Comics. (s17)

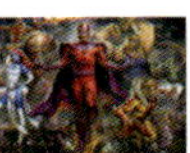

PAGE 106 | *Magneto & the Brotherhood of Mutants*
PROPERTY | Marvel
ARTIST | Ian MacDonald
PRINT SIZE | 18" x 24"
EDITION SIZE | 300
RELEASE DATE | September 2017
MEDIUM | Digital Mixed Media
PRINT | Fine art giclée
© Marvel

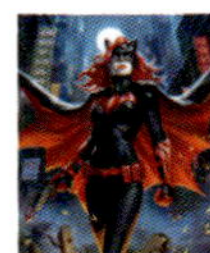

PAGE 108 | *Batwoman*
PROPERTY | DC Comics
ARTIST | Alex Pascenko
PRINT SIZE | 18" x 24"
EDITION SIZE | 300
RELEASE DATE | October 2017
MEDIUM | Digital Mixed Media
PRINT | Fine art giclée
BATMAN and all related characters and elements © & ™ DC Comics. (s17)

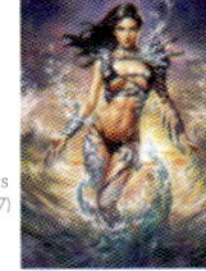

PAGE 110 | *Aspen*
PROPERTY | Aspen Comics
ARTIST | Ian MacDonald
PRINT SIZE | 18" x 24"
EDITION SIZE | 300
RELEASE DATE | October 2017
MEDIUM | Digital Mixed Media
PRINT | Fine art giclée
Michael Turner's FATHOM is ™ & © Aspen MLT Inc.

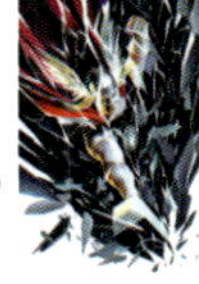

PAGE 112 | *Thor: Shattered*
PROPERTY | Marvel
ARTIST | Alex Ross
PRINT SIZE | 18" x 24"
EDITION SIZE | 300
RELEASE DATE | October 2017
MEDIUM | Gouache
PRINT | Fine art lithograph
Produced in collaboration with Alex Ross Art. © Marvel

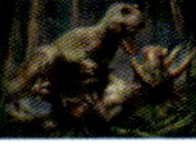

PAGE 114 | *T-Rex vs. Triceratops*
PROPERTY | Dinosauria
ARTIST | RJ Palmer
PRINT SIZE | 4" x 18"
EDITION SIZE | 200
RELEASE DATE | October 2017
MEDIUM | Digital Mixed Media
PRINT | Fine art giclée
© 2017 Sideshow Inc.

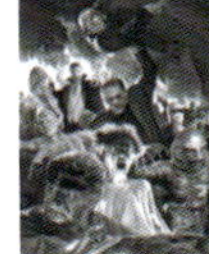

PAGE 116 | *The Mash*
PROPERTY | Universal Studios
ARTIST | Alex Ross
PRINT SIZE | 18" x 24"
EDITION SIZE | 100
RELEASE DATE | October 2017
MEDIUM | Gouache
PRINT | Fine art lithograph
Produced in collaboration with Alex Ross Art. UNIVERSAL and all related characters and elements © & ™ Comcast. (s19) Bela Lugosi name and likeness ™ & © 2019 Lugosi Enterprises. All rights reserved.

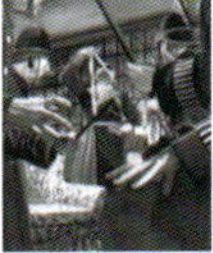

PAGE 117 | *The Invisible Man*
PROPERTY | Universal Studios
ARTIST | Alex Ross
PRINT SIZE | 18" x 24"
EDITION SIZE | 100
RELEASE DATE | October 2017
MEDIUM | Gouache
PRINT | Fine art lithograph
Produced in collaboration with Alex Ross Art. UNIVERSAL and all related characters and elements © & ™ Comcast. (s19) Bela Lugosi name and likeness ™ & © 2019 Lugosi Enterprises. All rights reserved.

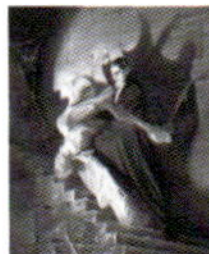

PAGE 118 | *Dracula*
PROPERTY | Universal Studios
ARTIST | Alex Ross
PRINT SIZE | 18" x 24"
EDITION SIZE | 100
RELEASE DATE | October 2017
MEDIUM | Gouache
PRINT | Fine art lithograph
Produced in collaboration with Alex Ross Art. UNIVERSAL and all related characters and elements © & ™ Comcast. (s19) Bela Lugosi name and likeness ™ & © 2019 Lugosi Enterprises. All rights reserved.

PAGE 119 | *Creature from the Black Lagoon*
PROPERTY | Universal Studios
ARTIST | Alex Ross
PRINT SIZE | 18" x 24"
EDITION SIZE | 100
RELEASE DATE | October 2017
MEDIUM | Gouache
PRINT | Fine art lithograph
Produced in collaboration with Alex Ross Art. UNIVERSAL and all related characters and elements © & ™ Comcast. (s19) Bela Lugosi name and likeness ™ & © 2019 Lugosi Enterprises. All rights reserved.

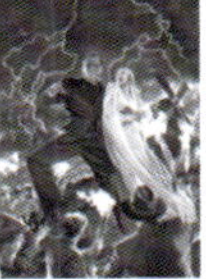

PAGE 120 | *Frankenstein*
PROPERTY | Universal Studios
ARTIST | Alex Ross
PRINT SIZE | 18" x 24"
EDITION SIZE | 100
RELEASE DATE | October 2017
MEDIUM | Gouache
PRINT | Fine art lithograph
Produced in collaboration with Alex Ross Art. UNIVERSAL and all related characters and elements © & ™ Comcast. (s19) Bela Lugosi name and likeness ™ & © 2019 Lugosi Enterprises. All rights reserved.

PAGE 121 | *The Bride of Frankenstein*
PROPERTY | Universal Studios
ARTIST | Alex Ross
PRINT SIZE | 18" x 24"
EDITION SIZE | 100
RELEASE DATE | October 2017
MEDIUM | Gouache
PRINT | Fine art lithograph
Produced in collaboration with Alex Ross Art. UNIVERSAL and all related characters and elements © & ™ Comcast. (s19) Bela Lugosi name and likeness ™ & © 2019 Lugosi Enterprises. All rights reserved.

PAGE 122 | *The Mummy*
PROPERTY | Universal Studios
ARTIST | Alex Ross
PRINT SIZE | 18" x 24"
EDITION SIZE | 100
RELEASE DATE | October 2017
MEDIUM | Gouache
PRINT | Fine art lithograph
Produced in collaboration with Alex Ross Art. UNIVERSAL and all related characters and elements © & ™ Comcast. (s19) Bela Lugosi name and likeness ™ & © 2019 Lugosi Enterprises. All rights reserved.

PAGE 123 | *The Wolf Man*
PROPERTY | Universal Studios
ARTIST | Alex Ross
PRINT SIZE | 18" x 24"
EDITION SIZE | 100
RELEASE DATE | October 2017
MEDIUM | Gouache
PRINT | Fine art lithograph
Produced in collaboration with Alex Ross Art. UNIVERSAL and all related characters and elements © & ™ Comcast. (s19) Bela Lugosi name and likeness ™ & © 2019 Lugosi Enterprises. All rights reserved.

PAGE 124 | *Hela: Goddess of Death*
PROPERTY | *Thor: Ragnarok*, Marvel Studios
ARTIST | Olivia De Berardinis
PRINT SIZE | 17.5" x 21"
EDITION SIZE | 200
RELEASE DATE | November 2017
MEDIUM | Acrylic
PRINT | Fine art giclée
© Marvel

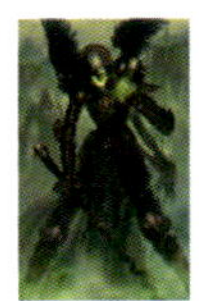

PAGE 126 | *Mortighull: Soldier of Cruel Purpose*
PROPERTY | *Court of the Dead*
ARTIST | Jimmy Xu
PRINT SIZE | 15.75" x 24"
EDITION SIZE | 100
RELEASE DATE | November 2017
MEDIUM | Digital Mixed Media
PRINT | Fine art giclée
© 2017 Sideshow Inc.

PAGE 128 | *Thor: Ragnarok*
PROPERTY | *Thor: Ragnarok*, Marvel Studios
ARTIST | Andy Park
PRINT SIZE | 18" x 24"
EDITION SIZE | 400
RELEASE DATE | November 2017
MEDIUM | Digital Mixed Media
PRINT | Fine art giclée
© Marvel

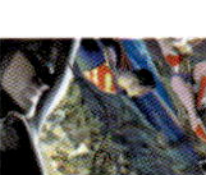

PAGE 130 | *Liberty and Justice: Trinity*
PROPERTY | DC Comics
ARTIST | Alex Ross
PRINT SIZE | 24" x 18"
EDITION SIZE | 300
RELEASE DATE | November 2017
MEDIUM | Gouache
PRINT | Fine art lithograph
Produced in collaboration with Alex Ross Art. JUSTICE LEAGUE and all related characters and elements © & ™ DC Comics. (s17)

PAGE 7, 132 | *Spider-Verse*
PROPERTY | Marvel
ARTIST | Mark Brooks
PRINT SIZE | 18" x 24"
EDITION SIZE | 400
RELEASE DATE | November 2017
MEDIUM | Digital Mixed Media
PRINT | Fine art giclée
© Marvel

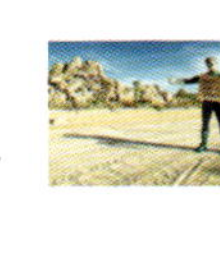

PAGE 136 | *Green Lantern: Deserted*
PROPERTY | DC Comics
ARTIST | Ian MacDonald
PRINT SIZE | 16" x 12"
EDITION SIZE | 200
RELEASE DATE | November 2017
MEDIUM | Digital Mixed Media
PRINT | Fine art giclée
GREEN LANTERN and all related characters and elements © & ™ DC Comics. (s17)

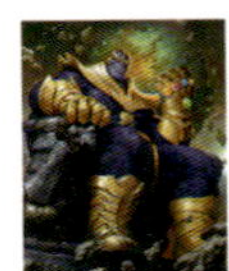
PAGE 138 | *Thanos on Throne Variant*
PROPERTY | Marvel
ARTIST | Doo-chun & Ian MacDonald
PRINT SIZE | 18" x 24"
EDITION SIZE | 500
RELEASE DATE | December 2017
MEDIUM | Digital Mixed Media
PRINT | Fine art giclée
© Marvel

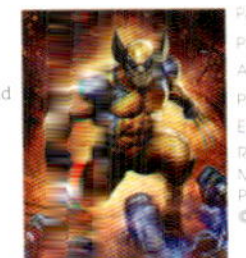
PAGE 140 | *Wolverine*
PROPERTY | Marvel
ARTIST | Dave Wilkins
PRINT SIZE | 18" x 24"
EDITION SIZE | 350
RELEASE DATE | December 2017
MEDIUM | Digital Mixed Media
PRINT | Fine art giclée
© Marvel

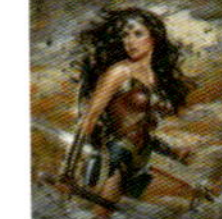
PAGE 144 | *Wonder Woman: Amazon Warrior*
PROPERTY | *Batman v Superman: Dawn of Justice*, Warner Bros.
ARTIST | Olivia De Berardinis
PRINT SIZE | 17.5" x 21"
EDITION SIZE | 275
RELEASE DATE | January 2018
MEDIUM | Acrylic
PRINT | Fine art giclée
BATMAN V SUPERMAN: DAWN OF JUSTICE and all related characters and elements (c) & (TM) DC Comics and Warner Bros. Entertainment Inc. WB SHIELD: TM & (c) WBEI. (s17)

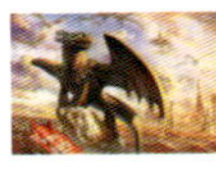
PAGE 144 | *Toothless & the Dragons of Berk*
PROPERTY | *How to Train Your Dragon*, Dreamworks Animation
ARTIST | Ian MacDonald
PRINT SIZE | 24" x 18"
EDITION SIZE | 250
RELEASE DATE | January 2018
MEDIUM | Digital Mixed Media
PRINT | Fine art giclée
DreamWorks Dragons © 2018 DreamWorks Animation LLC. All Rights Reserved

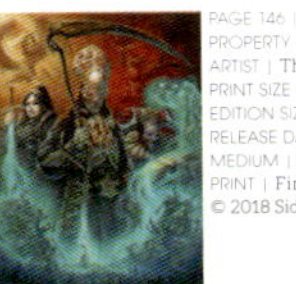
PAGE 146 | *The Underworld United*
PROPERTY | *Court of the Dead*
ARTIST | The Underworld United
PRINT SIZE | 18" x 24"
EDITION SIZE | 100
RELEASE DATE | January 2018
MEDIUM | Digital Mixed Media
PRINT | Fine art giclée
© 2018 Sideshow Inc.

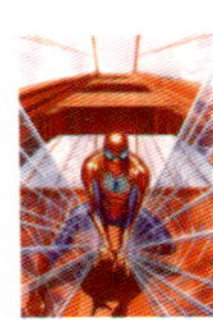
PAGE 148 | *Spider-Man: Trouble in San Francisco*
PROPERTY | Marvel
ARTIST | Alex Ross
PRINT SIZE | 18" x 24"
EDITION SIZE | 200
RELEASE DATE | January 2017
MEDIUM | Gouache
PRINT | Fine art lithograph
Produced in collaboration with Alex Ross Art. © Marvel

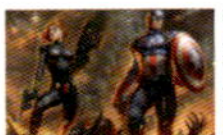
PAGE 150 | *Captain America & Black Widow*
PROPERTY | Marvel
ARTIST | Alex Pascenko & Ian MacDonald
PRINT SIZE | 24" x 18"
EDITION SIZE | 300
RELEASE DATE | February 2018
MEDIUM | Digital Mixed Media
PRINT | Fine art giclée
© Marvel

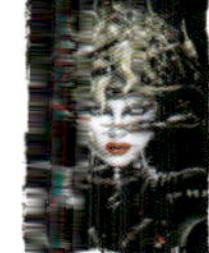
PAGE 152 | *Chat Noir*
PROPERTY | *Batman Returns*, Warner Bros.
ARTIST | Olivia De Berardinis
PRINT SIZE | 17.25" x 25.5"
EDITION SIZE | 250
RELEASE DATE | February 2018
MEDIUM | Acrylic
PRINT | Fine art giclée
BATMAN and all related characters and elements (c) & (TM) DC Comics and Warner Bros. Entertainment Inc. WB SHIELD: TM& (c) WBEI. (s18)

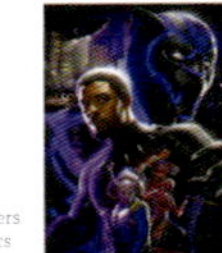
PAGE 154 | *Black Panther*
PROPERTY | *Black Panther*, Marvel Studios
ARTIST | Ryan Meinerding
PRINT SIZE | 18" x 24"
EDITION SIZE | 250
RELEASE DATE | February 2018
MEDIUM | Digital Mixed Media
PRINT | Fine art giclée
© Marvel

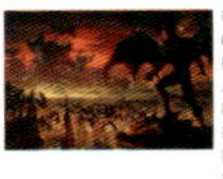
PAGE 156 | *Batman: Gotham City Nightmare*
PROPERTY | DC Comics
ARTIST | Fabian Schlaga
PRINT SIZE | 24" x 18"
EDITION SIZE | 150
RELEASE DATE | February 2018
MEDIUM | Digital Mixed Media
PRINT | Fine art giclée
BATMAN and all related characters and elements © & ™ DC Comics. (s18)

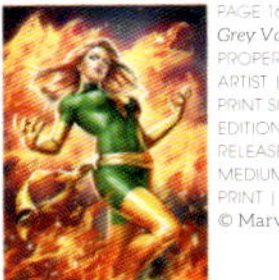
PAGE 160 | *Phoenix: Jean Grey Variant*
PROPERTY | Marvel
ARTIST | Ian MacDonald
PRINT SIZE | 18" x 24"
EDITION SIZE | 250
RELEASE DATE | February 2018
MEDIUM | Digital Mixed Media
PRINT | Fine art giclée
© Marvel

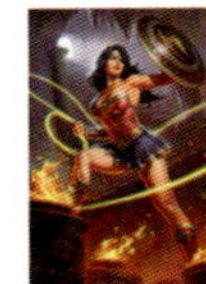
PAGE 162 | *Wonder Woman*
PROPERTY | DC Comics
ARTIST | Alex Pascenko & Ian MacDonald
PRINT SIZE | 18" x 24"
EDITION SIZE | 275
RELEASE DATE | March 2018
MEDIUM | Digital Mixed Media
PRINT | Fine art giclée
WONDER WOMAN and all related characters and elements © & ™ DC Comics. (s18)

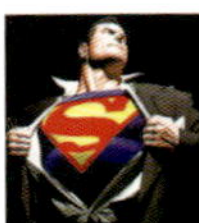
PAGE 166 | *The Man of Steel*
PROPERTY | DC Comics
ARTIST | Alex Ross
PRINT SIZE | 18" x 19"
EDITION SIZE | 200
RELEASE DATE | March 2018
MEDIUM | Gouache
PRINT | Fine art lithograph
Produced in collaboration with Alex Ross Art. SUPERMAN and all related characters and elements © & ™ DC Comics. (s18)

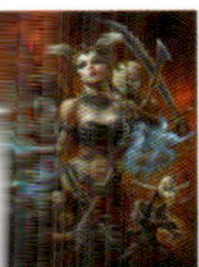
PAGE 168 | *The Impermanence of Flesh*
PROPERTY | *Court of the Dead*
ARTIST | Alex Horley
PRINT SIZE | 18" x 24"
EDITION SIZE | 100
RELEASE DATE | March 2018
MEDIUM | Acrylic and oil
PRINT | Fine art giclée
© 2018 Sideshow Inc.

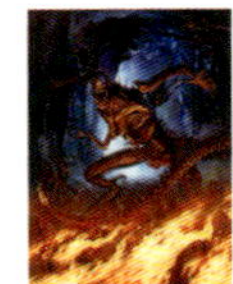
PAGE 170 | *Alien Queen*
PROPERTY | *Aliens*, Twentieth Century Fox
ARTIST | RJ Palmer
PRINT SIZE | 18" x 24"
EDITION SIZE | 250
RELEASE DATE | March 2018
MEDIUM | Digital Mixed Media
PRINT | Fine art giclée
Alien TM & © 2017 Twentieth Century Fox Film Corporation. All Rights Reserved.

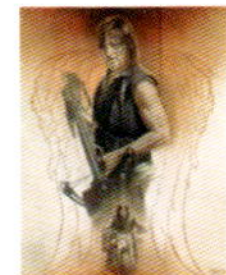
PAGE 172 | *The Drifter*
PROPERTY | *The Walking Dead*, AMC
ARTIST | Brian Rood
PRINT SIZE | 18" x 24"
EDITION SIZE | 200
RELEASE DATE | March 2018
MEDIUM | Digital Mixed Media
PRINT | Fine art giclée
The Walking Dead (c) 2018 AMC Film Holdings LLC. All Rights Reserved.

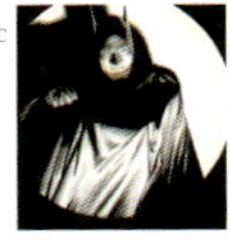
PAGE 174 | *The Batman*
PROPERTY | DC Comics
ARTIST | Alex Ross
PRINT SIZE | 18" x 24"
EDITION SIZE | 200
RELEASE DATE | April 2018
MEDIUM | Gouache
PRINT | Fine art lithograph
Produced in collaboration with Alex Ross Art. BATMAN and all related characters and elements © & ™ DC Comics. (s18)

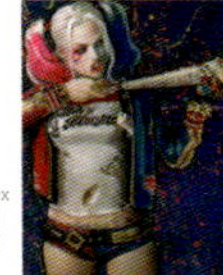
PAGE 176 | *Harley Quinn: Batter Up!*
PROPERTY | *Suicide Squad*, Warner Bros.
ARTIST | Olivia De Berardinis
PRINT SIZE | 17.5" x 21.75"
EDITION SIZE | 275
RELEASE DATE | April 2018
MEDIUM | Acrylic
PRINT | Fine art giclée
SUICIDE SQUAD and all related characters and elements (c) & (TM) DC Comics and Warner Bros. Entertainment Inc. (s18)

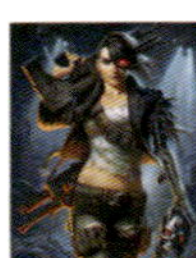
PAGE 178 | *Rebel Terminator*
PROPERTY | *Terminator*, StudioCanal
ARTIST | Alex Pascenko & Ian MacDonald
PRINT SIZE | 18" x 24"
EDITION SIZE | 150
RELEASE DATE | January 2017
MEDIUM | Digital Mixed Media
PRINT | Fine art giclée
The Terminator © 2018 Studiocanal S.A.S. ® All Rights Reserved.

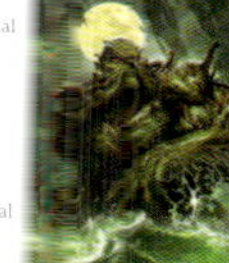
PAGE 180 | *Swamp Thing*
PROPERTY | DC Comics
ARTIST | Dave Wilkins
PRINT SIZE | 18" x 24"
EDITION SIZE | 250
RELEASE DATE | April 2018
MEDIUM | Digital Mixed Media
PRINT | Fine art giclée
All DC characters and elements © & ™ DC Comics. (s18)

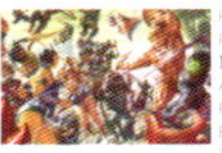
PAGE 182 | *Masters of the Universe*
PROPERTY | *Masters of the Universe*, Mattel
ARTIST | Alex Ross
PRINT SIZE | 16" x 20"
EDITION SIZE | 125
RELEASE DATE | September 2017
MEDIUM | Gouache
PRINT | Fine art lithograph
Produced in collaboration with Alex Ross Art. MASTERS OF THE UNIVERSE and associated trademarks are owned by and used under license from Mattel, Inc. (c) 2017 Mattel, Inc. All Rights Reserved. Under license to Classic Media.

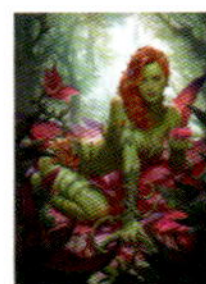
PAGE 184 | *Poison Ivy*
PROPERTY | DC Comics
ARTIST | Heon-hwa Choe
PRINT SIZE | 18" x 24"
EDITION SIZE | 300
RELEASE DATE | April 2018
MEDIUM | Digital Mixed Media
PRINT | Fine art giclée
BATMAN and all related characters and elements © & ™ DC Comics. (s18)

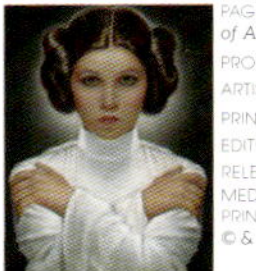
PAGE 190 | *Leia: Princess of Alderaan*
PROPERTY | *Star Wars*, Lucasfilm Ltd.
ARTIST | Leia, Princess of Alderaan
PRINT SIZE | 18" x 24"
EDITION SIZE | 500
RELEASE DATE | May 2018
MEDIUM | Acrylic
PRINT | Fine art giclée
© & ™ Lucasfilm Ltd.

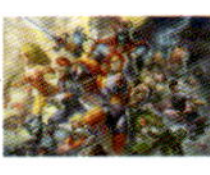
PAGE 192 | *ThunderCats*
PROPERTY | ThunderCats, Warner Bros.
ARTIST | Alex Pascenko
PRINT SIZE | 18" x 24"
EDITION SIZE | 275
RELEASE DATE | May 2018
MEDIUM | Digital Mixed Media
PRINT | Fine art giclée
THUNDERCATS and all related characters and elements ™ WBEI & © WBEI & Ted Wolf. (s18)

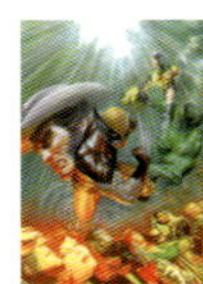
PAGE 194 | *The Death of Wolverine*
PROPERTY | Marvel
ARTIST | Alex Garner
PRINT SIZE | 18" x 24"
EDITION SIZE | 250
RELEASE DATE | Alex Ross
MEDIUM | Gouache
PRINT | Fine art lithograph
Produced in collaboration with Alex Ross Art. © Marvel

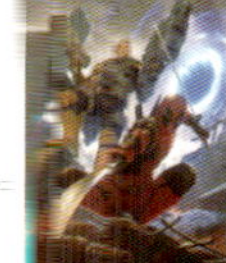
PAGE 196 | *Deadpool & Cable*
PROPERTY | Marvel
ARTIST | Alex Horley
PRINT SIZE | 18" x 24"
EDITION SIZE | 300
RELEASE DATE | May 2018
MEDIUM | Digital Mixed Media
PRINT | Fine art giclée
© Marvel

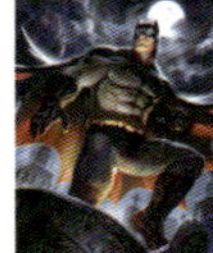
PAGE 198 | *Batman*
PROPERTY | DC Comics
ARTIST | Alex Pascenko & Ian MacDonald
PRINT SIZE | 18" x 24"
EDITION SIZE | 250
RELEASE DATE | May 20187
MEDIUM | Digital Mixed Media
PRINT | Fine art giclée
BATMAN and all related characters and elements © & ™ DC Comics. (s18)

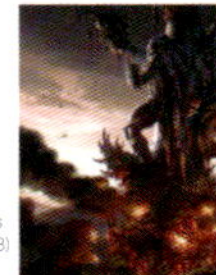
PAGE 200 | *Predator: Jungle Hunter*
PROPERTY | *Predator*, Twentieth Century Fox
ARTIST | Fabian Schlaga
PRINT SIZE | 18" x 24"
EDITION SIZE | 200
RELEASE DATE | May 2018
MEDIUM | Acrylic
PRINT | Fine art giclée
Predator TM & © 2018 Twentieth Century Fox Film Corporation. All Rights Reserved.

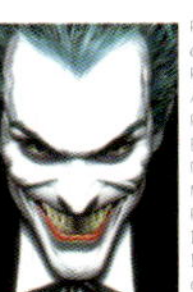
PAGE 202 | *The Joker: Portraits of Villainy*
PROPERTY | DC Comics
ARTIST | Alex Ross
PRINT SIZE | 18" x 24"
EDITION SIZE | 275
RELEASE DATE | June 2018
MEDIUM | Gouache
PRINT | Fine art lithograph
Produced in collaboration with Alex Ross Art. THE JOKER and all related characters and elements © & ™ DC Comics. (s18)

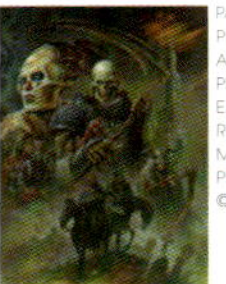
PAGE 204 | *The Strength of Bone*
PROPERTY | *Court of the Dead*
ARTIST | Alex Horley
PRINT SIZE | 18" x 24"
EDITION SIZE | 100
RELEASE DATE | June 2018
MEDIUM | Acrylic and oil
PRINT | Fine art giclée
© 2018 Sideshow Inc.

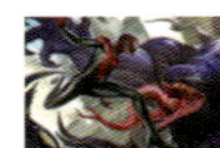
PAGE 206 | *Spider-Man: Miles Morales*
PROPERTY | Marvel
ARTIST | Anthony Francisco
PRINT SIZE | 18" x 24"
EDITION SIZE | 250
RELEASE DATE | June 2018
MEDIUM | Digital Mixed Media
PRINT | Fine art giclée
© Marvel

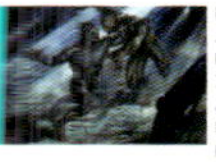
PAGE 210 | *Black Panther vs. Erik Killmonger*
PROPERTY | *Black Panther*, Marvel Studios
ARTIST | Adi Granov
PRINT SIZE | 24" x 18"
EDITION SIZE | 250
RELEASE DATE | June 2018
MEDIUM | Digital Mixed Media
PRINT | Fine art giclée
© Marvel

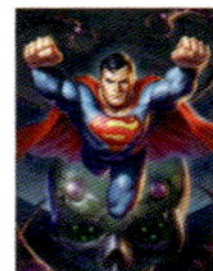
PAGE 212 | *Superman*
PROPERTY | DC Comics
ARTIST | Alex Pascenko & Ian MacDonald
PRINT SIZE | 18" x 24"
EDITION SIZE | 200
RELEASE DATE | May 20187
MEDIUM | Digital Mixed Media
PRINT | Fine art giclée
SUPERMAN and all related characters and elements © & ™ DC Comics. (s18)

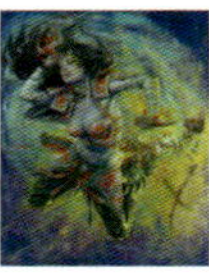
PAGE 214 | *Gallevarbe: Eviscerator*
PROPERTY | *Court of the Dead*
ARTIST | Olivia De Berardinis
PRINT SIZE | 17.5" x 21.5"
EDITION SIZE | 150
RELEASE DATE | June 2018
MEDIUM | Digital Mixed Media
PRINT | Fine art giclée
© 2018 Sideshow Inc.

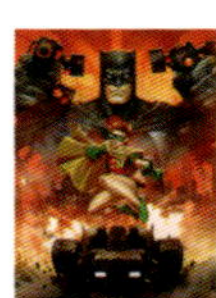
PAGE 216 | *Batman: The Dark Knight Returns*
PROPERTY | DC Comics
ARTIST | Dave Wilkins
PRINT SIZE | 18" x 24"
EDITION SIZE | 150
RELEASE DATE | June 2018
MEDIUM | Digital Mixed Media
PRINT | Fine art giclée
BATMAN and all related characters and elements © & ™ DC Comics. (s18)

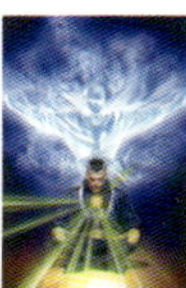
PAGE 218 | *Doctor Strange Omnibus*
PROPERTY | Marvel
ARTIST | Alex Ross
PRINT SIZE | 18" x 24"
EDITION SIZE | 150
RELEASE DATE | June 2018
MEDIUM | Gouache
PRINT | Fine art lithograph
Produced in collaboration with Alex Ross Art. © Marvel

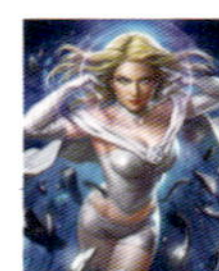
PAGE 220 | *Emma Frost*
PROPERTY | Marvel
ARTIST | Ian MacDonald
PRINT SIZE | 18" x 24"
EDITION SIZE | 300
RELEASE DATE | July 2018
MEDIUM | Digital Mixed Media
PRINT | Fine art giclée
© Marvel

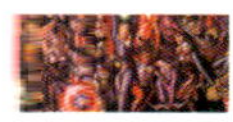
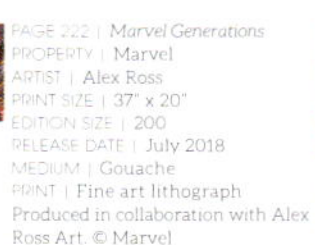
PAGE 222 | *Marvel Generations*
PROPERTY | Marvel
ARTIST | Alex Ross
PRINT SIZE | 37" x 20"
EDITION SIZE | 200
RELEASE DATE | July 2018
MEDIUM | Gouache
PRINT | Fine art lithograph
Produced in collaboration with Alex Ross Art. © Marvel

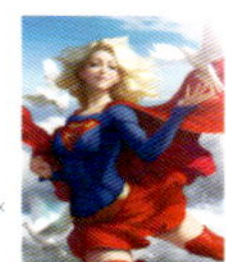
PAGE 224 | *Supergirl*
PROPERTY | DC Comics
ARTIST | Stanley 'Artgerm' Lau
PRINT SIZE | 18" x 24"
EDITION SIZE | 400
RELEASE DATE | July 2018
MEDIUM | Digital Mixed Media
PRINT | Fine art giclée
SUPERMAN and all related characters and elements © & ™ DC Comics. (s18)

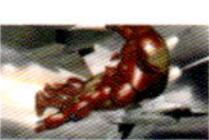
PAGE 226 | *Iron Man Mark III*
PROPERTY | *Iron Man*, Marvel Studios
ARTIST | Adi Granov
PRINT SIZE | 28" x 18"
EDITION SIZE | 200
RELEASE DATE | July 2018
MEDIUM | Digital Mixed Media
PRINT | Fine art giclée
© Marvel

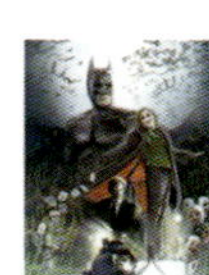
PAGE 230 | *Batman: The Dark Knight*
PROPERTY | *The Dark Knight*, Warner Bros.
ARTIST | Brian Rood
PRINT SIZE | 18" x 24"
EDITION SIZE | 300
RELEASE DATE | July 2018
MEDIUM | Digital Mixed Media
PRINT | Fine art giclée
THE DARK KNIGHT and all related characters and elements © & ™ DC Comics and Warner Bros. Entertainment Inc. (s18)

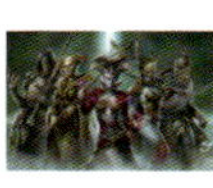
PAGE 232 | *Pillars of Rebellion*
PROPERTY | *Court of the Dead*
ARTIST | Ian MacDonald
PRINT SIZE | 24" x 18"
EDITION SIZE | 100
RELEASE DATE | July 2018
MEDIUM | Digital Mixed Media
PRINT | Fine art giclée
© 2018 Sideshow Inc.

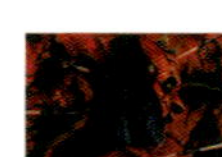
PAGE 234 | *Darth Maul: Dark Disciple*
PROPERTY | *Star Wars*, Lucasfilm Ltd.
ARTIST | Walter O'Neal
PRINT SIZE | 24" x 18"
EDITION SIZE | 500
RELEASE DATE | January 2017
MEDIUM | Acrylic
PRINT | Fine art giclée
© & ™ Lucasfilm Ltd.

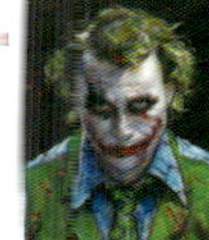
PAGE 236 | *Why So Serious?*
PROPERTY | *The Dark Knight*, Warner Bros.
ARTIST | Olivia De Berardinis
PRINT SIZE | 17.5" x 24.5"
EDITION SIZE | 350
RELEASE DATE | July 2018
MEDIUM | Acrylic
PRINT | Fine art giclée
THE DARK KNIGHT and all related characters and elements © & ™ DC Comics and Warner Bros. Entertainment Inc. (s18)

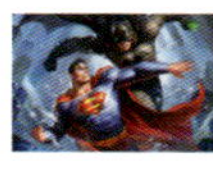
PAGE 238 | *Batman vs. Superman*
PROPERTY | DC Comics
ARTIST | Ian MacDonald & Alex Pascenko
PRINT SIZE | 24" x 18"
EDITION SIZE | 500
RELEASE DATE | July 2018
MEDIUM | Digital Mixed Media
PRINT | Fine art giclée
BATMAN, SUPERMAN and all related characters and elements © & ™ DC Comics. (s18)

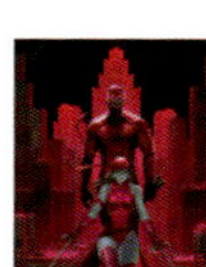
PAGE 240 | *Daredevil & Elektra*
PROPERTY | Marvel
ARTIST | Ian MacDonald
PRINT SIZE | 18" x 24"
EDITION SIZE | 250
RELEASE DATE | August 2018
MEDIUM | Digital Mixed Media
PRINT | Fine art giclée
© Marvel

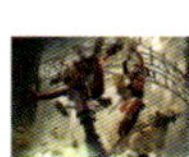
PAGE 244 | *The Joker & Harley Quinn: Arkham Asylum Breakout*
PROPERTY | DC Comics
ARTIST | Jon Foster
PRINT SIZE | 24" x 18"
EDITION SIZE | 275
RELEASE DATE | August 2018
MEDIUM | Digital Mixed Media
PRINT | Fine art giclée
BATMAN and all related characters and elements © & ™ DC Comics. (s18)

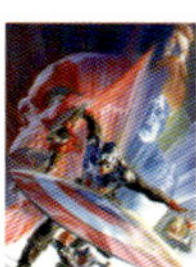
PAGE 248 | *Captain America 600*
PROPERTY | Marvel
ARTIST | Ian MacDonald
PRINT SIZE | 17" x 24"
EDITION SIZE | 175
RELEASE DATE | August 2018
MEDIUM | Gouache
PRINT | Fine art lithograph
Produced in collaboration with Alex Ross Art. © Marvel

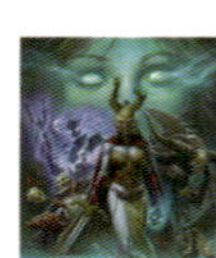
PAGE 250 | *The Transcendence of Spirit*
PROPERTY | *Court of the Dead*
ARTIST | Alex Horley
PRINT SIZE | 18" x 24"
EDITION SIZE | 100
RELEASE DATE | August 2018
MEDIUM | Acrylic and oil
PRINT | Fine art giclée
© 2018 Sideshow Inc.

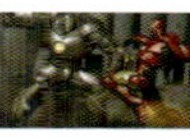
PAGE 252 | *Iron Man vs. Iron Monger*
PROPERTY | *Iron Man*, Marvel Studios
ARTIST | Adi Granov
PRINT SIZE | 28" x 18"
EDITION SIZE | 200
RELEASE DATE | August 2018
MEDIUM | Digital Mixed Media
PRINT | Fine art giclée
© Marvel

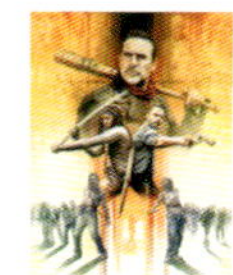
PAGE 254 | *My Brother's Keeper*
PROPERTY | *The Walking Dead*, AMC
ARTIST | Brian Rood
PRINT SIZE | 18" x 24"
EDITION SIZE | 150
RELEASE DATE | August 2018
MEDIUM | Digital Mixed Media
PRINT | Fine art giclée
The Walking Dead (c) 2018 AMC Film Holdings LLC. All Rights Reserved.

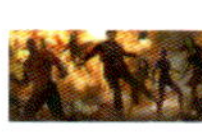
PAGE 256 | *Guardians of the Galaxy Vol. 2*
PROPERTY | *Guardians of the Galaxy Vol. 2*, Marvel Studios
ARTIST | Andy Park
PRINT SIZE | 28" x 15"
EDITION SIZE | 200
RELEASE DATE | August 2018
MEDIUM | Digital Mixed Media
PRINT | Fine art giclée
© Marvel

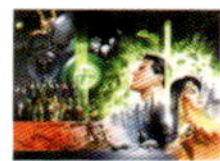
PAGE 258 | *History of the DC Universe*
PROPERTY | DC Comics
ARTIST | Alex Ross
PRINT SIZE | 18" x 19"
EDITION SIZE | 200
RELEASE DATE | August 2018
MEDIUM | Gouache
PRINT | Fine art lithograph
Produced in collaboration with Alex Ross Art. SUPERMAN and all related characters and elements © & ™ DC Comics. (s18)

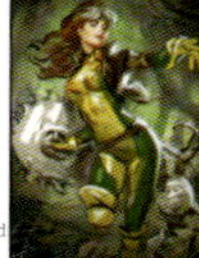
PAGE 260 | *Rogue*
PROPERTY | Marvel
ARTIST | Ian MacDonald & Alex Pascenko
PRINT SIZE | 18" x 24"
EDITION SIZE | 250
RELEASE DATE | September 2018
MEDIUM | Digital Mixed Media
PRINT | Fine art giclée
© Marvel

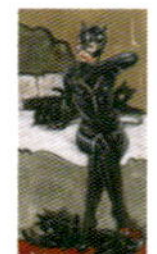
PAGE 262 | *Clawsplay*
PROPERTY | *Batman Returns*, Warner Bros.
ARTIST | Batman Returns, Warner Bros.
PRINT SIZE | 14" x 28"
EDITION SIZE | 150
RELEASE DATE | January 201
MEDIUM | Acrylic
PRINT | Fine art giclée
BATMAN and all related cha... and elements (c) & (TM) DC C... and Warner Bros. Entertainm... Inc. WB SHIELD: TM& (c) W... (s18)

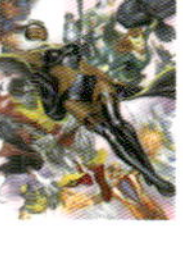
PAGE 264 | *Uncanny X-Men*
PROPERTY | Marvel
ARTIST | Alex Ross
PRINT SIZE | 16" x 24"
EDITION SIZE | 200
RELEASE DATE | September 2018
MEDIUM | Gouache
PRINT | Fine art lithograph
Produced in collaboration with Alex Ross Art. © Marvel

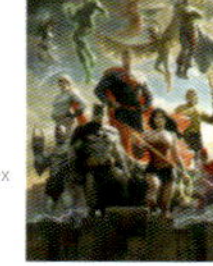
PAGE 266 | *Justice League*
PROPERTY | DC Comics
ARTIST | Paolo Rivera
PRINT SIZE | 18" x 24"
EDITION SIZE | 300
RELEASE DATE | September 2018
MEDIUM | Digital Mixed Media
PRINT | Fine art giclée
JUSTICE LEAGUE and all related characters and elements © & ™ DC Comics. (s18)

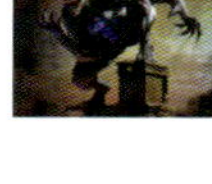
PAGE 268 | *Venom*
PROPERTY | Marvel
ARTIST | David Igo & Fabian Schlaga
PRINT SIZE | 24" x 18"
EDITION SIZE | 250
RELEASE DATE | September 2018
MEDIUM | Digital Mixed Media
PRINT | Fine art giclée
© Marvel

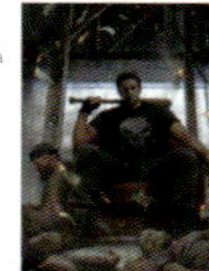
PAGE 270 | *Punisher on Throne*
PROPERTY | Marvel
ARTIST | Karla Ortiz
PRINT SIZE | 18" x 24"
EDITION SIZE | 1250
RELEASE DATE | October 2018
MEDIUM | Digital Mixed Media
PRINT | Fine art giclée
© Marvel

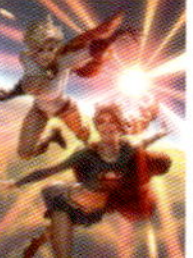
PAGE 272 | *Supergirl & Power Girl*
PROPERTY | DC Comics
ARTIST | Alex Garner
PRINT SIZE | 18" x 24"
EDITION SIZE | 250
RELEASE DATE | October 2018
MEDIUM | Digital Mixed Media
PRINT | Fine art giclée
JUSTICE LEAGUE and all related characters and elements © & ™ DC Comics. (s18)

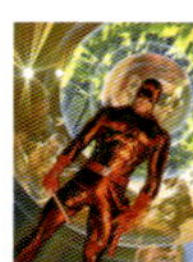
PAGE 274 | *Daredevil: The Man Without Fear*
PROPERTY | Marvel
ARTIST | Alex Ross
PRINT SIZE | 18" x 24"
EDITION SIZE | 150
RELEASE DATE | October 2018
MEDIUM | Gouache
PRINT | Fine art lithograph
Produced in collaboration with Alex Ross Art. © Marvel

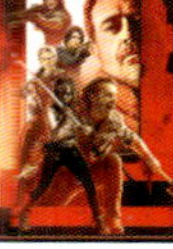
PAGE 276 | *The Last Stand*
PROPERTY | *The Walking Dead*, AMC
ARTIST | Brian Rood
PRINT SIZE | 18" x 24"
EDITION SIZE | 250
RELEASE DATE | October 2018
MEDIUM | Digital Mixed Media
PRINT | Fine art giclée
The Walking Dead (c) 2018 AMC Film Holdings LLC. All Rights Reserved.

PAGE 278 | *Mystique*
PROPERTY | Marvel
ARTIST | Jenny Frison
PRINT SIZE | 18" x 24"
EDITION SIZE | 275
RELEASE DATE | October 2018
MEDIUM | Digital Mixed Media
PRINT | Fine art giclée
© Marvel

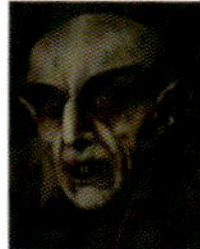
PAGE 282 | *Nosferatu*
PROPERTY | *Nosferatu*
ARTIST | Dan Colonna
PRINT SIZE | 18" x 22"
EDITION SIZE | 150
RELEASE DATE | October 2018
MEDIUM | Oil on canvas
PRINT | Fine art giclée

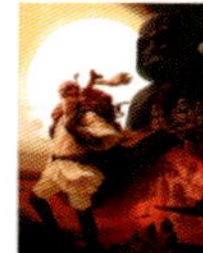
PAGE 284 | *Obi-Wan Kenobi: Desert Nomad*
PROPERTY | *Star Wars*, Lucasfilm Ltd.
ARTIST | Fabian Schlaga
PRINT SIZE | 18" x 24"
EDITION SIZE | 350
RELEASE DATE | November 2018
MEDIUM | Digital Mixed Media
PRINT | Fine art giclée
© & ™ Lucasfilm Ltd.

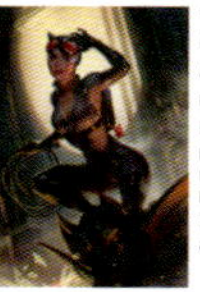
PAGE 286 | *Catwoman*
PROPERTY | DC Comics
ARTIST | Heon-hwa Choe
PRINT SIZE | 18" x 24"
EDITION SIZE | 275
RELEASE DATE | November 2018
MEDIUM | Digital Mixed Media
PRINT | Fine art giclée
BATMAN and all related characters and elements © & ™ DC Comics. (s18)

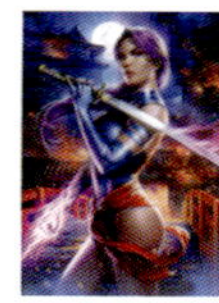

PAGE 288 | *Psylocke*
PROPERTY | Marvel
ARTIST | Ian MacDonald
PRINT SIZE | 18" x 24"
EDITION SIZE | 275
RELEASE DATE | November 2018
MEDIUM | Digital Mixed Media
PRINT | Fine art giclée

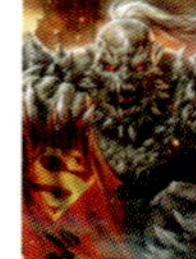

PAGE 290 | *Doomsday*
PROPERTY | DC Comics
ARTIST | Dave Wilkins & Ian MacDonald
PRINT SIZE | 18" x 24"
EDITION SIZE | 150
RELEASE DATE | November 2018
MEDIUM | Digital Mixed Media
PRINT | Fine art giclée

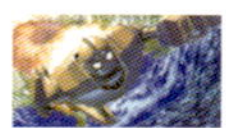

PAGE 292 | *Iron Giant: "No Atomo, I Superman"*
PROPERTY | *The Iron Giant*, Warner Bros.
ARTIST | Alex Ross
PRINT SIZE | 17" x 26"
EDITION SIZE | 100
RELEASE DATE | November 2018
MEDIUM | Gouache
PRINT | Fine art lithograph
Produced in collaboration with Alex Ross Art.

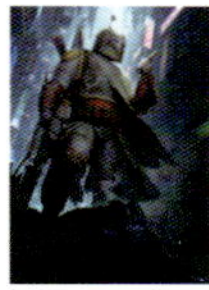

PAGE 294, 303 | *Boba Fett: A Force to Be Reckoned With*
PROPERTY | *Star Wars*, Lucasfilm Ltd.
ARTIST | Darren Tan
PRINT SIZE | 18" x 24"
EDITION SIZE | 300
RELEASE DATE | November 2018
MEDIUM | Digital Mixed Media
PRINT | Fine art giclée

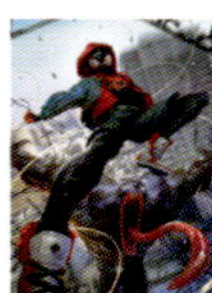

PAGE 296 | *Ultimate Spider-Man: Miles Morales*
PROPERTY | Marvel
ARTIST | Derrick Chew
PRINT SIZE | 18" x 24"
EDITION SIZE | 150
RELEASE DATE | December 2018
MEDIUM | Digital Mixed Media
PRINT | Fine art giclée

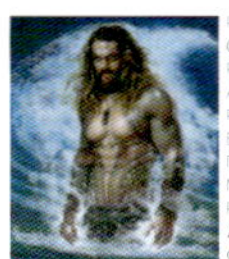

PAGE 298 | *Aquaman: Permission to Come Aboard*
PROPERTY | *Aquaman*, Warner Bros.
ARTIST | Olivia De Berardinis
PRINT SIZE | 17" x 22.5"
EDITION SIZE | 200
RELEASE DATE | December 2018
MEDIUM | Acrylic
PRINT | Fine art giclée

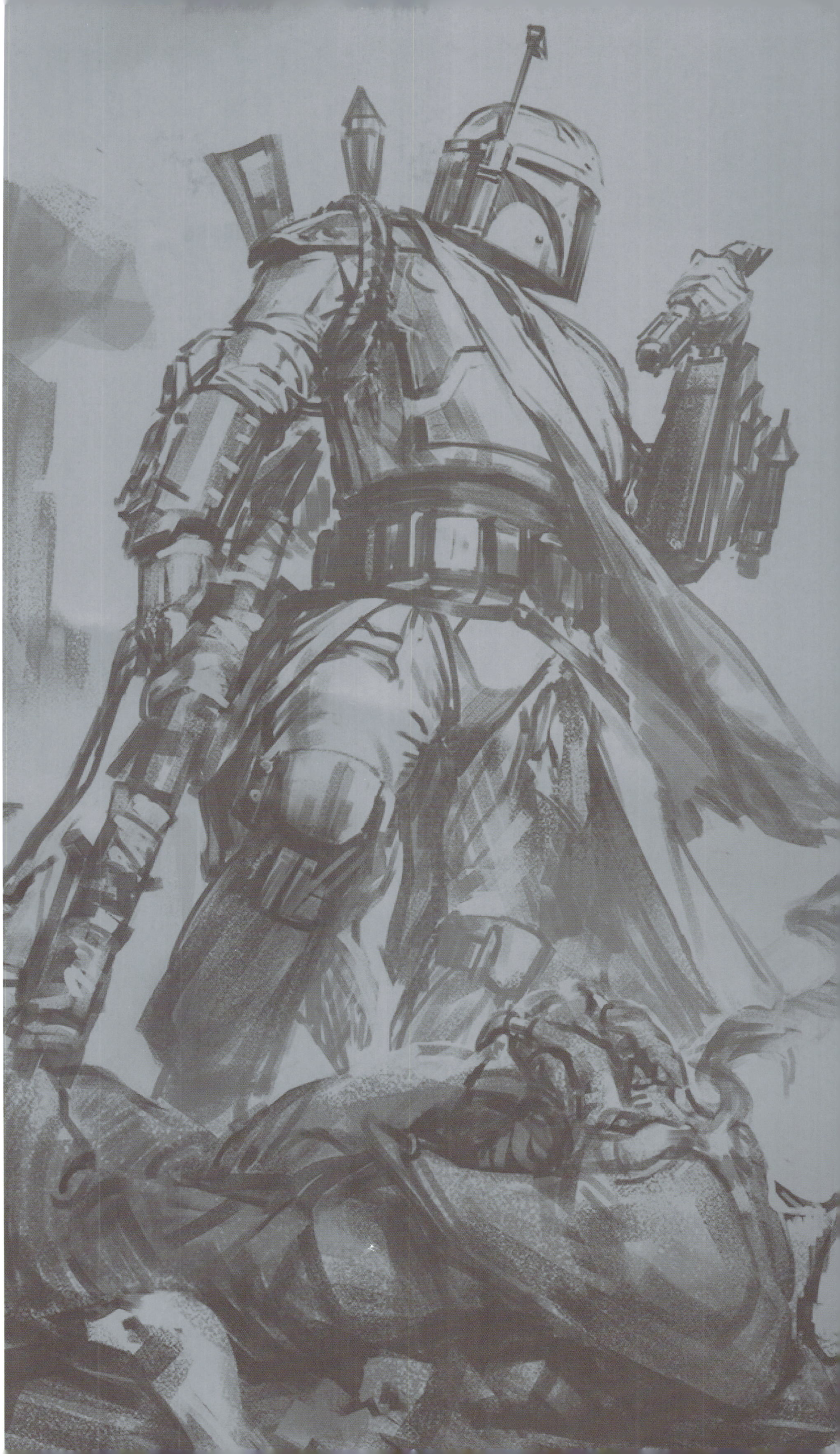

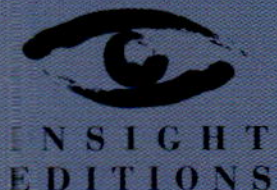

PO Box 3088
San Rafael, CA 94912
www.insighteditions.com

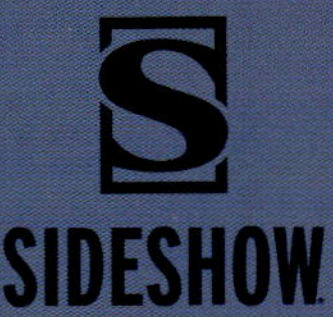

2630 Conejo Spectrum Street
Thousand Oaks, CA 91320
sideshow.com

Trade ISBN: 978-1-64722-425-7
Sideshow ISBN: 978-1-64722-580-3

Library of Congress Cataloging-in-Publication Data available.

INSIGHT EDITIONS

Publisher: Raoul Goff
VP of Licensing and Partnerships: Vanessa Lopez
VP of Creative: Chrissy Kwasnik
VP of Manufacturing: Alix Nicholaeff
Editorial Director: Vicki Jaeger
Sponsoring Editor: Harrison Tunggal
Managing Editor: Lauren LePera
Senior Production Editor: Elaine Ou
Senior Production Manager: Greg Steffen
Senior Production Manager, Subsidiary Rights: Lina s Palma

Also available from Sideshow Collectibles and Insight Editions:

Capturing Archetypes Volume 4: Demigods and Defenders: The Balance of Power
DC: Collecting the Multiverse: The Art of Sideshow
Star Wars: Collecting a Galaxy. The Art of Sideshow
Court of the Dead: The Chronicle of the Underworld
Shadows of the Underworld Graphic Novel
Inside the Sideshow Studio

SIDESHOW COLLECTIBLES

Creative Director
Tom Gilliland

Book Series Concept
Andrew McBride
Greg Anzalone

Design and Photography
Andrea Mendoza
Andrew McBride
Cassie Fuertez
Erick Torres
Jeannette Villarreal Hamilton
Katie Fernandez

Fine Art Program
Andrew McBride
Gracie Bifulco

Art Director
David Igo

To learn more about the studio's environments, the talented artists, and the unique Sideshow creative process, check out the behind-the-scenes videos at Sideshow.com

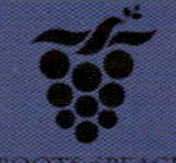

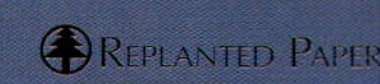

Insight Editions, in association with Roots of Peace, will plant two trees for each tree used in the manufacturing of this book. Roots of Peace is an internationally renowned humanitarian organization dedicated to eradicating land mines worldwide and converting war-torn lands into productive farms and wildlife habitats. Roots of Peace will plant two million fruit and nut trees in Afghanistan and provide farmers there with the skills and support necessary for sustainable land use.

Manufactured in China by Insight Editions

10 9 8 7 6 5 4 3 2 1

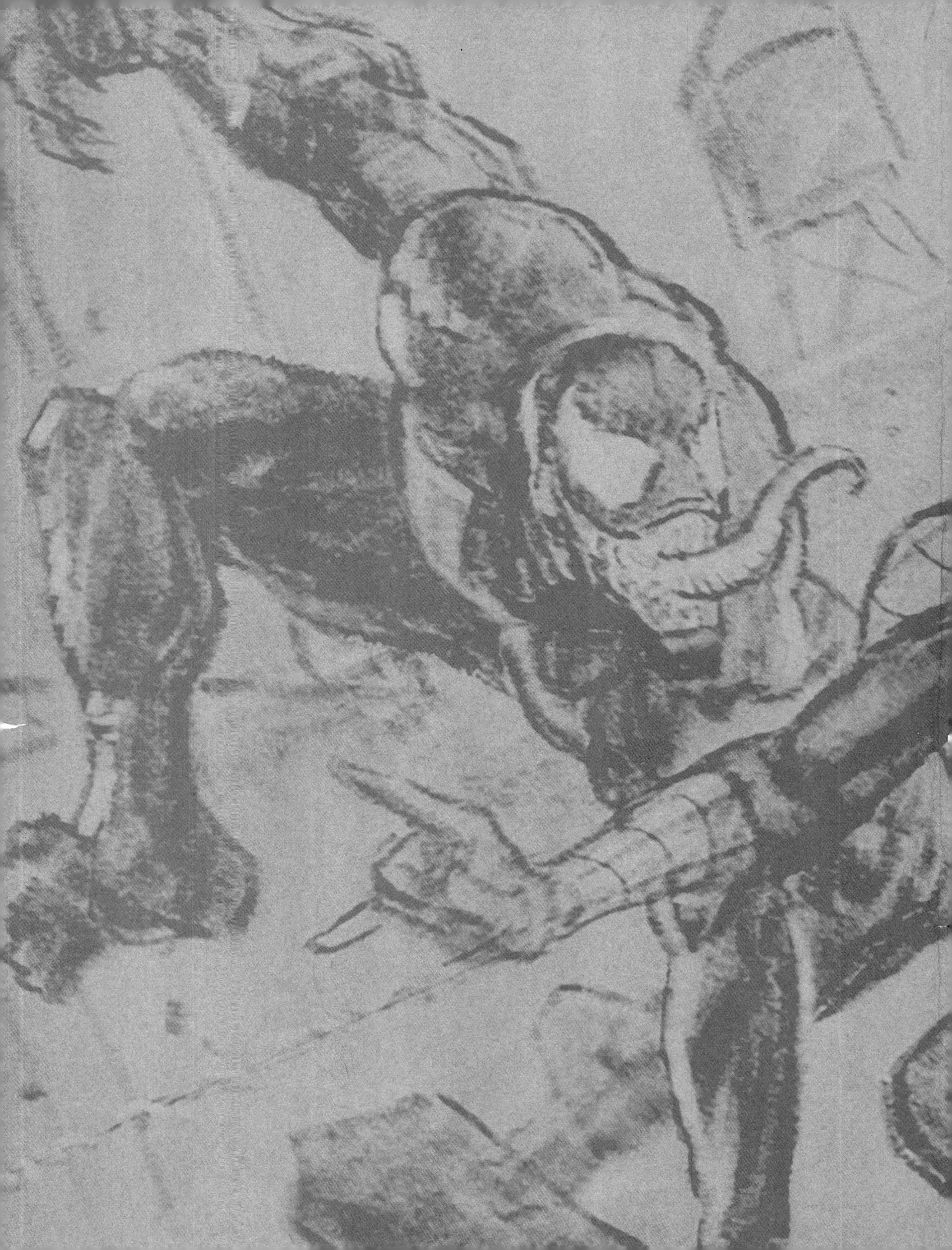